S0-ARK-280

Classics in Commercial Bank Lending

46 Practical, Time-Honored Articles Selected from *The Journal of Commercial Bank Lending*

Edited by William W. Sihler with a Foreword by P. Henry Mueller

rma

ROBERT MORRIS ASSOCIATES
The National Association of Bank Loan and Credit Officers
Philadelphia, Pennslyvania

While Robert Morris Associates believes the material contained in this publication is accurate, no opinion expressed on a legal matter should be relied on without the advice of counsel familiar with the facts in a particular case and the applicable law.

© 1981 by Robert Morris Associates

All Rights Reserved. Printed in the U.S.A.

Library of Congress Catalog Card Number: 81-83354

International Standard Book Number: 0-936742-03-8

Library of Congress Cataloging in Publication Data

Main entry under title:

Classics in commercial bank lending.

   1. Bank loans—Addresses, essays, lectures.
I. Sihler, William W., 1937-   . II. Journal of commercial bank lending.
HG1641.C56   332.1'753   81-83354
ISBN 0-936742-03-8   AACR2

Additional copies of this publication are available from the Order Dept., Robert Morris Associates, 1616 Philadelphia National Bank Bldg., Philadelphia, PA 19107 (215) 665-2850.

Table of Contents

iii

III. Loan Structure and Profitability Analysis

IV. Documentation and Legal Aspects of Lending

V. Problem Loan Management

VI. Credit Policy and Administration

VII. Aspects of International Lending

Foreword

Commercial banking, as part of the financial services industry, has been undergoing profound change and modernization. But in the area of lending, many strong links with the past must and should persist, especially when experience has taught that ignoring them heightens risk. Other guidelines may lose their relevance and become equally as dangerous if applied unthinkingly. For these reasons, the most important criterion used by Professor William Sihler to select articles for this collection was current usefulness.

As bank lending practices are brought into line with today's realities, it is tempting to speculate on what the future may hold. By way of perspective, current practices reflect deep-rooted influences on borrowers, depositors, and savers, as well as all lenders. Think of some of the more significant developments since the 1933 bank holiday:

- The heavy shift to term and cash flow lending, which started in the 1930s
- The introduction of the CD—the certificate of deposit—in 1961, a new vehicle by which banks could bid for reserves and lend despite money market conditions
- The burgeoning of Euromarkets, commencing in the mid-1960s, which enormously increased and facilitated the global transfer of financial assets
- Chronic inflation, which brought about extreme fluctuations in interest rates in the 1970s and 1980s
- The traumatic change in the cost of energy, dating from 1973, and its pervasive effects on borrowers and lenders
- The escalation of changing technology, with scientific knowledge doubling every five years
- The internationalization and cross-investment of business and banking
- The revolution taking place in the financial services market itself
- The growth and complexity of borrowers and the changes that have been occurring in their balance sheets and funding cycles

The loan officer's prime adversary—change—is constant, but more seems to have taken place in bank lending in the past five years than in decades. For this reason, the articles in this anthology should be viewed in the context of what influences lending and lending patterns.

Over time, the realities of the marketplace may well date some of the mechanics of lending discussed in these articles, but the basic principles should remain sound. What this book tries to do is to pull together valuable insights of the past and to provide a platform from which to consider the future.

What, then, are the potential issues that loan officers might face in the future? With respect to borrowers, here's a sampler:

- Corporations, so dependent on debt in general and short-term debt in particular, face an unprecedented challenge—the restoration of balance sheets to a reasonable level of normality. The current trend toward deteriorated balance sheets has reached serious proportions. Will the balance sheets be restored? Or, will the financial institutions find themselves unexpected participants in the borrower's equity?

• There are problems of evaluating management in an era characterized by complex organizational structure and environment; by the impersonality of borrowing and lending entities; and by the increasing number of individuals who are involved in specific transactions. Accurate evaluation of character and management has always been one of the loan officer's most demanding challenges, but the task will be more critical *and* more difficult in the future. How does one really get to know the borrower in today's fluid marketplace, with its mounting complexities and time pressures?

• The fetish for growth and earnings per share has exacerbated the pressures and demands on management at all levels and has also accelerated senior management turnover, merger, and acquisition. When these developments occur, how firm are the premises on which prior loans were extended? How do lenders cope with management and negotiating styles that have been nurtured by this environment? Suppose borrowers' objectives and businesses change mid-stream?

• What about the spread of comfort letters and other forms of unguaranteed support, including handshakes from parents?

With respect to lenders, there are other issues pending:

• Loan portfolios have become increasingly diverse, shifting from conventional direct lending to a variety of risk taking that includes the purchase of assets, the financing of leveraged buyouts, and the issuance of letters of credit to backstop third-party debt (or performance). Given the corporate merger movement, there has been a trend toward concentration of credit exposure to large corporations, as well as the loss of quality borrowers to the commercial paper market. Are bank portfolios headed toward "nonfunds lending?" What are the implications for bank earnings, leverage and funding, structure, and staffing?

• With capital increasingly a constraint on asset building, banks must earn profits sufficient to make returns to stockholders competitive with other investments. Risk-asset growth must be selective, and risk/reward characteristics of assets must undergo the closest scrutiny. What are the implications for pricing? Will adequate returns be available without a painful clearing of the marketplace?

• How can lending institutions protect loan officers' objectivity? What can be done to prevent their becoming jaded by either "profit-centeritis" or by overly close personal involvement with borrowers?

• How can loan officers get an accurate handle on a borrower's financial and operating controls? On what basis can judgment be made as to whether current management can perform well in adversity? How can loan officers be sure a borrower isn't selling the future short by pushing current performance? Should banks reevaluate their analytic approach and, perhaps, like institutional lenders, move more heavily in the direction of security and bond analysis techniques?

• What will be the long-term impact of the marketing and profit-center concepts in banking? How have they already affected recruiting and staffing? With greater and longer risks being taken by banking today, how do they square with banking's traditional credit culture? How should good lending be recognized? Do good lenders make good administrative officers? Is the reverse true? How can both functions be given proper incentives and rewards?

In the future, the external environment will assume even greater importance. As a result, loan officers will face many questions, including:

• How do borrowers and lenders adjust to inflation, energy economics, and accelerating technological change? Because it is impossible to predict the future precisely, what are the risk implications of long tenor in periods of economic instability?

• How have recent changes in laws and regulations altered lending risks, and how do banks defend against them?

• What can be done to improve the approach to workouts when syndicated credits or public debt is involved? How subordinate is "subordinated" debt in the case of serious deterioration? What about other classes of creditors? What have been the lessons to be learned?

• What are the risks for lenders created by accounting practices that have a regulatory focus rather than an orientation toward lenders' mutual interest? Shouldn't accountants be more accountable to lenders?

• What are the risk implications of extended tenors or project finance transactions when borrowers try to push risks off their balance sheets and onto the banks? Is it really proper for lenders to bear the borrower's business risks? Is banking leaning too far in the direction of quasi-equity lending?

• What will the commercial bank lending function be like in 1990?

The bankruptcy of Penn Central marked the postwar change in the risk-taking climate. We are in a testing period for management: Some will be winners, others losers. The management factor, which is second to the pervasive influence of the business cycle, is never to be underestimated.

Loan officers are also being tested by this shifting scene. They must understand the meaning of the times and relate to specifics. The articles in this book were selected to be of help. And, to paraphrase Clarence Day's classic comment, intelligence must never be permitted to outstrip wisdom.

P. Henry Mueller
Chairman, Credit Policy Committee
Citicorp and Citibank, N.A.
New York, New York

Preface

This collection of readings from *The Journal of Commercial Bank Lending,* 1970-1980, puts in one volume 46 classic articles on bank lending practices and procedures. Over the years, the *Journal* has been the leading publication covering these topics, but many practicing loan officers as well as loan officer candidates do not have ready access to back issues or may not have the time to research back indexes for references to subjects.

That is one of the reasons that as a banking professor, I have long felt the need for a collection of a variety of readings from the *Journal* to use as a text in banking courses. P. Henry Mueller, a distinguished New York City banker, shared my feelings about the usefulness of such a collection. He felt it would be of value to seasoned loan officers as well as to bank trainees just beginning their lending careers. This book therefore emanates from our desire to provide bankers and students alike with a collection of classic articles in commercial lending.

Because this anthology has been assembled for the convenience of the practitioner and banking student or trainee, the current usefulness of material was one of the important criteria used to select articles. Unfortunately, use of this yardstick has meant that many articles, which were outstanding in their time, have been omitted because their age has finally begun to show.

However, it was surprising how many articles have endured. The preliminary screening reduced the number of candidates to approximately 150. It was very difficult to reduce this number further, but space restrictions required a brutal use of the editorial pencil, painful though it was. In the final selection process, preference had to be given to those articles that best stood the test of time.

An additional objective was to provide a reasonable balance of the topics to be covered. This goal did not prove difficult to accomplish because, over the ten years that the anthology spans, a wide variety of articles has been published in the *Journal* on the important issues in the commercial lending field. Nevertheless, because this collection was not planned or written by one individual, it may lack the smooth transitions one expects in a work by a single author. The offsetting advantage is the insight that comes in seeing the same problem from different perspectives.

The book is divided into seven sections, moving gradually from the general to the specific. An overview section opens the book with a series of articles offering a broad perspective on credit analysis and the lending decision. A section treating more specific topics in credit analysis follows, reflecting the need for basic skills before addressing the credit analysis of special industries and lending situations.

The third section considers the problems involved in loan structure and profitability analysis, which have received considerable attention in recent years. Loan pricing as such, however, has not been included despite the many articles that have appeared in the *Journal* on this topic. The practices in this area have been changing so rapidly that published articles appeared either dated or were quickly becoming obsolete.

The fourth section covers documentation and legal aspects of lending. Surprisingly, articles relating to problem loan management, the topic of section five, were quite limited. The sixth section addresses questions of credit policy and credit administration. Finally, the seventh section contains articles on aspects of international lending.

I would like to acknowledge two individuals who have offered invaluable assistance in the preparation of this book. I have already mentioned Henry Mueller who supported this project from the beginning and contributed the Foreword. He also served on a review committee for the book with Hugh M. Durden, executive vice president at Wachovia Bank & Trust Company in Winston-Salem, North Carolina. These two highly experienced bankers reviewed the material for the book at various stages of development and made useful comments and suggestions throughout the selection and editorial process. I thank them for their significant contribution to this book.

My thanks go also to the 1980-81 Policy Division Council of Robert Morris Associates which approved and directed the preparation of the *Classics*.

William W. Sihler
Arthur J. Morris Professor of
Business Administration
The Colgate Darden Graduate School
of Business Administration
University of Virginia
Charlottesville, Virginia

X

Contributors*

Gary G. Anderson, Director
> Business Intelligence Program
> SRI International
> Menlo Park, California
> (Formerly Manager, Management Data Services, General
> Electric Information Services, Rockville, Maryland)

Herbert L. Ash, Partner
> Hahn & Hessen
> New York, New York

Hurd Baruch, Partner
> Winston & Strawn
> Washington, D. C.

C. Perry Bascom, Esq., Partner
> Bryan, Cave, McPheeters & McRoberts
> St. Louis, Missouri

Cass Bettinger, Vice President, Director of Strategic Planning
> Commercial Security Bank
> Salt Lake City, Utah

Grover R. Castle, Vice President
> Chemical Bank
> New York, New York

Douglas S. Clarke, Deceased
> (Formerly Vice President, Newark Trust Company,
> Newark, Ohio)

Eugene E. Comiskey, The Fuller E. Callaway Professor of Accounting
> Georgia Institute of Technology
> Atlanta, Georgia

C. Thorne Corse, Senior Vice President and Assistant General Counsel
> Bank of America N.T. & S.A.
> San Francisco, California

William P. Creamer, Vice President in the High Technology Group
> Bank of America N.T. & S.A.
> San Francisco, California
> (Formerly Manager, Capital Programming Unit,
> Girard Bank, Philadelphia, Pennsylvania)

---

* The list of contributors gives information about the current positions and affiliations of
all authors. If contributors held positions with other organizations at the time their articles
were published, that information appears in parentheses following the current data.

xi

John C. Cresci, Vice President
Philadelphia National Bank
Philadelphia, Pennsylvania
(Formerly Executive Vice President, Southeastern
Pennsylvania Development Fund, Philadelphia)
Jack R. Crigger, Executive Vice President
American National Bank and Trust Company
Chattanooga, Tennessee
Robert E. Davis, Senior Vice President
United Virginia Bank
Alexandria, Virginia
D. R. Denison, Vice President and Manager, Beverly Hills Office
First Interstate Bank of California
Beverly Hills, California
Stephen C. Diamond, President
Chase Commercial Corporation
Englewood Cliffs, New Jersey
(Formerly Senior Vice President, Walter E. Heller &
Company, Chicago, Illinois)
Margaret Hambrecht Douglas-Hamilton, Associated with
Sullivan & Worcester, Boston, Massachusetts, and
New York, New York
(Formerly associated with Bingham, Dana & Gould,
Boston, Massachusetts)
Cato Ellis, Jr., Senior Vice President
Munford Union Bank
Munford, Tennessee
(Formerly Senior Credit Examiner, First Tennessee
National Corporation, Memphis, Tennessee)
Thomas M. Flynn, Consultant
(Formerly Senior Vice President, Somerset Trust
Company, Somerville, New Jersey)
Edward F. Gee, Deceased
(Formerly Retired Chairman of the Board, United
Virginia Bankshares, Inc., Richmond, Virginia)
Jordan L. Golding, Partner
Peat, Marwick, Mitchell & Company
Certified Public Accountants
Boston, Massachusetts
Robert C. Higgins, Professor of Finance
University of Washington, and Educational Director
Pacific Coast Banking School
Seattle, Washington
James A. Hoeven, Associate Professor
Colorado State University
Fort Collins, Colorado

Charles B. Jarrett, Jr., Attorney
Pittsburgh, Pennsylvania
(Formerly Senior Vice President and Counsel, Mellon
Bank, N.A., Pittsburgh, Pennsylvania)

Lawrence T. Jilk, Jr., Executive Vice President
National Bank of Boyertown
Boyertown, Pennsylvania

Christopher M. Korth, Associate Professor of International Business
University of South Carolina
Columbia, South Carolina

D. J. MacDonald, Vice President
Community Bank
Los Angeles, California
(Formerly Vice President, Security Pacific National
Bank, Los Angeles)

Roderick M. MacDougall, Chairman
New England Merchants National Bank
Boston, Massachusetts

W. Thomas Maloan, Senior Vice President and Director of
Education and Training
Thunderbird Financial Corporation
Shawnee, Oklahoma
(Formerly Senior Vice President, Commerce Union
Bank, Nashville, Tennessee)

Charles F. Mansfield, Jr., Vice President, Harrison, New York Branch
Citibank
Harrison, New York
(Formerly with Citibank's Paris Branch)

Hubert C. Mott, Senior Vice President
United Jersey Bank
Hackensack, New Jersey

P. Henry Mueller, Chairman Credit Policy Committee
Citicorp and Citibank, N.A.
New York, New York

Jerome S. Oldham, Senior Vice President and Senior Loan Officer
Fidelity Bank of Denver
Denver, Colorado
(Formerly Commercial Loan Officer, Commonwealth
Bank and Trust Company, Williamsport, Pennsylvania)

Gerald D. Quill, President
Southeastern Pennsylvania Development Fund
Philadelphia, Pennsylvania

A. Bruce Schimberg, General Counsel, NCFC and Partner
Sidley & Austin
Chicago, Illinois

Nancy Seawahl, Assistant Vice President and International
Economist
Detroit Bank & Trust Company
Detroit, Michigan
Bruce D. Shuter, Esq., Partner
Drinker, Biddle & Reath
Philadelphia, Pennsylvania
Alford C. Sinclair, President, Jacksonville Region
Atlantic National Bank of Florida
Jacksonville, Florida
A. Thomas Small, Vice President and Counsel
First Union National Bank of North Carolina
Raleigh, North Carolina
Roger K. Soderberg, President, Ursus, Inc.
Also with Soderberg & Doll
Salem, Massachusetts
(Formerly with Exeter International Corporation,
Boston, Massachusetts)
Dev Strischek, Vice President
Southeast Bank
Ft. Lauderdale, Florida
(Formerly Vice President, Commerce Bank of Kansas
City, N.A., Kansas City, Missouri)
Peter J. Tischler, Vice President, London Branch
Mellon Bank, N.A.
London, England
Charles A. Tritschler, Associate Professor, School of Management
Purdue University
West Lafayette, Indiana
F. William Vandiver, Jr., Senior Vice President
North Carolina National Bank
Charlotte, North Carolina
Charles S. Zimmerman, Vice President
The Citizens and Southern National Bank
Atlanta, Georgia

xiv

Classics in Commercial Bank Lending

I. Overview

The articles making up this section of the book have been selected to introduce the reader to basic aspects of the commercial bank lending decision process from a broad perspective. These articles establish a context for the more detailed discussions that follow and provide a framework which helps define the responsibilities of the loan officer. They also suggest the types of psychological problems with which the officer must contend. The authors of these articles are all very experienced senior bankers.

The section begins with an article by P. Henry Mueller, "Learning from Lending," in which he draws on his vast experience to identify briefly the problem areas in lending. Two articles by Edward F. Gee follow, the first setting forth eleven basic rules for the loan officer. These rules may seem to be something like the Boy Scout oath, but Gee writes so engagingly, and the rules are so enduring, that the article was a natural for the collection.

The second article by Gee, "Constructive Lending in Constrictive Times," originally appeared in 1971, but the contents are just as relevant today as the title is. The interest rates he cites are tame by comparison with those of the late 1970s and early 1980s, but the 20 rules of thumb, covering a wide range of topics, are classics.

The final article in this section, "Some Thoughts on the Slings and Arrows of the Banking Profession" by Roderick M. MacDougall, focuses on a different aspect of lending: the seldom-addressed fact that bankers have the tough job of saying "no." In an amusing but perceptive article, MacDougall discusses the problems this responsibility creates for the banker and the ways they may be confronted if not entirely eliminated.

For information about the authors of the articles in Section I, refer to the List of Contributors on page xi.

1

Learning from Lending

by P. Henry Mueller

Traditionally, my "learning from lending" talks
have followed an Aesop's fable format to pinpoint problem areas in bank
lending, cite morals, and suggest remedies. Because 1974 saw banking probe the
limits of its lending capacity, my comments here are broader in scope. I shall
offer a few propositions for further thought on (1) how banks arrived at their
current lending postures, (2) the hairline risk/return balance which, unskillfully
weighed, makes banks investors rather than lenders, and (3) certain measures
Citibank is taking to manage present and future risks.

Aldous Huxley is said to have remarked: "I peered into the future and it won't
work." As a minimum, that's the equivalent of a I A classification of the world by
the national bank examiners. Lending officers can ill afford to embrace this view,
but I do suggest that circumstances make it fitting for them to reassess the
application of their skills and take a fresh look at their objectives before pressing
on.

This article is based on an address which Mr. Gee made during the Asset Management Conference sponsored by the Virginia Bankers Association.

2

Good times not synonymous with good loans

The years 1955 and 1974 were watersheds in commercial bank lending, but for opposite reasons. Loan officers went back into action in 1955 after hovering around for the preceding 20 or so years that securities portfolios exceeded loans. By 1974, after two decades of loan growth, climaxed by a spate of exuberant asset building, a striking change took place. Lenders at last found "for real" that loan volume, loan pricing, and loan quality do, in fact, impact capital and the ability to raise it. They also had a sensation of *déjà vu* as they witnessed the disarming effects of prosperity (a few rascals for borrowers), sound lending practice fallen into disregard and bad loans made in good times. The response was a tighter band around the lenders' money, with emphasis on asset selectivity, basic lending principles, and return on assets and capital.

Changes in bank lending patterns

The fundamental that has shaped bank lending from the 1950's, when banks were challenged to seek out new and profitable outlets, to the present, has been the shift from seasonal lending to the underwriting of term risks in banking's various markets. The evolution of lending philosophy, like Darwinian theory, is influenced by the impact of alterations in the environment it serves. Over time, marketing shifts and distribution changes that impacted the flow of goods and cash, obsoleted seasonal bank lending, set the stage for consumer lending by banks and finance companies, and perhaps ultimately contributed to the sourcing of loans with negotiable CD's, which have been upstaging the demand deposit.

Certainly the demand for ever-more-expensive machinery, aircraft, ships and plants was largely responsible for the mutant we call the term loan, which is really a high-technology version of the old asset-based bank loan, the critical difference being that the vestigial self-liquidating feature is sometimes so difficult to identify that one scarcely believes it is there at all. The banks' term lending philosophy as it evolved in the last 20 years has been impressively buttressed by parallel evolution in the thinking of accountants, financial executives and business schools.

The "3c's" still apply

All this has affected the nature of many of the loans commercial banks are called upon to carry. Credit quality has suffered from undue emphasis on finely tuned cash flow as the "way out" and too little attention to the goodness of the credit and how it is structured, whether its purpose is to meet a seasonal need, finance construction of a vessel, or provide for a consumer want. Time-tested principles and standards, from the 3 C's on up, still form the template to be placed against credit in any form, short or term.

Risk follows the outreach of maturity, and this calls for a keener feel of what the risks are. When short-term credit was the mainstay of the portfolio, loans supposedly were repayable in the current year, generally 60 or 90 days, and rarely beyond six months. Even so, there were demand loans and rotating bank lines which may have represented more permanent credit than some of today's term loans. The balance-sheet banker's chief interest was an evaluation of inventory and receivables, periodic bank and trade checkings, and the reputation and standing of the borrower. The figures describing a company needed only to extend from one year to the next, for lending was geared to a 2:1 liquidating concept rather than to underwriting a company's life tenure.

More to cash flow than meets the eye

There are more moving parts to credit extension when the span of exposure runs to several years. The basic lending technique used is, of course, the cash-flow approach, with debt repayment related primarily to a flow of funds which will permit regular amortization. A successful past record and proper ratios are still important, but it is essential to dig even more deeply behind the figures, consider the product line, the competitive position in the industry, the break-even point, the validity of projections, the character, competence, and experience of the management and how the competition views it, and the margin for contingencies, to cite a few points.

In this kind of lending bankers are considerably at the mercy of their informants—treasurers, comptrollers and others on whose word they may have to rely; hence, one must guard against becoming too compliant. When we do drift into problems it is usually because we have not gone sufficiently behind the figures or have been diverted by visions of attractive earnings opportunities. This, incidentally, does not seem to be so with institutional lenders whose risks extend beyond the bank lending range. Mr. Richard Dicker, vice president and associate general counsel of the Equitable Life Assurance Society of the U.S., stated a little over a year ago that "in some four decades of direct placement financing done by the Equitable on an unsecured basis for large and moderate-sized corporate business enterprises, involving many billions of dollars, there have been only two default situations in which a monetary loss has been sustained and in both of these cases the recovery exceeded well over 90 cents on the dollar." We obviously have much to learn.

Mistakes start in the mind, and false assumptions must lead to wrong decisions. Curiosity is an essential quality; unfortunately, we sometimes find out lots more about a company after it gets into trouble than before.

Look twice before you leap

Bankers have been almost exclusively cash-flow oriented for the past several years. There should never have been any question about the need for more than one way out of a loan of any type, but by 1974 the need to look carefully at the quality of each borrower's assets and liabilities, as well as income statement, took on fresh importance. What happens, for example, if sales should fall off 5%? 10%? 15%, or even plateau? Do costs also reduce proportionately? What is the impact of protracted high interest costs on highly leveraged borrowers? What is the borrower's capacity for further debt and where could it be obtained? Will you become the lender of last resort? In the current period, the small- to moderate-sized borrower is particularly vulnerable, although no borrower is immune.

Despite the sophistication that has been developed, a term loan is still best made to well established, successful enterprises with historically demonstrated cash generation to give every reasonable assurance of meeting the interest and amortization requirements of the loan, with ample margin for contingencies, including realistic net working capital, and leverage provisions to serve as a guarantee of performance of such requirements.

The increasing need for a safety margin

These are the highlights of our increasing move from seasonal, balance-sheet lending, where our knowledge had traditionally focused, into a broader, more complex variety of lending. But in our profession, things don't necessarily go by the book. A look at 1974 provides insight into the danger of removing one's self too far from the core principles of lending money.

While the principles and policies of term lending have generally been proven out over the span of some 35 years, the major business change we are now undergoing may well prove the necessity of providing even greater margins of safety. Unforeseen factors have always been a certainty, but the current scene points further to the peril of ignoring this axiom, whether the times are good or bad. There is no substitute for a well conceived loan that is well policed, and I should think lending officers would prefer to manage risks instead of vice versa. Where, in particular, did credits get off the track in '74?

Inflation effects

The unexpected double-digit inflation, with the high interest rates that accompanied it, introduced a critical element, especially since the strength of borrowers had been built in a history of price stability. Inflation erodes capital. Balance sheets and their normal ratios are distorted. Traditional financial reporting doesn't reflect changes in purchasing power, nor does the tax structure. Debt rises because, among other things, depreciation is inadequate and inventories are more costly to replace. Invested capital is understated, and profits are overstated, taxed away and, in any event, difficult to evaluate.

With our current inflation came expanded bank borrowings as borrowers and non-bank lenders were unwilling to enter into long-term commitments. With the leverage and liquidity of borrowers pushed to the limits, backstop lines that allegedly would never be used suddenly became real and, of course, there was in most instances no way to redress the balance sheet through the sale of equity. Other contingent liabilities, oftentimes in the past not viewed too seriously, came to life: "Takeouts" evaporated. "Take or pay" contracts became "pay" contracts. Traditionally liquid "bulletproof" credits congealed. On top of this, new business zeal in pursuit of market share caused lending officers to bore with too big an auger. In some instances, hog-sized hunks of credit had been extended to acceptable but actually marginal- or middle-grade credits.

A basic tenet of corporate finance is that permanent needs should be met with permanent money. Too often banks found themselves proxies for both the equity and long-term debt markets, having made no realistic provision for a second way out of their loans. A major shortcoming was lending to overleveraged, overambitious borrowers with excessive emphasis on cash-flow.

If they ever really existed, "the days of wine and roses" drew to a close, and some lending officers learned for the first time that, when a borrower is in trouble, his troubles become the bank's troubles. Hopefully both senior management and lending officers have learned that you don't get into a credit unless you're willing to live with it.

Longer commitment, longer thinking

Departing Eden, Adam is alleged to have remarked to Eve: "This, darling, is an age of transition." The exercise of credit judgment is self-evidently bound up with the business cycle. Longer commitments make it necessary for lenders to make longer bets on the management, earnings, and trade position of borrowers. Decisions must be made in the context of ongoing activity and the drift of events. I must admit to a road-map theorem of lending which postulates that the behavior of both borrowers and lenders is fairly predictable in any given phase of the cycle and that many lending mistakes repeat themselves when this is ignored. It is essential to anticipate the risks likely to arise when economic signals change.

A generation ago, the Marines—an outfit known to take a pragmatic approach—had an unwritten battle doctrine to the effect that if you get killed it's your own fault. They obviously didn't have in mind *force majeure*, but anything short of that was taken seriously and, when fundamentals taught in training were violated, survivors were appropriately disciplined. The results spoke for themselves. When lending mistakes repeat themselves, as they too frequently do, and we seek out clues as to why, too many are found to be of the lending officer's own doing for one reason or another.

Did, for example, the banks encourage the REIT's to paint themselves into a corner with cheap bank lines that ultimately became commercial paper backstop lines, which, in times of stress, were hard to hold together, by Eurodollar facilities, by documentary discount notes, by not being demanding enough about the competence of management, and by not looking to see where the money was going or to the source of repayment?

Tripping over pebbles

"Pilot errors" that deserve mention include accepting insufficient facts about a borrower and ignoring track records, financing start-up situations with immature management and entrepreneurial overcommitment, and depending upon continued economic growth. Failure to take collateral early, loans to holding companies—some of which didn't hold together, lack of understanding of various markets here and abroad, overgenerosity and loans for poor purposes are much too common for comfort. The influence of noises in the marketplace can lead the unwary to take unreasonable risks to maintain position.

Lending to companies too debt-heavy on the short end as opposed to the funded position; overcompensation in the direction of figures versus qualitative measures, including character; accepting more than normal risks in making capital loans involving new types of activities to managements unable to cope with enlarged scope; lack of well reasoned follow-up as opposed to nominal follow-up; deficient documentation; and waiving provisions of loan agreements too readily without weighing carefully explanations of deviations and thinking of the bank first (this would include material adverse change provisions) should be included in any list of faulty judgments.

The list is endless, but its message points to either a shortcoming in selection, training, or simply disregard of sound practice. The fact that much of it is not new is worrisome, and it also makes one wonder whether bankers take time to absorb the complexities of transactions and what can be done about them or, particularly, whether they think deeply about how liquid a loan will be before they undertake the engagement.

Bank lenders more frequently trip on pebbles—basics if you will—than on boulders. We must not lose sight of the fact that each lending officer influences the standards in the marketplace by the terms and conditions he either proposes or is willing to accept. It's pretty serious business, since lending money is still banking's primary earnings source.

Unfortunately, 1975 does not promise to be any more a forgiving economy than was 1974. The likelihood is that more marginal borrowers will run out of gas or be forced to the wall, and the name of the game, as always, will be to remain alert to ambush so as to be able to take remedial action before the options to do so are foreclosed. The most immediate task is to look carefully at our present portfolios, to identify and hand-hold credits that need bolstering or restructuring, in order to maximize recoveries in soft situations.

"Propriety" the necessary third dimension

Faced with the ongoing and increased need for banks to keep their liquidity in good repair, lending should be more than two-dimensional and go beyond the age-old test of asset coverage and cash generation plus profitability. The necessary third dimension is "propriety," which seems to have fallen by the wayside. Propriety doesn't relate to the goodness of the loan *per se*, nor to its return to the bank, but rather to its appropriateness from two standpoints: (1) is it consistent with the bank's overall loan portfolio objectives? and (2) is it really the most suitable financing vehicle for the borrower? This presses the lending officer's professional resources and diplomatic skills. How he or she handles these should be made part of the officer's evaluation.

The backdrop must, of couse, be provided by senior management itself, for in the '70's banks yielded to the temptation of trying to be all things to all borrowers. Many had mixed objectives and confused focus on where they should be headed. They need to pick their markets well, tool up for them, target the names, and not be diverted. Lending mistakes are bound to occur and be repeated unless the focus on corporate objectives at all organizational levels is clear.

In Citibank, the budgeting process, which is developed annually from the grass roots and reviewed quarterly, is the process by which objectives are identified, refined, and implemented on a unit by unit basis in terms of specific strategy. Each lending officer is committed to this, which then becomes one of several elements in evaluating individual performance. Volume and type of exposures are scrutinized by senior management in the annual and quarterly review process. Sovereign risk guidelines for some 100 countries in which we do business are derived through a process which is entirely independent of the budgeting of target loan volumes.

Delegation of responsibility and accountability

In terms of credit extension, accountability goes hand-in-hand with the delegation of responsibility. As banking grows, and becomes more complex, this should be tightened. It is also important that we break with the lending-mistakes-repeat-themselves syndrome. Too often credits are made riskier by the lending officer because of such things as poor structuring, lack of follow-through, or poor credit habits. We require at Citicorp certain reasonable standards and disciplines. We expect lending officers to be scrupulously provident and to act responsibly in evaluating risks and in negotiating terms, conditions, and position, and in the area of follow-up and credit housekeeping. This leaves no margin for miscast venture capitalists.

We don't weigh excellent or unsatisfactory performance on the basis of factors beyond the individual's control, but we do, for example, expect that a lending officer will grasp thoroughly the transaction and its details, that he or she will analyze its future variables and make adequate allowance for reasonable judgment of their impact. "Reasonable judgment" could prove to be wrong, but we want to be certain that a "reasonable judgment" was, in fact, arrived at. If satisfied as to the likely outcome, it is expected that the loan will be appropriately structured and buttoned up with documentation that will hold water.

We expect that our rules governing credit extension will be observed in spirit as well as word, that reasoned follow-through and credit administration will not be brushed aside by the more glamorous lure of growth and income, that pricing dynamics will be understood and nonincremental pricing avoided, and the consultation on contemplated commitments will be timely. A lack of perception of problems and an unwillingness to face up to them would not measure up.

By means of weekly meetings, at which examples are cited, the lending groups make clear what is considered satisfactory and unsatisfactory. And, in inspecting each domestic and overseas credit unit, our internal examiners, who report through the comptroller to the board of directors, comment on the structuring and policing of credits, on the adherence to policies, rules and procedures, and on credit ability, training and experience.

Backup and review

In order to learn from the past, a portion of each monthly meeting of senior staff credit officers is devoted to a critique of "bum" loans. Loans that are discussed underscore such aspects as these: knowing your borrower; letters of comfort; lending to regulated industries; guarantees; one-way out loans; lending to holding companies; family management—all critical areas. When something turns sour, we look for clues we might have had and then look at other credits that could move into comparable straits. We hope some of this preventive medicine will pay off.

Our lending mechanism provides strong backup to the delegated responsibility/accountability concept. Although we pursue a grass roots approach to lending, we have a clearly defined and operative centralized policy setting and review process. When credits under consideration in any part of Citicorp here or abroad embrace some ten or so features which experience has taught us may be fraught with enlarged risk, the lending officers involved must persuade Credit Policy Supervision that there are warranting factors. For example, it is mandatory to discuss credits beyond a certain tenor, amount, sovereign risk, or those which involve an increase to a classified loan.

Lending officers are expected to review their credit exposure on an ongoing basis, and it is also expected that they will identify a troublesome credit well prior to its being assigned a negative classification by any of the various internal or external examiners. The system works well.

When a loan is classified by any authority, its status must be reported monthly in the more serious categories, and otherwise quarterly. Projections of anticipated outstandings a month hence and at year-end, plus a statement of the strategy being pursued to remedy it, are provided. These are carefully reviewed at senior levels. The report reaffirms to the lending officer his or her accountability.

Training and retraining

Needless to say, credit training programs are reviewed regularly to ensure that they reflect our needs. The education and development of each junior lending officer is part of the daily responsibility of his or her more senior associates. I should add that management exhortations about this have their limitations, for some officers possess a skill for absorbing what comes and then going their own ways. However, for those who would succeed in credit, one's own efforts at self-improvement are critical. The best banker is the first to admit that he still has much to learn.

It always seems fruitless to see the wheel reinvented. This usually arises in instances where talent is long but experience short. Gaps in an individual's training may surface, too. The tuition paid in credit losses and management time is unacceptably high. Two things business schools have yet to underwrite are experience and common sense, and both are needed when problems walk off the pages of the book. One way to cure the first is to be sure that juniors work under the close supervision and guidance of mature and seasoned lending officers; the cure for the second is "selection out" of credit work.

Some wisdom that has already survived two generations in our bank is still apt: "It takes a credit officer of only average intelligence to make the right decision on a loan if he has all the facts. The difference between a smart lending officer and one who is not is that the former has the intelligence and takes the time to obtain all the pertinent facts before he reaches his decision.''

Eternal vigilance is the price

If banks are to make loans that will be good in all seasons, continuous hands-on management is necessary at all levels. Since bad loans are usually made in good times, there is no time out for relaxation. The 1974 experience implies something about concentration on volume and reaching for business at the expense of quality. The burden placed on the credit process, and on lending officers themselves, therefore needs close watching. Also important to follow is whether the bank's credit mechanism keeps pace with changes in organization and management style.

In sum, credit extension is hardly an exact science, but adherence to fundamental principles, found by experience to be sound, can provide reasonable assurance against loss. When you think of straying, watch out. If you get ''killed,'' it could be your own fault! ☐

Eleven Rules for Loan Officers

by Edward F. Gee

1. Condition yourself to look upon each loan request as a challenge and an opportunity—not a chore.

When a loan applicant approaches your desk, or calls you on the telephone, look at it this way: Here's an opportunity to put to work the things I know; to bring to bear the experience I've acquired; to function as the banker I'm supposed to be. Here's a challenge to my judgment; a chance to use my brain; a test of my discretion. Here's a problem to be solved; to be analyzed, evaluated and concluded to the advantage of the bank, the applicant and the community. Here, in all probability, is an opportunity to grow, to increase my effectiveness—by learning more about a man, a business, an industry and economic conditions generally.

Note: This article was first published 20 years ago in what was then known as the RMA Bulletin. However, because of the timeliness of the author's message, the article was reprinted in the November 1976 *Journal*.

2. Don't prejudge or pre-evaluate but listen attentively, intelligently, under-standingly and sympathetically.

This sounds easy but it is one of the most difficult things a human being can do. Failure to understand and observe this simple rule is the greatest barrier to effective communication between two people. We see, hear and understand others only in terms of our own frame of reference. We judge ourselves by our thoughts—others by their actions and words as interpreted by the varying meanings that such actions and words may have for us. We must strive to hear precisely what the other fellow says and then to understand why he said it and what he really meant. Only after we have listened attentively and sympatheti-cally and have understood intelligently should we attempt to judge or evaluate. Most of us don't listen—we get the gist of what the applicant is saying but are so busy thinking of what we're going to say, prejudging and pre-evaluating, that we fail to hear and understand him fully.

3. Don't pretend to have knowledge you don't have or about which you are doubtful.

The mark of a wise man is his acknowledgment of his limitations. He knows he has a respectable fund of knowledge about many things and so is never hesitant in asking questions about other things he doesn't know or about which he is doubtful. When an applicant assumes incorrectly that you know certain things about him or his business or his industry, or even about banking or law, it is tempting, but extremely dangerous, to let him proceed on that assumption. It's human nature to gloss it over and hope the point or the facts can be picked up later. Try never to yield to this weakness—stop him promptly, set him straight on your deficiencies, ask him questions, and don't proceed until you are abso-lutely sure of your ground. You'll command his respect, avoid any inkling of ever appearing a phony and achieve a far firmer base for your conclusions.

4. Keep pushing yourself back from the details (though they must be covered) in order to stand off and view the credit as a unified whole.

We can become so immersed in figures and details as to lose sight of, or give inadequate attention to, the broad strengths or weaknesses of the credit as a whole. We can get off on one limb and run it down to the tip of a twig while overlooking some other limb and failing to get a true over-all concept of the whole tree. Keep standing off for perspective to see that the picture is complete, that nothing has been left out, that no loose ends remain. Keep looking at the tree, the whole tree, and its place in the forest about it.

5. *Remember that, with respect to a loan, it's not simply "how good" but also "how liquid."*

A safe loan is a loan that, to the extent determinable, is free from ultimate loss. A sound loan is a safe loan that can be repaid within its maturity terms without hardship or stress on the borrower. It is not enough for a loan to be safe; it must also be sound. A borrower must not only have adequate statement strength or adequate security, he must also have adequate repayment ability. Bank loans are made to be repaid, not to employ funds permanently with each borrower. However strong the statement or however good the security, always ask yourself this question: "How is he going to pay it back?"

6. *Don't commit yourself prematurely before getting all the facts, considering all the aspects and deliberating adequately.*

On every loan desk, there might well be this reminder: "Of thy unspoken word thou art master." Don't speak the word until you're prepared to do so and until you're prepared to be bound by its consequences. Don't announce the outcome until all the votes are in. Be sure you have all the facts, that every consideration has been weighed, before you commit yourself on any point or in any way at any stage of the discussion. Once a statement is prematurely made, or a decision prematurely announced, you'll be so busy trying to justify your position, then and thereafter, that judgment and reason may well be ignored.

7. *Don't attribute the dirty work to "the loan committee" or "the board" or "the bank" or "the head office."*

If anything smacks of treason in banking, this is it—indicating or implying to an applicant that you might well agree with him but that the loan refusal or the rate increase or the request for security or endorsements, or some other dis-agreeable decision, is the work of "the loan committee" or "the board" or "the bank" or of "those people at the head office." No attitude is more to be deplored in a responsible banking official. You represent the bank; you are the bank; you must assume or share ("*we* think; "*we* have decided; "*we*" have concluded) full responsibility for any decision that is made by the bank however little you may have contributed to it and however little you may agree with it. Your responsibil-ity is to argue the merits of the decision within the bank; once it is made it becomes your decision also—as long as you remain a part of the bank. If it then needs defending, you must defend it as your own decision. Any other course is but little short of seditious.

8. *Never apologize or beat around the bush when, after mature deliberation on all the facts, you have to turn down a loan request or lay down a requirement or rate you suspect will be unhappily received.*

Timidity has no place in a loan officer's makeup. Be sure of your ground, evaluate carefully, then say straight out what your considered judgment dictates, without apology or hesitation because you suspect it may prove disagreeable. Make it a point to look the applicant straight in the eye when you say it—you don't have to be evasive or uncertain when you're convinced of the soundness of your grounds. On occasion, perhaps to your surprise, you'll have your judgment confirmed, then or later—an applicant will admit he would have thought you foolish to lend him the money, or that he really knew you were going to insist upon endorsements or collateral, or that he has simply asked for a 4% rate because he would have been perfectly happy with 5% and thought you were going to charge 6%.

9. *Accept full responsibility and make decisions promptly on your own when you know you have all the facts, have considered all aspects of the case and have sound reasons for the decisions you make.*

There is no reason to seek guidance from others or to share the responsibility with others when you are acting within your authority, when you are confident of your facts, and when you have confidence in your judgment. Seek counsel and guidance only when you are unsure—never simply to shift or dilute your responsibility. When you are certain, act. But see to it that your action is not motivated to any degree by a desire to show your authority or that you have the power to act without consulting others. Decisions affected by so pernicious an influence are more likely to be wrong than right.

10. *When you have concluded from the facts and your deliberations that you are going to say "yes," say it ungrudgingly.*

Most problems in life have shades of gray—they're neither all white nor all black. When you've concluded that you're going to grant a loan request, you must have decided that the white outweighs the black. Let it go at that and concede to the white as graciously as you can. Don't burden the applicant with the impression that you're doing him a rare favor or that he has talked you into doing something against your better judgment. If you're going to lend the money, don't taint it in the process. Weaknesses that might be helped through constructive comment should be discussed *before* the decision is reached; once reached, a favorable decision overrides such weaknesses and should be given positively and ungrudgingly.

11. Don't place too much dependence on any set of rules like this.

Lending money soundly and constructively is primarily a matter of applying intelligence to the facts in each case, based on the broadest possible background of knowledge and experience. Intelligence, in a way, is simply common sense—or perhaps uncommon sense. It is the inborn and God-given ability of an individual to apply his knowledge and experience, however limited or however great, to the successful solution of a new problem. To some extent, every loan is one of those new problems. Rules and suggestions may enrich your background but they won't make your credit decisions. Sound lending requires intelligence—making up rules like these is something anybody can do. I've proved it.   ☐

Constructive Lending in Constrictive Times

by Edward F. Gee

THIS AGNEW-ESQUE TOPIC is not of my own choosing although, I must say, I'm just square enough to like it. It was assigned to me some months ago when, from the standpoint of bank liquidity at least, the times were considerably more constrictive than they are at the moment. Aided by some Q-relief, some relative easing in loan demand, and a changed Federal Reserve policy that has resulted in an almost continuous increase in our money supply since February, there has been a remarkable turn-around in bank liquidity trends in just a relatively few months.

". . . the times are constrictive,
and . . . . are likely to remain so . . . . in the foreseeable future."

At the end of February, the 13,600 commercial banks in the country had aggregate loans amounting to about 71% of their aggregate gross deposits and had aggregate short-term borrowings in the $23 billion range. In the ensuing nine months, total deposits have been increased by about 10% while total loans have increased by about half this rate. As a result, the ratio of loans to gross deposits has eased down a little, and aggregate short-term borrowings by banks have been reduced significantly.

This article is based on an address which Mr. Gee made during the Asset Management Conference sponsored by the Virginia Bankers Association.

In short, the shoe still pinches, but the throbbing has eased, temporarily. With this new-found freedom from pain, the money-center banks began to feel they were back in bedroom slippers and promptly began to cut the prime rate—from 8½% to 8% in March, from 8% to 7½% in September, from 7½% to 7¼% in early November, and from 7¼% to 7% ten days later—an aggregate proportionate drop of about 18% over this period.

But the times, of course, are still constrictive, and I think the odds are that they are likely to remain so, relatively, in this business of lending throughout the foreseeable future. I think the days of those ridiculously low loan to deposit ratios of 20% to 25% that we saw in the '40s are gone forever (actually, as of the end of 1945, the aggregate loans of all commercial banks in the United States amounted to only 17% of their aggregate deposits). The days are gone forever of those 30% to 40% ratios we saw in the '50s and of those comfortable 50% to 60% ratios we saw in the early '60s. It's my guess that from now on we are going to see loan to deposit ratios that, in the aggregate, stay up in that 65% to 75% range. With a float factor that, for many banks, may average 20% or more of demand deposits and maybe 10% or more of total deposits, this means that we are talking about aggregate loans that may average from 80% to 90% or more of average daily usable deposits. For some time now, this has been and in my opinion, will continue to be, the neat tightwire balancing act for all bank managements—keeping fully loaned in an effort to meet demand and to maintain earnings in the face of constantly rising expenses and trying to keep from being knocked off the wire by unexpected deposit or loan fluctuations, including the unexpected use of existing lines of credit or of other express or implied commitments.

And certainly, from the standpoint of bank earnings, the times continue constrictive, if not equally, they are more so from the standpoint of the earnings of virtually all our business borrowers.

All these factors combine clearly to put a premium on constructive lending. And by constructive lending, I mean (1) lending that is good for the borrower, that will help him grow, and that can be comfortably repaid from his prospects *and* (2) lending that, from the standpoint of the bank, will not endanger its balancing act with an undue risk of poor loan quality or liquidity, and will not burden or endanger its future with inordinate loan losses. With the gross profit margin on the sale of our product confined to a relatively modest interest return, there always has been darn little margin for error, and there is even less so now.

With the fairly-full loan positions we are running today, and which seem likely to be our destiny for the future, the consequences of error can be far more drastic than when, as in 1945, we had over 80% of our total deposits in cash and Governments. The essentiality of loan quality to the soundness of our banks varies directly with our loan to deposit ratio. Today, it's a good four times more important for the soundness of our banks that we have high loan quality, keen lenders and alert loan officers than it was then. I'm not at all sure that the need has been recognized or that the requirement has been met.

**". . . more often than not
. . . losses are more the fault of the bank . . .
than the borrower."**

Constructive lending in any volume in any times will always involve a normal element of loss. The losses that can kill you, and often figuratively do, are those which are not normal, which arise from carelessness or negligence or inexperience, or from loans that clearly, from the beginning, violated every rule in the book. They are not the normal losses which may arise from the unexpected, but abnormal losses which arise from the should-have-been-foreseen. And more often than not, such losses are more the fault of the bank than they are the fault of the borrower.

They may arise, for example, from a loan that was supposedly adequately collateralized but against which, for some reason, a security interest was never perfected; from an unwarranted degree of dependence on collateral which, by its nature, would clearly have little or no value in the hands of the bank when the chips were down; from an unwarranted degree of dependence on an endorser whose worth, at the time, was clearly more fictional than real; or from collateral or endorsements that, while originally good, were permitted, for some reason, to deteriorate steadily without triggering any loan action. Losses can result from an unsecured loan to a business borrower who, for some reason, was permitted to delay in furnishing an annual statement that would clearly have shown him to be well on the way to bankruptcy; from financial statements that were received and filed but whose trends and significance, for some reason, were completely ignored; or from a loan whose repayment was clearly dependent on new capital but for which, for some reason, no underwriting or take-out commitment was first obtained. Sometimes they result from the bank's procrastination, for some reason, in obtaining security or endorsements when the need was evident and while the security and endorsements were available; from a loan that, clearly from the beginning, had no reasonable way of being repaid within the loan officer's lifetime; or from continuing and increasing loans to a borrower that simply encouraged him to continue beyond his depth and caused him eventually to drown in a sea of debt. In short, the bank is at fault when losses arise from loans that were made, from some reason, in an amount, for a duration, or a risk disproportionate to all common sense.

"... Forces at work
that can cause the unburnt loan officer ... to be trapped ..."

Unfortunately for banks, there seem to be forces at work that can cause the unburnt loan officer or credit analyst to be trapped into approving loans which should never have been approved in the first place. These forces would all seem to be completely innocuous and inconsequential in themselves, but experience has shown that they do seem to have a way of fuzzing up our thought processes.

"... the unfortunate fact that balance sheets balance."

First, there is the unfortunate fact that balance sheets balance. Assets on the one side and debts and net worth on the other, are all precise amounts that balance to the penny. This tends, to the unwary, to invest the figures with a precision and a solidity that are not warranted by accounting principles and practices. Estimates, approximations and judgmental values are always involved, principally in inventories but to some extent in receivables and liabilities. And when you get down below the current asset line, accounting conventions call for figures that may have no relationship whatsoever to realizable asset values. For example, in an accounting sense, fixed assets are, for the most part, simply deferred charges to future operations. The amounts at which these future operating charges are carried on the books are determined merely by cost-spreading accounting devices and not by any relationship to asset value. And accounting principles call for creating and assigning a value to certain other assets, unamortized bond discount, unamortized research and development costs, and so on that are openly and obviously without value of any kind in a debt-paying sense. So, it may be most unfortunate for the young credit analyst that balance sheets always balance.

"... with 'figure myopia,' they lose sight of the forest for the 'threes,' "

Secondly, there is the related force that we might call "figure myopia." Bankers and credit men, in considering loans, find themselves working constantly with figures. They get conditioned to figures, and eventually they get completely addicted to the figures. At that point, a sort of myopia sets in. They can see the figures and the figures only, not the assets the figures represent. They begin to think in terms of the inventory figure, not in terms of the racks of bolts, or shelves of goods, or stacks of materials or piles of junk that the inventory figure really is or may be. They begin to think in terms of the machinery and equipment figure, not in terms of the rusting machinery and unsalable equipment that the machinery and equipment figure really may be. They begin to think in terms of the real estate figure, not in terms of the special-purpose building or the low-lying swampland that the real estate figure really may be. In short, with figure myopia, they lose sight of the forest for the "threes."

". . . the net worth syndrome."

Then, there is what might be called the net worth syndrome. When you have a young man in your bank who begins to think or to talk or to write credit memos or to lend money in terms only of a borrower's or endorser's net worth, you may well have a sick loan man, or a sick loan, or both, on your hands. What he may have failed to focus on, and what you both may later wish he had, is that a $100,000 net worth is simply the mathematical difference between a hard total of $1,000,000 in debts and a mushy total of $1,100,000 in assets. Or that a $1,000,000 net worth is simply the mathematical difference between a hard total of $10,000,000 in debts and a mushy total of $11,000,000 in assets. So, it is always far from reasonable to assume that a man with a $100,000 net worth should certainly be good for a $5,000 loan or a $5,000 endorsement or that a business with a million-dollar net worth should certainly be a reasonable risk for a $100,000 loan or a $100,000 guarantee.

As of December 31, 1969, the Penn Central Transportation Company showed a net worth of $1,805,372,000.00. Six months later, as all banks know, and some very painfully so, it was bankrupt. The net worth figure should never be the focus of a loan decision.

The focus, of course, should always and clearly be first on the present and projected debts of the borrower, the endorser, or of the guarantor. How much do the debts aggregate now and with the proposed new debt, how do they mature, and how and from what source or sources can they be paid when they fall due? That obviously should be the first thought in considering a loan, in talking about a loan, or in writing a credit memo. The net worth figure is only a residual or an incidental consideration. When we find ourselves or others using it as the primary consideration, the net worth syndrome may be alerting us to a loan illness ahead.

". . . equalitarian semantics . . .
equating values in assets or collateral
to the names they are called . . ."

Next, there is the force that we might call equalitarian semantics. It tends to cause us to view all things with the same name as being equal. In looking at assets, and especially in lending against collateral, it traps bankers, particularly young bankers, into equating values in assets or collateral items to the names they are called: a savings account is a savings account, regardless of the soundness of the institution it is with; cash value of life insurance is cash value of life insurance, regardless of the size or condition of the company which issued the policy; an account receivable is an account receivable, regardless of the financial strength of the debtor; a stock is a stock, regardless of whose stock it is; a bond is a bond, regardless of who issued it; a take-out commitment is a take-out commitment, regardless of the size or condition of the permanent lender; a firm construction contract is a firm construction contract, regardless of the financial condition of the contractor which signed it; and so on down a treacherous list of unlikes being viewed as equals. None of these things has any value from its name alone; each requires that we consider individually the financial strength that backs it. If we fail to do so, we've fallen into the trap of equalitarian semantics.

". . . balance sheet bias . . .
the tendency to use the balance sheet alone
as the basis for a loan decision."

Lastly here, but by no means finally among these forces, is what might be called the balance sheet bias. If a one-day balance sheet, or a one-day statement of assets and debts, looks reasonably good, there is the tendency to use the balance sheet alone as the basis for a loan decision. Overlooked is the fact that that one-day point may now be well past, that nothing is static, and that in the intervening month, or three months or six months, the whole picture may have been changed completely.

With an individual, he may have, the very next day, mortgaged or sold his home, pledged or given away his stocks, or guaranteed some ill-fated venture that may make his name worthless, or certainly far less acceptable by the time you accept it or need it.

With a business, a series of past operating statements may have shown clearly that its substance was being depleted daily through operating losses and that, however strong its one-day balance sheet at some point in the past, you have no reasonable assurance that it won't be busted by the time your new loan matures. Normally, a business has but one function—to make money. If it is failing at that, it is obviously sick, and you can deal with it only at your peril. A balance sheet can tell you nothing of its health—it may be on the way up or on the way down, it may be as healthy as a cow, it may only have the sniffles or it may be eaten up by cancer. Only operating statements, and the trends they show, can tell you that. When we find ourselves or others using a past balance sheet as the be-all and end-all, we are fuzzing up our thinking with a balance sheet bias.

"The principles of constructive lending . . ."

The principles of constructive lending, as I have defined it, are precisely the same in constrictive times as they are in any times. Even if I knew them all, which I don't, and even if I could be certain of the soundness of the few I do know, which I can't, I couldn't begin to go into them all here. But I do have a few favorites, with which you may or may not agree, and I am going to use the rest of my time to try to list them briefly:

1. *Never ask for collateral or endorsements you don't need, but once you've asked for them don't waive the requirement.*

How many times have you heard, "He didn't want to give us collateral" or "He didn't want to ask his wife to endorse," and yet the loan was made? What the borrower wants or asks for becomes almost academic if, in the judgment of the loan officer, the need really exists. If it doesn't, the collateral or endorsement should never have been requested in the first place.

2. *Never wait until "next time" or until the "next maturity" to raise a rate or to get the collateral or endorsements you really feel are needed now.*

This is human nature at work—a tendency to take the easier course. But one postponement of a disagreeable step tends to make the next postponement easier, if not inevitable, and "next time" or "next maturity" may often prove too late. Eventually, when the fat's in the fire, the collateral or endorsements may be no longer available.

3. *Never reduce an existing loan rate at the time it is asked for, and never increase an existing loan rate that you are not prepared to make stick.*

If you reduce the rate when the borrower asks for it, you're really admitting that you've been gypping him all along. Preferably, you should review the fairness of all existing loan rates as frequently as you review existing loan quality and should adjust them promptly and voluntarily to the levels you are fully prepared to defend. This is heavenly theory, of course, but it can be hellish in practice.

4. *Always keep loan rates on long-term loans and on loan commitments as flexible as you possibly can.*

Banking's experience with old, fixed loan rates in 1966 and again in 1969 should cause it to be eternally wary of this trap in the future. In term-loan agreements or loan commitments, rates should be tied to the prime or to some other index of current money-costs—or never made firm in the first place except for some reasonable time. Mortgage papers might possibly be drawn with a right to review and and adjust rates at five-year intervals. Preferably, no fixed rate, in percentage terms, should ever be specified in naming a seasonal line of credit.

5. *Beware of equity-issue or debt-refunding repayment sources without firm underwriting or take-out commitments from responsible sources.*

No such loan should ever be made by a bank unless it is fully prepared to take the risk of a long-term payout from future earnings. Changed market or rate conditions may make this eventuality a reality despite the very best of intentions to fund-out later. If you are not prepared to be stuck with a work-out, you'd better get your firm commitment from a responsible source before, and not after, your loan is made.

6. *Never gamble on the stock market by making or continuing loans on thin margins to borrowers who have no substance or supplementary means of repayment.*

    Its been demonstrated that values in blue chips can be chipped away in the psychology of the marketplace as readily as they can disappear almost totally with the cats and dogs. And with such loans, particularly when the risk is compounded by a lack of quality or a lack of diversification, we are no longer lenders, we are clearly stock market speculators.

7. *Never make a business loan on the strength of a personal endorser without controlling, by agreement or otherwise, the disposition of his assets and the extent of his direct and contingent debts with others so long as the loan is outstanding.*

    On December 31, 1968, Lammot du Pont Copeland, Jr., showed, in a statement prepared by a certified public accountant, a personal net worth of $25,959,340.00. In October, 1970, according to the *Wall Street Journal*, he became one of the biggest personal bankruptcy cases on record, with his total debts reported at over $33 million in excess of all his indicated assets. About $40 million of his nearly $60 million in debts arose from his personal guarantee or endorsement on loans to his various business interests.

8. *Never fail to evaluate the financial statements of an endorser or guarantor as thoroughly as you would the statements of a borrower—what assets and/or earning power exist, and are they of a form and nature that can reasonably assure the repayment of all direct debts plus endorsed or guaranteed debts?*

9. *Never forget that, like faith, hope and charity, there are only three possible sources from which a loan to a business can be repaid: (1) from the conversion of assets to cash, (2) from earnings or other new capital, or (3) from the transfer of the loan to some other creditor.*

    Of these, the first, like faith, is the greatest. The second, like hope, is dependent on the future. The third, the least dependable of the three, may often literally be sheer charity.

10. *Never lend to a business without first seeing a current series of balance sheets and operating statements—and once you get them, don't ignore them; dissect them, compare them, and heed the story of their trends.*

    A balance sheet weakness can be acceptably offset by strong operating trends; few balance sheets can be sufficiently strong to outweigh the significance of a series of severe operating losses. A business with consistently strong earnings trends and prospects rarely gets into trouble that can't readily be cured.

11. *Never lose control of a credit—always keep in the driver's seat.*

Sometimes, unfortunately, that control doesn't exist from the beginning—there was, when you got in, no way you could get out without wrecking the vehicle and taking a loss. More often, it's lost during the course of the ride—through a failure to take action while you still had the power to do so. Try never to give up, through blind faith, carelessness or negligence, full control of the wheel.

12. *Never let a sleeping dog lie—look at him frequently and critically; if you don't you may stumble over him one day and find that he's dead.*

A formal program for reviewing all existing loans regularly, frequently, carefully, and critically is essential to the continued soundness of any bank's loan portfolio. Just because a loan looked good at the time it was made is no assurance it's going to remain good until it is paid. And, wherever applicable, this review procedure should include a thorough audit of the adequacy, currency and validity of all secured loan documentation.

13. *Beware of link-financing—account balances, as a rule, should always be in the borrower's name.*

14. *Never make or continue a loan against the assignment of accounts receivable without considering the risk of offsets, of sales returns and allowances, of non-performance, of lack of diversification, of weak or fictitious accounts and of a failure to follow and control all payments.*

15. *Always control your overdraft approvals as carefully as you control your new loan approvals and focus on your overdrafts as frequently and regularly as you focus on past-due notes.*

In more instances than one, the overdraft route has been the back door to a bank's vault and has led to substantial losses even when notes have been taken to cover. Why it is that a bank will pay over a customer's balance on a checking account when it wouldn't lend him another nickel on a new loan request is one of the intriguing mysteries of the banking business.

16. *Never forget in lending to contractors, that retainages and surety bonds are for the purpose of protecting the owner or the prime contractor—not the bank—and that mechanics' liens will, and a bonding company may, come ahead of the bank in its claims on a job.*

A favorite sport of the live-it-up loan officer is to lend against the assignment of contract receivables or contract retainages on uncompleted jobs as if they were money in the bank. There is no surer way to court disaster. And to have any feeling that the loan should be good because the contract is "bonded" is sheer absurdity unless, as is rarely the case, a special bond has been written for the protection of the bank.

17. *Beware of lending against equipment, particularly heavy or specialized equipment, on the strength of its cost value to the borrower.*

For some odd reason, its value is diminished on the day the bank takes its lien, and it's a rare down-payment that can offset the continuing diminution in value that becomes evident only when the bank has to offer the equipment for sale. It's clearly a case of a bird in the hands of the borrower being worth two in the hands of the bank.

18. *Beware the too-good deal.*

Risk tends always to increase proportionate to reward, and the loan proposal that offers the exceptionally-high rate, or the exceptionally-high balances, or the fat kicker on the side, always, like Mr. Lincoln's rathole, bears looking into.

19. *Never make a new loan to a business, or renew an existing loan, before a financial statement that is clearly due and should be available has been seen or at least discussed.*

A promise to bring in a delayed statement "next time" or to "send it down soon" is never as reliable as a view of the figures. Next best, and always indispensable in such instances, is a clear understanding of what the key figures actually show or are likely to show when they are received. We are faced now with a fairly significant loan loss because we failed to insist on the submission of a statement at the time it was clearly due and didn't find out until far too late that the business had lost much of its shirt and was continuing to lose the remainder.

20. *Never make a loan, regardless of all other consideration, without asking yourself, "How is he going to pay it back?"*

A loan is not a loan but a gift or an investment unless it is made to be paid back. Thus, even to know that we've made a loan, we've got to know how it's going to be repaid. That sounds so elementary as to be almost ridiculous but it's probably one of the most prevalent weaknesses in a loan officer's thinking. It's not enough for him to feel that a loan is good; to make a sound loan, he's got to know that it has a sound source and an acceptable-rate of repayment.

Throughout all this listing, I've been free with the use, primarily for emphasis, of a lot of "nevers." Of course, all of you know that, in this accelerating world of marvels and change, any rational person, particularly a banker, should never say "never." On some points, I'm willing to stick with being irrational; or others, you must remember that, in banking, there is never a "never" that never has an exception. But we've got to know our "nevers," of course, before we can know when and why we have made an exception.

That list was so long, I'm sure you thought it would never end. It hasn't—but I'm going to stop now because a speaker should never exceed his allotted time. ☐

Some Thoughts on the Slings and Arrows of the Banking Profession

by Roderick M. MacDougall

Shakespeare thought lending was an unpopular and unpleasant business. He would not likely change his mind if he looked at the banking industry today. So what's the compensation? Roderick MacDougall says it's professionalism.

We all know Shakespeare's admonition, "Neither a borrower nor a lender be." We are prone to forget, however, that the next line provides the reason for this advice: "For loan oft loses both itself and friend." In other words, don't lend money, because, first of all, you probably won't get it back, and, second, you will make an enemy in the process.

Much has been said over the last two years about the first problem—loan losses—which is an integral part of the banker's world. I don't intend to dwell on that too familiar subject. But I would like to review the other consequence of being a lender: unpopularity. I would like to discuss the ramifications of unpopularity for both lending officer and top management. I'll conclude by trying to convince you that such a lot is not all that bad.

This article is based on a speech given by the author to the RMA New England Chapter on April 19, 1977.

The no-win life of lenders

The primary function of a commercial bank is to serve as a financial intermediary which gathers the excess funds of individuals and businesses and reallocates those funds in ways that respond to the needs of individuals, businesses, and the community as a whole. Most important it ensures the return of the funds to the depositors when needed.

Given those guidelines and human nature being what it is, the effective lending officer has all the odds against him if his objective is to be popular and admired by all customers. Loan officers have the difficult job of separating the viable from the nonviable proposals. No statistics that I know of accurately reflect the number of loan requests made of the banking industry, but my guess would be that banks turn away two angry people for every one they satisfy.

The tough job of saying no

Aspiring entrepreneurs flock to commerical banks, convinced that their pet project is sound. Loan officers shoulder the tough job of pointing out that the shoe store they want to buy is located too far away from the heavy shopping areas, that they need to develop marketing experience before they set up an insurance agency, that the equity they have to invest is inadequate to absorb the projected first two years of losses, that their windmill needs to be perfected and patented before they borrow to produce it.

Certainly, most bank officers try to be constructive and helpful as they point out the fundamental weaknesses in a business proposal, but to most people on the other side of the desk, loan officers simply have neither vision nor faith. They are unimpressed when you tell them that there are between 10,000 and 12,000 business failures each year in the U.S. and that one-third of such failures occur in the first three years of operation.

Were you to tell loan applicants that approximately 93% of those business failures were due to the incompetence or inexperience of the owner or manager, it would have little impact. They wouldn't be at the bank unless they were convinced that their venture was bound to succeed and that they had the skills to make it work.

Most leave dejected, and more often than not, they tell their friends that the banker stymied their future. Sometimes they tell their Congressmen and state Representatives also. How is the politician to know that the constituent who complains to him about the lack of bank credit in his city represents a poor credit risk and that putting him in business could be a disservice to the community? Certainly the rejected borrower doesn't tell him.

It is unfortunately true that the opinions of governmental officials about commercial bankers are shaped to a great degree by disillusioned and unsuccessful businessmen. You contact your Congressman when you have a complaint, not when you want to throw bouquets. It is a rare customer who accepts the banker's logic behind the firm no. So, on balance, the scales are tipped against your popularity when you hang out a shingle that says, "Money for Sale."

Prudent advice not always well received

Judging new businesses is not the only battleground where loan officers pick up scars, however. Often it is necessary, though by no means easy, to tell a business borrower that he is growing too fast. "Slow down and consolidate progress" is often prudent advice. If his business disintegrates after you tighten the reins, then you're bound to be blamed for not letting him add the new product line or open the new outlet. If demand for his product booms, you'll probably be accused of causing him to run out of inventory and lose some profits. Often it is a no-win proposition, but that's the fate of the professional banker.

Even the great humorist Ogden Nash found the caution and conservatism of bankers grist for his mill in a poem which starts "Consider the banker." His choice lines are—

When with clients he was closeted
he was attempting to convince them that everything ought to be made do, worn out,
    eaten up, or deposited.
In a word, if you wanted to catch up with the Joneses or bust
you couldn't do either with the connivance of the First National Pablum Exchange
    Trust.

Criticism comes even from bad poetry.

The acid test

Sometimes the banker must step in and pull the plug on a company that should be placed in bankruptcy. If you're not prepared to pass that acid test, you're not prepared to live up to the full responsibilities of the profession.

A business failure is a tragic development affecting the lives of many people, including those indirectly involved in the business. But most failures must be identified as such and brought to a head by some responsible party to prevent even more serious damage to a wider range of people working for suppliers and users.

Someone must make the tough judgment that the financial resources and talents committed to a nonviable and declining business should be pulled away. Those resources should be recommitted to a purpose that will better serve the community before they are drained from the economy. Naturally, you won't win popularity contests if you choose a career that puts you in that critical position.

A colorful example of what some people think about bankers came to one of our senior officers 15 years ago in a letter from a down-easter. Describing the difference between a steam clam and a quahog, the author says, "The quahog is like a Boston banker: It never gets into anything very deeply, rarely risks being uncovered by the tide except at the full moon, sticks his short neck out only a teeny bit and, although accessible, is very difficult to get at."

As he continues, his comparison becomes painfully physical: "The anterior end of the quahog is short while the posterior is developed into a broad oval sweep." Bankers not only have to endure barbs about their credit judgments, but they also have to suffer assessment of their physiques.

The no-win life of top management

Now that I've made the lending officer's life seem bleak, let me move up the corporate ladder a little and sketch the no-win life of a bank's top management. Like the lending officer, the top manager finds that each decision produces two or more Bronx cheers for every "bravo."

The conflicting needs of many publics

You've undoubtedly read articles that speak to the management challenge of responding to the conflicting needs of the bank's customers, employees, and stockholders. Such a simplistic listing of the publics top managers serve and to whom they are accountable is grossly misleading and obscures the dilemma faced by the management of any highly regulated industry, particularly banking.

I recently tried to elaborate on that simple list of three publics to determine how many publics with potentially conflicting interests bankers are actually required to be conscious of as they conduct business. My list now numbers 21 different publics, each of which has its own drum to beat.

Employees

Let me go through that list with you. In terms of response to management decisions, employees can be divided into at least two categories: new or high-turnover employees and long-time career employees. If you increase pension benefits instead of putting the same dollars into free lunches, the long termers will be pleased; the short-termers won't.

Stockholders

Similarly, the stockholder whose primary interest is divided income reacts differently to some management decisions than does the stockholder whose primary interest is appreciation or whose tax bracket makes dividends meaningless.

Customers

Customers also must be broken out. I have come up with five different categories, each of which looks to the bank for different things at different times. The first category is the regular demand depositor. He might react negatively to closing a branch, for example, where other types of customers are happy to see overhead reduced.

The second category is the supplier of short-term funds, such as CDs and Federal funds, whose interest is rate and liquidity. The third category is the borrower whose viewpoint is obviously different from that of the others.

Then there is the personal trust customer who often resists change in an organization. Last, there is the operational service user. Such a customer could be a company whose only relationship with the bank is its payroll account. It demands performance. So employees, stockholders, and customers total nine different publics.

More publics

Bondholders are another of the publics. Their long-term interest in the safety of the institution very often makes them react favorably to a management decision that displeases stockholders.

Then there are the state and city governments, a public which management must consider when making decisions. Not only do they carry funds with the bank, but they make the laws that influence the banking business.

The press is another public which often reacts to management decisions differently from other constituents although it purports to represent the public in general.

When making decisions, management must also think about community organizations needing financial support. And, of course, consumer advocate groups are another important and vocal public, eager to react to all that banks do.

Within the banking industry, I have separated two other publics that management tends to think about as it makes decisions. First are competing banks, and second are the banking industry leaders in general. They are represented by general banking groups such as the fifty state banking associations and the

American Bankers Association. There are also the several specialized associations, such as Robert Morris Associates.

Last, there are five publics that could be lumped together under the general heading of regulators although each group has its own area of interest. These publics are the Federal Reserve System, the Comptroller of the Currency, the State Banking Commission, the Securities and Exchange Commission, and the U.S. Treasury Department with its responsibility for affirmative-action compliance.

So there's a list of 21 separate outside interests, all looking over bank management's shoulder and reacting negatively or positively to most management decisions. If it seems that I've exaggerated in arriving at 21 publics, consider these familiar names that banks deal with frequently and that are *not* included in my list:

(1) Federal Trade Commission
(2) Internal Revenue Service
(3) OSHA
(4) Department of Labor
(5) Department of Justice
(6) Social Security Administration
(7) Small Business Administration
(8) Department of Commerce

It is easy to see that each of these bodies would have different reactions to any given management decision and should be counted among the publics to which we pay attention. I didn't include them in my list because it was meant to prove the point, not be exhaustive.

Demonstrating that a bank can't please all of its publics all of the time

I recently had some fun with this list of 21 by asking each of 21 members of our Management Trainee group to assume the role of one of these publics. Each was to indicate on a form whether his reaction was positive, negative, or indifferent to a dozen fictional management decisions.

For example, one decision was an increase in the dividend of the bank. Another was a 4% across-the-board salary increase for all employees. Another, a 15% increase in trust fees. Another was to close two branch offices, and another was disclosure of a $50,000 contribution to the Boston 200 Bicentennial Fund. I even threw in a decision about a bank helping a city get through a financial crisis by buying its bonds.

The results were fascinating but not unexpected. I (the bank) announced 12 management decisions to this group. On the average, one-third of the 21 publics was indifferent to what the bank announced, one-third was positive, and one-third was negative.

The most popular of the 12 decisions among my 21 publics was to raise trust fees, with the only outside objection coming from the personal trust customer. The across-the-board salary increase was the least popular decision. Competitors didn't like it because they would have to match it. Consumer advocate groups, the press, and community organizations didn't like it because it could mean higher loan fees or lower contributions. Stockholders in for the quick gain would have preferred higher per share earnings. The borrowers wanted lower rates.

The reactions to the other decisions were similarly diverse. No clear pattern of responses emerged except that very few of the publics liked much of what I announced. None of the 12 decisions produced fewer than three negative reactions. This result supports the general belief that there is nothing a bank could possibly do that would receive universal approval.

If every time the management of a bank had to review and concern itself with the reaction of each of the 21 publics to all of its important decisions, few decisions would ever be made. Managers instinctively balance the negative and positive reactions of their publics to possible decisions. Those decisions must be made irrespective of the fact that a third of the publics will be unhappy with each and every one.

Management's decisions, like the loan officers' decisions, cannot be influenced by a concern for personal popularity. Not only is it unprofessional to have such concerns, but there are too many constituencies with different ideas about how management should behave.

Sticking with the fundamentals but selling them to the publics

The Louis Harris Polls measure the popularity of business and banking from time to time. When banking's score dips, a rash of articles appear in banking journals suggesting that banks must change their ways. I agree that banks must be concerned with the industry's unpopularity because the extreme consequence of increasing unpopularity is the nationalization of the industry. But banking's response to an unfavorable Harris rating should not be to alter the fundamentals of banking that history has proven to be in the best interest of the economy. Rather it should do a better job of explaining and selling those fundamentals to all the publics.

Banks cannot take for granted their place in a rapidly changing society. Many banking rules and practices have been modified and will continue to be modified to adjust to changes in society. But when bankers hold fast to fundamentals like the tools lending officers work with each day, they are obligated to continually justify and explain those fundamentals.

When a lending officer makes an extra effort to explain fully to the client the reasoning behind a rejected loan application, the officer may not be enhancing his own popularity. He is, however, playing a much-needed role in the educational process that is essential to the continued functioning of banks within the free enterprise system. The president of your bank is also playing his proper role when he explains the reasoning behind management decisions to any of the 21 protesting publics.

Compensation for unpopularity

At the beginning of this article I promised to offer some comfort as a counterweight to the burden of having a career that loses you friends, as Shakespeare tells us. The comfort is simply the knowledge that without such mixed blessings banking would be a trade, not a profession.

We all want the work to which we devote a major portion of our lives to be considered a respected profession. The outside world has always viewed banking with some skepticism. If bankers constantly strayed from the sound rules and convictions gained from long experience, they would not have the right to label their calling a profession. Plutarch said, "Those that are greedy of praise prove they are poor in merit." And Alexander Pope warned us, "Yet let not each gay turn thy rapture move/For fools admire, but men of sense approve."

Bankers' dedication to sound fundamentals, despite the protests of the client turned away and the unhappy constituent, will ultimately gain approval by thoughtful, sensible men and women. By dedication to a professional code, you will be recognized and accepted as a professional. Another reward for being a true professional is that uncommon and uncommonly pleasant experience of having the unhappy client, whose dreams he claimed you shattered, return to thank you. He shakes your hand with sincere appreciation for keeping him away from an investment that went sour or admits you were right about not buying the second machine tool.

There will always be those who are jealous of the banker's role. There will always be those who are convinced bankers are motivated by some sinister scheme to forestall progress or prevent the distribution of wealth or what have you. So get used to the slings and arrows. Learn from them even though you will never learn to enjoy them. ☐

II. Credit Analysis

The articles in this six-part section of the anthology emphasize the techniques of credit analysis. The first two articles address important fundamental aspects of the lending decision and specify the types of considerations that are essential to that decision. The second part contains one important article on statement interpretation. The third part, on financial analysis and funds forecasting, presents several important techniques for forecasting funds requirements. Gathering data with which to make and interpret forecasts is the topic of the fourth part. Because of their importance to many lending decisions and financial evaluations, inventory issues are the subject of the fifth part. The final part presents one article on the doleful subject of anticipating financial problems.

For information about the authors of the articles in Section II, refer to the List of Contributors on page xi.

A. Basic Considerations in Lending

Jack Crigger's article, "An Ocean of C's," is a classic and amusing summary of the C's of credit expanded from the traditional five or six into fourteen, covering not only the C's of the borrower but a number of the C's for the loan officer. P. Henry Mueller's "What Every Lending Officer Should Know About Economics" lays out the relationship between the stages of the economic cycle, the nature of a business' need for funds, and the lender's ability to meet these needs. It also discusses the behavior of the various parties to a loan and alerts the lender to combinations of the business cycle and behavior which can lead to financial trouble.

B. Statement Interpretation

Proper interpretation of financial statements is clearly the foundation of financial and credit analysis. The subject is far too broad to be treated in depth in this collection; complete coverage would be more appropriate in a textbook. One article was chosen for this anthology from a number of excellent candidates because it discussed important topics that may not be as evident as many other issues in statement interpretation. The article by Eugene E. Comiskey and Charles A. Tritschler, "On or Off the Balance Sheet—Some Guidance for Credit Analysts," reviews a number of pesky liabilities that can be tucked so far into the corners of financial statements that they may not be easily seen. These include such items as pension liabilities, leases, and deferred taxes.

C. Financial Analysis and Funds Forecasting

The articles chosen to cover this topic address basic skills and methods of financial forecasting. The first two articles introduce basic forecasting techniques. In "How Much Capital Does a Business Need?," Douglas S. Clarke shows how asset turnover ratios can be used to prepare an easy, quick estimate of funds needs. Robert C. Higgins offers further insight into the same topic in "Sustainable Growth: New Tool in Bank Lending." He demonstrates that problems arise if the growth in a firm's equity lags behind the growth in its sales.

Two articles then address cash flow estimation techniques. Dev Strischek's basic and comprehensive article, "Analyzing the Quantity and Quality of Cash Flow for Long-Term Borrowing," not only deals with mathematical insights but also contains comments on the interpretation of accounting conventions. "The Banker's Shell Game—Lending Against Cash Flow," by D. R. Denison, is a cautionary elaboration on the problems of defining what cash flow is and on the difficulties companies have in maintaining it.

Although the final article, "Evaluating a Firm's Liquidity and the Bank Credit Risk" by Peter J. Tischler, duplicates some of Strischek's contribution, it offers additional valuable insights into liquidity estimation.

D. Data Accumulation

An analysis based on inadequate or inaccurate data can be worse than having based the analysis on no information at all. The first of the two articles in this part, "The Role of Economic Information in Commercial Lending Analysis" by Gary G. Anderson, specifies data and factors the analyst should consider in developing the important economic environmental appraisal which underlies a credit decision. Anderson also suggests where the necessary information can be found to prepare the analysis. The second article, by Cass Bettinger, "Making a Plant Visit Pay Off," contains suggestions for the all-important "kick-the-tires" phase of credit evaluation and supplies a checklist for the analyst to use in planning an on-site inspection.

E. Inventory Evaluation

The amount written on the subject of lending against inventory testifies to the importance that subject has for the loan officer. The two articles included here lead from the general aspects of the subject to some very specific ones. William P. Creamer's article, "Looking at Management? Try the Inventory Window!," starts out on a technical note but quickly gets down to very pragmatic and basic insights into the different types of inventory and the purposes they serve in the production process. Creamer offers useful guidelines for the analyst and suggests questions the loan officer may wish to raise with management.

In "Retail Inventories and the Loan Officer," Jordan L. Golding discusses the retail method of accounting and warns of some of the dangers that can arise from the use of this technique. He also presents a thorough discussion of last-in-first-out inventory accounting.

F. Predicting Financial Problems

Avoiding troublesome loans is better than having an excellent workout department. Loan officers and analysts have therefore long been searching for simple, reliable ways to spot applicants with potential financial problems and to identify borrowers who are slipping into difficulty. However, the lender does not want to refuse all borrowers who *might* get into trouble. That would probably mean that very few loans would be made. The loans to be avoided are only those that are *very likely* to turn into problems.

The *Journal* has published a number of articles on this subject, but only the broadest of these has been selected for this anthology. James A. Hoeven, in "Predicting Default of Small Business Loans," develops a very technical approach. His article offers useful insights for structuring thoughts about the problem even if precise application of the technique may not be practical for all lenders. The article also includes a useful review of previously published literature on the topic.

An Ocean of "C's"

by Jack R. Crigger

LET US DISCUSS THE C'S OF CREDIT, even though bankers are quite familiar with what they are. However, it seems the trend in most everything is to nostalgia or back to the basics. What could be more basic than a group of bankers discussing the acceptance of a credit risk? That's what we do—accept—we don't extend credit. We accept the credit risk for an exchange of funds. Here I ask the indulgence of the more experienced lenders—I also ask you to think as we go along and see if you identify the C of credit that was perhaps the reason for a loan loss in your bank last year.

Character

Keeping in mind that there will be some overlapping of principles, let's start with Character. That's easy. Bankers do not accept credit unless the party has character—good character or bad character (we normally do not lend money to strangers). But let us ask a question: How many loans have we charged off and, when we really evaluated the reason for the loss, it may well have been the character of the borrower.

What is Character? There are many definitions. Basically, it means doing what is morally right; but then integrity and honesty, and a lot of other words consti-

40

tute character. It's easy to be honest and exercise integrity in good times; when times are bad, character is tested. A rat will fight if he is in a corner; an individual may turn on you in bad times.

How about corporations? Can we gauge their character? A company requests a 90-day $25,000 loan to pay income tax. A review of the records shows from financial statements they only owe $10,000, and you made a loan 90 days ago for the same purpose in that amount. Do you wonder about their integrity? What is the character of an entity like this? We have to go deeper; we have to go to the individuals. We say we do not make loans to individuals or companies without solid character; yet, we charge off many loans. Why? My guess is that character, honesty and integrity, either changes or, more likely, we do not properly evaluate this characteristic in the beginning.

Complacency

Let's look at a *C* that can, and does, spell trouble—let's be realistic.

Complacency—we're all guilty of this and it may be a cause of our not properly evaluating character. You know old Joe—he's been good for $10,000 many times. He appears at the bank and wants $10,000 for 90 days—you're busy and do not check on those rumors you've heard, so you let him have it! Or did he let you have it? Those rumors are true; you find out 90 days later his wife did sue him for divorce. He is hitting the bottle and your $10,000 went to Vegas and did not return. You didn't find out what the loan was for, or how it was to be repaid and from what source. You took things at face value; you were complacent, took the road of least resistance. Being complacent about accepting a credit risk can, and will, show up as a loan loss.

To another *C*—one we hear a lot about—

Capacity

Capacity, the ability to pay debt. For example, I want to buy a Cadillac. I have character, but I don't have the cash flow ability to retire the debt; therefore, I am a poor credit risk. Not to belabor a point, but every loan falls basically into one of two repayment categories, i.e., by working capital cycle (conversion of an asset) or as a term loan—it's the same for an individual or a company.

We're guilty too often of not properly evaluating this criterion. Sam's company requests a $20,000 working capital loan—says he will pay you in 90 days. Do we really question his capacity? Or he wants a 5-year $50,000 term loan to purchase fixed assets and/or equipment. Do we just take his word that he's worked out the payback, or do we really dig deep? Do we look at cash flow to determine that he can repay? Consider the individuals who borrow on stocks—

90 days, 6 months, 6 years, etc. Intentions are good at loan inception, but conditions change and so do priorities, intentions and promises. Earning power can be curtailed and committed income cannot pay new debt. You know the picture: we should not lend large sums of money to individuals who have limited worth and income to purchase stocks of a speculative nature, but it has happened many times.

Flip back to the other side, another trouble spot, another C.

Carelessness

Carelessness: poor records, poor documentation. Perhaps you've gone to court to realize on collateral and you find a serial or model number in error that can throw the case out of court—you can lose. Intent does not win court cases. As an example, an SBA guaranty states that their liability is predicated on the fact that all the conditions of the authorization are carried out or perfected.

Let's refer to another C here—Current financial statements. Do we fail to properly evaluate what we receive? A change in conditions, a change in accountants may alter our judgments. Financial statements, particularly company statements, generally are 6 weeks to 6 months old when we extend loans. Do we get careless about what has happened since the statement date? Do we exercise caution about exceptions in title policies, in abstracts? Are we careless or complacent about renewals or do we really ask proper questions? One good loan review system that is easy to follow is to treat every renewal as a new loan—would you make the loan now in light of present conditions?

Back to a C we use in our evaluation.

Capital

Capital—regardless of character and capacity, a company still needs capital. If a company or individual has strong character and sufficient capacity, we can temper the criterion of capital a bit. There is still a need for fixed assets and working capital, but $1 of capital will support only so many dollars of sales. When that point is reached, then the company must rely on creditors, either bank or trade creditors. With any new business venture, we need to evaluate what our position might be in relation to their capital structure. We could be in a frozen position with our loans.

Capital is a cushion, and the net worth position of either individual or company is nothing more than an arithmetic exercise. The residual figure—the difference between assets (subject to fluctuations) and liabilities (constant in terms of monetary units)—is at best an estimate. We should not rely on capital paying a debt. The borrower must first liquidate the business, or at least part of it, to pay.

How much do we expect to receive in forced liquidation? Capital will pay creditors only in liquidation. Think of statements you have seen showing net worth of individuals including household goods and equities of questionable values.

Yet another C will get us into trouble.

Contingencies

We could build a strong case for considering what might happen, but that's being negative; yet, we do need to consider whether this is a one-man show with no back-up, no continuity of management. If the borrower dies, okay, we have insurance. But suppose he's just incapacitated. There are other contingencies: accounts receivable and notes sold with recourse; the borrower is an accommodation endorser, warranties and guarantees, concentration of business, law suits, inadequate insurance coverage could deplete capital and your cushion, loss of an important business client, tax regulations, safety, pollution, unions (strikes), shortage of materials, Congress, controls, etc. How would the customer compete—could he survive?

Now one of the original C's.

Conditions

Conditions—of the economy within the country and within the industry. Can our customer weather an economic crisis? In loans to land and real estate developers, interest alone can be a problem. Is the customer vulnerable to an inventory position? Can the business survive a sales decline? What about substitutes for his major product? Is his service or product innovative or is management innovative (example, fads such as hoola hoops or plastics)? Is it a growth company? What about legislation relative to business—patents, leases, contracts? It seems to me one has to be an economist of sorts, a forecaster, a judge of current events. The impact of such events on the future of any particular business must be scrutinized relative to the conditions prevailing in agriculture, commerce and industry. We cannot have this expertise unless we remain a student of economy and banking. Definitely a C of credit, Conditions require constant attention.

And yet another C.

Collateral

Collateral—Probably the most important thing one can say about collateral is that we should not look to collateral to pay a debt. Properly it should be viewed as an alternative source of repayment—don't believe that we want our lobbies full of John Deere tractors! We must not look to equipment and stocks that have no market. Collateral takes many forms from the pledge of actual cash (coin collection) to the assignment of rental space in a garage. Correctly done, the pledge should be legally sound, properly documented and continuously checked as to its authenticity and value. Otherwise, we can wind up with an unsecured loan and a loss. For example, would you lend to a 70-year-old man who wants to speculate in the market? Look at the documentation of collateral as if you were in court. Remember we need a marketplace. When we must sell, who wants to buy?

Back to a *C* that ofttimes spells trouble.

Competition

Competition is one way we can let a loan get in trouble—just let our competition dictate our loan policies. You know the story: The customer makes a loan request and ends the conversation by saying, "If you don't feel comfortable, then the bank across the street will be glad to accommodate me. They've been soliciting my business for years, but I've told them you have always taken care of my loan requests at the best rate in town," or, "The rate or terms you offer are not as good as Bank 'A'." We need to evaluate the request properly, determine the ground rules and conditions, and stick by them.

Negotiation is fine, but don't let the competition dictate the terms. Giving in to competitive threats is a sign of weakness and encourages the customer to make more demands. Look at some of our loans now in trouble; they may well be some that we "took away" from our competitors.

Now a couple of *C's* that may be "plus" or "minus"

Circumstances

Circumstances like this: Joe Doe needs a loan—one he does not really qualify for—a speculative loan on stock or another kind of investment. The first inclination is to decline. But look at the circumstances—he is the beneficiary of a large trust in our bank or our competitive bank, but the trust does not mature for a few years. How do we react? Or he is the treasurer of a company, our customer or even our competitor's customer, and he controls a large bank account or he is instrumental in determining where the account is placed—a real problem! Or he is a professional man—a doctor, attorney, etc.—whose earning power is just beginning to mature.

Consider a company whose loan request is not justified by the statement of condition, but one owned and operated by men of ability whose field of endeavor is one of promise, but realistic repayment is impossible. Personal endorsements—yes—but when we have to call on individuals to repay company debts, we can lose customers. So the circumstances dictate that we counsel, negotiate, innovate and understand the terms and conditions of the loan request.

Communications

Communication . . . *good* communications are essential to sound loan administration. Poor communications can and often do get us in deep water. Tell the folks in your bank what is going on relative to your borrowing customers. I suggest some rather formal means—credit memos to your staff who are involved. Write it down, pass it around, let them know; then when you are away there is no doubt about your intentions relative to a loan. Communication goes a lot further; it goes into loan review. Someone in every bank should be looking at the loans after they are on the books—looking at documentation, repayment, etc. Good communications would tell any loan officer those things he needs to know when the original loan officer is away. Tell the board—don't let there be any surprises on loan losses!

A *C* that can cause trouble—one we must look at very carefully—

Civic responsibility

Civic responsibility, or social responsibility, means things like this: A loan for the public good or a community need (as an example, air or water pollution) is usually a rather sizable request, one that will not add to the productivity of the company, but one of civic necessity. This could well be a loan requiring considerable cash flow in a period of recession and could be a source of trouble. Don't get me wrong, I am for such things, but we need to be realistic about such extensions of credit. Evaluate the results, the problems generated, the losses sustained and the point is made. Without experience and ability such a loan can become a loss and the exercise of a civic duty by a lender can create a problem from an operational as well as a public relations standpoint.

Still another *C* to consider—

Continuity

Continuity of management, of statements and statement dates, of visits. Take management first—the customer is a one-man show, strong, good public relations individual, excellent salesman, a man who instills enthusiasm in his business, is experienced and capable. Where is his back-up man? Who takes his place if he dies or if he becomes disabled?

Let's consider statements. Look at each one you request very carefully, look at who prepared them, look at how long a time elapsed between statement date and the receipt of statement. Are the accountants the same? Is the reason for the statements the same, i.e., for management, for tax purposes, for a credit request? Obviously, customer visits are important and continuity here is imperative.

Look at another *C*.

Crooks

Crooks. Generally speaking, we charge off loans made to people we know. A crook who walks in off the street will have tough time extruding money or credit from experienced lenders. That being the situation, how do crooks "take" the banking establishment? Do you know what a counterfeit stock certificate looks like? I do—it looks just like the real thing. A person can purchase a blank form, use some fancy lettering, a gold seal, and approach you and me for a loan. Other con methods that have worked in the past include the double pledge of trust receipts on real estate loans; fraudulent statements with overvalued assets; fraudulent invoices (for example, fake accounts receivable), and if you don't control pledge payment, it becomes very easy for funds to dissipate.

And yet another C—

Control

Control, through loan review. There are all kinds of reviews from very limited to sophisticated, but every loan officer has some sort of review. It can be done by the Credit Department or it can be done by the loan officer. One very simple but effective review is to ask at least five (5) questions on a request for a renewal of the original loan.

1. Is collateral adequate and are all documents in order?
2. Is there an established repayment schedule, one that is realistic? (Capacity)
3. Are financial statements "current"? (Conditions)
4. Are your credit memos current? (Communication)
5. Would you make the loan now in view of present Circumstances?

I would suggest that we look closely at any loan on the books over a year. What was the original purpose, the terms and the collateral? How many of our loans would be classified as forever loans? Do we really control our portfolio of loans or do they control us?

Conclusion

We've looked at some of the "C's" of credit. There are others; get the dictionary, pick a few and add your own experiences. I guess the real point of these remarks is to say that we must be in constant touch with the basics of lending money, whether it be on a 90-day loan for buying cattle or a 9-year term loan for term working capital, or an equipment loan, or whatever.

When times are good, lenders can make mistakes without being hurt too much. When times are bad, money is tight and credit must be rationed, then we cannot make such errors, and if we do—we must accept the consequences.   □

What Every Lending Officer Should Know About Economics

by P. Henry Mueller

In the following article, Mr. Mueller discusses the important relationship between the economic picture and the loan decision. He may lead you to look at prospective borrowers in a somewhat new context.

The key to sound lending is perceiving and understanding risk and then protecting against it. In order to do this properly, considerably more than the intrinsics of the credit must be evaluated. There is a credit extension gestalt, and recognizing the linkage between lending money and the business cycle is part of it. This article—and the portion of the monograph on which it is based—describes how changes in general business affect specific industries and individual borrowers and how borrowers and lenders behave vis-à-vis the credit markets at various stages of the cycle in overall economic activity.

© 1978, Citibank, N.A. This article is based on a talk presented by the author at the eighth annual meeting of the Financial Management Association in Minneapolis on October 12, 1978. It is also based on part of a monograph co-authored with Leif Olsen, Chairman Economic Policy Committee, Citibank. The monograph, entitled *Credit and the Business Cycle*, is soon to be published by Citibank.

It is an effort to illuminate a critical dimension of credit extension with the aim of improving current practices and encouraging further research and study—seed material, perhaps, for books and doctoral dissertations.

Sound lending commences with a thorough evaluation of the borrower's honesty, integrity, viability, competence, and ability to complete a loan transaction in the manner proposed, plus a determination as to whether or not the transaction is feasible, economically and technically, and free of inordinate risk. This leads to a long view and understanding of the industry, its structure, economics, maturity, and place in the economy. Beyond this, sound lending practices lead to an appraisal of the industry standing of the borrower—risk is usually heightened as lenders finance borrowers in the lower industry reaches—and management's ability to cope with and manage growth since demands on management change with the size of a company.

Credit judgment is so tightly bound up with the recurrence of recessions and recoveries, boom and bust, that the behavior of both borrowers and lenders is predictable for any given phase of the business cycle. There are basic economic "givens"—verifiable propositions—which enable us to anticipate the risks likely to arise when economic signals change. Many lending mistakes repeat themselves when this is ignored. The passage of time has underscored that our approach to lending has been too limited. The 1973–75 recession again illustrated the major impact of the business cycle on the quality of bank assets. The cycle has more impact than does any single factor. A simple example would be the value of security, which depends upon the severity of a cyclical downturn. These considerations, critical to the quality of our lending, suggest that they should be spelled out. It is strange that so little attention has been given in the credit literature to the lending/business cycle relationship.

Lack of knowledge about the lending/business cycle relationship

The lack of applied knowledge about the lending/business cycle link can be traced to both the manner in which current lending practice has evolved and to the widespread failure of borrowers and lenders to appreciate fully that business decisions which they make or do not make are, in themselves, economic forecasts which may or may not be compatible with economic reality. In fact, only in recent years have economic developments drawn widespread attention. During the early 1930s, many academic students of credit problems were domiciled outside of university economics departments so that lending and the business cycle were literally separated. There was little macro theory and few macro statistics: current GNP numbers were introduced in 1941. Even in the 1960s economic understanding was limited. For instance, the relationship of persistent deficit spending to a nation's ability to meet its external obligations was grasped by few. There is still today an uneven, if not totally inadequate, understanding of economic relationships and interdependencies. Nonetheless, since loans must be collected, lending officers need to be high on the learning curve and clearly understand the fourth "C" of credit: the *conditions* of the times.

Business environment's accommodation of shift in loan patterns

The fundamental that has shaped commercial bank lending from the 1930s, when banks in quest of earnings were forced to explore new outlets for their funds, has been the shift from seasonal working capital loans to the broader, more complex, underwriting of term risks. This movement was accommodated by alterations in the business environment. Marketing shifts and distribution changes affected the flow of goods and cash, setting the stage for consumer lending. The need to finance war industry and increasingly expensive machinery and equipment, aircraft, ships, and plants led to widespread use of the term loan.

Evolution from balance sheet to cash flow lending

The term lending philosophy that has evolved has been buttressed by a parallel evolution in the thinking of accountants, financial executives, and teachers of business administration. Although most bankers perceived the greater risks to which they were exposing themselves, their general reaction was to offset them by structuring, covenants and default clauses, and by long range studies of the borrower, the industry, and its prospects. In the evolution from balance sheet to cash flow lending, some stumbled by stressing the profit and loss statement over the balance sheet. Credit quality suffered from undue emphasis on cash flow as the "way out" of a loan of any type. Borrowers themselves usually focused narrowly on what was happening to their own businesses rather than on what was happening to others around them—many a plant has been built just as a business cycle was cresting.

Term loan borrower requirements

Whereas loans for working capital purposes are tied to an analysis of the borrower's cash cycle, primarily the turnover of inventory and receivables, term risks require lending officers to make longer bets on management, earnings, and the borrower's trade position. There are more moving parts and enhanced risk when a credit runs to several years. And, since the bank credit market is not cold-nosed, a bank lender is not usually free to enter and leave a credit at will. Continued involvement and exposure, regardless of economic conditions, is part of the calculus. A term loan is still best made to well-established, successful borrowers with historically demonstrated cash generation. What is desired is a quality and quantity of cash flow that gives every reasonable assurance of meeting the interest and amortization requirements of the loan, with ample margin for contingencies, including realistic net working capital and leverage provisions to guarantee performance.

Ability to predict economic developments

Claims are made from time to time that the business cycle can be "fine tuned," but somehow unforeseen variables have a way of encroaching and making control a slim possibility if one at all. There is also some feeling that structural changes in the U.S. economy are lessening the importance of the business cycle, although historical comparison of the behavior of the current cycle does not seem to bear this out.

Economic activity is actually far more stable and its patterns of change more predictable than many believe. While it may not be possible to predict economic developments with the precision required for all business decisions, it is nonetheless possible to make accurate predictions about directions of change which can have great value when properly understood and used.

Consideration of loan prospects in context of economic picture

What is most obvious but perhaps needs emphasis is that each transaction must be considered in the context of its economic setting and the business cycle. Whether in the U.S. or abroad, the specific behavior of a borrower is affected by both the economic environment of the country itself and its particular cyclical problems. Additionally, if the lending is across borders, the means of repayment must not only be clear but so must the conversion risk. One needs to relate what's going on in a country to the specifics of portfolio exposure. A good credit risk is the first line of defense in sovereign risk; the first loans not repaid are the poor credits. We live in an era that responds worldwide to serious local trauma, economic or political, and lenders must constantly examine their borrowers' substance in terms of their ability to withstand shock. In sum, a lending officer must define risks accurately, looking beyond financial elements alone to determine an entity's viability. Variables can quickly offset past trends, and adequate allowance must be made for their impact. As lending officers bring their counsel to bear, borrowers will appreciate the banker's concern for the customer's long-term viability.

Probing the link between the credit and the business cycle

These are some questions that might be asked in probing the linkage between the credit and the business cycle:

(1) At which stage of the business cycle are we? How does the borrower relate to it?

(2) Does the borrower's business track the business cycle, or does its inherent volatility cause it to move independently? Does it lead or lag the business cycle?

(3) What is the life of the borrower's industry cycle, and at what stage is it now? Is there serious overcapacity? Is industry activity tapering off?

(4) Is the borrower in a new product business that is subject to booms and busts?

(5) What is the borrower's main business, and how does it relate to the industry cycle?

(6) Is the industry function performed by the borrower one that will endure, or is the borrower's role losing ground?

(7) Are industry consolidations taking place or likely to occur?

(8) What are the distinct risk characteristics of each of the borrower's business segments? What must the borrower do well to succeed?

(9) At what stage of the business cycle is the borrower most strongly affected? How is his performance affected by those cyclical pressures?

(10) What is the borrower's historic ability to weather recession?

The dynamics of the business cycle are explained in the portion of the monograph on which this article is based (see footnote, page 2). It is important to grasp them in a macro sense and then to identify the economic series which fits each borrower's activities. A sense of trend and timing is important so as to get an approximate fix on where the bank and the borrower are in terms of the cycle and how it would impact both.

What follows is an overview of the regular patterns of behavior of borrowers and lenders throughout stages of the cycle.

How Borrowers and Lenders Behave Over the Cycle

Stage of Business Cycle	Behavior of Borrower	Behavior of Lender
• Recession—unemployment and idle capacity.	• Liquidation in the case of marginal borrowers. • Faced with melting backlogs and order cancellations, repairs balance sheet liquidity; pares inventory and cuts production; receivables run off; cost-cutting programs undertaken; fixed costs are hard to trim quickly. • Reduces bank borrowing. • Defers nonessential capital needs.	• Repairs liquidity. • Excess liquidity, which erodes pricing; push for market share; irrational tendency to accept "caps" and fixed-rate deals. • Cautious on credit quality; security conscious.
• Recovery and expansion, commencing with pickup in consumer spending.	• Continues to repair balance sheet liquidity. • Inventory and receivables build. • Increases productivity and earnings. • Updates plant and equipment and contemplates future capital needs. • More liberal on wage settlements. • Overtime payments grow. • Introduces new products, and new ventures appear. • Large borrowers make extensive use of the commercial paper market.	• Loan volume shows signs of pickup in the face of excess bank liquidity. • Intense competition tends to push bankers into unsound deals. • Rates rise, and business borrowers turn to banks rather than to bond market.
• Boom—acceleration of inflation beyond economy's potential growth rate.	• Optimism mounts. Orders and prices soar above historic norms, often at unsustainable levels. • Raises wages sharply. • Reluctant to turn to long-term financing, increases short and intermediate credit substantially. Supply of internally generated business funds increasingly constrained by low rates of increase in productivity and slow rates of increase in physical output, which narrow profit margins. • Probes limits of physical capacity. Uses less productive facilities and workers; productivity declines.	• Optimism mounts. • Increasing amounts loaned against increasing cash flow; over generosity on the part of lenders. In some instances the liquidity supplied by the bank is all that's keeping the borrower afloat. • Susceptibility to euphoria and loss of perspective of what constitutes a good credit. Mania for growth, going down market to get it.

How Borrowers and Lenders Behave Over the Cycle

Stage of Business Cycle	Behavior of Borrower	Behavior of Lender
	• Backlogs increase as cycle ages. Builds inventory.	• High dependence on cash flow for collectibility.
	• Finds cost of replacing depreciated capital equipment rising. Acquisitions and tender offers more attractive.	• Demand for short-term funds increasingly strengthens.
	• Finds cost of replacing stocks of raw materials and components high.	• Lending for capital spending grows and heats up toward the end of a maturing "up" cycle.
	• Working capital needs rise to accommodate rising unit costs and inefficiencies.	• Acquisition loans increase.
	• Overall profit performance swells because of inventory profits.	• Banks tend to become proxies for the equity and long-term debt markets.
	• Profitable lines obscure weak performance of other lines.	• Wise lenders exercise caution—stress avoidance of exposure to weakening borrowers.
	• Fears credit controls. Anticipatory buying of supplies and raw materials. Increases prices wherever possible. Wages increased in anticipation of a freeze.	
	• Liquidity declines; leverage sometimes excessive.	
	• Large borrowers that have relied heavily on the commercial paper market return to banks for at least part of their short-term cash needs. In anticipation of a credit squeeze, borrowers negotiate revolving and other forms of committed credit.	
	• Marginal borrowers find it difficult to hold on.	
• Crunch—restrictive monetary policy, with restraint on the growth of bank reserves. Credit conditions and general frustration with inflation spawn proposals for credit allocation.	• Cuts production as backlog orders decrease.	• Cautious and selective in extending new credit.
	• To the extent possible, limits borrowing as credit restraint takes hold, although inflation usually accentuates demand for credit.	• Allocates funds formally or informally; basic needs of established business customers for normal operations met to assure production and distribution of goods and services.
	• Pressure on working capital affects debt servicing ability.	
	• Tries to improve collection of receivables as payments slow.	
	• Takes large write-downs in recognition that assets are in-	

How Borrowers and Lenders Behave Over the Cycle

Stage of Business Cycle	Behavior of Borrower	Behavior of Lender
	flated. This could precipitate further problems, depending upon how the marketplace interprets the action.	• Discourages loans for: 1. Purely financial activities—acquisitions or purchase of own shares. 2. Speculation. 3. Use outside domestic economy, funded from domestic sources. 4. Discretionary spending that might be deferred. • Displays less flexibility on moratorium or grace periods but more flexibility on repayments. • Raises interest rates and hardens fee structure.

Impact of other factors besides business cycle

In postwar years, banking has been somewhat *ad hoc* and opportunistic with respect to lending transactions. Perhaps the long era of prosperity which prevailed, except for some interruptions, from 1948 to 1973, contributed to this. We seem now to be moving into a period of greater cyclical velocity, and it's also one in which there are large numbers of political and other happenings that impinge on business. These developments, together with commercial banking's term orientation, demand a consistently high professional approach.

Quantitative analysis of credit has never been sufficient for decision-making purposes. The qualitative side of a credit sometimes has been shortchanged; we have not always known and evaluated managements sufficiently, for example. While this article indicates the need to link the credit cycle with the business cycle in our thinking, this hardly completes the scene. The impact of other exogenous factors must be taken into account.

Energy Crisis

One of the more critical of the other factors to consider in connection with the credit cycle is the unresolved impact of the energy crisis on the economics of a borrower's business. If his activity is energy intensive, can the borrower continue to use the same equipment? Must the borrower alter the product or the product mix? What are the financial implications? Environmental restrictions, unfunded pension liabilities, forced divestitures, accounting changes, and demographic shifts are among other important considerations. Such a comprehensive view helps in the early detection of weakening credit situations. Early problem recognition permits timely steps to be taken which might not otherwise be possible.

New products cycle

The business cycle is not the only cycle that invites trouble for lenders. Another one is generated by new products. When a company introduces a new product, it may initially enjoy a lead time over competitors. During this time, it can charge a price not only high enough to recapture development costs but to earn supernormal profits. Over time, however, this price attracts imitators, new entrants with lower or negligible research and development costs, and a willingness to accept a lower profit than the originator in order to garner a share of the market. As more producers enter the field, prices are forced lower. Total demand for the product increases as prices fall. Producers extrapolate the rising demand without correctly determining at what point the fall in price will impinge on their profits. Then there is a levelling off of demand. But most producers still don't realize the extent to which market shares are captured by charging prices that are too low to be sustained. To put it another way, producers have great difficulty in projecting accurately the product growth trend that will eventually be established. Yet production facilities are often rapidly expanded—usually with borrowed money—in what is not yet a stable market.

Finally, the competition begins to squeeze the marginal, less efficient producers out of business. In this way the industry is moving toward equilibrium in a cost-price structure that can be sustained only by the most efficient sellers. Obviously, the process of consolidation means bankruptcy for some borrowers and loan losses for some lenders. Examples of the hazards of lending in new product markets include computer leasing in the 1960s and, more recently, the fad for hand-held calculators, CB radios, and snowmobiles

Despite such hazards, lending on new products can be profitable. Moreover, the chances of avoiding trouble may be enhanced by facing up to the risks—scrutinizing balance sheets with extra care and applying conservative standards to borrowers. In the final analysis, ample liquidity is essential to survival in the consolidation phase of new product development, especially in the case of the new producers whose earnings flow solely from the new product line. Somewhat similar principles can be applied to any industry where volume suddenly explodes.

It is said that a bank is as sound as the intelligence and judgment of its decision-makers. Each lending officer is a decision-maker. Need more be added?   ☐

On or Off the Balance Sheet—Some Guidance for Credit Analysts

by Eugene E. Comiskey and Charles A. Tritschler

Professors Comiskey and Tritschler believe that credit analysts must go beyond standard liability definitions in deciding if several types of potential liabilities legitimately belong on or off the balance sheet. A firm's status as a going or troubled concern is one important factor they should consider in their analysis.

Financial ratios have inherent limitations as guides to the evaluation of leverage, liquidity, and profitability. In particular, current accounting standards limit the reliance placed on liability side ratios. This limitation results primarily from the *exclusion* of several items which appear to warrant liability status from a credit analysis perspective.

This article provides a brief overview of a number of areas in which current accounting standards result in exclusion of liability-type items. These areas include pension accounting (unfunded pension liabilities), lease reporting (uncapitalized operating leases), consolidation policy (unconsolidated debt of finance subsidiaries), and unconditional commitments (take or pay agreements). Deferred income taxes probably represent the only significant case where accounting standards currently call for *inclusion* of an item of questionable liability status, particularly in those cases where the likelihood of taxable income is in question.[1] The nature of deferred taxes and their liability status will be

---

[1] *Accounting Principles Board Opinion No. 11*, "Accounting for Income Taxes" (1967) calls for use of the deferred method. Deferred taxes are based on the tax rates in effect when the timing differences originate. No adjustments are made for future rate changes. The tax effects of timing differences which reduce taxes currently payable are technically considered to be deferred credits as opposed to liabilities. In this article, however, the effects are referred to as liabilities.

examined. Adjustments to include (or exclude) these items in liability ratio calculations are discussed and illustrated from a balance sheet position point of view. The effect on income and fixed charge coverage is not within the scope of this analysis.

In the development of adjusted liability ratios and the related analysis in this article, an effort is made to adopt a credit analysis perspective. Other papers in this much debated area reflect mainly the going-concern orientation of the financial analyst who is concerned with the valuation of equity shares and with risk from the perspective of the shareholder.[2] In this article, we acknowledge that the status of the firm may range from investment grade, to speculative, to troubled, or ultimately to that of reorganization or liquidation.

Our position is that the inclusion or exclusion of questionable liabilities (including the matter of their valuation) should be determined, in part, by the status of the firm. Classification as a viable going concern is the normal location for a firm to occupy on the financial-health spectrum. In their analysis of risk, credit analysts shift the center of interest to the potential claims on the borrower's resources in the event of distress. Current accounting standards are properly oriented to the going-concern concept for most purposes. Generally accepted accounting principles, to the extent that they are conditioned by the going-concern concept, result in the inclusion and exclusion of liabilities which are improper if the going-concern assumption is abandoned in a pro forma projection of worst-case effects for credit analysis. The discussion and illustrations which follow are designed to elucidate on this theme.

Inclusion of pension liabilities

Accounting Principles Board Opinion No. 8 (APB) entitled, "Accounting for the Cost of Pension Plans" (1966), outlines employer accounting requirements for pension-cost recognition.[3] More recently, the Employee Retirement Income Security Act (ERISA) of 1974 established other important requirements which center on funding, participation, vesting, and other features designed to make employee pension benefits more secure. Even though an employer follows the expense recognition standards of *APB Opinion No. 8* and conforms to the funding requirements of ERISA, the pension fund assets may amount to less

---

[2] For example see the excellent paper by Daniel A. Lasman and Roman L. Weil, "Adjusting the Debt-Equity Ratio," *Financial Analyst Journal*, Sept.–Oct. 1978, pp. 49-58. We acknowledge our debt to the Lasman and Weil article for prompting our interest in and providing essential background for the present study.

[3] For a detailed technical discussion of these topics, see Tom Fratar and Barry Gilbert, "Pension Cost Accounting and the Implications of Unfunded Vested Liabilities for Financial Statement Analysis, "*The Journal of Commercial Bank Lending*," July 1977, pp. 32-44.

than either the current actuarial pension liability (the present value of pension benefits earned to date from prior services) or even less than vested pension benefits. However, even under such circumstances, the financial statement of the sponsoring firm will reveal no pension liability.

Effect of ERISA

Prior to the passage of ERISA, the standing of unfunded vested benefits was less critical in credit analysis, since employee claims ran only to the pension fund itself and not the underlying employer organization. With ERISA, this situation was changed to permit a claim to be brought against the employer organization for the lesser of the unfunded vested liability or 30% of its net assets in the event of termination of the plan. An example of a company's commentary on this potential obligation is found in the 1979 Deere and Company *Annual Report:*

> The company would be liable in the event of termination of these pension plans for any guaranteed benefits in excess of trusteed pension funds. Such guaranteed benefits, assuming termination of the plans on October 31, 1979, would be no greater than the value of unfunded vested benefits at that date attributable to pension plans covered by the 1974 Employee Retirement Income Security Act.[4]

It is worth noting that the claim for up to 30% of net assets is brought by the Pension Benefit Guaranty Corporation (PBGC). In general, it appears that in case of a plan termination the guaranteed benefits will be less than the vested benefits for highly paid employees due to the application of ERISA limitations on the benefit guaranteed.[5] In the analysis which follows, we focus on unfunded vested benefits as a close approximation of guaranteed benefits in the absence of more complete disclosure.

Inclusion of unfunded vested benefits as liabilities

Like conventional debt, unfunded pension liabilities impose an implicit interest requirement on the firm and eventually require a cash outlay to discharge. For financially strong firms, the future cash flow burden will probably be borne without great difficulty. However, in the case of the weak (potentially non-going-concern) firm, the prospect of a plan termination does not provide the creditor protection but now raises the specter of a claim by the PBGC for up to 30% of a firm's net assets to satisfy the guaranteed benefits. Or, as Moody's

---

[4] Deere and Company, *Annual Report,* 1979, p. 22.

[5] For further background on the issue of vested versus guaranteed benefits, see Isidore Goodman, *Plan Terminations Under ERISA* (Chicago: Commerce Clearing House, 1978) and Frank G. Burianek, "Pension Plans: An Asset or a Liability," *Meidinger Update,* December 1977, pp. 1-5.

Investors Services concluded, ERISA ". . . had negative implications for the holders of marginally rated, unsecured debt issues of companies which have relatively large unfunded vested benefits."[6]

Whereas unfunded vested pension benefits (UVPB) are not booked as formal liabilities under current accounting standards, the benefits should be included in a comprehensive pro forma creditor liability analysis where the going-concern status is assumed subject to question and hence plan termination more likely. This is readily accomplished using pension data disclosed in notes to the financial statements. Inclusion of the unfunded vested pension liabilities calls for a deferred tax and retained earnings adjustment. Incorporating the liability for unfunded vested benefits into a liability analysis should reflect any tax benefit to be realized when and if the future disbursements become tax deductible. The inclusion of deferred tax credits on balance sheets is addressed as a separate issue shortly. For example, $10,000,000 of unfunded vested benefits would have the following balance sheet impact:

Liability increase	$10,000,000
Deferred tax benefit @ 46%	4,600,000
Retained earnings decrease	$ 5,400,000

Typically, the total unfunded pension liability will exceed the unfunded vested portion. In the analysis that follows, the smaller amount is included on the basis that this is an approximation of the balance elevated to near-liability status due to the ERISA provisions. Still another alternative amount to include would be the lesser of UVPB or 30% of stockholders' equity.[7] This latter amount would conform to a legal interpretation of the liability for vested but unfunded benefits and is probably most relevant where going-concern status is in doubt. Under a going-concern assumption, however, it is the total of the unfunded pension liability (of which vested is only a portion) which will need to be covered by future cash outlays.

In contrast to the troubled concern and credit analysis orientation adopted here, others, who have studied this issue from a going-concern and equity investor perspective, have included the entire unfunded pension liability in their revisions of liability ratios:

> We believe that the larger of the two amounts, unfunded vested pension benefits or unfunded prior service costs, constitutes an interest-bearing liability of the corporation.[8]

---

[6] "ERISA—A Bond Rater's View," *Moody's Bond Survey,* February 20, 1978.

[7] *Standard and Poors Ratings Guide* (New York: McGraw-Hill, 1979), p. 36. The guide discusses this alternative and indicates that it is the approach used in Standard and Poors' rating process.

[8] Lasman and Weil, p. 53.

Effect of UVPB inclusion—with and without 30% limitation

The impact of including UVPB, both with and without application of the 30% limitation, is demonstrated in Table 1 which is based on 1979 data for five steel companies. These companies are used for illustrative purposes only, and there is no implication that their status as going concerns is in question.

Table 1—Impact of UVPB on Five Companies

	Liabilities to Equity Ratio		
Company	Without UVPB	With UVPB	With UVPB and 30% Limitation
Republic Steel	.85	1.48	1.38
Armco	.90	1.07	1.07*
Bethlehem Steel	1.01	1.96	1.56
Wheeling Pittsburgh Steel	1.10	2.97	1.72
United States Steel	1.25	1.64	1.64*

* Given the amount of stockholders' equity of these two companies, the 30% limitation does not result in the exclusion of any of their UVPB.

Observe how the relative liabilities to equity ratios of the firms above are altered as the UVPB are included. Republic has the smallest ratio without UVPB but moves to second smallest when total UVPB are included in the ratio. All the other companies also have their relative standings on the liabilities to equity ratios altered as the alternative ratios are computed. By incorporating the UVPB, a clearer picture emerges of the relative liability position of these companies; further, comparability of the liability burdens is enhanced.

Inclusion of lease liabilities

The issue of proper lease accounting has been debated heavily for at least two decades. Primary attention has been devoted to the practices of lessees and that is the focus here. The key consideration has been the debt status of long-term leases. Currently, lessee reporting is guided by *Statement of Financial Accounting Standards No. 13,* "Accounting for Leases," issued by the Financial Accounting Standards Board (FASB). *FASB Statement No. 13* establishes tests for determining whether a lease must be capitalized. While the capitalization criteria have some intuitive appeal, they are inherently arbitrary in nature. Further, it is clear that many lessors actively work with lessees to "structure" a lease agreement in such a way that it does not meet any of the criteria which would call for its capitalization.[9]

Structuring leases to avoid meeting capitalization criteria

The upshot of the capitalization criteria game is that leases which are economically equivalent to other leases but which have *not* met one or more of the capitalization criteria are instead classified as operating leases. This means, of course, that they do not formally become part of the firm's liability picture. As long as lessees are motivated to keep certain leases "off the books," they will, in concert with lessors, find ways to structure leases creatively so as to avoid meeting any of the capitalization criteria. Over the longer term, the FASB will probably move in the direction outlined in the March 15, 1979, issue of the FASB's *Status Report* in which it was disclosed that:

> A majority of the Board members expressed the tentative view that, if Statement No. 13 were to be reconsidered, they would support a property-right approach in which all leases are included as 'rights to use property' and as 'lease obligations' in the lessee's balance sheet.

Capitalization of all leases for liability analysis

Whether they meet *FASB Statement No. 13* capital-lease criteria, all leases of property can be viewed as giving rise to property rights and obligations to pay rents on the part of the lessee. The leases represent a determinable asset and liability of the lessee properly included in the financial statements. Economic consequences of both capital leases and operating leases on a going-concern basis are in essence similar. Therefore, the classification of long-term noncancellable leases into capital and operating leases should be unnecessary; all leases would be capitalized for purposes of liability position analysis.

However, in line with the theme of this article, if the going-concern assumption comes in question, operating leases are probably the most subordinated of commitments. Their avoidability, albeit with some economic penalty, causes the operating lease obligation to take on equity-like characteristics in the event of financial difficulties. Therefore, while future lease accounting changes will (consistent with a going-concern viewpoint) probably call for more extensive capitalization of leases, the resultant liability to equity ratios, for the troubled firm, will overstate the claims on cash flows of these commitments.

---

[9] For an analysis of the capitalization criteria, and how in practice they are avoided, see Richard Dieter, "Is Lessee Accounting Working?," *The CPA Journal,* August 1979, pp. 13-19.

Illustrations using UAL, Inc. data

To illustrate the impact of including all leases in liability analysis, consider the 1978 Annual Report of UAL, Inc. Its leases cover aircraft, hotels, and airport passenger terminal space to name a few. Included in its 1978 balance sheet were capital lease obligations at a present value of $439,086,000. Total minimum lease payments under operating leases, disclosed in a note to the financial statements, were $634,594,000, and under capital leases, $717,354,000.

Inclusion of operating leases requires their present value amount whereas otherwise, disclosure would typically be confined to year-by-year minimums for five years with the ramainder beyond five years simply disclosed in total. Finding the present value of operating leases would ideally call for complete year by year outlay information, executory costs, and associated interest rates. Such data should be used if available to the credit analyst. In their absence, a conservative crude approximation is available. Operating leases can be reduced to present value by making the same proportional reduction represented by the present valuing of the capital leases. This is illustrated in Table 2 with 1978 UAL, Inc. data.

Table 2—Data for UAL, Inc. Showing Present Value of Capital and Operating Leases (In thousands)

	Present Value of Capital Leases	Present Value of Operating Leases
Total Minimum Lease Payments	$716,354	$634,594
Present Value of Minimum Lease Payments	$439,086	$389,006

The present value of operating leases was developed by applying the following formula:

$$\frac{\text{Present value of capital leases}}{\text{Total minimum capital lease payments}} \times \text{Total minimum operating lease payments} \quad \text{or}$$

using the figures in Table 2—

$$\frac{\$439,086}{716,354} = 61.3\%$$

$$61.3 \times \$634,594 = \$389,006$$

The impact of including the capitalized operating leases in a total liabilities to equity ratio for UAL, Inc. and four other airlines is outlined in Table 3.

Table 3—Impact of Including Capitalized Operating Leases on Five Airlines' Liabilities to Equity Ratio

Company	Liabilities to Equity Ratio	
	Without Operating Leases	With Operating Leases
UAL, Inc.	2.13	2.45
Pan American World Airways	2.16	2.51
American Airlines	2.34	2.72
Braniff International	2.42	3.05
Trans World Corporation	3.42	3.94

Capitalization of operating leases greatly affects the ratios in the preceding table. Companies which rely heavily on leasing, such as airlines, hotels, department stores, and fast food chains, will be most affected. The virtue of adopting an all-inclusive capitalization approach is that it promotes comparability among companies which vary in the extent of their reliance on leasing or which differ markedly in their use of capital versus operating lease arrangements. Further, for the going-concern, all-inclusive capitalization provides a more realistic index of the total financing in relation to a firm's equity base.[10] Finally, if the FASB eventually adopts a more inclusive capitalization standard, more energy can be focused on structuring leases based on fundamental financial factors and less on cosmetic accounting considerations.

Consolidation policy

Voting stock ownership greater than 50% usually provides the basis for consolidation of a subsidiary. However, current reporting standards provide for exclusion of subsidiaries from consolidated statements if they are in an unrelated line of business. The most frequently excluded subsidiaries are finance, insurance, or leasing subsidiaries of manufacturing companies.

Given the great variety in the operations of manufacturing subsidiaries, which *are* consolidated by diversified companies, exclusion of a small set of companies (finance, leasing, and insurance) is difficult to justify. The key re-

[10] In quite a different vein, one could argue that the most relevant dimension of capitalizing all leases appears on the asset side, since the firm's dependence on generating cash flow from readily withdrawn resources is displayed.

quirement for consolidation is effective financial control, and, in most cases, the excluded subsidiaries are 100% owned.

A common argument against consolidation of finance-type companies has been that the analytical value of the consolidated statements would be diminished through incorporation of units with significantly different asset and liability structures. However, as has been observed:

> With segment information now provided to unscramble consolidated statements which represent an aggregation of manufacturing and financing components, the justification provided in ARB 51 (Accounting Research Bulletin) for non-consolidation is somewhat diluted.[11]

Adjustment of parent liability-to-equity ratios to include financing on the separate unconsolidated statements of finance subsidiaries is made simple due to the use of the equity method of accounting for the subsidiary investment by the parent. Under the equity method, the parent has already adjusted its net assets (specifically its investment account) to pick up its share of the earnings of the financing subsidiaries (typically all of their income due to 100% ownership). This is commonly referred to as a one-line consolidation.

To develop the liability to equity ratios that produce the same results as with full consolidation of the financing subsidiaries requires simply adding subsidiary liabilities to those of the parent. The impact of such a revision is outlined in Table 4 for the 1979 statements of five heavy equipment manufacturers:

Table 4—Impact of Adding Subsidiary Liabilities to Those of Five Parent Companies

| | Liabilities to Equity Ratio | |
Company	Without Subsidiary Liabilities	With Subsidiary Liabilities
Allis-Chalmers	1.33	2.58
Clark Equipment	.76	2.31
International Harvester	1.44	3.54
Deere and Company	1.12	1.74
Fruehauf	2.03	3.03

Again, the adjusted ratios in Table 4 provide greater comparability of debt capacity employed when the credit analyst is assessing the extent of outside financing in a consolidated entity's total capital structure.

---

[11] *Arthur Young Views*, "Another look at the Consolidations of Finance Subsidiaries?," December 1978, p. 6.

Take or pay agreements

"Take or pay" contracts are representative of a class of off-balance sheet financial commitments which have been the subject of growing interest. Most recently, the FASB has issued an exposure draft of a proposed new standard entitled, *Disclosure of Guarantees, Project Financing Arrangements, and Other Similar Obligations* (March 1980). The proposal would expand disclosure requirements for financial commitments, particularly those unconditional obligations to make payments irrespective of whether a product or service is actually received.

The following is an example of disclosure of a take or pay agreement from the 1979 *Annual Report* of Armco, Inc.

> A subsidiary of Armco has entered into a completion and "take or pay" agreement under which it will take its share (40%) of the production of taconite iron ore pellets by Eveleth Expansion Company. Eveleth has outstanding $175,000,000 worth of 9½% and $43,200,000 worth of 10% First Mortgage Bonds due in 1995. Armco is committed to advance up to 40% of the funds needed for the continued operation of Eveleth, including amounts for depreciation and amortization at least equal to the amounts required to pay principal and interest on such bonds.[12]

In the example just given, it is not possible to determine precisely how much Armco will be required to pay in the future. The proposed FASB standard provides that ". . . for such contingencies an enterprise should disclose the aggregate commitment and the payments required in each of the next five years."[13]

In the case of a take or pay agreement, while perhaps variable in amount, future cash outlays are certain to take place. These commitments differ in this regard from guarantees which will call for a cash payment only if a particular event occurs, such as some other company's being unable to meet an obligation. As an example, the 1978 Republic Steel *Annual Report* reveals that:

> In the event certain companies are unable to make payments on their indebtedness (principally related to construction of facilities by companies supplying raw materials to the corporation), the corporation has agreed to pay specific amounts thereof aggregating $200,600,000 at December 31, 1978.[14]

---

[12] Armco, Inc., *Annual Report*, 1979, p. 38.

[13] Financial Accounting Standards Board, *Disclosure of Guarantees, Project Financing Arrangements, and Other Similar Obligations*, March 1980, p. 4.

[14] Republic Steel, *Annual Report*, 1978, p. 28.

The issue with respect to liability analysis is whether unconditional take or pay agreements should result in the recognition of assets and associated liabilities. In its exposure draft, the FASB has deferred any final determination on this matter until relevant portions of its project on the conceptual framework for financial accounting and reporting are completed. If the "taker's" operations are curtailed, the domino effect is apparent. The supplier must seek recourse against its customer whose troubles will then compound.

From a credit analysis viewpoint, take or pay agreements should be included in a complete liability position analysis, especially if going-concern status is in question. This contention stands irrespective of whether some future FASB standard includes take or pay agreements under the asset/liability umbrella. While executory in nature, take or pay agreements do have known, or estimable, future cash flow consequences. Whether they meet a going concern accounting liability definition is probably not a relevant consideration. The adjustment procedure would be similar to that illustrated for UVPB and is, therefore, not illustrated here.

Exclusion of deferred taxes

For years controversy has surrounded the proper accounting for income taxes when companies report differently to their shareholders and to the Internal Revenue Service. *Accounting Principles Board Opinion No. 11* entitled, "Accounting for Income Taxes" (1967) remains the central authoritative pronouncement in the area. It calls for application of comprehensive income tax allocation for all timing differences. Timing differences reflect disparities between profit reported to shareholders and the Internal Revenue Service which will reverse over time. If profit reported to shareholders is greater than tax-return profit initially, then sooner or later tax-return profit will exceed shareholder profit and vice versa.

Efforts to eliminate permanent deferrals

In many cases, the application of comprehensive income tax accounting results in the recording of additional taxes that become an almost permanent fixture in the company's balance sheet. Given future prospects of taxable income for a company, the deferred taxes recorded essentially become permanently deferred. However, without positive taxable income prospects, the deferred tax liability will over time disappear. In response to the common prospect of permanent deferral of taxes recorded on timing differences, a new tax reporting standard has recently been issued in the United Kingdom.[15]

---

[15] *Statement of Standard Accounting Practice No. 15*, "Accounting for Deferred Taxation."

Under this standard, deferred taxes are recorded only if there is a reasonable probability that they will reverse (mature) within the foreseeable future. The response to the new standard by U.K. companies has been to reduce drastically or to eliminate altogether the recording of deferred taxes.

It is difficult for a bank credit analyst to determine which deferred tax items are likely to require a cash outlay. Judging from the recent U.K. experience, however, it seems reasonable to adopt the general view that most deferred taxes are, under a going-concern assumption, permanently deferred and they should be eliminated from the firm's liabilities and restored to equity. Should a large deferral originate from an identifiable source with a known maturity pattern, such an item should not be excluded. However, an effort should be made to reduce its carrying value to a present value amount.

Even where going-concern status becomes questionable, liability classification for deferred taxes is not indicated. Often the troubled firm incurs operating losses of such a magnitude that they must be carried forward (the carryback feature is exhausted and losses still remain or persist). The current reporting standards permit recognition of the carryforward tax benefits through reduction of deferred tax liabilities that would otherwise reverse during the loss carryforward period.[16] The liability reduction is accomplished without a cash outflow and is, therefore, no real burden.

Unlike the other items discussed in this article, deferred tax liabilities represent a case where the proper treatment in credit analysis is the same in general for both the going and troubled concern. Liability elimination, as is now the dominant practice in the U.K., is indicated.

Impact of excluding deferred taxes

The impact of excluding deferred taxes from the liability to equity ratio is illustrated in Table 5 from the 1978 data (1977 for J. C. Penney) of five large

---

[16] *APB Opinion No. 11*, "Accounting for Income Taxes," pp. 172-75.

Table 5—Impact of Excluding Deferred Taxes
from the Liabilities to Equity Ratio of Five Companies

	Liabilities to Equity Ratio	
Company	With Deferred Taxes	Without Deferred Taxes
Sears	1.15	.85
J. C. Penney	.89	.56
Carter Hawley Hale Stores	1.63	1.25
R. H. Macy and Company	1.30	.79
Allied Stores	1.18	.98

retailers. The major sources of deferred taxes for these companies are depreciation accounting (straight-line in shareholder reports and accelerated in the tax return) and installment sales accounting (all profit taken into the shareholder report in the year of sales with the tax return reporting the profit as cash is collected on the installment basis).

Summary and conclusion

As banks increasingly adopt computerized procedures for generating standard financial ratios, there is the potential that credit analysts will accept too uncritically liability definitions based on current accounting and reporting standards. This article has provided a brief overview of some key areas in which the analyst must go beyond standard liability definitions for balance sheet recognition. In addition, attention has been directed to varying interpretations of commitments (liabilities) based on a firm's status as a going versus troubled concern.

Pensions, leases, consolidation policy, and take or pay agreements were identified as areas where the nature of conventional accounting standards typically require the credit analyst to consider the status of the firm before deciding whether to include or exclude a liability or other commitment in assessing a company's overall liability position. Only in the case of deferred taxes do current reporting standards call for inclusion of an item as a liability that in almost all cases should be excluded. A summary of the impact of all previously discussed adjusments is presented in Table 6 for four companies.

Whereas the analysis in this article has focused on what many call *off balance sheet* liabilities, much could also be said about the recognition and valuation of off

---

Table 6—Summary Impact of Liability Adjustments on Liabilities to Equity Ratios

Company	Ratio on an As Reported Basis	UVPB*	Independent Impact of			Net Adjusted** Ratio
			Operating Leases	Finance Sub-sidiaries	Deferred Taxes	
Sears (1978)	1.15	+0.05	+0.03	—	−0.29	.92
Allis-Chalmers (1979)	1.33	+0.79	—	+1.25	−0.18	3.26
Armco (1979)	.90	+0.17	—	+0.53	−0.22	1.31
American Airlines (1978)	2.34	—	+0.38	—	−0.53	2.13

* UVPB limited to 30% of stockholders' equity.
** Since some of the adjustments alter the amount of owners' equity, the row elements do not sum across the table. They should each be interpreted as the independent impact of each adjustment on the liabilities to equity ratio.

balance sheet assets in relation to unrealized elements of the equity to liabilities ratios.

In fact, in its recent *Annual Report,* Armco weighted its off balance sheet assets and liabilities and concluded, "We estimate that as of December 31, 1979, the value of off-balance-sheet assets exceeded obligations by a substantial margin."[17]

Especially now, with the new reporting becoming available under *Statement of Financial Accounting Standards No. 33,* new data are more widely available on the current cost of companies' assets.[18] Further, LIFO companies are now reporting the spread between the LIFO valuation and the current cost valuation of their inventories without jeopardizing their LIFO election. However, the recoverable amounts of long-term assets are bound to be lower than current cost of replacement for firms in financial distress. The write-up of LIFO inventories is the most prevalent and reliable of resources available off the balance sheet in the event the going-concern basis comes in question. In the future, a complete adjustment of the conventional liabilities to equity ratios will probably require the incorporation of some of these new data.   □

---

[17] Armco, *Annual Report,* 1979, p. 27

[18] *Statement of Financial Accounting Standards No. 33,* "Financial Reporting and Changing Prices," September 1979.

How Much Capital Does a Business Need?

by Douglas S. Clarke

ONE OF THE SIGNIFICANT QUALIFICATIONS of a bank commercial loan officer is that he be a competent business financial counselor. All businesses deal with banks, and, many times, the selection of a particular bank may hinge upon the counselling a bank loan officer may provide.

The average businessman knows how to "make" and "sell," but he knows little about finances. All he knows, at a particular time, is that he needs "money." The kind or type of money, or its ultimate source, is quite beyond his thoughts at this initial stage. Naturally, his first inclination is to lay his problem before his commercial banker. The banker must be prepared to analyze the problem and advise the customer as to appropriate solutions.

First, the problem must be defined. What is the job to be done? At the root of all analysis is the nature of the business.

Trading assets—working capital

Each business has its own characteristics; and the nature of the business and the practices in the industry determine the turnover of each important element in the balance sheet.

Let us look at two diverse examples from the *RMA Annual Statement Studies*[1]—for bakeries, on the one hand, and book publishing, on the other hand.[2]

	Bakeries (a)	*Book Publishing (b)*
Receivable Turn (days sales) (c)	22 days	55 days
Inventory Turn (days sales—cost) (c)	16 days	90 days

From the income data it will be seen that cost of sales is 61.5% of net sales for bakeries and 62% for book publishing. Instead of looking at turnover of inventory, we wish to find, "how many days sales are represented by inventory?" Therefore, we divide the respective inventory turnover figures by the cost percentages—61.5% and 62%—and we have inventory expressed in terms of days sales. Then inventory is exactly comparable to the receivables figures which are already expressed in terms of days sales. The revised figures would be:

	Bakeries	*Book Publishing*
Receivables—days sales	22 days	55 days
Inventory—days sales	26 days	146 days
Trading Cycle—Days Sales	48 days	201 days

Of course, with the customer's statements in front of him, the loan officer will not have to convert inventory turnover (cost basis) to the equivalent of sales days. He would figure it directly, the same as he figures receivables. The result tells him how many days sales it would take, from the time inventory is purchased, processed, sold and receivables are collected, until he gets his money back. The above illustrates that bakeries have a cycle of "cash to cash" of 48 days sales and book publishers have a cycle of 201. Certainly this means something in terms of capital need. For example, if we assume each company does business at the rate of $1,000 per day, the baker would need $48,000 in net trading assets and the book publisher would need $201,000 *to do the same volume of business.*

Trade credit

However, there are compensations. It will be noted from our industry figures that amounts "Due the Trade" are considerably different in the two industries. Bakers accounts payable[3] average 11.2% of the composite balance sheet, while accounts

---

[1] 1971 Edition.

[2] (a) Bakeries, p. 16
    (b) Book Publishing, p. 49
    (c) Median figures from "All Sizes" category.

[3] The "all sizes" figures may range from cash (sight draft) to 45 days. Flour millers prefer the sight draft method of sale.

payable due the trade for book publishers are an average of 9%. The inventory figures are, respectively, 13% and 23.1%. In other words, accounts payables for bakers are 86% of inventory and for book publishers, 39% of inventory. By inference, therefore, the composite accounts payable, in terms of daily sales, would be 22 days for bakers (86% of 26 days) and 56 days for book publishers.

Again, the loan officer could obtain the accounts payable carry, in terms of average daily sales, directly from the customer's financial statements without the above conversion. The amount of financing provided by trade accounts payable is, of course, important in analyzing the financial need. The financing support provided by trade accounts payable is important to our problem since we see that the net cash cycle (cash to cash) is considerably improved:

	Bakeries	Book Publishing
Trading Cycle (sales days)	48 days	201 days
Accounts Payable (sales days)	22 days	56 days
Net Cash Cycle	26 days	145 days

It is evident that, on a net cash cycle basis, it takes over six times as much money in net trading assets to be in the book publishing business as it does to be a baker. Further, as long as a company is in active business, receivables and inventory must be thought of as just as permanent an investment as bricks and mortar. Think of receivables and inventory as oil in a pipeline. The pipeline must always be full (while we stay in business) before anything comes out of the other end of the line.

If there were no seasonal fluctuation in either of the two businesses, bakers or book publishing, the investment capital needs of each business would be permanent and would be determined by the level of sales. In other words, if we assume a sales level of $5,000 per day, the capital need in the bakery business for trading assets would be $130,000 ($5,000 x 26 days) and $725,000 ($5,000 x 145 days) for book publishing.

The financing support given by trade creditors cannot be overestimated, and the banker should be familiar with the Terms of Sale offered by suppliers in each industry. A summary of Terms of Sale is periodically published by Dun & Bradstreet, and they vary all the way from sight draft (auto companies and some flour millers) up to 70 days for cotton goods with discounts up to 8% allowed for "anticipations."

It is also important to note the breadth of discounts given by suppliers since this can be an important cost, or cost saving as the case may be. For example, the usual steel terms are ½%, 10 net 30, and missing a discount is equivalent to paying 9% for the privilege of being financed for 20 days (terms net 30). It is cheaper to borrow from a bank, in most instances; however, the banker must carefully observe the trade record, first to see that the customer is not borrowing in two places—the bank and the trade—and second to see that the customer is not abusing trade credit to the point where his supplies (credit) may be reduced or cut off. Being placed on a C.O.D. basis by suppliers is usually fatal.

Trading assets, how much are needed?

How much should be invested in trading assets? The above illustrations presume a stable volume, but businesses fluctuate in season. While permanent capital investment should cover the low periods of volume (the permanent investment), bank credit can be employed at seasonal peaks and may be self-liquidating when business recedes again.

If we assume that there is sufficient invested capital to cover the needs of the business at its seasonal low point that five days sales "till cash" is sufficient, we might project a seasonal loan requirement for our baker as follows: (000 omitted)

	January	March	July	September	December
Sales Per Day	$ 1	$ 2	$ 3	$ 2	$ 1
Cash	5	10	15	10	5
Accounts receivable	22	44	66	44	22
Inventory	26	52	78	52	26
Current (Total Assets)	$53	$106	$159	$106	$53
Bank Loan	$ -0-	$ 31	$ 62	$ 31	$ -0-
Accounts payable	22	44	66	44	22
Net Worth	31	31	31	31	31
Total	$53	$106	$159	$106	$53

In the above example we see the classical seasonal "self-liquidating" loan. The loan finances the seasonal increase in receivables and inventory and is paid out when receivables and inventory are reduced in the low volume periods of the year. Of course, at July, when sales are $3,000 per day, the company's debt is $128,000 against a net worth of only $31,000 and the risk is high, momentarily. It is a question of judgment whether a banker should make a peak loan, even temporarily, at such a high risk. If not, then (a) more capital is needed or (b) the baker's volume must be restricted to more reasonable levels.

The decision in the latter case might be that the bank would lend up to $31,000, the condition at March and September, because at those points we have $54,000 of "quick" assets, cash and receivables, and would have to go into inventory only $21,000 or 40% to pay current (and total) debt. This is a fair short-term risk. The situation at July is 60% into inventory and, even for a couple of months carry, is a lot of risk—particularly with perishable products. How much additional capital would be needed? Enough to bring the risk down to, say 40% into inventory or an additional 20% of inventory or about $15,000. In any event, insurance for fire, water, business interruption and other hazards would be a necessity.

Perhaps the owner wants to do a volume of $3,000 a day (the July peak) and could protect the bank by "outside" assets such as cash value of life insurance or with securities he can temporarily pledge. The point is to keep the risk within reasonable bounds or else refuse to make the loan. These alternatives can be explained to the customer very simply so he can see the risk. He cannot guarantee against catastrophe, and he should not expect to have the bank—or other creditors—face a certain loss from his "overtrading" position should a serious accident occur. The point is (a) analyze the problem, (b) explain the problem, (c) point out the risks, (d) explore alternatives and (e) make a decision on the facts.

Overtrading

In discussing the July balance sheet, above, reference was made to "overtrading." This is a condition where the employment of debt is so great that any inadvertence will, almost surely, wipe out net worth and creditors will sustain a loss because of inadequate equity protection. Overtrading invites financial failure and loss to creditors.

There are four elements of risk associated with overtrading:

1. Serious depletion of profit margin,
2. Organization failures associated with high volume,
3. Receivables losses and
4. Inventory risks

Depletion of margin. Sales minded managements who pursue sales volume at the expense of margin of profit, invariably run into the following situation: Sales of $100,000 at 10% yields $10,000 in profits, but sales at a 9% margin require an increase of sales of 11% to make the same profit. Similarly:

> 8% requires 25% more sales to equal the same profit,
> 7% requires 43% more sales to equal the same profit,
> 6% requires 67% more sales to equal the same profit, and
> 5% requires 100% more sales to equal the same profit.

Therefore, from the standpoint of net return, the decision to increase sales primarily through the device of cutting prices or profit margins is a rapidly self-defeating exercise.

Organizational failure. Handling more inventory, receivables and all the collateral problems of higher volume not only can be expensive in an organizational expansion sense, but the risk of a "snafu" raises its head very quickly. Consider the receiving, vouchering, warehousing, stock control, production and servicing aspects of suddenly increasing volume. Unless the organizational adjustment is well planned and gradually indoctrinated into the personnel, resulting in a smooth functioning organization, a sudden increase in volume may mean disaster.

Receivables loss. An attempt to increase volume in a short space of time (shades of the credit card experience) means taking on new customers, not on a small order trial basis, but in wholesale quantities and amounts. While larger amounts of capital will be needed to carry larger receivables (and inventory), there will undoubtedly be an additional capital need because of a materially slower turn in trading assets. Receivables may go from 30 to 45 days, and if weak credits are sold in the process, a real risk of credit loss is entailed despite an expanded, alert, but expensive, credit staff.

Inventory risk. Inventory risk is always related to the nature of the product, but, nevertheless, the risk seems to expand by the square of the deficiency in working capital to cover the inventory investment. While the 60% into inventory risk in the July statement, above, has been pointed out, what would happen if the customer tried to expand volume to $4,000 per day or $5,000 per day? At the latter figure, there is no margin of protection at all!

In other words, if sales are going to be dramatically increased, the capital protection of creditors must likewise be increased. We have the industry figures published by RMA and D&B as testimony that the turnover of accounts receivable and inventory cannot be materially improved over the averages. A management must be extraordinary to be better than the average and excel over industry performance to any significant degree. Therefore, the only safe answer is to increase capital and reduce the risk to creditors.

Fixed and non-trading assets

The area of commercial bank lending is largely concentrated in the financing of trading assets. Ideally, a banker should not be heavily involved, short-term or long-term, where current assets do not cover total debt.

This may seem a severe caveat but its violation considerably increases the risk to a lender. Certainly if it is violated, the security of a cashable nature should be adequate to justify the risk. Ideally, the banker should be in such a position that a recession in volume of sales reduces inventory and receivables which turn into cash to pay the banker's loans. Of course, this reckons without losses which usually accompany a recession and some allowance (margin of collateral or liquidable assets) must be made in measuring the risk.

If trading assets are strictly construed—as they should be—to be only cash, receivables and inventory—then all other assets are "nontrading." Hence, such items as prepaid insurance, prepaids generally, cash surrender value of life insurance or investment securities are nontrading and will remain so until management makes a decision to convert them to trading assets either by sale or use as collateral resulting in cash which can be used in trading.

In our illustration of the baker, above, consideration was given solely to the capital needs of his trading position, and that should remain in focus, no matter the size of the balance sheet. Certainly our baker was already short of trading capital at the July peak period. Suppose, now, he wants to purchase a $100,000 building and some $50,000 of equipment.[4] Assuming the proper earning power (or cash gain) to amortize a debt of 60% of the building and, say, 75% of the equipment, the additional liquid capital requirement would be a total of $58,500 to provide the equity over the respective mortgages. Now, however, our baker has an additional $91,500 of debt— way out of proportion to the net worth ($31,000)—and we have added a substantial interest and amortization factor which prevents even a high earning operation from increasing working capital and restricts the company's ability to trade and grow.

Further, the company has put itself in such a debt position that the banker cannot help, even for presumably seasonal short-term loans. The risk at the seasonal peak would, obviously, be unconscionable. It will be observed that although $58,500 of net worth may be added to provide the equity for the real and chattel mortgages, not one cent was added to the company's trading assets. Obviously additional capital is needed. How much? Now we fall back on our rule of thumb that current assets should cover total debt—at least for the basic requirement at the low season of the year. If they cover debt at that point, they will always cover provided succeeding loans are made strictly for working capital purposes.

A quick proforma statement shows that if we have total trading and non-trading assets of $203,000 ($53,000 + $150,000), we must inject new liquid capital of $119,000 (instead of the $58,500) in order to satisfy the premise that current assets cover total debt at the seasonal low (basic capital). To the extent of the increased liquid capital of $119,000, the proforma debt would be reduced accordingly and also the requirements for interest and debt amortization. This means our customer can pay cash for his machinery (reducing the higher interest and fast amortization) and additionally reduce his mortgage requirement to $31,000. Now the customer, with fair earning power, has a chance to add to working capital out of earnings rather than have earnings absorbed in debt service. The resulting balance sheet proforma would be:

---

[4]RMA figures, *op. cit.* show bakers "all sizes—92 cases" to have 52.5% of assets in "fixed" and 7.2% in "all other—noncurrent." To this I would add "all other—current" of 1.5%. Therefore, 61.2% of assets are "non-trading."

Proforma Balance Sheet
(At low point January—000 Omitted)

Sales per day .... $ 1

Cash..........................	$ 5	Bank Loan	$ -0-
Accounts receivable	22	Accounts payable	22
Inventory	26		
Current Assets	53	Current debt	22
		Term debt (mtg)	31
		Total debt	53
Plant	100		
Machinery	50	Net worth	150
Total	$203	Total	$203

If it is protested that a $100,000 building could carry a larger mortgage than $31,000, say up to $60,000, the banker would most certainly agree, provided cash gain will support the debt with significant additions to working capital during the life of the loan and—significantly—if the increased borrowing of $29,000 went exclusively into working capital. This would reduce borrowing needs at the peak periods and substantially reduce risk to all concerned. At July, total debt, proforma, would be only $130,000 (proforma $159,000 less $29,000) and be more than covered by current assets, an entirely comfortable position.

Conclusion

As in all such rules of thumb, there is bound to be some give and take within reasonable limits, but there must be some guideposts. Loans are not made because there is collateral, but because they can be paid in a comfortable manner which assists the customer in his normal growth. If collateral is relied upon solely because of its value, then the way the loan will be paid is liquidation of the collateral and the customer's business. That, certainly, is not the objective of the bank officer in making the loan.

The area of commerical bank lending is in the working capital area. This applies to term loans also. Beyond the point where current assets (proforma) do not cover total debt, other financing sources of an investment nature are usually indicated. However, it must be remembered that an outside secured lender has a first claim on his security and then shares equally with the unsecured banker in what is left.

The commercial banker has a great responsibility to advise unsophisticated customers. A properly financed, healthy customer means a constructive, healthy bank.

□

Sustainable Growth:
New Tool in Bank Lending

by Robert C. Higgins

The sustainable growth rate is a useful concept not only for evaluating loan requests, but in handling client relations and new business prospects. So says Professor Higgins who shows how to calculate and interpret this valuable equation.

It takes money to make money. Nowhere is that old saw more applicable than in financing rapidly growing enterprises. Although every additional dollar of sales adds a few cents to profits, growth also requires significant new investment in receivables, inventories, and fixed assets. Sometimes this required investment can be financed internally through retained profits on new and existing sales. However, for rapidly expanding companies, the need for new investment capital can easily exceed internal sources. In this situation, increasing amounts of external capital are required to finance the growth in sales.

Rapid growth and a prudent balance

If the rapidly growing company can maintain a prudent balance between debt and equity sources, this reliance on external capital creates no problem. However, in too many instances, rapid sales growth, coupled with modest profit margins and an inability to sell new equity, forces the company to rely increasingly on bank credit. Rapid growth then leads to increasing debt ratios and increasing banker headaches.

Aware of the interplay between rapid growth and balance sheet strength, the lending officer should attempt to answer two questions when contemplating a loan to a rapidly expanding firm:

1. Is the applicant in balance? Given the customer's growth targets and financial policies, will the company be able to maintain a stable debt ratio over time, or will it be forced to rely increasingly on debt?

2. When can the bank expect repayment of the loan? Is the requested amount sufficient over the long run in light of the firm's growth targets, or is the contemplated loan likely to be just the downpayment on a much larger commitment?

Definition of sustainable growth rate

To help answer these questions, it is useful to calculate what I will call the firm's *sustainable growth rate*. Assuming the loan applicant wants to maintain a constant dividend payout ratio without selling new shares, sustainable growth is the annual percentage increase in sales which is consistent with a stable capital structure. Sustainable growth is a single number: If the company expands at any rate greater than its sustainable growth rate, it will be out of balance. Unless remedial action is taken, the applicant's debt ratio will rise steadily over time.

Calculation of a loan applicant's sustainable growth rate is by no means a substitute for detailed financial projections in evaluating loan requests. However, used before or in conjunction with a detailed projection, the sustainable growth calculation has several appeals.

1. Unlike detailed projections, a company's sustainable growth rate can be calculated by hand in a few minutes. As discussed in more detail later, this simplicity and ease of calculation means that the sustainable growth expression can be useful to the lending officer in new business development.

2. The sustainable growth expression focuses directly on those variables which are most important to the banker and the financial manager. This is in contrast to detailed forecasts where one can easily lose sight of the forest for the trees.

3. The sustainable growth expression gives the banker and the manager a simple way to coordinate the company's growth objectives and its financial policies to assure that future growth can be financed.

In the following pages, I will develop a general expression for sustainable growth in terms of a company's financial policies and its operating characteristics. I will then show how this expression can be used in several common lending situations. My conclusion will take a brief look at the impact of inflation on financing growth and on the use of the sustainable growth expression in new business development.

How to calculate a firm's sustainable growth rate

Consider a company which wants to maintain a stable dividend payout ratio and capital structure without selling new shares. Given these common corporate goals, Figure 1 illustrates an important fact about growth. Rather than an independent variable to be maximized, an enterprise's growth rate is determined by certain financial policies and industry characteristics which together form a closed system.

A given target debt-to-equity ratio and a target dividend payout ratio are set by financial policy. A given profit margin and a capital-output ratio are determined by industry characteristics. The firm's sustainable growth rate in sales closes the loop.

Figure 1
The Sustainable Growth Loop

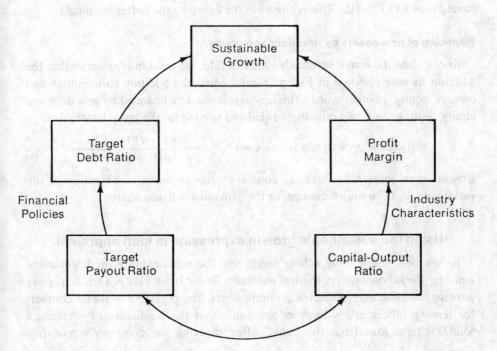

The mathematical symbols in the sustainable growth equation

To derive the sustainable growth expression, we need only equate annual sources of company cash to annual uses. It will help to define the following symbols.

p = the firm's profit margin on sales
d = the target dividend payout ratio [$(1 - d)$ is therefore the target retention ratio]
L = the target total debt-to-equity ratio
t = the capital-output ratio, defined as total assets divided by net sales
s = sales at the beginning of the period
Δs = the increase in sales during the year.

The basic idea is illustrated in Figure 2. Assuming that p and t are the same for new sales as for existing sales, the new assets required to support increased sales of Δs are $\Delta s(t)$, shown as the cross-hatched rectangle in Figure 2. On the other side of the balance sheet, total profits for the year will be $p(s + \Delta s)$, and additions to retained earnings will be $p(s + \Delta s)(1 - d)$. This is shown in the figure by the shaded rectangle. Finally, because every dollar added to retained earnings enables the company to borrow $\$L$ without increasing its debt-to-equity ratio, new borrowings equal $p(s + \Delta s)(1 - d)L$. This is shown in the figure by the dotted rectangle.

Financing of new assets by new debt and equity

To calculate the firm's sustainable growth rate, we need only observe that the addition to assets shown in Figure 2 must equal the addition to liabilities and owners' equity. In other words, the new assets must be financed by new debt and equity. Setting these two quantities equal and solving for the growth rate, $\Delta s/s$,

$$\text{sustainable growth rate in sales} = g^* = \frac{p(1 - d)(1 + L)}{t - p(1 - d)(1 + L)}$$

Unless actual growth in sales, g, equals g^*, one or some combination of the variables p, d, L, or t must change, or the firm must sell new shares.

Using the sustainable growth expression in loan appraisal

To see how the lending officer might use the sustainable growth equation, consider the following hypothetical example. Radar Industries is a small, rapidly growing manufacturer of electrical components. The president of Radar contacts the lending officer at his bank of account about the possibility of securing a $500,000 term loan from the bank. After studying the company's proforma

Figure 2
Calculating Sustainable Growth

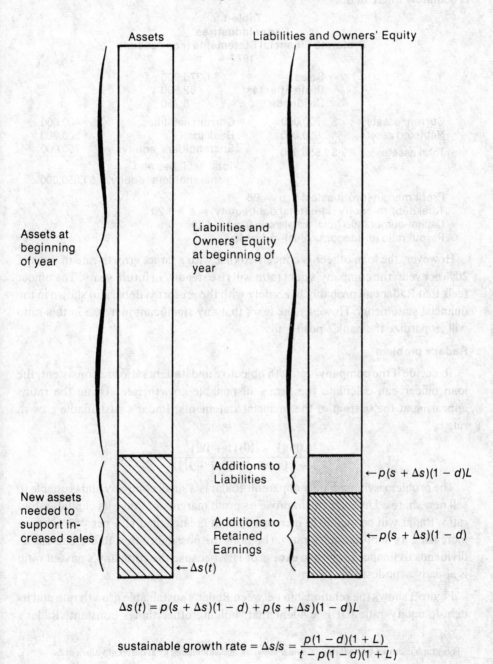

Assets   Liabilities and Owners' Equity

Assets at beginning of year

Liabilities and Owners' Equity at beginning of year

New assets needed to support increased sales

Additions to Liabilities   ←$p(s + \Delta s)(1 - d)L$

Additions to Retained Earnings   ←$p(s + \Delta s)(1 - d)$

←$\Delta s(t)$

$$\Delta s(t) = p(s + \Delta s)(1 - d) + p(s + \Delta s)(1 - d)L$$

$$\text{sustainable growth rate} = \Delta s/s = \frac{p(1 - d)(1 + L)}{t - p(1 - d)(1 + L)}$$

financial statements for 1977, reproduced in condensed form in Table 1, the banker is definitely interested.

Table 1
Radar Industries
Proforma Financial Statements (condensed)
1977

	Sales	$1,375,000	
	Profit after tax	82,500	
	Dividends	8,250	
Current assets	$ 700,000	Current liabilities	$ 400,000
Net fixed assets	950,000	Bank loan	500,000
Total assets	$ 1,650,000	Shareholders' equity	750,000
		Total liabilities and shareholders' equity	$ 1,650,000

Profit margin (profit/sales) = p = .06
Total debt-to-equity ratio (total debt/equity) = L = 1.20
Capital-output ratio (total assets/sales) = t = 1.20
Payout ratio (dividends/profits) = d = .10

However, the loan officer is concerned that with a target growth rate in sales of 20% per year, the company's debt ratio will rise steadily in future years. The officer feels that Radar can probably live safely with the proforma debt ratio shown in the financial statements. However, he fears that any significant increase in this ratio will jeopardize the bank's position.

Radar's problem

To decide if the company's growth objective and its debt ratio are consistent, the loan officer can calculate the firm's sustainable growth rate. Using the ratios appearing at the bottom of the financial statements, Radar's sustainable growth rate is

$$g^* = \frac{(.06)(1 - .10)(1 + 1.2)}{1.2 - (.06)(1 - .10)(1 + 1.2)} = 11\%$$

The problem is immediately apparent. Radar is a small company and is unable to sell new shares. Unless it can improve its profit margin or reduce its capital-output ratio, Radar will be unable to increase sales at greater than 11% per year without increasing its debt-to-equity ratio. (I ignore the possibility that Radar can cut its dividends to finance growth in excess of 11% because the company's payout ratio is already a modest 10%.)

Figure 3 shows the relationship between Radar's sustainable growth rate and its debt-to-equity ratio.[1] It is evident that, holding other things constant, Radar's

---

[1]This graph is drawn by holding p, t, and d constant and calculating g* at different values of L.

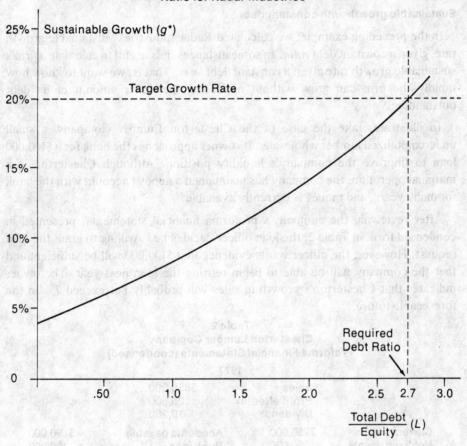

Figure 3
Sustainable Growth Rate as a Function of Debt
Ratio for Radar Industries

debt-to-equity ratio must rise from 120% to 270% before its 20% growth target and its capital structure are in balance. (This 270% figure can be calculated directly by setting $g^* = 20\%$ in the sustainable growth expression and solving for L.)

In a matter of minutes, the sustainable growth equation indicates that unless remedial action is taken, achievement of Radar's growth objectives will significantly weaken the company's balance sheet. This information should help the loan officer in appraising the loan request and, perhaps more important, in counselling the client. For if the client can be made to understand the interdependence between growth targets and financial policies, it may be possible to bring the company back to a sustainable growth path. At the same time, the loan could be made attractive.

Sustainable growth with constant debt

In the preceding example, we calculated Radar Industries' sustainable growth rate, given a constant debt *ratio*. In some instances, it is useful to calculate a firm's sustainable growth rate given a constant debt *level*. That is, we want to know how rapidly the firm can grow without increasing the dollar amount of its debt outstanding.

To illustrate, take the case of the Chesterton Lumber Company, a small undercapitalized lumber wholesaler. Its owner approaches the bank for a $100,000 loan to improve the company's liquidity position. Although Chesterton is a marginal operation, the company has maintained a deposit account with the bank for many years, and money is currently available.

After reviewing the company's proforma financial statements, presented in condensed form in Table 2, the loan officer decides he is willing to grant the loan request. However, the officer wants evidence that $100,000 will be sufficient and that the company will be able to begin retiring the loan next year. The owner indicates that Chesterton's growth in sales will probably not exceed 7% in the foreseeable future.

Table 2
Chesterton Lumber Company
Proforma Financial Statements (condensed)
1977

Sales		$850,000	
Profit after tax		25,500	
Dividends		10,200	
Current assets	$250,000	Accounts payable	$ 90,000
Net fixed assets	90,000	Bank loan	100,000
Total Assets	$340,000	Shareholders' equity	150,000
		Total liabilities and shareholders' equity	$340,000

Profit margin (profit/sales) $= p = .03$
Nonbank debt-to-equity ratio (nonbank debt/equity)$= \hat{L} = .60$
Capital-output ratio (total assets/sales) $= t = .40$
Payout ratio (dividends/profit) $= d = .40$

To decide whether Chesterton could repay the loan in the near future, we can use a modified version of the sustainable growth expression. The original expression was derived assuming that the firm's total debt would grow in proportion to the increase in shareholders' equity. In the present case, we want to calculate the firm's sustainable growth rate assuming that only the firm's nonbank debt grows in proportion to the increase in equity. By construction, the firm's bank debt is to remain constant. Defining

$$\hat{L} = \text{the target nonbank debt-to-equity ratio,}$$

the revised sustainable growth expression becomes

$$\hat{g}^* = \frac{p(1-d)(1+\hat{L})}{t - p(1-d)(1+\hat{L})}$$

If actual growth in sales, g, exceeds $\hat{g}^*$ and if p, d, t, and $\hat{L}$ stay constant, the firm will be unable to pay existing bank debt and will, in fact, need more bank credit.

Growth-financing problems reduced by low capital-output ratio

Looking at Chesterton Lumber's proforma financial statements, we see that the firm's only source of nonbank credit is accounts payable. $\hat{L}$ is therefore only .60. Substituting this and the other ratios appearing at the bottom of Table 2 into the revised sustainable growth expression,

$$\hat{g}^* = \frac{(.03)(1 - .40)(1 + .60)}{.40 - (.03)(1 - .40)(1 + .60)} = 7.8\%$$

This is the evidence the lending officer seeks. Because the sustainable growth rate without additional bank debt exceeds the forecast growth rate, Chesterton's internally generated cash should be sufficient to finance growth and to begin repayment of the loan. As is true of many nonmanufacturing concerns, Chesterton's growth-financing problems are reduced by a low capital-output ratio. If Chesterton's capital-output ratio equaled Radar Industries', its sustainable growth rate without new bank debt would be only 2.5%.

Sustainable growth and inflation

In recent years, it has become common to distinguish between real and inflationary growth. Real growth comes from an increase in the physical volume of goods and services sold, whereas inflationary growth is due entirely to an increase in prices.

In many contexts, it is proper to argue that real growth is the variable of primary interest and that inflationary growth is entirely illusory. Bankers and managers should realize, however, that the impact on an enterprise's financing needs is almost identical, regardless of whether the growth is real or inflationary.

Financing the increase in current assets

Consider first the firm's current assets. During inflation, the dollar value of a company's investment in accounts receivable and inventory will rise even if the physical volume of merchandise represented by these accounts stays constant. A small part of this added investment can be financed by the inflation-induced increase in reported profits. But as already noted in the opening paragraphs, internal sources are often insufficient. In these cases, external capital must be provided to finance the increase in current assets. The situation is the same as if the growth were real instead of inflationary.

The impact of inflationary growth on fixed asset investment is more circuitous, but the result is much the same. In the initial stages of inflation, the firm's need to increase its investment in fixed plant and equipment is unaffected by inflation, depending only on the real increase in physical volume. However, as existing fixed assets are replaced, the price of new fixed assets, capable of producing the same physical volume, will be higher.[2]

If depreciation were based on an asset's replacement cost instead of its historical cost, companies could finance this increased fixed asset investment out of depreciation cash flows. The fact that depreciation must be based on historical cost, however, means that depreciation cash flows will be insufficient to maintain existing assets even at the same physical volume. Additional financing must then be secured.

Two important conclusions

There are two important conclusions to be drawn from this discussion. The most obvious is that inflation worsens financing problems because it superimposes a second type of growth on the firm. This growth does not add to the real value of the firm, but it must be financed almost as if it were real. Particularly frustrating is the fact that inflationary growth is outside the control of an individual company. Management has some control over its firm's real growth rate through its pricing and other policies; however, inflationary growth is created almost entirely by factors which are external to the firm.

The second important conclusion is that the sustainable growth expression presented earlier is applicable — at least as a first approximation — for inflationary as well as real growth. That is, with inflation, the sustainable growth equation applies broadly to the firm's observed, or nominal, growth rate (where the observed growth rate is composed of a real portion and an inflationary portion).

To illustrate, consider a company whose sustainable growth rate, based on reported financial figures without adjustment for inflation, is 15%. If the general inflation rate is 5%, then the firm's *real* sustainable growth rate is only about 10%. If the company increases the physical volume of sales at greater than about 10%

---

[2]For the sake of argument, this ignores the possibility that, due to improved technology and design, less equipment would be needed to produce the same volume.

per year, its financial policies and growth objectives will be out of balance. Moreover, if the inflation rate rises to 10%, the maximum increase in physical volume falls to about 5% if balance is to be maintained.

Briefly then, the concept of sustainable growth and the sustainable growth equation are even more important under inflationary than under noninflationary conditions.

Sustainable growth and new business development

In addition to use in loan evaluation, the sustainable growth expression is potentially useful in client relations and new business development. A primary virtue of the sustainable growth concept is that it focuses on a critical element in company planning in a very straightforward manner.

There exists, particularly among managers of many smaller firms, the presumption that as long as the company is profitable and growing, its financial problems will take care of themselves. The sustainable growth expression gives the banker or financial consultant a simple way to demonstrate the fallacy of this reasoning. It also shows a manager the interrelationship between his firm's financial policies and its growth rate.

The sustainable growth concept can be used creatively in customer relations and new business development. It can give the loan officer a forum for discussing a company's financial policies, its growth objectives, and the extent to which the bank can help the firm to reach its objectives.   ☐

Analyzing the Quantity and Quality of Cash Flow for Long-Term Borrowing

by Dev Strischek

Both quantitative and qualitative considerations are important in term loan cash flow analysis. In the following article, Dev Strischek discusses five different ratios for evaluating a firm's solvency position. In his opinion, the major problem in using these types of ratios is how to compare tax-deductible expenses with nondeductible funds outlays. The five ratio formulas he presents all allow for making this comparison.

The importance of earnings quality becomes author Strischek's focus in the latter part of the article as he demonstrates how various accounting practices can distort the earnings picture.

As commercial borrowers' needs have become more complex, bankers have had to extend their time horizons for debt repayment. It used to be that seasonal lenders presumed repayment to flow from the current assets' cash cycle. But today's commercial lenders increasingly must deal with firms whose borrowings must be repaid from cash flow.

Our national obsession with growth, for better or for worse, permeates our business community and is reflected in decisions stressing revenue and profit expansion. This expansion, in turn, requires increases in minimum levels of working capital and fixed assets. Earnings cannot completely fund the desired growth, and the equity markets have never been accessible to most of America's corporate borrowers.

A number of financial institutions have risen to the challenge. Insurance companies, finance companies, and investment firms have been long-term lenders for years; it is the commercial banking industry that has been the laggard in term lending. The trend from lines of credit to revolvers to outright term loans is clear to any observer of credit markets. The task before bankers is to develop the quantitative and qualitative tools necessary to assess the volume, stability, and quality of cash flow.

Reasons for long-term borrowing

A basic tenet of finance is that short-term assets should be financed with short-term debt and long-term assets with long-term debt and equity. In other words, we fund the uses with sources of equal duration.

The typical reasons for long-term borrowing, then, are generally uses associated with sales and operations expansion such as:

(1) An increase in noncurrent assets, usually new fixed assets.

(2) An increase in the minimum or permanent net working capital levels.

(3) Repayment of long-term debt.

Repayment obligations

Ultimately, the lender expects that earnings from operations will fund these uses because the primary purpose of the expansion is to generate profits. If there are no profits to be made, there is no reason to expand. Economists are very quick to tell us that we only increase production as long as the extra costs required to expand are covered by extra profits; economists say that when marginal profits equal marginal costs, the firm is maximizing its profits.

Permanent current assets and liabilities

Creditors and, in turn, owners commit funds to a firm with the reasonable expectation that the firm will repay loans plus a fair rate of interest to the creditors and will declare satisfactory dividends for the shareholders. Moreover, the firm has internal financial responsibilities to maintain its productive assets at optimal efficiency.

While the term "permanent assets" is primarily restricted to capital assets and other noncurrent assets, it should also be recognized that the firm must carry a minimum level of current assets. This minimum level is properly part of the permanent assets, and that portion of current liabilities carried year around should be considered permanent debt. These permanent current assets and liabilities do not have directly associated servicing requirements. But their expansion and contraction should theoretically be funded through corresponding changes in debtors' equity, that is, by liabilities and owners' equity.

Firm's ability to service six primary obligations

Being able to service its obligations means the firm is able to pay interest expense on outstanding debt, meet the debt repayment as scheduled, pay adequate preferred and common stock dividends, and set aside a portion of earnings through depreciation and amortization to replenish the firm's productive assets. In addition, where leased facilities and equipment are a significant proportion of productive assets, the lease expense's fixed contractual payment is a relevant factor in appraising the firm's ability to service its permanent obligations. These six outlays—interest expense, debt repayment, preferred dividends, common dividends, capital expenditures, and lease expense—are the principal uses of funds generated by operations. A firm unable to fund its permanent obligations will be unable to maintain its assets. One definition of solvency is the ability of a firm to repay its long-term obligations.

We can quantitatively judge a firm's solvency through ratios comparing various sources of funds with various uses.

Introduction to solvency ratios

There are several ratios by which to judge a firm's solvency position, but they all share the same approach. Earnings and/or cash flow (earnings plus depreciation) are compared to various expenses and outlays associated with a firm's permanent debt, owner's equity, and permanent assets. The funds available for paying the various outlays are usually divided by the outlays; thus, the higher the ratio, the better is the coverage of the outlays by the funds from operations. A ratio of less than 1.00 means that, within the context of the ratio, funds from operations are less than outlays being compared. Therefore, the coverage as defined by that ratio is inadequate.

Before-tax outlays vs. after-tax outlays

The major problem in using solvency ratios is how to compare tax-deductible expenses with nondeductible outlays. Under corporate tax laws, lease payments, interest, and depreciation are deductible expenses; however, dividends, debt repayments, and capital expenditures are not tax-deductible. Therefore, nondeductible outlays require a greater before-tax portion of earnings than the tax-deductible expenses.

For example, a $5 common stock dividend declared by a company in a 48% corporate income tax bracket has to earn $9.62 in order to have a sum after taxes equal to the declared dividend:

$$\begin{bmatrix} \text{Earnings before} \\ \text{taxes required} \\ \text{to pay a \$5.00} \\ \text{dividend} \end{bmatrix} \times \begin{bmatrix} 1-48\% \text{ income} \\ \text{tax} \end{bmatrix} = \begin{array}{l} \text{\$5.00 dividend} \\ \text{after taxes} \end{array}$$

$$\begin{bmatrix} \text{Earnings before} \\ \text{taxes required} \\ \text{to pay a \$5.00} \\ \text{dividend} \end{bmatrix} = \frac{\text{\$5.00 div. A. T.}}{(1.00 - .48)}$$

$$\begin{bmatrix} \text{Earnings before} \\ \text{taxes required} \\ \text{to pay a \$5.00} \\ \text{dividend after} \\ \text{taxes} \end{bmatrix} = \text{\$9.62}$$

It is clear from this example that the corporate income tax rate distorts and consequently precludes logical comparison of tax-deductible expenses with after-tax nondeductible outlays. Meaningful analysis is possible only if the data are comparable. Hence, one outlay must be converted to the tax position of the other.

The preferred approach is to convert nondeductible outlays to their pre-tax earnings equivalent. A before-tax basis eliminates the difference in the tax rate often encountered in comparative analysis of small and large companies. Moreover, even internal analysis is affected by the year-to-year differences in corporate profits and the concomitant income tax rate.

Simple formula

The formula for converting after-tax amounts to before-tax amounts can be stated in shortened form as follows:

$$\textbf{(Before \$)} \ (1.00 - r) = \textbf{(After \$)}$$

$$\textbf{(Before \$)} = \frac{\textbf{(After \$)}}{(1.00 - r)}$$

The logical proof behind the formula was presented in the $5 dividend example. Here it is again stated in the shortened form just given:

$$\textbf{(Before \$)} \ (1.00 - r) \ = \ \textbf{(After \$)}$$

$$\textbf{(Before \$)} \ (1.00 - .48) = \ \$5.00$$

$$\textbf{(Before \$)} = \frac{\$5.00}{(1.00 - .48)} = \frac{\$5.00}{.52} = \$9.62$$

Solvency ratios

With the mechanics of the solvency ratios perfected, the solvency ratios per se can now be discussed. Each of the following five ratios has its strengths and weaknesses, but all five conform to the general principles and quantitative mechanics presented in this section.

Times-interest-earned ratio

One of the most widely used solvency ratios is the times-interest-earned ratio. The increased use of long-term debt, its senior position over owners' equity in the capital structure, and the resultant practice of highlighting interest expense in financial statements make this aspect of solvency appraisal hard to ignore and easy to calculate.

Both long-term creditors and owners concentrate attention on the portion of the earnings stream to which they are entitled. But present and prospective long-term creditors examine the operating statement to see how adequately their interest return is covered by the pre-tax operating income. Bondholders, banks, insurance companies, and other long-term creditors usually enjoy a variety of protective convenants. Such covenants ensure that the debt will be repaid at the promised time and compensate the lender for the use of his money by the payment of an interest charge. A breach or violation of a covenant usually gives the lender the right to accelerate the date of maturity or some other privilege unfavorable to the debtor. In view of these undesirable remedies, the analyst may sensibly assume that at least one basic solvency guideline is the ability of a firm to cover its interest expense at least once.

The times-interest-earned ratio is calculated as follows:

$$\text{Times-interest-earned} \ = \ \frac{\text{EBIT}}{\text{Interest expense}}$$

where EBIT equals earnings before interest and taxes.

A minimum solvency guideline of 1.00 more was suggested earlier. However, a typical guideline is 3.00 to 8.00 because of the variations in earnings and interest expense from period to period and also because of differences between various lines of business. For the sake of comparison, Moody's and Standard and Poor's bond ratings of top rated Aaa/AAA industrial companies show a 16.84 average, and their medium grade industrial companies, a 4.21 average coverage for the 1973–1978 period.

Fixed charges coverage ratio

Besides applying funds to the payment of interest expense on its long-term debt, a firm must also commit funds to repayment of the debt principal. Scheduled repayments of principal are just as mandatory as interest payments. Any failure to pay according to the debt agreement would normally subject the firm to the same unfavorable circumstances as encountered in default on the interest expense. Although scheduled debt repayments can be delayed, they inevitably must be repaid. A conservative analytical approach is to assume that the debt will be repaid as agreed. Scheduled debt repayment is equally as important in appraising a firm's solvency as is the interest expense factor.

Debt repayment is the reduction of a liability and therefore cannot be considered a cost of doing business any more than the original proceeds of the loan can be counted as income. In a sense, a portion of the earnings must be retained in the business to repay debt. Debt repayment is not tax-deductible and must be converted to its pre-tax earnings equivalent to use it in this ratio.

Current maturities of long-term debt. For practical purposes, the balance sheet item shown as "current maturities of long-term debt" under the current liabilities classification is satisfactory for use as the scheduled debt repayment. The desired approach is to match the scheduled debt repayment of the previous accounting period with the outlays of the present period—the period during which the debt repayment would presumably occur. If this approach is impractical, then the current period's long-term debt maturities is acceptable provided that this amount is applied consistently in all the ratios and throughout the trend series.

Preferred dividend. A second outlay that tacitly functions as a fixed burden is the preferred dividend. Theoretically, the preferred stock combines the limited obligation of a bond with the flexibility of common stock. In exchange for his first claim to dividends, the preferred stockholder's priority in dividends is generally limited to a fixed percentage of the par value of the stock or a fixed number of dollars per share for no par stock. However, the security of his preferred position is usually reinforced with the "cumulative" feature; before any common dividend can be paid, not only must the current preferred stock be paid but also any unpaid preferred dividends declared in previous years.

The prior claim of the preferred stockholder does not guarantee a fixed, regular rate of return. The claim only establishes an order of priority by which the board of directors will pay dividends if it decides to declare dividends at all. The fixed nature of the claim sets a definite upper limit to the preferred shareholders' claims on earnings. The prior position of preferred stock also usually extends to the disposition of assets in event of liquidation but only with respect to common stock. The senior position of creditors remains unaffected.

The pressure for a regular, consistent common dividend record virtually assures the preferred dividend's prior claim on dividends as a fixed burden. The common stock's market performance is not enhanced by a history of unpaid preferred dividends. If a firm cannot effectively compete in the equity capital market for additional funds with new common stock offerings, management inevitably treats the preferred stock as if it were a bond issue and regularly pays the full preferred dividend.

Tax laws interpret preferred dividends as a distribution of net profits to owners rather than as a business cost. Thus, preferred dividends must be converted to the pre-tax earnings equivalent to be on the same basis as interest expense.

Lease expense. A third item that should be included in the fixed charge coverage is lease expense. FASB 13 and its amendments have essentially eliminated off-balance sheet financing by promulgating the concepts of capital leases and operating leases. A capital lease asset is capitalized and its obligation recorded as a liability. Operating leases are still expensed and are the obligation under discussion in this paragraph. Capital lease repayment is a long-term debt reduction, and if the firm could not pay the rent on its leased productive assets—facilities and equipment—the company could not continue operations. While this argument could conceivably be extended to other operating expenses, lease expense is exceptional in that it is usually contractually fixed at an agreed-upon sum over a period of time. Lease expense essentially functions similarly to debt repayment and is in fact the servicing of an obligation, capitalized or not.

Since lease expense is recognized as a legitimate business expense, it is directly comparable with interest expense. No conversion to a pre-tax basis is necessary because lease expense is already on a before-tax basis.

The fixed charges coverage ratio is simply the times-interest-earned ratio expanded to include lease expense, debt repayment, and preferred dividends compared to earnings, all on a pre-tax basis:

$$\frac{\text{Fixed charges}}{\text{coverage}} = \frac{\text{EBIT} + \text{lease expense}}{\underset{\text{exp.}}{\text{Interest}} + \underset{\text{exp.}}{\text{Lease}} + \frac{\text{Preferred Dividends}}{(1.00 - r)} + \frac{\text{Scheduled Dbt. Repay.}}{(1.00 - r)}}$$

Obviously, the fixed charges coverage ratio shows a lower quantitative coverage than does the times-interest-earned ratio. This lower coverage is due to the inclusion of more factors in the solvency appraisal. The lower ratio is probably a better indicator of the solvency position than simply the times-interest-earned ratio.

Debt repayment coverage ratio

This ratio is one of few solvency ratios published among industry statistics; it is calculated and printed in RMA's *Annual Statement Studies.*[1]

The debt repayment coverage ratio compares cash flow to current maturities of long-term debt:

$$\frac{\text{Debt repayment}}{\text{coverage ratio}} = \frac{\text{Net profit after taxes + depreciation}}{\text{Scheduled debt repayment}}$$

Cash flow or "throw-off" is the primary source of regular long-term debt repayment, and this ratio purportedly measures the cash flow coverage of such debt service. However, the two components of cash flow, depreciation and earnings, have other uses. Depreciation expense is ideally reserved for fixed asset replacement, and a portion of net profits is supposed to pay dividends. Nevertheless, cash flow is also the primary source of funds for repayment of debt.

The debt repayment coverage ratio lacks the detailed analytical scope of the fixed charges coverage ratio, matches debt repayment with the inappropriate operating period, and assumes that earnings plus depreciation represents the true cash flow. Nevertheless, this ratio does provide a rough approximation of the firm's ability to retire debt each year from cash generated by operations. Both cash flow and scheduled debt repayment are on an after-tax basis which eliminates the necessity of pre-tax conversion. Although depreciation expense is a tax-deductible expense, it is also a noncash consuming expense. Thus, the full portion of revenues reduced by depreciation is additional cash earnings theoretically available for capital expenditures. However, inflation has rendered depreciation reserves practically useless as the sole source of funds for capital asset replacement. *Value Line* recently reported that depreciation expense covered only 68% of the estimated replacement cost of productive capacity in 1978 for 175 companies in 14 industries.

Comparison with industry statistics, such as RMA's *Statement Studies,* would provide a guideline for judging the adequacy or inadequacy of the quantitative values of these ratios.

---

[1] Published annually. Available from RMA, 1616 Philadelphia National Bank Building, Philadelphia, PA 19107. Contact RMA for pricing information.

Debt and capital expenditures coverage ratio

The addition of capital expenditures to the scheduled debt repayment to be covered by cash flow yields a ratio employed by the bond rating services in evaluating public offerings:

$$\frac{\text{Debt \& capital}}{\substack{\text{expenditures} \\ \text{coverage}}} = \frac{\text{Net profit after taxes} + \text{depreciation}}{\substack{\text{Scheduled debt} \\ \text{repayment}} + \substack{\text{Capital} \\ \text{expenditures}}}$$

The major rating services consider .5 to be acceptable for this ratio. Here we have combined two major uses of funds and compared them to the available cash flow. A norm of 50% suggests that the average industrial firm can only rely on its internal cash flow for 50% of the funds needed to add new plant and repay old debt.

Both the debt repayment coverage ratio and the debt and capital expenditures coverage ratio are relatively easy to compute because of their after-tax position. Both ratios also have limited industry statistical data for external comparative analysis. Unfortunately, neither ratio recognizes the pre-tax burdens of interest, lease expense, and dividends on cash flow.

Funds flow ratio

The funds flow ratio is an attempt to consolidate the conceptual advantages of all the preceding ratios into one ratio. The ratio comprises the six major outlays—interest expense, lease expense, scheduled debt repayment, preferred dividends, common dividends, and capital expenditures—on a pre-tax basis compared to the corresponding pre-tax cash flow. The only component not in the other four ratios is common dividends.

Common dividends are not an enforceable commitment, but common stockholders have residual equity. They are entitled to consider as theirs all earnings after prior charges whether or not distributed as dividends. Moreover, in the discussion of preferred dividends, it was stressed that a company seeking additional equity from time to time is obliged to maintain a fairly regular dividend policy on both classes of stock.

The funds flow associated with common dividends must be converted to the pre-tax earnings equivalent because the law does not permit common dividends to be considered a cost of business.

The funds flow coverage ratio formula is shown below:

$$\frac{\text{Funds Flow}}{\text{Coverage}} = \frac{\text{EBIT} + \substack{\text{Lease} \\ \text{expense}} + \substack{\text{Depreciation} \\ \text{expense}}}{\substack{\text{Int.} \\ \text{Exp.}} + \substack{\text{Lease} \\ \text{Exp.}} + \substack{\text{Sched. Dbt.} \\ \text{Repay.}} + \substack{\text{Pref.} \\ \text{Div.}} + \substack{\text{Common} \\ \text{Div.}} + \substack{\text{Capital} \\ \text{Expend.}}}{(1.00 - r)}$$

The lack of industry statistics precludes external comparative analysis, as is the case with three of the other four ratios. As a tool for internal analysis, the funds flow coverage ratio summarizes the trends reflected in the other four ratios for measuring the quantity of cash flow available for the six major outlays.

Systematic calculation of the solvency ratios

The data to calculate the ratios should be organized in logical order and the ratios themselves should be arranged so that they reflect more and more obligations to cover. If so done, the computation and interpretation of the ratios will be simpler and easier to understand.

Hypothetical data for Nationwide Airlines, a fictitious national airline, is presented below. Note its poor performance in 1974 and 1975 and its general recovery after 1975.

For the year ended 12/31:

Given and Expressed in $MM		1974	1975	1976	1977	1978
1. Interest expense		63.9	67.2	64.7	90.4	79.4
2. Lease expense		152.3	162.5	167.4	87.2	97.7
3. Debt repayment		67.2	93.5	49.3	120.2	97.5
4. Preferred dividends		1.0	-0-	-0-	1.0	1.0
5. Common dividends		1.1	-0-	-0-	9.3	10.6
6. Capital expenditures		216.7	106.4	98.1	97.7	190.2
7. Federal income taxes		.8	(17.2)	25.3	16.0	5.9
8. Profit after taxes		(23.6)	(86.3)	36.8	64.8	86.6
9. Depreciation expense		122.2	128.2	130.5	133.5	190.8
Calculated and Expressed as ( )						
10. Tax rate (r)	(%)	3.3	(16.0)	40.7	19.8	6.4
11. Cash flow	($MM)	98.6	41.9	167.3	198.3	177.4
12. EBIT	(X)	41.1	(36.3)	126.8	171.2	171.9
13. Times interest earned	(X)	.64	(.54)	1.96	1.81	2.16
14. Fixed charges coverage	(X)	.71	.41	.75	1.04	.88
15. Debt repayment coverage	(X)	1.47	.47	3.39	2.01	2.85
16. Debt & cptl expenditures cov.	(X)	.35	.21	1.14	.91	.46
17. Funds flow coverage	(X)	.61	.68	.83	.81	.91

Interest coverage has generally increased since the 1975 loss year. The fixed charge coverage ratio and the debt and capital expenditure ratio fell in 1978 because of the heavier capital expenditures. The funds flow ratio was not so affected because capital expenditures were tax-factored and debt repayment was lower. Since the funds flow ratio is the most inclusive of the group, the overall trend seems to be one of the generally increasing coverage.

Summary of quantitative analysis

Five ratios have been offered and explained for use in determining a firm's solvency position. All five are mechanically similar in that earnings and/or cash flow available to pay certain outlays are compared to the various outlays. The individual differences in the ratios are the result of the outlays considered and their tax position in relation to the funds flow available to cover them. Industry statistics are relatively scarce, so external comparative analysis is limited for the most part. However, the five ratios do provide a good base of data for internal solvency trend analysis.

This discussion of solvency analysis has been limited to a historical approach. That is, past results have been assumed to be a reasonable basis for predicting the firm's present and future solvency position. Indeed, this is an implicit assumption in all trend analysis. Nevertheless, we still need reasonably formulated projections of earnings, debt repayment schedules, capital expenditures, and dividends to derive a balanced appraisal of a firm's probable future solvency.

At best, the techniques discussed in the preceding pages provide data for a static appraisal of solvency in the current time period. At the worst, these ratios may not be inclusive enough to reflect the firm's solvency position. The ratios give only quantitative values of various relationships. The qualitative appraisal of the firm's solvency requires a closer look at the rules of generally accepted accounting.

Qualitative considerations

We have assumed that the quality of earnings is not strained, or less poetically, is solid 100% cash. In fact, there are some accounting practices which can lead to considerable differences in the quality of cash flow between two companies with the very same dollar cash flow.

Earnings quality is appraised by an evaluation of a company's accounting practices. The more conservative a company's reporting methods are within generally accepted accounting principles (GAAP)—that is, the more likely the company is to minimize reported profits regardless of the level of underlying earning power—the higher will be the quality of reported earnings. Companies that use accounting techniques designed to increase reported earnings have low quality cash flow.

The conglomerate excesses of the '60s resulted in a revived awareness of how profits can be a function of accounting ingenuity rather than solid business success. The accounting profession, federal regulators, corporate officers, investment bankers, and securities analysts all became aware of the need to curb accounting gimmickry and illusions once the '60s' bubble burst. The accounting profession's AICPA and FASB and the SEC deserve praise for bold measures such as the Accounting Principles Board Opinion No. 15: Earnings per Share (APB Opinion No. 15). APB No. 15 was designed to compel more complete corporate disclosure and assist investors in pinning down earnings.

Earnings quality is very much related to balance sheet quality and overall corporate financial strength. It is possible for a troubled company to report a quality income figure. However, it is not likely that a corporation with a poor profit quality will have a high-quality balance sheet because individual accounting practices generally affect both the income statement and the balance sheet. Evaluation of earnings quality or inferiority, therefore, is a way to understand the overall soundness of a company's financial statements and a way to analyze the conservative or liberal nature of accounting practices employed in drawing up the statements.

LIFO vs. FIFO

The LIFO (last in, first out) inventory accounting method signals higher earnings quality than FIFO (first in, first out) when prices are rising because reported profits under LIFO are minimized by the higher current costing of inventory used to calculate the cost of goods sold. However, accumulating LIFO inventory profits may reflect a change in conditions warranting a reconsideration of the inventory method. For instance, during a depression when prices are supposed to be falling, FIFO would be the better method.

Accelerated depreciation vs. straight-line depreciation

Accelerated depreciation accounting for stockholder reporting purposes is preferred over the straight-line method because accelerated depreciation puts aside more funds for plant replacement and simultaneously reduces reported earnings. Depreciation has traditionally been considered part of cash flow because it is a noncash-using expense charged to operations. Any method which increases depreciation expense also increases cash flow, and since accelerated depreciation charges more depreciation to operations than straight-line depreciation in the early years of an asset's useful life, accelerated depreciation results in more cash flow as well as a lower income tax liability because of the lower earnings. However, keep in mind that when a company stops growing and depreciation booked on an accelerated basis slips below straight-line depreciation, the method is no longer so conservative.

Income deferral

It is also better to defer income while flowing through expenses within the framework of GAAP. Therefore, when a company defers a chunk of plant start-up costs, the reported profit is probably overstated. However, when it defers the benefits of, say, investment tax credits, profits are probably understated.

Tax rate

Companies which employ flow-through accounting methods and generate timing differences in financial reporting and tax reporting are likely to show low tax rates. Companies with higher, more normal income tax rates in the 45% to 50% range are likely to have better quality earnings.[2] Investment credits, capital gains tax rates, and percentage depletion allowances are vulnerable to changes in tax laws. Companies that base their profit strategies on the permanence of these tax reducers will find themselves only dependent on what may be at best a temporary and variable source of funds.

For example, the investment tax credit was introduced in 1962, was suspended for a period of time, and then increased sharply. The investment tax credit may be subject to reduction or elimination, however, because of its controversial political status, its use as a counter-cyclical incentive for investment, and the need for a sustained level of capital expenditures each year. Capital-intensive industries benefit most from the investment tax credit, and they are also sensitive to business cycles. It is not hard to imagine the Congress' indifferent attitude toward auto makers' pleas for bigger tax credits in the third or fourth year of an expansion phase of a business cycle.

Likewise, the capital gains tax feature and the percentage depletion deductions have come under increasing political pressure as tax shelters for already profitable big business. The high profits of oil companies in 1979 have not made depletion popular among individual taxpayers or some members of Congress. What is particularly appealing or appalling, depending on one's political and economic philosophy, is that the percentage depletion deductions for natural resource exploitation can cause the tax return deduction for depletion to exceed permanently the book depletion deduction and create a permanent differ-

---

[2] A certain irony would seem to exist here. While the author identifies a 45% to 50% tax bracket as high quality, he also judges cash flow to be high quality when accelerated depreciation and quick write-offs are used. However, faster write-offs would seem to reduce earnings and therefore possibly reduce the company's tax bracket.—Ed.

ence between book and tax return income. Thus, oil companies and lumber companies will carry deferred tax liabilities which will never have to be repaid—unless the law changes. And the law could change if these permanently deferred liabilities become too large and too publicized to ignore.

Full consolidation

Fully consolidated reports that assume a parent company and its subsidiaries are a single entity usually make analysis easier and eliminate intercompany sales and profits. It is important, however, to know also what part of the subsidiaries' incomes can be used by the parent for corporate purposes and dividend payments.

Summary of how accounting practices can distort earnings

There are several common accounting practices which may distort a firm's earnings, that is, understate or overstate earnings. A banker should view an understated cash flow as conservative and as affording a margin of protection for repayment of his credit. Conversely, overstated earnings lead to undue optimism and great expectations by unwary lenders. These accounting practices are summarized below in terms of understating or overstating cash flow.

Cash flow quality

Qualitative aspect	High quality	Low quality
1. Inventory valuation	LIFO understates profits in inflationary period	FIFO overstates profits in inflationary period
2. Depreciation method	Accelerated depreciation more accurately matches replacement cost	Straight-line depreciation under-reserves funds for fixed assets replacement; thus, it overstates earnings
3. Deferred assets	Intangibles are written off as quickly as possible	Expenses are capitalized and earnings are overstated
4. Deferred income	Income is deferred while expenses are flowed through; for example, benefits of investment tax credits are deferred	Expenses are deferred; for example, plant start-up costs and tax credits are taken immediately

Cash flow quality

Qualitative aspect	High quality	Low quality
5. Tax rate	"Normal" effective tax rate, such as 45% to 50%, usually reflects minimal reliance on various tax deferral methods—investment tax credits, capital gains credits, and percentage depletion deductions—and therefore, better quality	Low effective tax rate, such as below 40%, usually reflects reliance on various tax deferral methods which may be vulnerable to reduction or elimination; the lower effective rate suggests low quality because of the potential for change in the tax deferral methods.

Therefore, if you must choose between two borrowers with an equal earnings of say, $100,000, pick the one that values its inventory on a LIFO basis, accelerates its depreciation, amortizes its intangibles as quickly as possible, defers income, and carries the higher tax rate.

Conclusion

Cash flow is the pool of funds available for preferred and common dividends, capital expenditures, and debt repayment. We must expand the concept to a before-tax basis to recognize tax-deductible costs associated with servicing a firm's permanent obligations—that is, interest expense and lease expense. To ignore any of these uses, before-tax or after-tax, is to overestimate cash flow available for debt repayment. Prudent banking dictates appraising *all* the uses which a pool of funds is expected to service. Attempts to maximize cash flow to rationalize a marginal credit risk invites delinquencies, losses, and write-offs.

Next, the firm's accounting practices must be reviewed. Earnings are probably overstated where there is FIFO inventory valuation, straight-line depreciation, slow intangible asset amortization, immediate income recognition, and unusually low income tax rates.

If bankers are to be good term lenders, they must be able to quantitatively and qualitatively analyze a firm's cash flow and solvency. I hope this article provides a method of performing this dual analysis.   □

The Banker's Shell Game— Lending Against Cash Flow

by D. R. Denison

CASH FLOW—NO PHRASE IS MORE AMBIGUOUS NOR ANY CONCEPT MORE ELUSIVE. Once cash flow has been named as the primary source of repayment, the adept loan officer can manipulate numbers to prove its adequacy with a facility equal to the manual dexterity of any carnival gamesman. While the process can result in self-delusion and bank loan losses, a far more frequent loser is the borrower. No con man's mark is ever more neatly gaffed than the victim of a "creative lender."

Many young bankers see so few true seasonal loan requests that it is hard for them to believe that commercial lending was once limited to such activity. It is a hallowed axiom that seasonal loans are preferable to term loans, but the reasons offered to support this axiom often emphasize liquidity rather than risk. With the deposit stability of the FDIC era, banks have been able to extend average maturities somewhat without causing major liquidity problems. But the absolute risks of loans repayable from future profits remain.

This article was originally written as a submission in the 1975 RMA National Paper writing competition, where it earned third-place honors for its author.

Forms of credit repayable

Several forms of credit are primarily repayable from profits or non-cash charges or both. Term loans, to finance either working capital or fixed assets, leap immediately to mind. But many other forms of credit imply that the true payout will come from profits, at least in the long run. Most revolving credit arrangements can be so classified.

The definition of cash flow is integral to its problems. Manipulators like to argue ad infinitum over the propriety of including in their calculations quasi-non-cash charges such as deferred income tax, but this is not a meaningful issue. Every first semester accounting student learns that cash flow is net profit plus depreciation, but the only kind of cash flow that can truly be used to repay debts is "cash available for discretionary expenditure, in a checking account of the entity that owes the debt." Anything less is insufficient. Sometimes this amount, which will be referred to as "discretionary spendable," will equal net profit plus depreciation—but not often.

Lending against non-cash charges is particularly tenuous, since they exist as charges to income precisely because a future commitment or detriment is implied. To lend against them for unrelated purposes (such as to provide additional working capital) may well be perfectly safe from the bank's point of view, but may have dire implications for the borrower long after the loan is paid. The potential dangers of loaning against cash flow are magnified in these times of heavy inflation. Not only are non-cash charges suspect, but even profits are not necessarily available as discretionary spendable if they are inflation-generated.

Bankruptcy as a secondary source of repayment

One of the biggest disadvantages in using cash flow as a primary source of repayment is that it is then unavailable as a secondary source. Many very marginal loans to support asset or liability fluctuations have been repaid only because a strong economy bailed out the lender by providing even mediocre entrepreneurs with enough profit to repay indebtedness.

The typically named secondary source of repayment for loans payable primarily from cash flow is "asset liquidation." This is fine if assets can truly be liquidated without destroying a business's viability. But far too often the only way that significant asset liquidation can take place is to shut down the business. Collateralized loans exacerbate the problem. With the reduced values realized in a pledgee's sale, speedy liquidation is achieved only by wiping out whatever equity exists. It is not at all rare that the proximate cause of a business bankruptcy be a cash flow lender seeking to force asset liquidation.

Economic cycles are two-edged swords, and slumps can wipe out the profits of the best entrepreneurs. If nondisruptive asset reduction is the primary source of repayment, loans can be repaid whether or not profits exist. When these two sources of repayment (asset reduction and cash flow) are reversed in priority, asset reduction may prove to be "disruptive" or worse!

Buy now—pay later

Three basic types of loans are payable from cash flow: loans repayable basically from profits, loans related to non-cash charges and revolving loans. Each type has the common element of capital substitution. The loan permits the acquisition or support of assets that would otherwise, and must eventually, be supported by retained earnings. Just as the philosophy of consumer debt is to permit enjoyment of an object while funds are acquired to pay for it, so the equivalent corporate loans pledge an uncertain future income stream to support current investment. The hazards are similar.

Depreciation must be considered

An installment-basis car buyer finds his paid-for car does not provide a high enough trade-in allowance to cover the down payment on his next car. The reason is inflation. Similarly, replacement prices for fixed assets rise constantly. The tax code permits depreciation only of historical cost, so replacement requires the partial support of after-tax dollars as well as the reinvestment of depreciation. Loans based only on the recapture of historical cost thus wind up escalating over time.

Depreciation is a non-cash charge only in the short run. To justify a "going-business" approach to financial analysis, one must recognize replacement needs. Insurance companies active in the long-term (10–20-year) debt market commonly ignore depreciation as a source of debt coverage, looking strictly at the relationship between profits and fixed payment requirements. This practice is fully justifiable when one recognizes that most depreciable assets are subject to replacement in a 20-year time frame.

Bankers, too, should recognize the replacement problem in their term loan analysis, particularly when loans are to provide working capital. Even if major replacement needs occur after the final payout date, the borrower should not be allowed to treat his potential future requirements too lightly.

Repayment from charges other than depreciation

Some loans are paid from non-cash charges other than depreciation. An example is the loan to finance an annual expenditure: taxes, annual mortgage payments, insurance premiums and the like. Amortization merely spreads out the cash payments required to fund the expenditure and do not necessitate increased (or, in some instances, any) profits for repayment. Even very short-term loans to discount payables can be thought of as being repaid from non-cash charges if the effective source of repayment is the reaccrual of accounts payable rather than any true reduction in current assets.

All loans are repayable primarily from cash flow

It may not be quite as obvious that all revolving loans are repayable primarily from cash flow. There is a tendency to think of "collection of receivables" as the primary source of repayment for an accounts receivable financing line of credit. But in the long run the company will either improve or deteriorate, and the revolving credit will be repaid either by retained earnings or by enforced liquidation. To establish any revolving line and justify its inclusion in a bank loan portfolio, it is necessary to anticipate that the entire credit will be replaced by retained earnings in the long run.

A meaningful item for analysis is the ratio of bank debt to profits. How many years will it take to repay bank debt from profits, even in a no-growth environment? This question makes the definition of "discretionary spendable" more meaningful. It is one thing to *choose* to invest discretionary spendable in future growth; it is quite different to be *unable* to repay bank debt from meager profits. Many revolving credit arrangements are secured, and there is a tendency to overemphasize collateral in the analysis of these credits rather than to weigh the likelihood of eventual payout.

Now you see it; now you don't

The arcane formulas for calculating cash flow coverage can deceive the user into overconfidence by their sheer complexity. To read a learned article, struggling with the problem of whether credit should be given for the tax benefit of interest and lease expenses at the accrued tax rate or at the cash-paid tax rate, one must assume that such a calculation will provide an analytical tool of great accuracy.

Leakage the biggest problem

In reality, the biggest problem with cash flow is leakage. Cash flow does not always show up in the borrower's checking account as discretionary spendable just because it has been duly certified as AICPA-approved cash flow. A banker may finally grasp the leakage problem when, halfway through the payout period on his term loan, the borrower returns for additional funds or a program modification.

Growth is the most frequent villain in such situations, but leakage occurs even when a company is standing still. Inflationary increases in fixed-asset replacement costs have already been discussed. In addition, inventory replacement can also be subject to the pressures of inflation; stagnating sales may result in slowing receivables; payables terms can be shortened. All these factors can provide leakage, but sales growth is more important.

Sales growth as factor

Sales growth can be a discretionary phenomenon and then is not leakage per se. The cash to repay a loan may indeed have once been in the checking account—and was then consciously diverted to support sales growth. Such a sequence of events does not change the amount of discretionary spendable. What does change it is sales growth that is not truly discretionary, a growth that is unavoidable within the historic pattern of operation. Therefore, far more attention should be placed on the inevitable changes in receivables, inventory and fixed assets than on such minutiae as deferred income tax.

The inventory trap

Of the three assets mentioned, inventory is the most difficult to analyze because of the judgmental factors inherent in its quantification. The definitions of receivables and of fixed assets are not free of loopholes, but each is rock solid when compared with the hunk of Swiss cheese that passes for a definition of inventory. Cost allocation is highly arbitrary, and the accounting profession tends to permit excesses to continue for years until they collapse under their own weight. By then the poor banker may be buried in the rubble.

Publishing industry as example of cost allocation problems

Extreme examples of cost allocation problems are sometimes seen in the publishing industry. Printing is a high-fixed-cost/low-variable-cost business. It makes much economic sense to seek long press runs to minimize costs. A textbook or a fine-art print may have a market lifespan of several years, and it is not an unreasonable entrepreneurial decision to print a 2- or 3-year supply based on expected sales. But how should the costs of that press run be allocated to the units as they are sold?

Imagine that a run of 50,000 units costs $50,000. Analyzed chronologically, perhaps the first unit cost $25,000.50, while each succeeding unit cost only 50¢. These are the parameters that must be considered by the entrepreneur in deciding how long to make a press run, but they do not reflect the format of cost allocation used on financial statements. Very frequently, the total cost is spread evenly at $1 per unit, even though the press run is a 3-year supply. "Well and good," says the banker, "as long as the merchandise doesn't become stale."

But look at the temptation available to the entrepreneur, especially the manager of a public company or the owner of a company who desires to sell out. He may estimate 20,000 units in first-year sales, 15,000 units in the second year and again in the third year and *perhaps* another few years at 5,000 per year. If he increases his press run from 50,000 to 70,000, he increases his total cost from $50,000 to $60,000. But his average cost will decline to 85.7¢ and his first-year reportable pretax profit will increase by $2,860—not because he sold more but merely because he produced more. If the final 20,000 prove unsalable, the total profit on the run will be $10,000 less; but this won't be noted by the CPA's until they make the company write off the "stale" inventory four or five years later. "You see," says the CPA, "we always catch them in the long run." But, as Keynes said, "In the long run, we all are dead." Especially bankers who do not get suspicious of slowing inventory turnover rates!

The pocket problem

Why is it necessary to include the phrase ". . . in a checking account of the entity that owes the debt" in the definition of discretionary spendable? The importance of this qualification is well noted by creditors of failing conglomerates. Complex corporate organization is an inescapable feature of our laws and tax codes; but sometimes the corporate treasurer finds himself in the position of a man whose clothes have many pockets, only some of which have money in them and only some of which he has ready access to. His total cash may look impressive but it may be in the "wrong pocket" to pay maturing debts. For this reason, consolidated financial statements may not give a complete picture of the debt servicing ability of a complex corporate organization.

Consider, as an example, an imaginary conglomerate consisting of a parent and five subsidiaries. The parent is basically a holding company owning certain fixed assets plus the stock of the various subsidiaries, each of which is run independently. Subsidiary A was acquired under an agreement calling for a purchase price determined in part by future earnings; its cash cannot be transferred in contravention to the "earn out" provisions of the purchase agreement. Subsidiary B has an outstanding issue of debentures with strict covenants on ratio maintenance and dividend payments. Subsidiary C has negative retained earnings and a tax loss carry-forward that will expire soon. Subsidiary D is in an industry in which the parameters of growth are very unfavorable. To limit growth to that which would be supported by internally generated cash would require great forbearance. Both subsidiaries C and D also have minority shareholders, with minority interests less than 5%. Subsidiary E needs to borrow money, but cannot support its loan request alone. The parent company offers to guarantee or even to borrow directly for Subsidiary E's needs.

Consolidated statements must be analyzed for the money "pockets"

The consolidated financial statement of the conglomerate may look impressive, both as to profits and as to cash position. But a consolidating statement must be analyzed to determine whether the money is in the right "pockets." Cash can move from subsidiary to parent via dividend, loan or fee. Each of these methods may be restricted by some circumstances. Earn-out agreements and the covenants of other lenders may restrict cash transfers of any kind. The protection of minority shareholders limits the amount of cash that can be transferred by means other than dividend payments. Tax considerations may affect the amount of intercompany fees that should be charged. Dividend payments are limited by retained earnings. The impact of growth on cash availability may vary greatly from subsidiary to subsidiary.

For all these reasons, it may happen that our imaginary conglomerate will be unable to pay back a bank loan to Subsidiary E, even though it has double the amount of the loan showing as "cash" on its consolidated financial statement. Credit to the parent must be analyzed on the basis of the very illiquid asset structure of the parent corporation itself. It may be that the only secondary source of repayment for the risky loan to Subsidiary E is the sale of some other subsidiary. The situation described above is contrived; but it illustrates several problems that occur in real situations.

When the music stops

Providing a revolving credit arrangement is a lot like playing musical chairs. It is necessary to keep a careful watch on the places in which to sit down. Many formal revolving credit arrangements are collateralized, and many of those that are not do at least have covenants calling for collateralization in the event of default. It was pointed out above that profits, rather than the turnover of collateral, should be considered the primary source of repayment for revolving loans. Similarly, "liquidation of collateral" should not be considered the secondary source.

It is hard to learn the pitfalls of collateral liquidation without experiencing some of them. The claims for credit adjustments that materialize as soon as a trade debtor learns that a bank is now the holder of his account payable can be very educational. Similar knowledge comes from attending bankruptcy auctions, not to watch the bidding but to watch the people not bidding. A businessman who would be ecstatic to be offered inventory at 50¢ on the dollar by a supplier will, without malice or collusion, fail to overbid a competitor bidding 24¢ on the dollar at a bankruptcy sale of the same inventory. He has come to the auction with a preconceived idea of the type of "bargain" such a sale should entail, and psychologically he cannot change that concept.

Availability of another lender vital

What then is the proper secondary source of repayment for revolving credit arrangements? In most cases, it is the availability of another lender to take the bank's position. The continued willingness of the other lender to do so is the "chair" that must be watched to prepare for the day the music stops.

The most frequent outlet for deteriorating bank loans is the commercial finance house. These lenders have their own hierarchy. It is not uncommon to see a borrower move from short-term unsecured bank debt to bank accounts receivable financing, to Finance Company A, to Finance Company B, to Finance Company C, as his position deteriorates. Interest rates increase along the way and it is finally Finance Company C, perhaps charging 30%, who actually has to liquidate the collateral.

When to call a loan?

There are two important points to note in considering this process. First, it is essential for a banker to keep track of the requirements of various finance companies. The loan office must be prepared to call a loan before it deteriorates beyond those criteria. If Finance Company B will lend X% of receivables and Y% of inventory only as long as payables are no more than 30 days past due, then it is imperative that the banker insist on a position significantly better than those terms so that any future operating losses will not cause them to be exceeded. If the position today is only marginally better than the minimum criteria, then the loan should be called now. By the time the banker learns of any further deterioration, it will be too late to seek a finance company.

The second important point to note is the role of Finance Company C, the "Thirty Percenter." This player in the game is not really a lender, he is a liquidator. Very few companies can make 30% on invested capital, so it is likely that most of this finance company's customers are in a negative leverage situation. A major portion of the 30% gross yield goes to cover liquidation losses. This fact is of importance to the banker who shows an ethical interest in a customer's well-being. Many customers see such liquidation losses as a reason for the bank to continue to carry their loans rather than insist that they move to Finance Company A or B when the situation gets marginal. But this is not the issue.

The customer's risk–reward relationship must be considered

The opportunity for ethical decision-making occurs much earlier. Perhaps at the time the decision was made to use a bank accounts receivable financing program other options were available to avoid liquidation as capital substitution. Could expansion have been curtailed? Could part of the business have been profitably sold off? The decision to use revolving credit in lieu of capital should not be made lightly. Even though bank interest rates may provide positive leverage, there is always a statistical chance that adversity will force a change to a higher rate—negative leverage—lender. Any potential benefits should be worth that risk.

A key measurement in such a decision is the ratio of profits to bank debt. The longer that the "temporary" capital substitution must be relied upon, the greater is the risk that future adversity will be leveraged into catastrophe. Bankers should not become so swayed by the profitability of revolving credit that they ignore or obscure its impact on their customers' risk–reward relationship.

The impact of inflation

Old habits die hard, and most of us are finding it painful to accept the new ground rules necessitated by steep inflation. Accountants grapple with the problem of "standard accounting units" following decades of using dollars as a synonym. The rush of companies to convert from FIFO to LIFO inventory valuation should make suspect those who do not. The use of FIFO inventory valuation creates a new source of "leakage" of cash flow: income taxes. On a FIFO basis, the company which is standing still will show a pretax inventory profit equal to inflation, merely by keeping the same units in stock. If half of this is taxed away, the company has an operating loss in constant dollars. Thus a FIFO company must have cash flow at least double its inventory valuation profits to have *any* discretionary spendable at all!

The use of LIFO is not a panacea; it merely helps. Sound entrepreneurial decisions are based on NIFO (Next In, First Out), and a valid calculation of discretionary spendable must allow for inventory replacement at higher future prices, just as equipment replacement at higher prices must be allowed for. The impact of this problem cannot be minimized. Many long-profitable companies recently have failed to price their products properly, while their managements have deluded themselves with record paper profits which have been totally absorbed by taxes and by inventory replacement. Casual cash flow lending to such a company does a disservice to both the borrower and his bank.

The shell game

In using the shell game as an analogy for cash flow lending, it is easy to conceptualize the banker as the mark. When the shell is lifted, the pea is not there: the anticipated discretionary spendable has not materialized. But the banker is the mark only if the borrower palms the pea, diverting the cash flow. If there were never any discretionary spendable in the first place, it would be the banker's fault. The borrower is the mark.

Throughout this article, there has been a recurrent theme: the banker's ethical obligation to save the borrower from himself. This should not be taken lightly. Clear thinking and definitional accuracy are essential to analyze cash flow properly. The tradition that borrowers should rely on their bankers for advice as well as money seems to be fading in these days of go-go money managers. But the banker's professional and ethical obligation remains. Your customer may wish to promise you money he will not have, pledging cash flow that is not true discretionary spendable. Don't let him pledge something that is not there. Don't let him play the shell game! □

Evaluating a Firm's Liquidity and the Bank Credit Risk

by Peter J. Tischler

THE PURPOSE OF THIS ARTICLE is to examine several prevailing misconceptions in bank credit risk analysis and to suggest some preferable alternative analytical procedures. It is claimed in particular that:

1. The debt payment capacity of the firm is not properly defined and the credit risk and the liquidity indicators are not properly interpreted.
2. The firm's refinancing ability is infrequently evaluated.
3. Excessive importance is given to the "liquidation concept" which produces misleading results.

Bank credit risk analysis is concerned predominantly with the liquidity of a borrower. Liquidity is, therefore, the main concern of this paper. We will first examine the flow concepts—income flow and cash flow—and other indices used by bank credit analysts, such as net working capital and the current ratio. We will then proceed to the presentation of several real cases and examples, including one complete credit situation, to demonstrate the shortcomings of the traditional analytical methods and to justify the adoption of methodology. Finally, a methodological framework for credit risk analysis and evaluation is presented.

Flow concepts—their content and information value

Flow concepts[1] are continually used by corporations and their analysts to evaluate certain aspects of the performance of a business firm in a given period of time, whether past, present, or future, and to explain a change in the firm's financial standing from one reporting date to the next. While the accounting profession always makes a clear and sharp distinction among these flows, others—especially security analysts—have brought considerable confusion to the subject.

The problem is as follows: It is taken for granted that income (as reported in financial statements) represents or is equal to cash inflow and that, correspondingly, income from operations plus depreciation is equal to total cash inflow from operations in the same reported period of time. Some analysts, disregarding extraordinary gains and losses, go so far as to call net income and depreciation "cash generated from operations." On the other hand, hardly anybody fails to understand that net cash inflow is the difference between cash receipts and cash outlays and that net cash inflow from operations is the difference between cash receipts and cash outlays related to operations.

What undoubtedly causes difficulties and becomes a source of misunderstanding is the standard accounting practice, according to which changes in net working capital (NWC) and in income are recorded at the same moment of time. Since income is recognized at the same time a receivable is created, reported income is accrued (realizable) income and not cash (realized) income. Understandably then, cash generation must lag behind NWC and accrued income flow.

For readers who might wish to refresh their knowledge of accounting, standard accounting textbooks should provide enough information on this subject. Otherwise, the following summary should prove to be useful:

1. NI + D $\neq$ change in NWC from operations $\neq$ net cash inflow from operations.
2. NI + D $\neq$ total change in NWC $\neq$ total net cash inflow.
3. NI + D $=$ change in NWC from operations $\pm$ book gain or loss.

Because: NI before extraordinary items + D = change in NWC from operations and change in NWC from operations $\neq$ net cash inflow from operations.

Consequently: NI before extraordinary items + D $\neq$ net cash inflow from operations.

---

[1]For extensive treatment of this subject see: R. K. Jaedicke, R. T. Spouse, *Accounting Flows: Income, Funds and Cash.* (Prentice Hall, Inc., 1965), particularly Chapters V, VI and VII. This book also contains numerous references.

The extension of these accounting principles should lead to a recognition of the basic fact that although net cash inflow is conditionally dependent upon income generation, income (operating income) may be reported, but net cash flow (from operations) simultaneously can be of either a positive or negative value. Moreover, although a loss (operating loss) may be reported, net cash flow (from operations) may be of either a positive or negative value.

This basic theoretical conclusion is of extreme practical importance because it bears a direct relationship to the methodology of financial analysis. In fact, a failure to recognize the differences between income flow, net working capital flow and cash flow decreases the information value of historical analysis and, when used to project future trends, will have undesirable implications for the quality of various financial decisions.

Before proceeding, let us further define our terms:

1. Net Income and Depreciation will be referred to as NI + D.
2. Net Profit after Taxes before Extraordinary Items plus Depreciation will be referred to as Operating Income plus Depreciation and abbreviated as OI + D.
3. This OI + D after adjustments converting its accrued nature into OI + D on a cash collection and disbursement basis will be called "Real Net Cash Proceeds from Operations" and abbreviated as RNCPO.
4. The term "Cash Flow from Operations" (often understood to be equal to NI + D) will not be used at all in this paper.
5. The abbreviation I + D will be understood to be Income + Depreciation and used in such instances where no special indication as to the content of the income is necessary.

Income flow versus cash flow

When evaluating the ability of a firm to meet its debt obligations, the analysts focus on determining the firm's internally generated cash inflow. Traditionally, NI + D is considered to be a reliable indicator of the firm's internally generated debt payment capacity.

The accrued nature of income does, however, suggest that accrued income and true cash income might be quite different monetary values. Therefore, it is advisable to determine how much these two values may differ and then to ascertain which of these values is a more reliable indicator of the firm's debt payment capacity. The method for converting accrued income into cash income[2]

---

[2]For extensive treatment of this subject see:
   M. Moonitz, L. H. Jorday, *Accounting, an Analysis of its Problems*, Revised edition, Volume I. (Holt, Rinehart and Winston, Inc., 1966), particularly Chapter 4, p. 82.
   Statement Analysis. A Programmed Training Unit. (American Bankers Association) Book V. page 103.

(i.e. accrued OI + D into OI + D on a collected cash basis) involves the derivation of "Real Net Cash Proceeds from Operations" (RNCPO) from the usual data supplied by balance sheets and income statements through conversion of accrued items to cash items using the following procedure.

Add: Sales revenue
                + Decrease (− increase) in accounts receivable
                Cash collections on sales
                + Other income (adjustments made later)
        Total cash collections from operations

Deduct: Cost of goods sold
                + Increase (− decrease) in inventories
                + Decrease (− increase) in trade accounts payable
                Operating expenses
                Interest and other expenses
                + Increase (− decrease) in accrued assets
                + Decrease (− increase) in accrued liabilities
                Income taxes
                + Decrease (− increase) in accrued taxes
                + Decrease (− increase) in deferred taxes
        Total cash payments for operations

Equals: Real Net Cash Proceeds from Operations (RNCPO)

The same result can be obtained by using an "indirect method." Sales revenue, other income, cost of goods sold, operating, interest and other expenses and income taxes on the income statement would produce net profit before extraordinary items plus depreciation. This figure must then be adjusted for the changes in accrued assets and liabilities and in deferred income taxes as indicated above. Obviously, the results should be identical.

For example, the sales revenue figure on the income statement is equal to the amount of newly created receivables during that particular business year. If, then, the year-end figure for accounts receivable is greater than the figure at the beginning of the year, the difference represents an increase in uncollected receivables and should be deducted from the sales figure to determine how much has been collected as opposed to how much has been billed. A similar approach should be applied to other items in our formula.

The (OI + D) figure prior to adjusting for accrued assets and liabilities and deferred income taxes will naturally be different from the figure reached after adjustment. The extent of these differences might best be demonstrated by the figures in Exhibit I and the corresponding graph in Exhibit II. (The figures are real, the names of the companies have, however, been disguised.)

Exhibit I

Income Flow vs. Cash Flow

A) Historical Data (in millions)

Company A	1966	1967	1968	1969	4-Years Total
1. NI + D	$ 22.6	$ 44.8	$ 30.4	$ 34.8	$ 132.6
2. OI + D	45.1	44.8	43.6	42.2	175.7
3. RNCPO	6.1	50.2	100.6	25.8	182.7
4. Difference (3-2)	−39.0	5.4	57.0	−16.4	7.0

Company GL	1968	1969	1970	1971	4-Years Total
1. NI + D	$ 98.7	$ 113.5	$ 87.5	$ 96.2	$ 395.9
2. OI + D	98.7	92.4	87.5	95.9	374.5
3. RNCPO	−117.8	−49.0	25.3	160.5	19.0
4. Difference (3-2)	−216.5	−141.4	−62.2	64.6	−355.5

B) Forecasted Data (in millions)

Company's H Cash Budget	1972	1973	1974	1975	1976	5-Years Total
1. NI + D = OI + D	$ 0.7	$ 1.0	$ 1.4	$ 1.9	$ 2.8	$ 7.8
2. RNCPO	0.8	0.7	0.9	0.7	0.4	3.5
3. Difference (2-1)	0.1	−0.3	−0.5	−1.2	−2.4	−4.3

(Note: It is interesting to read this budget both forwards and backwards)

Company GH Pro forma forecast developed by a bank	1972	1973	1974	1975	4-Years Total
1. NI + D = OI + D	$112.8	$120.0	$129.1	$139.6	$501.5
2. RNCPO	82.4	86.4	95.8	104.4	369.0
3. Difference (2-1)	−30.4	−33.6	−33.3	−35.2	−132.0

Company T

Theoretical forecast developed under the assumption of all ratios (like Sales/Receivables; CGS/inventories, etc.) being constant while sales substantially fluctuate.

	1971	1972	1973	1974	1975	1976	1977
1. OI + D	$ 40	$ 60	$ 80	$100	$ 80	$ 60	$ 40
2. RNCPO	0	20	40	60	120	100	80
3. Difference (2-1)	−40	−40	−40	−40	40	40	40

	1978	1979	1980	1981	11-Years Total
1. OI + D	$ 60	$ 80	$ 60	$ 80	$ 740
2. RNCPO	20	40	100	40	620
3. Difference (2-1)	−40	−40	40	−40	−120

EXHIBIT II

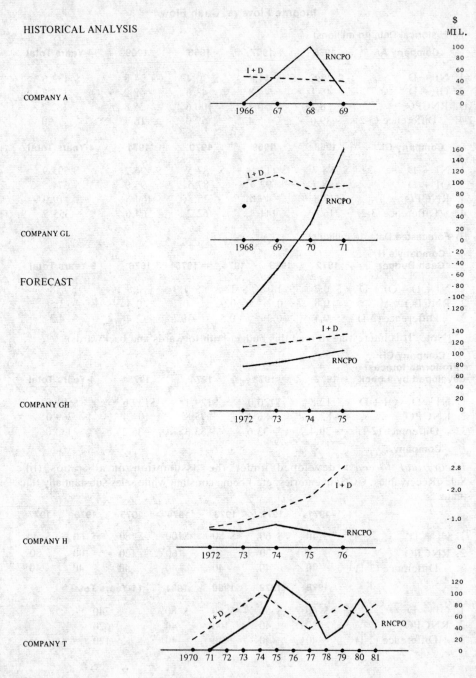

HISTORICAL ANALYSIS

COMPANY A

COMPANY GL

FORECAST

COMPANY GH

COMPANY H

COMPANY T

Systematic examination of these differences reveals that:

1. In historical analysis of the correlation between NI + D or OI + D and RNCPO:
   (a) I + D in any given year differed substantially from RNCPO;
   (b) In every year, the historical cash flow curve changed its slope independently of the I + D flow curve; and consequently, in a short- or medium-term period any correlation between income plus depreciation flow and RNCPO was non evident.

These findings suggest that the NI + D or the OI + D figures do *not* indicate whether the company is or is not experiencing a period of liquidity ease or liquidity strain.

It should be emphasized that the lack of correlation between the income flow and cash flow refers to the past, present or future of any company under analysis and that the analyst should not be misled by his findings in his forecast as they appear in our Exhibit I and Exhibit II and as they are explained below.

2. In the pro forma forecasts, the relationship between the I + D and RNCPO figures and flows changes from a very erratic one into a relationship in which:
   (a) The RNCPO flow curve generally appears to change its slope in direct dependence upon changes in the slope of the income plus depreciation flow curve.
   (b) However, the changes in the RNCPO flow curve lag behind the changes in the I + D flow curve.
   (c) Consequently, in periods of corporate growth I + D will be greater than the RNCPO, while in periods of decreased sales, the firm's I + D will be smaller than its RNCPO.

In a forecast, the relationship between I + D and RNCPO figures carries a high correlation due to the fact that the credit analyst must assume certain constant relationships between, for example, sales and receivables, cost of goods sold and inventories, etc. His chances of arriving at a very close estimate of the accrued income figure may be quite good; yet, as the historical evidence suggests, his chances of approximating the RNCPO figure are relatively small.

Now we seem to stand at a crossroad. The value of the (I + D) figure can be predicted with an acceptable degree of error. This concept, however, measures the general business success of the firm rather than the firm's immediate liquidity. On the other hand, the RNCPO figure represents a true debt payment capacity of the firm. Its figure, however, cannot be predicted with a reasonable degree of accuracy. Which concept, then, to use?

To elaborate upon this apparent conflict, a case is presented of a term loan agreement.

Traditionally used methods of evaluating the firm's liquidity and their effect upon the quality of credit decision making

Traditionally, the credit decision of commercial banks is a result of careful examination of the company's NI + D flow, its net working capital (NCW) flow and its current ratio. While NI + D is understood to be cash flow, the current ratio (CR) is considered to be a good measure of the corporation's ability to pay off its maturing debt.

The most difficult of all credit decisions involves term loans. At this point we present an elementary (yet complex) example demonstrating that even under conditions of complete certainty in which the actual performance would exactly coincide with the projected trend, the following may be observed:

1. Favorable NI + D flow does not guarantee a repayment of the term loan according to the repayment schedule based upon such NI + D flow even if a substantial margin of safety against the NI + D flow is introduced.
2. The level of NWC and changes in the same give no indication as to whether the firm already is or in the near future will become illiquid.
3. The value of the current ratio and changes in its value are not a measure of the corporation's ability to pay off its maturing debt either at a certain point of time or in the future. Current ratio in that sense has no predictive information value.

The case of Company X

Company X desired to improve its profit picture both in volume and margin and planned to invest in new production facilities to support larger sales and to achieve economies of scale. The management considered borrowing $200, servicing the debt by the proceeds from its total business. Before calling on the bank, the treasurer prepared and submitted the following justification:

1. NI + D in the year 1970 (base year) equals $20, of which $10 is net income and $10 is a straight-line depreciation charge on present facilities.
2. The new facility of $200 acquisition value will have an annual straight-line depreciation charge of $20.
3. Assuming that the bank regards potential increase in net income as a safety margin, this still leaves 5 times the 1970 NI + D of $20 plus 5 times additional depreciation charge of $20 equal to $200 to amortize the entire loan in five years through NI + D.

The bank questioned the company on its projected sales and cost and devel-

Table I

Company X Income Statement
(pro forma and actual)

	1970 Actual 1	1971 Forecast 2	1972 Forecast 3	1973 Forecast 4	1974 Forecast 5	1975 Forecast 6	Total 1971-1975 Forecast 7
Sales	$500	+ $25 $525	+ $25 $550	+ $25 $575	+ $25 $600	$600	$2,850
CGS	480	+ 15 495	+ 15 510	+ 15 525	+ 15 540	540	2,610
Gross Profit	$ 20	+ 10 $ 30	+ 10 $ 40	+ 10 $ 50	+ 10 $ 60	$ 60	$ 240
Depreciation (old equip.)	10	10	10	10	10	10	
(new equip.)		20	20	20	20	20	150
Net Income	$ 10	$ 0	$ 10	$ 20	$ 30	$ 30	$ 90
Net Income	$ 10	$ 0	$ 10	$ 20	$ 30	$ 30	$ 90
Depreciation	10	30	30	30	30	30	90
NI + D	$ 20	$ 30	$ 40	$ 50	$ 60	$ 60	$ 240

Statement of Sources and Uses of Net Working Capital
(pro forma and actual)

	1970 Actual 1	1971 Forecast 2	1972 Forecast 3	1973 Forecast 4	1974 Forecast 5	1975 Forecast 6	Total 1971-1975 Forecast 7
Sources							
NI + D	$ 20	$ 30	$ 40	$ 50	$ 60	$ 60	$ 240
Proceeds of Long-Term Debt	—	200	—	—	—	—	200
Total Sources	$ 20	$230	$ 40	$ 50	$ 60	$ 60	$ 440
Uses							
Capital Expenditures		$200				—	$200
Decrease in Long-Term Debt		30	40	50	60	—	200
(transfer to current maturities)							
Total Uses		$230	$ 40	$ 50	$ 60	—	$400
Beginning NWC	$ 60	$ 60	$ 60	$ 60	$ 60	$ 60	$ 80
Change in NWC						+ 60	+ 40
Ending NWC	$ 80	$ 60	$ 60	$ 60	$ 60	$120	$ 120

oped the pro forma income statement shown in Table I on the preceding page. Following a very conservative approach in developing the sales and cost figures, the realistic NI + D total for the years 1971-1975 amounted to $240 (see last column), which was 20% more than the debt service requirement of $200.

To maintain the margin of protection, the schedule of installments was designed as follows: (Take down 1/1/71, $200; payments, December 31 annually.)

	1970	1971	1972	1973	1974	1975	(Total) 1971-1975
NI + D	$20	$30	$40	$50	$60	$60	$240
Installments		20	30	40	50	60	200
Safety Margin		$10	$10	$10	$10	—	$ 40

Table II
Company X Balance Sheet
(pro forma and actual)

	Actual 12/31/70	Pro Forma 1/1/71	Actual 9/30/71	Actual 12/31/71	Actual 9/30/72	Actual 12/31/72
	8	9	10	11	12	13
Cash	$ 10	$ 10	$ 16*	$ 0	$ 15	$ (5)
Accounts Receivable	100	100	104	105	109	110
Inventory	50	50	62	65	73	75
Total Current Assets	160	160	182	170	197	180
Fixed Assets	100	300		300		300
Minus: Depreciation	(50)	(50)		(80)		(100)
TOTAL ASSETS	210	410		390		370
Accounts payable	80	80	80	80	80	80
c/m of LT Debt	—	20	20	30	30	40
Total Current Liabilities	80	100	100	110	110	120
Long Term Debt	—	180		150		110
Capital Stock	80	80		80		80
Retained Earnings	50	50		50		60
Total Liab. + Equity	210	410		390		370
NWC	$80	$60	$82	$60	$87	$60
Current ratio	2.00	1.60	1.82	1.54	1.79	1.50

*Sales 393, minus CGS 372, minus increase in accounts receivable 4, minus increase in inventories 12, plus beginning cash 10, equals 16.

Next, a pro forma balance sheet as of January 1, 1971, was developed (see Table II, column 9) to give effect to the loan take down as of that date. Since both the current ratio and the tangible worth/total liabilities ratio looked reasonable, a pro forma statement of sources and uses of funds (i.e. NWC) based upon the opening statement as of January 1, 1971, was developed (see Table I). NWC was found to remain fairly constant through out the next four years and, consequently, the dollar value of "the margin of protection offered to the bank as well as other current creditors" was considered to be satisfactory.

The bank approved the loan, stipulating that various restrictive covenants be written into the loan agreement. These included retention of all earnings in the business and submission of quarterly statements.

Routine analysis of the quarterly statements indicated that everything was proceeding according to forecast. As of 9/30/71, the "cash generation" (i.e. NI + D for nine months of the year 1971) was proportionately equal to the projected annual figure, and receivables and inventories kept their previous relationship to sales and cost of production. It was noted with satisfaction that NWC increased to $82, and the current ratio rose to 1.82. Moreover, the quick ratio approached 1.2. There were few who expected difficulties at year-end, when the first installment would fall due.

The installment was paid, and for the 120 days following the company's year-end, nobody was concerned with the credit of Company X. When the annual report as of 12/31/71 was submitted, it was noted with surprise that there was no cash balance quoted. However, the bank's deposit journal showed a reasonable recovery since that time, and no credit agreement covenants were violated.

The bank then received quarterly statements as of 3/31/72, 6/30/72, and 9/30/72. Constant progress and improvement were noted. For example, as of 9/30/72, 75% of projected annual income was generated, and the company revealed an impressive current ratio and NWC.

On December 31, 1972, the company reported it was unable to pay the full $30 installment and proposed a $25 payment instead.

Although we have already dealt with the difference between NI + D flow and real cash flow, it still might prove helpful to show how it worked in this particular case:

		1971	1972
	Sales	$525	$550
MINUS:	Increase in Accts. Rec.	(5)	(5)
	Cash Collections	$520	$545
	Cost of Goods Sold	$495	$510
PLUS:	Increase in Inventories	15	10
PLUS, MINUS:	Change in Accts. Pay.	0	0
	Cash Payments	$510	$520
	RNCPO	$ 10	$ 25
PLUS:	Cash Balance as of Jan.	10	0
MINUS:	Repayment of Debt	20	30
	Cash Balance as of Year-End	$ 0	$ (5)
	RNCPO	$ 10	$ 25
	NI + D	30	40

The lesson of the Company X case appears obvious. The I + D flow should not be used for credit decision making when estimating the debt payment capacity of the firm. Correspondingly, it should not be employed to structure the term loan installment schedule, either to determine the maturity of the loan for a given amount or to determine the amount to be lent for a given period of time. In summary, the I + D flow concept for bank credit decision making is a concept which should be avoided because it works with an irrelevant data base.

Methodologically advanced banks today have well-developed skills to generate pro forma balance sheets for the period of a term loan under consideration, and the so-called "Funds Deficit" on a computer forecast printout indicates the point at which the company would become illiquid. But where computer-facilitated forecasting is impossible or unavailable, the liquidity of the firm is too often judged and measured in terms of its NI + D flow, NWC, the NWC flow and in terms of the current ratio. Moreover, even if the computer facility is available, the above-mentioned concepts represent the basic categories of the current analytical approach.

To many analysts, perhaps these concepts do reveal a great deal about the liquidity of the firm. It is difficult, however, to justify the use of accrued (realizable) income and an excess of current assets over current liabilities as indicators of the debt payment capacity of the firm.

Critical appraisal of the most commonly used methods of evaluating the firm's liquidity

The liquidity of a firm is its ability to pay off maturing debt in full and on time.

This widely used definition is so broad in its meaning that it will be useful to structure the problem of liquidity more exactly.

The firm's ability to pay off maturing debt can be judged from two basic aspects:

1. The aspect of the time when the firm is expected to pay may be viewed as of a certain moment of time or during some period of time.
2. The aspect of available resources may apply to assets on hand (money, highly liquid assets, or other assets) or assets accumulated and obtainable during a certain period of time (RNCPO + current liquidity balances + new borrowings, etc.)

The aspect of time and of available resources reflects itself in two concepts of liquidity—the "liquidation concept" and the "going concern concept."

When we use the liquidation concept of liquidity, we evaluate the firm's ability to pay off its debt from its available resources on hand at a certain moment of time. A comparison of the firm's immediately payable liabilities with the firm's liquid assets on hand would then represent a logical approach. In case of liquidation of the firm, we would compare the liquidation value of assets with the respective groups of liabilities in descending order of their priority of claim satisfaction. Unfortunately, a generally accepted liquidity hypothesis offers us the notion that positive NWC and a current ratio superior to 1.0 represent a "margin of protection to current creditors." (For reference, see: *ABA Program Training Unit*, Book II, pages 13 and 33.) This statement is false from at least two points of view.

First, it is difficult to imagine that any creditor would consider NWC (i.e., the excess of current assets over current liabilities) offered to him in any other form than a good debtor's check as a due execution of repayment. At a given moment of time, it is absolutely immaterial whether the firm demonstrates positive or negative NWC. In either instance, it may or may not be able to pay off the immediately maturing liability.

Second, should the liquidation of the firm take place, NWC would not constitute a "margin of protection to current creditors" because: (a) It is probable that not all current assets would be sold first. (b) Bankruptcy laws state that a commercial bank's unsecured claim ranks behind the government's tax claims, claims of the employees and claims of secured creditors in priority. The bank's claim ranks equal to the claims of other unsecured and unsubordinated short-term and long-term creditors. Therefore, if any unsecured bank creditor considers NWC and a favorable current ratio as a margin of protection, he is (to say the least) overestimating the real probability that the loan will be repaid.

In summary, the liquidation concept of liquidity, as traditionally related to the concepts of NWC and the current ratio, lacks any rationale.

The going concern concept of liquidity involves the evaluation of the firm's ability to pay off its maturing debt from newly generated resources of its own or resources borrowed during that period of time. One would compare, then, the actual or potential inflow of cash with the actual or possible outflow of cash. This concept, however, has not been universally adopted.

What we have been offered instead is the notion of the flow concepts, which can be summarized as follows: "Current assets are at various stages in the cash conversion cycle. They will be converted into cash during the next operating cycle and, hence, become available to pay current liabilities." Although this is a correct statement drawn from the microeconomic theory of the firm, it seems to suggest to some analysts that the cash conversion cycle functions smoothly and without interruptions. Realistically assuming that wages and taxes are routinely satisfied first, it would be incorrect to assume that NWC (i.e. the excess of current assets over current liabilities) must necessarily, through the cash conversion cycle, result in timely satisfaction of all other claims (including bank debt) without a necessity of refinancing. In most instances this is not the case since the firm's continuous ability to retire all its liabilities and debts is conditionally dependent upon the changing width and speed of the cash conversion cycle stream. On top of that, newly acquired assets to replace the sold ones need financial coverage as well. Simply, NWC is not excess cash continuously available for (bank) debt retirement. Exhibit III on the next page proves this point very clearly.

Exhibit III also offers additional information based upon some historical data of the GL Company. For example, at year-end 1968 the company showed NWC of $469.6MM and a current ratio of 2.0. The following year, however, the company's RNCPO (i.e., its internally generated debt payment capacity) was minus $49.0MM, indicating that the company not only had to refinance all of its maturing debt, but an additional $49.0 had to be borrowed. Needless to say, capital expenditures and investments, if any, were also financed by newly acquired debt. At year-end 1970, the company showed NWC of only $417.0MM and a current ratio of only 1.8. The next year, however, its RNCPO amounted to a positive $160.5MM available for debt retirement (without refinancing necessity), dividends and capital expenditures.

In summary, it is necessary to state that NI + D flow, NWC and current ratio are unreliable indices for making a credit decision as:

1. Not considering reborrowings, the only internal source of the loan re-

payment are the RNCPO and *not* accrued income plus depreciation, which represents additions to NWC. In every particular year those two figures are substantially different.

2. Changes in NWC do not indicate when the company will become illiquid (NWC can be comparably strong but the company illiquid).
3. Current ratio is not a measure of the firm's ability to pay off its maturing debt (without reborrowing) either at a certain point of time or during a future period of time. (CR lacks any predictive information value).

Exhibit III
Company GL

Financial Position

Fiscal years ending 7/31	1968	1969	1970	1971
Operations and Efficiency				
1. Sales revenue	1,313.9	1,563.6	1,629.6	1,566.3
2. Net income	69.8	72.1	44.8	55.6
3. Net income %	5.3%	4.6%	2.7%	3.5%
Capital Ratios				
4. Tangible Net Worth		513.8	509.8	542.2
5. Total Debt/Tangible Net Net Worth		2.8	2.9	2.6
Liquidity Ratios				
6. NWC	469.6	576.5	417.0	478.4
7. Current Ratio	2.0	2.2	1.8	2.4
8. Quick Ratio	0.8	1.1	0.7	0.9
Funds Generation & Liquidity				
9. (NI+D)	98.7	133.5	87.5	96.2
10. Real Net Cash Proceeds from Operations	− 117.8	−49.0	+25.3	+160.5
11. Bank loans and current maturities of LTD as of the end of the year	166.5	226.2	282.5	105.0
12. Suggested Liquidity Ratio (10 ÷ 11) or "Current Refinancing Independence"		$\frac{-49.0}{166.5}=-0.29$	$\frac{25.3}{226.2}=0.11$	$\frac{160.5}{282.5}=0.57$

The information value of the NWC and of the current ratio consists of indicating the general healthiness of the firm's financial structure at a certain point of time. Specifically, a good current ratio indicates that the refinancing needs of the firm cover only a part of current assets, while noncurrent assets and a remaining portion of current assets are financed by long-term funds. In such a situation, if internally generated cash and/or the proceeds of reborrowing are insufficient, the forced sale of assets might not reach a volume at which bankruptcy would occur. In other words, heavy concentration of the firm's liabilities into long-term debt creates a favorable situation—the firm's "debt payment capacity" (i.e., its RNCPO) may be relatively low because the firm's refinancing needs are kept at a reasonable level.

As an alternative for using current ratio and NWC as the measure of the firm's liquidity, it is the author's opinion that the liquidity of the firm on a going concern basis would be better evaluated when using the following ratio.

$$\frac{\text{Liquidity}}{\text{Ratio}} = \frac{\text{RNCPO (Debt Payment Capacity of the Firm)}}{\text{Generated during the Year X}}$$
$$\frac{}{\text{Bank and other Monetary Debt Listed among}}{\text{Current Liabilities at the beginning of Year X}}$$

This ratio represents the firm's "current refinancing independence." (Example: Exhibit III, lines 10, 11, and 12)

Various facets of the credit risk[3]

Financial risk is uncertainty on the part of a firm's creditors as to whether they will be paid both the principal and the interest on their loans on time and in full. Bank credit risk is a similar uncertainty on the part of a bank.

The creditors of the firm are not really interested in the source of repayment after their loans have been paid off. However, before extending the loan, the creditors reveal a strongly defined pattern of preferences as to the source of repayment because with each of these repayment sources there is associated a different degree of risk. The source of repayment creating the least risk appears first on the preference function list that follows. New risk elements are added at each subsequent step.

1. Internally generated funds
2. Refinancing
3. Enforced liquidation of assets
4. Injection of owner's capital

---

[3]Of the very little that is available on that subject, the following two publications take a more comprehensive approach:

R. I. Robinson: *The Management of Bank Funds*, Second Edition (McGraw-Hill Book Co., 1962). Chapter 9.

A Banker's Guide to Commercial Loan Analysis, (The American Bankers Association, Ninth Printing, 1971).

Internally generated funds involve the least amount of risk because the financial success (i.e. the profitability of the firm) is the only and the basic credit risk element. The financial success of the firm is a product of an objective variable, external environment, and a subjective variable, management. External environment includes the general economic and political conditions of the country in which the firm is located, future prospects for the firm's industry and the firm's standing in its competitive environment. In the management variable we may include protective diversification and the product and marketing strategy as well as other related subjective variables. Financial success of the firm as a basic risk element can be assessed only if measured in real monetary proceeds from operations. The credit risk can be assessed only if these monetary proceeds from operations (RNCPO) are compared with the total amount of maturing debt as suggested earlier.

In reality, the RNCPO are rarely used for debt repayment since most corporations, especially the growing ones, experience increasing financing needs to support a larger volume of business. For the growing concern, there is no debt-free point since using the RNCPO for debt repayment would result (at best) in the stagnation of the firm's business activity. To avoid such a situation, maturing debt is paid off through refinancing. The refinancing ability of the firm is a function not only of the firm's general business and financial success (the basic risk element) but also of the general or particular conditions in the financial markets. Financial market conditions are the added risk element here.

In assessing the firm's *refinancing ability,* one must determine the following:
1. Which segments of the financial market are generally available to the firm?
2. Which segment or segments of the financial market are most likely to be employed?
3. What are the particular creditors' requirements in that financial market segment, and how can the firm meet these requirements?
4. What is the supply or demand condition in that particular market segment?

For example, in 1971 Company GL (to which all financial markets would normally be available) had no access to the long-term subordinated debt market because current issues were rated B, and it had questionable access to the long-term unsubordinated debt market because of its poor credit standing at that moment of time (see Exhibit III above). Furthermore, the company's commercial paper rating was not published by S & P, an indication of its poor rating. In fact, the company withdrew from the commercial paper market at that time and put its sole reliance on commercial banks. The company's stock was considered a speculative placement.

To illustrate the point of the creditors' requirements, let us look at what S & P considers the most important decision variables for an appraisal of the credit risk related to commercial paper and long-term open market borrowings:[4]

Commercial Paper	Long-Term Borrowings
1. Current ratio, quick ratio	1. Protective value of indenture
2. Rating of long-term debts	2. Earnings
3. Access to reborrowing	3. Current ratio, Debt/Equity, Tangible net worth
4. Trend in net income and in NI + D	4. Management
5. The firm's reputation	5. Access to reborrowing

Obviously, the degree to which various firms satisfy these requirements will result either in open access to or unavailability of the funds traded in a given market segment.

As indicated above, an appraisal of the firm's refinancing ability should also include a forecast for the financial markets. Specifically, this should indicate whether the financial market to be entered for reborrowing will be experiencing a period of monetary ease or monetary restraint at the time of repayment. The competitiveness of each individual firm in obtaining refinancing must be appraised, particularly in the periods of tight monetary policy. As different segments of the financial market will experience a different degree of monetary tightness, the creditors' selection criteria may alter. For example, in a tight money period, commercial banks will tend to place extreme importance on the customer's deposit history, and customers who are otherwise good credit risks, may not pass the test. Clearly, appraising the firm's refinancing ability is a crucial matter which requires careful dissection; Firms incapable of refinancing their debts have to liquidate their assets and, hence, cannot be considered good credit risks.

If the firm is forced to *liquidate* some portion of its assets, proper questions might be:

1. How much of the assets will have to be sold?
2. What might be the liquidation proceeds as opposed to the book value?

---

[4]*Financial Executive*; "How Corporate Bonds and Commercial Paper are Rated," September, 1971, Brenton W. Harries.

3. How much damage of this kind can the firm sustain without approaching a complete situation of bankruptcy?

4. How much additional capital might the owners be willing to bring in to save a collapsing venture:

Although logical, the above questions are more difficult to answer than the following ones.

5. What would be the particular creditor's position in the distribution of the proceeds of liquidation?

6. What would be the liquidation proceeds?

7. How deep is the equity cushion?

Finally, an *injection of the owner's capital* was listed as the last and least preferable alternative for the loan repayment. It is the most risky one; it depends on both the availability of and the willingness to supply such capital. Credit risk appraisal, giving weight to this factor, makes sense only inasmuch as collateral on the owner's personal property or personal guarantees are obtained and analyzed. Naturally, in cases of large publicly-owned corporations, such arrangements are out of the question.

The foregoing discussion was based primarily on the theory that the process of the credit risk evaluation should follow the creditor's preference function in the sequence suggested above and should use proper analytical procedures related to each individual risk element.

Finding the "most likely" source of repayment should steer the analysis in a very realistic direction. For example, the commercial paper market places greatest importance on the firm's short-term refinancing ability since the extent of borrowing through commercial paper is usually too large to be serviced by RNCPO generated in the respective periods of time. Available unused bank lines are required to provide a safe source of funds should the firm be suddenly unsuccessful in the commercial paper marketplace. On the other hand, the long-term creditors face a substantial degree of uncertainty as to what the most likely source of repayment might be. They are interested rather in the projected income as an indication of the long-term business prospects of the firm, considering debt roll-over to be a necessary assumption for the firm to be a going concern. Unlike commercial paper creditors, the long-term creditors look closely at the net worth or net worth plus subordinated debt cushion.

Framework for credit risk analysis on a going concern basis

Given the fact that banks extend new credit only to such corporations whose future existence (at least at the present level of sales and profitability) is unquestionable, a going concern approach to credit analysis procedure should be applied as follows:

1. Determine the debt payment capacity of the firm,
2. Determine the degree of the firm's refinancing independence or dependence,
3. Appraise the firm's refinancing ability (refinancing risk). If refinancing is unlikely, the firm under consideration cannot be considered a going concern and the loan request should be turned down,
4. Conduct a comparative analysis with the firms in the same industry.

In determining the debt payment capacity of the firm, the RNCPO figure is the variable on which to focus one's attention. The RNCPO represent the difference in what the firm has collected from and what it has paid for its operations in a given year. This is the amount of internally generated cash that is available for the following uses during that year:

1. Current debt repayment (without refinancing),
2. Capital expenditures (financed internally),
3. Dividends (financed internally),
4. Advanced retirement of long-term debt (without refinancing),
5. Retirement of equity shares (without refinancing).

The competing uses for the RNCPO have been listed in the order reflecting a preference in which the company shall satisfy them once it gets into a liquidity strain. This kind of financial behavior would reflect the "Cash Outlays Rationing Function." Correspondingly, the bank credit risk assessment should be based upon evaluating the firm's ability to service its maturing debt from its RNCPO which represent the debt payment capacity of the firm.

If the debt payment capacity of the firm is larger than the firm's current debt, the difference represents cash available for capital expenditures, dividends, advanced retirement of long-term debt or of the equity shares. In this situation, the loan repayment is not dependent upon refinancing or upon other sources of cash (liquidation of assets), and the company is an unquestionably excellent credit risk.

If, on the other hand, the debt service capacity of the firm is lower than the firm's current debt, the difference (deficit) shows the extent of the firm's refinancing needs. Obviously, nothing is left for capital expenditures, dividends, etc., all to be financed by increased indebtedness. In a deficit situation like this, the credit risk increases in direct relationship with the size of the deficit in the coverage of the debt payment requirement on the firm. Consequently, evaluating the firm's refinancing ability is necessary.

A comparative analysis can be conducted and the results placed on the "Bank Risk Indifference Function" curve. Every particular level of risk would then suggest:

1. Which loans are preferable,
2. Which loans are undesirable (the "Bank Risk Indifference Function" indicates the unacceptable risk level),
3. Which interest rate is to be charged for a given level of risk

Any "Risk Indifference Function" the analyst or a decision maker might develop is a subjective variable and would differ also in respect to different situations under consideration, but it is still a convenient way of organizing the review of the results of any analysis.

Below some pertinent data regarding Company GL are repeated and the results are plotted on the graph which follows. The Company GL case is quite instructive, hence, we are taking a liberty of using the company trend analysis instead of an intercompany comparison, which should be employed as a matter of correct procedure.

	(in millions)		
	1969	1970	1971
1. Debt payment capacity	$- 49.0	$+ 25.3	$+160.5
2. Current debt payment requirement	166.5	226.2	282.5
3. Difference (1−2):			
Available for other uses (+)			
Refinancing necessity (−)	−215.5	−200.9	−122.0
4. Liquidity ratio (1 ÷ 2)	− 0.29	0.11	0.57
5. S & P's long-term debt rating	B	B	B

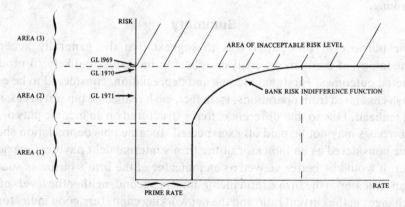

Area 1 covers those situations where our liquidity ratio is equal to or better than 1.0 or, if lower, such ratio can withstand the comparative test if subjected to an intercompany analysis within the particular industry. Corresponding loans should be priced at prime rate.

Area 3 covers those situations where our liquidity ratio is at an unacceptable level and there are serious doubts about the refinancing ability of the firm. Here, our "Bank Risk Indifference Function" flattens out, indicating that loans to such corporations are unacceptable whatever rate might be charged.

Area 2 covers those situations where either the liquidity ratio is good but the refinancing ability questionable or an opposite situation where the refinancing ability is good but the liquidity ratio poor. There is certainly enough space to play with the interest rate here.

In each area, "safety margins" should be considered as well. It should also be noted that the refinancing ability of the firm (best appreciated by learning current ratings of the firm's debt instruments) changes post fact (i.e. after the results of the previous period's operations are published).

Making a judgment as to what weight should be assigned to the firm's refinancing ability introduces an obvious complication. Logically, the better the liquidity ratio the less weight should be assigned to the firm's refinancing ability and vice-versa. In our particular Company GL situation, where unchanging long-term debt rating functions as a constant, we are left with only one variable—the liquidity ratio. An attempt was made to locate the GL's situation on the vertical axis as regards its 1969, 1970 and 1971 liquidity strength. Using the suggested going concern approach, the reader is invited to use the NI + D and the current ratio figures for relevant years as they appear on Exhibit III and to locate the GL's situation on the vertical axis using these traditional indices. The difference is striking.

Summary

The purpose of this paper was to suggest that the generally accepted methodology of bank credit analysis relies on indicators unlikely to produce expected outcomes. First, net income and depreciation, considered to be equal to cash generated from operations, is, in fact, cash realizable but not necessarily cash realized. Due to that difference, loans structured on an income plus depreciation basis may not be paid off as expected. Income plus depreciation should not be considered as an indicator of the firm's internal debt payment capacity; rather, it would be better viewed as an indicator of the firm's business success and an indicator of the firm's refinancing ability. Second, neither the levels of nor the changes in the current ratio and the net working capital are good indicators of the firm's internal debt payment capacity. Particularly, they have no predictive information value in that respect. The current ratio would be better regarded as an indicator of the firm's long-term funding and of the extent of the firm's refinancing needs.

An alternative approach was suggested whereby the firm's internal debt payment capacity is judged based upon the value of the "Real Net Cash Proceeds from Operations." The value of it can be reached by adjusting the operating income and depreciation figure for changes in various current assets and liabilities related to the firm's operations. If the value of the firm's RNCPO is compared with outstanding debt, the strength of the firm's internal debt payment capacity or the firm's "refinancing independence" can be evaluated. Subsequently, the firm's refinancing ability should be carefully appreciated because a firm unable to refinance its debts has to liquidate its assets.

An apparent conflict arises from the fact that the value of the RNCPO can hardly be predicted with an acceptable degree of accuracy while the income figure can. Since the level of and the changes in income are only indirectly related to the firm's internal debt payment capacity, if this is what we are interested in, the use of the RNCPO is the only available alternative. As Exhibit II indicates, the RNCPO is a methodologically correct and practically indispensable concept for both a historical analysis and for projection of future trends of the internal debt payment capacity of the firm. □

The Role of Economic Information in Commercial Lending Analysis

by Gary G. Anderson

When combined with standard financial analysis, economic information can be used to evaluate loan proposals and to reduce risks. What information about the economy will be relevant and how to use it in connection with a specific loan applicant comprise part of the author's discussion. He rounds out his presentation with some guidelines for using economic indicators and a description of those that can be meaningful for the commercial lender.

Due to unforeseen economic events, the past four years have been extremely difficult for all areas of business planning. Droughts, freezes, and crop and fishing disasters have combined to put pressure on prices of food commodities worldwide. International trade conditions, most notably the oil embargo and subsequent increases in energy costs, have radically changed the world supply and demand patterns for many goods. Finally, attempts by governments to correct for the results of these problems have often gone awry, intensifying rather than solving world economic problems.

In an increasingly interdependent world economy and one where governments are expanding their role in managing their economies, it seems unlikely that the next four or five or ten years will be any smoother or any easier to plan for than the past four years have been. Murphy postulated that if anything

This article is based on a presentation made by the author to RMA's Mountain States Chapter Loan Management Seminar on May 4, 1977 in Salt Lake City, Utah. At that time, Mr. Anderson was a senior economist with Merrill Lynch Economics, Inc. in San Francisco.

could go wrong, it would. Some businessmen now seem to be planning as if Murphy were an optimist.

Affected by radical changes in business conditions brought on by the events just mentioned and others, commercial loan officers, as much as any other group of business managers, have had difficulties in coping with a volatile and unpredictable business environment. The purpose of this discussion is to develop the general theme that the risks involved in business planning, particularly those inherent in commercial lending under uncertain economic conditions, can be reduced if economic information is used in conjunction with other standard methods of commercial loan analysis.

In the first portion of the presentation, the various criteria used in evaluating a loan proposal and the contribution that economic analysis can make to these evaluations will be discussed. The second portion of the presentation will deal with the relationship between the individual company and general economic conditions and the methods by which this relationship can be identified. The third portion will describe the various time horizons over which economic information will be utilized and the means by which the differing information requirements imposed by these horizons can be obtained and applied. The final portion will suggest how the individual loan officer can personally monitor current information on the economy as an indication of trends and issues which may affect the loan client and will provide a short list of specific economic indicators which are most appropriate for this purpose.

Economic change and loan evaluation criteria

At the risk of oversimplifying a complex and highly involved process, the evaluation of a loan proposal might be categorized under three major criteria. First, what is the current financial situation of the prospective client? Second, what are the future prospects of the project for which the loan is being requested and for the company if the loan is granted? Third, has management taken and is it likely to continue to take prudent measures to minimize risk and assure the success of the project?

Using these three criteria as a general outline, we can explore the impact that economic events can have on the project and the role that economic information and forecasts can play in evaluating the proposal in terms of the three major criteria.

Evaluation of the current financial structure

This analysis is based upon balance sheet data and past income statements, and standards are usually well-defined. Relationships among line items in these documents can be computed in terms of levels, ratios, and percentages and evaluated against specified standards for acceptability.

This approach might be called a "rear-view mirror" approach to loan analysis since it relies on the past for information about events which will take place in the future. The past several years have taught us that much of what affects a corporation may be beyond the control of the individual manager and may be totally unforeseeable. Acknowledging this points up a major reason for analyzing the firm's current financial position.

The ratios and levels contain information on the corporation's vulnerability to unforeseen change. Are cash and liquid assets, for example, sufficient to weather a short downturn in the market for the new product the company is bringing out? Given the potential for such a downturn, or for increased inflation, are inventories, particularly of finished goods, closely controlled so that they are high enough to hedge against raw material price increases but not so large as to produce injurious carrying costs should demand be hit hard for a short period?

Even when compared against similar companies and standard measures of acceptability, the financial criteria will not tell with certainty the future condition of the firm. But they at least convey some information on how well the firm or project is protected from abrupt or unforeseen economic change. If, in addition, economic analysis can suggest the specific nature of potential problems, then the evaluation of the firm's current financial position can be a hedge against future risk as well as a view of the past.

Prospects for the proposed project

The second criteria relates to the future of the project and the company over the term of the loan. Here the loan officer generally relies on cash flow projections as a means to structure information on the proposal. In the cash flow statement, the increased cash available from the loan plus cash generated can be compared against the obligations—raw materials, marketing costs, labor, debt servicing and repayment, and so forth—imposed by the project and undertaken by the company. The net obligations can be compared against the projected revenue stream to verify the potential for a successful outcome.

Economic information can make its most significant contribution to this aspect of the evaluation since each projection is likely to be affected by changes in the economy, from the projection of production costs through anticipated unit sales to price and net revenue. For example, is the market going to grow as fast as the client's demand projections? Or is an assumption being made based on sales projections that an increasing share of market is going to be obtained, even though prospects for the market itself are not promising. What about costs of raw materials or energy? Are raw materials going to be available in the quantity and at the price assumed, or are they likely to be subject to shortages or price increases? If the costs of goods sold are subject to inflation, will the market support similar increases in selling prices or might the consumer substitute another cheaper product for the more expensive product marketed by the loan applicant?

Each of these questions can only be answered by a corresponding assumption—explicit or implicit—on what some aspect of the economy is likely to be doing in the future. It is in this area that the loan officer must become, and assist the client in becoming, at least a part-time economist.

Evaluation of management quality

Finally, the third criteria has to do with management quality. Awareness that economic change is likely to take place over the term of the project is important. As one aspect of evaluating management's ability to assure a successful outcome, the loan officer may wish to look for economic awareness in the strategies presented by the management. Alternative strategies might properly be requested which are available should the economic assumptions underlying the baseline projections change. For instance, could assets be redeployed to other areas? Or could the new product be sold to other markets should the primary market be hit hard by an abrupt downturn? For example, if the primary buyers of the new product are home builder contractors and assumed strength in the housing market doesn't develop, could the product be marketed to individuals who are repairing present homes because they can't afford to buy new ones?

In general, the question to be asked of management is whether or not the business plan allows for the probability of economic change. Furthermore, is management allowing for unexpected economic change by including contingency plans in the overall strategy to compensate for potential problems?

The importance of overall economic conditions

In the foregoing, the assumption was made that economic factors beyond the control of the individual company will affect it and thus should be taken into account in evaluating the loan request. A forecast of demand for the company's product, for example, is a logical request for a proposal to fund a new product; what is suggested here is that it may be important to examine the potential for the overall market in the context of general economic conditions.

Is this a valid assumption? Is it really worth the loan officer's time to devote attention to economic conditions and projections, particularly when dealing with a small company or a limited market? The question might be restated in the opposite sense: Is there ever such a company or a project which is truly isolated enough, or insulated enough, so that changes in the overall economy won't have a measurable effect or so that the effects can be easily compensated for?

It is true that relationships may often be distant or indirect. National conditions affect different regions in different magnitudes. Individual industries do not always change in lockstep with aggregate economic change. Individual companies can prosper while their industry or market is suffering. Finally, connections may be difficult to trace when an individual company supplies goods or services to other companies which themselves may be at least partially insulated from individual events.

However, the critical point is not that each individual company or project will move exactly as its market or as national trends move. Rather, it is suggested that it may be difficult to achieve increased sales, for example, when the overall market is declining. On the other hand, if overall trends are upward, then an individual project is that much more likely to prosper. The relevant questions then might be ones of adequate capacity and assurance of raw material supplies rather than assurance of strong demand.

In general, adding economic conditions to the list of important loan criteria can be justified simply as a matter of providing guidelines against which to evaluate the myriad of projections required in a loan proposal and as a means of alerting the loan officer and the client to potential sources of problems.

Relating the company to the economy

Accepting the general principle that external economic events will have some impact on business and that they will affect the prospects for any business venture requiring loan support, the obvious problem is twofold: The loan officer must first determine the relationship between the individual company and the economy. Then relevant economic information must be secured and applied.

The first step in evaluating a loan should be a detailed analysis to determine what business the client is in and how the prospective venture fits into this business. To whom does the client sell the product or service, and what are the characteristics of that business? If applicable, to whom, in turn, does the client's customer sell?

As an example, if the client's product is a machine tool, is it sold to an automotive manufacturer or to an aerospace company? The relevant factor to be evaluated in the first case would be consumer spending and in the second case, government defense spending.

How the client's product fits into the production cycle also might be a relevant question. If the product is an industrial fastener rather than a piece of production equipment, it may be more directly tied to short-term cycles in the purchaser's market rather than to the long-term growth trends which generate need for additional production capacity.

These examples point to another justification for economic analysis. Often the small company is at the very end of a chain of circumstances put into motion by economic change. Because of the relatively small size of the company or its lack of diversification, for instance, it may be much more affected by change than a larger company. With the larger company, the relationships may be clearer, but the company's ability to weather setbacks in any one market segment is greater.

Within many banks, particularly larger ones, it may not be necessary for the individual loan officer to do this analysis of the company and its relationship to economic factors. The economics department may be a useful source for assistance in translating the information which the loan officer obtains from the applicant into a basis for selecting important economic information.

In any case, this micro-economic analysis, coupled with logic and common sense, is the key to selecting pertinent and required economic information.

Categories of economic information

Accepting the use of economic information as a possible means for minimizing some of the risks inherent in loan decisions and with a basic understanding of the relationship between the client company and its markets and suppliers, we may then go on to these next questions: What type of information is relevant to various aspects of the loan evaluation, and where can relevant information be obtained?

Economic events can be divided by the timing of their impact on the corporation into three major categories. First, there are current conditions in the economy, and these can be expected to have an impact in the very short run, that is, three to six months or less. Second, there are economic events which are a part of the current cycle, but which are not yet fully in motion and which might affect the corporation in the foreseeable medium term; that is the period from three months to perhaps two years out. Finally, there are economic issues which are not going to have their full impact on the project or company until a five- to ten-year period has elapsed.

In evaluating and allowing for these economic circumstances, the loan officer must combine personal monitoring of present conditions with the use of outside sources. These sources can provide forecasts over the short to medium planning horizon and analysis of possible issues and events which might have implication for the long term.

Short-term economic information

In many cases, the success or failure of a proposed project may be determined in the first three to six months of the project. Personal monitoring of current economic conditions by the loan officer can be one means of anticipating and avoiding potential near-term problems. Also, monitoring economic conditions as they develop during the life of the project might give the three to six months' warning necessary to develop and put alternative strategies into play before the project is lost.

Two applications of current economic information can be suggested. First, the choice of timing in beginning or entering a critical phase of the project is important, particularly in a volatile economic climate. Starting a project soon after the market for the product has turned upward can ensure immediate returns. On the other hand, entering a market that has just begun a downturn might produce immediate cash flow problems which may doom the project before long-term growth in the market can be exploited.

Second, economic information can suggest strategies to minimize current risks. For instance, the stage of the market cycle may not be clear, or doubt may exist as to when there may be a more positive environment, but postponement may mean lost opportunities. In these situations, awareness of the potential risks suggested by current data might indicate a strategy allowing for higher cash needs or slower return or a strategy of avoiding higher levels of finished goods inventories until the path of the cycle is clearer.

These determinations are not necessarily limited to the inception of the project. Most projects consist of a stream of small decisions, each predicated on the condition of the project at that time and in the next period of time. Hence the contributions to project success which can be made by monitoring economic conditions at the beginning of the project are equally valid throughout the life of the project.

Awareness of economic conditions and allowance for them in project strategies do, however, require more than an overall outlook for the general economic cycle. It is well understood that some industries and some regions recover later or with less strength than other sectors of the economy. In the current cycle, for example, retail spending, particularly for automobiles and single family housing, showed strength very early in the recovery. Capital spending remained weak for almost a year after the turnaround, and construction of new plants was still improving at a very slow pace well into the second year of the recovery. By that time, construction of single family housing was already beginning to plateau. Thus it is necessary to identify what sectors of the economy most closely relate to the project at hand and then determine how those sectors specifically are performing in the current period.

Knowing the stage of its cycle that the relevant market or industry has reached and determining immediate market prospects can be achieved through analysis of current data. Since this analysis can be done effectively by the loan officer, I will return to this topic later in the discussion to suggest a list of specific indicators which can be monitored for this purpose and to provide some general guidelines for their use.

Forecasts of mid-range economic conditions

Current economic conditions can provide the loan officer with a great deal of information concerning immediately foreseeable events and some indication of risks to the successful beginning of a proposed loan project. It is also necessary to extend the economic horizon out to cover a longer portion of the loan term. For this reason, forecasts of impending economic change are required. However, the development of valid forecasts, in the detail required to estimate their impact on the individual firm, is probably not an effective use of the loan officer's time, even if it is within his or her capability.

It is generally better to rely on an outside source for economic forecasts so that the major portion of the officer's attention can be devoted to the specific issue at hand. In most banks, an economics department is already in place and can provide economic forecasts if requested. For smaller banks, it may be possible to arrange for such services, perhaps from a larger correspondent bank or from a commercial economic consulting service. There are some general guidelines worth mentioning for the individual loan officer's use of this resource.

First, the forecasts should be sufficiently detailed so that the general outlook can be translated into its implications for the specific markets or sectors which the officer has identified as important through analysis of the company. This means that information such as consumer spending by category, capital spending by industry, corporate profits by industry, housing activity by type of dwelling unit, and construction by type of project will be useful.

Second, all of these detailed forecasts should be secured from the same source so that the loan officer is assured that they are consistent with one another and with the overall outlook for the economy. Prices, interest rates, and personal income, for instance, are all interrelated and related to equally interrelated estimates of consumption, production and spending. A consistent outlook, updated frequently to allow for changes, is far superior to a piecemeal collection of information.

For instance, planning a shopping center depends on estimates of positive conditions in the local housing market as well as on continued good retail spending which may rely on the employment and salary conditions in a significant local industry. If forecasts for one of these elements are drawn from an optimistic analyst while forecasts for another are drawn from an alarmist rumor obtained from another source, the loan officer will not have the necessary assurance that the situation is promising, nor will he or she be sensitive to the implications of economic changes which might alter the outlook.

Third, the outlook should be updated often and compared with actual data as released so that if it is necessary to modify expectations, this necessity can be recognized. This situation may even be relayed to the client soon enough to alert him to the need for a change in strategy. There is an informally accepted motto in our profession which says that if you must forecast, forecast often. The loan officer and the loan client might do well to do the same. Plans should be reviewed and updated as often as conditions change.

Fourth, use other sources of economic information such as newspapers, magazines, the trade press, and personal contacts sparingly and carefully and only in the context of the overall economic outlook being used. These sources can be useful to provide information on current conditions, but they can be unreliable when they venture into the area of interpretation or prognostication. And they usually do venture into that territory. For the sake of increasing the newsworthy nature of an article, journalists will often venture in where economists would fear to tread.

It is often mentioned that economists have not been noted for the accuracy of their forecasts over the past four years. Some of their performance may be attributed to the fact that the most significant economic events during those years have been ones that were unforeseeable in advance. It is not surprising, for instance, that inflation forecasts for 1974, which were published before the announcement of the oil embargo in 1973, proved inaccurate. However, professional economic forecasters, who forecast a detailed outlook and update it regularly, are usually the best source of information on the true significance of an unexpected event once it has occurred. Further, over a short-term horizon, four to five quarters into the future, the accuracy of professional forecasts is usually quite dependable.

Analysis of long-term economic conditions

If economic projections are important for the short term and for the first years of a loan project, then projections of economic change are no less important over the longer term, particularly when evaluating loans which may have a three- to five-year life or longer. However, the purpose and the technique for utilizing long-term economic analysis is quite different.

In the longer term, the primary application of economic analysis should be to isolate, as far in advance as possible, those issues which may be sources for potential difficulty. The longer-term analysis can provide potential alternative economic outlooks and information on immutable trends such as changes in age group size. It can thus be quite useful as a tool for the manager securing the loan and for the loan officer who will grant the loan and who will have a responsibility for monitoring it.

Generally, the information provided by the longer-term analysis will apply either to projects with a long lead time between beginning and the first payout or to an investment in assets with a long payback period. These types of commitments require a great deal of advance warning if any adjustments are to be made in strategies.

The same caveats suggested for obtaining middle range economic forecasts apply equally to obtaining and applying discussions of long-term trends and issues. It is best to rely on a full-time economist, department, or consulting firm for these as well. The contribution here is in providing detailed discussions of the long-term issues as a backdrop for assisting in development and evaluation of contingency strategies in the business plans of the applicant.

Measuring the present:
The use of economic indicators

It was suggested earlier that information on current economic conditions can be useful in loan decisions affecting such questions as the timing of the beginning of a project or identifying immediate risks which can be hedged against.

To monitor current economic conditions, economists long ago developed the concept of "leading economic indicators." These indicators, nothing more than measurements of such things as numbers of building permits requested or changes in personal income, are watched with all the attention and reverence that Greek prophets once devoted to the entrails of chickens. Unlike the entrails of the ancients' chickens, however, leading economic indicators can be used by any loan officer or business manager. Their use requires simple common sense and some basic business knowledge. Furthermore, since they are published in readily available government releases and reported in the business press, these indicators are generally easier to obtain than chicken entrails.

These indicators are valuable because they can be measured with relative accuracy, they can track important sectors of the economy, and by their nature, they tend to act as useful predictors of subsequent economic changes. For example, housing permits are a good indication of conditions in the home building market. In addition, since new homes when occupied generate some demand for new furniture and appliances, they are also a useful leading indicator for consumer durable purchases.

General guidelines for using economic indicators

In this concluding section of my presentation, I will suggest a list of some eight or ten such economic indicators and their specific applications. Before doing that, I would like to suggest some basic guidelines for the general use of economic indicators.

First, a specific set of indicators should be selected, and that set should be followed consistently. By doing this, familiarity with the characteristics of the indicators and their relationship to economic conditions will increase over time.

Second, it is useful to learn as much about the individual indicator as possible. Find out the detailed definition of the series, rather than simply relying on its title. Learn something about the way the series is sampled and how often it is subject to revision since, of course, all series are actually reported as the result of samples rather than being directly measured. They are subject to revision as time permits the agency publishing the data to take a broader sample.

Third, it should be remembered that no indicator will move in one direction on a continuous, month by month basis. All indicators will to a greater or lesser extent display month by month variations while still reflecting a general trend. For this reason, it is essential that the given period's report be placed in a general perspective by comparing it to previous levels and movements in the series. A graph of the series which will show trends over several past business cycles, and the normal period to period movement is usually the best way to avoid attaching too much significance to a given period's change. Also, if the most current report not only departs from the apparent trend but also seems to contradict the forecast being used, it may be necessary to wait for a second or third period's report before making any changes in strategy.

Fourth, always evaluate the indicator against the current overall outlook which has been obtained from the bank economist or outside economic source. This guideline has already been mentioned, but it should be stressed again as a separate point. If the report is in disagreement or the interpretation of the report as published in a newspaper or magazine contradicts the overall outlook, it is usually wise to check the assumptions of the outlook and compare the report with other reports and with personal observations before acting on the new information.

Finally, any publication of a given indicator, such as industrial production or wholesale prices, is usually supplemented by breakdowns by specific category. These subaggregate measures are usually of more use than an overall indicator, particularly when relating general business conditions to a specific company. As a result, the detail underlying a current trend should receive as much or more attention as the overall indicator.

Useful leading indicators of economic behavior

Following a small group of leading indicators as they are reported, if done properly, can be a very useful way of relating general economic trends to specific industries as well as giving some firsthand information on the economy. The following indicators are by no means all-inclusive, but they are widely available, generally dependable, and are good measures of present and projected near-term behavior for specific industries and markets. While similar data are often not available for the region or locality, these indicators can also serve as a guide as to what local conditions to watch.

Personal income—Data on personal income are available in both current dollars on a monthly basis and in "constant dollars" each quarter. (Constant dollars are adjusted for inflation using an inflation index to give a measure of purchasing power change as opposed to increases due to inflation which don't increase purchasing power.) Because consumers do not change purchasing patterns as quickly as their income changes, this indicator can tell a great deal about potential changes in volume of purchases which can be expected over the next several months. It is also published monthly, though with somewhat less accuracy, on a state-by-state basis in some sources.

Employment—Changes in the employment situation also have an impact on consumer behavior, often with a greater lead time than changes in personal income. They also have an indirect effect through influences on consumer sentiment, which will determine the extent to which consumers are willing to take on debt to finance large purchases. There are several ways of measuring employment, and unfortunately, the one that gets the greatest press, the overall unemployment rate, is the least useful. More useful on a national basis is the *layoff rate in manufacturing,* particularly when compared with the accession or hiring rate in manufacturing. When the layoff rate starts increasing, particularly when compared with the hiring rate, this can be a distinct signal that manufacturers are being forced to draw down their activity. This drawdown is often due to large inventories, lower profitability, and the expectation that things are not going to improve soon enough to justify keeping even experienced workers.

A good indicator for strength in the consumer sector, the layoff rate is also often the first signal of impending downturns in business spending and expansion. Supplementary indicators such as employment ads for the region, changes in state unemployment rolls, or personal information on local companies can help relate national employment trends to the state or local picture.

Changes in consumer debt—Extensions and repayments of consumer installment debt are perhaps the best direct indication of consumer sentiment and an indirect indication of other business activity. These companion indicators measure the extent to which consumers are willing to commit themselves to future payments or the extent to which they feel the need to draw down their debt obligations. Thus they are a good check on the current health of the consumer sector.

By comparing the level of repayments and extensions against past history, it is often possible to derive some indication of how long currently strong sales might continue. An extreme rise in the ratio of debt extensions to repayments may suggest an impending need to reduce borrowing through a reduction in purchases of large-ticket items. Similarly, once the level of debt extensions drops below the level of repayments, it generally indicates that the correction in the consumer's financial situation has been completed. This is usually a reliable indication that consumer spending can be expected to show good improvement in the near future.

Information on consumer debt extensions and repayments is also often available, at least informally, on a local basis. Comparisons between national and regional consumer conditions can be used to draw inferences on prospects for local businesses, particularly retail establishments selling large-ticket consumer durable goods.

Capacity utilization rates—There are several indicators which will assist in anticipating changes in business spending. Among them is the measure of the percentage of productive capacity currently in use in manufacturing, in total and in specific industries. This estimate is controversial because it is based upon a factor that is not really observable or measurable. Nevertheless, when used in conjunction with other measures, it can give some indication of anticipated spending. Regardless of current business conditions or profits, businessmen seem unlikely to expand capacity if a substantial portion of it is unused in relation to historical usage levels. On the other hand, with any confidence at all, business managers will find the means to expand capacity if it is likely to be in short supply.

In using this indicator, it is important to compare it with historical levels. For example, current capacity usage is reported to be running between 80% and

85% after running below 70% at the trough of the recession. By comparison, during the past business expansion in 1973–1974, bottlenecks and shortages were encountered by the time capacity began exceeding 85%, and it has never exceeded 90%.

Manufacturers' appropriations for capital spending—Capital spending is a long process, and as a result, it can be checked at several points in the life of the decision. The manager won't make a decision to invest until demand looks as if it will exceed current capacity for a sustained period. Only at that point is capital appropriated; that is, a decision is made to purchase a piece of equipment or to build a new plant.

The actual decision is sampled by the Conference Board once each quarter by asking managers of the thousand largest U.S. corporations what they are committed to spend. Other groups, such as Merrill Lynch Economics, Inc., McGraw-Hill, and the U.S. Department of Commerce, also publish quarterly, semi-annual, and annual surveys of capital investments. Taken on average, these surveys are the first signal of actual spending intentions. Hence they tend to lead actual spending by six to nine months, the time it takes to get a project from the board room decision to construction or orders.

New orders for producers' durable goods—The final step before spending actually takes place is the placement of the order for equipment. Without this order, the previous samples mentioned will have been meaningless. At the same time, if new orders are increasing faster than previous appropriations or are being made at low levels of capacity utilization, they may only signal a more drastic turndown later. When this series moves in the same general direction as capacity and appropriations, however, it is the best signal that business expansion is actually taking place and with it, employment prospects, income prospects, and general economic health are improving. However, this indicator is one of those which can move in a very volatile fashion from month to month and thus has to be viewed in conjunction with the readings of several previous months before interpretation is likely to be accurate.

Housing—Housing is an important part of the economy, not only because it is a primary generator of jobs and purchases of material but also because it is a good measure of secondary activities. Purchases of furniture and appliances and requirements for services such as retail stores and restaurants in new areas are examples of such secondary activities. Two indicators are useful at the national level in measuring housing.

Net flows into savings and loan institutions—A variety of leading economic indicators measure overall health in the housing industry, but the most reliable indicator is the availability of mortgage funds. This indicator must be used with some care, however, since it is not always consistent on timing. However, it is a good precondition to housing industry change. That is, if net flows into S & L's are not positive, then it is unlikely that mortgages are going to be readily available at stable rates and, as a result, it is unlikely that increases in housing are going to take place or be sustained in the near future. On the other hand, rises do not necessarily mean that housing is going to increase with certainty at a specific point in the near future. If S & L flows are negative or decreasing, they generally are an advance indication of weakness in the housing industry. This indicator works well on a local basis as well where the information is available.

Housing starts and permits—The best indicator of activity in the housing industry is data on the beginning of construction of housing units. From the beginning of housing unit construction to completion, the construction time required is relatively fixed. Generally, a single family home is completed about five to six months after it is started, while multiple family structures require just over a year on average from start to completion. The actual length of time for completing a multiple family dwelling varies with the number of units in the project. As a result, since housing both benefits and is benefited by business activity in a region, monitoring housing by watching the number of units initiated can be valuable and can provide advance warning of one quarter to as much as a year of changes in conditions in various markets and areas of economic activity.

In addition to the sales of materials and construction wage increases generated directly by new housing construction, housing activity also generates demand for appliances, furniture, carpeting, and drapes upon completion and occupancy. Housing activity also tends to produce requirements for stores, restaurants, and other service facilities when concentrated in a new area. As a result, housing activity can indicate something about potential success of new business ventures in a given area with a lead time of six months to a year.

It is of course important, when evaluating this indicator, to take into account other information such as local occupancy rates or stocks of unsold houses. It is also important to look at the breakdowns of construction into types of units, that is, single family, two to four unit buildings, and five or more unit buildings. Strong activity in the single family housing market generates demands for different types of goods and services than does activity in apartment house or condominium building. On a local basis, the size and quality of the units being built can also be of help in assessing the impact on a particular business venture.

Two indicators of housing activity are available on a national basis. Data are reported on the number of housing units started on a regional and national basis, referred to as "housing starts." Data are also reported by communities whose building codes require housing permits before construction can begin. Housing permits tend to run in tandem with housing starts, but housing permits are perhaps the better indicator of the two to watch on a continuing basis. Local data are usually available on construction by number of permits granted, and thus national and local trends can be easily compared, particularly in conjunction with other national/local comparisons.

Sources of information on economic indicators

The single most useful source of current economic measures is the *Business Conditions Digest,* published by the Bureau of Economic Analysis of the Department of Commerce. This source is published monthly and is available by subscription. Providing a comprehensive set of economic data on various categories of economic indicators, this source has the added advantage of providing the data in graphic as well as tabular form.

Also published by the Bureau of Economic Analysis, the monthly *Survey of Current Business* is the other standard source of economic data. The data are, for the most part, the same as published in the *BCD,* but the survey does not present data in graphic form. On the other hand, its articles on current economic conditions can be a useful resource. The *Survey* is also available from the Department of Commerce by annual subscription.

Various newspapers and business magazines also publish and report on different sectors of the economy with a greater timeliness than government publications. When reading these sources, it is worthwhile to remember that they both report changes in economic data and also comment upon the implications of the change. In the former, they are useful and readily obtainable information sources. In the latter, their analysis should be reviewed with care since it represents opinion in the same sense that the analysis by government and private economic forecasters does and hence should be interpreted in the context of other sources of information. The two best sources for economic data on a daily and weekly basis are the *Wall Street Journal* and *Business Week* since they provide comprehensive coverage in a defined format and are, as a result, easy to check quickly for releases of current data.

Finally, several time-sharing computer systems specializing in services for the business community provide access to commercially maintained data bases of national and regional economic data which are updated daily. These sources, coupled with the analytical software maintained by the companies, are particularly useful for quantitative research requiring calculations, production of tables, and preparation of charts. These tools may be beyond the requirements of the individual loan officer but can be extremely useful in evaluation and development of loan policy.

Summary

As a summary, the following points can be reviewed. First, in applying standard loan criteria of current financial stability, projections of the relevant future, and management quality, it is useful to add economic conditions to the issues considered to minimize risk and hedge against unforeseen problems.

Second, background analysis of the commercial loan applicant should include its relationships to its markets and sources of supply as a means to determine the economic factors which are likely to affect its business.

Third, monitoring of current economic conditions, forecasting of near to mid-term economic prospects, and analysis of long-term economic issues should be used to obtain economic information which will assist in identifying and anticipating specific changes bearing on the success of the project.

Finally, the loan officer should personally monitor current economic conditions on a continuing basis, using a limited number of readily available economic time series as indicators to anticipate economic change and respond to it as it occurs.   □

Making a Plant Visit Pay Off

by Cass Bettinger

Cass Bettinger feels that loan officers frequently do not take the time to plan their calls on borrowing customers. And he believes that, in many cases, they do not know what to look for during a plant visit. In the following article, he suggests what the officer should focus on to get the most out of the valuable time spent making customer calls.

As we all know, regular plant visits are a normal part of a commercial loan officer's responsibilities. Nevertheless, commercial lenders are busy individuals, and plant visits can easily take up from half a day or more, depending on where the plant is located. For this reason, many loan officers find that time constraints often seem to make annual plant visits impossible. Even in those cases when the visit is made, however, that precious time is frequently not used wisely, and a good deal of potentially valuable information is overlooked.

Perhaps the first thing to remember about a plant visit is that its primary purpose is not to make a social call but to obtain information—any and all information—that will aid in assessing the firm's credit-worthiness. It is, therefore, essential that the visit be thoughtfully planned. Meetings should be scheduled with *several* key individuals in the organization. And the calling officer should have a list of carefully conceived questions relating to the firm's major activities. Naturally, every firm is unique, and variations on the fundamental approach will be necessary. The purpose of this article is to suggest a basic analytical format designed to make a plant visit really pay off.

Objectives of plant visit

The first area that needs careful consideration is management. The calling officer should schedule time with the general manager or president of the firm.

Evaluation of management

The calling officer should be interested in ascertaining the extent to which management clearly understands the firm's purpose and strategy. It is often taken for granted that existing management activities are oriented around a clearly defined and carefully articulated purpose. Unfortunately, however, this is not always the case.

"Probably the skill most nearly unique to general management, as opposed to the management of functional or technical specialties, is the intellectual capacity to conceptualize corporate purpose and the dramatic skill to invest it with some degree of magnetism." [1] Peter Drucker contends that, "Only a clear definition of the mission and purpose of the business makes possible clear and realistic business objectives." He further states, "That business purpose and business mission are so rarely given adequate thought is perhaps the most important single cause of business frustration and business failure." [2] The relevance of this matter to the credit decision should not be underestimated.

Time should also be scheduled with managers of major functional areas. According to *The Business Failure Record,* published annually by Dun and Bradstreet, business failure is generally attributable to some form of management deficiency. "Unbalanced experience" is defined as "Experience not well rounded in sales, finance, purchasing, and production on the part of the individual in case of a proprietorship, or of two or more partners or officers constituting a management unit." It is given as a cause of failure in 23% of the reported cases. It is, therefore, important to make sure that competent management exists throughout the business entity. This can only be accomplished by meeting and questioning the managers of major functional areas. It is also quite helpful to obtain biographical information on those key individuals.

Gaining familiarity with board of directors

In addition to evaluating management, it is often important to develop insight into the composition of the board of directors. Whenever necessary, the plant visit should be used as an opportunity to meet one or more of the board

---

[1] Daniel J. McCarthy, Robert J. Minichiello, and Joseph R. Curran, *Business Policy and Strategy: Concepts and Readings* (Homewood, Ill.: Richard D. Irwin, Inc., 1975).

[2] Peter F. Drucker, *Management: tasks, responsibilities, practices* (New York: Harper and Row, 1973), pp. 75 and 78.

members. This is especially important when the borrowing company is located in another city, thus making familiarity with board members more difficult. The calling officer should attempt to determine what types of expertise the board members bring to the company. Is this expertise compatible with the challenges facing the firm? Are there any apparent conflicts of interest?

Risk management

A third area that deserves attention yet is seldom considered is that of risk management, which has been defined as, "the identification, measurement and treatment of property, liability and personnel losses."[3] The American Management Associations (AMA) stresses the importance of risk management in its "Risk Analysis Questionnaire." The questionnaire consists of 43 pages covering the basic risks facing a business enterprise which should be identified and controlled.

Illustrating the importance of risk management in today's environment is an article entitled "Risk Management: New Ways for Business to Insure Against Loss," appearing in the November 1977 issue of *Nations Business*. In that article, it states that, "A short time ago, the Warner-Lambert Company, Morris Plains, N.J., and four of its executives were indicted on charges of second degree manslaughter and criminally negligent homicide. The charges grew out of an explosion in November 1976, that wrecked the company's chewing gum manufacturing plant in Long Island City, New York, killing six persons and injuring others." In today's world, risk management is absolutely essential to the proper operation of any business entity. Yet it is an item that is often neglected by management and by the commercial lender.

Analysis of product lines, competition, and research and development

Other items that need to be analyzed are product lines, competition, and research and development. The plant visit is an excellent time to review the company's products with top management. The calling officer will want to know what the market share is for individual products and the trend of that market share. The officer will also want to know the answers to these questions: To what extent are sales dependent on one or two products? Are the company's products in a growth stage, or are they being overtaken in the marketplace by a superior or a substitute product? In some cases, an entire industry can be adversely affected in this regard. It is the calling officer's responsibility to understand fully what is happening in this important area, for

---

[3] C. Arthur Williams, Jr. and Richard M. Heins, *Risk Management and Insurance* (New York: McGraw-Hill Book Company, 1976), p. 176.

"Tomorrow's banker will have to concentrate more on identifying the borrower's needs by understanding in depth the borrower's business."[4]

Assessment of company's capacity to respond to technological change

We live in a world of rapid and profound change, and only those firms which are creative will survive. According to *Business Policy and Strategy,* "Fifty-seven of the one-hundred corporations which dominated U.S. industry in 1918 had within the succeeding fifty years either gone out of business or suffered a drastic reduction in importance. In most of these 57 cases, the deterioration of these organizations has been traced to their inability to organize for and adapt to a changing business environment."[5] With technological changes occurring at an increasingly rapid pace, it is critical that the commercial lender fully appreciate the impact of technological change on a borrower's activities and the extent to which that borrower can respond creatively to that change. Research and development management should, therefore, be queried about any new technology which might ultimately affect the industry. The calling officer will want to know what new products are being developed by the borrower and how they relate to those offered by major competitors. He or she will also want to know how the company's expenditures on research and development relate to industry standards.

Examination of quality control procedures

The plant visit also presents a convenient opportunity for the calling officer to examine the quality control procedures being followed within the company and to question quality control personnel about reject rates, returns, and product recalls. To emphasize the importance of investigating this area, a recent article reports that, "Last year, a record total of more than 50 million products—from foods, drugs and cosmetics to autos, appliances and toys— were recalled by their manufacturers, either voluntarily or under pressure from one of the four major government agencies empowered to police the marketplace for dangerously defective products. (Products that are defective but not hazardous are not recalled.) And the prospect is for an even bigger recall year in 1979."[6]

---

[4] Peter F. Nostrand, "Tomorrow's Banker: Commercial/Financial Adviser," *The Journal of Commercial Bank Lending,* 59, September 1976, p. 52.

[5] Daniel J. McCarthy, Robert J. Minichiello, and Joseph R. Curran, *Business Policy and Strategy: Concepts and Readings* (Homewood, Ill.: Richard D. Irwin, Inc., 1975), p. 175.

[6] "A Record Year for Recalls," *Dun's Review,* January 1979.

Evaluation of marketing strategies

Another area of extreme importance is marketing. The calling officer should take time to meet with the marketing manager to assess his or her experience and capabilities and to evaluate the marketing strategies of the firm. This provides a unique opportunity for evaluating the extent to which marketing research is being used and the quality of that research. Marketing is an area that is often overlooked by the analyst. Yet the attitude of marketing management and of senior management as it relates to marketing activities and to customer needs can often mean the difference between success and failure. As Theodore Levitt stated in his classic article about the decline of the railroads, "They let others take customers away from them because they assumed themselves to be in the railroad business rather than in the transportation business. The reason they defined their industry wrong was because they were railroad-oriented instead of transportation-oriented; they were product-oriented instead of customer oriented."[7]

Is the borrower truly customer-oriented? Are the marketing strategies compatible with management's concept of purpose? These are often critical questions relevant to the continuing viability of the firm.

Meeting financial management personnel

Finally, the plant visit gives the calling officer a chance to meet with financial management. The banker will already have a great deal of information about the company's financial condition from normal credit analysis procedures. In many cases, however, the loan officer has never met anyone other than the controller or financial manager. For the purpose of determining management depth and quality, the plant visit provides the opportunity to become acquainted with several of the individuals responsible for the firm's accounting and financial operations. The banker can observe, among other things, the extent to which automated equipment and procedures are being utilized and the types of financial reports being prepared as management tools.

Summary

In summary, a well-planned plant visit can be an invaluable tool for the commercial lender. A tremendous amount of vital information *available no other way* can be obtained through a plant visit. The all too common practice of relying almost exclusively on financial analysis in arriving at the credit decision

---

[7] Theodore Levit, "Marketing Myopia," *Modern Marketing Strategy* (Cambridge, Mass.: Harvard University Press, 1960, 1964), reprinted in *Insights for Marketing Managers* (Santa Monica, Calif.: Goodyear Publishing Company, Inc. 1977).

can be a costly error for any banker. A complete analysis should include a written report covering a well planned plant visit.

The following is presented as a basic format for that visit. The questions listed are suggested as those which can provide the commercial lender with the information necessary to make the best possible credit decision. Naturally, the format in each case will depend on the particular industry and on the firm itself. Other areas such as human resource management, engineering, logistics, social responsibility (consumerism), and labor relations may need to be covered. The truly important thing is that the calling officer do the planning which will make the plant visit really pay off for borrower and lender alike.

Questions to Be Covered in a Plant Visit

A. *General Management*

1. Are the purposes and strategies of the firm well conceptualized?

2. Is there broad management experience and skill in all major functional areas? (Obtain biographical data whenever possible.)

3. What are the extent and quality of management depth?

4. What are the outstanding characteristics of top management that have propelled the company to its current position in the industry? Are these characteristics still in evidence?

5. Who is responsible for planning? What does planning entail in the subject company? To what degree are profit plans utilized as management tools?

6. What is the extent of executive turnover?

7. What types of management information systems are being used?

B. *Board of Directors*

1. What skills and expertise do the directors bring to the firm?

2. What is the extent of their influence and control?

3. Are there any apparent conflicts of interest?

C. *Risk Management*

1. Who is responsible for risk management in the firm? (If the answer is "What's risk management?"—look out!)

2. Is management aware of the AMA's "Risk Analysis Questionnaire"?

3. Has insurance coverage been increased to keep pace with inflation?

4. Are the firm's premises clean and well-organized? Are there obvious hazards of any kind? Are OSHA guidelines being observed?

5. Are property, liability, and personnel exposures all covered?

6. What are the product liability exposures facing the firm? Are they adequately covered?

7. Does the firm have competent legal counsel?

8. In the case of partnerships, does a buy-sell agreement exist? How is it to be funded?

9. Where the need exists, has keyman insurance been purchased?

D. *Product Lines, Competition, and Research and Development*

1. What are the major products of the company? What is the corresponding market share of each product? In what stages of the product life cycle are the various products? What strengths and weaknesses have characterized the firm's product lines? Are the product lines compatible? To what extent are they vulnerable to economic fluctuations?

2. To what market(s) are the products directed? Are these markets expanding or contracting? At what rate? What are the technological characteristics of the industry, and how is the firm rated from a technological standpoint compared with the competition?

3. What successful new products have been developed by the firm? How recently?

4. What percentage of gross income is devoted to R & D? How does this compare to industry standards? What is the depth of the firm's research and development capabilities? What new products are planned for the future? Timing? How do they fulfill market needs? What is the reliability record of existing products? How adequate are the quality control procedures? Are the facilities, equipment, and manufacturing processes technologically up-to-date compared with the rest of the industry? Does manufacturing meet deadlines, or are there apparent conflicts with the marketing department?

E. *Marketing*

1. Is the marketing capability compatible with the diversity and complexity of the company's products?

2. What types of marketing research are being used? Quality?

3. What channels of distribution are being used?

4. How successful has the marketing department been at developing new markets for the firm's products? Are the marketing strategies compatible with the overall strategies articulated by top management?

5. What are the key elements of competitive strategy for the firm? Are they compatible with market or industry realities?

F. *Financial and Accounting*

It is recognized that questions relating to these matters will generally result from normal financial analysis. The plant visit can also offer the opportunity to observe the extent to which modern, up-to-date equipment is used, to meet individuals in addition to the vice president of finance, and to determine the extent to which the accounting and finance areas assist top management for planning purposes.   □

Looking at Management?
Try the Inventory Window!

by William P. Creamer

Bristol, Pa.—Things were finally starting to look a little rosier at Paterson Parchment Paper Co., a big office-supply and paper concern.

At the end of the first nine months of 1972, Paterson Parchment showed a small operating profit, compared with a year-earlier loss.

However, things didn't turn out as well as expected. Last month Paterson Parchment announced that the company had another big loss in 1972 despite the encouraging gains of the first nine months. The reason? A chagrined management explained that accountants at a key division, in effect, had been counting the same inventory more than once. The blunder made it necessary to write down earnings in the three years since 1970 by a whopping $1.3 million.

Paterson Parchment's woes may be extreme, but inventory problems are hardly uncommon, as increasing numbers of companies seem to have discovered lately. One dramatic example: Whittaker Corp., a big Los Angeles conglomerate, was recently forced to buy back two subsidiaries it had sold to another company when a $6.3 million inventory shortage in the subsidiaries' accounts was uncovered.

Inventory problems appear to be cropping up more frequently, and some experts warn they may intensify as the economy heats up.

The *Wall Street Journal* article (4/25/73) quoted above brings into a focus a problem which is the thesis of this article—the specter of inventory mismanagement.

It is of paramount importance for investors and creditors to have an effective method for accurately evaluating and forecasting management's future success. A widely used procedure has been to evaluate a firm's continued profitablity in terms of future sales expectations and product differentiation (a function of market demand). While this method has credence, it ignores a basic prerequisite—namely, profit maximization is a function of effective management. In this regard, the outsider has sought to satisfy himself by focusing on bottom line figures (after tax profit, PE ratio, etc.), as a proxy for management merit. In times of rapid economic growth, this credulous practice may prove fallacious.

One approach which I have found to be reliable as a management measurement test (for both analyzing the past and predicting the future) is econometric model building. A primal behavioral model reflecting management's acumen can be developed by examining how management manages its inventory.

The sum and substance of this approach is to construct simplified representations of the economic and financial behavior of the firm. These representations are called models. The model becomes econometric when mathematical and statistical techniques are applied to the investigator's observations which are quantified algebraically in the model. With an econometric model, periodic reports of income and expenditures can be related over long periods, allowing the investigator to establish an Historical Management Margin of Error (please see "Key role of inventory analysis" section of this paper for further comment) used in modifying company forecasted sales and profits, (hence a proxy for measuring management expertise).[1]

It is beyond the scope of this article to pursue the above statistical methodology in any greater depth. However, it is germane for effective credit analysis to discuss the qualitative rational underlying the statistical evaluation process.

The ensuing discussion of four topics will delineate these aspects:

- Key role of inventory analysis
- Nature of the system
- Impact
- How the outsider knows

It is my intent to pinpoint the areas of concern, and to discuss those ques-

---

1. The main function of Girard Bank's Capital Programming Unit.

tions which will furnish the information necessary in order to evaluate management and which are of special significance to the bank credit/loan officer. How these answers are translated into a statistical measurement process will not be pursued at this time. It is sufficient to say that the intuitive knowledge needed for management evaluation can be obtained by attention to the points and questions raised in the following pages.

Key role of inventory analysis

I have chosen the manufacturing industry for purposes of this article for three reasons. First is the sheer size of the manufacturer's inventory investment and its importance to him. Second, the analogy can be extended to other industries. Third, most manufacturing operations are subject to rapid change and the dynamic quality of their inventory problems makes them a regular customer for seasonal financing.

The key role of inventory analysis is revealed by its ability to serve as a leading indicator for determining:

- Management's skill at estimating demand. (This serves as a test of their market knowledge.)
- Future cash requirements needed to carry inventory.
- Indicated idle money. (If inventory level is too high, the company is warehousing dollars at zero return.[2])
- Historical Management Margin of error factor (HMM). Realizing that the scheduling of production is equivalent to the forecasting of sales, one could attest management's long run profitability expectations by ranking their past frequency of success or failures. This can be done by applying a discount factor (HMM) to company forecasted sales.[3]

The effect of past distortions on future earnings

Profit and loss statements are not static but continuous in nature. Identifying trends of marginal erosions should be an early warning sign to the analyst.[4] Economically speaking, a firm should seek to maximize its posi-

---

2. Firms whose resources are limited must be particularly wary of the risks to their liquidity. Indeed, both the firm's solvency and the bank's charge-off rate may hinge on limited capital's being tied to hard-to-move inventories.

3. The statistical rationale and formula derivation of HMM will not be discussed in this article. This is one of the factors developed in my "Reliable Management Measurement test."

4. Marginally increasing inventories of time period$_{1,2 \ldots n}$ to marginally declining sales in time period$_{1,2 \ldots n}$.

tion by reaching equilibrium of supply and demand. If we think of supply as inventories and demand as manifested through sales, then we can readily see that inventory carry-forward could put downward pressure on price and deflate the creditor's collateral. The key to good and efficient management of a firm is maximum dollar utilization—i.e., proper inventory levels.

Nature of the system

Since inventory is the heart which pumps the system (production-stock accumulation—A/R—cash), it is of paramount importance to understand its component cells. Assuming that information is available, or can readily be obtained from the customer, concerning the breakdown of inventory into raw materials, work-in-process and finished goods, several questions should be considered.

How much raw material? Our first key.

Realizing that raw material inventories are necessary to insure smooth production runs, the analyst should not view large inventories as excessive or conservative. The key element is to gauge the level needed to provide maximum return on investment.[5] Hence, our first indication of management's ability to achieve internal controls.

For purposes of financial planning and cash forecasting, both the financial officer of the firm and the credit analyst of the bank should show particular concern to the cashflows connected with inventory. Since business concerns normally don't pay cash at the time of purchase but defer payment by increasing their accounts payable,[6] cash outflows resulting from purchases of raw materials can be planned for by setting up a schedule of future payments. Obviously the existence of such a schedule is one indication to the credit analyst that management is truly aware of the hidden powers of inventory management.

What type of questions should the analyst ask himself, and the company,

---

5. This is equivalent to using marginal analysis to find the last unit worthy of being ordered.

6. In times of cash stringency, the marginal firm often overlooks the payment terms (2-10 @ 30) because he can get a greater return than 2% by internal use of the cash for an additional month. This becomes an academic opportunity cost decision when viewed in terms of 2% discount vs. 98% cash loss for 20 days. This does not mean the firm goes to the extreme of running a bad credit rating but implies, in strict accounting terms, he does not consummate purchases via cash but through scheduled payables.

in order to ascertain that the optimum level of raw materials is being pursued as a company goal?

- What level of stocks are held for possible shortages?
- What type of budgets are established for purchases of raw materials?
- Are purchase prices pegged on the basis of anticipated economic patterns or on unrealistic, lagged, historic company patterns?
- Does the level of stocks seem realistic in light of anticipated production and sales volumes?
- What is the cost of carrying the stocks?

How much work in process?

It is at this point that a tremendous amount of knowledge can be gained by the analyst. A careful study of the incremental costs change of Work-In-Process inventory can be analogous to reading a master plot describing a particular drama. I will not discuss the intricacies of inventory pricing for costing sales. However, it should be noted that the level of costs which flow into W-I-P inventory establishes management policy and practice and indicates their success or failure in achieving internal cost control. The asset value of W-I-P inventory reflects the accumulative costs of production (direct & indirect)[7] associated with the partially completed products.

When a multiperiod analysis is performed, one can ask:

- Are costs rising faster than sales, thus narrowing profit margins?
- How much of the rise is due to increased purchase price of raw materials vs. internal cost increases?
- How effective or efficient is the firm at recognizing cost rises, and what steps are being taken to counter the rises?
- How successful has the company been at taking down into gross and net profit a higher percentage of total revenues, indicating higher profits were not solely the result of high-priced sales but also related to effective cost management? This would be a particular asset in depressed times.

The volume of production can also play a major role in the firm's profit maximization plans. Although the number of units produced is information usually foreign to the analyst, certain relationships should be stressed:

- Production downtime will cause rising costs and will also serve as a measure of plant inefficiency.
- Investment in W-I-P fluctuates with the volume of production.

---

7. Such as consumption of raw materials, utilities, wages, supervision, etc.

- Volume of production will have a greater correlation to anticipated sales rather than actual sales.
- A plant producing at a low level of capacity will have higher unit costs relative to sales; thus, costing increasingly more to produce the constant volume necessary for sales support.
- Capacity constraints can also be caused by an inefficient plant, machinery, lower production yields,[8] etc.

All of the above will cause a higher ratio of cost of goods to sales.[9] Action must be taken by the firm to offset these inefficiency costs in order to preserve profit margins.

How much finished product?

Realizing that overestimating production results in the warehousing of dollars (storing idle money) and that underestimating sales results in stockouts, the analyst can readily gauge management's acumen for reconciling, or finding, a saddle point[10] of equilibrium. Seldom can production be cut back, or expanded rapidly, without severe organizational strains and higher unit costs which produce diminishing returns to scale.[11] Management's judgement plays a critical role at this juncture.

Since the firm pegs its production to estimated future sales, one should ask:

- What techniques are employed in estimation?
- How sophisticated are these techniques—does management know the key economic variables which influence their sales and their predicted direction?
- Do sales show a normal or erratic trend?

Many manufacturers have experienced severe cash stringency, sometimes

---

8. For example: Formerly it took 25 units of ingredient A to produce product B; now it takes 35 units of A to produce B.

9. Assuming: (1) constant sales level, (sales level remains fixed in short run), (2) the manufacturer is not a price dictator—cannot pass along cost inefficiencies via increasing selling price.

10. In the above context, saddle point refers to equilibrium between maximum returns with minimum losses associated with several alternatives.

11. We can define the short-run period of time as a period during which the firm can change its output but cannot change its capacity. Short-run analysis is associated with the principles of diminishing marginal and average returns to variable inputs. In the long-run, the firm can change its existing capacity. Thus in the long-run, all inputs are variable—therefore, long run analysis is related to the concept of returns to scale.

leading to business failure, as a result of freezing too much of their resources in finished goods for which expected orders failed to develop.

The critical role of sales forecasting in effective inventory management can hardly be over-emphasized. More precise sales forecasts would permit a closer meshing of production schedules with demand and an economizing on inventories. If sales developments could be predicted with greater precision, it might be possible to avoid much of the overtime and other costs occasioned by abrupt readjustment of production schedules. Increased efficiency and predictablity can be gained by utilization of econometically-applied industry models.[12]

Impact

As mentioned previously, the impact of marginally declining sales is usually a deferred one. Since cash and receivable collections are a function of current and previous period sales, a firm may not notice the vice tightening until collections from continued decreasing sales periods fall due.

As for the immediate effects, the practice of fixing objectives and measuring results by reference to a given rate of return on capital employed places a special emphasis on inventory. Since the rate of return produced by a given profit figure varies inversely with the amount of capital employed (including inventory), the higher the investment, the lower the rate of return. Because the amount invested in inventory may be subject to far greater short-term fluctuations than the amount invested in assets, success or failure in management's inventory outlay decisions can have a more immediate and significant effect on rate of return comparisons (which biases decision making for the firm and presents a distorted picture to the investor). This indicates the appreciation the loan officer must have for the dynamic characteristics of inventories in one period (t_1) to sales/profits in later periods $(t_2 \ldots n)$.

There is an inherent degree of risk in all inventories which is a function of our dynamic economy. Changing styles, prices, etc., can render inventories unsalable and nearly worthless. If creditors are holding finished inventory as collateral, a drop in price of the finished product will effectively devaluate this collateral. If lenders are to rely to a great extent on inventory at liquidation, certain elements must be satisfied to protect against holding a can of worms:

---

12. The Capital Programming Unit of Girard Bank utilizes this technique to both gauge success and offer alternatives.

- Salability—liquidity.
- Stability—is it a trend item?
- What portion of the total inventory is RM, W-I-P and FP—how salable is each group?
- Is the market demand relatively elastic or inelastic?

It makes quite a difference whether you are lending against gold inventory (firm mining gold) or against an inventory of which 80% is raw materials and has no market attraction until it is completely finished.

How does the outsider know

Efficient management of inventories is well recognized as a vital link in the chain of business operations, requiring the exercise of considerable commercial and managerial skill and judgement. The costs of mismanagement can be high, substantially affecting the results of the business. Because of the paramount role this asset group plays in determining a firm's outcome, the investors, lenders and stockholders have a vested interest in discovering and understanding the significance of inventory movements. Further analysis should be performed to discern whether changes in inventory can be equated to changes in sales.

For example, an increase in inventory levels, substantially beyond that which might be expected from an increase in sales, should stimulate the analyst to question whether the unexplained increase is the result of: accumulation of unsold merchandise; inventory speculation in raw materials; price level changes not reflected in selling prices; or some other factor. Certain questions and observations may provide valuable insight. In summary we can ask:

- Are inventories maintained at appropriate levels; adequately safeguarded against loss or misuse and properly applied in the operations of the business?
- Are inventories duly accounted for?
- Can management identify slow-moving, obsolete or defective goods?
- What arrangements/adustments, if any, are made in order to market or otherwise make use of these items?
- Does management periodically write down inventory which is obsolete, surplus, or for any other reason unusable for production?
- Does the firm keep perpetual inventory records or make periodic physical inspection?

- How often does the firm reconcile its book to physical inventory for each stock location?
- Has management recently switched accounting methods—revalued its inventory?
- Is the firm's production cycle a continuous or discrete nature? Which does the industry market follow?
- Is management aware of the company's seasonal sales patterns? Does their production *chase the crest* (i.e., erratic production-stock piling) or ride with it?
- Does the firm price out goods on a standard cost basis? If so, how often are its standards updated? How close do they come to actual?

Conclusion

Any good loan officer or credit analyst must not be fooled by the apparent success of a company during boom periods. The long run success or failure of any enterprise is couched in effective management. Many business failures are due to management's concern for revenue expansion and neglect of cost contraction.

In the final analysis the financial officer's, as well as the bank administrator's, role should be more than that of an observer. Good inventory management is good financial management. When the bank supplies the heart of a firm's money, it should also take a close look at its blood pressure!

Retail Inventories and the Loan Officer

by Jordan L. Golding

INVENTORIES HAVE BEEN OF PRIME IMPORTANCE to loan officers in almost all commercial borrowing situations. Furthermore, many industries have peculiarities surrounding their inventories and their valuations which must, of necessity, be understood by the bank officer dealing with customers in that particular field. The retail trade is one such area where a thorough understanding of the accounting procedures relating to inventories becomes a definite necessity.

In analyzing the financial statements of retailing establishments, one readily finds that inventories usually comprise the largest single asset on the balance sheet. Indeed, the 1971 edition of the *Annual Statement Studies* published by the Robert Morris Associates, indicates that inventories, classified by various industries, range anywhere from approximately 20% to over 60% of the total assets of the merchandising companies.

Despite the dominant position held by many of the well-established retail chain and department stores, our economy has also seen the emergence of many new retail operations which often open three to ten branches within a period of one to three years, representing a total annual sales volume of anywhere from $1 million to $5 million. As these successful new enterprises emerge and strive for even more branch locations, the requirements of carrying additional merchandise to support their operations invariably bring requests for additional debt financing from the companies. This, together with the normal seasonal need for funds, often strains the established borrowing limit of the company.

To the extent that the loan officer is confronted with applications for substantial debt financing, and given the premise that inventories are generally the largest single asset of the retailing establishment, then a thorough understanding of the process leading to the valuation of the inventories appearing on the balance sheet becomes a basic requirement of the loan officer dealing in the merchandising field. It is important for him to know not only the total dollar value of the inventory, but also the method by which the value was determined. Primarily, he should be satisfied that the inventory figure includes proper adjustments for markdowns, slow-moving or obsolete merchandise and damaged goods. In stores where fashion or style merchandise is significant, it becomes critical that due care be taken to reflect markdowns on a prompt basis. Typically, style merchandise more than one season old should be marked down from 25% to 50%. In addition, it is important for the loan officer to be assured in some manner that the inventory level is proper for the particular establishment and that excessive stocks do not present a liquidity crisis in the form of exposure to substantial further markdowns.

The question of markdowns, obsolescence, etc., although of prime importance in retail inventories, is not unique to the merchandising field. Many companies in manufacturing and distribution, faced with similar style, market and obsolescence problems, must likewise insure that their inventories reflect cost or market, whichever is lower, for purposes of reporting financial condition and operating results in accordance with generally accepted accounting principles. Yet, the loan officer must be aware that lower of cost or market, from a merchandising standpoint, is too narrow a definition and does not always apply to the retail establishment since this industry has often applied two modifications to the customary valuation methods. One is the so-called retail inventory method which affects the method by which the valuation is ultimately placed on the inventory. The other is LIFO, the procedure under which the value of the goods on hand is pegged to a base price devoid of inflationary factors.

The retail method of inventory accounting

The retail inventory method is basically a system by which merchandise inventories are priced at current selling prices and then reduced by a percentage reflecting the adjusted cumulative markons to bring it to an amount which realistically approximates the lower of cost or market. The retail inventory method requires that all purchases of merchandise be recorded on the books at current marked selling prices and that the accounts be relieved by the dollar amount of sales, markdowns and other adjustments. For financial statement purposes, this selling price inventory is reduced by an amount reflecting the cumulative markon percentage which has been placed on the merchandise, giving effect to the markons, markdowns and shrinkage. When this method is utilized, the balance sheet usually describes it as:

Merchandise Inventories—at the lower of cost (principally by the
retail method) or market.

It is not the purpose of this discussion to review all the technical computations that
enter into the retail inventory method; rather it is to describe the significance and
implications of the method. Probably the single greatest aspect is the fact that the
adoption of this method gives the company a continual book inventory at selling price
which can be reduced to estimated cost at any given moment by the application of the
adjusted cumulative markon percentage. The advantages flowing from having a book
inventory at retail are as follows:

1. At any given period the company can generate interim financial statements
   without the need to have a physical inventory count of the merchandise.

2. At such times that physical counts of the merchandise are taken, there is a book
   figure against which the actual count can be compared in order to accurately
   determine shrinkage and other variances from the book figure.

3. It is a simple matter to keep the inventory figures broken down by branch
   stores, departments or merchandise class so that internal financial information
   can be generated by store or department on a monthly, semi-annual or annual
   basis. Accordingly, it allows management to evaluate the performance of any
   given unit or department on an interim basis without waiting for the results of
   an actual physical inventory at the annual or semi-annual closing.

4. The fact that the retail method provides a book inventory at selling price by
   store or department allows for the internal audit department to take a physical
   inventory at any given time for control purposes and have a book figure against
   which this can be compared. Thus, it allows for greater flexibility and overall
   internal control programming.

5. In addition, the retail inventory method provides great advantages to the
   merchandising manager and the various buyers who can control the investment
   in their stock on a month-to-month and even week-to-week basis. In fact, the
   retail method is almost essential to a proper controlling of stock levels by the
   respective buyers or departments. The availability of the continuous book figure
   at retail allows them to monitor the results of current sales activities against
   budget, open-to-buy, planned markdowns, etc.

Thus, the retail inventory method not only has tremendous advantages from the
standpoint of management control of the retail establishment, but also provides a
significant degree of assurance to the loan officer who is concerned about the management and administration of the inventory to which the proceeds of his loan are often
applied. It also gives the loan officer the satisfaction of knowing he can request

monthly or quarterly financial statements without causing the customer to take the time and expense to actually have a physical count of merchandise.

Accordingly, the retail inventory method provides many advantages which may be beneficial from the standpoint of the interests of both the manager of the business and the bank lending officer. Apart from its value as a tool which is economical to operate, flexible with respect to the number of sub-divisions or departments to which it can be applied and its ability to generate frequent information, its key value from the standpoint of the loan officer is its ability to provide management with a device to control inventories. The control aspects apply not only to those elements which relate to shrinkage, markdowns, etc. but also in keeping the overall inventory within a manageable range.

Problems under the retail inventory method

Because the retail method is a procedure by which the retail book inventory is ultimately reduced by the weighted average of the purchase markon percentages, the method will usually produce a figure slightly higher than the lower of cost or market method applied to individual items. This results from the fact that in a store or a department having varying rates of markon, the average markon based on cumulative figures for the fiscal period may not be representative of the markon prevailing on goods actually in stock at a given time. Typically, the lower markon merchandise will tend to turn over faster or sell more rapidly than the higher markon merchandise because of its special promotional nature, whereas the closing inventory may in fact have less of the lower markon or promotional merchandise because it has sold faster. For example, at the end of any given accounting period, the department or store may have purchased two or three times as much of the promotional (low markon) merchandise as the high markon merchandise; however, the closing inventory might contain an equal amount of both items. The high rate of sales of the low markon merchandise will reduce the average cumulative percentage of the overall merchandise in stock. Thus, when this percentage is applied to the closing inventory, there will be a slight inflation of cost because of the application of a lower markon percentage produced by the faster turn in that merchandise.

Obviously, this distortion would not appear in the unlikely situation where all merchandise in the store or department had the exact same markon. It is also a situation which can be minimized by fragmenting the retail inventory method by departments which are categorized by more consistent markons for the merchandise within the applicable departments. In any event, this distortion produced by the averaging factor will tend to be consistent from year to year, assuming the merchandising policies of the store or departmental buyer remain consistent.

Certainly, the management and control benefits accruing from the retail inventory method far outweigh any disadvantages by virtue of the slight distortion caused by the averaging factor.

Finally, the increasing acceptance of the retail method is illustrated in the 1971 edition of *Accounting Trends and Techniques*, published by the American Institute of Certified Public Accountants, which contains a survey of the various accounting practices utilized by 600 companies with published annual reports. The following tabulation shows the total number of merchandising companies included in the survey, together with the number utilizing the retail method. During the three year period, 1968 to 1970, the percentage of the number of retail concerns in the study employing the retail method increased from 41% to 50%.

	Merchandising Companies Surveyed	Number Utilizing Retail Method	Percent Utilizing Retail Method
1970	54	27	50%
1969	53	24	46%
1968	52	21	41%

LIFO

LIFO or "Last-In, First-Out" is a method of inventory valuation under which the first item of merchandise sold is considered to have borne the most recent cost of the same article. Thus, those items remaining in inventory are deemed to be the oldest and bearing the oldest possible cost attributable to the item. This procedure has as its principal advantage the fact that the base inventory is devoid of inflationary factors. Therefore, to the extent that the cost of the items has risen over the years due to the general inflation within the economy, then no profit is taken on this inflationary factor and, accordingly, no taxes are payable on the inflated profit for those items remaining in inventory.

LIFO, therefore, must be considered primarily a tax tool which allows the taxpayer to eliminate inflationary factors from inventories and to reduce the tax liability accordingly. The following example illustrates the substantial savings which can be affected by the adoption of LIFO in an inflationary economy. It assumes a 4% constant inflationary factor and an effective corporate income tax rate of 50%:

	Inventory (Constant Units)	4% Inflation Factor	Tax at 50% on Inflation Factor
Beginning	$1,000,000	—	—
End year 1	1,040,000	$ 40,000	$ 20,000
2	1,081,600	41,600	20,800
3	1,124,864	43,264	21,632
4	1,169,858	44,994	22,497
5	1,216,652	46,794	23,397
Total		$216,652	$108,326

In the foregoing example, which assumes no change in the physical size of the inventory, inflation would add $40,000 to the value in the first year alone, on which the company in question would have a tax liability of $20,000. With no increase in the physical size of inventory, the 4% inflation rate would raise the inventory dollar value by $216,000 or 21.6% in just five years, with a resulting tax of $108,000 on the added value. Obviously, if inflation is expected to be of long duration and of a significant rate, then the adoption of LIFO is worthy of serious consideration. On the other hand, in the absence of inflation, the LIFO method would lose the tax benefits described above and could even produce adverse effects.

There is no question that in an economic environment which is continually beset with inflation, LIFO can produce substantial tax benefits to the merchandising client while enhancing his cash flow and working capital position. On the other hand, LIFO also presents certain extreme difficulties with respect to the interpretation of the financial statements as compared to companies using the conventional FIFO or "First-In, First-Out method." Section 472 of the Internal Revenue Code is quite specific with respect to the fact that it prohibits taxpayers who have elected the LIFO method of inventory from utilizing any other method of inventory pricing in inventorying such goods to ascertain the profit or loss of the company. The section of the code specifically precludes supplementary financial reports or statements employing any other valuation for purposes of reporting to "shareholders, partners or for credit purposes."

Thus, the company electing to adopt the LIFO method of inventory for purposes of tax savings now finds itself in the position where it cannot issue any other financial statements, either to stockholders or creditors, which effectively reconciles the LIFO inventory with that of the conventional first-in, first-out method. Loan officers are therefore confronted with a situation where their customer may be enhancing his own financial condition and cash flow by virtue of the fact that he is not paying income taxes on that portion of his profit arising out of price inflated inventories; nevertheless, the banker cannot obtain financial statements based on accounting procedures which account for the inventories on a first-in, first-out basis.

Although the Internal Revenue Code precludes those who have adopted LIFO from restating earnings on any other basis, the applicable section of the Code refers only to the Profit and Loss Statements, per se. It does not prevent the electing company from disclosing in the footnotes the value of the inventory computed on the basis of first-in, first-out inventories. Where this alternate valuation for both opening and closing inventories is disclosed in the footnotes or other supplementary financial information, the loan officer is in a position to compute earnings on a conventional FIFO basis. In order to accomplish this, he must not only substitute the appropriate inventory values, but also take into account the applicable federal and state income tax provisions on the earnings differential.

If supplementary FIFO valuations are not available, the loan officer must have an understanding of the LIFO method in order to attempt to interpret the financial statements. For example, if the physical inventory on a unit basis remains constant, then irrespective of any price inflation, the financial statements of his customer would reflect a dollar inventory which also remains approximately constant. In this instance, the net profit or loss figure reflected in the statements would be one which measures the operating profit, devoid of any earnings resulting out of changes in the price level of the inventories.

In situations where the physical volume of inventories has increased, then the incremental volume in any given year will be priced at the new or current cost value added on to the base LIFO inventory. Thus, any increase in the dollar value of the inventory between the opening and closing figures necessarily indicates an increase in the physical volume of goods at current year prices. The loan officer should determine whether the increased physical inventory can be justified by tangible business reasons such as the expansion of the business or the addition of new merchandising lines.

On the other hand, if inflation continues and the dollar value of the LIFO inventory or the statement decreases, then the company is obviously decreasing its physical inventory and is thereby realizing inventory profits based on the fact that the base inventory, priced at the historical cost, is being depleted at a current, or inflated, selling price. If this change occurred in a company where the operating profits remained constant or declined, then it would appear that the situation might be serious and that the profits could be eroding at a rate faster than that indicated by the profit and loss statement since the stated flat or declining earnings were actually shored up by the infusion of inventory profits arising out of the decline of the physical base stock priced at historical cost.

Although the level of physical goods in a retail company may increase or decrease as the overall company expands or contracts, the quality of merchandise in a given store or department will tend to remain stable (assuming no change in the size of the store or department). From a management or control standpoint, therefore, LIFO has the advantage of stating inventories on a common dollar basis for a period of years which affords the vantage point of looking at the profit and loss statements in the absence of inflationary factors. Thus, one can feel that the net profit figures reflect true profit margins and are not tainted by "unearned" inflation in the base stock inventories.

The balance sheet effect of LIFO is to value inventories at lower than replacement cost. By the same token, the liability side will not reflect any provision for the taxes on the portion of profit eliminated by virtue of the lower inventory valuation. The net result is to understate the current ratio and net worth by the amount of inventory devaluation, less the applicable income tax liability thereon.

The brief examples described above should illustrate the need for the loan officer to exercise great care in analyzing the financial statements containing LIFO inventories. In summary, LIFO is an inventory procedure developed to eliminate the effects of inflation of inventory valuations and thus to save on income taxes applicable to the inflationary portion of the price changes in inventory. Although this method has been utilized in the past to save taxes and retain cash in the corporate enterprises, it also has the effect of making the interpretation of financial statements based on this method substantially more difficult.

Summary

The loan officer dealing with retail accounts, especially, those of emerging and growing chains, should be aware of the overall implications of the method of accounting utilized by the company in connection with its inventory valuations. It is not sufficient to be sure that adequate provision for markdowns has been taken. The loan officer should be aware of whether or not the company is employing the retail method of accounting; if it is not, he should ask why the adoption of such a method is not being considered by the company. Likewise, it might be of great benefit to a particular customer to utilize the LIFO inventory method; in this case the loan officer will have to be very diligent in his interpretations of the financial statements of the company. □

Predicting Default of Small Business Loans

by James A. Hoeven

The study reported on in the following article indicates that, in general, multivariate analysis is not very useful in determining the quality of small business loans. The author presents this conclusion, among others, after reviewing previous studies on the same subject and discussing the details of his own study. These details include the study's data base and analytical framework, the organization of the data and financial variables in a factor analysis, and the multivariate discriminant tests used and their results.

There is a long history of evaluating the financial performance and the financial condition of business firms by means of financial ratios. However, more recently, a number of studies have been concerned with the usefulness of a combination of modern statistical techniques and financial ratios to predict the future success or failure of business ventures [(1), (3), (4)—numbers in parentheses refer to the sources listed at end of article, page 60.]. The presence and availability today of pre-assembled statistical computer programs have increased the practicality of employing more sophisticated techniques such as multiple discriminant analysis in the prediction of business success or failure.

The essence of these studies, whether univariate or multivariate analyses, is to select financial variables out of any number of possible financial ratios that will be most predictive with respect to future success or failure. In multiple discriminant analysis (MDA), a function is developed that takes the form of

$$Z = X_1c_1 + X_2c_2 + X_3c_3 \ldots X_nc_n$$

where Z is a discriminant score for a particular data sample that predicts either future success or failure according to its value; X_1 through X_n reflect the values of selected financial ratios (most predictive of success or failure); and c_1 through c_n are coefficients of the chosen financial variables X_1 through X_n, respectively.

The purpose of this article is to expand the knowledge of this predictive approach as it applies to small business firms and specifically to the predictability of default on commercial bank loans. In addition to the basic concern of predictability of default on commercial bank loans, the article examines the relative effectiveness of static versus percentage change in financial ratios as predictors of default. Finally, the study looks beyond the general category of small business to several subsets relating to different types of business operations, such as manufacturing, retailing, service, and construction.

Why a study on small business

A study on small business seemed appropriate because the incidence of business failure and default on business loans is much greater among smaller sized firms. Furthermore, smaller firms do not have the staying power during adverse business conditions, and a serious deterioration of financial condition can take place in a fairly short period of time. Also, the diversity in types of small business operations leads to quite different values in terms of financial ratios; consequently, it seemed necessary to examine subsets of small businesses to determine the consistency of the financial ratios selected as being the most predictive.

The two critical questions that must be asked regarding the usefulness of such an analytical tool are—

(1) *How consistent are the discriminant functions that are generated from different groups of small businesses (populations) or different sample data?* The populations may differ for any number of reasons such as time period, size of firms, type of business, etc. The implications of this question are rather obvious to the practitioner who intends to use a given discriminant function to make an ex ante decision[1] on a new set of data.

(2) *What is the degree of accuracy in the classification of the sample firms?* If one assumes a naive model with a random sample would be correct 50% of

---

[1] Based on assumption and prediction and being essentially subjective and estimative.

the time, then the discriminant model must do better than this to be useful. However, the typical loan officer, whether he is considering new loans or loans already in his portfolio, likely faces a much lower probability than 50/50 in terms of loans that will eventually default. Some form of grading of loans by lenders upon inception or in review is no longer uncommon. Realization that other forms of discrimination among loans already exists places a demand for even greater accuracy upon any new predictive model.

The balance of this article takes the following form. First, it reviews two previous studies on the same subject. The review provides background for this article and a comparison of the nature of those previous studies and their findings. Second, the article presents the data base and analytical framework for my own study. Third, it examines the organization of the data and the financial variables in a factor analysis. Fourth, it develops the multiple discriminant analysis tests and their results, and finally, it presents conclusions drawn from the study.

Previous studies

As mentioned above, a number of studies have examined the ability of financial ratios in a multiple discriminant analysis to predict business failure in one form or another [(2), (1), (3), (4)]. Their criteria of failure have ranged from inability to satisfy a financial commitment to technical and legal bankruptcy.

Much discussion in these papers and in subsequent reviews focused on the methodology of multiple discriminant analysis and the possible bias that could be reflected in their findings because of the statistical techniques employed. The review presented here, which focuses on the studies by Edward Altman (1) and Robert Edmister (4), will concern itself principally with the basic nature and findings of these two studies rather than with repeating the details of the statistical techniques employed. The Altman and Edmister studies were chosen for review, in part, because the study reported on in this article has followed a statistical approach that is similar to the approach used in their studies. Somewhat later in this article, some of the major limitations of the analyses involved in this study and the studies by Altman and Edmister will be summarized.

Altman's study

Edward Altman's study, which was concerned with the ability of financial ratios to predict corporate bankruptcy, consisted of a sample of 66 corporations. Of these 66 firms, 33 were known to be legally bankrupt and 33 were not. The mean asset size of the bankrupt firms was $6.4 million, ranging from $.7

million to $25.9 million. Since the bankrupt group was not homogeneous either by size or type of industry, Altman carefully selected the nonbankrupt group to make paired samples. From numerous computer runs, he selected five ratios that did the best job of classifying the actual firms into their respective groups of bankrupt and nonbankrupt firms.

Altman made "no claims regarding the optimality of the resulting discriminant function." Four of the ratios represented in his function included one each from the well-known categories of liquidity, activity, profitability, and leverage ratios.[2] The fifth ratio in the function was retained earnings/total assets which says something about the seasoning of the firm and its demonstrated ability to generate and accumulate profits.

Altman's criteria for selecting the financial variables were—

(1) Measures of statistical significance of alternative variables and the relative contribution of specific variables to their overall function.

(2) A test of intercorrelation between the variables chosen.

(3) The predictive accuracy in actual classification tests by different functions.

(4) The author's judgment.

Altman's model had a 95% accuracy score in classifying the two groups correctly on data from financial statements one year prior to bankruptcy. His model achieved an even higher 96% accuracy level on a secondary sample of later bankrupt firms. The accuracy of his model declined to 72% when financial data two years before bankruptcy were used.

Edmister's study

Robert Edmister published a study in 1972 using the same statistical model but based upon small business firms. The source of his sample was SBA files with a mean value of assets and sales of $165,000 and $407,000 respectively. Forty-two borrowers from the files had statements for three years prior to the date that a loan had been granted while statements were available on 562 borrowers one year before the date of the loan. No mention is made of how long a period elapsed before a loan defaulted. The use of SBA files as a data source by Edmister is understandable given the difficulty of securing adequate and complete data on small business loans; however, the exclusive use of such a source did interject a special characteristic into his data sample other than simply small business loans.

---

[2] Altman's function was given by $Z = .0012X_1 + .014X_2 + .033X_3 + .006X_4 + .999X_5$. $X_1 =$ working capital/total assets. $X_2 =$ retained earnings/total assets. $X_3 =$ earnings before interest and taxes/total assets. $X_4 =$ market value of equity/book value of total debt. $X_5 =$ sales/total assets.

Edmister allowed different types of financial variables to enter his discriminant function other than the financial ratios' actual level. For example, he introduced a three-year trend ratio and also allowed both of these type ratios to be compared to industry norms. He, too, was concerned about the potentially high intercorrelation of financial ratios originating from a common set of financial accounts. A variable was not permitted to enter the function in the normal step-wise procedure if its simple correlation coefficient with a variable already in the function was greater than .31. The results of this study indicated that no function based upon only one year's statements proved accurate in predicting loan default on either a validation or a subsequent holdout secondary sample. However, a function based upon sample data over three years of financial statements correctly classified 39 out of 42 cases for a 93% accuracy rate on the validation sample.

Data base and analytical framework

In my own study which I will now report on, the sample base of small business loans employed were provided by 12 different independent banks in the Denver, Colorado, metropolitan area. All loans were non-SBA, small business commercial bank loans. The mean asset size and sales of the business firms in the sample were $447,000 and $800,000 respectively. For every defaulted loan a nondefaulted loan was provided in a like type of business (i.e., manufacturing, retail, etc.), with very similar asset and sales size.

The criteria for loan default were practical. It was not necessary that the loan be written off although this was the result in most cases. Neither did it matter whether the banker knew the loan proceeds could be recovered via liquidation of the collateral or by some personal guarantee. All that mattered was that the loan was already in default with respect to principal payments and that in the opinion of the banker there was no chance of the business' recovering on the strength of its own internal operations.

Data profile on loans and financial statements

Requests were made for financial statements on all loans, one, two, and three years prior to the date of loan default on both the defaulted and good loans. A certain numer of loans were accepted into the sample that did not have three full years of financial data; however, each individual financial statement on each firm served as a separate case from which discriminant functions were developed. Acceptance of loans that had only one prior year's financial statements served to increase the number of cases, and furthermore, separate classification tests could be run on only the one year prior to default statements.

After many months of requests to the banks participating in the study, the data profile on loans and date of financial statements was as follows:

	Defaulted	Nondefaulted	Total
Financial statements 1 year prior	58	58	116
Financial statements 2 years prior	48	41	89
Financial statements 3 years prior	28	14	42
			247

Difficulty in acquiring suitable financial data

Before proceeding to a discussion of the analytical framework, a brief comment on the sample data is warranted. I encountered extreme difficulty in securing adequate and comprehensive financial data. Commercial banks in the area simply did not have that many defaulted small business loans for which they could supply financial statements.

Typically, banks have difficulty in obtaining financial statements from small business and especially from those firms who may sense they are in financial trouble. There is the further problem of consistency in financial accounts and their treatment which can be due to several reasons such as the lack of understanding on the part of the preparer, the desire to condense financial information, or perhaps, because certain financial items do not exist uniformly throughout the different types of business operations. This inconsistency of financial accounts had a distinct impact on the study which will be discussed later in the article. However, the difficulty encountered in securing adequate and consistent financial data in this study does suggest to me the probable impracticality of anyone's or even several commercial banks' attempting to develop a predictive model of the type developed here on the basis of their own sample loans.

The statistical models

The statistical models employed in my study for the preliminary factor analysis and subsequent multiple discriminant analysis tests were developed by the Vogelback Computer Center at Northwestern University. While its SPSS (Statistical Package for Social Sciences) program for developing and testing discriminant functions provides several statistical approaches, the essential criteria for the functions were that they (1) be as highly predictive as possible within the minimum constraints of sample size and (2) satisfy statistical tests of significance—that is, each variable should be as uncorrelated as possible to other variables in the function, yet add to the overall predictive power of the function whose combination of variables does the best job of separating the mean values of the two groups of defaulted and nondefaulted loans.[3]

The Vogelback SPSS program for discriminant analysis is a stepwise selection process that chooses one variable at a time, maximizing an F value (statistical test of significance) for the combination of variables chosen for the function. Initially, the F value criteria for inclusion was .01 and for deletion was .005 to permit both easy entry and exit of all possible variables. As in the previous studies cited, prior probabilities in terms of being selected as a default or a nondefault loan were equal.

Each financial statement, of which there were a total of 247, served as an individual case. The program as designed does not require a paired number of default and nondefault cases for statistical validity. When a ratio was missing for a particular case, as noted earlier, the program was told to drop out such a case (statement) and move on to the next statement. The effect of this was to drop out samples whenever a financial ratio entered and stayed in the function but a particular statement did not possess that ratio. This alternative, which cut down on sample size, was preferred to that of letting the program discriminate against "0" for any given case. Therefore, the study had to compromise between the best selection of variables and the sample size that resulted from this procedure.

I selected 38 financial ratios to be used in the study. A complete list of these ratios is found on page 54.[4] The chosen ratios represent each of the well-accepted categories of liquidity, activity, profitability, and leverage, as well as all ratios found to be significant in previous studies.

Factor analysis (Test 1)

The purpose of this analysis was to classify the sample data used in the study and to determine whether such a preliminary classification would assist in the selection of variables for a subsequent discriminant analysis. It is a method to explain the most information with the fewest number of independent relationships included in the original data. The analysis groups those variables most correlated and separates variables with the least or even negative correlations. For example, factor analysis in this study placed all 38 financial ratios in one of

---

[3] Alternative statistical tests included Wilks Lambda, Raos V, and Max-Min, all of which revealed essentially the same results in terms of classification and the statistical significance of the variables and functions involved.

[4] For each static financial ratio found in the list of ratios, a percent change in the ratio was also calculated to be used in a separate test for the predictability of the loan default. The percent change was calculated on the change that took place in the respective ratios between the earliest and latest statement date.

Ratios Used in the Study

$$R\ 1 = \frac{\text{Net Working Capital}}{\text{Assets}}$$

$$R\ 20 = \frac{\text{Inventory}}{\text{Current Liabilities}}$$

$$R\ 2 = \frac{\text{Retained Earnings}}{\text{Assets}}$$

$$R\ 21 = \frac{\text{Net Income}}{\text{Sales}}$$

$$R\ 3 = \frac{\text{EBIT}}{\text{Assets}}$$

$$R\ 22 = \frac{\text{Current Assets}}{\text{Current Liabilities}}$$

$$R\ 4 = \frac{\text{Net Worth}}{\text{Assets}}$$

$$R\ 23 = \frac{\text{Accounts Payable}}{\text{Sales per Day}}$$

$$R\ 5 = \frac{\text{Sales}}{\text{Assets}}$$

$$R\ 24 = \frac{\text{Net Working Capital}}{\text{Sales per Day}}$$

$$R\ 6 = \frac{\text{Current Assets} - \text{Inventory}}{\text{Current Liabilities}}$$

$$R\ 25 = \frac{\text{Other Accruals}}{\text{Sales per Day}}$$

$$R\ 7 = \frac{\text{Net Worth}}{\text{Sales}}$$

$$R\ 26 = \frac{\text{Current Bank Debt}}{\text{Sales per Day}}$$

$$R\ 8 = \frac{\text{Net Working Capital}}{\text{Sales}}$$

$$R\ 27 = \frac{\text{Current Liabilities}}{\text{Sales per Day}}$$

$$R\ 9 = \frac{\text{Inventory}}{\text{Sales}}$$

$$R\ 28 = \frac{\text{Net Income}}{\text{Total Liabilities}}$$

$$R\ 10 = \frac{\text{Cash Flow}}{\text{Current Liabilities}}$$

$$R\ 29 = \frac{\text{Cash Flow}}{\text{Current Bank Debt}}$$

$$R\ 11 = \frac{\text{Cash} + \text{Marketable Securities}}{\text{Current Assets}}$$

$$R\ 30 = \frac{\text{Cash Flow}}{\text{Total Liabilities}}$$

$$R\ 12 = \frac{\text{Accounts Receivable}}{\text{Current Assets}}$$

$$R\ 31 = \frac{\text{Cash Flow}}{\text{Net Working Capital}}$$

$$R\ 13 = \frac{\text{Inventory}}{\text{Current Assets}}$$

$$R\ 32 = \frac{\text{Cash Flow}}{\text{Assets}}$$

$$R\ 14 = \frac{\text{Cash} + \text{Marketable Securities}}{\text{Sales per Day}}$$

$$R\ 33 = \frac{\text{Cash Flow}}{\text{Current Assets}}$$

$$R\ 15 = \frac{\text{Accounts Receivable}}{\text{Sales per Day}}$$

$$R\ 34 = \frac{\text{Net Worth}}{\text{Total Liabilities}}$$

$$R\ 16 = \frac{\text{Inventory}}{\text{Sales per Day}}$$

$$R\ 35 = \frac{\text{Net Worth}}{\text{Current Liabilities}}$$

$$R\ 17 = \frac{\text{Current Assets}}{\text{Sales per Day}}$$

$$R\ 36 = \frac{\text{Net Income}}{\text{Assets}}$$

$$R\ 18 = \frac{\text{Cash} + \text{Marketable Securities}}{\text{Current Liabilities}}$$

$$R\ 37 = \frac{\text{Retained Earnings}}{\text{Current Liabilities}}$$

$$R\ 19 = \frac{\text{Accounts Receivable}}{\text{Current Liabilities}}$$

$$R\ 38 = \frac{\text{Net Income}}{\text{Net Worth}}$$

eight distinct factor groups which explained 100% of all the variation in the original data sample. Five of these factor groups identified 88.6% of the total variation.

The next step was to select one variable from each of the five factor groups with the highest relative contribution to its group, which is called its factor loading, and then to recheck the correlation coefficients of the chosen variables. The variables chosen by this analysis did not follow any particular pattern of acknowledged groupings such as liquidity, activity, profitability, or leverage ratios. It tended to group ratios that had common accounts such as those with sales in the denominator, etc. Four of the five ratios selected from the factor groups that explained 88.6% of the total variation in these data indicated a strong significance of liquidity type variables. This result proved interesting because one might hypothesize that the liquidity position of small business firms might be most indicative of probable default or nondefault on business loans. In spite of the high factor loadings for five variables chosen and their low correlation coefficients, (all below .300), the discriminant function developed from this source of variables correctly classified only 62% of the known cases.[5]

Discriminant analysis tests

Test 2—static variables on all cases

The second discriminant analysis utilized all 247 cases and the 38 selected ratios. This analysis involved the Wilks Lambda version of the Vogelback SPSS program performing the stepwise selection process. This initial test with low entry and exit criteria selected 31 variables to predict a 96% correct classification. However, the original 247 cases had been cut to just under 100 using these 31 financial ratios. This was the first example of many computer runs wherein chosen variables selected by the program threw out cases in the sample whenever any one of the variables could not discriminate for a particular financial statement due to the absence of a financial account. After numerous runs, the best results from a seven-variable discriminant function was 65% correct classification. The final function included 56 cases from the default group and 110 cases from the nondefault group.

The available appendix, presenting all of the actual functions developed in the study (see footnote 5), indicates the discriminant functions developed in each of the tests that were run. It provides a description of the financial ratios

---

[5] For those interested, an appendix presenting all of the actual functions developed in this study may be requested from the author, Prof. James A. Hoeven. Please write Prof. Hoeven at the Department of Finance and Real Estate, Colorado State University, Fort Collins, Colo. 80523, and include a self-addressed, postage paid envelope.

chosen, their relative contribution to the function, and their respective F in/out values. The only common variable chosen by this stepwise Wilks Lambda procedure and the factor analysis is the net working capital-to-sales ratio. The three most consistent financial ratios for all the discriminant analysis tests performed in this study are found in this function. They are the activity ratio of sales/total assets, the capital adequacy ratio of net worth/sales, and the liquidity ratio of net working capital/sales. The relatively high significance of these three ratios is similar to the findings of Altman and Edmister.

Test 3—percent change variables on all cases

In the initial run with the same low entry and exit criteria, 20 variables predicted 100% accuracy in the classification of known default and nondefault loans. The original sample on which percent change ratios were to be calculated contained 75 cases. Twenty-five of these cases were dropped out by the program because of the absence of a financial account required to calculate a percent change ratio. However, when the function was reduced to the best eight variables, the classification score fell to 86% on the basis of 52 known cases.

This improved score in classification indicated that percent change variables were better predictors of default than static ratios. In part, this finding is similar to that of Edmister whose final function included a trend ratio and who found that no function that was developed on only one year's data was able to do an adequate job in classification.

Test 4—static variables tested on statements one year prior to default

The study next examined whether predictive accuracy would increase when functions were applied to those financial statements only one year prior to default. The function was developed on all statements, from one to three years, but applied to only those one year prior to default. It is desirable to develop the function over a longer time period to avoid any bias in terms of the economic conditions of a particular year. Furthermore, a useful function would have to be applied in this way since it is expected to deal properly with the future.

On the one hand, one would expect the accuracy of classifications to improve the closer the year to actual default, but if the characteristics of the statements tested differed significantly with the sample used to develop the function, then correct classification could be lower. A five-variable function was able to classify correctly only 67% of the 100 cases that remained in the program which began with 116. This result indicates that the classification score rose only slightly from the 65% classification when all three years' data were used. In spite of testing statements only one year prior to default, the improvement in classification was only slight, presumably because the sample from which the function was developed differed from the sample to be classified.

Test 5—static variables on service businesses one year prior to default

An additional concern, as noted in the introduction of this article, was the possible lack of homogeneity among the subsets of small businesses. Therefore, a discriminant analysis was next run on only the service firms, the largest sample by type of business (40 cases) of the 247 cases. The intent of this test was to see whether there would be a change in the variables found in the function, as well as the possibility of a higher classification score, due to a more homogeneous sample.

An all-service industry sample of six variables produced a quite different discriminant function and when tested on statements only one year prior to default correctly classified 70% of the known cases. This again was only a slight improvement over the classification score of the previous test that included all types of businesses. However, one could, perhaps, hypothesize that it would be more difficult to discriminate between default and nondefault service firms on the basis of financial ratios because of their relative labor rather than capital asset intensity.

Test 6—static variables on 20% holdout samples

A major concern in discriminant analysis is the validity of classification scores when using the same sample as used to develop the discriminant function. For this reason, five different 80% samples of the original 247 cases were assembled to develop functions that then could be tested against the remaining 20% holdout samples. These samples were chosen at random by the computer.

Once again the study revealed the discriminant functions or choice of discriminant variables were very sensitive to change in the sample. For example, out of five different functions using six or seven variables, there was only one variable that appeared in all five functions, one that appeared in four, and one other variable that appeared in three functions. In all, fifteen different variables appeared in the five different functions.

There was a corresponding lack of consistency in the ability of the chosen functions to classify the holdout samples correctly. In general, the centroids (means) of the two groups, default and nondefault, were too close together, and the discriminant scores on the holdouts tended to be clustered. Similar to the Altman and Edmister studies, three areas of classification were designated. The first area (I) was for all scores below (to the left of) the centroid of default loans.

The second area (II) designated all scores above the centroid (to the right) of the nondefault loans. In between the two centroids was area III called a gray area where the margin for error in an incorrect classification is narrow, particularly given the narrow spread of the two centroids.

For example, in Sample 1 there were 11 correctly classified loans out of a total sample of 18 for a 61% correct classification. If three of the incorrect classifications are removed from the calculation of the percent correct calculation because they fall in the gray area, then the percent correct rises to 73%. The results of all five samples based upon a total and an elimination of the gray area classification are as follows:

		Total Sample		Total Nongray Area Sample	
Sample	Correct	No.	% Correct	No.	% Correct
# 1	11	18	61	15	73
# 2	13	21	62	18	73
# 3	15	22	68	18	83
# 4	18	28	64	27	66
# 5	20	29	69	26	77

While the classification improves with the designation of a gray area, the improvement is not great. An additional important aspect of these sample classifications was the number of type I versus type II errors in the incorrect classifications. A type I error is a more serious misclassification, from a practical point of view, for it has called a default a good loan. A type 2 error, on the other hand, which has called a good loan a default, might only result in some unnecessary credit analysis by a loan officer. Except for sample # 4, over 50% of the errors in these samples were of the type I variety.

Summary and implications

One of the major problems in the use of multivariate analysis for the purpose of determining the quality of small business loans, new or existing and based upon financial criteria, is the inadequacy of usable financial information. In this respect, I believe that the experience of this study is not unique.

Although previous studies have suggested that a few selected variables that are representative of different financial aspects of the business (that is, liquidity, profitability, activity, and leverage ratios) may be the most discriminant variables, this study shows no such consistency whether using factor analysis or a statistical stepwise selection process. Based upon the findings of the study, the percent change or trend variables are better predictors of default than static financial ratios.

Discriminant analysis functions based upon small business loan financial data are extremely sensitive to changes in samples, whether the change is a representative change in terms of type of business in the original sample or a change in the mix of different types of small businesses. In spite of the variability of different functions from different samples, there are a few financial variables that repeat themselves most often. These are, in the order of their frequency in the different functions, sales/total assets, net worth/sales, and net working capital/sales. The fact that they occur most frequently in this study does not suggest any special explanation.

Although one would expect that classification based on financial data one year prior to default would be superior to similar data on earlier years, the findings of this study do not indicate a marked improvement. Neither did the use of holdout samples and the elimination of gray area misclassifications improve classifications to any significant degree.

In general, this study indicates that multivariate analysis is not very useful in determining the quality of small business loans. In spite of some reduction of sample in the program runs, the samples for this study were sufficiently large to conclude that there is no consistency in terms of the variables that best predict the quality of such loans. This finding means that potential users cannot depend upon a particular function developed by others to be an effective classifier of their own loans.

Possible reasons for this study's findings begin with the questionable dependability of the information provided in the financial statements of small business firms. Furthermore, the differences in the financial characteristics of a sound or weak small business may not be as dramatic as the differences found by Altman in his prediction-of-bankruptcy study which dealt with large corporations. A weak financial condition of a small, closely held firm may not reveal other financial resources possessed by its owner(s) that can become quickly available when needed. On the other hand, other financial resources are generally not as available to small businesses. Thus, small firms may not have the same staying power through an adverse business climate as their larger corporate counterparts. Therefore, a good loan to a small business firm can become bad more quickly than one to a large business firm. □

List of sources

(1) Altman, Edward. "Financial Ratios, Discriminant Analysis and the Prediction of Corporate Bankruptcy." *Journal of Finance*, September 1968, pp. 589–610.

(2) Beaver, William H. "Financial Ratios as Predictors of Failure." *Empirical Research in Accounting: Selected Studies*, 1967, supplement to Vol. 5, *Journal of Accounting Research*, pp. 71–102.

(3) Deakin, Edward. "A Discriminant Analysis of Predictors of Business Failures." *Journal of Accounting Research*, Spring 1972, pp. 167–179.

(4) Edmister, Robert. "An Empirical Test of Financial Ratio Analysis for Small Business Failure Prediction." *Journal of Financial and Quantitative Analysis*, March 1972, pp. 1477–1494.

(5) Harrigan, James O. "A Short History of Financial Ratio Analysis." *The Accounting Review*, April 1968, pp. 284–294.

(6) Meyer, Paul, and Howard Pifer. "Prediction of Bank Failures." *Journal of Finance*, September 1970, pp. 853–868.

(7) Sinkey, Joseph F., Jr. "A Multivariate Statistical Analysis of the Characteristics of Problem Banks." *Journal of Finance*, March 1975, pp. 21–36.

(8) Thiel, Henri. "On the Use of Information Theory Concepts in the Analysis of Financial Statements." *Management Science*, May 1969, pp. 459–480.

III. Loan Structure and Profitability Analysis

The subjects grouped under this heading range from relatively straightforward ones such as secured lending and structuring loan agreements to the more esoteric such as loan participations and project financing. The last three articles in this section focus on profitability analysis and negotiating a price. Readers are urged to review also the articles included in the sections on legal aspects of lending and problem loans for further insights regarding the implications of loan structure.

This section begins with a discussion of topics that are often basic to structuring a loan agreement: determining what security is available and how to obtain it. In "Some Considerations about Secured Lending," authors Quill, Cresci, and Shuter first work their way down the left side of the balance sheet, commenting on the values various assets might have as security and how the values might be estimated. They also mention off-the-balance-sheet assets such as insurance and suretyships. The dangers of recorded and unrecorded liabilities are covered, and the article concludes with tips on policing security and danger signs that the borrower may be in trouble.

Charles S. Zimmerman's article, "An Approach to Writing Loan Agreement Covenants," is far from a collection of boilerplate terms. It includes comprehensive definitions and thoughtful discussions of various types of covenants, their purposes, and the way they can be combined into an effective package to protect the lender. The author includes an extensive checklist, with sample provisions, cross-referenced to show the purpose the covenant would serve.

The problems of negotiating agreements between banks has not received as much attention as working out agreements between borrowers and lenders. F. William Vandiver, Jr., writes about the former topic in his article, "Loan Participations—Upstream/Downstream." He illuminates the considerable subtleties in this area, which is one of increasing importance, and includes a number of checklists to use in reviewing a participation proposal.

Even smaller firms can become quite complex if their owners elect to disperse assets and, perhaps, risks. Stephen C. Diamond brings the experience of a com-

195

mercial finance lender to his cautionary article, "Structuring a Secured Loan to a Multi-Corporate Organization." While it is narrowly focused on technical points, the article briefly introduces the types of problems that lenders can encounter in attempting to control funds and obtain a solid claim on valuable assets.

Project loans are the subject of Grover R. Castle's thorough essay, "Project Financing—Guidelines for the Commercial Banker." The author provides a comprehensive summary of the analytical techniques that should be followed in evaluating a project lending opportunity—be it in natural resources, real estate, or industrial construction—according to the type of project financing being considered. This article is included in the loan structure section of the anthology because many of the author's observations have direct implications for structuring the terms of a loan.

The next two articles deal with a common subject: analysis of loan profitability, a subject which has become increasingly critical as spreads have narrowed. The first of the two articles, Thomas M. Flynn's "Loan Profitability—A Method to the Madness?," offers a quick survey of the problems of evaluating the profitability of a loan. The approach he suggests is not sophisticated and thus is suitable for a bank that does not have an elaborate cost analysis system or for an officer who is doing an analysis on the back of an envelope.

A more sophisticated approach is provided by "Commercial Loan Profitability—Pricing Analysis," by James A. Hoeven and Jerome S. Oldham. These authors outline a much more complex formulation although their specific pricing recommendations as such may no longer be as valid as when the article was originally published.

Regardless of the pricing technique used, however, the problem of achieving a good spread always exists. Lawrence T. Jilk, Jr., draws on the general insights offered by recent contributions on the sociology of negotiating in his article, "The Art of Interest Rate Negotiating." He makes a number of suggestions for general strategy as well as for tactics that will help the banker win the terms desired.

For information about the authors of the articles in Section III, refer to the List of Contributors on page xi.

Some Considerations about Secured Lending

by Gerald D. Quill, John C. Cresci, and Bruce D. Shuter, Esq.

The secured lender's best friend is an accurate valuation of collateral. Here are some guidelines for obtaining such a valuation and protecting the collateral position once it is established.

Business collateral seems to have the least value exactly when it is needed most. Markets disappear as equipment suddenly becomes usable only in a depressed industry, account debtors quickly find flaws in goods delivered by a

This article is based on a symposium given by the authors at the National Convention of Business Development Corporations at Colorado Springs, Colorado on June 23, 1976.

borrower in liquidation, and yesterday's valuable work-in-progress rapidly becomes today's junk. Accordingly, the secured lender must evaluate, understand, and police his collateral thoroughly and effectively or its value may decline so swiftly the unprepared lender will face a serious loss.

Cooperation between borrower and lender

Cooperation by the principal of a borrower corporation is likely to be at its lowest ebb when such cooperation is most needed by its secured lender. Few lenders have the technical know-how to complete work-in-progress or the personal contact to collect accounts from account debtors hoping to avoid paying in full for merchandise.

Lenders are dependent on the help of their borrowers to realize the full value of their collateral, but why should a corporate officer undertake such an effort when the benefit will inure solely to the lender? Therefore, to insure such cooperation, the secured lender must consider a guarantee or the officer's personal collateral.

There is no substitute for carefully considered and prepared documentation in connection with a secured loan. The most honorable borrower will exploit every loophole or flaw when faced with a desperate struggle to survive, and even if the borrower wishes to cooperate, the lender may have to contend with an uncooperative trustee in bankruptcy.

Accurate valuation of collateral

The secured lender's best friend is a solid and accurate valuation of the borrower's collateral. If a lender is sure of the amount his collateral will return, everything else falls into place. Rate, structure, term, and restrictions on the borrower all flow easily from the confident knowledge of return on collateral in the event the borrower fails. But how does one obtain an accurate valuation?

Appraisals

The appraiser

A reliable appraisal is the foundation of successful secured lending, and a reliable *appraisal* begins with a reliable *appraiser.* The best test of an appraiser is the test of time. How have his appraisals stood up in liquidation situations? In time a lender's own good experience with particular appraisers will lead to confidence.

Of course, when a lender chooses an appraiser for the *first* time, past experience is non-existent. In such cases, the lender should consider recommendations of respected members of the financial community based on their *own* experience, if possible, and the appraiser's general reputation.

In seeking recommendations, a lender should keep in mind the type and location of the collateral. All appraisers are not necessarily expert in all kinds of property or in all local practices and customs, but often they specialize.

Another important factor is the integrity of the appraiser. Unfortunately, some borrowers, in their anxiety to obtain loan approval, have been known to offer "incentives" to the appraiser to establish high values. There is little the lender can do to protect himself, except to select only appraisers with high reputations for honesty.

The method of appraisal

Equally important as a reliable appraisal is understanding the basis of the appraisal. Broadly speaking, valuations are made on the following basis:

1. *Market value.* The price to be paid by a willing buyer on sale from a willing seller.

2. *Income.* The amount that will be paid for particular property so that the yield from the property will equal current rates for the type of investment involved.

3. *Replacement.* The cost to replace particular property at current prices.

4. *Liquidation.* The price property will bring at a distress sale.

While the first three methods will provide valuations important to a lender, the key values are liquidation values. The fact that a machine may be worth $500,000 on the open market often will have little relationship to the amount a lender can realize when the borrower has failed. Usually the machine must be sold by the end of the month or it will have to be moved or stored. And the market for that particular machine is soft because the industry in which the machine is used is depressed, or new technology has resulted in the machine's becoming obsolete.

Contents of an appraisal

An easily readable, complete, and concise report is most desirable. If the report is complete and contains sufficient detail, such as serial and model number and manufacturer of each item of equipment, it can later be used to police the collateral during the life of the loan, form the basis for legal documentation, and guide the lender in developing inventory lists for the ultimate liquidation of the property if that becomes necessary.

Analysis of accounts receivable, contract rights, or other similar intangibles

No appraiser can foretell the value of accounts receivable (referred to here as "accounts"), rights performed under contracts ("contract rights"), or other intangibles for which money is or will eventually be due to the borrower (as in the case of leases, for example). Accordingly, the lender must self-appraise.

Some of the keys to determining the value of accounts are:

1. *The tradition of the account debtor's industry for payment.* For example, some large institutions are slow in paying; in other industries, account debtors are typically small and financially shaky and unreliable.

2. *The type of product.* For example, some borrowers are engaged in long-term completion of large and expensive, specially made items, and their accounts are often collected only after completion. Such situations are subject to disputes as to quality or fitness of the product's purpose.

3. *The ability of the lender to engage in collection of the type of account involved.* For example, does the lender know enough about the product to judge disputes? Can the lender cope with collecting hundreds of small accounts?

The same considerations are involved in the valuation of other similar intangibles. The lender must be able to isolate the problems surrounding the borrower's conversion of the asset in question into cash.

The nature of the collateral

The value of a particular property on a given day is only a starting point for a lender. As suggested earlier, the only day collateral is really important to the lender is the day of sale. Certain types of high-priced, high value machinery, such as computers, can lose much of their value almost overnight when a new, more comprehensive model is introduced. In other words, the lender must be in a position to take the appraisal and estimate how the passage of time will affect the appraisal value.

Analyzing equipment collateral

This is certainly not an exact science, but there are steps the lender can take to protect his position. Equipment collateral must be analyzed and fully understood.

There are a whole series of questions that should be asked beginning with — Where is it? In a remote location that will require expensive transporting or in a loft which will require extensive rigging in the event of a sale? Or is it highly movable, or located in an attractive plant that a prospective user might acquire so that it can be sold in place?

Is the equipment usable for a single purpose or single industry only, so that when the borrower fails, prospective buyers are also suffering financial reverses and are not expansion-minded? Or is the equipment multi-purpose and, like a drill press, usable by many industries for many purposes?

Are there other special problems? Equipment is subject to limitations made by potential obsolescence or the seasonal nature of the product, or it can be self-consuming, such as a transportation company's truck tires.

Is the lender in a position to police the equipment? Policing is the only way to assure proper maintenance and prevent disappearance.

Evaluation of real estate

Real estate must be similarly evaluated but with a different emphasis. *Location* is the key to real estate. Property values are based on the general value of surrounding properties. For example, will the area decline or will it develop? Will transportation improve or will a key rail line be abandoned?

Adaptability is important. Is the structure single- or multi-purpose? One has only to count vacant gasoline stations to appreciate this problem.

That it is not highly liquid is another problem of real estate. The lender must be prepared to bear costs of protection and maintenance before sale, particularly for commercial property. If there are tenants, the lender must be prepared to cope with their problems.

Inventory evaluation

Inventory raises many of the same considerations as equipment, but it also generates a few others, such as:

Is it fungible? That is, is it indistinguishable from other goods of its type and grade such as grain, lumber, or pork bellies? If it is, it probably is most valuable in its raw state.

Is it work-in-progress? Partly finished goods are often of less value than the raw materials and have a fraction of the value of the finished product. Accordingly, can the lender physically complete the work? What will be the expense, and does the lender have the capacity to market the finished product?

Is the inventory perishable, unstable, or difficult to handle? How many lenders are in the position to deal with quantities of foodstuffs that can be maintained only for short periods or for which extended maintenance can be expensive?

The foregoing is not meant to be a definitive list of the problems a lender must take into account, but it is designed to stimulate thinking. Basically, the lender should examine his collateral with this thought in mind: What is the exact process to be completed if faced with liquidation of the collateral sometime in the future?

There are no conclusive tests or crystal balls, but fuzzy thinking about these questions before a loan may eventually result in significant loan losses.

Prior liens

One other consideration should be kept in mind even if the initial values are present, and it is likely they will be sustained until maturity. The lender must be assured that prior claims on the collateral by third parties will not absorb more than a tolerable amount of its value.

Uniform Commercial Code

The most common type of lien for the lender to be concerned with regarding personal property is a consensual lien obtained under the UCC. The existence of such liens can be easily determined by a search of the appropriate public records. Care must be taken, however, in determining the amount of any such lien.

Consider the following example: Lender A files a financing statement under the UCC against all the assets of borrower B, but does nothing more. Lender C finds A's filing, but learns nothing has been loaned. C then files against all B's assets and advances $50,000 to B.

Subsequent to C's loan, A advances to B $200,000. B defaults and becomes insolvent. All of B's assets are worth $100,000. C wisely appraised B's assets and situation and was confident those assets would be worth $100,000 on liquidation. C felt doubly safe because C had advanced only 50% of a conservative, but accurate estimate of collateral.

Held: A was entitled to the entire $100,000 of assets. The UCC is a notice statute, and advances relate back to the date of filing the notice. C gets nothing.

Moral: Do not advance funds to any borrower on a secured basis when there is a prior UCC filing covering the same collateral, unless the prior filer has agreed to subordinate or limit advances.

Mortgage liens

For the lien of a mortgage to be perfected, the mortgage must be recorded in the local land records of the jurisdiction in which the property is located. Obtaining searches of these records is not difficult, although qualified searchers should be carefully selected.

In cases where real estate collateral is being relied on (rather than being used just as "sweetener") and in areas where it is available, perhaps the best approach is the use of *title insurance*. Title insurance is a guarantee, up to a stated limit, by a land title researcher that is financially reliable, at least to the extent required by law. The land title searcher confirms that title to a particular property is actually as represented in the report of their search.

A mortgage lender thus receives the assurance that if a previously undisclosed defect in the title or prior lien impairs the lien of the mortgage as insured, the title insurance company will indemnify the lender against any loss.

A word of caution. It is the loss caused by the defect that is recoverable, not the loan. Thus, if the searcher fails to discover a $2000 prior lien, the title insurance company is not obligated to the lender for the amount of the loan, only the $2000, plus any penalties that may have accrued. Similarly, if the property is not worth $2000, the title company would be liable only up to the actual value even though the lender has insurance in excess of that amount.

Title insurance premiums can be substantial and the lender usually requires that they be paid by the borrower. On balance, title insurance is probably a good idea when available and practicable.

Leases

If property that a lender includes in his appraisal does not belong to the borrower, the valuation will obviously be inflated. Yet, such will be the case if the lender fails to determine if any property on the borrower's premises is leased from others.

There is no easy way to make this determination. One source is to ask the borrower specifically about any leased equipment and to ask the appraiser to similarly check the borrower's records. This may not be helpful if the borrower is less than candid or his records less than accurate.

The only other protection available to the lender is to examine the equipment to determine if a lessor's name is affixed or to know the borrower's trade and the practices of the local area so that the presence of the type of property that is usually leased can be questioned. Checking public record information may also be helpful.

Another word of caution. Just because a transaction is called a lease does not make it a lease under the UCC. A "lease" which is really a financing will be treated as a financing, and the "lender's" right to take back the property for nonpayment can be perfected against the secured lender *only* if a financing statement covering the property has been duly filed by the so-called "lessor."

Tax and mechanics' liens

State law often grants liens in real and personal property to state and local governments or material suppliers and artisans. Because these liens differ so much from state to state, it is not possible to comment specifically in this article, except to say that such liens can cause the value of collateral to be substantially less than anticipated for the unaware. Local counsel should be consulted about such liens.

Federal tax liens can be discussed more fully, but are a complex matter and should be discussed with the lender's counsel. However, a few things can be stated that will be helpful to the lender dealing with collateral.

Generally, liens perfected under state law will have a priority over *unfiled* tax liens so that a lender can rely on a search of the tax lien records. However, after forty-five days from the filing of the tax lien, property acquired by the borrower becomes subject to the tax lien, even if the lender holds a lien in so-called after-acquired property.

The effect of this on an inventory or accounts lender is quite clear. As new inventory is obtained by the borrower and new accounts arise, a tax lien can become prior in right once the forty-five-day period expires. Similarly, if future advances are covered, and the lender makes a nonobligatory advance past forty-five days after filing, the tax lien will have priority over that advance.

Thus, the inventory and accounts lender should consider a search every forty-five days, and all secured creditors a search within forty-five days of non-obligatory advances, unless the lender is sure the borrower has no federal tax liability.

Purchase money liens

Purchase money liens, like tax and mechanics' liens, can jump ahead of previously established liens. Purchase money liens arise when a creditor finances the purchase of particular goods and takes a security interest in those goods. With the exception of inventory, such liens can occur without notice to prior lien holders. However, financing statements must be promptly filed.

The theory is that prior lien holders cannot be damaged because additional assets are coming into the borrower's hands, and even if the purchase money financier comes in ahead, the prior lien holder has a second position in the new assets. Purchase money inventory liens, however, require notice because it is anticipated a prior inventory financier will expect to be secured by a first position in new inventory as it arrives.

A lender can protect against purchase money liens by being alert to the borrower's purchasing activity. If a borrower has a new machine, the lender should know how the borrower paid for it. Also, a periodic check of the financing statement records will reveal purchase money liens.

If a lender does not want purchase money liens to exist, the loan documents should prohibit them. Then if such a lien is discovered, the lender can insist on its being removed or can call the loan.

Subordination

Subordination or limitation of prior liens, while not a prior lien itself, is discussed here to point out that the secured lender need not refuse to make a loan because of prior liens. Such liens may be subordinated or limited to an acceptable level.

Other collateral

To complete a preloan evaluation of a particular borrower's collateral, it is desirable to see if there may be some other collateral aside from the typical categories of equipment, contract rights, accounts, inventory, and real estate. Several other forms of collateral will be mentioned briefly. The purpose of the discussion is not to suggest that any one or all will be appropriate for all lenders and all loans, but to indicate that in certain situations, a careful lender can take additional steps to further protect itself.

Documents of title

In cases where a borrower stores inventory in public warehouses or receives goods that are shipped by common carriers, it is possible to take the documents issued by the warehouseman or shipper as collateral. The result is that the lender is secured even while the goods are shipped and stored. He is assured that the collateral cannot be obtained by others.

Bank letters of credit

In certain situations a borrower may be able to obtain what is known as a "standby" letter of credit that is good, for example, in the event of a loan default. While there may be some legal questions concerning such devices, they are becoming increasingly popular and more widely used.

Credit balance with account lender

Occasionally, secured lenders deal with borrowers who have financed their accounts with a prior lender on a factoring basis. Usually, such an accounts lender will hold a credit balance out of the collections of the accounts for further security. Often in liquidation cases, however, the entire credit balance is not used because account debtors continue to pay for merchandise delivered before liquidation.

There is no reason why the commercial lender cannot enhance his collateral with a junior lien on such credit balances. The key is to obtain the consent of the accounts lender to turn over the credit balance. Otherwise, experience indicates there is little chance the lender will ever see any of the cash. The same principle can be applied to bank deposits if the senior lender is a bank.

Trade names, trademarks, and other intangibles

These intangibles have limited value by themselves, and there is some legal question as to whether they can even be sold alone, without the assets of the business that used them. Nevertheless, a security interest in such intangibles can be important.

Such types of collateral to be considered include molds which cause the borrower's tradename or trademark to be indelibly imprinted on the finished product. If the lender is in the position to sell not only the mold for a product, but a recognized trademark as well, the value of the mold is enhanced. Without the ability to sell the trademark, the mold may have little value.

Consigned inventory

In certain industries it is common practice to place substantial amounts of inventory in the hands of distributors for sale on the following basis: The distributor will only "pay for" the items when and if sold or will return the goods after some period.

This method of distribution poses a problem for the lender of the supplier. Such goods will usually be considered property of the distributor by the creditors of the distributor, unless the supplier takes certain steps to prevent this result. Filing of a financing statement under the UCC would be such a step. Accordingly, a lender of the supplier can have the benefit of such inventory as collateral if the lender causes the supplier-borrower to take the appropriate steps.

Insurance

Finally, having appraised the value of the collateral, considered the effect of the passage of time on its value, checked for prior liens, and obtained every ounce of available collateral, the lender is faced with one of these considerations: The loss or destruction of the collateral or the untimely death of a key management person.

Life insurance

Most businesses depend on one, two, or three key persons. In smaller concerns, there typically is an inside manager who runs the operation and an outside marketing man responsible for the company's sales. The sudden death of either party can devastate the profitability of the company and impair the borrower's ability to repay a loan.

The answer is life insurance in an amount that would reduce the loan so that after the insured person's death, the borrower's reduced capacity would still be adequate to service the remainder of the loan.

We will skip a major discussion of all the various types of life insurance. However, a lender should know if a policy is *term insurance,* whereby the only value of the policy is a face amount payment on death, or *whole-life,* which features a cash surrender value. The surrender value is itself collateral and can be used if default occurs and there has been no death. Of course, the premiums are higher for this type of policy. Term insurance may feature level payments and a declining face value, which should not decline faster than the loan, or increasing premiums and level face amount.

Hazard insurance

Of course, a lender should insist on insuring insurable collateral in adequate amounts against loss by destruction, theft, or disappearance.

What may be less well known is that the lender should insist that a loss-payee clause be added to the policy, which usually demands no additional premium. This provision requires that the lenders be paid directly for any loss covered by the policy, even if the borrower breaches the policy and cannot collect himself. The insurer should be required to agree not to cancel the policy except for non-payment of premiums and then only after the lender has a thirty-day notice period to pay the premium on behalf of the borrower.

The agent

If the borrower's insurance agent is not competent, it will be difficult even to obtain a proper loss-payee clause. But more seriously, an incompetent insurance agent can hurt a lender and a borrower by not providing adequate coverage or by duplicating coverage.

If duplicate coverage does not sound like a problem for a lender — besides the burden of unnecessary duplicate premiums on the borrower — imagine waiting for a recovery while several large insurance companies squabble over which one should bear a certain loss.

Business interruption insurance

Every lender should be aware that borrowers can buy insurance to protect against the event of an interruption in the borrower's business caused by unforeseen disasters, such as fire. This new insurance form has been aptly called *disability insurance for companies* and is worthy of consideration as part of the preloan evaluation.

Suretyships (guarantees)

While not strictly collateral, suretyships can be viewed as an additional repayment source, and in that sense, sureties do secure a loan. In addition, suretyships can themselves be secured by all types of property.

The primary source of collateral for a suretyship is equity in the residential real estate of the surety, since sureties are generally the individual principals of a corporate borrower. Other common collateral are stocks and bonds. Furs, jewelry, or stamp or coin collections are also desirable because, unlike most other personal belongings, they have high liquidity.

Suretyships inspire cooperation

Possibly the main value of the suretyship is that it binds the sureties to the borrower so that the surety-principals will not abandon their company when it is not successful or fails. As any experienced lender will know, the corporate principal's cooperation, necessary to a successful liquidation, increases dramatically with the introduction of a suretyship agreement. Cooperation is more vigorous when the surety has assets behind the suretyship that he wishes to protect.

The Fed's position on requiring the spouse's signature

Similarly, because most people's assets are held jointly with their spouse, unsecured suretyships have little "bite," especially for cooperation purposes, unless joined in by the spouse. Federal Reserve Equal Credit Opportunity Regulations, presently prohibit requiring the spouse's signature in most such cases. In a revision of the regulations which was due to become effective March 23, 1977, the Federal Reserve has significantly relaxed this position. However, before requiring a spouse's signature on a suretyship, counsel should be consulted.

Securing the suretyship, usually with a second mortgage on the principal's home, protects the lender even more. It should be considered, especially when the corporate assets are suspect.

Policing the loan

Having carefully evaluated the situation and applied the techniques discussed above, the lender has now advanced funds. The goal remains the same, however: assuring that the collateral will realize sums sufficient to repay the loan and the lender's expenses if liquidation becomes necessary. The following methods may serve as ways of achieving this goal.

Inspections

Benefits of personal visits. Personal visits and inspections to the borrower's operation serve many purposes. First, the borrower will appreciate the lender's interest in the collateral. Since borrowers usually will try to please their creditors, the borrower will "read" the interest and will make protection of collateral a high priority. A borrower will also be less likely to defraud a lender who inspects his or her premises frequently.

Second, the lender will gain a feeling for the borrower's operations and will be able to sense subtle changes on subsequent visits, particularly if some visits are made on a "surprise" basis. In this way, deterioration can be detected early and remedied more easily. The lender can take the opportunity to update collateral lists on each visit as equipment is replaced or increased or inventory changes in nature or amount.

Incidently, surprise visits should be made part of every policing program because only in this way can the borrower's true operations be observed.

Attending board of directors meetings. The lender might also consider the desirability of attending meetings of the board of directors. This can be very useful, especially where there are outside directors that the lender might not meet otherwise. On the other hand, attendance at such meetings may lead to participation or even joining the board, and while this may offer additional benefits, each lender should be aware of possible legal complications that can be created. Consultation with counsel on this point is urged before taking any action.

Visiting the borrower's auditors. Personal visits with the borrower's auditors will supplement inspection of the borrower's operations. Also, discussions with the auditors will help the lender get the maximum information from the borrower's financial reports.

Audit reports prepared by senior lenders, if any, should be obtained. It is clear that any lender should continue to review the borrower's financial reports after making a loan; no one would seriously disagree, yet some lenders overlook the value of studying financial reports.

Special reports

In certain situations the lender should consider supplementing the standard financial reports. One type of supplement is complete certificates as to accounts and inventory, including aging. An experienced lender will be able to tell much about a borrower's business from that type of report. This is not appropriate in all cases, but in some cases it is so important the lender should insist that such reports be made by the borrower's auditors.

Searches

Some financial reports are enhanced by public record searches. Subsequent liens are a tip-off of problems, and foreclosure of even a junior position can terminate a work-out preferred by the senior lender. Regular examination of judgment and lien records published in legal periodicals will alert a lender to liens as entered. This measure is inexpensive and can be most helpful. Discovering liens, when entered, highlights the borrower's problems when there may still be time to help.

Detectives

The most drastic cases call for the most drastic measures. When a lender has a reason to believe his borrower is actually defrauding him, the use of a private detective is often desirable. When confronted with the information gathered by a detective, the borrower will often cease fraudulent practices and become cooperative. Also, collateral can be traced and later recovered if its whereabouts are known.

Updates on appraisals

A lender cannot rest on his appraisals even if they are well-prepared and accurate. Very little remains forever, so updates on appraisals are important. Certain situations are obvious, such as when the borrower is asking for additional credit for expansion. Other times, updates are not so clearly indicated, but possibly may be even more important.

We consider an update mandatory when a serious adverse development occurs, and it is likely the borrower's financial structure will need some change. In any event, it is probably more important to update appraisals on bad news than on positive developments.

Danger signs

The next question then is what is bad news, how does the lender know when things are about to go awry? The following discussion of some early warning signs are not given as mechanical triggers to be pulled whenever they occur. Rather, they are presented as a guide to things that appear when a business may be experiencing trouble.

Slow-pay

If payments are late, especially if this occurs suddenly, there may be a liquidity problem developing. Of course, it could also be a new bookkeeper, but it is a signal to be alert.

Changes in management

Whenever management changes occur, beware. A change may ultimately be positive, but it is a sign that the lender should be alert and should fully investigate. This is especially true when an active manager becomes an absentee.

Sudden credit requests

Like most danger signs, sudden needs for cash can be quite innocent, but they can also be signs of poor financial planning. Every lender should be aware of the reasons for a credit crisis. If sudden credit requests become chronic — watch out!

Financial statements

An obvious place to look for problems is the company's own financial statements, especially if independently prepared. Such statements should be examined until the lender is thoroughly familiar with them. In particular, a lender should be concerned if the accountant will not give a so-called "clean certificate," if periodic statements are delinquent or late, or if the loan proceeds do not appear to be disbursed in accordance with the supposed purpose of the loan.

Failure to pay other debts

Often a borrower will keep the most important creditor happy at the expense of the other creditors. A lender in the most important category can be fooled unless a close watch is kept on payables. Also, since overdrafts are a generally unanticipated form of credit, lenders should investigate if they occur.

Take-down extended

If a credit is based on a series of advances within a specified time, and the borrower asks for an extension of that time, a lender should be careful. Such extensions are a sign that the borrower's business is off-schedule, which can lead to serious problems.

Failure to pay withholding tax

Aside from the fact that failure to pay taxes can create tax liens as already mentioned, failure to pay withholding means that the borrower is borrowing from his employees. This situation is present in almost all business failures, and if spotted early, the lender may be able to accomplish corrective action.

Borrower becomes hostile

Borrowers are usually cooperative with their creditors. When a borrower turns defensive, it likely stems from worry that the lender will find out something the lender will not like. While this can be a most difficult situation, the lender must determine what has happened in order to know what action to take.

Conclusion

By accurately valuing and understanding the nature and priority of collateral, a secured lender will be in the position to properly assess and structure a loan. By policing and insuring the collateral, a lender can best protect his or her position and eliminate any costly surprises. A lender with a solid collateral position is better able to serve the borrower with confidence.

Finally, a properly secured lender is a lender constantly in the best position to liquidate the collateral. The cooperation of corporate officers, reinforced by their suretyships, contributes greatly to being in such a position.

This article is not meant as a definitive checklist, but rather to stimulate thought on the subject. There is no substitute for thoughtful, careful analysis at any stage of a loan. If the reader is now motivated in that direction, the article has accomplished its purpose.   □

An Approach to Writing Loan Agreement Covenants

by Charles S. Zimmerman

LOAN AGREEMENTS ARE A SOURCE OF CONFUSION AND MISUNDERSTANDING to many bankers. Frequently, the reader of loan agreements is not aware of their objectives and limitations, and further, is bewildered by the legal jargon of the numerous qualifying clauses.

Essential to the creation of effective loan agreements are the affirmative and negative covenants, which specify what the borrower must and must not do to comply with the agreement. The thrust of this paper is to facilitate the understanding and use of covenants in loan agreements. The use of covenants will be

This article was the first place winner in RMA's 1975 National Paper Writing Competition.

discussed in detail following an overview of the purpose, characteristics and basic composition of loan agreements.

Purpose of loan agreements

Large amounts of time, effort and money are spent in the development and implementation of loan agreements. They provide protection and communication for the parties involved and a general stability for the loan relationship through greater understanding among the parties. Further, should the borrower have other long-term debt, the loan agreement coordinates any legal or procedural interface with the debt and its associated creditors.

Where several banks are participating in a large credit, the loan agreement specifies the rules which govern the loan administration, and the responsibilities and liabilities of each bank.

As a major objective, the lender is interested in protecting its loan and assuring timely repayment. Through the loan agreement, the bank creates a clear understanding with the borrower as to what is expected of it. In doing so, the bank establishes its control of the relationship and provides for several basic functions to effect that control.

The lender attempts to ensure regular and frequent communication with the borrower by using certain covenants in the loan agreement. The communication results in an up-to-date assessment of the borrower's financial situation and its general management philosophy.

When the bank requires that the borrower maintain certain financial ratios, it is accomplishing several objectives. On the surface these covenants provide triggers or early warning signals of trouble, which will allow the bank to take rapid remedial action. The borrower is made aware of where the minimum performance cutoffs are. However, the banker is also helping the borrower set reasonable goals in terms of financial condition and growth. In some cases, a "growth formula" is created which states that until a specified set of financial conditions is met, the borrower may not be eligible for further debt.

All these controls—required ratios, ratio goals, required actions and forbidden actions—may seem arbitrary or restrictive; but applied wisely, they are not. The process lets all parties know where they stand, thus reducing the number of unknowns or uncertainties in the loan relationship.

Characteristics of loan agreements

When asked to describe the salient characteristics of loan agreements, most bankers will use adjectives such as "long" or "dull" or "confusing." While many agreements may be thus described, other definitions are certainly more informative.

The loan agreement is one of the most important loan documents in that it provides the basis for the entire banking relationship, establishing intents and stating expectations. It relates all the basic loan documents to one another and creates the means of control and lines of communication which are important in protecting all parties involved.

It follows then that only three main courses of action are open to the bank in the event of a default by the borrower. The account officer may waive, either temporarily or permanently, the condition which has been violated. This is frequently done in the case of financial ratios, although too lax an attitude in this respect can lead to a loss of control and an ineffective covenant and/or loan agreement. An alternative is for the banker to have the agreement rewritten to make it more viable. The rewrite is also a tactic used to obtain a much tighter hold over the borrower, if needed, by using as a bargaining tool the bank's legal right to call the loan. The third, and most drastic, approach for the bank is, of course, to declare the borrower in default, call the loan and, if necessary, file suit against the borrower.

The implications of the nature of a loan agreement are extremely important. As an example, assume that a loan has been made on an unsecured basis and one covenant forbids the pledging of assets to anyone. This is obviously an attempt to maintain the strength of the bank's unsecured position in the event of liquidation. However, let us further assume that in violation of the agreement, the borrower pledges its assets to another lender. The bank certainly retains its option to call the loan, but the other lender holds the security. If the bank does call the loan, forcing liquidation, it remains an unsecured creditor vying for those assets which remain after satisfaction of the first lienholder.

The loan agreement, then, is not a substitute for security. If a loan should be secured in the absence of an agreement, then security should be taken with one. In fact, a loan agreement is not a substitute for anything. If the situation does not satisfy the five C's of a loan decision—character, capacity, capital, conditions, and collateral—then the loan should not be made.

Composition of a loan agreement

There are seven basic sections of standard loan agreements, any of which may be modified, depending upon the purpose of the loan.

1. **The loan**—This section describes the loan by type, size of commitment, interest rate, repayment schedule, and security taken, if any. Also

specified are all participants and their roles plus terms of participation if more than one lender is involved. Any definitions of financial, accounting or legal terminology to be used in the agreement are stated here.

2. **Representations and warranties of borrower**—Basically, this section is an attestation to the lender that certain statements are true. For instance, the borrower may warrant that it is a corporation, that it is entering into the agreement legally, that financial statements supplied to the bank are true, and that no material change has occurred since their preparation. The company may attest to the nature of its business, that it does own its assets as represented, and that it currently is not under litigation. In other words, the company reaffirms in writing all those things about its current state of existence which have been known or assumed throughout the negotiations.

3. **Affirmative covenants**—In contrast to the warranties, which attest to existing fact, affirmative covenants state what action or event the borrower must cause to occur or exist in the future.

4. **Negative covenants**—Negative covenants state what action or event the borrower must prevent from occurring or existing in the future.

5. **Conditions of lending**—This section states that, prior to the lending of any money, all documents and notes must be in proper form, that both the borrower's and the bank's counsel must approve the entire arrangement, and that the borrower's auditor, or at least its chief financial officer, must certify current compliance with all conditions of the loan agreement.

6. **Events of default**—Conditions which will be considered events of default are specifically stated. Such conditions might be delinquent payment, misrepresentation, insolvency proceedings, change in ownership, or other occurrences which could jeopardize the company's viability and/or the bank's position. All covenant violations are considered events of default, although many are designed to be used in correcting a situation rather than in calling the loan. In any event of default, timing is crucial. For instance, it may be that default does not occur until a covenant has been violated for 30 consecutive days.

7. **Remedies**—The remedies section spells out what the bank may do in the event of default. The bank's rights may include several potential actions, but always include the right to accelerate payments, a term which means to call the loan. Timing is important. The borrower may have a certain period of time to correct the default prior to the enforcement of a remedy.

In a credit with several participating banks, the remedies section also defines procedures for calling the loan. For example, the agreement may require banks representing 70% of the commitment to call the loan.

Approach to the covenant package

Prior to writing a set of covenants for a loan agreement, it is necessary to have a systematic approach to developing them. One must ask questions ranging from an assessment of basic objectives and risks to types of protections and remedies which must be provided to ensure the successful attainment of the objectives.

Since covenants are the heart of a loan agreement, setting the objectives is a process very similar to that of defining those for the total agreement. The bank is obviously hoping to be repaid on a timely basis, but, as a secondary set of objectives, would like to maintain or improve upon the financial position, cash flow, growth progression and general financial condition of the borrower. Once goals have been set for the mutual benefit and protection of all parties, the lender must reassess the risks involved from a point of view different from that in the initial loan decision.

Determination of risk

No longer is the lender looking for a yes/no decision. The aim at this point is to define the risks involved and to determine their magnitude. The account officer needs to ask, "What conditions or events could block the accomplishment of my objectives?" In other words, "Where is the loan vulnerable?" Weaknesses may lie in poor cash flow, thin net worth or other financial statement items. It may be that the industry is volatile and highly subject to strikes or public fancy. Perhaps the company is small, or it has a short track record, so that much of the loan decision is based upon projections.

Whatever the risks, it is now the task of the loan agreement writer to prevent or minimize the consequences of those risks as well as possible, in a form which remains as flexible as possible.

Scope of covenants

The lender's effort to safeguard the loan against known and unknown risks will take the form of loan covenants. In asking what triggers exist and what actions may reasonably be taken and enforced once a risk materializes, the scope of potential covenants is almost limitless. Triggers may range from financial ratios and limits on financial statement accounts to restrictions on corporate, or even management, activities.

Furthermore, methods of treating a specific item are quite flexible in order to obtain the appropriate coverage. For example, it is possible to restrict a financial statement item to a minimum or maximum of

—a fixed dollar amount
—a dollar amount increase or decrease per time period
—a percentage of total assets, tangible net worth or some independent indicator
—a percentage change per time period.

As a special case, businesses subject to seasonal variances may have the above modifications fluctuate with the peaks and troughs of the cycle to more closely approximate actual conditions.

With so many potential requirements and restrictions, however, it becomes evident that the key to an effective loan agreement is *not* to see how many activities or conditions can be covered; it is to obtain the most protection in the simplest, most efficient manner.

Simplicity and efficiency

To devise a simple and efficient network of covenants, it is imperative that the writer have a thorough understanding of the company, its management, and loan-associated risk in conjunction with a realistic attitude. This combination will result in covenants which allow the borrower maximum flexibility within the constraints necessary to provide the bank maximum protection.

Effective covenants are stated in terms which are well-defined and measurable. Consider the difference in ease of enforcement between the following two affirmative covenants:

(1) Borrower will maintain adequate cash flow.
(2) Borrower will maintain a ratio of cash flow to current maturities of long-term debt of 1.5 to 1 on a fiscal-year basis.

The necessity for a realistic attitude dictates that a covenant also be such that the borrower is able to comply with it and the lender is willing to enforce it. Should either of these conditions not be met, a covenant may be frequently waived, thereby losing its psychological and, perhaps, legal control.

The essence of a loan agreement covenant is that it is simple, well-defined, measurable, risk-reducing, efficient and reasonable. In short, it is the creative development of protection in the loan situation. As an aid to the direct application of these principles, a working guide to the construction of loan agreement covenants follows.

Working guide for loan agreement covenants

This guide consists of two cross-referenced sections: Functional Objectives and Covenants.

Functional objectives

The keyed, numbered objectives shown on the grid are more fully described in the numbered paragraphs following:

1. **Full disclosure of information**—To make competent, ongoing lending decisions, the account officer must have an intimate understanding of the borrower. Full disclosure also aids the lender in maintaining regular contact with the borrower and close control over the loan relationship.

2. **Preservation of net worth**—The borrower's basic financial strength and ability to support debt and absorb downturns lie in its net worth. The purpose of related covenants is to assure the growth and continued strength of that net worth.

3. **Maintenance of asset quality**—Asset value represents two major factors of importance to the lender—earning power and liquidation value. In either case, it is to the bank's advantage to require high standards of asset quality.

4. **Maintenance of adequate cash flow**—In the case of normal repayment of a loan, the lender is repaid from the borrower's cash flow. In such cases, it is imperative that the lender closely monitor the cash flow and attempt to maintain its quality.

5. **Control of growth**—As a definite drain upon cash flow, working capital, fixed assets, management energies, and capital funds, excessive growth has been recognized as the cause of numerous charge-offs and bad loans in the past few years. It is obviously in the interest of both banker and borrower to maintain growth in an orderly fashion, although the two parties rarely see eye to eye on this matter. The bank's objective is to reach a clear understanding with the borrower on the limits of its growth.

6. **Control of management**—In any loan situation, but particularly if the loan is unsecured, the success of the total relationship depends heavily upon the borrower's management. The bank, then, hopes to ensure the continuing quality of management.

7. **Assurance of legal existence and concept of going concern**—The purpose of devising covenants such as these is to ensure the bank of a viable entity which may produce the conditions necessary to repay its loan.

8. **Provision for bank profit**—Banks lend money in return for an expected profit, and, therefore, are interested, not only in protecting the principal amount of the loan, but also the profit, whether it be interest, servicing income, or other.

Covenants

The terms of the covenants are given in roman in the guide, followed by an interpretation of their applicability (in italic type face).

Using the guide

The basic objectives formulated by the user for any particular agreement can be grouped into one of the eight functional objectives previously described. These are then cross-referenced to the covenants which will help achieve these objectives.

Having identified the applicable covenants, the loan agreement writer may then apply any needed modifications and limitations.

Where a covenant satisfies a particular functional objective, an X is found in the appropriate numbered column corresponding to the applicable objective. Two examples will clarify the use of the grid.

(1) To locate those covenants which apply to the functional objective "Control of Growth," search for X's in column 5, since "Control of Growth" is the fifth objective in the grid.

(2) To determine which functional objectives are satisfied by the covenant "Casualty Insurance," look at the numbered grid beside the covenant heading and then match these numbers to the corresponding functional objectives.

**Functional
Objectives***

Disclosure	Net worth	Asset quality	Cash flow	Growth	Management	Going concern	Bank profit	
1	2	3	4	5	6	7	8	
		X	X					
	X	X	X			X	X	
							X	
		X	X					

Affirmative Covenant

Affirmative covenants state conditions that the borrower must fulfill until the loan has been paid in full.

Casualty insurance

Insurance, equal in amount to the book value of all assets, naming the bank as loss payee, must be maintained and evidence thereof furnished.

If any assets are uninsured and are destroyed or in any way lose their value, the bank's position is weakened should liquidation occur. Insurance is necessary whether or not the loan is secured.

Life insurance

"Key man" life insurance on Mr. Principal must be in an amount no less than the total commitment, naming the bank as beneficiary.

Frequently, the loss of a principal in a closely held business will bring about the forced sale or ineffective management of the business, seriously jeopardizing the bank's position. The situation is remedied by "key man" life insurance, naming the bank as beneficiary.

Corporate existence

Corporate existence shall be maintained.

The legal existence of the borrower is necessary to protect the effectiveness of the promissory note.

Liens

The borrower must comply with all applicable statutes and pay all obligations which, if unpaid, might result in a lien, except those obligations which are being contested in good faith.

Like the covenant on "Tax Liabilities," this covenant is intended to prevent any erosion in the bank's claim to assets through legal proceedings.

*See pages 8 and 9 for discussion of objectives.

1	2	3	4	5	6	7	8
	X	X	X				
X					X		
X					X		

Tax liabilities

All accrued tax liabilities must be paid as they become due.

Actually a subset of the "Liens" covenant, this assures compliance with tax regulations to avoid any liens upon or seizures of assets.

Financial statements

Within 90 days after the fiscal year-end, unqualified, audited fiscal statements, with an auditor's letter stating whether or not default has occurred, must be supplied.

The borrower's financial statements supply detailed information relating to its progress and financial condition. Lenders generally request quarterly and audited fiscal statements and, depending on the industry, other statements as applicable. Also, a provision is usually made for the submission of additional statements at any time on request. Essentially, statements and their structure depend upon the company. The basic fiscal and quarterly statements may be requested on any or all of several bases such as: consolidated, consolidating, comparative, with or without final adjustments, and audited or unaudited. Additional statements requested may include: pro forma statements, historical cash flow, cash flow and sales projections, construction status reports, and individual statements of the principals.

Accounting procedures

These shall be substantially the same generally accepted accounting standards currently in use, and, should a change become necessary, the bank is to be notified in writing prior to the change of the nature of and reasons for such change.

It is essential that the lender have complete financial information and that he understand it. Furthermore, much of the analytical value of the statements and the use of their ratios as "triggers" is lost if accounting procedures are changed. Frequently, a change in accounting procedures is a sign of trouble within the organization, and an effort on the part of management to conceal it.

1	2	3	4	5	6	7	8	
	X	X	X					**Working capital**

Working capital shall never be less than $100,000 and, in any event, at a current ratio of not less than 1.5 to 1.

As a strong indicator of liquidity, working capital is frequently set by varying means. Often working capital is defined in variance with the traditional "current assets less current liabilities." For instance, prepaid expenses may be excluded from current assets, or inventory allowed at only 80% of book value. Further, the minimum working capital amount is often coupled with a minimum current ratio. The working capital required may vary according to several risk-related factors, such as growth, cyclicality, total assets and cash flow.

1	2	3	4	5	6	7	8	
X	X		X					**Net worth**

Tangible net worth shall never be less than $200,000 and total debt to tangible net worth ratio no more than 2 to 1.

Net worth is a measure of what would be left if all of a firm's assets were sold at book value and all liabilities paid in full. To obtain a slightly more accurate net worth figure, the bank may require the borrower to maintain a tangible net worth of a certain amount, or a debt to tangible net worth ratio of at least a specified value. The use of tangible net worth is designed to eliminate from the ratio those assets, such as goodwill, which do not have a liquidation value.

Financial ratios

Generally considered to be good "triggers," there are numerous usable ratios, depending upon the desired effect. The ratios listed below appear frequently in covenants, in addition to the working capital and net worth ratios.

1	2	3	4	5	6	7	8	
X	X	X						*Quick ratio*
		X						*Times interest earned*
		X						*Fixed charges coverage*
		X						*Sales to receivables*
		X						*Purchases to payables*
	X	X						*Cost of goods sold to inventory*
	X							*Sales to assets*
X								*Sales to net worth*
		X						*Profit to assets*
X								*Profit to tangible net worth*
X	X							*Debt to depreciated capital assets*
			X					*Cash flow to current maturities*

1	2	3	4	5	6	7	8
		X					
X	X		X				
X	X	X	X		X		
X						X	

Property, plant and equipment
Property, plant and equipment shall be maintained in good repair.

As with the "Insurance" covenant, the bank is attempting to maintain the integrity of its collateral position against misuse.

Inspection
Persons designated by the bank shall be permitted to inspect any or all records and property to verify the authenticity of furnished statements and actual physical condition of assets.

As a matter of procedure, the bank should inspect the actual books and property of the borrower. The inspection is not intended to "catch" the borrower; it is merely a routine audit on the part of the bank. However, without this covenant, attempts to examine the borrower's properties could be refused or be construed to be harassment.

Contingent liabilities
The bank is to be informed of any actual or probable litigation, or changes in contracts or the status quo, which might materially affect the business.

This covenant is designed to assure full disclosure of information which might affect the quality of assets or net worth, which would in turn affect the status of the loan. In closely held corporations, this covenant would also apply to the principal, including such matters as divorce settlements.

Banking services
Principal checking accounts shall be maintained with the bank.

This covenant aims at gaining revenue-producing business of the borrower in addition to the actual loan. Having the accounts in-bank also allows a monitoring of the accounts and, if necessary, an offset of the account.

1	2	3	4	5	6	7	8
							X

Attorney's and printer's fees

All attorney's fees and printer's fees in connection with this agreement shall be paid by the borrower.

Typically, the bank charges to the borrower all out-of-bank expenses associated with the loan, allowing a more certain calculation of risk versus return for the bank.

Functional Objectives*

Disclosure	Net worth	Asset quality	Cash flow	Growth	Management	Going concern	Bank profit
1	2	3	4	5	6	7	8
	X		X	X			
	X	X	X			X	

Negative Covenants

Negative covenants describe prohibitions to which the borrower is subject until the loan has been paid in full.

Borrowings

Debt other than short-term debt shall not at any time exceed $75,000, plus debt incurred in the normal course of operating the business.

Generally, borrowings of a long-term nature are not allowed due to potential impairment of the borrower's financial situation and loss of control. Short-term borrowings, in addition to trade debt, are frequently allowed up to a specified amount, generally required to meet seasonal fluctuations.

Sales of assets

The borrower shall not dispose of assets valued at an aggregate amount exceeding $25,000 during any fiscal year, excluding sales transacted in the ordinary course of business.

It is essential to maintain control of cash flow and any changes in asset strength. Limiting the sale of assets is one such way. As a "trigger," a sale of assets could indicate liquidity problems.

---

*See pages 8 and 9 for discussion of objectives.

1	2	3	4	5	6	7	8
		X	X	X			
		X	X	X			
		X	X				
		X	X				

Capital expenditures

Capital expenditures in any fiscal year shall not exceed total depreciation in that year.

Controlling capital expenditures allows the bank to limit growth and control cash flow. Typically, the bank may limit asset growth to a specific dollar figure or a percentage increase per year.

Leases

The aggregate of all lease or rental payments shall not exceed $1,500 monthly.

Related to the restriction of asset increases, leasing limitations prevent off-balance sheet financing and growth. Leases may be limited by aggregate rent payments, aggregate lease commitments, a limitation upon capitalized leases plus capital assets, or other appropriate measures.

Investments

Purchase of any stock or obligations other than U.S. Government obligations is prohibited.

The bank's position could be seriously jeopardized either by a shortage of cash due to investments or a deterioration in the value of the investment made. U.S. Government obligations are generally acceptable due to their liquidity and low risk. Further exceptions might be stock of major corporations, CD's with major banks, or stock of subsidiary companies.

Loans

Any loans made, except those to officers of the company or to subsidiaries, shall not exceed $30,000 and $150,000 respectively.

A borrower who is making loans is, in effect, lending the bank's money to someone the bank does not know, which certainly increases risk to the bank. If the borrower has excess cash, it is either not managing its short-term money needs well, or, if the excess is truly temporary, could be investing the funds in lower-risk debt instruments.

1	2	3	4	5	6	7	8
	X		X	X	X		
	X		X	X	X	X	
X	X	X	X	X	X	X	
	X		X				

Change of business

The borrower shall not engage in any business other than that in which it is engaged as of the date of this agreement.

The bank has made a loan to a specific company for a specific purpose. Any change, such as the nature of basic business philosophies or product line, would require a reconsideration of the loan decision.

Mergers

The borrower shall not enter into any merger or consolidation or acquire all or substantially all the assets of any entity.

This covenant is similar to the "Change of Business" covenant; if a merger occurs, the entire character of the loan changes. In such a case the bank would want the prerogative of withdrawing from, or changing, the agreement.

Change in management or ownership

Any change in management or ownership which might materially change the character or operating philosophy of the company is prohibited.

The loan is extended based upon certain existing facts, among which is management. To change actual management or operating philosophy, such as expansion or product line, could be disastrous in terms of the viability of the entire company. Specific management personnel, particularly principals, may be required to stay with the borrower to prevent default.

Dividends

Dividends shall not be paid except out of net earnings accrued after the date of this agreement, and in no calendar year can they exceed 50% of net earnings after deducting all current debt service requirements.

Dividends are restricted to maintain control over cash flow and net worth. They may be disallowed or allowed in the amount of a specified per cent of some measure of earnings.

1	2	3	4	5	6	7	8
	X		X				
	X		X		X		
	X		X				

Repurchase of stock

The borrower shall not repurchase any of its own stock.

Although it may in some cases be desirable to retire stock, generally the cash drain incurred and decrease in net worth make such purchases undesirable.

Officer salaries

Compensation for company officers in an aggregate amount shall not exceed $150,000.

This covenant is frequently used in closely held companies where a large salary account could severely affect cash flow and net worth. Officer salaries could be set at a specific amount or tied to a measure of profitability.

Deferred compensation

No stock option or other deferred compensation plan not in effect as of the date of this agreement shall be established.

This is one of the several covenants designed to plug any possible leaks in the cash flow cycle to avoid any diversion of cash from the operation of the business and repayment of the loan. □

Loan Participations— Upstream/Downstream[1]

by F. William Vandiver, Jr.

Before entering a loan participation, a bank should arrive at an independent credit decision about the loan. So advises the author who also instructs the prospective participant to apply the same fundamentals of credit analysis to this loan decision as it would in a direct lending situation.

Loan participations are an integral part of our banking system although they are quite often neglected and misunderstood. They are neglected because bankers often enter into a loan participation as a buyer or seller far too casually, and they are misunderstood due to the often complex legal questions involved. There is a tendency to say, "If XYZ is in the credit, then it must be okay." But we have all learned some hard lessons in recent years and have found in hindsight that problems occurred due to inadequate credit review by the purchasing bank, a poorly drawn participation agreement, and inadequate consideration of legal implications.[2]

I would like to put some of these problems in perspective by looking at the nature of participation loans, the risks involved, and the ways to minimize these risks.

---

[1] This article is based on a speech delivered by the author at the spring 1977 meeting of RMA's Carolina-Virginias Chapter.

[2] Readers may also be interested in a 1975 booklet entitled, "Guidelines for Upstream/ Downstream Correspondent Bank Loan Participations," published by Robert Morris Associates.

How do participations arise?

There are four broad categories of loan participants:

(1) *Correspondent banking.* The banking business itself breeds dozens of opportunities for large and small banks to develop joint lending situations.

(2) *Large, complex credits.* These situations arise as banks spread risk through credit or absolute dollars.

(3) *Banks with commercial finance companies, factors, or SBA loans.* By participation with another financial intermediary, a bank can logically satisfy the needs of its customer.

(4) *Early maturities with insurance company.* Banks many times take the first few years of a 15- to 20-year note.

There are hundreds of variations within each of these categories, but the opportunity is ever-present for a bank to participate in such a loan.

The issues facing participating banks

The first issue facing participating banks is the issue of credit. How does a participating bank go about making the credit decision? I contend that there is one principle that must be reiterated: *The basic fundamentals of direct lending must be applied in loan participations.* These fundamentals are covered in the following questions:

(1) What is the purpose of the loan?

(2) From what source will I be paid?

(3) Is the borrower credit worthy?

(4) Is the loan structured properly and realistically?

(5) How good is management?

(6) What is the nature of the borrower's industry?

Pointers for arriving at an independent credit decision

However, we must recognize that these questions are more difficult to answer when we are a participant because we may be one step removed from the borrower. Here are some pointers that could help in arriving at a sound credit decision as a participant:

(1) Before entering the participation, the prospective participant should ask the following questions:

(a) Who are you buying the participation from?

(b) What is their lending record?

(c) What is their lending philosophy?

(d) How do they react to difficult situations?

(e) What is their financial condition?

(2) The participant should insist on as much lead time as possible. The participant needs the same chance to review the credit as the originating bank.

(3) Whenever possible, the participant should have direct contact with the borrower.

(4) The participant must be furnished with *full* financial information on the borrower.

(5) The participant should have a direct say about the structure of the loan, the agreement, and other essential documents.

(6) Control of the credit must be dictated by size, complexity, and terms of credit.

(7) The participant *must* look at the total credit—not just at his share.

(8) Is the participant on a LIFO basis or full term? The nature and duration of the credit will dictate this.

While there are many other points to consider, the preceding are some of the more important. Of course, what all of this means is that as a participant, *you must make your own independent credit decision.*

Handling documentation

Once the credit decision is made, the second issue is documentation. This is particularly important in secured transactions or more complex loans involving loan agreements.

There are several ways to handle the documentation. The originating bank may simply sell or assign an existing note with or without recourse to a participant. This is a clean, simple, and fairly common way of doing business, particularly in the correspondent banking business. This form of participation gives the purchaser the ability to proceed directly against the borrower if the need arises. However, as a participant, you are subject to the terms of the seller's note; therefore, you should be cautious.

By far the most common method of documenting loan participations is through the *participation agreement* and *participation certificate*. In this procedure, the borrower executes a note with the originating bank, which then, through the use of a participation certificate, sells a prorata share of the loan to a participant. There is generally no mention of the participant in the note, loan agreement, or security documents. The borrower does not necessarily know that the participant exists, and only the money owed the originating bank is reflected on the books of the borrower. The participation agreement is an extremely important document because it outlines contractually the entire arrangement between the originating bank and the participant.

A typical participation agreement goes something like this:

(1) It names the buyer and seller. (That sounds easy enough, but I have seen some where the wrong names were used.)

(2) It should clearly define the note and the underlying transaction. Here again, problems can develop if the seller has multiple notes to a borrower.

(3) It should clearly stipulate how payments are to be made, who gets how much, and when.

(4) The seller will generally add some disclaimer regarding the collectability or validity of the note. The participant must not overlook this; he should make sure that the selling bank has obtained proper borrowing resolutions.

(5) The agreement should clearly outline the circumstances under which the note can be modified. Many participants and sellers have run into problems here because they failed to read this particular covenant.

(6) The agreement should stipulate who can enforce the obligation.

(7) The agreement should contain language governing the payment of legal fees, the release or substitution of collateral, and termination provisions, if appropriate.

A third type of documentation stipulates that all participants are parties to the loan agreement and named in all documents relating to the loan. Each participant might have its own note or could simply buy a participation from the lead bank. In this case, the borrower has entered into an agreement with each bank, and there is little doubt about the intent of the parties.

Handling secured transactions and the agent arrangement

Now let's turn to *secured transactions*. The element of security adds a new dimension to the subject, and this is the third issue.

Under the straight participation arrangement, the originating bank is the secured party. The public records do not indicate that there is a participant, and all documentation is handled by the originating bank. Recognizing this, the participant should insist on copies of all UCC filings, deeds of trust, mortgages, security agreements, etc. The participant must assure himself that the originating bank has properly perfected the security interest. The point I stress again is that in this particular arrangement, the participant is *not* the secured party and *must* look to the originating bank for payment.

The agent arrangement was mentioned earlier. This is quite common in larger, more complex credits involving multiple participants. A secured loan involving an agent is typically characterized as follows: All participants may negotiate the terms of the loan with the borrower and each other. The participants then elect an agent bank whose duties are to represent the participants in dealings with the borrower. An agency agreement establishes the duties and responsibilities of the agent and the relationship between the participating banks. The loan agreement, security agreement, and other documents would normally be signed by the agent although it is common for each participant to sign these documents with the agent. Each bank may or may not have its own note, depending upon the nature of the credit itself.

The agent agreement generally will indicate that the company has pledged the collateral to the agent for the benefit of the banks. It will also stipulate that the agent has the right to manage, perform, and otherwise enforce the terms and provisions of the obligation. Most agent agreements require the agent to use "reasonable prudence and judgment" in carrying out its duties. Who determines "reasonable prudence and judgment?" The agreement will stipulate that the agent will not be liable for the consequences of any oversight or error in judgment nor answerable for any loss, except through gross negligence or willful misconduct. You need to think about that one! And finally, there will be a clause stating that the agent makes no representation or warranty and has no responsibility for the financial condition of the company nor the enforceability of the agreement nor any instrument connected with the loan. The agent obviously has a very difficult and precarious role; he wears two hats, as participant and as agent.

Some interesting cases have emerged involving agent banks, the most recent of which involves several participants in a large loan who are suing the agent. The participants charge that—

(1) The agent withheld essential information on the borrower.

(2) The agent misled the participants about the credit worthiness of the borrower.

(3) The agent neglected its *fiduciary* responsibilities to the participants.

That last point is important. If the courts rule in favor of the participants, a precedent could be set for placing all agents in the role of a fiduciary. This would send our attorneys scrambling to alter the language in all existing participation agreements! It is becoming fairly commonplace to see a "nonreliance" clause in agent agreements which says that the participants have not relied on statements or information furnished by the agent in entering the transaction.[3]

Risks

Having dealt with the general aspects of loan participations, we should now examine some of the risks to a participant and an originator.

Participant risks

(1) In most participations, you are looking to another party to administer, document, and collect the loan. Being one step removed from the borrower adds to your risk.

(2) You cannot legally proceed directly against the borrower if something goes wrong. Your recourse is against the originator.

(3) If the lead lender goes into receivership or bankruptcy, you *could* become an unsecured creditor of the trustee or receiver. Several recent cases have upheld this, even when the loan was secured and there was an underlying agreement which clearly outlined the intentions of both parties.

(4) Your rights to terminate, modify, or in any way affect the loan may be limited by a poorly drawn participation agreement.

Originating bank risks

(1) You may be bound by the desires of participants which could restrain your ability to take action that you deem appropriate.

(2) You are obliged to keep participants fully informed about the borrower. Adequate and complete disclosure of facts is essential; the risks of incomplete disclosure include being sued, losing a correspondent relationship, or having to repurchase a share of the loan that could violate your lending limit.

Some ways to minimize risk

(1) You should know from whom you are buying a participation: What is the seller's financial condition, track record, and integrity?

---

[3] Readers are referred to a booklet just published by Robert Morris Associates entitled, "Guidelines for Domestic Agented/Agreement Credits."

(2) Where possible and practical, you and each participant should be a party to the loan agreement and be named in the security documents.

(3) You should ensure that the participation agreement *clearly* outlines the intentions of the parties. Make sure there are no clauses that you do not clearly understand.

(4) You should ensure that the originating bank has taken all steps necessary to document the loan properly. If an agent is involved, make sure that the borrower acknowledged the agent's role.

(5) Above all else, you should guard against *complacency*. Legally, there is no such thing as, "Don't worry, we'll buy it back."

My comments have dealt primarily with bank to bank participations. However, the same principles and problems apply when participating with other financial institutions. But one key difference would be the perspective of the other party. For instance, when participating with a commercial finance company, remember that it is basically an asset lender. A deteriorating income statement in that situation might not be the cause for alarm that it would be in our business. Therefore, differences can arise. Check your termination rights; these clauses vary with the industry, and you should know exactly what your rights are.

Summary

Loan participations represent a legitimate and commonplace method of extending credit. There are problems involved, as with other forms of lending, and there is no "right way" to handle all of the various types of loan participations.

Being aware of the risks is crucial: Know what you are getting into and do not assume anything. On the other hand, do not overreact. Examine each situation on its own merits and structure the deal accordingly. Above all, use sound judgment to reach your own independent decision. ☐

Structuring a Secured Loan to a Multi-Corporate Organization

by Stephen C. Diamond

Can a subsidiary legally guarantee an obligation of its parent? And if it can, is the creation of a security interest in the sub's collateral enforceable against the creditors of the sub in the event of its bankruptcy? These are just two of the legal questions which Stephen Diamond explores in discussing how to structure secured loans to multi-corporate organizations.

When several corporations are part of a single corporate "family," the way in which a loan to such an organization is structured can quite often have a significant legal impact on the lender. In today's commercial loan environment, it is increasingly common for a corporate borrower to have a corporate affiliate, parent, or subsidiary. Yet each corporation is, in fact, a legal entity and must be dealt with accordingly. The problems that this condition creates are highlighted when a lender seeks corporate collateral to secure a loan. Whether that collateral is sought at the time the loan is made or subsequently due to deterioration of the borrower's financial strength, the legal issues are quite complex. The intent of this article is to highlight these problems from an operating standpoint.

Major pitfalls in structuring a secured loan

The major legal pitfalls one faces in structuring a secured loan are—

(1) Failure to comply with applicable state law affecting security interests (such as the UCC in all states except Louisiana).

(2) Failure to comply with applicable provisions of the state Business Corporations Act.

(3) Failure to comply with applicable provisions of the Federal Bankruptcy Act. The sections of the Bankruptcy Act that are most germane to the structuring of secured loans are Section 60a (the preference section, which we will not discuss), and Sections 67d and 70e which relate to fraudulent transfers. Although these sections are not necessarily applied in a uniform manner by the courts, the problems they present to lenders can best be analyzed in light of what their most probable results would be, and we will proceed on that basis.

Examples of problems lenders can face

A recent example of the type of problems secured lenders face involved a corporate parent with over 40 operating subsidiaries. The parent had $33 million of unsecured bank lines in use and $14 million of commercial paper outstanding, not backed up by unused bank loans. The company found itself unable to roll over its commercial paper and faced an immediate default. It approached its banks to increase their lines by $18 million—$14 million to cover the commercial paper and $4 million for additional working capital.

The banks did not feel that the company could support a $51 million unsecured line of credit and sought to take collateral. An in-depth analysis of the company indicated that while the consolidated statement reflected over $100 million in face amount of accounts receivables and inventories, almost all of this potential collateral existed at the subsidiary level—while the bank and commercial paper obligations were at the parent level. The parent itself had relatively little in assets, except for the stock of the subsidiaries. The immediate question was how the banks could collateralize the loans at the parent level with collateral which was at the subsidiary level. A possible approach was to merge all of the subsidiaries into the parent, but the time element made this option unacceptable.

Less complex hypothetical case

Before we reveal what actually happened in this case, let's explore the issues involved by looking at a similar but less complex hypothetical situation. For illustrative purposes, let us assume that a lending officer is looking at the following corporate structure:

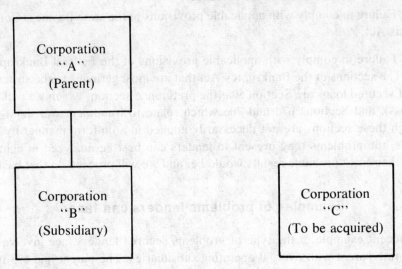

We will also assume that (1) the appropriate provisions of the UCC will be complied with, (2) "A" holds as its sole asset 100% of "B's" common shares, (3) "B" has a net worth of $1 million of which $750,000 is in various capital accounts and $250,000 is retained earnings, and (4) the lending officer's credit judgment indicates that would-be borrower "A" is entitled to a $500,000 line of credit, provided the lender can get a valid first lien against "B's" accounts receivable and inventories.

"A" seeks to borrow $500,000 for the purpose of acquiring 100% of the common stock of Company "C." Should the structure be to (1) lend the money to "A" secured by "B's" collateralized guarantee, (2) lend the money to "B" and have it upstreamed to "A," or (3) do neither (1) or (2)?

The answer to the first of the proposed structurings rests on the resolution of the following issues:

(1) Can a subsidiary, under applicable state corporate law, legally guarantee an obligation of its parent? In most states it cannot, and if such is the case, option 1 falls.

(2) Assuming, however, that such a guarantee is permissible, is the creation of such a security interest in "B's" collateral enforceable against the creditors of "B" in the event of "B's" bankruptcy? The answer to this turns on whether "B" received adequate consideration within the meaning of Section 67d of the Federal Bankruptcy Act.

Receipt of adequate consideration

In our hypothetical situation, what value did Corporation "B" really receive? While "B" permitted a security interest to be taken in its current assets to induce the lender to lend $500,000 to its parent, it received no direct benefit. In terms of financial statement analysis, "B's" financial statement would have shown no increase in assets and a $500,000 increase in contingent liabilities as a result of the transaction. How, then, can it be successfully argued that "B" received adequate consideration? The answer is that it cannot.

"Unreasonably small capital" as a result of transfer

Assuming that there is no adequate consideration, transfers can be set aside under various provisions of Section 67d of the Bankruptcy Act. The provision of that section that is most relevant in this instance states that if "B" becomes bankrupt within one year after the date of the transfer and its remaining assets constitute "unreasonably small capital" (that is, working capital), the transfer may be voided. This applies even if "B" was solvent at the time of the transfer. Nor is it dependent on any bad faith or improper intent on the part of the lender. Thus, if "B" is shown to have "unreasonably small capital" as a result of the transfer, the transaction—"B's" pledge of collateral to the lender—can be set aside.

Bankruptcy within the proscribed period

Courts generally seem to apply hindsight with respect to what an "unreasonably small capital" is, with the result that "B's" bankruptcy within the proscribed period creates a presumption that capital was, at the time of the transfer, unreasonably small. Even if "B" avoids bankruptcy for a period of longer than one year after the date of transfer, the transfer may be set aside under Section 70ę if it is within the time-frame established by the appropriate state's Fraudulent Conveyance Act. This section essentially permits a trustee in bankruptcy to void a transaction that violates the Fraudulent Conveyance Act of the applicable state. Most states provide that a fraudulent conveyance can be set aside for up to a five-year period.

In short, this proposed structuring will leave the lender vulnerable for at least one year and, in most cases, for a longer time period. The lender's counsel would no doubt tell the lending officer that he should not structure the loan in this manner if part of his credit judgment is based on the value of "B's" collateral.

Lending officers are a hardy lot, however, and after thinking a few choice thoughts about whether there would *ever* be any loans made if all lending officers were attorneys, our hypothetical hero will try again. Why not, he may say, pursue option 2: Lend the money to "B" directly, have the funds upstreamed to "A," and thereby permit "A" to acquire the stock of "C"? Why not indeed?

Whether the transfer of dollars from "B" to "A" is booked as a dividend or as creation of inter-company debt, it should be analyzed as if it were a dividend for the purpose of determining the validity of the transfer. Since the amount upstreamed would exceed the amount of "B's" retained earnings, the first question is whether the applicable state law would permit a company to pay a dividend out of its capital accounts. In most states, such a "dividend" would be improper, and a lender facilitating such a payment would not be permitted to benefit by it: That is, he would be denied "B's" collateral.

Even if, under applicable state law, such a dividend could be paid, the question would still exist as to whether the transfer would be effective in the event of the subsequent bankruptcy of "B." As with the first approach, these are the issues: Was there adequacy of consideration, did the transfer leave "B" with an "unreasonably small capital," and did "B's" bankruptcy take place within the proscribed period set forth in the Bankruptcy Act or the applicable state Statute of Frauds? Again, our lending officer would be denied.

A structure defensible against Section 67d

Now, somewhat bloodied and bowed, our persistent lending officer must seek another structure. What if, instead of lending the money to Company "A," collateralized by "B's" guarantee, or lending the money to Company "B" and upstreaming it to "A," the lender lent money to Company "B" and "B" acquired the stock of "C"? In this situation, there would be no upstreaming of dollars, and "B" would be receiving adequate consideration, assuming the acquisition of "C's" stock is an arms-length, fair value transaction. An analysis of the financial statement immediately after the transaction would indicate a $500,000 increase in "B's" assets (representing the investment) and a $500,000 increase in "B's" liabilities (representing the loan). Thus, even if "B" went bankrupt, the lender should be able to successfully defend against a Section 67d attack. If the lending officer felt it was useful, "A," as "B's" parent, could guarantee the obligation; the parent's guarantee of the obligation of its subsidiary is perfectly valid.

As this case indicates, the validity of a lender's lien on collateral can stand or fall, even with superficially identical economics, based on different loan structures. Let us see how this type of reasoning was applied in the case we presented at the beginning of this article.

Solution to more complicated case: separate loans to each of the subsidiaries

The banks recognized that they probably could not get a lien on the subsidiaries' collateral to cover their existing $33 million line on a basis that could withstand a Section 67d argument. Recognizing that the value of their collateral—the stock in the subsidiaries—was a function of the subsidiaries' continued viability and not wanting their client to go into bankruptcy, they realized that the consolidated operation had to have the opportunity to borrow the needed additional $18 million. Because of the marginal nature of the operation, they did not want to supply the $18 million, even on a secured basis.

What happened is that a new group of lenders was allowed to provide the funding. Loans were made to various subsidiaries that had both sufficient collateral and sufficient retained earnings to permit a part of the loan to be upstreamed. The arrangement was not structured as a joint-and-several obligation of all the subsidiaries but as separate loans to each of the subsidiaries.

This structure was dictated by an unrelated previous case: a secured lender's joint-and-several lien had been attacked on the basis that if the loan proceeds were in fact used for the parent's benefit, there was no adequate consideration passing to the joint obligor-subsidiary, thus leaving the pledge of its collateral subject to attack under Section 67d. Cross-corporate guarantees were not sought where the issuance of such a guarantee would have rendered the subsidiary technically insolvent, since the creation of such an insolvency could present a trustee in bankruptcy with an additional basis for attack under Section 67d of the Bankruptcy Act.

Of the $18 million loan, $14 million was upstreamed to the parent to cover its commercial paper obligation and the balance was upstreamed and, in turn, downstreamed to some of the subsidiaries for working capital. Within a period of three years after the making of the loans, the secured debt had been repaid in full, and the bank loans, which by then had been paid down to under $10 million as a result of the sale of certain unprofitable operations, were refinanced. It was a happy story for all concerned.

Conclusion

The lesson is fairly clear. Because of the increasing complexity of multi-corporate organizations, the structuring of a secured loan, in a large number of cases, involves legal issues as well as credit issues. A commercial lending officer will be more effective if he can structure a loan in a manner that minimizes both the legal and credit risks rather than in a manner that relates only to the credit side of a problem. When all is said and done, a lender needs to look to his collateral only when the borrower's business is no longer economically viable. And at that time, a lender must know that he is legally entitled to the collateral that was the basis for his credit decision. □

Project Financing—Guidelines for the Commercial Banker

by Grover R. Castle

"**P**ROJECT FINANCING" OR "PROJECT LOANS" have become increasingly popular in recent years, and commercial banks are being asked to consider more and more of such financing. However, the analysis of this type of loan is quite different from the analysis of a loan to a financially sound corporation based on the company's balance sheet. For this reason Chemical Bank did a study of project loans in an attempt to be more sophisticated in our approach to them. As part of this study, we examined 29 project financings for which information was available. In this article I shall describe project loans and set forth the guidelines we developed, as an aid to credit officers who might have occasion to analyze this type of financing.

Definition of "project financing" or "project loan"

The terms "project financing" and "project loan" commonly describe the various methods that banks and institutional lenders use to finance the construction of new projects on a basis whereby payout is anticipated from the revenue stream generated by the project. A project financing often involves a loan to a new entity formed specifically to own the project.

242

The analysis of a project loan proposal is quite different from the analysis of other term-loan proposals since it involves a credit decision based on the review of a projection or forecast rather than of historical earnings and/or it involves the reliance on contractual obligations of third parties.

Lenders are asked to assume the added risks associated with project loans because:

1. Project financing may permit a company to obtain additional leverage. It is possible for companies to arrange financing on a project basis that could not be arranged as a direct borrowing. For example, a company may not be permitted to borrow more money directly, due to a limitation in a bond indenture. However, a project financing can sometimes be negotiated on a basis not prohibited by the indenture.

2. Often the sponsors of, or the stockholders in, the project are seeking an off-balance-sheet financing. For example, 11 of the 29 projects in our study were arranged on an off-balance-sheet basis and one showed on the balance sheet as a deferred income item. An off-balance-sheet financing, for the purpose of this article, is a financing which does not show as a direct liability on the balance sheet of the sponsors of or stockholders in a project.

3. Projects are often located in a foreign country. The financing is arranged so that the lenders assume the political risk on the loan because many companies rightly believe that this arrangment affords a degree of insulation from political risk not otherwise obtainable.

4. Many projects are jointly owned by several sponsors. This form of financing lends itself well to a situation where a new entity is formed to own a project and do the borrowing.

Project loans can be used to finance a variety of activities including development of iron-ore deposits and associated pelletizing plants; development of coal reserves; construction of pipelines, alumina plants, fertilizer plants and refineries; etc. The specific areas of analysis can be quite different, depending upon the type of project being financed.

It is important, therefore, to classify the proposal according to the type of project, and also by the nature of the financing—nonrecourse financing, financing covered by a guarantee of completion and financing supported by an undertaking lasting for the life of the financing. I will discuss each of these types in more detail later, but first, I should like to make some general comments about the risks involved in new projects.

The project risk

Experience indicates that there is a high probability that any new project will experience some form of trouble. For example, of the 29 projects in the study, only 17 can be evaluated from a performance standpoint. The other 12 either have not matured to the point where they can be evaluated or information on performance is insufficient. Of the 17 that could be evaluated, 14 (82%) have run into some form of trouble. Analysis showed, the most frequent types of problems encountered were:

• *Cost overruns*—This proved to be the most common difficulty associated with new projects and, in my opinion, the greatest risk. Of the 17 projects in my sample, 12 (71%) experienced cost overruns. These overruns ranged from 300% to 5% of original cost; 8 projects (47%) had overruns of more than 20%. I believe that the problem is actually worse than these statistics indicate because the projects in the sample are all mature and were completed before the current inflation and materials shortages. These factors have aggravated and will continue to aggravate the cost-overrun problem.

• *Completion delays*—Another problem probably as common as cost overruns is inability to complete a project within the time span originally anticipated. Of the 17 projects evaluated, 10 (59%) experienced completion delays. The delays ranged from as long as 20 months (ignoring an extreme case where one project was abandoned) to as short a time as a month, and 5 projects (29%) were delayed for 6 months or longer. The average construction period in the projects that were delayed was about 33 months.

• *Actual annual cash flows not equal to original projections*—Of the 17 mature projects 6 (35%) did not generate the cash flow originally projected. Reasons for the variances included interference by a foreign government, underestimation of operating costs, low productivity of foreign labor, miscalculation of the characteristics of an ore reserve, more frequent equipment replacements than originally projected, and changes in parities of currencies. (A foreign project with sales contracts in U.S. dollars will suffer if there is a dollar devaluation.)

• *Market problems*—A project may be initiated to meet a legitimate demand for a particular product in short supply but, by the time completion occurs, the shortage has been overcome by competing projects. As a result, the selling price of the product drops below what was originally projected. This proved to be a problem in one project of the sample.

• *Reserve miscalculations*—Obviously if the project involves development of a mineral deposit and if the payback is dependent solely upon minerals in the ground, then reserve evaluation is critical. A miscalculation of the reserves became a problem in one project.

• *Political risk*—Overseas projects involve added risks because foreign governments may take action that will affect the projects. In addition to the usual political risks such as expropriation, war and inconvertibility, a number of more subtle actions may also cause trouble. Some of these are:

—Increased taxes or royalties.

—Requiring equipment to be purchased within the host country.

—Imposition of import duties on raw materials needed for the project.

—Delays in completion caused by the time needed to obtain import licenses or required parts.

One project in my sample experienced foreign government interference.

• *Project inefficiency*—Obviously the most extreme case of inefficiency is one in which the process does not work at all, and I know of only one such situation. However, an inefficient process can have a serious effect on overall economics, and can also adversely affect repayment of a loan dependent, for example, on ore reserves. In such a case, a larger than anticipated percentage of ore could be used up because of refining inefficiencies.

Of the 17 matured projects in the study, 9 (53%) had what I would describe as severe trouble (2 ended in bankruptcy and 6 others did not generate enough cash flow during some period of the financing to cover payments of principal). This, I believe, is a high incidence of trouble.

Despite the dismal picture that I have just described, in only one of the 17 projects did the lenders take a loss, and then they lost money only after the project sponsor went bankrupt.

The lenders fared well in spite of the statistics because they were able to shift many, if not all, the risks to others. If all the risk is not going to be shifted, then it is important to analyze carefully every potential area of weakness in any new project to be sure that you are covered when and if trouble occurs. For this reason, I believe that the analysis of a project loan requires a high degree of sophistication in more than one area and is best accomplished by a team effort. For example, a project involving the development of a mineral reserve in a foreign country should require:

1. A project financing specialist to negotiate the financial terms and help structure the deal.

2. A qualified engineer to appraise the mineral reserve.

3. An international specialist to analyze country risk.

The three types of project financing

Nonrecourse project financings

In this case the lenders can look only to the project for a payout since there are no backup undertakings from the stockholders. This type of financing is quite rare because of the high degree of risk involved, and in fact, I could only find three cases in the study that would properly fall into this category. This method of financing should probably be confined to projects where no new technology is involved or where special circumstances (such as a high percentage of equity) reduce the risk.

The analysis of any nonrecourse project financing should consider the following points:

1. Equity—Probably the first and most important question in any nonrecourse project financing is the amount of equity that should be required. There is no established rule of thumb as to the precise equity required since it should vary with the nature of the risk. However, I wish to emphasize that a large equity investment is of vital importance, although it may gradually become less important as the undertakings from the stockholders become stronger.

The average equity in the three nonrecourse project financings in my sample was 59% (computed as a percentage of original estimated cost) and ranged from a high of 93% to a low of 35%. In the project with a 93% equity, outside collateral was contributed to the project to support the financing and the 93% was computed by assigning a value to this collateral.

Those projects in the study that were supported by a guarantee of completion had an average equity of 35%, with a range from 67% to 18%. The projects supported by an undertaking lasting for the life of the financing had an average equity of 27%, with a range from a 67% to 2½%.

While the amount of equity is determined primarily by the type of financing and the type of project, other factors also enter into its calculation. These factors include the financial strength of the stockholders, the coverage "for the life of the reserves" (discussed later), the type of geological formation, the geological characteristics of the minerals, etc.

2. Feasibility study and economic projection—A feasibility study and economic projection should always be required if for no other reason than to force the sponsors to think through all the problems involved. The feasibility study should confirm that the project can be completed to meet technical specifications at the estimated cost. The economic projection should forecast the amount of production, sales, operating costs and earnings that will be generated over the life of the project.

It is preferable that both the feasibility study and the economic projection be prepared by a well recognized and independent engineering firm, but it is not always possible to insist on this. If an independent study is not available, I usually attempt to verify the figures to the extent that it is possible. This might be done by checkings or by comparisons with other similar projects. The analysis of the project should include a computation of coverage on an annual basis.

Annual coverage measures the ability of the project to cover the required payments in each year. This coverage is computed by dividing cash flow in each year by the amount of required debt service in that year. It is also advisable to do an *average coverage of the debt service* during the payout of the loan to get an idea of how the coverage looks for the entire term. This average can be arrived at by simply averaging all the annual coverages.

Consideration should be given as to whether the cost figures and market assumptions used in the forecast are reasonable. A review of historical as well as future markets might be appropriate to determine whether to revise the forecast using a lower price per unit and/or arbitrarily assuming increases in costs. Furthermore, if the project is located in a foreign country it might be appropriate to see what would happen to the coverages if the host country increased taxes or if there were a devaluation of either the dollar or the local currency.

It might also be useful to know what the *breakeven level* is on a project. The average coverage during the payout of the financings in the study ranged from 1.10× to 4.77×. I do not like to see a coverage of less than 1.50× because, as proved to be true of the projects analyzed in the study, there is too great a chance that maturities will need to be extended.

3. Reserve analysis—With projects involving the development of a mineral reserve or the construction of a facility such as a pipeline dependent on mineral reserves, it is customary to require verification of the reserves to be developed or to be dedicated to the pipeline by an independent technical expert. The only exception to this rule would be if the documents include an undertaking by financially responsible third parties to indemnify the lenders if the reserves are not as extensive as originally estimated.

Our bank has the technical staff and is equipped to "analyze the reserve risk" (i.e., the risk that the oil or other mineral is not as extensive as orginally estimated), without requiring an outside independent study, except in large projects which would require a large engineering department to do the study. However, we prefer to simply verify an independent study. Such a verification involves starting with an independent reserve report and reviewing the calculations that have been made and the methods used by the outside consultant. Verification of reserves is important in order to be certain that, by our standards, there is a coverage for the payout on the financing during the life of the reserves.

The life of the reserve coverage is different from the annual coverage and average coverage discussed earlier. Chemical Bank's minimum criterion is that our analysis must indicate that, at the time the loan is projected to pay out, at least half the reserves and at least one half the future net revenue are still remaining.

Let's take an example of a mineral deposit with 45 million tons of ore reserves and a project financing projected to pay out in its eighth year. The projection indicates that 17,350,000 tons of ore will be consumed during the first eight years, which amounts to 39% of the total 45 million tons. Furthermore, the projections indicate that a total of $343,990,000 of future net revenue (cash flow) will be earned during the life of the reserves and only $133,568,000 (39%) of the total future net revenue will be used during the first eight years. This project fits within our standards because more than 50% (61%, in this case) of the reserves and future net revenue are remaining at payout. This coverage for the life of the reserves is critical because all oil and gas or mining proposals involve wasting assets that, once depleted, are gone forever. Thereafter the project is no longer viable after the reserves are used up.

"Proved producing" is an important consideration in mineral projects. We are reluctant to make loans against mineral properties except in cases where the reserves are thus classified. Obviously a rigid policy in this regard would not permit financing the development of any new mineral reserves without a guarantee or some other third-party backup. We commonly relax this rule in the case of hard-mineral projects provided we receive a guarantee of completion (which will be discussed on page 25) and provided further that such reserves, though nonproducing, are classified as proved.

We feel that it is acceptable to loan against proved nonproducing hard-mineral reserves on this basis because it is relatively easy to determine with a high degree of accuracy the extent and composition of an ore body. The more difficult part of a hard-mineral project lies in producing a concentrate or refined product that meets design specifications as to quality and quantity, and producing the concentrate within estimated cost limits.

Proved nonproducing petroleum reserves in a few cases have been financed without a guarantee or other backup, but each of these exceptions has been reviewed very carefully. I am reluctant to take the development risk in a project loan based on potential oil or gas reserves because it is much harder to define the true extent of petroleum reserves than it is of hard minerals. On the other hand, the products produced can be sold more easily and with almost no processing, and normally producing costs are a less significant part of sales.

To summarize: when a project loan involves taking the so-called "reserve risk," I would not suggest a nonrecourse project financing unless the reserves are classified as proved producing. This effectively means that such financing is not really possible in a situation where the proceeds of the financing would be used for development of the properties. If the financing is backed by a guarantee of completion and the reserves are classified as proved nonproducing, it is not unusual for the lenders to take the reserve risk in a project loan if a hard-mineral reserve is being developed. It is possible—but more difficult—to arrange such a financing if the mineral is oil and gas.

Classification of a mineral deposit as proved requires that a well or a number of wells must have been drilled to define an oil and gas property, or core holes trenches or shafts, etc. in the case of a hard-mineral deposit. A banker not technically trained and/or without experience should not attempt to classify a mineral deposit, but should rely on experts. The type and nature of the mineral deposit dictate the extent of exploration necessary to define the mineral deposit.

To classify oil and gas accumulations as proved nonproducing requires the drilling of enough test wells to verify the magnitude of the reserves and that quantifiable reserves can be recovered. Typically, this would include an accumulation in a "thick pay section" with a rather uncomplicated trapping mechanism (i.e., a consistent indication of oil or gas without faulting). In the case of hard minerals, there should be core holes enough, not only to outline a hard-mineral deposit, but also to give good data as to the analysis of the ore. The number of core holes obviously depends upon the geology and can vary from as much as 600-foot centers to a 5-meter grid.

4. Market—The lenders must be satisfied through either market studies or long-term sales contracts that a market is available for the project output. In all the nonrecourse financings in the study the lenders were protected by a dedication of a substantial percentage of the output under minimum-price sales contracts with an acceptable party, under terms running until well after the final payout.

Nonrecourse financing analyses should include a careful review of the terms of the contract and particular attention should be paid to the following features:

—*Obligor:* How strong is the purchaser?
—*Term:* Does it extend beyond payout?
—*Quantity:* What percent of design capacity is covered by the contract? Are the projections based on contract quantities?
—*Quality:* What quality requirements are in the contract?
—*Force majeure* provisions.

—*Default provisions:* Under what conditions can the buyer refuse to take under the contract?

—*Price:* The sales price should compare favorably with the price used in the economic projections. Also it is preferable to have price escalation to cover increases in operating costs.

5. Political or country risk—If the project is located outside the United States and if the financing is structured so that the lenders assume the political risk (i.e., any undertakings from the stockholders or others do not indemnify the lenders against war, expropriation, inconvertibility, changes in taxes, etc.), the analysis of the proposal takes on a whole new dimension. A decision has to be made as to whether the lender wishes to assume this political risk, and this would presumably involve a country study by the territorial officer in the international division of the bank.

Assuming that a bank is willing to take the political risk in the foreign country where the project is to be located and further that the financing is structured in such a way that the lenders take the political risk, then the following steps ought to be taken:

- Demand a copy of the concession and review it looking for provisions relating to:
  —*Term:* If the concession runs for only 15 years, then the computation of the coverage for the life of the reserves should include only reserves projected to be produced during the first 15 years.
  —*Taxes* and/or *royalties* that need to be paid to the host country.
  —Basis for *cancellation* or *default*.
  —Required development *schedule*.
  —Host-country *participation* in ownership.
  —Host-country right to take *output*.
  —Transfer out of the host country of *proceeds* of sales of output from the project.

- Require a letter from the government of the host country addressed to the bank and stating:
  1. That there shall be no change in the provisions of the concession (including those relating to taxes) during the payout of the financing.
  2. That the project shall be given its fair share of goods and services within the host country.
  3. That the host country is aware of the terms of the financing and that the host country shall not take any action that will have an adverse effect on the payout of the loan.

Obviously, the requirements in any such letter—in fact the actual requirement of such a letter—basically depend upon the confidence that the lender has in the host country. In eight of the projects used in the study, the lenders took the political risk and in only two of those did the lenders obtain such a letter. In one case, the letter took the form of a virtual guarantee of payment by the host government. Five of the projects were in countries considered politically stable. In one case no letter was required because nationals from the host country owned a fairly large equity interest in the project.

- Require a letter from the central bank of the host country guaranteeing the transfer out of that country of proceeds of sale in convertible currencies in amounts needed to cover the payments on the project's debts. This should be a standard and routine requirement in some form in connection with any project financing in which the lenders are taking the political risk.

6. Environmental considerations and governmental clearance—The lenders must be satisfied that all governmental approvals have been obtained and that there is no risk or only minimal risk of environmental suits. Environmental actions can delay or halt construction of new projects.

For example, through November 1972, Con Edison had spent over $21 million on its Storm King project for a pumped-storage hydroelectric plant at Cornwall, N.Y., and the project has been held up since 1963 by environmental suits. In May 1973, Con Edison estimated that the cost of the project has been increased by $292 million as a direct result of this delay. Another well publicized example is the TAPS pipeline from the North Slope of Alaska to Valdez. This involved a five-year fight over environmental issues before Congress authorized construction.

Obviously a lender would not wish to advance funds on a nonrecourse basis before all clearances have been obtained. An analysis of the environmental issues should include the following:

- Determination of the aspects of the project requiring government clearances, such as air emission, emission into streams or water bodies, diversion of streams, disposition of waste or noise emission.
- Determination of the particular governmental body that has jurisdiction over each aspect of the project—state, Federal or local.
- Examination of the procedural aspects of the clearance.
  —*Nature of approval:* The Environmental Protection Administration

and many states often require filing for approval a written impact statement (prepared either by the sponsors or by the governmental authority) on new projects. Other agencies may require only oral hearings or a petition.

—*Timing of approval:* Some authorities require approval in stages with an initial approval based on the plans, followed by intermediate approvals based on the implementation of these plans and a final approval based on actual operation of the project.

- Study of new legislation. Be alert to current and impending legislation trends. The environmental aspect is a new and popular problem with new legislation being enacted every day.

7. Supply contracts—The lenders should be satisifed that all feedstock and power required by the plant or project are available at costs which do not exceed those in the economic projections. It is preferable that both feedstock and power be covered by long-term fixed-price contracts, and these should be analyzed just like a sales contract.

8. Builder—The builder of the project is always important and particularly so when no guarantee of completion is available. The analyst will wish to make a thorough check of the builder's reputation and performance. Proper analysis of a nonrecourse project financing should also include a careful review of the construction contract to examine such provisions as:

—Is it a fixed price?
—Is there a requirement that the project be completed prior to a fixed date?
—Are there penalties for delay?

9. Title—Title is a particularly important consideration in projects involving reserves of oil, gas and minerals or the construction of a pipeline and should be considered in connection with any new project. The lenders should be satisfied that the project has "good and marketable" title to the land on which the project is to be located and the mineral reserve to be mined. The most common way to satisfy this requirement is with a title warranty from a financially responsible party, but in a nonrecourse financing this might be accomplished by title opinions from an independent law firm. It is also possible to obtain title insurance from a title insurance company.

10. Insurance—During those periods when the lenders are not protected by undertakings, the project should be protected by insurance with a loss-payable clause in favor of the lenders. Some obvious risks to be considered are: builders' risk, property damage, comprehensive general liability, workmen's compensation and employers' liability, automobile liability, boiler and machinery coverage and, where appropriate, excess (umbrella) coverage. This is a very specialized field and it is best to seek technical advice from qualified specialists.

11. Operator—Careful consideration should be given to the operator's financial strength as well as demonstrated ability to operate the project. A review of the operating agreement is an integral part of the analysis of a project financing.

Project financing covered by a guarantee of completion

Many of the more common risks can be eliminated from a project financing if the lenders negotiate a guarantee of completion whereby the project stockholders agree to complete the project. After completion, the lenders are essentially on their own, relying only on sales contracts, supply contracts and the project itself.

Because the lenders are on their own after completion, all eleven points discussed above under nonrecourse project financing are also pertinent here, except that title can usually be covered by a warranty rather than title opinions or title insurance.

The form of the guarantee of completion is very important. Ideally it should cover the following elements:

1. Completion date and overrun costs—The obligation of the guarantor to complete by a certain date and to cover all overrun costs in the form of equity should be stated. Of the 11 projects in the study where financing was covered by a guarantee of completion, 6 (55%) required completion by a certain date usually somewhat later than the projected completion, and 8 (73%) specifically obligated the guarantors to cover all overruns with equity.

Occasionally the completion undertaking will only be a simple covenant by the stockholder to complete without a date. However, in such a case if the project is delayed due to governmental action or an environmental suit and the stockholders decide to fight these actions in the courts, the lenders would probably be forced to stand by during this period with no recourse to the guarantors.

2. Definition of completion—Completion should be defined as the time when the project shall have operated for a *period* (to be negotiated) according to the specifications in the feasibility study and during that period have produced a specified *quantity* of output which meets a specified *quality* test at a *cost* no greater than indicated in the economic projections.

If a refining process is involved, the guarantee might also require a certain degree of efficiency. For example, the definition of completion of a plant might require that it operate for 90 consecutive days and during that period produce 100,000 barrels a day (90% of design capacity) of product which meets a predetermined specification (usually the specifications in a sales contract) with an operating cost per barrel of no more than 50¢ per barrel. One completion guarantee that I am familiar with contained the points mentioned above plus a requirement that, during the initial consecutive three-month period of operation, the project earn 80% of the amount of cash flow set forth in the economic projections.

However, only 6 (55%) of the 11 projects in the study sample contain any operating test at all and only 2 (18%) contained a cash-flow test in the definition of completion.

The definition of completion sometimes contains a requirement that the project have a minimum amount of working capital on the date of completion. Two (18%) of the 11 study projects contained such a provision.

3. Maturities prior to completion—Of the 11 completion guarantees in the study, 5 (45%) contain a continuing obligation of the guarantors to cover any maturities on the loan prior to defined completion; one provides the guarantors with an option of purchasing the notes. In the absence of this type of provision, the lenders could be forced to sue stockholders for damages and, to prove damages, the lenders might be required to go through a foreclosure proceeding to establish the amount of their loss.

Three of the five undertakings mentioned contain an obligation of the stockholders to pay off the loan if the project is not completed prior to a certain date well beyond the expected completion date.

4. Acceleration provisions—If the loan accelerates prior to completion, it is preferable to require that the obligation to pay under the completion guarantee also accelerates. However, this is difficult to negotiate; in fact, only 3 (27%) of the 11 guarantees among the study projects contain such a provision. In many situations the obligation to meet the maturities is confined to the original maturities, regardless of acceleration against the borrower.

5. Bankruptcy or default—In the event the obligor under the completion guarantee goes into bankruptcy or defaults under another agreement, it is preferable to have acceleration of the obligation under the completion guarantee regardless of the status of the project. This feature is difficult to obtain with large triple A guarantors, and only 2 (18%) of the 11 guarantees in the sample contain such a feature.

6. Financial covenants—It is possible to include financial covenants restricting the guarantors in the completion guarantee. This is not a common feature and was included in only one of the completion guarantees in the study.

7. Environmental clearances—The definition of completion can also require that all environmental clearances have been obtained before completion occurs. This is most important in domestic projects, and more important with some projects than with others. Only 2 (18%) of the 11 guarantees in the study contained such a provision.

8. Prohibition of sale of interest—The completion guarantee can also require that the guarantors will not sell their interest in the project. This is a fairly common requirement. Of the guarantees contained reviewed 8 (73%) included such a provision, and one of the three exceptions provided for a default in the loan agreement (against the borrower) if the stock was no longer owned by the sponsors.

9. Title warranty—Whenever appropriate, the completion guarantee can also contain a warranty of title to the reserves of oil, gas or minerals being developed.

As you can see from this discussion all completion undertakings are different. The final product is the result of a variety of factors such as the complexity of the project, the amount of lender's confidence in the sponsors, the type of project and how well the lenders negotiate the terms of the proposal.

Project financing supported by an undertaking for the life of the financing

It is possible to shift all or substantially all the risk to the sponsors of the project through various types of undertakings which go far beyond the obligation to complete. In these cases, it is still contemplated that the financing will pay out from the project's cash flow, but, if the cash flow doesn't cover debt service, the lenders have recourse against the sponsors. Most of these undertakings make unnecessary the eleven points discussed under nonrecourse project financing. Some forms of these undertakings are :

• *Minimum working capital undertaking or working capital maintenance agreement*—Under this type of arrangement, the sponsors agree to maintain at all times a minimum working capital in the borrower to assure the lenders that the borrower shall have sufficient funds to meet maturities on financing. If working capital as defined falls below a specified level, the agreement requires stockholders to make subordinated advances (usually on a pro rata basis) in amounts sufficient to increase working capital to the required level. This type of undertaking was used in three projects in the sample studied. In two of them the financings were off balance sheet, and the third has not been taken down as yet.

• *Cost company arrangement*—Under a cost company arrangement, the stockholders are unconditionally obligated under an operating agreement assigned to the lenders to provide the cost company with their pro rata share of all amounts needed to pay operating costs for the project plus principal and interest on the project's borrowings as they become due. Funds are furnished by the stockholders in proportion to their stock ownership. The arrangement is usually off balance sheet for the stockholder.

This arrangement is common in connection with iron-ore projects. In a typical case, each stockholder received from the project a pro rata share of the ore produced. The cost company does not sell any ore and has no net income, and each stockholder includes in income statements a pro rata share of the cost company's production and operating expenses.

• *Throughput arrangement*—Pipeline projects are often supported by throughput agreements assigning amounts due the pipeline. Each stockholder is severally obligated to ship or cause to be shipped through the pipeline, in proportion to stock ownership, liquid hydrocarbons in a total amount which will provide sufficient cash to pay all the pipeline's expenses and liabilities as they come due.

If for any reason, including failure to complete the line and cessation of operation, the pipeline has insufficient cash to pay all expenses and liabilities, the stockholders shall contribute on a several basis an amount sufficient to augment such cash deficiency to meet all liabilities and expenses.

So long as there is sufficient cash from other shippers to pay all expenses and liabilities, no stockholder will be obligated to ship its full requirement as described above. Throughput-agreement financing is usually off balance sheet.

• *Tolling contracts*—Alumina and other plants often obtain financings based on the assignment of a tolling contract whereby the participants in the projects are unconditionally obligated to pay their pro rata share of amounts needed to meet the principal and interest on financing. A tolling contract is very similar to the so-called "take or pay contract" whereby the purchaser is obligated to pay for purchases regardless of whether the seller is able to deliver or not. The tolling contract is usually off balance sheet.

General comments on structuring of project financings

Interest rates

Usually lenders are able to demand a higher interest rate on project financings than on direct loans made to the sponsors. A nonrecourse project financing would be expected to carry a higher rate than a financing backed by a guarantee of completion. A financing backed by an undertaking for the life of the financing would carry the lowest rate of the three types of loans. A comparison of the rates charged in the projects studied bears this out, as shown below:

Type of Project	Average Rate*
Domestic Dollar Financings	
Nonrecourse	16.67%
Covered by Guaranty of Completion	15.79%
Covered by Continuing Undertaking	15.53%
Eurodollar Financings	
Nonrecourse	None
Covered by Guaranty of Completion	12.55%
Covered by Continuing Undertaking	12.25%

*All rates computed using the following assumptions:
1. Prime assumed to be 12% on the date the loans were negotiated for the life of loan on domestic dollar financings.
2. London Interbank rate assumed to be 11% on the date the loans were negotiated for all Eurodollar financings.
3. All rates are computed on a no-balance basis.
4. All computations are calculated without provision for reserve requirement.
5. All fixed-rate financings are related to prime on the date the loan was negotiated. The average rate is computed by using the same absolute spread over a 12% prime as the fixed rate was over prime on the date the loan was negotiated.

Maturity

It is important that the maturity schedule be set up so that it fits within projected earnings. For example, in some projects the projected cash flow will not support equal payments over the term of the loan, and, therefore, a balloon payment is sometimes set at the final maturity, or the payments might start out low percentage-wise and gradually increase in later years. When there is a balloon payment or when the later maturities are weighted more heavily than early payments, it is customary to provide for an earnings recapture clause (sometimes called a mandatory prepayment provision) whereby a percentage of cash flow exceeding a certain level is applied against the loan in the inverse order of maturity to reduce the balloon payment. Five of the projects in the sample had such clauses.

Often a flexible maturity schedule provides that payments commence three months after completion, whenever that occurs, with a requirement that these maturities start no later than a certain date regardless of the date of completion.

With all loans where the lenders take the reserve risk, it is preferable that the financing pay out through a dedication of a percentage of gross revenue with a minimum payment schedule rather than through fixed maturities. For example, where total future net revenue is approximately 57% of total ore value (gross revenue or sales) we would attempt to get a dedication of 55% of gross revenue (ore value) commencing with completion of the project. This dedicated revenue would be applied against the financing first to interest and then to principal on a monthly or quarterly basis.

This type of payout preserves the coverage in the life of the reserve test (see page 20), even if the oil, gas or other mineral is extracted faster than originally projected. If the mineral is extracted faster than originally expected and the financing pays out with equal quarterly maturities, then obviously fewer reserves would remain at final maturity than anticipated.

It is also possible to provide that if the dedicated percentage does not pay down the loan in accordance with a minimum schedule, then the percentage dedicated increases to the extent necessary to meet that schedule.

Covenants

Generally speaking, the loan agreement confines the borrower's activities to the operation of the project, which means that a full set of financial covenants are enforced against the borrower.

Events of default

In addition to the usual events of default relating to the borrower, it is customary to have an event of default if:

—The project is not completed by a certain date.
—There is a default under a supply or sales contract or other key contracts such as tolling contracts or throughput agreements.
—If any of the stockholders become bankrupt, breach a loan agreement or dispose of their stock in the project. This is appropriate where there is an undertaking that runs for the life of the loan. It is also appropriate prior to completion where there is a guarantee of completion. It is often difficult to negotiate this provision if the project is jointly owned by several major companies, and it is sometimes acceptable to have acceleration of only a defaulting stockholder's pro rata share of the loan.

While the above types of default are customary, there are cases where the only defaults relate to the borrower and there is no default if the plant is not completed by a certain date.

Collateral

The collateral usually includes an assignment of any supply contract, sales contract and other key contracts such as tolling contracts or throughput agreements, and often also includes a mortgage on the project plus a pledge of the stock of the borrower. Furthermore, it is often appropriate for the lenders to be named as beneficiary under any insurance coverage on the project. ☐

Loan Profitability—
A Method to the Madness?

by Thomas M. Flynn

The underlying concept of loan pricing and profitability is the achievement of a return on the loan portfolio that is in line with management's planned objectives. Thomas Flynn describes a basic, easy-to-follow method of profitability analysis that may contribute as much to this effort as other, more complicated systems now in use.

Probably one of the most interesting and perhaps most confusing topics in banking today is the concept of loan profitability analysis. In recent months, many articles relating to the subject have appeared in banking and financial publications. Unfortunately, there is little uniformity among the theories proposed. All seem to be tailored to their own specific goals. As a result, the banker in the loan administration capacity at a medium size regional bank sits quite perplexed with as many loan pricing and profitability theories as he has loans. He is faced with the insurmountable task of choosing the best for his particular circumstances.

As regional bankers know, responsibility for loan pricing and account profitability is but one of several important hats the loan administrator wears. Thus, he faces quite a dilemma. He can "stop the clock," pick the best parts of all available theories, and face the long and arduous job of developing his own system. Or he can continue on the "blind shooting" path in loan pricing and profitability. By the way, the latter cannot be all that bad since banks have spent decades doing just that, with no real detriment to profits.

259

The intent of this article is *not* to confuse the loan administrator with further involved theories on profitability. Instead, the purpose is to present a basic, simple format on loan profitability which I feel has at least as much validity as systems presently on the scene.

Identifying the concept problems

A brief presentation of the concept problems is appropriate in setting the scene. These are presented in what I feel to be their order of importance.

A common standard.   As already explained, the numerous approaches and theories presently available serve to confuse the potential user and, at best, create conflicting standards in loan profitability and pricing. This situation casts a slight shade of embarrassing confusion to the regional banking industry. You will catch a glimpse of the problem and its implications if you will consider for a moment the commercial borrower discussing rates and pricing with two or three competing banks in a particular market area, all of which ascribe to a different theory.

The common denominator.   This is the standard on which one bases the net profit of a loan transaction. Should it be based on return on capital, investable funds, pool funds, or gross funds provided?

All, of course, create a very different result as well as answer a very different question, not necessarily about the profit on a loan.

Cost components.   What costs go into pricing a loan? How much "double dutying" of costs is there? Are all related costs captured? These questions are vital to the profitability analysis.

Funds costs.   These costs amount to our inventory of "finished goods." Is the inventory priced on replacement costs? Average time deposit costs? Market-oriented costs? Each of these, and many others, will create very different results.

Setting the proper standard—the intent of the system

What are the objectives in loan profitability? It appears that these can be covered in four basic steps:

(1) Determine, as closely and realistically as possible, the *true profit contribution* of the lending function and, in particular, of each specific loan transaction.

(2) Provide the portfolio managers with a day-to-day tool with which to gauge loan performance, that is, to price their product.

(3) Offer the portfolio manager a *realistic* goal or standard to aspire to in pricing his products.

(4) Assure senior bank management of a return on the loan portfolios in sufficient amounts to create the desired return on bank capital set forth in the "profit plan."

This approach is basic. In essence, loan portfolios are charged with creating a profit level which fits into the overall pre-established plan of the bank, usually based on senior management's desired return on capital employed. In formula, this approach says—

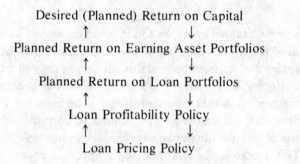

Desired (Planned) Return on Capital

Planned Return on Earning Asset Portfolios

Planned Return on Loan Portfolios

Loan Profitability Policy

Loan Pricing Policy

In normal bank practice, senior bank management, through its profit planning objectives, sets an overall profitability goal. From the senior management level, this goal is usually, and quite logically, based on the desired return on capital employed. To achieve this desired yield, the profit planning area computes the return on various earning asset portfolios necessary to produce the overall goal. It mathematically translates this objective to a percentage return on each specific earning asset portfolio. The loan portfolio manager then is left with his standard challenge—to produce a specific yield on his loan dollars. This, then, can be considered the overall standard concept in loan pricing and profitability: to achieve a return on loan portfolios in line with senior management's planned objectives.

The common denominator

One very real problem in loan profitability today is the use of an irrelevant denominator with which to gauge the loan profit. For example, we see many profitability systems with the overall objective of the profitability report structured to show the loan profit expressed as a percentage return on capital. This basis is normally removed from the loan officer's scope of responsibility and, in some cases, from his interest, since it is traditionally the grounds of senior management planners. Moreover, it results in the essence of product pricing, the yield, being related to a "foreign" base—capital.

Relationship of net yield to dollars loaned

In simple terms, the return on a product is related to the product itself—the dollars loaned out. As any other free enterprise business bases its profit and loss on the selling price of its product (net profit on sales), so should the loan officer base his profit and loss on his product, the loan portfolio. The universal standard of profit and loss reporting holds as true as ever in bank lending. I submit, therefore, that the net yield on a loan must be identified as a percentage of the loaned dollars to have any relevance at all to the profit of the loan function.

It appears to me that net profit on a loan when expressed as a percentage of pool funds used or capital allocated or investable funds provided, creates the proverbial apples and oranges comparison. It serves only to confuse the loan officer, the customer, and perhaps the banking industry in general. Consider for a moment the confusion that would prevail if your main borrowing accounts began reporting their net profits as a percentage of cost of goods sold or gross margin or general and administrative expenses, or even worse, each on a different basis. This I fear is regional banking's apparent course in profitability analysis.

Only one true measure

I certainly do not mean to imply here that computing loan profitability on the various bases mentioned is not informative and perhaps critical to certain banks. Rather, I suggest that these various expressions of loan profitability are intended for supportive ratio analysis and reviews and *not* as the basic standard of determining the profit on a particular product.

The only true standard or measure of the overall results of selling your product (loans) is determined by dividing the net profit, after all related costs, by the total dollar value of the product sold. Only this mathematical computation identifies the clear results of your efforts in "selling" your product.

The profitability report format

A prime guideline often ignored in banking is that banks, as any other business, must price their products uniformly for all potential purchasers. The only variances in the general pricing scheme should be represented by other profit and cost implications incidental to a specific account relationship. Notwithstanding these support service functions, specific loan prices differ only in relation to the three prime ingredients of any loan—balances, term, and risk.

The sample profitability review on page 8 displays a basic, easy to follow profitability analysis. The following is a descriptive commentary on this review in "flow" sequence.

Flow of funds

By now, the universal method of computing net balance contribution of a borrowing account seems to have settled in. The only remaining variances are represented by differences in float fields of the particular bank and their effect on the net collected balance. This format also follows the widely accepted and quite logical theory that a borrower first uses his own net available funds to finance his loans, with the residue being supplied from the bank's "pool" of available funds. Adding credence to this theory is the fact that it probably gives the best treatment to a "compensating" balance relationship. In essence, the balances reduce, dollar for dollar, the funds loaned and, consequently, the cost of borrowing.

The net result of the flow of funds section is, of course, to identify the net product sale, that is, the dollars loaned.

Profit and loss

This section again follows a very simple format. It computes the loan yield for the period under review and the amount, if any, of yield on excess balances (surplus of balances over funds loaned), computed at the average yield of earning assets, since this is where the funds are employed (the "pool" concept).

The other income area provides for an accounting of miscellaneous support income, that is, service charges, loan fees, etc. In our bank's particular system, the income derived from service charges on an account is not identified as a profit item because the total service charge income is treated, in its entirety, as a reduction to cost of funds. Therefore, service charge income is already considered as a cost offset instead of a profit contribution.

Expenses

Cost of funds. Clearly the most critical factor in the analysis is the cost of funds or the "cost of goods sold" in industry terms. The many approaches and short-cuts to this factor presently on the scene certainly serve to confuse the average regional bank loan administrator.

Probably the largest error in judgment which can be committed by the regional banker is to follow the "big brother" concept and use the prime rate factors or average money market rates in pricing his funds. He then, in a word,

_____ Net Creditor

_____ Net Debtor

_____ Nonborrower

Profitability Review

XYZ Corporation

Data — $100,000 revolving credit line — full use
        — Average balance — current six-month period — Ledger $25,000
                                                        Collected $21,000
        — Rate — Base + 1.5%

(A) *Funds Flow*

Average Ledger Balances	$ 25,000
Less: Uncollected	(4,000)
Reserves @ 11.8%	(2,950)
Investable Funds Provided	18,050
Less: Average Loaned Funds	100,000
Net Funds Provided (Used)	$ (81,950)

(B) *Profit and Loss*

Income:

Yield on Loaned Funds @ 9%	$9,000
Yield on Excess Funds Provided @ _____ %	—
Other Income (Net)	—
Total Income	$9,000

Expenses:

Cost of Funds @ 5.85% (81,950)	$4,795
Loan Overhead* @ 1.50% of Loaned Funds	1,500
Total Expenses	$6,295
Net Return	$2,705
Return on Loaned Funds	2.7%
Desired Return	3.0%
Profitability Index	90%

* Commercial Demand Note

prices his quite different product at someone else's costs. To make matters worse, the someone else in this case represents a money center bank whose time/demand mix on deposits varies substantially from the regional banker's! Given the large variances in time/demand mix between money center banks and regional banks in recent years, one can readily see the folly in this approach. For instance, consider a 65%/35% (time/demand mix) regional bank using the same funds cost factors as a 45%/55% money market center bank.

As a side comment, this very real consideration can create chaos for an efficient, well-systematized regional bank which attempts to place a realistic price on its loan portfolio while competitors ascribe to money market center cost and pricing standards. While quite interesting in its repercussions, this involved subject is treated lightly here since it is somewhat removed from our main topic.

For purposes of loan profitability, I can only say that each bank must be the master of its own destiny. It must price its funds to the very best of its ability under the most effective method it can devise. We are fortunate in that our bank operates under a basic profit center cost accounting system which provides us with the true, all-inclusive cost of funds each and every month.

For a bank with less organized cost systems or no system at all, perhaps a fair approximation of cost of funds can be derived by using true cost (interest) of time funds. This cost approximation can be coupled with the very informative and useful statistics of overhead costs for time and demand funds put out by the Federal Reserve in their annual "Functional Cost Analysis" studies. These two components can be combined in certain mathematical considerations to produce a good bench mark for cost of funds. However, it still only approximates your most important cost element.

I would strongly recommend, therefore, that each loan administrator place on his current objectives list the development of an effective profit center cost accounting system. This method, at least through our own experience, produces the closest approximation of true cost of funds.

Loan overhead. This category includes all expenses for originating, carrying, and maintaining a loan on the bank's books. Again, through our profit center cost accounting system, components to compute this factor are readily available. Less sophisticated banks can perform a basic cost accounting study encompassing the cost of loan support functions, lending officers, clerical assistance, and all other costs incidental to the lending function. Use of standard statistics available in the aforementioned Federal Reserve studies can be quite helpful along these lines. At the very least, an approximation of average overhead costs by loan functions is available in these studies and can be utilized in place of any lacking internal data. For simplicity, this expense component is computed and reported as a percentage of dollars loaned.

The "activity costs" category, which seems to appear in the majority of available profitability formats, is missing from the expense area in this format. In my opinion, an effective cost of funds is all-encompassing. That is, the cost of obtaining, maintaining, and servicing deposits is already reflected in its entirety in the cost of funds charge. To penalize the account further for activity charges creates a double charge for the same costs.

As a matter of information, astute businessmen have asked me about this quite obvious double dutying of costs reflected in many banks' profitability reports. Perhaps this practice is a result of the overall confusion in producing profitability reports on nonborrowers as well as borrowers. Our profitability system includes both borrowing and nonborrowing accounts. The format for the latter is slightly different, of course, and is intended to identify particular activity costs to the specific account. This, again, is another topic treated quite lightly here.

Net return.   As explained previously, our net return is expressed as a percentage of dollars loaned—the only real barometer of loan profitability as far as the portfolio manager is concerned. He then compares the overall profitability result to his desired goal, as set by senior management, and makes any adjustments necessary. With the simplicity of the format, a change in the interest rate charged on the loan will create the identical change in the profitability report's net return.

Pricing versus profitability—the conflict

Once a portfolio manager has set profitability standards and chosen a profitability format, he must then determine its relationship to pricing the particular loan. One must not forget that profitability is an *effect:* It depicts the *results* of an interest rate charged and is not intended, nor should it be used by itself, to determine the rate to charge on a loan. A projected profitability review will, of course, be very helpful to the loan officer in computing an acceptable rate, but I do not think it should be the determining factor in quoting interest rates.

What then does one use to quote rates? An effective loan pricing system's most vital ingredient is its cost of funds figure. When this is added to the loan overhead factor, the result is the break-even price on the loan transaction; hence, you have the starting base for loan pricing. The interest rate to be charged on a particular loan is then computed by applying the three basic variables in lending—balances, term, and risk.

It is only logical to state that the return on a loan portfolio is composed of the results of individual pricing techniques on all loans in the portfolio. Some of these have rates significantly higher than the desired yield level due to the risk, balance, and term factors, and some have very nearly break-even yield due to these same factors. To apply a standard profitability percentage to a loan portfolio and subsequently to apply the identical interest rate to each individual loan is, to say the least, ridiculous and is not the intent of a profitability system.

In summary, a profitability system is intended to determine the ultimate effectiveness of a loan pricing policy, not to set the pricing policy—that is another job. □

Commercial Loan Profitability—
Pricing Analysis

by James A. Hoeven and Jerome S. Oldham

MEASUREMENT OF LOAN PROFITABILITY is an area of commercial loan administration which has been given considerable attention in recent years. Many larger banks have already developed a system of measuring the profitability of the corporate-customer borrowing relationship. It is likely, moreover, because of the continuously restrained profit margins on loans, banks of all sizes

At the time this article was written, Mr. Oldham was a graduate student and research assistant at Colorado State University, Fort Collins, Colo.

will become increasingly aware of the need to determine the profitability of customer borrowing relationships. Such an awareness is necessary to ensure the most efficient allocation of banking's most important product.

In order that proper "margins" may be maintained, however, it is of critical necessity that banks also become aware of the need to systematically determine the proper nominal interest rate to be charged. Furthermore, the loan officer has to appreciate the changing market demand for product, i.e., credit, and this change in market demand requires, as it does in any other competitive business, flexibility in pricing technique.

Many articles have been written in the past on loan profitability analysis. The complexities of those analyses and types of considerations given have varied considerably. It is our belief that the formulation of many of these analyses has been overly general and, therefore, not very suitable for a given purpose such as the pricing of loans. For example, a loan profitability analysis that is meant to be integrated into a complex and full-absorption cost accounting system will not be particularly useful as a means for pricing loans. If the purpose is to evaluate and price commercial loans, there is no need to include all income and expense considerations (whether computed on cost or price) that are extraneous to loans, even though they are part of the total customer relationship. On the other hand, an analysis suitable for loan pricing can be compatible with a profit-center accounting concept. The profit center is, of course, the commercial loan department, and the price set on loans, as well as all relevant departmental costs, should be included in the profitability analysis.

Profitability and pricing considered within same analytical framework

Given this compatibility, there is no reason why loan profitability and loan pricing should not be considered within the same analytical framework, a practice that has not been apparent to date. After all, the purpose of analyzing loan profitability is to establish a price that will provide a desired return, not simply to evaluate the relative profitability of loans in the total loan portfolio. Even today, many banks which employ profitability analysis proceed through a laborous task of determining a new loan's potential profitability contribution without making provisions within the analysis for actually pricing the loan. The analytical procedure presented in this article conveniently considers loan profitability and price determination as important products of one analysis.

With these thoughts in mind, the discussion that follows will be directed toward these objectives: (1) to present a method of evaluating the profitability, or yield, of a commercial loan on both a projected and an historical basis; (2) to subsequently establish the appropriate nominal interest rate to assess the loan customer and (3) to consider alternative methods of evaluating loan yield and the pricing of loans under differing market conditions that call for flexibility in the pricing technique of commercial loans

General acceptance criteria, theory, and objectives

For any method of profitability analysis to be acceptable, it must satisfy certain basic criteria or suffer the consequences of misuse or obsolescence. Generally, the following requirements or conditions must be satisfied:

- The method used must be able to analyze a customer's borrowing relationship in terms of the potential profit at the time a new relationship is initiated, as well as be equipped to analyze an existing relationship in terms of the actual profit derived. Within this context, new loans are analyzed and profitability is predicted, while existing loans are analyzed (reviewed) and past profitability is determined. By analyzing a loan both when it is initiated and later, while it is a bank asset, the loan department should be able to ascertain whether the original profit goal is being met. If it is not, a rate change may be necessary. Moreover, by also analyzing the loan after it has been terminated, the loan department will be able to determine the final profitability of the loan and relate this to the rate of profitability that was originally predicted. In this context the analysis serves the purpose of budgetary review and control.

- The results must be expressed in terms which are consistent with management's normal objectives, policies and vocabulary. They must measure profitability in terms of *income* and *yield,* as bank loan officers are accustomed to working with profitability in these types of terms.

- The profitability analysis method must be equitable and, above all, objective. Because the analysis will be used by various loan officers to measure the relative profitability of different customer borrowing relationships, it is important that the method chosen for analysis exclude the possibility of natural bias which may unintentionally influence the derived profitability or price.

- The method of analysis should be straightforward and precise for those who use and rely upon it. It should be easily understood and relatively easy to use. Ideally, the analysis should be able to be completed while the customer is sitting at the loan officer's desk, or possibly during the period of time between an initial and subsequent interview. In this way, it becomes a definite marketing tool, and the customer realizes that a rate is not based upon the loan officer's best guess as to that it should be. The analysis should be no secret to the customer, but rather evidence of having been treated fairly and equitably in rate determination.

• The method of analysis should be adaptable to changing economic conditions without format alteration. It should be a flexible tool which can be used on an ongoing basis.

• Finally, the method of analysis should be adaptable to automation. It should be programmable so that its use can ultimately be expedited to bring about the most efficient decisions possible.

The importance of these criteria will be shown as the methodology and format of the analysis are discussed.

Methodology

The method of loan analysis presented calculates the return on funds employed and compares this yield to a projected (or desired) departmental profit goal, which is also expressed in terms of a percentage yield. This is done to ascertain a loan's relative profit contribution and then to determine the required nominal rate which must be charged to achieve the desired profit contribution.

Throughout the discussion of methodology, it will be beneficial to refer to the Commercial Loan Yield Analysis Worksheets, Exhibits A and B. While these worksheets provide a systematic format by which the objectives of profitability analysis are accomplished, specific headings and subheadings deserve additional explanation and examination.

Sources of funds employed

The first section of loan profitability analysis derives all the sources of funds necessary to support the average outstanding balance of the loan under consideration. Part of these funds is contributed by the borrower through his compensating balances; however, the majority of these funds is normally supplied by the bank's general available "pool of funds."

The *Average Loan Balance* (line 1)*, in the case of a new loan request, represents a realistic estimate of what the loan's average outstanding balance will be from the date of inception to the date of termination. In the case of an existing or terminated loan that is currently undergoing review, this balance represents the loan's actual average balance over the period of time under consideration.

The *Total Deposit Contribution* (line 5) provided by the borrower is determined in order to give proper credit for all compensating balances. Note that the bank's reserve requirement on deposited funds is subtracted, reflecting only the

---

*All line references apply to both Exhibits A and B unless otherwise indicated.

portion of the deposit considered to be loanable. If figures are available, the average "collected" demand deposit balance should be used in computing the *Demand Deposit Contribution* (line 2) since the amount of float may differ greatly between depositors. However, since provisions are not always made by banks to calculate the collected balance, the average balance is considered to be acceptable for purposes of analysis.

It has been suggested by some authorities that an earnings credit be applied to the income or yield calculation for that portion of the loan proceeds supplied by the borrower, rather than subtracting it from the average loan balance. We believe the latter is preferable since it does not involve an extra calculation and it does not require an arbitrary judgment about the earnings rate assumed for these funds, which obviously will vary over time for the commercial bank.

The *Net "Pooled Funds" Required* (line 6) simply represents the portion of funds necessary to support the average loan balance which the borrower has not already provided. The term "pooled funds," which is often used when discussing loan profitability, simply refers to the toal of all the bank's available sources of loanable funds (i.e., checking and savings accounts, certificates of deposit, Federal funds and other nondeposit sources of funds, including bank capital).

Again, certain authors on loan profitability analysis have suggested alternative ways of handling "pooled funds" required. For example, some suggest that a certain percentage allocation of the funds required comes from bank capital and this portion of the total is set aside from the other "pooled funds." Then later, in the expense calculation, separate charges are made for capital allocation and for the cost of other "pooled funds." We believe this is an unnecessary calculation and that it has very little meaning. Except under special circumstances cited later, there is normally no direct application of sources of funds to particular investment uses.* Putting it simply, acceptance of an investment by a bank, or any other business firm, requires that the return on the use of funds is greater than the annual percentage cost of the source of funds. To be sure, this includes an adequate or desired return to capital; however, there is no explicit need to separate the return to capital on each and every commercial loan. As will be seen later, our analysis implicitly provides for a desired yield on capital in the nominal rate calculation of a given commercial loan.

In summary, it is important to consider "pooled funds" and "borrower-contributed funds" separately when determining the sources of funds employed for three basic reasons. First, and most obvious, the borrower's contribution

---

*A definite exception to this statement is the investment in government securities required to be pledged against public deposits.

must be netted out in order to give proper credit for compensating balances. Second, "pooled funds" must be considered separately in order that the actual funds required may later be calculated (on line 10). Finally, by calculating the borrower's deposit contribution, the loan analyst is required to take more than a casual look at the customer's total bank relationship.

Total loan income

This section of the profitability analysis simply lists all sources of income derived or expected to be derived from the customer's loan relationship. The actual dollar amounts in this section are determined straightforwardly and involve very little investigation on the part of the analyst. *Loan Interest* (line 7) includes all interest accruing on the loan during the period being analyzed. For a new loan, the interest would be that expected at some arbitrary rate of interest. *Service Charges and Other Fees* (line 8) represent actual charges or fees collected as a matter of practice which are necessary to offset specific or extraordinary costs of the loan (i.e., legal recording or appraisal fees). Additionally, these charges or fees may be collected simply to upgrade overall yield. Although seldom assessed in commercial lending, "points" or "front-end" fees represent an example of this type of income.

Total loan expense

The third major section of the Commercial Loan Yield Analysis Worksheet derives the bank's total expenses (or expected expenses) associated with servicing the loan customer's relationship.

The *Cost of Funds Required* (line 10) represents the expense incurred through the use of the bank's available "pool of funds." The calculation of this expense obviously requires that the bank's accounting system provide an average "pooled cost of funds" rate on an on-going basis. This method of allocating the expense is appropriate because the bank cannot normally judge that a particular source of funds supports a particular credit. If it did so arbitrarily, then it would discriminate between credits since different sources have different explicit costs. An exception to the above would be a situation where the bank is completely "loaned up," and it is clear what the cost would be of any marginal funds necessary to support a new loan. This situation calls for a marginal costing approach rather than an average costing approach; more, however, will be said about this situation later in this article.

Time Deposit Interest Expense (line 11) must be considered when applicable so that the borrower's time deposit contribution may be assessed its appropriate cost to the bank. Nonrecurring *Loan Servicing Costs* (line 12) represent "extraordinary" expenses incurred by the bank in the process of making or administering the loan. Specifically, expenses falling into this category may be either *Initial Costs* (line 12-A) or *Term Costs* (line 12-B). Initial costs, such as extraordinary loan documentation expense or legal fees, result from the initial processing of the loan request. Term costs, such as Small Business Administration fees or other premium servicing fees, result from the administration of the loan after it has become a bank asset. It is important to note that although loan servicing costs are considered extraordinary or unique, they are usually predictable and measurable at the time the new loan is being analyzed for profitability and during subsequent reviews.

Departmental Overhead Expenses (Exhibit A, line 14) are routine expenses which are necessary to carry on the general operating business of the department. Departmental overhead consists of a variety of costs such as department payroll expense, materials, supplies, maintenance, depreciation of equipment, rent allocation (if appropriate), phone, etc. It is attached to the loans indirectly by means of a factor that can be directly related to each loan being analyzed. The allocation of departmental overhead for the purpose of profitability analysis may be accomplished in a variety of ways; however, the allocation must be such that each loan contributes realistically to the total departmental overhead expense. Acceptable methods of allocation include the following:

TRANSACTION METHOD: Using this method, the expense is allocated according to the number of notes used by the customer annually. An "Average Cost per Note" factor is developed based upon the total yearly budgeted departmental overhead expense divided by the total number of notes used annually. This factor, which is then applied to all loans being analyzed, is multiplied times the number of notes used by the customer under consideration. The equations used for these calculations are:

Average Cost per Note (ACPN) =

$$\frac{\text{Total Budgeted Departmental Overhead Expense (\$'s)}}{\text{Total Number of Notes per Year}}$$

Allocated Departmental Overhead Expense =

ACPN × Number of Customer Notes Used

Allocating expenses strictly on a transaction basis, however, *may* tend to treat unfairly the smaller borrower, whose loan may not actually be as costly to administer as the larger borrower.

LOAN BALANCE METHOD: Using this method, expenses are allocated on the basis of the customer's average outstanding loan balance. An "Overhead Allocation Factor" is developed based upon the total yearly budgeted departmental overhead expense divided by the total average loan portfolio. This factor, which is then applied to all loans being analyzed, is multiplied times the customer's average loan balance. The equations used for these calculations are:

Overhead Allocation Factor (OAF) =

$$\frac{\text{Total Budgeted Departmental Overhead Expense (\$'s)}}{\text{Total Average Loan Portfolio (\$'s)}}$$

Allocated Departmental Overhead Expense =

$$\text{OAF} \times \text{Average Loan Balance}$$

Allocating in this manner, however, ignores the fact that the costs actually incurred *may* have little correlation with the size of the loan. That is, there may even be an inverse relationship between a loan's departmental overhead expense and its size (average balance).

COMBINATION TRANSACTION–LOAN BALANCE METHOD: An alternative to allocating on a transaction basis or loan balance basis is to combine the two methods. The equation used for this calculation is:

Departmental Overhead Expense =

$$\tfrac{1}{2}(\text{ACPN}) \times \text{Number of Customer Notes Used} +$$
$$\tfrac{1}{2}(\text{OAF}) \times \text{Average Loan Balance}$$

Since overhead expenses may vary with the quality of the credit, a special extra allocation of overhead could be assessed in reviewing an existing or terminated loan.

Risk (Exhibit A, line 15) is treated as an expense within the framework of this analysis in order that the bank may provide for realistic exposure to loan losses. In effect, this expense represents the probability of eventual write-off on a new loan or the exposed risk of a possible write-off on an existing loan undergoing review. One recommended technique to asses the amount to be expended is to classify each loan according to the loss experience of its type, assign an appropriate risk rate factor, and then multiple the risk rate factor times the average loan balance of the loan under consideration.

While it is difficult to treat risk as explicitly as suggested here, we believe that every attempt should be made to follow some such procedure. Every loan officer, at one time or another, has made an upward adjustment in his mind on the interest charged to a loan applicant on the basis of risk and risk alone. If this is true, it would be preferable to make that adjustment in as objective a fashion as possible.

Demand Deposit Activity Costs (Exhibit A, line 16) are actual servicing costs, as measured by excessive account activity, which are not recovered from the borrower by assessing service charges.

Net loan income and yield

This section of the analysis calculates the *Net Loan Income and Yield* (Exhibit A, lines 18 and 19). The net loan yield provides a measurement of whether a loan is profitable relative to other loan situations and whether a loan is profitable relative to predetermined departmental yield projections.

In order that the net loan yield computation be used to offer the most benefit, it is essential that management compare the calculated yield to what it considers to be a desirable yield. It is imperative, therefore, that management previously establish a range of desirable yields for different types of loans. This should be done *before* the results of profitability analysis are interpreted in order that they can be compared to a realistic standard.* Regardless of the method chosen to establish the desired yield, it is imperative to have such a rate in hand if loans are to be priced correctly on a day-to-day basis such that profit projections are realized. The development of realistic desired yields is essential to our loan pricing technique that is developed in the final section of the Commercial Loan Yield Analysis Worksheet (Exhibit A, lines 20 through 22).

Nominal rate calculation

This section of the analysis (Exhibit A, lines 20 through 22) is likely to be the most important. Although it represents the essence of practical loan pricing, it is often neglected in loan profitability analysis.

After a loan's profitability has been measured, it is essential to establish a rate which realistically supports the desired departmental yield projections. If a new loan request is being analyzed, then this calculation will assist in determining the proper rate to charge the customer. If an existing loan or a terminated loan is currently undergoing review, then this calculation will provide insight into what

---

*There are different ways to establish desired yields on loans. They may result simply from a sampling of loans considered to be typical of those in the loan portfolio. However, a preferred method is one that results from an annual budgeting procedure. The procedure begins with a target or goal of annual dollar profit for the department that is checked to see that its contribution to overall bank profitability will yield adequate return on stockholder equity or a desired earnings per share figure. From this point on, it often become a trial-and-error procedure, for given the direct costs involved in commercial lending, the dollar loan volume is in part a function of the rate established for the desired yield. Also, looking a year in advance, changes can be made in departmental overhead. Finally, the dollar loan volume and types of loans must fit into the bank's overall policy with respect to asset and liability management.

may be a proper rate change or what may have been a more realistic rate at the time the loan was made.

As with the loan yield calculation, it is important to note that the proper rate determined by this analysis is, at best, a relative indication of a realistic rate. It must be realized that this analysis is a formal and objective tool that determines the appropriate nominal rate to be charged for a particular loan request based upon certain explicit quantitative income and expense considerations. However, other qualitative considerations such as competition, the liquidity or reserve position of the bank, or possible spillover benefits to other departments in the bank may logically demand an alteration of the actual nominal rate that is charged.

Pricing loans under changing market conditions

The demand for loans and prevailing interest rates normally follow the change in general economic activity. Furthermore, few authorities would contest the proposition that interest rates on commercial loans are vary sensitive to factors of supply and demand and that they are one of the most competitive prices found in our economy. Being aware of these facts, the commercial loan officer must be willing to adapt to changes in the demand for loanable funds. While prime rate quotations by major banks give some indication of general trends of interest rates, each commercial bank may have its own individual demand and supply situation. This article has presented thus far an objective framework for evaluating profitability and the pricing of loans under normal conditons; however, adjustments are required in the pricing technique for the more or less extreme conditions of an excess or shortage of loanable funds.

Maximum cyclical ease or an excess of loanable funds

The principal adjustment in the pricing of loans under these conditions is the adoption of the well known theory of contribution. A commercial bank with excess loanable funds is only slightly different from an industrial firm with excess production capacity. A commercial bank does have the alternative of placing its excess supply of loanable funds in securities. If it invests in long-term securities in a period of maximum cyclical ease, it does so at distinct market risk. If it keeps its maturities short, then it is a question of the margin between the rates it can secure on these securities in a depressed capital market and the rates that can be charged in an equally competitive loan market.

Under these conditions, the competitive rate that can be charged on loans may well be below a rate that covers all overhead expense and also provides a desired return on capital. The absolute minimum rate is one that covers all direct or variable costs of the loan including the cost of "pooled funds." As noted above, the opportunity cost of rates on short-term securities may set a minimum above the contribution rate; nevertheless, any rate charged on loans above this minimum would definitely make a contribution to overhead and be better than holding excess cash reserves. Exhibit B is an alternative worksheet that can be employed to calculate the minimum required rate on loans necessary to provide a contribution. While loan officers under similar conditions have set rates on loans below the rate required to cover all overhead and provide a desired return to capital, it is important that such a decision be objective and be supported with a sound economic rationale.

Maximum cyclical tightness or a loaned-up condition

This other extreme calls for still another adjustment in the pricing of commercial loans. The adjustment in this case is one of adopting a purely "marginal costing" concept. Under normal conditions the commercial bank is utilizing all its sources of funds to make loans. There is no need to make direct allocations from specific sources to uses and, as suggested earlier, it would discriminate among loans if different costs had to be covered simply because the funds were presumably provided by more or less expensive sources.

Under normal conditions or during cyclical ease, the cost of funds is a weighted average cost of the "pooled funds." However, when the commercial bank is truly loaned-up, then marginal costing is appropriate. Under these conditions, any new incremental dollar to be loaned must be secured externally at a new incremental dollar cost. The source of funds could be certificates of deposit or some other nondeposit type of bank borrowing, but, whatever the source, it is identifiable *at the margin* and its specific cost must be covered.* All that is required to incorporate this concept of marginal costing into our yield analysis worksheet is to use this rate in the *Cost of Funds Required* (line 10) in place of the weighted average rate, which otherwise would be used.

Floating interest rates

Some consideration must be given to the situation when both the bank and the customer wish to establish an interest rate on a loan that floats on the basis of some selected market or prime rate. The customer is guaranteed a continuous competitive rate and the bank is assured a margin protection between the interest earned on the loan and the cost of its pooled funds on a current basis. This consideration, however, does not require an alteration in the format for

---

*A strong case in point is the past situation at Franklin National Bank that failed to recognize this important consideration. See article in *Fortune*, October 1974, p. 118.

EXHIBIT A
NORMAL MARKET CONDITIONS
COMMERCIAL LOAN
YIELD ANALYSIS WORKSHEET

Borrower's Name _____

☐ New Loan   ☐ _____ Review   Date _____

SOURCES OF FUNDS EMPLOYED
1. Average Loan Balance $ _____
2. Demand Deposit Contribution (Average
   Balance x (1 − Reserve Requirement _____%)) $ _____
3. Time Deposit Contribution (Average
   Balance x (1 − Reserve Requirement _____%)) $ _____
4. Other Deposit Contribution (Average
   Balance x (1 − Reserve Requirement _____%)) $ _____
5. Total Deposit Contribution (Total of
   Lines 2 through 4) $ _____
6. Net "Pooled Funds" Required (Line 1 − Line 5) $ _____

TOTAL GROSS LOAN INCOME
7. Loan Interest (Line 1 × Interest Rate
   Charged _____%) $ _____
8. Service Charges and Other Fees $ _____
9. Total Gross Loan Income (Line 7 + Line 8) $ _____

TOTAL LOAN EXPENSE
10. Cost of Funds Required (Line 6 × Appropriate
    Cost Rate _____%) $ _____
11. Time Deposit Interest Expense $ _____
12. Loan Servicing Costs (Non recurring)
    A. Initial Costs $ _____
    B. Term Costs $ _____   TOTAL $ _____
13. Total Direct Expense (Subtotal of Lines 10
    through 12) $ _____
14. Departmental Overhead Expense $ _____
15. Cost of Risk (Line 1 × Appropriate Risk
    Rate Factor _____) $ _____
16. Demand Deposit Activity Costs $ _____
17. Total Loan Expense (Total of Lines 13
    through 16) $ _____

NET LOAN INCOME AND YIELD
18. Net Loan Income (Line 9 − Line 17) $ _____
19. Net Loan Yield (Line 18 ÷ Line 6)   _____%

NOMINAL RATE CALCULATION
20. Required Net Loan Income (Line 6 × Desired
    Yield on Pooled Funds Employed _____%) $ _____
21. Required Gross Loan Income (Line 20 + Line 17) $ _____
22. Interest Rate Required (Line 21 ÷ Line 1)   _____%

EXHIBIT B
EXCESS LOANABLE FUNDS CONDITIONS
COMMERCIAL LOAN
YIELD ANALYSIS WORKSHEET

Borrower's Name _____

☐ New Loan   ☐ _____ Review   Date _____

SOURCES OF FUNDS EMPLOYED
1. Average Loan Balance $ _____
2. Demand Deposit Contribution (Average
   Balance x (1 − Reserve Requirement _____%)) $ _____
3. Time Deposit Contribution (Average
   Balance x (1 − Reserve Requirement _____%)) $ _____
4. Other Deposit Contribution (Average
   Balance x (1 − Reserve Requirement _____%)) $ _____
5. Total Deposit Contribution (Total of
   Lines 2 through 4) $ _____
6. Net "Pooled Funds" Required (Line 1 − Line 5) $ _____

TOTAL GROSS LOAN INCOME
7. Loan Interest (Line 1 × Interest Rate
   Charged _____%) $ _____
8. Service Charges and Other Fees $ _____
9. Total Gross Loan Income (Line 7 + Line 8) $ _____

TOTAL LOAN EXPENSE
10. Cost of Funds Required (Line 6 × Appropriate
    Cost Rate _____%) $ _____
11. Time Deposit Interest Expense $ _____
12. Loan Servicing Costs (Nonrecurring)
    A. Initial Costs $ _____
    B. Term Costs $ _____   TOTAL $ _____
13. Total Direct Expense (Subtotal of Lines 10
    through 12) $ _____

CONTRIBUTION LOAN INCOME AND YIELD
14. Contribution Loan Income (Line 9 − Line 13) $ _____
15. Contribution Loan Yield (Line 14 ÷ Line 6)   _____%

NOMINAL RATE CALCULATION
16. Minimum Required Loan Contribution (Line 13) $ _____
17. Minimum Interest Rate Required (Line 13 ÷ Line 1)   _____%

pricing a loan that is presented in this article. An appropriate rate must still be
established at the time a new loan is made and then can be allowed to float on the
basis of some other agreed upon market or prime rate. Analyzing the profitability
of a loan based upon a floating interest rate poses no particular problem since the

considerations are still the actual interest earned on the average net funds employed after deducting the actual average cost of funds to the bank over the period under consideration.

Summary

There are two critical facets of the loan pricing problem: first, the measurement of loan profitability, and, second, the application of a loan pricing technique sufficiently flexible so that it is applicable for changes in the market demand for loans. In the future, bank profitability will become increasingly dependent upon management's ability to more efficiently determine the actual profit contribution of each borrowing relationship and assess the proper interest rate accordingly.

The method of analysis presented in this article appropriately considers loan profitability and price determination within the framework of one analysis. While satisfying the appropriate basic acceptance criteria, it also accomplishes the following three major objectives:

- It assesses the relative profitability of any commercial loan relationship.

- It assists the loan officer in his need to determine an appropriate nominal rate on any given commercial loan.

- It provides a valuable marketing tool to assist in selling a bank's most profitable product—credit.   □

The Art of Interest
Rate Negotiating

by Lawrence T. Jilk, Jr.

*"Confusion," "delay," and "feinting" may sound like foot-
ball maneuvers, but, in this article, they refer to some specific
techniques of interest rate negotiating. Larry Jilk discusses
these and many other techniques as part of a bank's overall
loan pricing program.*

One of the major innovations in the commercial banking system in the 1970s
has been the development of the art of loan pricing. Dozens of articles on loan
pricing have appeared in the *Journal* and other banking publications. Most
major and medium-sized banks have developed their own loan pricing systems
which consider the value of the various income streams, as well as the several
cost components of each loan. However, knowing the "correct" rate is the
easy part of our battle to improve net margins. Negotiating the rate with the
customer is the hard part! It is in the area of "rate negotiating" that I feel the
next innovations in the field of loan pricing will occur.

Components of rate negotiating

Rate negotiating is a rather broad topic that can be sliced into two major
components: establishing the proper mental attitude and learning and applying
negotiating tactics.

The proper mental attitude

Establishing the proper mental attitude is a must for both bank management and the loan officer. Bank management must be prepared to support a rate negotiation program. This means that occasionally some business must be lost to competition. And when business is lost, the loan officer must have the active support of management. Furthermore, for those banks that have reached the point of applying MBO techniques to loan officers, increases in *net* profitability must be considered along with outstandings.

Finally, management's most precious resource—time—must be fully committed to loan pricing. Consider all the time spent in your organization maintaining the quality of loans: credit department time, loan officer time, loan committee time, and board of director's time, not that all this effort is wasted. It pays off in the high quality of most portfolios.

At most banks, net loan losses might amount to ½% of loans. But reflect for just a moment on the effect on your average loan rate if, say, only *half* of the time spent on maintaining loan quality were devoted to loan pricing. Could you increase your average return ⅛% to ¼% after several years? I would think so! How many banks review *all* compensating balance deficiencies on a quarterly basis at their loan committee? How many banks review loans secured by marketable securities, certificates of deposit, or passbooks at least annually—not for credit but for profitability? How many banks review at a senior management level the profitability of *all* commercial loans? How much time is spent in face to face rate negotiation by bank management?

Loan officers must similarly be prepared to support a rate negotiation program. How many times has an officer, when asked to get a rate higher than he feels is necessary, responded by saying, "OK, but if I can't get it, can I come down ¼%?" Nine out of ten times he won't get the desired rate because he doesn't believe in it; and, either consciously or subconsciously, he won't fight for it.

Line loan officers must fully support, believe in, live, eat, and sleep a rate negotiation program or else it's doomed! This line officer involvement, while not quite requiring a company song, does necessitate the full involvement of the line officer in the development of the rate and his understanding of why the rate is fair, both to the bank and to the customer. Relating line officers' salaries to increases in loan yields is also a most remarkable method of assisting line officers to fight for the bank rather than opt for the pleasant way out!

Learning and applying negotiating tactics

The second part of any rate negotiating program is for account officers to learn and apply rate negotiating tactics. These tactics are simply adaptations of tried and true methods used in labor-management negotiations, as well as in acquisition, husband-wife, or parent-child negotiations. There's nothing sneaky or unethical about learning and using negotiating tactics anymore than saying "please" or buying flowers for your wife on your anniversary. Not everyone will feel comfortable using all negotiating tactics, but at least they should be learned. Your customers are going to use them on you to get lower rates or better terms. That's a guarantee!

Most seasoned lenders are familiar with the more common negotiating techniques, having picked them up by trial and error over the years. They are used successfully by these lenders in the never-ending battle to increase (or maintain) profit margins. Why shouldn't the lending industry recognize the benefits to be gained from developing negotiating skills and train young (and old) lenders in these talents.

Training can take various forms:

(1) Several good books are available on negotiating. They are primarily oriented to labor-management, but the concepts remain constant.

(2) Courses in negotiating are taught by a couple of professional organizations, such as the AMA, as well as by local universities. These courses are well worthwhile and should be considered by every loan officer desiring to increase his or her skills as a well-rounded loan officer.

(3) In-house courses can be developed utilizing the experience of your senior personnel.

Selection of location

Learning negotiating techniques and developing a proper mental attitude are the two major components of a rate negotiating program. Two additional, minor considerations are the location of the rate negotiation discussions and the selection of the personnel involved.

The selection of physical location generally narrows down to either the bank's or the borrower's shop. Each should be considered and each has its advantages:

The bank. Many of our banks and offices are imposing. We should capitalize on this expense, which at least according to our architects, is designed to subconsciously place the borrower on the defensive—overwhelmed at the magnificence of this mighty, mortgaged mausoleum. Furthermore, the chairman can usually be persuaded to drop by unexpectedly, say "hello," and welcome the applicant to the new bank or ask the applicant and spouse to the next concert or simply talk about this, that, and the other thing.

The customer's place.   By negotiating away from the bank, line officers can usually avoid getting trapped into making a decision. They don't have all the balance information or loan history, or they aren't empowered themselves to approve a rate. Furthermore, their visiting the borrower may be interpreted as a sign of the bank's willingness to conclude the negotiations.

Selection of personnel

The selection of negotiating personnel is equally important. Banks may wish to consider a team concept with a "good guy" and a "bad guy" or possibly a single loan officer. The use of senior management is generally reserved for the coup de grace, but in certain instances, the president may be equally effective early in the game.

Specific techniques of negotiating

We have introduced the concept of negotiating loan rates. Let's look at some specific techniques:

(1) *The Dating Game or "a little bit at a time?"*   Let's agree that we want ¼% more from a customer. Why not get him to commit to a given compensating balance or profit margin over the next year? If he makes it, agree to no rate change. If he doesn't, the customer agrees in advance to pay the higher rate. It might take a little longer, but eventually your goal rate is achieved, or else the credit has improved to where the present rate can be justified.

(2) *Adverse comparisons.*   Compare your rate to the rates charged by finance companies, equipment suppliers, second mortgage lenders, or additional equity sources.

(3) *Nonrate Concessions.*   If you desire say 9% from a particular credit and your customer only wants to pay 8.75%, try to work the deal around to where it's worth 9%—extend terms, ease collateral, etc. (Obviously, you don't want to go *too* far with this one.)

(4) *Confusion.*   In a credit where you know the borrower is "shopping," don't quote the deal. The only winner will be the borrower. Change the deal. Make a direct rate comparison difficult. Increase the amount, change the repayment schedule, etc. But don't get caught in a direct rate battle with competition. You can only lose!

(5) *This is the way it is!*   When it comes time to quote rates, pull a well-worn rate chart from under your blotter, study it for a minute, look the customer squarely in the eye, and say, "The rate for this type loan is x%." Who can argue with the system?

A variation of this approach is to avoid rate discussions altogether, and when the note arrives, simply put it on at a fair rate. Our customers use this approach too. How often do we receive notes with the rate already typed in when no rate discussions were held?

(6) *Delay.*   Postpone making rate decisions until all other points are ironed out. The customer will hesitate to begin negotiations from scratch with another bank. Furthermore, customers often are placed under pressure to procure the funds—for added working capital, new plant, etc.—so their negotiating stance frequently weakens as time passes.

(7) *Side step artificial deadlines.*   How many times have we heard, "But we have to agree (on a rate) because I need the money tomorrow?" O.K., if the credit's good, put it on—at your rate. Tell the borrower that when time permits, you and he will get together and continue rate negotiations, and any adjustments in the borrower's favor can be made retroactive. You'll be surprised how often that's the end of negotiations as other matters take precedence.

(8) *Feinting or "Charge Onward Carefully."*   This technique entails pressing ahead for the desired interest rate but in an oblique manner avoiding head-on confrontation. We can feint either to the right (positive) or left (negative).

(a) A positive feint would consist of playing up the terms of the credit itself—the amount, the maturity, or the collateral—and openly reflecting on how favorable they are to the borrower. Or, along the same line, there can be conversations on what the borrower will be able to do with the requested funds—how much money he will be able to make. Under these circumstances, the borrower obviously has a good deal and how can he also ask for rate concessions?

(b) A negative feint consists of downplaying the consequences of agreeing to the bank's suggested rate. The after-tax dollar difference in interest expense can be calculated and used as an indication of how really minor this particular point is in the entire discussion. Or, the borrower can be asked to explain how he could possibly let the rate differential jeopardize the deal, and if a ¼% point is that critical, maybe the project (loan) should be reconsidered.

(9) *Surprise or "You've got to be kidding."*   There's a little ham in all of us, and, upon occasion, we should not hesitate to play our parts. When confronted with a suggested rate well below our normal return, a surprised "What??" will

do wonders in putting the legitimacy of that rate in its proper perspective. What respectable borrower would dare but accept the bank's normal rate! For those more talented in this technique, some waving of the arms or possibly even a quick departure from our chairs may be helpful.

(10) *Reversal or "Putting the cart before the horse."* A dangerous technique but sometimes helpful. Usually a cardinal rule of banking is to quote the rate last—after all, the terms and conditions of the deal are known. In some rare instances, however, you may know enough about the borrower and the deal to quote early in the game—hedged as necessary, of course, to provide for contingencies. By doing so, you can structure the deal around the rate. In these instances, the borrower begins negotiations knowing the cost and is hard pressed to bring up rate concessions after all the other terms have been agreed upon.

(11) *Agreement or "Let's work this out together."* This technique emphasizes areas of agreement between the borrower and bank. Not only should the agreed upon terms be rehashed, with all their favorable consequences for the borrower, but you, the loan officer, and your bank should be presented in a favorable light. Your knowledge of the borrower's industry should be highlighted; your desire to be a creative banker and your bank's particular interest in financing this particular company should be emphasized.

(12) *On again, off again.* This technique puts the borrower on the defensive by inferring the loan is not possible at the borrower's suggested rate—but stops short of taking a position from which the banker cannot retreat. Several methods of accomplishing this setting are—

(a) When a rate impasse occurs, change the subject to a topic as far away from banking as possible. This tactic implies that you cannot make any further rate concessions and that further negotiations will be fruitless. It makes the borrower re-establish rate conversations which almost requires a concession on his part.

(b) Start conversations pertaining to an entirely new approach to the financing need, such as, "If we can't lend you money (at our desired rates) one way, let's try another." The fear of a whole new set of negotiations is likely to extract rate concessions from the borrower. He will again want to get back to the original deal, and to do so, he will have to offer something.

(c) For new borrowers, start reflecting on the beautiful relationship that could have developed . . . if only the borrower would be reasonable on rates. You and he, together, can conquer the world if only . . . . .

(13) *"Take it or leave it" or "the ultimate negotiating technique."* Unfortunately, we will have occasions when all else fails. In these circumstances, the

bank must be prepared to draw the line. What would we think of our borrowers if they booked 100% of the business they quoted. We should not expect to get 100% of our quotes. If we do, we're quoting too low.

These are just some of the more common techniques. There are numerous others. You may not like using any one of these approaches. But in the interest of your bank's future profitability, you should learn them and use those techniques with which you're comfortable.

Conclusion

The art of loan pricing has progressed to the point where most loan officers or at least their management can properly determine the "correct" rate. Emphasis and time must now be placed on training our loan officers in negotiating the correct rate. Yes, not only must we be a business developer, a credit analyst, and a pricing technician all rolled into one, we must also be skilled in the art of negotiating. The next innovation in the exciting area of loan profitability is —rate negotiating!   □

IV. Documentation and Legal Aspects of Lending

The articles in this section cannot substitute for good legal advice at appropriate times. The purposes of the section are instead to alert the lender to common legal problems, to help the lender be aware of the need to consult counsel, and to make the communication between the lender and the lawyer more productive. The section thus starts with a discussion of some relatively common legal aspects of the loan relationship and concludes with comments on emerging developments and the new Bankruptcy Code. The reader should be aware that the material in this section can become obsolete faster than most other articles in this book as a result of new legislation and court decisions.

"Commercial Lending Can Be Fun" is a true statement, but it is a somewhat misleading title for Perry C. Bascom's amusing romp through two basic lending legal topics: documentation and security. The article is thus an excellent companion to several of the articles in the loan structure section. (Some of the references to Chapters X and XI of the old Bankruptcy Act may be out of date as a result of subsequent legislation, but the overall contribution of the article is valuable.)

Two articles on special topics follow. First, Hurd Baruch has written "Risks in Loans Collateralized by Securities," which covers in considerable detail the problems of using securities as collateral. A. Thomas Small discusses an increasingly popular financial instrument in "Letters of Credit for the Commercial Lender." He reviews the types of transactions that give rise to a letter of credit, discusses pertinent federal and state legislation, and comments on problems that can arise in a transaction.

The final three articles in this section deal with relatively recent legal developments. "Legislative and Judicial Developments Affecting Commercial Lending, 1978-1979" by A. Bruce Schimberg is one of a series on the subject that the *Journal* has run. This particular contribution was included because of its coverage of a number of critical and developing areas, such as security interest, the lender's liability under the securities act, and participations. Many of these topics will be familiar from the section of this book on loan structure.

The remaining two articles in this section discuss the new bankruptcy legislation. "The Bankruptcy Code from the Viewpoint of the Secured Commercial Lender," the second article by A. Thomas Small in this section of the book, presents a survey of the Code's terms, identifying the important differences and similarities between the Code and the older Act. In "The Preference Provisions of the Bankruptcy Code of 1979," Herbert L. Ash reviews in depth an important but narrower part of the new legislation.

For information about the authors of the articles in Section IV, refer to the List of Contributors on page xi.

Commercial Lending Can Be Fun

by C. Perry Bascom, Esq.

> *Mr. Bascom refers from time to time to local situations and to Missouri law. Even though the RMA* Journal *goes to readers throughout the country (throughout the world, really), we've published his thoughts essentially "as are," in order not to compromise their overall integrity and style. We think you'll appreciate the conversational approach of this skillful bank counsel.*

WHAT DOES A COMMERCIAL LOAN OFFICER DO? A commercial loan officer is a problem solver. A lot of times I think all of us get bogged down, take a pretty narrow view and say, "Well, all I really do is mark up forms or make bad loans." Look again, there is a lot of creativity in being a good commercial loan officer. A lot of imagination can go into servicing the customer and doing a good job. Banking is a service industry, and if you and I are delivering the product that we are supposed to be delivering to our customers or clients we are getting the job done. But if we don't bring a little creativity to the job, I don't think we can do what we are supposed to be doing. Speaking strictly

---

This article is based on an address presented during a meeting of the RMA St. Louis Chapter.

of the legal aspects of commercial lending, bankers cannot have all the answers just as lawyers, even though sometimes they talk as if they have the banking answers, don't.

I think, though, that if you can recognize the problems, if you know enough about a subject to know when a problem is arising, if you have a vocabulary of basic legal words—just as lawyers who deal with bankers have to develop a vocabulary of banking words, if you can ask the question, you are going to get more mileage out of your lawyer. You are going to provide better service for your customer and you are going to get the job done better.

The tools of our trade are infinitely variable

What I would like to do is to review some of the possibilities. I would like to talk about the tools you have to work with. I would like to talk about some of the kinds of security that you can take for loans, about enforcing loans—bad loans (fairly current and choice these days!). I will run through all this quickly, with the idea of just throwing these things out—putting them in your minds to think about.

The tools are all the forms you have to use, the different mechanics of putting loans together. I think you can see that the combination of possibilities that you can use to service your customer is practically infinite. Instead of approaching a problem saying, "Can we make this loan?" I think that the approach should be: "*How* can we make this loan?" Let me give you an example.

A year or so ago a client wanted to make a loan to a subsidiary of an insurance company. Well, the subsidiary's credit was not very good and the question came up: "Well, why can't the bank just have the insurance company guaranty the loan?" We lawyers doubted that an insurance company could guaranty a loan. An insurance company is a certain kind of corporation and, by and large, corporations have only the powers that they are given in the statutes pursuant to which they are incorporated. The laws relating to insurance companies didn't expressly permit insurance companies to guaranty debts. So we didn't know whether this corporate guaranty by this insurance company would be any good.

However, someone came up with a bright idea. Instead of having the insurance company guaranty the note, why not have the insurance company agree to purchase its subsidiary's note if the subsidiary should go bad and the loan should go into default? That was the solution.

I think it was a creative solution. The loan was made, and everyone was happy although the loan would have been shaky from a legal point of view if it had been made simply on the basis of the insurance company's guaranty. By using the note purchase instead of the guaranty, we didn't have to approach the commissioner of insurance for authority and we didn't have to ask anybody for a legal opinion. The deal became very simple and legally "clean." Now maybe the difference between the note purchase and the guaranty seems like only a difference in form, but we, as lawyers, felt it was a significant enough difference in substance so we could tell our client that it was okay to go ahead and make the loan.

Documentation

In approaching any situation, be it unusual or not, the more creativity as opposed to rigidity that can be brought to it the better off everybody's going to be. Documentation is, of course, one of the basic things. Lawyers make a lot of money with documentation—preparing a bunch of papers that apparently don't mean anything once the loan goes into default. There are reasons for documentation, though.

I frequently say to myself: "Look, this guy's either going to pay or he's not going to pay—if he's going to pay, all we should need is a promissory note to tell him the terms he's got to make his payments on. If he's not going to pay, a stack of documents four feet high isn't going to make any difference because he's just not going to pay." Well, that's true and it's not true. As between you and the borrower, it may have some truth. However, as a loan goes along, the borrower may have a difference of opinion with you about how the loan is supposed to be administered, what his net capital requirements are supposed to be, whether he is entitled to merge, whether he is entitled to declare a certain dividend on his stock. So even as between you and the borrower, the reason for good documentation goes beyond just "is he going to pay or is he not going to pay." Proper documentation at the beginning will be helpful both to you and your borrower.

Perhaps even more important, once a loan is in trouble, and particularly if it's a secured loan, you're going to have to fight off all kinds of people. At that point the borrower is the least of your worries—you want to hold on to your security and what you've got. You're going to be fighting off other creditors, you're going to be fighting off other banks, you're going to be fighting off maybe even the feared trustee in bankruptcy. At that point, that's where it is absolutely necessary that the documentation for the loan be there and be there right.

Categories of documentation

Essential documentation can be divided into three categories. First is the **primary documentation.** This is the documentation of what the deal is between you and your borrower. I think a *commitment letter* is a very good thing, particularly in loans that involve security or have terms and conditions beyond simply a million dollars payable on demand at 9½%. The commitment letter lays the basic groundwork for what the relationship between you and your borrower is going to be.

The commitment letter may or may not be followed by a *loan agreement*. If the letter is sufficiently detailed, maybe a loan agreement doesn't have to follow. The loan agreement is a kind of rule book for what's going to happen in the next year or two years, or five years, or however long your relationship is going to last.

And, of course, the other piece of important primary documentation is the *promissory note*. Without that you don't have any promise from the fellow to pay you back.

There's a whole bunch of **secondary documentation** that all bankers are familiar with. These are agreements between the bank and someone other than the borrower which backstop your loan. There are guaranties and there are note purchase agreements.

A *note purchase agreement* is nothing more or less than the agreement of a third party to purchase the borrower's note if the borrower should go into default. Note purchase agreements can be very useful in place of a guaranty in certain circumstances. There are also *subordination agreements* that you can use to lock in someone else's debt and make it a form of equity.

There are many additional documents you may request of your borrower—for one, *corporate authorizations*. It all depends on how far you want to go into the corporate authorization and the power and good standing of the borrower. You may ask for nothing more than a certified copy of the corporate borrowing resolutions, but, on the other hand, you may want to go back and read minutes book for the last five years. You may or may not want to ask for a *certificate of incumbency*. How far you will go with this secondary documentation—how much you will ask for—is to some degree a judgmental matter depending on how well you know your customer and how firmly you feel and how deeply you feel you ought to go into this.

Other secondary documentation could include *lien searches*—a very common type of lien search is a certificate of title, used if real estate security is involved. *Letters of credit*—more and more we are seeing letters of credit used to backstop the lack of equity in a loan, to step in in place of a guaranty. They can be very, very useful.

Negative pledge agreements can also be very useful. I don't think they provide much by way of security, but they are another tool. What I mean by a negative pledge is that the fellow will simply agree that, although he is not granting you a security interest in anything, he's not granting and he won't grant anybody else a security interest either so long as your loan is outstanding. Now that doesn't put you in a secured position, but with a pretty good borrower that might be enough for you to go along with.

There's **tertiary documentation,** which is getting pretty far down the line. *Participation agreements* are necessary if you are going to sell off part of your loan to another bank. Participation agreements can be in different forms. Frequently you'll see the participation receipt itself constituting the form of agreement because it'll have lots of terms and conditions in small print on it. Or the participation agreement can be a separate, written-out participation agreement with just a very simple receipt issued along with it. I think bankers tend to short-sell the importance of the participation agreement. If you've ever been in a participation situation with another bank and the lead bank has somehow messed up and you start wondering what your rights are and what his responsibilities are and you find you have no participation agreement, then you'll know what I mean when I say I think they are very important.

Forms are always around—use, don't abuse

Most of the things that I've just mentioned can be reduced to forms—you always have forms lying around. Subordination agreements—there are always some of those lying around. Forms are useful. Forms can also be abused. I think it is almost malpractice for a lending officer to use these forms—the guaranty form, the collateral pledge form or any other form—without having taken a half an hour to sit down and go through the fine print and understand exactly what it means. I think it would certainly avoid a lot of questions asked of lawyers that you could have answered yourself if you had read the fine print in the guaranty form.

So you think you have a guaranty—for what?

Forms can be abused and blind use of them can get you in trouble. I'll give you an example: The common form of guaranty that's in use in the St. Louis area is that so-and-so guarantees the loan of ABC Corporation to the extent of $100,000—you fill in the blank $100,000. Well, next week the borrower wants $100,000 more credit, so you make out another guaranty for $100,000; a week later, he wants $50,000 more, so you fill out another form for $50,000. Okay, now you've got three forms, two for $100,000 and one for $50,000.

Which one of those forms is the guaranty? Is it the last one? No, it shouldn't be, but it's arguable that it is, and instead of having $250,000 guaranteed, you find that some guarantor's lawyer is making the argument that that last $50,000 guaranty is all you've got. That's the kind of thing that a blind use of forms can get you into because there are forms that will "cure" any problem. So I caution you against a blind use of these forms.

Which collateral pledge?

Let me give you another example—the collateral pledge agreement. You are going to find some overlap in Missouri's new usury laws. The first one came along allowing any rate of interest on a demand note for the purchase of securities—that'll require one form of collateral pledge. Another form of collateral pledge will be required under the new usury law permitting any rate for a loan exceeding $5,000 which is simply secured by stock collateral. The collateral pledge provisions in those two loans will be different, and you'll have to watch out for them and you'll have to recognize them and know how to deal with them.

Care and feeding of lawyers

Lawyers, believe it or not, are human beings. And, believe it or not, they usually do like to try to help their clients. You can make it a lot easier on your lawyer if you keep a few thoughts in mind. Helping him means it's going to take him less time to do his job and, since lawyers charge by the hour, it's going to cost you less money to have him do a good job.

You make his job a lot easier if, in setting up a loan, you provide him with a commitment letter if you've written it yourself. Even better, ask your lawyer to write the commitment letter for you, because bringing him in at the beginning of a deal and letting him work his way through it, pursuing the ins- and- outs with you, is going to make him a lot more effective than if, after the deal is all concluded, you dump a bunch of papers on his desk that he hasn't read and he hasn't drafted and ask him what he thinks of them.

If it's going to take him 5 or 6 hours to go through some leverage lease agreement that you've asked him to look at, it probably would have been more economical—and certainly you would have gotten a better response—if he had been in at the very beginning.

Is your security secure?

Indirect security loans

One form of security that is very useful but potentially dangerous is the indirect real estate loan. What I call an indirect real estate loan is where you have a collateral note like a stock or bond note with a collateral pledge agreement on the back of it, and the collateral for that note is a deed of trust note. You may think that you have security on your note of real estate but you don't. Your security for an indirect real estate loan is a promissory note.

These indirect real estate loans have caused a lot of problems in Missouri recently. They've really come to the fore in the Lake St. Louis bankruptcy. Some of you may also remember the Stuckenberg bankruptcy a couple of years ago. A lot of these indirect real estate loans were floating around in both of those bankruptcies.

"Bona fide" and "dummy" notes—In an indirect real estate loan, the pledged deed of trust note may be a "bona fide" note—that is, a note made by a third party that actually evidences an advance of funds to the third party—or it could be a "dummy." A "dummy" note is made by the person who is borrowing from you on the collateral note or by someone who is simply acting for the borrower who does not intend to procure any advance on the "dummy" note. In any event, the "dummy" note doesn't represent any real advance of money, at least until you indirectly advance on it by making an advance on the collateral note.

The "bona fide" note is more of a true warehousing situation. The "dummy" note is used because, under Missouri law, you can't safely make future advances on a real estate mortgage without bringing the title down prior to each advance. A mechanic's lienor or a second deed of trust or a judgment creditor, any of them could, by intervening, become prior to you on your secondary advance. Thus, we always have a record check to be sure no one has sneaked in who could get priority to us on our secondary advance.

Do your record checking—I am not at all sure using a "dummy" note in an indirect real estate loan cures this problem. What I'm saying is that if your borrower pays his collateral note down and then you make him another advance but he has given someone else a second deed of trust in the meantime (and you made no record check prior to advancing more money to him so you didn't find out about it), you may not have the security you thought you did. This practice, I know, is very common but be careful. I don't know what the law is and I don't think this priority problem has ever been litigated. I'd prefer to avoid the litigation by taking the simple precaution of having a record check. If something shows up, either you don't make the advance or you find some way of insuring your position, perhaps by getting the intervening lienor to subordinate.

Remember the statute of limitations—There is also a bad statute of limitations problem when the deed of trust note pledged to you as security is a demand note, as it usually is. After 10 years from the date of the demand note pledged to you as security, it is no longer enforceable and your security is gone. The statute of limitations on the deed of trust securing that demand note you took as collateral is 20 years—fine, but it secures a note which can't be enforced. That's no good.

Double foreclosure is double trouble—You should also be very careful to recognize the "double foreclosure" problem in indirect real estate loans. When your collateral note defaults, you simply foreclose on the real estate, right? Wrong! You have no right to do that because, remember, your collateral is not real estate but a deed of trust note that is, in turn, secured by real estate. You must first foreclose and have a public sale of the note that is your collateral—if you buy it in and if it's in default, then you can foreclose on the real estate. A different procedure can get you into trouble. Double foreclosure can be avoided if proper language is added to your collateral pledge agreement to authorize one foreclosure. It's simply language, but be sure it's there before you try to skip a step.

Because they're useful I don't advocate stopping the use of indirect real estate loans. Just be sure you are not abusing them or relying on the security you think you have without taking a few simple backstopping measures.

Accounts and contract rights

Another kind of security that can get you in more trouble than it's worth unless you police it and stay on top of it, but it can be a very good thing for you if you do watch it, is accounts and contract rights.

There's nothing worse for a lawyer than to be told: "Look, we want to start collecting this borrower's accounts because he's in default, and now what are we going to do?" And the lawyer says, "Well, you have the right to send out notices to all the account debtors." And the banker agrees, but when the lawyer asks why hasn't the bank sent them out, the banker admits, "We don't know where they keep their accounting records." How does the borrower do his accounting? Is it on a computer somewhere? The banker doesn't know. A lawyer can't be very much help in going through the mechanics of writing nasty letters to account debtors unless you, the lending officers, do know. On the other hand, if you have the proper information and you can go out to the borrower and grab his computer printout and churn out a lot of form letters over a day or two, you're going to have a very, very high rate of success in grabbing those accounts, and that's good.

Funny collateral can be excellent if . . .

One other kind of collateral that can be excellent collateral, but I would put a bug in your ear about watching out for it, is what I call funny collateral. And the reason I call it funny is because you have to perfect your liens on it in ways different from those you use to perfect liens through the Uniform Commercial Code.

Aircraft—An example is airplanes—you have to perfect your lien on them, as you probably know, by going through Oklahoma City. This can be a bit confusing and time-consuming and you need lead time here. The chain of title to an aircraft is very much like a chain of title to real estate. For a lawyer to be able to tell you that you have a good lien on an aircraft before you advance your funds, he really needs 15 or 20 days of lead time. Now that's very frequently impractical, but it's something to keep in mind because if it's at all avoidable to run any risk you want to get as much lead time on something like that as you can.

Ship mortgages—Ships are another kind of funny collateral. They're funny because you perfect them with the Coast Guard. A lot of Missouri bankers know Commander Scott, a very fine person up at the Coast Guard offices. I understand that if you go to other Coast Guard documentation officers you don't necessarily get the same help and assistance as you do from him. So if you're perfecting any ship mortgages elsewhere than in St. Louis, don't expect to get the same expedited treatment.

More funny collateral—You should also watch out when you have rolling stock as collateral—you may have to perfect with the ICC. Also, there's a trap in the Missouri Uniform Commercial Code here and you may have to perfect under it, too.

Beware also of other collateral that you may have to perfect on in more than one way. For example, if you took a lien on the inventory of an automobile leasing firm you'd want to perfect by filing on "inventory" and, of course, by perfecting your lien on the title of each automobile.

Letter stock is yet another funny collateral. Some stock becomes, in effect, letter stock even though it's not legended, as where a borrower pledges its own stock or that of an affiliate. Unless you recognize this and plan properly, you may have trouble disposing of what you thought were readily marketable securities.

Finally, as regards perfection, be careful when you're taking assignments of real estate leases or fixtures—special kinds of filings may be necessary.

Funny borrowers, too—In this area of funny collateral, also remember that there are some funny borrowers also and that some regulated companies need the approval of the agency supervising them to borrow money or issue debt securities.

Have you kept your records up to date?

Some of this collateral—well, when the smoke has cleared, you really wonder if it's worth having. An example would be those accounts that you have taken but that you haven't thought much about. You find that when it comes time to notify the account debtors, it's going to take a considerable amount of hurry and concentrated effort to develop the proper information. You may have two or three of your people on this and you wonder whether you really wanted to rely on this kind of collateral or whether you wouldn't have been better off picking up some real estate and paying the cost of the mortgagee's insurance. On the other hand, if you are up to date and have policed your borrower's accounts, it's a pretty easy procedure—you have the accounts and you're glad you didn't take the real estate because you might have had to become a landlord overnight.

Legal aid for the promise to pay

From time to time, the promise to pay does need some legal aid by way of lawyers or by way of the bankruptcy court.

Self-help

I recognize three basic kinds of enforcement of the promise to pay. One is self-help. That simply means that you go out to the motel that you've got a defaulted real estate loan on, you storm in the door, you make yourself a mortgagee in possession and you hope nobody comes around and starts swinging at you. Basically you self-help. You go in and you start running the operation and collecting the rents yourself.

Judicial help

The second kind of aid for the promise to pay is judicial help. That's simply going to a court, looking for an order of replevin, looking for an injunction against the borrower to keep him from interfering with the accounts that have been assigned to you.

Debtor's relief or creditor's rights laws

The third and perhaps most unhappy method of enforcement is use of the so-called debtor's relief or creditor's rights laws. Basically, this means bankruptcy or receivership, procedures pursuant to which the debtor is put under the protection of the court and folks like bankers are kind of made to stand back.

It's better to keep talking—A good friend of mine puts it: Litigation is nothing more or less than the total breakdown of human communications. That may at first seem kind of glib, because there does come a time when you've got to take your big stick and go out and drag an uncooperative deadbeat to court—that's what they put steps on the courthouse for. But the more I see of workout situations, the more I'm convinced that as long as you can keep talking to your customer you're a lot better off than if you drag him up the courthouse steps, because that is simply an admission that you failed in trying to work the situation out with him. Sure, sometimes there's no other way. But the time demands of litigation and the expense are such that I think litigation should be avoided.

A lawyer, no matter how well you've equipped him, no matter how well you have documented your loan and no matter how well you know your debtor—a lawyer cannot walk into court and wave a magic wand and have a cornucopia pouring down dollars and cents to pay off your loan. It just doesn't work that way. It takes time, it means delays, it means personnel will have to be testifying instead of being at work, and meanwhile collateral is dissipating and the debtor's condition is degenerating. However, as long as you and your borrower are still talking, together or through lawyers, you have a chance to avoid such waste. Most people are honest and will try if given a chance.

Filing involuntary petitions—You may be faced with the proposition where you have to decide whether you are going to file an involuntary petition against one of your customers. I don't think you should be afraid of filing an involuntary petition, but I think the single biggest consideration should be what's in it for you. If I'm going to go to the bankruptcy court, if I'm going to put up with the hassle of filing an involuntary petition, what's in it for me?

Basically, the only reason for putting a debtor into involuntary bankruptcy is that you think you're going to be better off after he's declared a bankrupt than you are now. And that comes down to one thing—that's the power of the trustee to pull back into the bankrupt's estate fraudulent transfers and preferential payments that that bankrupt has made. If he's paid off everybody in sight but you in the last four months and now has nothing left, you may very well be better off putting him into bankruptcy, having the trustee grab these assets back into the estate and paying you off 20¢ on the dollar. But, again, you've got to have the information about whom he's paid, what for, when the payments were made, whether that payee has security. There's no substitute for your having a good enough grip on your borrower so that you can answer those questions.

Chapters X and XI—As to reorganization proceedings—of which we're seeing more and more—Chapters X and XI are absolute anathema. Supposedly in Chapter XI the rights of a secured creditor cannot be affected. That's so much baloney, because the first thing that happens when a Chapter XI petition is filed under the Bankruptcy Rules is an automatic stay of any lien enforcement. If you have a foreclosure notice being published, if you have repossessed part of the debtor's inventory and you're getting ready to sell it, don't do it. Technically, you're in contempt of court if you do. What you do then is you sit there and you wait, and your lawyer goes to court sessions, nothing happens, and your collateral sits there and deteriorates. You're entitled to your collateral by contract and Chapter XI isn't supposed to affect your rights but it does—you can't foreclose or take possession unless the court says you can.

The basic distinction between a Chapter X and a Chapter XI is that, in a Chapter X, the rights of all creditors secured and unsecured and the rights of stockholders can be affected. Ordinarily, a Chapter X will only come about with a larger, more publicly held or semi-publicly held corporation. In Chapter X you actually have a trustee in possession of the debtor's operations; in a Chapter XI you do not. The debtor remains in possession unless a receiver is appointed, which a debtor usually will resist pretty strongly. The other interesting thing about a Chapter X is that you will frequently find the SEC coming in. It's a requirement that the SEC get involved where the bankruptcy involves liabilities of more than $3,000,000.

It all hangs together

The first seven to ten years I was practicing law, it seemed like I never did anything more than once. Every problem was new. And it may sound as if I'm telling you to approach every one of your problems as a brand-new fresh problem. It's not really that way.

There was a fellow who opened up a law office in Concord, N.H., and he was destined for great things. His name was Daniel Webster. The first day he was there, he hung up his shingle. Pretty soon the village blacksmith came in and he asked Daniel to take his case, and Daniel said he would. He tried the case and he lost it, he appealed it to the intermediate court and he lost it, he took it all the way to the Supreme Court of New Hampshire and he won the case. The next day he sent the village blacksmith a bill for $10. The village blacksmith stormed into his office, threw the bill down on the desk, said it was the most ridiculous bill he'd ever seen, he wouldn't think of paying it. So Daniel put that one away for future reference, went on to the United States Senate.

Many years later, after he had established his fame and reputation, he was sitting in his law office in Boston. The president of the New York, New Haven and Hartford, which was then an important railroad, came into his office and told Daniel he had a little problem—in fact, it was a very significant problem and the president pleaded with Daniel to take it. Daniel thought it sounded kind of familiar and said he'd take the case.

The president left and Daniel went back into his office and found the brief that he'd written for the village blacksmith 50 years before. He dusted it off a little bit, checked the cases and rewrote the brief—total elapsed time about two hours. Daniel went to the Supreme Court of Massachusetts and won the case. He sent the railroad a bill for $10,000.

The next day the president came in, threw the bill down on the table, said it was the most ridiculous thing he'd ever seen, he wouldn't think of paying less than $20,000 for the job that Daniel had done for the railroad. So Daniel went into the back of his office, pulled out his ledger book and went back to the first page—to the bill of the village blacksmith—and he wrote across it "Paid in full."

These things happen. They've probably happened to you. They've happened to me and it's fun when they do. That's why putting in the maximum effort and imagination on every new problem pays off in the kind of service we give. □

Risks in Loans Collateralized by Securities

by Hurd Baruch

Like Cinderella's coach, securities held as collateral can turn into a pumpkin right before your eyes. So warns Counsel Baruch who discusses the various legal aspects of bank securities lending, including new SEC regulations and requirements. He also provides warning signals and recommended procedures for the lender with securities collateral who wants to live happily ever after.

Happiness, for a lawyer, is having a bank for a client. Not only do banks pay their legal fees, they are exceptionally ethical clients in other ways. Banks rarely request a lawyer to chart a path for them through the thin, gray zone between legality and illegality in business dealings. Moreover, the attorney for a bank can be confident that his client will provide him with a continuous stream of problems requiring his services.

This article is based on an address which the author presented at a meeting of the RMA Pittsburgh Chapter on October 28, 1976.

303

Causes of banks' legal problems

The causes of legal problems for banks are not hard to find. Banking in the United States today is the most regulated business in the history of the world. I doubt that, with the best of faith and the greatest diligence, bankers could comply fully with all the various laws and regulations which govern their activities. Indeed, it is difficult for a bank officer even to be fully aware of all of the applicable laws and regulations pertaining to his business, so fast do they change and from so many sources do they come.

In addition, the marked proliferation of attorneys in recent years has no doubt led to an increase in litigation against banks, not all of which is well-founded, to say the least. The recent economic downturn has also resulted in litigation. Suits are brought in an attempt to collect defaulted loans which would have been written off in better times.

Three ways of doing things

Although such general causes of bank problems cannot be dealt with successfully on an individual basis, one cause should be singled out for attention. Those of you who have been in the army will perhaps understand that cause better if you recall the old army joke about the three ways of doing everything: the right way, the wrong way, and the "army way"! It seems to be the same at some banks with regard to forms, policies, and procedures: There is a right way, a wrong way, and the bank's way!

A prime example is the way many banks handle loans collateralized by securities. Being paid the prime rate or higher for a "riskless" loan seems almost too good to be true — and, in some cases, it is. Unfortunately, there is a great temptation for a bank to bend its standards in making a loan that seems so secure: Warning signals are disregarded, and the loan officer happily carts the collateral off to the vault, where the securities remain until the borrower defaults and the collateral must be sold. At that point, the loan officer all too often learns that the securities cannot be sold because they were stolen or counterfeit. Or the officer finds that the securities are subject to restrictions pursuant to contract or to the Federal securities laws.

A summary of problems with securities collateral

It is the purpose of this article to set forth in summary form the various problems that can beset a loan officer who is offered securities as collateral. Also included will be a list of warning signals and recommended procedures to prevent such collateral from turning, like Cinderella's coach, into a pumpkin before your eyes.

The problem of stolen securities

The stolen securities problem began in the late 1960's when there was a complete breakdown in the flow of paper work which both recorded and directed the flows of money and securities in the brokerage houses. Physical custody of the securities broke down, and the securities were left lying about on tables, on floors, in shoe boxes, in stairwells, etc. It has been estimated that as much as $1,500,000,000 in securities were stolen in the 1968-1972 period, in what one assistant district attorney of New York City called a "free-for-all."

Where did these securities go? They went primarily to financial institutions in this country and abroad, and many of them are still there. Organized crime, the dominant factor in the thefts, found that it could best avoid scrutiny by using the securities as collateral directly or indirectly. For example, it used securities as "window dressing" on balance sheets of borrowers.

The failure of Sci-Tek

Ultimate solutions were debated, especially the immobilization of stock certificates and their eventual elimination. However, such solutions were viewed as being far in the future. In the meantime, there was immediately available a partial solution of great promise known as "Sci-Tek." It was a computerized information retrieval system allowing users to obtain up-to-the-second information on all missing, stolen, or counterfeit securities reported to the system. Some of the largest brokerage firms on Wall Street joined the system, but the major banks did not. So despite its clear technological feasibility and its low cost of operation, Sci-Tek was a financial failure.

Why didn't the banks subscribe to Sci-Tek? One possible reason, in my opinion, was the banks' fear that if Sci-Tek became readily accepted, a purchaser would have to make inquiries to protect his status as a bona fide purchaser. General use of the system might subsequently reveal that a significant amount of the collateral in bank vaults was stolen or counterfeit.

The bona fide purchaser doctrine

The bona fide purchaser doctrine set forth in Section 8 of the Uniform Commercial Code is central to any bank's policies concerning the acceptance of securities collateral. The doctrine is vital because it provides that a "bona fide purchaser" takes a security free of all defenses such as theft, fraud, and forgery. Those of you who are familiar with the "holder in due course" doctrine set forth in Section 3 of the Uniform Commercial Code, relating to negotiable instruments, will recognize this as a parallel doctrine.

Here is the fundamental question which loan officers must ask themselves in accepting securities as collateral: Is the bank a bona fide purchaser of these securities? To be a bona fide purchaser, one must be a purchaser for value, in good faith, and without notice of any adverse claim.* In addition, a bona fide purchaser must take delivery of a security in bearer form or in registered form issued to him or endorsed to him or in blank.

Ordinarily, there will be no question that the bank is a purchaser for value, nor will there be any question about the delivery. Thus, the key to being a bona fide purchaser and to taking the collateral free from all defenses is that the collateral be taken "in good faith and without notice of any adverse claim."

Good faith and bad faith

The term "good faith" in the statutory definition of a bona fide purchaser does not mean affirmative good faith as you might imagine it. It is a legal term and has a special meaning, namely the absence of bad faith. What is bad faith? Bad faith is either guilty knowledge (knowledge of some illegality) or the failure to make inquiry when an inquiry is clearly called for because of suspicious circumstances.

I am sure that you will have nothing to do with securities which you know to be stolen or which you know to bear forged endorsements or which you know to have been obtained by fraud. Your problem will arise if you are aware of peculiar or suspicious circumstances suggesting further inquiry, which you are unwilling or unable to make for one reason or another.

Ordinarily, you are under no duty to make inquiries that might reveal a defect in the title to the securities offered by your borrower. Courts are most reluctant to impede the flow of commerce by imposing a duty of inquiry on purchasers of securities, including lenders.

The Pennsylvania bank case

Just how far some courts have gone in protecting loan officers is evident from a recent case involving a bank in Pennsylvania. The bank made a loan to an individual and the company he controlled which was collateralized by debentures. The debentures turned out to have been stolen. The true owner of the debentures argued in court that the bank should bear the burden of the loss because the bank did not act in good faith. He pointed to the following facts in particular:

1. The bank did not require proof that the borrower owned the debentures.

2. The bank failed to check with the transfer agent, the issuer, the FBI, etc., to see if the debentures were stolen.

---

*"Purchaser" is defined to include a lender who takes securities as collateral.

3. The borrowers were strangers to the bank, yet the bank did not check out either the borrowers' financial condition or their reputation.

4. The debentures had overdue interest coupons attached.

5. The amount of the debentures tendered bore no relation to the size of the loan since they were about three times the size of the amount borrowed.

6. The bank never inspected the premises of the corporate borrower or saw how the proceeds were utilized.

The court in the Pennsylvania bank case said there was nothing irregular in the transaction which served to arouse the loan officer's suspicions. Obviously a thorough investigation might have revealed the suspicious character of the borrower's possession, but the bank had no investigative duty to discharge.

While a court will not require loan officers to make an investigation in the absence of irregularities which serve to arouse the suspicion of a reasonable person, it is well-established that loan officers cannot deliberately close their eyes to suspicious circumstances. If they do so, they will be held to have knowledge of all facts which would have been uncovered by a reasonable inquiry. In short, if the danger signals are flying, and a loan officer ignores them, he will be found to have acted in bad faith, and the bank will not be a bona fide purchaser of the collateral.

Danger signals surrounding a loan collateralized by securities

Quite obviously, it is important for a loan officer to recognize the danger signals or suspicious circumstances surrounding a loan collateralized by securities. The danger signals may vary from case to case, and no list has been furnished in any treatise or court opinion. But a study of the cases reveals that the following circumstances have led to losses by banks:

1. **A stale (overdue) security.** Since the principal amount of a debt instrument is normally collected when it is due, there is a presumption of irregularity when a stale security is put up as collateral. Indeed, under Section 8-305 of the Uniform Commercial Code, where a security is obtained more than six months past the due date of the principal, the purchaser *cannot* be a bona fide purchaser. (Note that the doctrine of staleness only applies where the principal is overdue; it does not apply to overdue interest.)

2. **Purchase at a steep discount.** Just as it is expected that the buyer will be suspicious if offered a diamond ring at a bargain price in an alleyway, it is expected that a bank will be suspicious if offered the opportunity to obtain securities at a very steep discount. Whether such an acquisition would be through an outright purchase or by means of foreclosing on a collateralized loan that the borrower is not expected to repay, the circumstances are questionable.

3. **An obvious break in the chain of title.** This may occur, for example, where collateral has been pledged by third parties pursuant to hypothecation agreements which have not been fully completed. The lender should be suspicious where the borrower comes in with third party collateral but does not have authority to pass title because his name has not been filled in as the one authorized to rehypothecate the collateral. In this situation, the lender should ascertain the borrower's authority by contacting the third party owner of the collateral.

4. **A restrictive legend on the certificate.** A restrictive legend is notice not merely of the particular restriction which it may recite or refer to, but also of other possible restrictions on disposition and even defects in the title. Specifically, a lender cannot take for granted that the only restriction is the one noted on the face of the certificate; he must ask the issuer or transfer agent to determine whether there are additional restrictions or defects including theft or forgery.

5. **A warning of defects in the chain of title.** If this "warning signal" seems superfluous, I ask you to consider the case of certain Treasury bills stolen from Morgan Guaranty Trust Company in New York. The Treasury bills were subsequently accepted as collateral for a loan by a bank in Massachusetts which wanted to sell them when the loan went into default. It came out in court that Morgan had flooded the financial community with notices of the stolen Treasury bills and that the lending bank itself had gotten such a notice.

When notices of lost or stolen securities were received by the lending bank, they were routinely sent to its larger branches and to the trust and collateral department. There they were placed in a file by a collateral clerk. However, the loan officers did not check the collateral against that file because they weren't even aware that their bank had such a file! Ultimately, the Massachusetts bank had to return the collateral and eat the loss.

6. **Special capacity of the borrower.** Where the borrower would have access to the securities of an issuer or third parties in the course of his employment, a loan officer should be particularly vigilant to insure that the borrower has not misappropriated the securities. Borrowers in this special category include persons such as —

   a. The treasurer of a corporation, where the securities offered as collateral are issued by that corporation.

   b. An officer or employee of a financial institution, particularly where the securities offered as collateral are bearer securities or securities registered in a "street name."

   c. Persons acting in a fiduciary capacity, particularly where the securities offered are registered in the name of a fiduciary.

The problem is exemplified by a famous case in Pennsylvania in which a bank made a loan to the treasurer of a corporation which was collateralized by bonds issued by that corporation. It later turned out that the treasurer had misappropriated the bonds, and the court had a very easy time in determining that the bank was not a bona fide purchaser because it overlooked an obvious circumstance calling for inquiry.

7. **The "smelly deal."** Most loan officers with a few years' experience have probably been offered at least one deal with a peculiar aroma. Such a deal generally is put together with great haste due to the urgent needs of the borrower — for some reason, the loan must be closed that day or that week. The borrower needs the money to close a big deal, the details of which are not exactly clear, and he just can't wait. Indeed, he might even ask that the funds be wire-transferred out to a different bank at the closing.

The deal generally also involves a borrower not previously known to the bank. Frequently, the unknown borrower is from out of state and may have no permanent residence. Such a borrower may also be unwilling (unable?) to provide financial information and credit references. Moreover, the securities probably are not registered in the borrower's name — they are bearer bonds or "street name" certificates. And, if questioned about some or all of these points, the borrower, instead of meeting the objections head on, suggests that the loan can be collateralized with still more securities!

A loan officer unlucky enough to walk into such a deal might ultimately discover that the borrower's willingness to "sweeten the pot" was prompted by the fact that the securities were stolen and had cost him only $.15 on the dollar.

Recommendations on how to avoid problems

The discussion of the major warning signals associated with securities collateral would be incomplete without recommendations for heading off problems. Of course, what I am about to recommend should be viewed only as a general guide to be modified in each case according to the bank's organization chart and personnel involved.

My first recommendation is that the loan officer be required to investigate situations where he has encountered one or more suspicious circumstance. The inquiry should include the following steps:

1. Check the bank's central file of lost or stolen securities notices.

2. Check with the issuer or transfer agent of the securities involved.

3. Make a *detailed* record of the checks made to verify the circumstances. The officer should note, for example, the date on which he called the transfer agent, the

name of the person he spoke to, that person's position, the certificate number the transfer agent furnished, and the transfer agent's response that there was no stop order against the certificate number.

4. Demand proof of the borrower's purchase of the securities, unless they are registered in the borrower's name. (Confirmation slips from a broker are excellent for this purpose, and they must have been retained by the purchaser for his tax records.)

5. Obtain proper documentation as to the chain of title *and* as to the bank's authority to dispose of the collateral in the event that the loan is not paid. (These may well require separate documents.)

My second recommendation is that the bank's central records custodian should be responsible for maintaining notices from other institutions of lost and stolen securities. Also, lending officers should be aware of the notice file and how to use it.

My third recommendation is that the securities custodian at the bank should be responsible for re-registering stock or bond collateral in the bank's name immediately upon receipt. A bank takes a wholly unnecessary risk when it maintains collateral in the borrower's name, even though it may have a stock power signed in blank.

Consider, for example, the litigation which would result from an unscrupulous borrower writing to the transfer agent of the securities, stating that he had lost the securities and requesting replacement certificates. In such a case, the bank would find a stop order against the certificates if it tried to sell them.

New legislation affecting the handling of collateralized securities

New duties imposed by Federal securities laws

Soon, the preceding recommendations will have to be supplemented to take into account the duties newly imposed on banks by the Federal securities laws. Prompted in part by the financial failure of the Sci-Tek system described previously, Congress enacted reform legislation in 1975. This legislation affects every member of the Federal Reserve System and every bank insured by the FDIC, as well as brokers, dealers, transfer agents, and clearing agencies. These entities are to perform two new duties regarding securities in their custody or control or for which they are responsible or in which they are effecting, clearing, or settling a transaction. They are to —

1. Report information about missing, lost, counterfeit, or stolen securities in accordance with regulations of the Securities and Exchange Commission (SEC).

2. Make such inquiry as the SEC prescribes to determine whether securities have been reported as missing, lost, counterfeit, or stolen.

Rule 17f-1

In January of 1976, the SEC proposed Rule 17f-1, under Section 17(f)(1) of the Securities Exchange Act of 1934. The Rule, as adopted in December 1976, will require the following:

1. **Reporting the theft or loss of securities.** In the case of U.S. Government and government agency securities and securities issued by certain international agencies, reports must be made to the Federal Reserve System through its nearest bank or branch. In the case of all other securities, reports must be made to the SEC. The reports will be due within one business day where criminal activity is suspected and within three business days otherwise.

2. **Inquiry of a computerized data bank regarding every security which comes into its possession or keeping, whether by pledge, transfer, or otherwise,** to ascertain if such security has been reported as missing, lost, counterfeit or stolen, *unless —*

   a. The security is received directly from its issuer at issuance.

   b. The security is received from another reporting institution.

   c. The security is registered in the name of the customer or the nominee of such customer.

The new rule goes into effect on a pilot basis between March 1, 1977, and February 28, 1978. During that period, the Commission will not require reports or inquiries on corporate securities without assigned CUSIP numbers and on transactions involving less than $10,000.

Those of you who have had occasion to fill out the new Form U-1 statement of purpose of a stock-secured extension of credit, published in 1976 by the Board of Governors of the Federal Reserve System, will be familiar with the following provision in part II of the form:

> *If any of the securities described above in tables 1 and 2 that directly secure the credit have been or will be physically delivered to the bank,* the undersigned officer further certifies that he or she (a) has examined, or will examine, the physical aspects of such securities and performed, or will perform, such validation procedures as are required by bank policy and government regulations promulgated under section 17(f) of the Securities Exchange Act of 1934, as amended, or has been informed that another employee of the bank has performed or will perform such functions, (b) if any of such securities are not or will not be registered in the name of the borrower or its nominee, has examined the written

consent of the registered owner to pledge such securities, and (c) is satisfied to the best of the officer's knowledge and belief that such securities are genuine and not stolen or forged and their faces have not been altered.

Using the new system, a bank employee will be able to make an inquiry by furnishing the name of the security, the certificate number, and other pertinent data. The employee will receive an instantaneous report as to whether that particular certificate has been reported as stolen, lost, counterfeit, etc.

In the eyes of many banks, the saving grace of the SEC rule is the exemption from the need to make inquiry in the case of securities received by one reporting institution from another. However, although such an inquiry will not be demanded for compliance with the securities law, *it may still be required if a bank is to meet the bona fide purchaser test* in those cases where the loan officer has knowledge of suspicious circumstances. (For example, a loan may be shifted from one bank to another bank under circumstances that suggest that the first bank has reservations about the borrower's integrity.)

It is too early to tell just how the verification system will work. However, it is important that your bank be aware of it and that you adapt your procedures to it when it becomes effective, in practice, in the near future.

Restrictions on the disposition of securities

The loan officer who safely negotiates the peril of the stolen securities problem must also avoid the danger of restrictions placed upon the disposition of securities by contract and by the Federal securities laws. Restrictions are often placed on the disposition of securities (1) covered by a buy/sell agreement or voting trust agreement between an officer or large stockholder and his company or other stockholders or (2) which were obtained directly from the issuer by way of original issuance at the formation of the company or by way of a merger, acquisition, stock option, or bonus.

The danger signals are important and should be recognized by the loan officer. They include the following:

1. A legend on the certificate.

2. Stock of a closely held company.

3. Stock owned by a present or former officer, director, or employee of the issuer.

4. A block of stock which is substantial in comparison to the outstanding number of shares.

The loan officer should attempt to obtain a written statement from the company itself that there are no contractual or SEC restrictions on disposition of the stock should any of the warning signals be discovered. If there are restrictions, they should be specified in detail. In addition, the bank's securities custodian should be responsible for "freeing-up" restricted securities as soon as the restrictions lapse. This will enable the bank to dispose of them promptly upon a default, instead of having to wait weeks or even months for the necessary action on the part of the transfer agent after a decision has been made to sell them.

In the case of restrictions imposed by the Federal securities laws, there can be no guarantee that securities which are restricted can *ever* be freely sold by the pledgee bank. This applies in particular to the registration requirement imposed by Section 5 of the Securities Act of 1933. Where a pledged security is restricted because it was obtained by the pledgor without a registration, the security can be sold by the pledgee bank only by registration. However, the security can also be sold pursuant to an exemption from registration which is generally a sale under Rule 144 of the Securities Act of 1933 or a sale by "private placement."

Sale by private placement

An owner of restricted stock has no right to require that his shares be registered by the issuer, absent a contractual provision to that effect. Inasmuch as registration is a costly and time-consuming process, most restricted securities are issued without any commitment by the company to register the shares in the future. And the exemption from registration, which is granted under the securities laws to a holder who resells in another "private placement," is limited to cases where the purchaser is knowledgeable and can bear the financial risk of loss.

A private placement, by definition, does not include a resale on a stock exchange or to members of the general public through a broker. Moreover, in a private placement, the purchaser gets a security which is still restricted and which he must hold for at least two years before reselling absent another exemption in the securities laws.

Sale under SEC Rule 144

Many loan officers believe that securities restricted under the Federal securities laws can readily be sold under the "dribble out" provision of SEC Rule 144. While it is true that many restricted securities can be sold under that rule, it should be carefully noted that all securities are eligible for sale thereunder and that eligibility can vary from one week to the next.

The rule requires that a certain specified amount of current information about the issuer company be available publicly. Ordinarily, the holder of restricted stock has no contractual right to insist that the issuer make the appropriate information available. And there is always the possibility that a company, particularly one whose securities are not listed on a stock exchange, will not be in full compliance with SEC reporting requirements at the time the pledgee desires to sell the stock. Next, there is the requirement of a two-year holding period which may not, in some cases, include the period of time the pledgor has held the stock.

Moreover, there is a limitation on the amount of stock which can be sold within a six-month period. The stock sold cannot exceed 1% of the total number of shares outstanding of that class or the average weekly trading volume based on the four previous weeks of trading, whichever figure is *lower*.

The volume limitation which is imposed on the sale of shares by the pledgee bank is a limitation which applies to all shares held by the pledgor or obtained through him, even by persons other than the pledgee bank. In other words, if the pledgor has himself sold a certain number of shares during a given six-month period or if other pledgees have sold shares of the same security which they have obtained from the same pledgor, the pledgee bank in question may be foreclosed from selling part or all of its shares during that six-month period.

To complicate matters further, a sale under Rule 144 can only be made in a "broker's transaction"; that is, the sale cannot be negotiated by the broker but must be one where the purchase order is unsolicited. This may put the bank in a Catch-22 situation because it may be difficult, if not impossible, to arrange a sale of a sizable block of stock in a closely held company without negotiation by a broker.

From the preceding comments, which fall far short of covering the subject, it should be clear that a loan officer cannot blindly rely on being able to sell restricted securities under Rule 144. Even an opinion of counsel that restricted securities can be sold freely at one time cannot be relied upon as an opinion that the same collateral will be freely saleable under Rule 144 in the future.

Conclusion

My purpose in describing "security risks" in detail is not to discourage you from accepting securities as collateral. Rather, it is to help you avoid the once-in-a-lifetime loan collateralized by stolen or restricted securities that could wipe out the profit from years of prudent lending. By keeping an eye out for the warning signals and by adhering to the recommendations given in this article, you should be able to demonstrate that the prime-plus loan, fully collateralized by readily marketable securities, is not too good to be true!   □

Letters of Credit for the Commercial Lender

by A. Thomas Small

Letters of credit can be very useful in commercial bank transactions, but they require a certain amount of knowledge on the lender's part. In the following article, Thomas Small describes the various types of letters of credit, pertinent state and federal laws, and many other important aspects of these popular instruments with which a lender should be familiar.

Over the past two decades, the variety of ways in which letters of credit are used has increased dramatically. Letters of credit were once used only in connection with international sales. But now letters of credit are used to assure football players of the payment of their salaries, mortgage lenders of the payment of their commitment fees, foreign governments of the soundness of equipment purchased, and in other similarly innovative ways. As a result, banks look increasingly to letters of credit for repayment of their loans. Generally, letters of credit are considered to be prime collateral for commercial loans. But unless lenders are knowledgeable and cautious in this area, letters of credit may prove to be of little benefit.

Types of letters of credit

Commercial letter of credit

The typical and traditional letter of credit transaction involves a seller of goods who wants to be sure that he is paid for his goods. The purchaser (called

315

the "customer") causes the purchaser's bank (called the "issuer") to provide a letter of credit for the benefit of the seller (called the "beneficiary"). Ordinarily, the letter of credit requires the issuer to honor drafts presented against the credit by the beneficiary, provided the draft is accompanied by documents which conform to the terms of the credit. Usually, the documents are evidence that the goods have been shipped.

This arrangement creates a contractual relationship between the issuer and the beneficiary, entitling the beneficiary to look directly to the issuer for payment as long as the beneficiary can provide the documentary evidence required by the letter of credit. The beneficiary is entitled to payment even if the customer is insolvent and even if the customer is challenging the quality of the goods sold.

This type of letter of credit, involved in the traditional buyer-seller situation, is often called a "commercial" letter of credit. Ordinarily, the intention of all parties to the commercial letter of credit is that the letter of credit will be drawn upon. The process is simple: The beneficiary makes shipment, draws drafts, and presents all documents to a bank (usually his own) which then negotiates the drafts and forwards documents. The issuing bank examines all documents for full compliance and honors the drafts presented. Reimbursement is then obtained from the customer.

Standby or guarantee letter of credit

In the past 20 years, however, with increasing frequency, the letter of credit has been used as a surety device to assure the beneficiary of the performance of the customer's obligations. The "standby" or "guarantee" letter of credit, as such a credit is called, assures the beneficiary that in the event of nonperformance or nonpayment of an obligation, the beneficiary may request payment from the issuing bank. Typically, the beneficiary is able to draw under a standby letter of credit by presenting a draft with the evidence, required by the letter of credit, that the customer has not performed an obligation.

Unlike the commercial letter of credit in which all parties anticipate that the letter of credit will be drawn upon, all the parties to a standby letter of credit anticipate that the customer will perform its obligation and that the letter of credit will not be drawn upon.

When the issuer is called on to honor drafts under a standby letter of credit, the customer frequently cannot perform the obligation to the beneficiary and cannot perform its obligation to reimburse the issuer for payments made under the credit. In those circumstances, an issuing bank inevitably scrutinizes its liability to the beneficiary. The beneficiary is apt to suffer losses unless it has been careful to examine the terms of the credit and protect itself in advance.

Clean letter of credit

Both commercial and standby letters of credit usually require that drafts presented under the credit be accompanied by documents. However, if the letter of credit "conspicuously states that it is a letter of credit or is conspicuously so entitled," the drafts will be honored without being accompanied by documents, in the absence of a requirement spelled out in the letter of credit to the contrary.[1] This type of letter of credit is called a "clean" letter of credit. Both commercial and standby letters of credit can be clean letters of credit.

What law applies

The law relating to letters of credit is intricate. Moreover, it has been developing rapidly as a result of the litigation deriving from increased letter of credit usage. Obviously, it is important for lenders to keep abreast of legal changes in this often confused field.

The law applicable to letters of credit is derived from many sources. Article 5 of the Uniform Commercial Code (UCC) applies to letters of credit, but, by its own pronouncement, Article 5 is subject to rules and concepts "developed prior to this chapter" and those which "may hereafter develop."[2]

In addition, as is the case with other UCC articles, the provisions of Article 5 are supplemented (to the extent not specifically excluded) by general principles of law, including, for example, fraud, estoppel, principal, and agent.[3] Also, UCC Section 1-205(5) makes "usage of trade" available for interpreting the terms of the letter of credit. Furthermore, pursuant to UCC Section 1-102(3), the effect of some provisions of the UCC may be varied by agreement of the parties, and pursuant to UCC Section 1-105(1), the parties may in some circumstances choose which state's laws apply.

Many letters of credit are issued by New York banks. Therefore, it is important to realize that the UCC as adopted in the state of New York contains a provision stating that the Uniform Customs and Practices for Documentary Credits (U.C.P.) and not Article 5 is the controlling law if the letter of credit (by its terms or by agreement of the parties) says that the letter of credit shall be

---

[1] UCC Sec. 5-102(1)(c).

[2] UCC Sec. 5-102(3).

[3] UCC Sec. 1-103.

subject in whole or in part to the U.C.P.[4] Most letters of credit issued by New York banks specifically say that they are governed by the U.C.P. As will be seen later, it can make a significant difference in some instances whether the UCC or the U.C.P. applies.

In most states other than New York, a statement in the letter of credit that the U.C.P. controls means that both the UCC and the U.C.P. are applicable; but, in the case of conflict, the UCC will control when the UCC provisions are mandatory.[5] Generally, the UCC and the U.C.P. complement each other, but there are some conflicts, a few of which will be mentioned as follows.

National Banking Act or UCC

In recent years, national banks have further complicated problems for beneficiaries. To keep from having to honor standby letters of credit, some national banks have resorted to the argument that the standby letter of credit was in fact a guarantee, which is beyond the powers of a national bank. This *ultra vires* position has not enjoyed much success, however. Courts in most cases have held that issuing standby letters of credit, even ones serving strictly a guarantee function, is nevertheless a proper activity for a national bank if in fact the transactions are truly letters of credit.

An Interpretive Ruling of the Comptroller of the Currency says that a national bank can issue a letter of credit permissible under the UCC or U.C.P. to or on behalf of its customers.[6] A standby letter of credit is defined by the Comptroller of the Currency in Interpretive Ruling 7.1160 as a letter of credit which represents an obligation to:

(1) Repay money borrowed by or advanced to or for the account of the account party or

(2) Make payment on account of any indebtedness undertaken by the account party or

(3) Make payment on account of any default by the account party in the performance of the obligation.

While the issue of the validity of a national bank's guarantee letter of credit has been buried, it is possible that the *ultra vires* argument with respect to a national bank will work for the issuing bank if in fact a letter of credit does not

---

[4] New York UCC Sec. 5-102(4). Missouri, Alabama, and Arizona have followed the New York lead. See Uniform Customs and Practices for Documentary Credits (1974 rev., International Chamber of Commerce Publication No. 290).

[5] White and Summers, *Uniform Commercial Code*, Sec. 18-3, p. 611.

[6] Comptroller of the Currency Interpretive Ruling 7.7016; 12 C.F.R. 7.7016.

exist. A letter of credit (involving a bank as issuer) is defined in UCC Article 5 as an engagement by a bank (in writing and signed by the issuer) at the request of a customer to honor drafts or other demands for payment upon compliance with the conditions specified in the credit if:

(1) The credit requires a documentary draft or a documentary demand for payment or

(2) Conspicuously states that it is a letter of credit or is conspicuously so entitled.[7]

A transaction may fall outside the Comptroller's definition of a standby letter of credit and still be a letter of credit under the UCC. The transaction may also fall outside the bounds of what constitutes a letter of credit under the UCC (or U.C.P.), and in that event, the *ultra vires* argument may have some vitality, notwithstanding the inclinations of most courts to compel banks to honor their argreements.[8]

It has been argued that a national bank can refuse to honor its obligations under a letter of credit if the advance, when coupled with other loans to the customer, would exceed the bank's lending limit in violation of 12 U.S.C. 84. That argument has been properly rejected.[9]

State banking law or UCC

The *ultra vires* ploy has also surfaced with respect to state banking law limitations. The issuing state banks have not, for the most part, been able to convince the courts that issuing guarantee letters of credit is an *ultra vires* act. However, varied state laws and state courts might enable them to do so.[10]

Needless to say, the beneficiary, especially in the more unusual and imaginative transactions, should be certain that the transaction does in fact constitute a letter of credit.

---

[7] UCC Secs. 5-102, 5-103(1)(a) and 5-104(1).

[8] *Republic National Bank of Dallas* v. *Northwest National Bank of Fort Worth*, 24 UCC Rep. 939; 566 S.W. 2d 358 (Tex. Civ. App., 1978), rev'd. 25 UCC Rep. 832; 578 S.W. 2d 109 (Tex., 1978), but in *Witchita Eagle & Beacon Pub. Co.* v. *Pacific Nat'l Bank*, 493 F. 2d 1285 (9th Cir., 1974), the issuing bank was held liable notwithstanding the fact that the document was a guarantee and not a letter of credit.

[9] *First America National Bank of Iuka* v. *Alcorn, Inc.* 24 UCC Rep. 1240; 361 So. 2d 481 (Miss., 1978).

[10] See Clark and Squillante, *Bank Deposits, Collections and Credit Cards*, Supplement p. 117; *Bank of North Carolina, N. A.* v. *Rock Island Bank*, 23 UCC Rep. 715; 570 F. 2d 202 (7th Cir., 1978); In *International Dairy Queen, Inc.* v. *Bank of Wadley*, 407 F. Supp. 1270 (M.D. Ala., 1976), a letter of credit was invalid because it exceeded the state bank's loan limit.

How banks get involved in letters of credit

As lenders, banks may be involved in letters of credit in three ways. Each of the ways has its own characteristics.

Assignment of a letter of credit

The first way a bank gets involved with a letter of credit is by assignment of the letter of credit under which the borrower is the beneficiary. Section 5-116 of the UCC says that the "right to draw" under a letter of credit can only be assigned when the letter of credit is designated by its terms as being assignable. Even though the right to draw under the letter of credit may not, unless specified, be assigned, the proceeds of the letter of credit may always be assigned.[11]

Interestingly, the assignment of a letter of credit's proceeds is governed by Article 9 (Secured Transactions) of the UCC as if the assignment were an assignment of an "account" except that certain steps spelled out in UCC Sec. 5-116(2) must be met before the security interest is perfected. What is not clear is whether the steps are the only actions required for perfection or whether they are *in addition* to the requirements of Article 9 relating to accounts.

Since there is some confusion on the subject, the safest course to take in perfecting the lien on proceeds of a letter of credit is to file the financing statements required by Article 9 with respect to accounts and, in addition, to follow the requirements of UCC 5-116(2), which are:

(1) Delivering the letter of credit to the assignee,

(2) Giving to the issuer notice (which must contain a request to pay assignee) of the assignment signed by the beneficiary, and

(3) If requested by the issuer, exhibiting the letter of credit to the issuer.[12]

Does delivery of the letter of credit mean that the assignee must retain possession of the letter of credit as part of the perfection requirements? Some authorities believe that is the case.[13] If the borrower is performing under a construction contract in a foreign country, it may not be convenient for the lender-assignee to retain possession, especially when the credit calls for pre-

---

[11] In accord, see U.C.P. Article 47. Under U.C.P. Article 46e, a transferable credit can be transferred only once.

[12] See UCC 9-302(e) for when filing is not required with regard to the assignment of accounts.

[13] Gilmore, *Security Interests in Personal Property*, Vol. I, Sec. 11.3 p. 343 and White and Summers, *Uniform Commercial Code*, Sec. 18.9 p. 633. UCC Sec. 9-305 says that perfection with respect to letters of credit *may* be by possession.

sentment of the letter of credit with each draw.[14] Could the assignee have "constructive possession" of the letter of credit through the possession of a third party bank in the foreign country which processes the drafts for collection? The answer is not clear under the UCC.

The extreme scarcity of cases construing the perfection requirements regarding the assignments of proceeds of letters of credit is reason for caution. The prudent commercial lender should take the conservative approach. He should follow the requirements of Article 9 and Article 5 and retain possession of the letter of credit or run the risk of a major disappointment at the hands of the assignor's trustee in bankruptcy.

Of course, as with the assignment of any contract right, the right to payment of the assignee of the proceeds of a letter of credit is only as good as the ability of the original beneficiary to perform the obligations underlying the letter of credit.

Lender as holder in due course

The second way a lending bank may be involved in a letter of credit is as a holder in due course. Although a letter of credit can be transferable, it is not negotiable. On the other hand, the drafts drawn under the letter of credit may be negotiable and, as such, may be negotiated to a holder in due course.

When dealing with drafts presented by a holder in due course, the issuing bank's defenses to payment are severely limited. Significantly, the defense of fraud in the transaction underlying the letter of credit is not available against the holder in due course.[15] An assignee of the proceeds of a letter of credit would not be a holder and would be subject to the defense of fraud in the underlying transaction. Obviously, if the holder has had notice of the defense prior to negotiation, he cannot qualify as a holder in due course.

Bank as beneficiary of standby letter of credit

Finally, a lending bank may be involved in a letter of credit as a beneficiary of a letter of credit issued for the purpose of assuring payment by the borrower.

Typically, the letter of credit will require drafts presented against the letter of credit to be accompanied by a statement signed by an officer of the lender certifying that a certain loan to the customer is in default. Although some courts

---

[14] The example is similar to but different from the "notation credit" described in UCC Sec. 5-108 under which the party seeking payment of the draft may include a signed statement that an "appropriate notation" had been made on the letter of credit.

[15] *Banco Español de Credito* v. *State St. Bank & Trust Co.*, 6 UCC Rep. 378; 409 F. 2d 711, 35 A.L.R. 3d 1397 (1st Cir., 1969); UCC Sec. 5-114.

have been somewhat lenient in determining compliance by the beneficiary in wrongful dishonor cases against the issuing bank, the beneficiary clearly should be certain that the requirements of the letter of credit can be met.[16] Also, upon drawing under the letter of credit, the beneficiary's certification should as much as possible follow the language of the letter of credit itself.

Other pertinent facts about letters of credit

Time is of the essence

By using theories of estoppel and waiver, some courts have extended the time in which the issuing bank must honor drafts beyond the time stated in the letter of credit. Nevertheless, in the absence of inequitable conduct on the part of the issuing bank, the expiration date of the letter of credit will be strictly applied.[17] The lender-beneficiary must be aware of the expiration date and be certain that the date gives the lender sufficient time to present drafts. A letter of credit which expires on the same date as the maturity of the underlying loan may be worthless. Similarly, an expiration date 15 days past the loan's maturity may not help if the loan has a 30-day notice and cure provision.

Revocable and irrevocable letters of credit

Both the UCC and U.C.P. say that letters of credit can be either revocable or irrevocable.[18] The UCC is silent as to whether a letter of credit is revocable or irrevocable in the absence of a specific designation in the credit. Given the court's usual inclination to enforce contracts, however, it is a fair bet that silence in the document would render the letter of credit irrevocable.[19] Under U.C.P. Article 1c, however, silence in the letter of credit as to revocability or irrevocability will cause the letter of credit to be revocable.[20] A revocable letter of credit, of course, should be unacceptable to a lender-beneficiary who should insist that the letter of credit specifically state that it is irrevocable.

Some letters of credit can be terminated by the customer upon presenting certain documents to the issuing bank (for example, a customer certificate that the loan has been paid). Courts have strictly construed these customer termina-

---

[16] Some courts are not lenient. See *Courtaulds North America, Inc.* v. *North Carolina National Bank,* 18 UCC Rep. 467; 528 F. 2d 802 (4th Cir., 1975); and *Venizelos, S.A.* v. *Chase Manhattan Bank,* 425 F. 2d 461, 7 UCC Rep. 719 (2d Cir., 1970).

[17] *Hyland Hills Metropolitan Park & Recreation District* v. *McCoy Enterprises, Inc.* 20 UCC Rep. 488; 554 P. 2d 708 (Colo. 1976).

[18] UCC Sec. 5-106 and U.C.P. Article 1a.

[19] *West Virginia Housing Dev. Fund* v. *Sroka,* 20 UCC Rep. 154, 415 F. Supp. 1107 (D.C.W.D., Pa., 1976).

[20] See *Beathard* v. *Chicago Football Club, Inc.,* 20 UCC Rep. 164; 419 F. Supp. 1133 (D.C.N.D., Ill., 1976).

tion requirements, but a provision permitting customer terminations in the letter of credit can only mean trouble for the lender-beneficiary.[21]

Modification of underlying transaction

The modification of the terms of an irrevocable letter of credit by the issuer and the customer cannot affect the rights of the beneficiary without his consent. On the other hand, a modification of the underlying contract between the customer and the beneficiary may, without the consent of the issuer, very well relieve the issuing bank from its obligations under the credit.[22] Would an extension of time for payment or the release of collateral by the lender-beneficiary relieve the issuing bank of its obligations? To be on the safe side, all modifications should be approved by the issuer.

Defenses by issuing bank

When the unexpected happens and the standby letter of credit is drawn upon, the customer may be insolvent, and the issuing bank may be scrambling for a reason not to honor the draft. Under UCC Section 5-112(a), the issuing bank has until the third banking day following receipt to defer honor. Under Article 8d of the U.C.P., the issuing bank has a "reasonable" time to examine documents and to determine if they are in accord with the terms of the credit.

Under UCC Section 5-114, the issuer must honor a draft which complies with the terms of the credit. If a conforming document is in fact forged or fraudulent or if there is fraud in the transaction, the issuing bank may, if acting in good faith, pay or not pay when dealing with the original beneficiary. When the issuing bank is dealing with a holder in due course of the drafts, however, the drafts must be honored even if forgery and fraud in the transaction are present.[23] One exception is the ever popular injunction which shall be discussed later.

Remedies for wrongful dishonor

The beneficiary's remedies for wrongful dishonor by the issuing bank are set out in UCC Section 5-115. Unfortunately, the remedies speak primarily of breaches of the commercial letter of credit. The beneficiary can recover the face amount of the draft together with incidental damages under UCC Section 2-710 plus interest less recovery on the resale of the goods which were the

---

[21] See *Witchita Eagle & Beacon Pub. Co., Inc.* v. *Pacific National Bank of San Francisco,* 14 UCC Rep. 156; 493 F. 2d 1285 (9th Cir., 1974).

[22] *AMF Head Sportswear, Inc.* v. *Ray Scott's All-American Sports Club,* 23 UCC Rep. 990; 448 F. Supp. 222 (D.C. Ariz., 1978).

[23] UCC Sec. 5-114(2)(a).

subject matter of the transaction. What are the damages for the standby lender-beneficiary? Certainly, the face amount of the draft should be recovered, probably with interest at the "legal rate."[24] Are attorney's fees recoverable? Probably not, unless specifically included in the letter of credit.[25] A careful beneficiary would require that the letter of credit provide for interest at the underlying contract rate and attorney's fees in the event of wrongful dishonor.

Customer defenses against beneficiary

The letter of credit transaction is supposed to create an obligation directly from the issuing bank to the beneficiary, who is to be paid even if the beneficiary has not performed to the satisfaction of the customer. Of course, if fraud in the transaction is present, the issuing bank may, at its option, honor or dishonor the draft when no innocent third parties (such as holders in due course) are involved. If no innocent third parties are involved, the customer will be entitled to an injunction prohibiting honor of the draft by the bank.

The injunction based on an allegation of fraud is a popular customer technique (with at times some help from the issuing bank). Some courts have been reluctant to enjoin honor of the drafts without a clear showing that fraud permeated the entire transaction.[26] On the other hand, other courts have granted injunctions on less than overwhelming evidence of fraud.[27]

Situations involving unusual facts can sometimes lead to unusual judicial decisions. One recent case that falls in that category might be some concern to the lender-beneficiary of standby letters of credit.[28]

The facts of the case are as follows: Bank A was the beneficiary of a letter of credit that had been issued by Bank B and that could be drawn upon by Bank A presenting drafts accompanied by "Certified and true photostatic copy of each instrument causing this establishment of credit to Thomas O'Grady to be called upon." Bank B's customer brought an action to enjoin Bank A from drawing under the letter of credit because, he alleged, the letter of credit was given in connection with a loan to X, Y, and Z. In fact, Bank A had only made the loan to X and Y. The customer made no allegations of fraud in his com-

---

[24] *Bossier Bank & Trust Co.* v. *Union Planters National Bank of Memphis*, 21 UCC Rep. 254, 550 F. 2d 1077 (6th Cir., 1977).

[25] *Id.*, also see *New York Life Ins. Co.* v. *Hartford Nat. Bank & Trust Co.*, 22 UCC Rep. 761, 378 A. 2d 562 (Conn., 1977) in which the beneficiary had to prove damages in a wrongful dishonor case.

[26] See *Intraworld Industries, Inc.* v. *Girard Trust Bank*, 17 UCC Rep. 191, 461 Pa. 343, 336 A. 2d 316 (1975) and *Werner* v. *A.L. Grootemaat & Sons, Inc.*, 23 UCC Rep. 136; 80 Wis. 2d 513, 259 N. W. 2d 310 (1977).

[27] See *Dynamics Corp. of America* v. *Citizens & Southern Nat. Bank*, 12 UCC Rep. 317; 356 F. Supp. 991 (D.C.N.D. Ga., 1973) and *NMC Enterprises, Inc.* v. *Columbia Broadcasting System, Inc.*, 14 UCC Rep. 1427 (N.Y. Sup. Ct., 1974).

[28] *O'Grady* v. *First Union Nat. Bk of NC*, 296 N.C. 212; 250 S.E. 2d 587 (1978).

plaint, saying only that drawing under the letter of credit was conditioned *by the customer* (the issuing bank did not know of the condition) upon the loan being to X, Y, and Z.

Nevertheless, the Supreme Court of North Carolina said that if the letter of credit were procured by the customer on the condition that the loan be to X, Y, and Z, then Bank A's drawing under the letter of credit in connection with a loan to only X and Y would amount to a presentment of fraudulent documents.[29] The Supreme Court of North Carolina sent the case back to the trial court to determine if the customer had communicated the condition to the beneficiary. The case was settled before re-trial.

If this case should be followed, the results could be disastrous for a lender-beneficiary. Real estate lenders will remember the imaginative defenses raised to delay a mortgagee's foreclosure (for example, breach of oral loan modification, failure to fund). It seems that in North Carolina, at least, the customer can allege oral conditions imposed by the customer, which, if communicated to the beneficiary and not complied with by the beneficiary, would render draws under the letter of credit fraudulent and thereby be subject to injunction.

The bankruptcy court and injunctions

If the lender-beneficiary's borrower-customer becomes insolvent, it is possible that the injunction issues may be raised in a bankruptcy court. Under the Bankruptcy Act of 1898, it has been held that a bankruptcy court did not have summary jurisdiction to enjoin the payment of a letter of credit by the issuing bank.[30] The Bankruptcy Reform Act of 1978, however, expands the jurisdiction of the bankruptcy court to include all civil proceedings "arising in or related" to cases under the Bankruptcy Code.[31] The argument can be made that the bankruptcy court still does not have jurisdiction since the dispute is between only the beneficiary and the issuer, but, as is the case with many other Bankruptcy Reform Act issues, the answer will come from the courts.

Conclusion

An uneducated or careless lender may be lulled into a false sense of security when a letter of credit is a source of repayment for a loan. Letters of credit have their limitations and require great care. Nevertheless, if lenders are cautious, letters of credit can be a safe source of security. ☐

---

[29] The court said that there was no fraud in the transaction but rather presentment of fraudulent documents.

[30] *In re Marine Distributing, Inc.,* 18 UCC Rep. 183, 522 F. 2d 791 (9th Cir., 1975).

[31] Bankruptcy Reform Act of 1978 Sec. 241(a); 28 U.S.C. 1471(b).

Legislative and Judicial Developments Affecting Commercial Lending, 1978–1979

by A. Bruce Schimberg

This article is a review of some of the legislative and judicial developments during the past year which are of special interest to loan officers—not only those in commercial finance companies but in commercial banks as well. It is based on a report given by the author as part of the program presented at the National Commercial Finance Conference, Inc. (NCFC) Annual Meeting in Dallas, Texas on October 31, 1979.

This annual review highlights some of the legislative and judicial developments during the year which are of special interest to the commercial financing industry.

There were two matters which attracted much of the industry's attention. One was The Bankruptcy Code of 1978 which became generally effective this past October. The other was the *Kimbell Foods* decision of the U.S. Supreme Court in which NCFC continued its successful efforts as *amicus curiae* in cases of national importance.

Cases involving Article 9 of the UCC continued to appear in large numbers, but there are only a few which seem to warrant special comment. There is little doubt that for the commercial financing industry, the new Bankruptcy Code will dominate our interest and time in the judicial arena for quite awhile.

Competing government security interests—
the *Kimbell Foods* decision

In a decision of considerable importance to the commercial finance industry, the U.S. Supreme Court rejected, by unanimous decision, an attempt by the government to establish a federal rule of priority that would have favored government-held security interests created under the UCC over privately-held security interests. Instead, the Court in *United States* v. *Kimbell Foods, Inc.,* 59 L. Ed.2d 711 (1979) ruled that the law of the states, primarily the UCC, should be used to determine the relative priority of security interests held by the SBA and private secured lenders. The NCFC filed a successful brief in the case as *amicus curiae* in support of the private secured party, Kimbell. In a companion case decided by the same opinion, *United States* v. *Crittenden*, the Court also concluded that state law should be relied upon in priority disputes between state statutory liens and government security interests.

Summary of the case

The facts of the *Kimbell* case were described in my article last year. (See the article entitled, "Legislative and Judicial Developments Affecting Commercial Lending, 1977-78," in the January 1979 *Journal,* page 55.) Briefly, Kimbell had the first perfected security interest in the debtor's existing and future equipment and inventory. The security interest covered some existing notes and all future advances in the form of continuing inventory sales on credit by Kimbell to the debtor. After perfection of Kimbell's security interest, the debtor obtained a bank loan of which 90% was guaranteed by the SBA. This loan was secured by the same collateral and perfected by filing after the Kimbell filing. Some of the proceeds of that loan were used to pay the notes held by Kimbell. But the proceeds were not used to pay the balance owing from the credit sales which Kimbell continued to make after the filing of the bank's security interest.

Eventually, the debtor defaulted on the bank loan, and the SBA honored its guarantee and received an assignment of the bank's security interest. At that time, the entire Kimbell claim consisted of future advances made after the bank loan. Both Kimbell and the SBA claimed priority for their security interests.

The trial court ruled that the SBA, as a federal agency with a security interest, was a holder of a federal lien and had priority over Kimbell's prior perfected security interest [*Kimbell Foods, Inc.* v. *United States,* 401 F. Supp. 316 (N.D. Tex. 1975)]. The Kimbell claim, derived from future advances, was found to be "inchoate" because, at the time the bank's security interest (later assigned to the SBA) was perfected, the Kimbell advances had not been made, and therefore the claim was not then certain.

The choateness doctrine

The choate lien test was a rule that had been created in the context of the old federal insolvency priority statute, 31 U.S.C. §191. It was designed to help determine the relative priority of government and private claims in insolvency proceedings. The doctrine was later applied to any lien or security interest competing with a federal tax lien.

The NCFC successfully participated as *amicus* in the *Crest Finance* case [*Crest Finance Co.* v. *United States*, 368 U.S. 347 (1961)] which upheld pre-UCC accounts receivable financing arrangements when attacked by a federal tax lien under the choate lien test. That case was followed by the Federal Tax Lien Act of 1966 which substantially eliminated the choateness doctrine in the tax lien area.

Generally, the choateness doctrine required that before a lien or security interest would be given priority over a federal lien, the amount of the debt, the identity of the obligor, and the property subject to the lien had to be certain. These requirements were so interpreted by the courts that, in almost all instances, the private security interest or lien was held to be inchoate and the government prevailed. *Kimbell* appears to be the first case in which the choateness doctrine was used to determine the priority of two competing Article 9 security interests.

On appeal, the Court of Appeals for the Fifth Circuit reversed the district court's ruling that the SBA had priority. It held that the time of perfection under the UCC, rather than the requirements of the choate lien test, should be used to determine which security interest was first in time. The government took the case to the U.S. Supreme Court.

The Supreme Court's decision

The Supreme Court ruled that Kimbell's security interest had priority over the SBA security interest regardless of the fact that the Kimbell future advances were made after the SBA perfected its security interest. No federal statute existed which resolved the priority question. Therefore, following the federal common law rule of "first in time, first in right," the Court looked to Article 9 of the UCC, rather than the choate lien doctrine, to decide who was "first."

Mr. Justice Marshall's opinion contains much that is of value to the commercial finance industry. The Supreme Court takes the position that banks and other lenders have a vital interest in the stability and certainty of state commercial law, which would be undermined by imposing a federal super-priority rule over the existing state UCC rules. In this sense, the *Kimbell* decision can be viewed as a major victory for those who rely upon Article 9 of the UCC in conducting their business.

It is important to understand that this decision did not necessarily adopt Article 9 in its entirety as the federal common law rule governing the priority of all government-held security interests. There are exceptions to the first in time concept in Article 9, such as the priority given to purchase money security interests which may be subsequent in time. And these exceptions may not be recognized in future cases of competing federal security interests. Many federal loan or guarantee programs are similar to that of the SBA. However, other statutes may provide special priority rules for those programs, and other agencies might require a more uniform federal rule, making *Kimbell* inapplicable in those unusual cases. Finally, the Court indicated that insofar as nonuniform Code provisions or other state statutes may prejudice the equal treatment of federal interests, such statutes will not be adopted as federal common law.

Kimbell and priority questions in an insolvency proceeding

The *Kimbell Foods* case did not decide or even consider the relative priority of federal and private security interests in an insolvency proceeding. The federal insolvency-priority statute (31 U.S.C. §191) declares that in some insolvency proceedings, all debts owing to the government must be paid first. The scope of this statute is not entirely clear. It might mean that private senior perfected security interests could become junior to government claims, whether secured or unsecured. Two cases decided by the Fifth Circuit Court of Appeals on the heels of *Kimbell* held, however, that the *Kimbell* reliance upon state law is also the proper approach for deciding priority questions in an insolvency proceeding [*United States* v. *S.K.A. Associates, Inc.,* 600 F.2d 513 (5th Cir. 1979); *United States* v. *Burlington Industries,* 600 F.2d 517 (5th Cir. 1979)]. The court concluded in *S.K.A. Associates*:

> [t]he Supreme Court's meticulous rationale in *Kimbell* . . . makes so much good sense that it should be applied effectively. To hold that federal law adopts state commercial law in a dispute between lienholders when the debtor is solvent, but not when he is insolvent, would deprive private lenders of equanimity when it is most needed. We, therefore, reject the argument that § 191 gives the Government as a secured lienholder a priority over other lienholders that it would not enjoy under state commercial law [600 F.2d at 516].

This treatment of the insolvency priority statute may stretch the *Kimbell* case too far. Whether the decision will be adopted by other circuits remains to be seen.

The new Bankruptcy Code

The enactment last year of The Bankruptcy Code of 1978, which completely revised the familiar Bankruptcy Act, is clearly the most significant development for commercial lenders, factors, and equipment lessors. Because the Code became effective only this past October, there are, of course, no judicial developments as of this writing.

A summary of most of the key provisions of the Code affecting the commercial financing industry was included in my article in the January 1979 RMA *Journal*. That was followed by special NCFC programs on the Code in New York, Chicago, and Los Angeles, and later by an important article in the NCFC *Journal*.

I will make no further comments on the Code until the first cases appear on the scene.

Treatment of security interests in bankruptcy proceedings—current cases

Post-petition collateral for pre-petition debt

The common practice of seeking post-bankruptcy collateral to secure pre-bankruptcy claims as part of a financing program in a Chapter XI proceeding was attacked and considered in two cases discussed in last year's article. This year, one of those cases was reversed by the Court of Appeals for the Second Circuit [In re Texlon Corp., 596 F.2d 1092 (2d Cir. 1979)].

In a very thoughtful opinion, the Court of Appeals held that such cross-collateralization was similar to an illegal preference and "contrary to the spirit of The Bankruptcy Act. . . ." It suggested that there may be occasions when this practice would be appropriate but only after notice and hearing and if financing could not be made available on other terms. This result may be expected under the new Section 364 of The Bankruptcy Code, which was cited by the Court of Appeals in its opinion.

Marshalling of assets and liens

Secured lenders may be compelled in some cases to pursue guarantors and collateral securing a guarantee before resorting to collateral of a bankrupt borrower. The Court of Appeals for the 8th Circuit, *In re Jack Green's Fashions*, 597 F.2d 130 (8th Cir. 1979), reached that conclusion under the old common law doctrine of marshalling. Normally, that doctrine is applied for the benefit of a junior lien creditor whose collateral would be insufficient unless the senior lien creditor resorted to other collateral from the same debtor. Here it was applied to help unsecured creditors when the liens were given by two different entities.

In the *Jack Green* case, the lender had a security interest in all the business assets of a bankrupt borrower and liens on real estate owned by guarantors, who happened to be the principal shareholders of the borrower and were also bankrupt. The court accepted the view, without objection from the secured creditor, that unsecured creditors would receive nothing unless the secured creditor looked first to the guarantor's collateral.

The secured loan had been made initially to the guarantors who later authorized the borrower to take over the loan one year before bankruptcy. These facts may have caused the court to assume that if the guarantors paid the lender and then asserted subrogation claims against the borrower's bankrupt estate, the stockholder-guarantors would have been subordinated to other creditors.

Effect of a guarantee upon the determination of a guarantor's solvency

Intercorporate guarantees from a parent, subsidiary, or affiliated corporation are common in commercial financing transactions. We know that granting security interests or liens as collateral for these guarantees may constitute fraudulent conveyances or preferences. One of the key issues is often whether the guarantor was insolvent at the time of the transfer of collateral to the lender.

Until recently, there was little or no authority as to whether all, some, or none of the contingent guarantee liability should be included in that computation. The guarantor's rights of subrogation against the borrower and contribution from other guarantors have not received much attention in the cases.

The Court of Appeals for the Second Circuit has resolved these problems in a well reasoned opinion [*In re Ollag Construction Equipment Corp.*, 578 F.2d 904 (2d Cir. 1978)]. A subsidiary had guaranteed a secured loan made to its parent. After the parent corporation experienced financial problems, the lender, to secure the guarantee, obtained a security interest from the guarantor subsidiary in its inventory and equipment. The parent corporation filed a bankruptcy proceeding, and within four months from the date the security interest was granted by the guarantor-subsidiary, bankruptcy proceedings were commenced against it. The trustee in the subsidiary bankruptcy successfully attacked the transfer of collateral by the guarantor as preferential.

The case was returned by the Court of Appeals to the trial court for further findings about the guarantor's solvency. The heart of the opinion is that for purposes of The Bankruptcy Act, any calculation of a guarantor's solvency must take into account not only the full amount of the guaranteed liability but the off-setting value of the guarantor's subrogation claim against the borrower and the value of contribution claims against any other guarantors.

Uniform Commercial Code—security interests

Progress of Article 9 Amendments

The Uniform Amendments to Article 9 of the UCC were adopted in Hawaii, Rhode Island, New Hampshire, Florida, and Massachusetts this year. This brings to 30 the number of states which have adopted the 1972 Amendments to Article 9.

Priority issues

Returned merchandise relating to a factored account. In an interesting opinion, the Alabama Supreme Court considered an unusual priority dispute concerning returned merchandise. The dispute was between a factor with a perfected interest in accounts as well as returned merchandise relating to the accounts and a secured party with a security interest in inventory perfected by filing [*Citizens and Southern Factors, Inc.* v. *S.B.A.*, (Ala. Sept. 7, 1979)].

The factoring agreement appeared to be in customary form. It provided not only for the purchase of accounts but contained an assignment of the debtor's interest in returned goods. The factor filed with respect to accounts and the debtor's rights in returned goods. Two years later, a bank made a loan to the debtor. The loan was guaranteed by the SBA and secured by inventory and proceeds for which an appropriate financing statement was filed.

The Court held that as between the factor and inventory lender, the factor must be given priority under the "first to file" rule of § 9-312(5). The factor had taken an express security interest in returned goods and had filed before the bank filed. The suggestion by the SBA that § 9-306(5) should govern was rejected. That section provides that a security interest in accounts continues in returned goods but is subordinate to an outstanding security interest in inventory which attaches to the goods upon their return by the account debtor. The Court construed § 9-306(5) to be applicable only if the factor had filed merely as to accounts and was seeking a security interest by statute, rather than by a filing, upon the returned goods.

The case confirms the important understanding in the factoring industry that having received an express grant of a security interest in returned goods and having filed, factors are entitled to priority over secured parties with subsequent filings. Any other result, noted the Court, "is clearly undesirable in that it could portend the demise of accounts receivable financing."

Consignments–knowledge of a secured party. A recent case decided by a federal district court in Pittsburgh involved an ordinary priority dispute between the supplier of inventory on consignment and a secured party with a prior perfected security interest in inventory [*GBS Meat Industry PTY Ltd.* v. *Kress-Dobkin Co.,* No. 76-897 (W.D. Pa. August 23, 1979)]. Disputes of this kind are decided routinely under UCC Section 2-326 in favor of the secured lender. That Section provides that the interest of a consignor in the consigned goods is subject to the interests of creditors of the consignee-debtor unless the consignor:

(1) Complies with applicable law requiring the posting of signs,

(2) Establishes that the consignee is generally known to be selling goods on consignment, or

(3) Complies with the filing provisions of Article 9.

Unfortunately, the court created a fourth exception to Section 2-326. It decided the case on the theory that if the secured party knew, or should have known, of the subsequent consignment, then its perfected security interest would be junior to the consignor's claim. Instructions to this effect were given to the jury without objection by the secured party. The jury concluded that the secured party had knowledge of the consignment, and the court held in favor of the consignor. An appeal has been taken to the Court of Appeals for the Third Circuit, but the procedural questions in the case may interfere with a reversal on the merits of the case.

Foreign accounts

The standards for perfecting security interests in foreign accounts owing by a U.S. resident are considered only rarely by the courts. In a recent decision of the District Court for the District of Columbia, *Walter E. Heller Canada Ltd.* v. *Buchbinder,* Sec. Trans. Guide (CCH) ¶ 53,236 (D. C. Cir. 1979), a foreign secured party, which received an assignment of accounts from a foreign debtor, duly perfected the security interest in accordance with the laws of the foreign country. In addition, the secured party notified the account debtor, a U.S. resident, of the assignment and directed the account debtor to pay only the secured party. Later, a creditor of the assignor-debtor attached the account in the U.S. and claimed priority over the secured party.

While the Court held that perfection in a foreign country does not constitute notice to U.S. residents, the direct notification by the secured party to the U.S. account debtor perfected the security interest in the U.S. As a result, the attaching creditor's lien was held to be junior to the interest of the secured party. The Court relied on UCC Section 9-103(5) which clearly states that if a foreign seller does not keep records in the U.S., then perfection of a foreign account is accomplished by notice to the account debtor.

Enforcement by assignee of voidable equipment leases and other claims

The effect of receiving as collateral, or otherwise acquiring, void or voidable accounts, chattel paper, leases, or similar intangibles was clarified in *Bankers Trust Co.* v. *Litton Systems, Inc.*, 26 UCC Rep. 513 (2nd Cir. 1979). The case is particularly interesting because it involves commercial bribery, conduct which many states treat as a crime.

Office equipment leases were arranged by a salesman for a manufacturer who received kickbacks from a lessor. The leases were assigned to banks to secure the credit extended to the lessor to enable it to purchase the equipment. There was no evidence that the banks or the lessee knew of the commercial bribery. Following a default, the lessee attempted to avoid a judgment and loss of possession of the equipment on the ground that the leases were unenforceable.

The applicable New York law declares that commercial bribery is a crime. In the view of the Court of Appeals, the kickbacks, not the leases, were illegal. And while the leases may be unenforceable as between the original parties, a holder in due course, such as the banks, would not be subject to this defense for two reasons. One is that the lessee had agreed not to assert against an assignee such defenses as may exist against its lessor. The other is that the defense of illegality is not effective against a holder in due course, under UCC § 3-305, unless the underlying paper is null and void rather than merely voidable. The court held this paper to be enforceable by the assignee since it was merely voidable between the original parties.

The tenor of the opinion is that protection of innocent third parties, such as secured lenders, is of paramount importance. As the Court stated:

> It would be poor policy for courts to transform banks and other finance companies into policing agents charged with the responsibility of searching out commercial bribery committed by their assignors.

Duty to preserve collateral—problem of declining value

Two cases during the last year considered the secured creditors' exposure for failing to sell collateral which is declining in value [*FDIC* v. *Webb*, 964 F. Suppl. 520 (E.D. Tenn., 1978); *Dubman* v. *North Shore Bank*, 90 Wis. 2d 266, 279 N.W.2d 455 (1979)]. Both cases involved the question of whether a pledgee's duty to preserve collateral under UCC § 9-207 means that a secured party is obligated to preserve the collateral's market value. Both cases held that secured creditors do not have a duty to sell collateral merely because it is declining in value.

The *FDIC* case was unusual in that the stock pledged to the lender was issued by the lender's parent corporation. The pledgor claimed that the lender knew of the declining value although the pledgor had no such information. The court said that mere negligence by the lender in its business operation would not be sufficient to impose liability, but evidence of intent by the lender to diminish the value of the collateral could create liability. The court also confirmed the view that no notice of the collateral's declining value is required to be given by a secured party unless by agreement or conduct, the secured party undertakes to give such notice.

The *Dubman* case added another facet to the problem of declining value of collateral. It held that a pledgor's request to sell collateral in a declining market may be justifiably ignored by the secured party unless the pledgor is prepared to satisfy the entire loan balance at the time of sale.

Lender liability under the Federal Securities Act

Pledges as "sales" of securities

In my article last year, I noted that the Court of Appeals for the Fifth Circuit had concluded that a pledge of securities is not a "sale" within the scope of the Securities Acts [*National Bank of Commerce* v. *All American Assurance Co.*, 583 F.2d 1295 (5th Cir. 1978)]. During the past year, two other courts of appeals offered conflicting opinions on this subject [*Lincoln National Bank* v. *Herber*, No. 78-2388 (7th Cir. August 20, 1979); *Mansbach* v. *Prescott, Ball, Turber* (1979 Transfer Binder) Fed. Sec.L.Rep. (CCH) ¶ 96,861 (6th Cir. 1979)]. The score at this time appears to be two circuits (5th and 7th) holding that pledges are not sales under the Federal Securities Acts and two circuits (2nd and 6th) holding to the contrary [See *Mallis* v. *FDIC*, 568 F.2d 824 (2nd Cir. 1977), *cert. dismissed*, 435 U.S. 381 (1978)].

The *Lincoln Bank* case involved a commercial loan secured by a pledge of stock later determined to be counterfeit. Recovery was sought by the lender against another bank and a bank officer for their conduct in connection with the pledge of stock. The court found that the pledge was not a "sale" within the scope of the Federal Securities Acts. Accordingly, it held that no federal claim for securities fraud existed, expressly disagreeing with the *Mallis* case in the Second Circuit.

The *Mansbach* case from the Sixth Circuit involved a pledge of securities by a customer to a broker-dealer to secure liabilities arising from securities transactions.

The customer sued the broker-dealer under the anti-fraud provisions of the Federal Securities Acts. The Court held that the pledge was a "sale" sufficient to bring the fraud claim under the federal law, following the reasoning of the *Mallis* case. This case may not necessarily be in conflict with the cases holding that pledges relating to commercial loans are not "sales." As the Court noted, the bank loan cases may have no direct impact on the securities industry unlike the conduct of a broker-dealer in this case.

Financing the purchase of securities

The exposure of lenders for aiding and abetting a violation of the anti-fraud provisions of the Securities Acts was confirmed again in *Tucker* v. *Janota*, [1979 Transfer Binder] Fed.Sec.L.Rep. (CCH) ¶ 96,701 (N.D. Ill., 1978). The case arose out of the collapse of a firm which sold partnership interests in tax shelters to physicians in violation of the anti-fraud provisions. The firm had arranged with two banks to provide loans to the physicians to finance the purchase of these tax shelter interests. Both banks were later made defendants in a action by investors claiming that the banks aided and abetted the seller's violation of the Securities Acts.

The court found that the banks, through their credit programs, facilitated the sales of these tax shelter interests which qualified as "securities" under the Acts. Credit was almost always granted to any requesting purchaser, and the banks did not seek other collateral or recourse against the borrower.

The court also determined that the banks knew the important aspects of the selling proposals—the expected return on investment and the calculated tax advantages. In addition, it found that to increase sales, the banks' willingness to extend credit for this program was presented by sales personnel as evidence of the attractiveness of the investment. Apparently, the banks made no effort to learn if the securities which they were financing and accepting as collateral were properly registered.

These circumstances were held to be sufficient, if established at trial, to impose liability on the banks as aiders and abetters of fraudulent sales of securities under the Securities Acts. The court made clear that proof of actual knowledge of the fraud by the banks was not required. Evidence of a reckless disregard of facts which could have provided knowledge of the fraud was all that the court held necessary to impose liability on the secured lenders.

Participations
Liability under the Federal Securities Acts to participants

The courts are divided on whether a participation is a "security" under the Federal Securities Acts. The last case we reported to you, *Union Planters*

National Bank v. *Commercial Credit Business Loans, Inc.*, No. C-75-76 (W.D. Tenn. September 14, 1978), held that a participation was not a security. That case is now on appeal and was followed this year by *Provident National Bank* v. *Frankford Trust Co.*, [1979 Transfer Binder] Fed. Sec.L.Rep. (CCH ¶ 96,858 (E.D. Pa. 1979), which also held that a secured loan participation was not a security.

The *Provident* case involved a loan secured by a real estate mortgage to finance the construction of townhouses. The lead and participating banks each had a 50% interest. When the project failed, the performance and completion bonds were found to be forgeries. The participant claimed that the lead bank had misrepresented several key matters about the credit at the time the participation was entered into, and it sued to recover its investment under the Securities Acts.

The court looked at the "economic realities" of the participation and found that it was a routine commercial financing arrangement rather than an investment. It noted that there was no expectation of capital appreciation but simply of repayment of a commercial loan that was secured at a fixed rate of interest. It also observed that the profits, which are interest payments in a participation, result not from entrepreneurial management of others but merely from routine loan monitoring by the lead lender.

It is interesting to note that the *Provident* case rejected the approach of the court in *CDC* v. *Lincoln First Commercial Corp.*, 445 F. Supp. 1263 (S.D.N.Y. 1978), which held that a participation in a commercial financing transaction was a security.

Liability for mismanagement of a participated loan

Litigation among participating lenders usually has involved claims that the participant was fraudulently misled into purchasing a participation. In a somewhat rare case, a participant sued a lead lender for abusing its discretion granted under the participation agreement. The case thus provided a judicial review of some commonly used participation terms [*Carondelet Savings & Loan Ass'n* v. *Citizens Savings & Loan Ass'n*, No. 78-2119 (7th Cir. August 31, 1979)].

The loan in *Carondelet* financed the construction of a student dormitory and was secured by a mortgage. About four years later, following a decline in demand for dormitory space, the borrower requested an extension of the maturity date, a reduction of the amount of each installment, and the capitalization of the interest for 10 months. The participant objected and asked that foreclosure be commenced. However, another participant acquiesced to the modification, and the lead lender reduced the monthly payments. A year later, the loan was in default again, and the lead made a separate loan to the borrower secured by a second mortgage. Other defaults occurred, moratoriums were granted, and reductions made to required monthly payments. Finally, foreclosure was begun.

The participant claimed that the modifications made over its objections and the failure to undertake a prompt foreclosure constituted a breach of contract. The participation agreement gave the lead lender the

> exclusive right to decide how to service such loans and what to do and how to do it and . . . when to foreclose. . . . The Buyer (participant) shall not be authorized to give directions to the Seller in connection with these matters.

The objections in the participation agreement relating to the foreclosure were:

> In the event of the inability of the Seller to collect any of said loans after exercising reasonable efforts to do so, Seller agrees to give prompt notice to Buyer, and to proceed to foreclose.

The court construed these terms to mean that the lead lender was not required to foreclose immediately upon the first default but only after it had exercised reasonable efforts to work out of the credit and collect the loan. In addition, the lead had the right, over the participant's objections, to make the type of modifications noted here. In general, the court saw the agreement as a poor attempt to grant broad discretion to the lead lender which was not abused or exercised in bad faith.

Usury

Two events this year were of particular interest in the usury area. One was the successful revision of the Florida usury laws in which the NCFC was active. The other was the opinion of the California Appellate Court holding that the various California usury limitations, as they apply to commercial loans, are constitutional.

The revised Florida usury statute is applicable to loans made on or after July 1, 1979. Under the new law, the general distinction between corporate and noncorporate borrowers was eliminated. The maximum interest became 18% on loans of $500,000 or less and 25% on loans exceeding $500,000. Special interest statutes will remain in Florida with respect to regulated lenders.

The trial court in *Committee Against Unfair Interest Limitations* v. *California*, CCH Consumer Credit Guide ¶ 98,039 (1978) had held that the 10% California interest limitation was unconstitutional as it applied to commercial and other nonconsumer loans. Several months ago, the California Court of Appeals rejected the holding of the trial court and decided that the California usury laws were constitutional after all.

Conclusion

The legal framework of the commercial finance industry is exceptionally strong so that the trends and highlights of this year were easily taken in stride. Our initiation into the new Bankruptcy Code and the possibility of a recession could make next year a difficult but important one. In any event, it will be interesting. ☐

The Bankruptcy Code from the Viewpoint of the Secured Commercial Lender

by A. Thomas Small

Should secured lenders be rejoicing over the new Bankruptcy Code or resigning themselves to more of the same problems they faced under the Old Act? While Thomas Small doesn't have the answer, he does have a great familiarity with the provisions and issues of the new law. He shares his expertise in the following article.

Many creditors are anxiously awaiting the effective date of the new Bankruptcy Code (Bankruptcy Reform Act of 1978). Some of these creditors, especially the real estate lenders, see October 1, 1979, as the date which marks the end of unfair "cram downs," the end of unreasonable delays, and in general, the beginning of better treatment for the commercial lender in the bankruptcy court. Perhaps these creditors should wait awhile before celebrating.

Undoubtedly, the new Bankruptcy Code contains provisions which are intended to benefit the commercial secured lender. The extent of that benefit, however, will not be known until the bankruptcy courts have the opportunity to rule on such items as "adequate protection" and "indubitable equivalent." It is also true, on the other hand, that the Bankruptcy Code offers changes that will make the creditor's plight more difficult. This article will discuss, from the perspective of a secured lender, some of the advantages, disadvantages, and open questions presented by the new Bankruptcy Code.

The pro-debtor bankruptcy court

There is a widespread belief among creditors that many bankruptcy courts, especially in rehabilitation proceedings, have a definite pro-debtor bias. This feeling may be in part the result of creative interpretations of the Bankruptcy Act. These have been used by some courts to defeat the secured lender's attempts to frustrate the debtor's plan of arrangement or reorganization. But, whether or not this prejudice exists, the appearance of partiality is built into the present system. In addition to having judicial functions, the bankruptcy judge is responsible for and actively participates in bankruptcy administration. If the trustee or debtor-in-possession is the chief executive officer of the distressed company, the bankruptcy judge may appear to the secured creditor to be the chairman of the board.

Experiment to relieve bankruptcy judge from administrative duties

The Bankruptcy Code has, as a five-year experiment, created the office of U.S. Trustee for several test districts to relieve the bankruptcy judge from administrative duties. In those districts not included in this pilot program, the bankruptcy judge will no longer preside at the first meeting of creditors, and there will be more delegation to the bankruptcy clerk's office. Nevertheless, the bankruptcy judge will still have the ultimate responsibility for the administration of bankruptcy cases.

Extension of terms for bankruptcy judges

While the bankruptcy law has been changed by the new Bankruptcy Code, the bankruptcy judges will, for the most part, remain the same for at least five years. In fact, all judges serving at the time of the Code's enactment have had their terms extended to March 31, 1984. Unless replaced for incompetency, each will serve until that date or until a successor has been appointed. Beginning March 31, 1984, bankruptcy judges will be appointed by the President with the advice and consent of the Senate for 14-year terms.

Jurisdiction of bankruptcy court

The jurisdiction of the bankruptcy court under the new Code has been greatly expanded; the bankruptcy court will have jurisdiction over all proceedings arising or relating to bankruptcy cases. The bankruptcy courts will have exclusive jurisdiction over the property of the debtor wherever located. The difference between summary and plenary jurisdiction will be eliminated.

The trustee will be able to litigate matters relating to the bankruptcy in the bankruptcy court without having to bring separate state or Federal court proceedings. The result should be a more expeditious and economical administration of bankruptcy cases, but the secured creditor who wants the dispute decided in another forum is out of luck.

Under present law, the creditor, if not otherwise subject to the jurisdiction of the bankruptcy court, could object or consent to that court's jurisdiction. Under the new Code, that option is no longer available. The increased jurisdiction of the bankruptcy court will unquestionably make matters more difficult for the secured creditor in the ongoing struggle with the bankruptcy trustee.

Automatic stays

One of the most difficult tasks of an attorney representing a secured creditor in a rehabilitation proceeding is explaining to the client why it takes so long to extricate collateral from the grip of the bankruptcy court. To the secured lender, especially those secured by real property, Chapters X, XI, and XII are synonymous with delay. The new Code promises some much needed relief in this area, but past abuses provide a basis for skepticism.

Easy access to court for creditors seeking relief from stay

Prior to the effective dates of the bankruptcy rules, it was the practice of most bankruptcy judges to enter orders in Chapter X, XI, and XII cases enjoining the secured creditor from enforcing lien rights with respect to the collateral during the proceeding. Rules 10–601, 11–44, and 12–43 made the stay against lien enforcement automatic upon the filing of the debtor's petition. Armed with the automatic stay, debtors have extracted countless concessions from their fearful secured creditors.

Each of the present stay rules contains procedures designed to give the creditor seeking relief from the stay quick access to the court. In the past, easy access has often been the exception rather than the rule. In some jurisdictions, courts have taken a wait-and-see attitude. Under the new Code, creditors' requests for relief from stays should be heard more quickly. The stay will be terminated within 30 days after the request has been made unless the court, after notice and hearing, orders the stay continued pending a final hearing. In that case, the final hearing must be commenced within 30 days after the preliminary hearing.

Attempt to balance debtor's needs and creditor's rights

The new Code has attempted to balance the needs of the debtor to use collateral in a rehabilitation proceeding with the rights of the secured creditor to have the value of the security protected. Relief from the automatic stay of Section 362 of the Code can be granted at the request of the secured creditor for the following reasons: (1) if the debtor does not have an equity in the property and the property is not necessary to an effective reorganization or (2) for cause shown, including the lack of *adequate protection* of the secured creditor's interest. The burden of proof for all issues, except the issue of equity in the property, is on the party opposing relief.

Adequate protection

Adequate protection is one of the most important concepts under the new Code. It is clear that Congress intended *adequate protection* to safeguard the interests of the secured lender. Ironically, *adequate protection* might turn out to be the secured creditor's nemesis, depending upon its interpretation by the bankruptcy courts.

Periodic payments and replacement liens

Adequate protection, set forth in Code Section 361, may take several forms. It may include *periodic* cash payments to the secured creditor as compensation for any decrease in value to the secured creditor occasioned by the trustee's action. This sounds equitable; however, the term *periodic* is not defined, there are no guidelines set as to the frequency of payments, and there is no requirement that such payments be made in advance.

Adequate protection under Section 361 can also be accomplished by granting an additional or replacement lien to the extent of the decrease in value. Again, this seems fair, but there is no requirement that the replacement lien be in the same type of collateral or have the same priority. Theoretically, a creditor with a first lien on prime collateral could be adequately protected by having that security replaced with a second (or lesser) lien upon collateral of a type which the lender would consider undesirable and unacceptable under normal lending circumstances.

Indubitable equivalent

Finally, adequate protection can be, in addition to periodic payments and replacement liens, in *any* form if it will result in the *indubitable equivalent* of the creditor's interest in the property. That's right, *indubitable equivalent!*

Short of requiring the bankruptcy judge's personal guarantee, the language of the Code could not be stronger. In reality, any valuation is based upon conjecture, and the degree of speculation necessarily increases when the value is dependent upon the success of the debtor's rehabilitation.[1] There are no guarantees when dealing with collateral values, and there are, unfortunately, no indubitables.

Use, sale, and lease of collateral

If authorized to operate the debtor's business, the trustee (or debtor-in-possession) may use, sell, or lease collateral other than *cash collateral* in the ordinary course of business. A secured creditor may object to such use, sale, or lease if he is not receiving adequate protection, and the trustee will have the burden of proof on that issue. Other uses, sales, and leases are not permitted except after notice and hearing.

Furthermore, the trustee may sell property free of liens only if—

(1) Applicable nonbankruptcy law permits the sale of such property free and clear of such interests.

(2) The sale price is greater than the liens' aggregate value.

(3) There is a *bona fide* dispute concerning the lien.

(4) The secured party could be compelled in a legal or equitable proceeding to accept money in satisfaction of such interest.

Section 363 defines *cash collateral* as cash, negotiable instruments, documents of title, securities, deposit accounts, or other cash equivalents in which the estate and any entity other than the estate have an interest. The trustee may not use cash collateral unless the secured creditor consents or the court authorizes the use after notice and hearing.

A trustee authorized to operate the debtor's business would be able to sell inventory without the necessity of notice and hearing because inventory is not within the definition of cash collateral, and because Section 9-307 of the UCC provides that inventory can be sold free of liens to a buyer in the ordinary course of business. The trustee could not, however, use accounts which the sales generated without obtaining the approval of the court after notice and hearing.

These new sections will provide some comfort to the secured creditor and at least will give him an opportunity to be heard before the liquid collateral is dissipated. The ultimate issue, however, will be adequate protection.

---

[1] See *In re Muriel Holding Corp.*, 75 F.2d 941 (2d Cir.1935) and *In re Georgetown Apartments*, 3 Bankr. Ct. Dec. 512 (M.D. Fla.1977) for cases discussing *indubitable equivalent*.

Chapter 11 reorganizations

Chapters X, XI, and XII of the old Act are consolidated under the new Code into Chapter 11, titled "Reorganizations." [2]

Under Chapter 11, the debtor will in most instances be a debtor-in-possession. The trustee will be appointed only upon the request of a party in interest after notice and hearing for cause (including fraud, dishonesty, incompetency, or gross mismanagement) or if the appointment is in the "best interests of creditors."

The new Code's preference for retaining the debtor-in-possession should have the effect of encouraging more debtors to use this form of relief. As an added safeguard for creditors, the court can, upon request, appoint an examiner to look into the debtor-in-possession's affairs.

A Chapter 11 case can be converted into a liquidation proceeding upon the request of a creditor after notice and hearing if in the best interests of the creditors and upon a showing of cause. Causes, among others enumerated in Section 1112, can include:

(1) Continuing loss to or diminution of the estate and absence of a reasonable likelihood of rehabilitation.

(2) Inability to effectuate a plan.

(3) Unreasonable delay by the debtor that is prejudicial to creditors.

(4) Failure to propose a plan within the time fixed by the court.

(5) Denial of confirmation of every proposed plan and denial of additional time for filing another plan.

A secured creditor may have its rights impaired by a plan if the other members of that creditor's class accept the plan (by vote of ⅔ in amount and 51% in number). In addition, it must be determined that the class would receive under the plan an amount which is the same or more than the class would have received in a liquidation. A plan also may be confirmed over the objection of a class of secured creditors if the class is not impaired by the plan as defined in Section 1124.

Cram downs

The dreaded *cram down* is a term used to describe a bankruptcy court's ability to confirm a plan of reorganization in Chapter X or a plan of arrangement under Chapter XII over the objection of a class of secured creditors.

---

[2] Please note that the new Bankruptcy Code uses Arabic numbers rather than Roman numerals which were used in the old Act.

The cram down usually involves the modification of the secured creditor's rights without the creditor's consent. Although infrequently litigated in the past, the cram down has been common during the middle 70s. Most early cases cite *Wachovia Bank and Trust Co.* v. *Harris,*[3] in which the construction lender became, to its dismay and over its objection, a permanent lender with a 20-year loan. More recently, the case most often referred to in discussions of cram downs is the case of *In re Pine Gate Associates, Ltd.*[4]

Old and new provisions for cram down

Under the old Bankruptcy Act, the cram down could be accomplished in four ways:

(1) Transfer or retention of property by the debtor subject to secured debts.

(2) Sale of the property free of liens for the fair upset price and transfer of the lien to the proceeds.

(3) Appraisal and cash payment (the type of cram down tried in the *Pine Gate* case).

(4) Any method which "equitably and fairly" provides adequate protection for the creditor. The problem, of course, has been that the secured creditor and the bankruptcy court often did not agree as to what was adequate protection.

Under the new Code, the cram down provisions can be found in Section 1129 (b) (1). It says that the court shall confirm a plan even though creditors' rights have been impaired and each class has not accepted the plan if the plan "does not discriminate unfairly and is fair and equitable with respect to each class of claims or interests that is impaired under, and [which class of claims] has not accepted the plan."

What constitutes a fair and equitable plan under new Code

A plan can be fair and equitable under the new Code if—

(1) The lien is retained and a creditor receives *deferred* cash payments totalling at least the value of the holder's interest,

(2) The collateral is sold and the lien attaches to proceeds, or

(3) The creditors realize the indubitable equivalent value. As with adequate protection, there is no insurance that the indubitable equivalent will in fact be realized. It is still a matter of judgment.

Before a plan can be confirmed under the new Code, at least one class of creditors must have approved the plan. Also, nonconsenting creditors must be

---

[3] 455 F.2d 841 (4th Cir. 1972).
[4] Bankr. Ct. Dec. 1478 (N.D. Ga. 1976).

in at least as good a position as they would have been in a liquidation under Chapter 7 of the Code.

The intent of Congress should be clear, and it is to be hoped the trend that has concerned so many secured creditors during the past few years will be reversed. But the ultimate test, the indubitable equivalent, remains.

Strong arm provisions

Section 70 (c) of the old Bankruptcy Act gave to the trustee the benefit of all defenses available to the bankrupt against third parties. The so-called *strong arm* provisions of that section gave the bankruptcy trustee the status of a hypothetical lien creditor as of the date of the bankruptcy petition. With that power, the trustee could avoid improperly perfected security interests.

Section 544 of the new Code retains the strong arm provisions. It also adds to the trustee's list of honorary titles that of a creditor extending credit to the debtor and that of a *bona fide* purchaser of real property, both as of the time of the commencement of the bankruptcy case.

Section 544 also retains the little-used *omnibus* clause of Section 70 (e) of the old Act. This clause gives the trustee the right of an actual existing unsecured creditor who could have avoided the secured creditor's lien.

Creditors secured by purchase money security interests should note that Section 546 enables such a creditor to perfect the lien in accordance with UCC Section 9-312 (4) even after the commencement of a bankruptcy case.

Preferences

The typical preference situation involves the payment of an unsecured creditor prior to bankruptcy, but it may also include the granting of a security interest. As will be discussed later, the floating inventory or accounts receivable lien can in some circumstances under the Code be attacked.

Limited good news regarding preferences

The recipient of a potential preference will be glad to know that the Code reduces the preference time from four months to 90 days. Unfortunately, that is the extent of the good news with respect to preferences. As previously discussed, the jurisdiction of the bankruptcy court has been expanded so that all preference matters may be heard in bankruptcy court. Under pre-Code law, a trustee often had difficulty establishing that the debtor was insolvent at the time of the transfer and that the creditor had "reasonable cause to believe" that fact. The Code now establishes a rebuttable presumption of insolvency during the first 90 days and eliminates the need to show that the creditor had "reason to know" of the insolvency.

Extension of preference period for insider

If the transferee of the preference is an *insider,* the preference period is extended to one year. In seeking to avoid a preference against the insider, a trustee will not have the benefit of the insolvency presumption beyond 90 days preceding insolvency and will have to show that the insider had reasonable cause to believe the debtor was insolvent.

One potential problem in this preference area is the definition of insider, which includes in that category a "person in control" of the debtor. If a trustee can establish that a creditor, by its actions, "controlled" the debtor, then with respect to that creditor the preference period may be one year rather than 90 days.

Floating lien on inventory or accounts as a preference

Although there is a dissenting minority view, most courts have held that the floating lien on inventory or accounts is not in itself preferential.[5] Since the new Code says that no transfer is made until the debtor has acquired rights in the collateral, those cases validating the floating lien are in effect overruled. The Code, however, provides that the floating lien is only preferential to the extent that unsecured creditors are prejudiced. It is also only preferential to the extent that the creditor's position as of the date of the filing of the petition has been improved from the date which is either 90 days prior to the filing (one year if the creditor is an insider) or the date the creditor has given new value.

On its face, the improvement test seems simple. However, proving the value of inventory or accounts 90 days or a year prior to the filing may be no easy task for the trustee. On the other hand, the creditor will no doubt have difficulty disputing any evidence offered by the trustee in that regard.

The arbitrariness of the improvement test will at times yield inequitable results. For example, normal cyclical fluctuations in inventory or accounts could cause a floating lien position to become preferential if the low point was attained on the pre-petition date of determination.

In any event, the secured lender relying on inventory and/or accounts as collateral should keep Section 547 of the new Code in mind when making or monitoring such loans.

---

[5] *DuBay* v. *Williams,* 417 F.2d 1277 (9th Cir. 1969) and *Grain Merchants, Inc.* v. *Union Bank & Sav. Co.,* 408 F.2d 209 (7th Cir. 1969) represent the majority view; *In re Tempco Business Services, Inc.,* 3 Bankr. Ct. Dec. 446 (E.D. Mich. 1977) represents the single dissent.

Fraudulent conveyances

Although there is little modification in the fraudulent conveyance area, the new Bankruptcy Code offers two significant changes which will cause secured creditors to be more receptive to problem loan workouts.

Elimination of *Dean* v. *Davis*

First, the concept of *Dean* v. *Davis*[6] which was incorporated under old Bankruptcy Act Section 67 (d) (3) has been eliminated. Under that section, a creditor who made a secured loan to a borrower who went into bankruptcy within four months of the creation of the security interest could lose that security interest, even though the security interest was taken contemporaneously with the granting of the loan. If the lender knew at the time of the loan that the borrower was insolvent, that the borrower intended to seek relief in the bankruptcy court, that the proceeds of the loan would be used to prefer one unsecured creditor over another, and if the transaction occurred within four months of the filing of the bankruptcy petition, then the lien could be avoided. Because of the trustee's ability to avoid the security interests of the lender who had "financed the preference," lenders were reluctant to make loans to distressed borrowers for working capital purposes.

A transfer such as that in the case of *Dean* v. *Davis* might, for example, involve a debtor who gives his brother-in-law a security interest in his house to secure a loan, the proceeds of which are used to pay a bank that has threatened to have the debtor prosecuted on forgery charges. Such an action could still be set aside under the new Code as being a transfer with the "actual intent to hinder, delay, or defraud" creditors.

Fair consideration

Second, under the old Bankruptcy Act a transfer made at the time the debtor was insolvent could be set aside if the transferee did not provide a *fair consideration*. The term fair consideration was more than just a dollar-and-cents test since its definition contained the element of good faith. At least one court has decided that a compromise of a debt in which guarantors were released did not constitute fair consideration, even though the debt relinquished exceeded the amount paid. This decision resulted because someone else benefited from the transaction, that is, the guarantors, and consequently there was no good faith.[7]

Since most deeds in lieu of foreclosure transactions involve the release of guarantors, lenders aware of such decisions have been reluctant to enter into

---

[6] 242 U.S. 438 (1917).
[7] *Bullard* v. *Aluminum Company of America*, 468 F.2d 11 (7th Cir. 1972).

these compromises. The new Code has substituted the term *reasonable equivalent value* in place of fair consideration, and good faith is not a part of this definition.

Executory contracts

Under the new Code, the trustee, with the concurrence of the court, may assume or reject an executory contract or unexpired lease of the debtor whether or not there exists in the contract or lease a *bankruptcy termination* clause.

Under the old Bankruptcy Law, one problem facing the real property lender secured by the lessee's interest in a ground lease had been the possibility that the lessor's trustee in bankruptcy would reject the lease to the detriment of the innocent lessee and the lessee's innocent subtenants. The new Code solves that problem. It provides in Section 365 (h) that if there is a rejection of a lease, the lessee may remain in possession for the term of the lease and any renewal extension period. The lessor in those circumstances would not be required to perform its affirmative obligations under the lease. However, the lessee would be entitled to offset, against the rent reserved, the damages arising from the lessor's failure to perform.

The bankruptcy termination clause no longer terminates an executory contract *ipso facto*. However, one important exception that will please the commercial lender is that the trustee cannot assume a contract to make a loan to or for the benefit of the debtor.

Certificates of indebtedness

When a debtor seeks rehabilitation relief from the bankruptcy court, an immediate need is to borrow additional funds. The secured lender's worry is that the court will approve a loan to the debtor and give the new lender a lien having priority over the original lender's security interest. Generally, this priority over existing liens, at least in Chapter XI, could not be given unless the proceeds of the loan would be used to preserve the original lender's security.[8]

Unreasonable extensions of credit to a distressed debtor

Some secured creditors anticipate that new Code Section 364 will prevent unreasonable extensions of credit in Chapter 11 proceedings. Section 364 provides that priority over existing liens will be given only if the trustee is otherwise unable to obtain the loan, and adequate protection is provided to the original lien holder. The burden is on the trustee to show adequate protection.

---

[8] *Collier on Bankruptcy* (14th Edition), Vol. 8, Section 7.2.

Not only is the benefit theory of old Chapter XI no longer applicable, the secured creditor runs the risk of being adequately protected by the bankruptcy court. Since most lenders will not lend to a distressed debtor without obtaining the first lien, the last resort test is not much protection.

Hypothetical situation involving adequate protection

Consider the following hypothetical situation. Lender A has a lien on accounts receivable but refuses to lend additional funds to the Chapter 11 debtor. Lender B will lend but requires a first lien on the accounts. The court awards Lender A adequate protection by giving him an additional second mortgage lien upon developed real property (perhaps in another state) having an equity value, after deducting the first mortgage loan, equal to the value of the accounts receivable. The debtor gets the loan, the new lender gets prime collateral, and the original secured creditor gets adequate protection. Not a very happy prospect, indeed.

Other aspects of the new Code

Turnover of assets

Under the new Code, third parties, including secured creditors, in possession of the debtor's property are required to turn over property to the trustee whenever the debtor has a legal or equitable interest therein.

Post-petition interest

The new Code resolves conflicting decisions regarding the allowance to secured creditors of post-bankruptcy petition interest. Section 506 (b) says that interest in connection with an allowable claim together with fees, costs, or charges provided under the loan documents shall be included in the claim to the extent that the property securing the claim has sufficient value to cover the principal, interest, and other fees, costs, and charges.

Post-petition collateral

Basically, a security interest in proceeds and products continues as to those items acquired after the commencement of the bankruptcy case. However, Section 552 could present some serious problems in that regard. Upon notice and hearing, the court, based upon the equities of the case, may modify or eliminate the security interest in the after-acquired property. This might occur in a situation in which the debtor added substantial value to the collateral during the Chapter 11 proceeding.

Adequate Information under Chapter 11

One of the best ideas incorporated in Chapter 11 is the requirement of *adequate information*. This term as defined in Section 1125 (a) (1) would enable a hypothetical reasonable investor to make an informed judgment about any proposed plan. The holder of a claim or interest must also be provided with the plan or a summary of the plan when the claimant's acceptance or rejection of a plan is solicited.

The bankruptcy court must approve, after notice and a hearing, the transmitted adequate information.

Chapter 11 creditors' committees

Unsecured creditors' committees are to be appointed by the bankruptcy judge at the beginning of a Chapter 11 case. Secured creditors' committees may also be appointed at the request of the party in interest. In the past, some creditors have been reluctant to serve on creditors' committees because of the potential of securities law violations. The new safe harbor provision of Section 1125 (3) alleviates some of those fears.

Setoff

The improvement test previously discussed under the section on preferences will also apply to the bank's right to setoff against a customer's account. In addition, the automatic stay of Section 362 applies to setoffs, but the bank can seek relief from the stay if it does not receive adequate protection.

Conclusion

In passing the Bankruptcy Reform Act of 1978, Congress has obviously attempted to achieve a more even balance between the rights of the secured creditor and the needs of the distressed debtor. Whether the imbalance which the secured creditor has loudly protested will be rectified depends upon the individual bankruptcy courts. If bankruptcy judges implement Congress' manifest intent, secured creditors have reason to celebrate; if not, the secured creditor can expect continued inequities in the name of debtor rehabilitation. ☐

The Preference Provisions of the Bankruptcy Code of 1979

by Herbert L. Ash

Herbert Ash analyzes what has probably been the initial cause of greatest concern to credit grantors studying the new Bankruptcy Code: the preference section.

The Bankruptcy Code of 1979 is the first substantial revision of the federal law relating to bankruptcy in 40 years. It is comprehensive. The narrow purpose of this article is to provide a guide for the loan officer concerning one of the changes from prior law. By way of caveat: The basic role of attorneys is and always will be to give legal advice in order that business conduct be guided accordingly. However, in order to do so, it must be possible to anticipate reliably the legal consequences of such conduct. What follows is inherently limited by the lack of case law and practical experience under the new Code.[1]

Preferences in general

Preferences are not illegal outside the federal Bankruptcy Code or similar state debtor and creditor law or other law regarding insolvencies. Absent such statutes, any debtor can prefer any creditor or group of creditors. The first question then is why does the Bankruptcy Code create a difference? It is simply

---

© 1980 by Herbert L. Ash.

[1] Footnotes have been eliminated. However, citations are available from the author.

because the primary goal inherent in the Code is equality of distribution among creditors. The possibility that one creditor will obtain more than another due to better leverage or quicker action is to be avoided. Thus there is a preference section which commentators call the most important of all the trustee in bankruptcy's avoidance powers.

The six elements of a recoverable preference

Section 547 of the new Bankruptcy Code is the so-called preference section. For the purposes of this article, we can consider preferences as having six elements. Let us compare those six elements with the elements under the old Bankruptcy Act which is still in effect for cases filed before October 1, 1979:

(1) A transfer of the debtor's property to or for the benefit of a creditor (outright or by way of collateral security) is the same in both the old and new laws.

(2) Under the old Bankruptcy Act, bankruptcy must have followed within four months of such transfer. Under the new Bankruptcy Code, except in one circumstance, there is a 90-day period. (That one circumstance is described under "Insiders and the importance of control" on page 60.)

(3) At the time of the transfer, the debtor must have been insolvent. This has not changed.

(4) The transfer must have been on account of an antecedent debt. This has not changed.

(5) The effect of the transfer must have been to prefer the creditor obtaining the transfer over other creditors of the same class. This has changed to the extent that class is no longer a consideration. The only question now is whether the creditor will receive more as a result of the transfer than it would have received if the debtor were liquidated under the Bankruptcy Code and the creditor obtained the liquidation value of its allowable claim in such proceeding.

(6) The trustee in bankruptcy no longer must prove the transferee creditor had reasonable cause to believe the debtor was insolvent at the time of the transfer. There is an exception in one circumstance. (It is discussed under "Insiders and the importance of control" on page 60.)

Insolvency

While this element has not changed, there is now a legal presumption that the debtor is insolvent during the 90-day period immediately prior to bankruptcy. This presumption can be rebutted by testimony on behalf of the transferee creditor. For the purpose of the new Code, insolvency is defined in terms of the debtor's debts versus the debtor's assets at fair value, that is, a balance sheet test.

Reasonable cause to believe

The early study groups on, and draftsmen of, the Bankruptcy Code concluded that the requirement that the trustee prove knowledge by the transferee of the imminent insolvency of the debtor effectively rendered the preference provisions of the old Bankruptcy Act ineffective. It was pointed out that the presence or absence of knowledge of the debtor's insolvency had nothing to do with the promotion of equality and the state of mind of the transferee creditor was irrelevant to such goal. In addition, the evidentiary hurdle created by the necessity to prove reasonable cause to believe more often than not protected creditors who were well aware of the debtor's situation. Such creditors were often perceived as having the ability to scramble in order to leave only the tag ends of unencumbered assets for other creditors.

Effect of eliminating requirement

Reasonable cause to believe is no longer an evidentiary hurdle. Therefore, absent any statutory exceptions, all transfers on account of antecedent debts within 90 days of bankruptcy will be the probable target of preference lawsuits by trustees in bankruptcy. Also affecting this area is the considerable expansion of the jurisdictional powers of the Bankruptcy Court. It will now be possible for preference suits to be brought in the Bankruptcy Court even if the transferee creditor fails to file a claim in such court or otherwise explicitly consent to the court's jurisdiction. As a result, credit grantors will not be able to assume a payment has come to rest until 91 days after it has been received.

The six exceptions to the general recovery process

There are six exceptions to the general recovery powers just discussed. They are designed to allow certain kinds of transactions to take place without fear of attack.[2] They are:

(1) *Contemporaneous exchange.* Where the transfer was intended by both parties to be contemporaneous and where it was for new value and where it in fact took place on a substantially contemporaneous basis, there is no preference. For example, payment of a debt by means of a check (normally a credit

---

[2] No consideration is given in this article to other trustee remedies, for example, fraudulent conveyance.

transaction) is protected where the check is presented in normal course, as the intention of the parties is determinative.

(2) *Payment within 45 days in the ordinary course of business*. Where a transfer is in payment of a debt incurred in the ordinary course of business of both the debtor and the creditor and where such payment was made within 45 days of the time such debt was incurred and where the transaction was in the ordinary course of business or financial affairs of both parties and according to ordinary business terms, it will be protected. Query: If a creditor or its representative calls to demand payment, would it eliminate this exception? Suppose such call was strictly routine in nature, for example, from a factor's credit department. We do not know. What about longer selling terms? These are not protected. The statutory period is arbitrary, and the exception requires exact adherence. This type of transaction was protected for the most part under the old Act because of the difficulty of proving the reasonable cause to believe element. There will probably be considerable litigation over the various ordinary business elements required by this exception.

(3) *Enabling loans*. Purchase money security interests, although technically transfers for antecedent debts, are protected to the extent such transactions are perfected within ten days and the funds can be traced as used by the debtor to acquire the purchased property. Adequate records should be maintained.

(4) *New value credit*. Present law has been codified to allow an offset to the extent new value is given after a preferential transfer. However, such new value must not have been secured or otherwise repaid.

(5) *Accounts receivable and inventory*. Under the guise of a fifth exception, a new test for recovering from lenders secured by accounts receivable and inventory has been created. The secured creditor with such a security interest is subject to attack to the extent its position is improved to the prejudice of other creditors holding unsecured claims during the 90-day period before bankruptcy.

The Code creates a two-point test. Point 1 is the deficiency or the debit balance in the account as it existed 90 days before the petition. Point 2 is the date of the filing of the petition. Intervening days are irrelevant. To the extent that the deficiency decreased (or the secured creditor's position improved) during that 90-day period, there is a preference. (If new value was first given during that 90-day period, then Point 1 is the date on which the new value was first given. Intermediate dates remain irrelevant.)

No preference is involved if a creditor was fully secured 90 days prior to the filing date. In that event, there could not have been an improvement in position. Case law will determine how the concept of fully secured will be measured and how collateral will be evaluated for purposes of this section. As of this writing, we are also not sure of the effect of the words "to the prejudice of other creditors." They seem intended to prevent the inclusion of the entire amount of an unsecured deficiency as a preference where the estate has not been depleted; but whether seasonal fluctuations or increases in market value will have impact cannot be stated with certainty. At any rate, lenders against the security of accounts receivable and inventory in a deteriorating situation will now have to measure their desire to assist the debtor through a trying period against the possibility that an improvement in position will subject them to preference attack.

(6) *Statutory liens.* Statutory liens, such as perfected mechanics liens, will not be vulnerable to preference attacks.

All exceptions are available on a cumulative basis. That is they may be used by the allegedly preferred creditor in the aggregate.

Insiders and the importance of control

The Bankruptcy Code's new preference section incorporates a new concept—that of the insider. Basically, if the borrower is a corporation, an insider would be a director, an officer, or a person otherwise in control. This would include those who control 20% of the borrower's voting stock. Similar definitions apply where the debtor is an individual, a partnership, or other entity. Control is not defined either in the Bankruptcy Code or in its legislative history. We must therefore use analogies to other areas. For example, the regulations to the Securities Exchange Act of 1934 define control as "possession, directly or indirectly, of the ability to direct or cause the direction of the management and policies of a person, whether through the ownership of voting securities, by a contract or otherwise."

At any rate, if a lender is found in control, then such lender is an insider. And for an insider, transactions outside of the ordinary 90-day preference period but within one year prior to the filing of the petition are also subject to attack as preferences. As a trade-off for the extension of the statutory period, the trustee must establish that the transferee insider had reasonable cause to believe the debtor was insolvent at the time of the transfer. The trustee no longer has the benefit of a presumption that the debtor was insolvent for such extended period. The justification for the longer period is that the insider might be able to arrange it so the preferential transfer takes place just outside the 90-day period.

When does the concept of control suffice to make a lender an insider? For example, a commercial finance company providing the day-to-day capital needs of the borrower, holding the personal guarantees of the principals, with collateral consisting of accounts receivable, inventory, machinery, equipment, and real estate, is arguably "in control." It strikes me, however, that this is proving too much and something more must be necessary. How will the performance of periodic field examinations in the commercial finance industry affect this area?

Summary

It can be argued that creditors can more readily petition debtors into bankruptcy—acts of bankruptcy are no longer required, merely proving that the debtor is generally not paying its debts as they mature. (This test is more difficult of objective realization than may initially meet the eye.) Also, the Bankruptcy Court now has expanded jurisdictional powers. As a result, there will be many more preference lawsuits. The practical effect may be lower advances compared to collateral base, an earlier cutoff of credit in times of adversity, and insulation, if not isolation, from the affairs of a borrower to prevent insider status. This may cause distress situations to reach the courts more readily and in greater quantity than in the past. From some points of view, that was the preferred result.

From the other side, given time and the ability to handle the workout, a larger estate might be created for all creditors. Such a result would be better and more economic and one which would keep the courts less congested. This area must be viewed in the overall context of the new Bankruptcy Code—which does not use the epithet "bankrupt," but the more palatable "debtor"—in which bankruptcy is a right which has been considerably expanded and not a condition to be avoided if at all possible.   ☐

V. Problem Loan Management

Surprisingly, the *Journal* has published only a limited number of articles on the subject of problem loan management, which undoubtedly reflects the success of Robert Morris Associates' educational effort. Four of the relatively few published articles have been selected for this section of the book.

D. J. MacDonald's approach, outlined in "Problem Loans: Their Prevention, Handling, and Cures," appropriately puts a great deal of emphasis on precautionary actions as the easiest way of avoiding remedial ones. Having laid out useful rules of thumb, MacDonald points to early warning signals that can alert the loan officer that action should be taken while it may still be effective. Finally, he discuses how to cure a problem loan.

"Problem Loans—Revisited" by Alford C. Sinclair is a sequel to an earlier contribution on this subject, and it brings even more experience to the topic than the earlier article. Like most lenders, Sinclair strongly favors problem prevention to problem cure, and he outlines a watch list procedure to help identify problem situations at an early point. In the event these precautions are for naught, the article contains a detailed discussion of workout procedures through to the settlement or charge-off stage.

Assuming that the borrower is in serious financial difficulty, Roger K. Soderberg has useful suggestions about what type of help might be needed and where it can be found. His article, "Assistance to Financially Troubled Companies," reviews in detail the various types of problems a company in financially straitened circumstances may encounter, what solutions may be available, and the nature of outside assistance that could be called on to help implement a solution. He also includes an in-depth discussion of liquidation and winding up a company's affairs.

Finally, Margaret H. Douglas-Hamilton, in "Troubled Debtors: The Fine Line Between Counseling and Controlling," focuses on the important but technical point of how far the lender may go in directing the affairs of the debtor without running the risk of exercising undue influence and losing creditor status. Although her comments are directed to the lender in a problem situation, the observations are important ones for all points of a lending relationship.

For information about the authors of the articles in Section V, refer to the List of Contributors on page xi.

Problem Loans: Their Prevention, Handling, and Cures

by D. J. MacDonald

No one can deny that an ounce of prevention is worth a pound of cure, especially in a lending situation. The author points out the areas that lenders should be alert to when a loan is being negotiated as well as those they should follow closely once the loan is on the books. But if the loan still ends up on the sick list, he also offers some remedies to ease the accompanying pain.

The Special Assets Department of Security Pacific National Bank deals with problem credits that originated elsewhere in our system. We handle these credits in two ways: First, we assume primary responsibility for the administration of these accounts and attempt to restore them to a healthy status so that they can be returned to their point of origin as a viable credit once more. If this is not possible, we try to recover our advances, to the extent that we can, by one of these measures:

(1) Having another financial institution or party assume our creditor position.

(2) Resorting to those legal remedies available to us.

(3) Liquidating collateral held.

(4) Liquidating the borrower's assets (business) in rare and difficult cases.

This article is based on remarks presented by the author at the RMA Western Regional Conference held in Santa Barbara, California on May 20, 1977.

Second, we make ourselves available to credit personnel throughout our system and act as a sounding board in helping resolve their problems locally (or even better, help prevent a problem from occurring) by sharing with them experience we have gained from contending with troublesome issues in the past. By sharing this experience, the bank can resort to preventive medicine and thereby obviate the need for corrective surgery, which is always more painful and sometimes fatal.

Why loans become problem situations

Because of the uniqueness of our function, we are blessed with a distinct advantage—*hindsight!* Because hindsight is nearly always 20/20, we can usually look backward from our vantage point and discern the causes of problems. From our observation, there are four principal reasons credits get into trouble:

(1) Lack of overall management balance.
(2) Lack of secondary repayment sources.
(3) Faulty documentation.
(4) Lack of early identification of warning signals.

Management balance

Let's discuss lack of overall management balance first. I recently had the opportunity of listening to an expert in the field of business management practices talk about the causes of financial trouble in which companies large and small frequently find themselves. It was the expert's experience that businesses finding themselves in trouble have usually followed this pattern:

(1) Most of them were originally founded by entrepreneurs who possessed fine *technical* "know-how."
(2) They develop a good product or service for which there is a real demand.
(3) They grow initially, in spite of themselves, out of the sheer momentum of supplying this demand, but—
(4) They soon outgrow their *overall management* capabilities.

The expert said that's where the trouble starts, and how right he was! In his view, this type of situation presents a real challenge to us as bankers. I agree with him.

Now, how can we as lenders eliminate this kind of problem? I believe one excellent way we can try to assure a profitable relationship for our customers and ourselves is to consciously evaluate a borrower's (or his management team's) total management capacities at the inception of the credit discussion and analysis. After all, we lay great stress on obtaining and analyzing financial statements, profit and loss statements, various forecasts, agings, credit agency reports, and bank and trade checkings. But all these efforts become useless if we don't first assess the ability of our borrower (or his team) to properly run the business in question.

In this regard, we must first understand what type of business we are lending money to. Having established that, we must then deliberately determine the range or ranges of management talent necessary to run the company properly and successfully. Once we've identified the necessary management slots, we then have to satisfy ourselves that each of those slots is manned by a competent incumbent. If we find that any required element of management talent is lacking, either because it never was supplied or because of incompetence, we must discuss this situation candidly and openly with the borrower so that the problem can be overcome to our satisfaction and to the company's benefit. If the borrower is unwilling or unable to agree with our assessment of insufficient management capacity, it is probably in our best interest to decline the loan unless or until the problem is solved to our satisfaction.

In appraising company operations which reflect management skills, what are some of the questions we should ask and some of the basic considerations we should investigate? I suggest the following points are pertinent but certainly not all-inclusive:

(1) Are successors in view if any member(s) of the existing team retires, becomes ill, or dies?
(2) Are lines of communication, authority, accountability, and responsibility well-defined and clear-cut?
(3) Is there a proper balance and coordination between the various functions and levels of the company so that one element is not overly dominant?
(4) Have power groups been allowed to form? This can lead to cliques and be devisive and damaging to a company's progress.
(5) Is there a formal "R & D" function? (If pertinent.)
(6) Is there a product and design function? (If pertinent.)
(7) Is there an engineering function? (If pertinent.)
(8) Is there a well thought out and implemented sales and marketing policy/strategy?
(9) Is the company's product or service properly costed?
(10) Are financial and accounting controls adequate?
(11) Are management and overhead controls adequate?
(12) Are manufacturing, distribution, and quality controls adequate?
(13) Is the business plant properly located as to site, transportation, and labor supply?

(14) Is there a satisfactory industrial relations and personnel function that can deal with personnel, labor union, and affirmative action problems?

(15) Have past expansions and acquisitions been leveraged rather than built on equity or retained earnings?

In addition to the preceding points, there are, of course, other specific questions and considerations to be explored in the light of the type of business the borrower is engaged in and whether he is a manufacturer, wholesaler, distributor, or retailer. We've got to be imaginative enough to determine those specific points and ask the appropriate questions. If we receive positive responses on all or most of the foregoing points, chances are our prospective borrower represents a well-managed company and, thus, a reasonable credit risk.

Secondary repayment sources

Now let's evaluate the consequences that flow from not considering secondary repayment sources at the inception of a credit. I believe all of us have been guilty at one time or another of indulging in the following scenario in discussing a possible loan to a customer:

(1) The customer comes in and describes what he considers to be his problem. At this point you or I should not merely be a reactionary listener. You must start the mental analytical engine going so that you can satisfy yourself that your customer is indeed describing his actual problem and not merely the symptom of a larger or deeper problem of which he might not even be aware.

(2) Assuming that upon your analysis you agree that the problem is actually as the customer describes, you then discuss the amount of money necessary to solve the problem. Here again, you have to analyze whether the amount your customer thinks he needs is sufficient or too little or too much for his needs.

(3) Once that amount is determined, you then negotiate repayment terms that are feasible from the standpoint of your borrower's abilities and your bank's particular policies.

(4) Then you have the usual, inevitable discussion of what is or isn't an appropriate interest rate. The customer usually lets you know he thinks you're a bandit. However, just remind him that your corporate objective is the same as his—to operate at a profit.

(5) Once all these items have been settled, the next obvious question to be resolved is the primary source of loan repayment. Often, once you've both agreed on this, the lending officer's analytical engine shuts off—and that's the very point when the lender can trap himself into booking a loan that becomes a

problem in the future. Why? Simply because very often, and for reasons beyond either the borrower's or lender's control, that primary source of repayment fails and a secondary source of repayment has not been considered and identified.

For example, we all have loans in our portfolio which were to have originally been repaid from the sale of securities or real property. There is no need to remind anyone of the roller coaster these two markets have undergone in recent years. Two recent cases of ours illustrate this.

In one case, our lending relationship stretched back over many years to an officer of a local business which had been founded by his family. The company stock was traded on the NYSE, and from time-to-time, we loaned our borrower money for personal investments. These advances were usually secured by a pledge of his company's stock and usually repaid from salary, bonuses, or sale of securities. However, in later years, the borrower began investing heavily in speculative real estate ventures, and our advances reached almost three quarters of a million dollars.

Along about this time, our customer retired and his income-producing ability shrank accordingly. This problem was compounded by both a decline in the stock market and a shuddering halt in real estate movement in the areas in which he was invested. He was consequently unable to repay our loans on the basis originally negotiated. Although we had collateral, it was not sufficient to satisfy our loan.

If we had sold our customer out, we would have severely damaged him in two ways: We would have eliminated his largest source of dividend income and, at the same time, created a huge capital gains tax problem for him because his acquisition costs, through inheritance and exercise of options, were very low. Fortunately, his family was able to arrange other financing for him so that eventually we were paid in full as to principal with some discount of earned interest. However, in retrospect, we went to sleep by not considering the consequences of our borrower's retirement and the heavy burden that event placed on the primary repayment sources' remaining viable. When these failed, we had insufficient *secondary* sources to look to.

In another instance we loaned money to a manufacturer for capital improvements. This loan was to have been repaid from cash flow and refinancing. No other repayment sources were explored or considered. When economic conditions caused a softening in our customer's markets and cash flow dwindled and refinancing became unobtainable, we were both trapped in an extended workout situation.

These two cases, I believe, illustrate the real need for identification of secondary repayment sources at the *inception* of a credit negotiation. This is especially true if the proposed primary source is volatile, represents undue risk, or requires that equities be converted to cash.

Faulty documentation

This brings us to the third problem area: faulty documentation of loans. Improperly prepared or a total lack of necessary documentation often inhibits or even precludes our being able to recover money loaned. For example, in our handling of problem credits, we frequently see improperly prepared guarantees or guarantees taken without requisite consideration having been received by the guarantor which, of course, may invalidate that guarantor's liability. This is especially true of upstream or cross-guarantees involving corporations and their subsidiaries.

It is also essential that any change in the original credit negotiation that the guarantor agreed to be bound by, be made known to him at once and his agreement to continue to be bound be obtained. Otherwise, you lose his liability. This pertains to changes in amount, rate, terms, and whether you move from a secured to an unsecured position. If the guarantor is not so informed, recent court cases have been decided in the guarantor's favor on the theory that he was not a party to the transaction subsequent to the original arrangement and hence had no opportunity to defend himself. We have also seen many cases where corporate guarantees have been obtained but which had not been authorized by the requisite corporate resolution. The guarantee in such an instance is valueless.

We have also seen instances where subordination to our position should have been obtained but wasn't. This can work to our detriment in a bankruptcy or liquidation proceeding, especially if we are in an unsecured position and the other party is secured. An illustration of this is the case where we are advancing unsecured credit for working capital needs and a finance house has a perfected position on the borrower's fixtures and equipment. If we have failed to obtain a subordination of the finance company's position to ours, the finance house would rank ahead of us in a bankruptcy or liquidation. Advances by officers to their company should also be subordinated to us for the same reason. There are many other situations where it is essential that we insist upon subordination of others' positions to ours so that we are not adversely affected in our ability to recover our advances.

The advent of the Uniform Commercial Code has also posed some serious problems for lenders. For example, under the requirements of the Code, it is mandatory that our security interest in assets be perfected by an appropriate filing with the secretary of state (and other government entities in some instances) or our supposed secured position is rendered invalid. It is also essential that we search for prior filings by other lenders before we advance our funds so that we can ascertain that we are, in fact, in a senior position. If checking reveals other creditors are on file ahead of us, we should obtain that creditor's subordination to our position or his termination or release of collateral he claims an interest in, or we will remain junior to his position.

The extremely technical attitude of the courts today also places a premium on proper document preparation. It is therefore necessary to know and understand what kind of documentation is required and, further, to prepare and file such documentation properly. Failure to do so can invalidate what we had thought was a secured, perfected position and can lead to needless losses.

Early identification of warning signals

Finally, let's discuss early problem identification with respect to our borrower's business. It is imperative that we as lenders be alert to the signals of problems as soon as they manifest themselves so that we can both protect ourselves and our borrower from loss or serious problems. But first, to properly gauge the significance of these, it is necessary for us to understand thoroughly the nature of the customer's enterprise and the meaning and nuances of the signs we are reading. In short, we should know our customer's business as well as he himself knows it! This is no easy task and requires a great deal of intensive analysis, research, and questioning to achieve such a position.

Once having attained this position, what are some of the sources and signals we should be reading and monitoring for hints of possible problems? The basic sources of information are our customer's balance sheets, profit and loss statements, and various forecasts. Provided these bodies of information are accurate (and professionally prepared), they can, if read properly, give us hints of possible problems and enable us to join with our customer in heading them off. A few of these signs can be categorized as follows:

(1) *Cash:* Is it adequate for the company's needs? Does it represent a proper proportion of the company's working capital position? Are cash controls of the business effective? Is excess cash invested in short-term obligations to maximize profits?

(2) *Accounts receivable:* Does their aging represent a satisfactory condition? What is bad debt write-off experience? If heavy, is this due to rejections of the product or inability to service accounts? Are reserves adequate to cover

possible write-offs? Are collection procedures and controls adequate? If A/R totals are building, is this due to slowing collections, unposted credit memos, delays in shipping, or simply increased sales volume?

(3) *Inventory:* Is the turnover factor satisfactory in relation to the borrower's type of business? Is inventory properly costed? What is the pricing method? Is the inventory obsolete? How is this obsolescence controlled and guarded against? Are purchase controls adequate and effective?

(4) *Machinery, Fixtures, and Equipment:* Are these items efficient and sufficient for the customer's needs? Is there an excess of downtime for machinery and equipment? Are replacement parts available? What is the age of machinery and equipment in relation to its expected useful life? Are reserves for depreciation adequate?

The preceding categories and questions are only a few of the areas of a borrower's balance sheet and P & L statements we must become familiar with. We have to evaluate all of our borrower's assets *as well as his liabilities* in this same fashion so that we are certain we have a real grasp of his overall financial condition and ability to succeed in his business.

As mentioned, another invaluable tool all lenders should employ in spotting trends, good or bad, in the operation of a borrower's business are various forecasts and how well or poorly the borrower meets these forecasts. This is an excellent test of a given management's ability to forecast its efforts and results of those efforts. Required forecasts should, as a minimum, include sales and pre-tax profits with adjustments to come to cash flow.

We should also know the assumptions used by our customer in preparing these forecasts. An earnings forecast for an average firm made twelve months prior to year-end usually tends to deviate only about 10 to 15%. This deviation rate is ordinarily acceptable in a loan situation. Certain industries such as automotive, aerospace, and steel are more difficult to forecast than other industries such as food, oil, and drugs. But the point is, if forecasts are consistently met, met closely, or exceeded, we usually can feel comfortable in management's ability to manage. When forecasts are consistently missed, we have a problem on our hands, and we must move quickly to identify it and solve it.

How to cure a problem loan

One excellent way for a lender to bring a problem into proper focus is to involve a borrower's board of directors in a mutual exploration of the situation. This practice has not been heavily resorted to in the past. But in the light of today's heightened awareness of board members' legal responsibilities and accountabilities to their company and shareholders, most boards seem to welcome this sort of involvement. This type of joint effort at problem solving, or problem averting, can pay rich dividends to lenders, borrowers, their boards and shareholders.

Many times it is also appropriate to seek outside help in the form of expert, qualified management consultants who can bring specific areas of expertise and objectivity to bear on an issue. Calling on their past experience in solving identical or similar situations, they can usually identify the problem areas quickly, provide suggested reasonable courses of corrective action, and help implement those actions on a prompt, effective basis. We have had good success in the use of this technique in several situations in which our bank has been involved. I admit that some borrowers may initially resist this suggested approach on your part. But if you are deft in your approach and graphically illustrate the advantages of employing a qualified consultant to all parties to the transaction, the results are usually rewarding to all concerned.

Requirements for debt restructuring

At times, however, it is too late for either the involvement of the board or outside consultants to be helpful in averting a troublesome situation and the lender must resort to other remedies. One technique we employ is restructure of the borrower's debt. But this technique requires the existence of two positive factors:

(1) There must exist a market for the customer's product or service.
(2) There must be a sufficient amount or number of viable assets to work with in liquidating the borrower's various liabilities.

With respect to the first factor just mentioned, there is not much sense in reorganizing a company and restructuring its debt if no market exists or can be acquired for its product or service. In one recent case of ours involving a loan to a manufacturer of a computer software program, we found to our dismay that this one program constituted his entire product line. The company had not indulged in R & D, and competition was rapidly rendering its product obsolete. In this case, the company was fortunate enough to be acquired by another organization which had a use for its program and could improve upon it enough to make it competitive. But we had to compromise our loan balance considerably and write off both a portion of our principal and interest.

But if you do have a market, a good product/service base, and assets to work with, you can restructure provided, again, that management is competent. In a restructure, you are looking at these twin questions: What assets are there to satisfy existing liabilities or how can these liabilities be reformed to match available assets? There are many ways to do this and the scope of this article does not allow time for discussion and detailed analysis of case studies. Suffice it to say that your approach must entail a program that existing assets can support and that anticipated cash flow can service. Often this approach entails some forgiveness of debt; conversion of debt to various forms of equity; creation of new equity; modification or extension of remaining debt; acceptance of certain assets in consideration of debt extinguishment; selling, liquidating, or consolidating unprofitable operations; or a combination of all the foregoing. While the doing of these things sometimes becomes convoluted, the final objective should always remain clear and simple: to restore the borrower to a healthy financial condition.

Another source of financing or legal remedies

In instances where a restructure may not be advisable, your borrower can sometimes find another source of financing to replace your credits. We've had some luck with this technique, although in recent years this solution has not been as readily available as in the past. A variation of this approach is the combination of credit where you share borrowings with a commercial finance house or factor. This can be expensive for your borrower and imposes a heavy load on his cash flow/profit trend.

Finally, if you can't restructure, can't find another lender to replace you or join you, it is sometimes necessary to resort to those legal remedies available to you to maximize your recovery and minimize your loss. This is usually the least attractive of the courses of action available to a lender. However, in certain instances involving fraud or misrepresentation, for example, it is the most prudent course to follow to protect your position. This presupposes, however, that your documentation can withstand challenges in litigation and that there are assets available to satisfy any judgment you obtain through litigation.

Summary

Looking backward from our experience platform, we believe that lenders can enhance their loan portfolio by being alert at the inception of credit negotiations and by consciously evaluating management balance and secondary repayment sources.

When a lender has decided to proceed with a loan, it is absolutely essential that he document it properly and indulge in appropriate filings when necessary. And once the loan is booked, part of the loan administration technique must include proper reading and interpretation of warning signals pertinent to the borrower's business.

If, in spite of all these precautions, the loan still becomes a "problem situation," don't hesitate to acknowledge it as such. Move quickly to implement an appropriate "cure" from the several I have suggested or develop whatever other remedy you deem appropriate depending upon the issues involved. If you do, your chances of loan restoration or recovery will be enhanced. At the very least, your loss will be reduced. I wish you all the best luck!   ☐

Problem Loans—Revisited

by Alford C. Sinclair

Mr. Sinclair focuses on the prevention and reassignment of problem loans, settlements and long-term payouts, and charge-offs, among other topics. Perhaps the highlight of the article is his discussion of the tie between loan officer performance and problem loans. We think you will find that he has liberally sprinkled the article with his own shrewd and invaluable insights.

Some days turn out much better than others. Sometimes a day gets off to a good start and then goes to hell by mid-day. But other times you can just sense a feeling of doom when you wake up. Let me share with you a few signs of a bad day.

You know it's going to be a bad day when you turn on the news and the broadcaster is displaying emergency routes out of your city.

You know it's going to be a bad day when your only son tells you he wishes Anita Bryant would mind her own business.

You know it's going to be a bad day when you read in the morning newspaper that your biggest loan customer declared bankruptcy yesterday.

You know it's going to be a bad day when you realize on the way to work that you and those fire engines are headed for the same building.

You know it's going to be a bad day when you open your mail and see that half of your past due notices have been returned with the message "Addressee Unknown."

This article is based on the author's presentation as part of the 1979-80 RMA Loan Quality Control Workshop.

You know it's going to be a bad day when you call "Suicide Prevention" and you're put on hold.

Any discussion of things going wrong always brings to mind Murphy's Law: "If anything can go wrong, it will." There are several variations of Murphy's Law. A few of them are:

(1) Nothing is ever as simple as it seems.

(2) Everything takes longer than you expect.

(3) If several things can go wrong, the thing that will go wrong first will be the one which can do the most damage.

(4) Left to themselves, all things go from bad to worse.

(5) If everything seems to be going well, you have obviously overlooked something.

Finally, there is Murphy's Law for bankers: *A bad loan is always worse than you think it is.*

Loan officer's need for realistic attitude

If what I have written so far leads you to believe that bank loan officers should be dyed-in-the-wool pessimists, I don't mean to create that impression. It's just that you need a good streak of realism to offset the boundless optimism invariably displayed by borrowers. If you could deal only with AAA prime rate borrowers, you wouldn't need all the documentation with which you burden yourselves and your borrowers and enrich your attorneys. You wouldn't need an endless program of loan review. Every loan could be simply an I.O.U. signed on a postcard. Wouldn't that be great?

But life isn't that way. You and I are not perfect judges of people's character and capacity to repay. We are not true prophets who can foretell what effects may be brought about by our constantly changing economic climate. Both our borrowers and we are fallible human beings who want desperately to have everything work out okay. But we must approach every lending opportunity with one big question in our minds: What are we going to do if everything does not work out okay?

Problem prevention

That's why we need loan agreements and collateral and co-signers and constant follow-up. That's why we need secondary and tertiary sources of repayment.

If your lending program is properly structured, losses in your consumer loan portfolio should be a minor and predictable cost of business, offset by the higher rates you charge for these loans (during normal times, that is). Losses in your commercial and real estate loan portfolio should be practically non-existent.

Please understand that I am not saying that your bank should have *no* losses nor take any chances. You have an obligation, both moral and legal, to meet the credit needs of your community. You have an equally strong obligation to your depositors and stockholders to protect their funds and their investments. You have a delicate balancing act to perform. But I contend that a good banker *can* meet the credit needs of his community without giving the shop away.

This balancing act calls for intelligence, training, experience, and hard work. But that's what we are paid to have and do. The introduction to my bank's lending policy states that we expect and allow for occasional errors in judgment, but we will not tolerate sloppy or careless lending practices. These errors in judgment and inability to foresee the future sometimes make us wish that we had not made a given loan. But proper planning and good workout procedures have enabled us to get out of some very sticky situations without losing anything but some sleep and some administrative expenses. (I will have more to say about those administrative expenses and the *real* cost of a loan workout a little later on in this text.)

Being prepared

My purpose in writing this article is not to talk about loan documentation and loan review procedures, but it's difficult to overemphasize their importance. Most battles, you know, are won or lost long before they take place. A couple of years ago, I bought a copy of the best-selling book by Robert J. Ringer, *Winning through Intimidation*. I hoped to find in it some magic formula for success. There isn't any magic formula, of course. Mr. Ringer's formula was simply to do his homework more thoroughly and be better prepared than the person with whom he would be dealing. That's always a winning formula, whether you're selling real estate (as Mr. Ringer was) or playing a football game or collecting a problem loan.

In problem loan situations, your opponent is *not* usually the borrower. You and he should be teammates, working closely together to solve your mutual problem. Your opponents, the people you want to be better prepared than, are usually the borrower's other creditors. A problem borrower, almost without exception, has other creditors—usually *many* other creditors—who are, or should be, just as eager as you are to be repaid. Your job is to get there first and get more than your share, since there probably are not enough assets to meet all the borrower's liabilities. (If there were, he wouldn't have a problem).

If you think that getting more than your share is greedy and unChristian, let me ask you this: How many of you would be satisfied to earn just the per capita income in your state? You want to do better than average, don't you? Nothing wrong with that.

You want your bank to do better than average, too. And the way to accomplish that is to *be prepared* when trouble starts.

Being prepared implies having all documents in order and having a loan review program which spots problems early. These problems include:

(1) Disturbing trends in the borrower's financial condition.
(2) Lateness in receiving financial statements.
(3) Lateness in receiving payments of principal or interest.
(4) Turnover of management.
(5) Changes in the personal habits of the borrower or the borrower's key managers.

Keeping tabs on the borrower for signs of trouble

Particularly in a small- to medium-size bank, the main responsibility for keeping an eye on the borrower should be that of the loan officer. You may have a person or a department responsible for keeping current financial statements and analyzing them. But any business borrower or large personal borrower is clearly the responsibility of the assigned loan officer. That loan officer should have sufficiently frequent contact with the borrower to sense trouble before it really develops. Just as a mother can usually detect impending illness in a child before it becomes apparent to anyone else, so a loan officer should be able to detect small changes in a borrower that signal trouble ahead. If the borrower is a business, the loan officer should visit that business regularly. Every business has a certain rhythm about it—a change in that rhythm should be investigated.

Using a watch list to identify problem loans

In our bank, we have a Watch Loan List. It includes loans classified by bank examiners, nonaccruing loans, loans which are delinquent more than 15 days, and loans which appear to warrant more than normal attention because of collateral deterioration or some other problem. An explanation of our watch list procedures is included in Exhibit 1.

A loan may be placed on the watch list by our loan review department. But we really expect it to be placed there by the responsible loan officer. He or she is certainly the person who should first be able to spot any impending problem. As a matter of management policy, we are quite disappointed if the loan officer

Exhibit 1—Watch List Procedures

Purpose ·

The stated purpose of listing a loan on the watch list is not to criticize our borrowers or our loan officers. The main purpose is to identify those loans that require more than normal review and attention to ensure they remain viable assets of the bank. Moreover, any noted deterioration in quality through continuous review will allow prompt and timely action.

Procedures

The watch list will be divided into four categories:

(1) Watch-classified
(2) Watch-nonaccrual
(3) Watch-past due (only those past due 15 days or more)
(4) Other watch loans

All loans over $50,000 will be subject to listing as watch loans, and we will require a memo at each month-end indicating current status.

A file on each category will be maintained listing all loans that fall within the aforementioned categories. In the file we will list the following information: loan details, review dates, account officer, internal and external rating and classification, and special comments or actions.

We will update the watch list monthly after receipt of our monthly status report.

The watch-classifieds, nonaccruals, and past dues are all self-explanatory. The category name signifies their nature and constitutes their placement. The fourth category, other watch loans, is much more open and allows and encourages objective input. A loan listed as simply an "other" watch loan will fall within the following broad definition: A loan having an obvious weakness such as current financials showing adverse operating trends, highly leveraged capital position, lack of quality or marketability in pledged collateral, or clear inadequacy of margin of collateral protection. Further, it will include loans not of the aforementioned character but which require more than normal management attention.

A loan can be placed on the watch list by being classified, placed on nonaccrual, or past due in excess of 15 days. Watch loans will be placed on the list by the loan officer, watch loan review committee, loan review officer, loan evaluation committee, or other necessary responsible loan administration parties.

For a loan to be removed from the watch list, it must pay out, no longer fall within the previously mentioned criteria, or be approved by the watch loan review committee chaired by the CEO.

The maintenance and responsibility for the watch list will be that of the bank's credit administration. But it will be maintained in a cooperative effort with all those involved in commercial and real estate lending at the bank.

does not blow the whistle on his own loans. As long as the loan is on the watch list, the loan officer must file a written monthly report detailing the status of the loan and what is being done to collect it or restore it to better condition.

Reassignment of problem loans

Once a problem loan has been identified, the vexing question remains of whether to leave it with the assigned loan officer or reassign it to a collection specialist or special department. In a relatively small bank, there may not be any other department to which the loan can be reassigned, so the loan officer may have to keep the loan himself and collect it as best he can. But in every bank, no matter how small, there is *someone*, usually more experienced, who can be turned to for help.

Reasons for keeping loan officer involved

As a generalization, I recommend keeping the assigned loan officer actively involved in the loan because he knows the details of the loan and he knows the borrower. Remember, the bank and the borrower are teammates in trying to solve a mutual problem. It's hard to overemphasize that point.

There is never a reason for a banker to adopt an adversarial position unless the borrower is completely dishonest. Fights between the lender and borrower rarely produce worthwhile results. You don't have to carry the adversarial position very far before you end up in court, and that's just where you don't want to be. Being in court wastes time and wastes money. Being in court means that you have lost control of the situation. You don't want to lose control. You want to call the plays, set the pace, keep the confidence of the borrower, and treat him fairly. You want to create in that borrower a state of mind that will cause him to bring you any money he gets his hands on.

Reasons for involving specialists

Back to the question of reassigning the loan. I've already expressed my belief that the loan officer should be kept closely involved whenever it is practical to do so. At the same time, you can improve your chances of collecting most loans by involving persons who are specialists in liquidating whatever kind of collateral you have. For example, if your collateral is a half-completed apartment development, you'd better seek the help of a person who knows the building contracting business. That person can accurately project the cost of completing the project and selling it. He or she can oversee the actual construction to make sure that a bad situation isn't made worse.

Advancing additional funds

This observation leads to the question of how much additional money should be advanced while you are trying to collect a problem loan. If it is a business loan, you always have the opportunity to advance more funds for payroll and to pay for more inventory so the borrower can stay in business a while longer and try to make a recovery.

Business people in trouble are usually like football coaches. No football coach worth his salt ever gets beaten. He just happens to be behind when time runs out. Given another quarter, his team could make a comeback. Of all the problem borrowers I have ever talked to, I can't remember one who admitted that he got in trouble because of his own lousy judgment or lack of management ability. In the borrower's mind, it is always a matter of being deserted by his banker or being cut off by his chicken-hearted suppliers or being a victim of some other circumstance beyond his control.

You have to understand this about borrowers. Most of them are entrepreneurs who never would have gone into business in the first place if they hadn't had a large dose of ego and a strong belief that they could succeed. What I'm saying is that most problem borrowers will keep on borrowing as long as you will keep on lending.

Determining why loan went bad

What you need to do is carefully evaluate each situation before you lend *any* more money. Make realistic projections on paper. Determine the factors which made the loan go bad in the first place. Was it the economy? Was it some unforseeable technological change? Usually it was poor management. The longer I stay in the banking business, the more convinced I become that quality of management is the key to the success of *any* business. If you don't believe that, analyze your past business loan losses or personal loan losses, for that matter. See if lack of adequate management was not the *key* element in the failure of the business almost every time.

If that be true, how can you justify lending more money to the same managers who got both of you in trouble? Your analysis may show that the addition of a strong financial manager may be sufficient to get a business back on the track. I make that suggestion because most businesses are started by sales personnel or people who have invented a new or better product or service. Very few businesses are started by financially oriented persons. Therefore, when the business suffers growing pains, it is frequently because of the inability of the entrepreneur to manage his financial affairs adequately.

You can rarely replace management completely because management usually owns the business. Even if you have the stock of the business assigned to you as collateral, you may not want to take on the potential liabilities which would become yours if you took over the business.

Need for caution

Not only can it be dangerous to take over a business completely, but it can cost you plenty if you advance money for payrolls. As you probably already know, a bank which advances funds for paying employees of a business can easily find itself liable for payment of withheld tax. A troubled borrower will *rarely* set aside these withholdings and send them to the government. Yet they must be paid. It has been held in a number of cases that, by advancing payroll funds, a bank becomes liable for these taxes.

To summarize the matter of advancing more money, I would suggest extreme caution before entrusting more money to borrowers who have already demonstrated their lack of ability to repay loans. A smart poker player doesn't risk much money trying to fill an inside straight.

Settlements and long-term payouts

Since few problem borrowers have the ability to repay a loan according to its original terms and conditions, you will frequently find yourself negotiating settlements and long-term payouts. If the borrower is fortunate enough to have some cash on hand or available to him, he may offer you x cents on the dollar in lieu of full payment. If that should happen to you, lock the front door and don't let him out until you can confer with your associates and calculate whether your bird in the hand is better than the two in the bushes.

Advantages of cash settlements and how to calculate their return

Cash settlements have some real advantages. They are a sure thing versus an uncertainty. They allow you to settle a problem and get on to other matters. They allow an embarrassing situation to become a matter of history rather than a continuing headache. As you certainly recognize though, all these advantages have a flip side. And part of your responsibility is to be sure that you don't settle too quickly just to get that embarrassment out of the way. As before, you need to calculate carefully the return to your bank of a *certain* partial settlement versus an *uncertain* full collection in the future.

A handy tool to use in your calculation is a present value chart. It measures the value, in today's dollars, of money collected in the future. A dollar due in the future is not worth a dollar today. But its present value is the sum today which will grow to that dollar in the future at a given interest rate. For example, a present value table indicates that a dollar collected over a 10-year period is worth only 55¢ today, assuming that you could invest the funds at 6% as you receive them. One good booklet on the subject is distributed by Financial Publishing Co. of Boston. It's entitled, *Financial Combined Mortgage and Corporate Financing Tables,* Publication No. 57.

Need for collateral and flexibility

Unfortunately, not many busted borrowers have enough cash on hand to make a reasonable settlement. So you usually have to settle for repayment over an extended period of time. If that is the case, let me suggest strongly that you get all the collateral you possibly can to secure the workout extension. Arranging an unsecured long-term workout is like repainting an old rotten chair. It's still rotten, and it's likely to break the first time you sit in it.

A second suggestion is that you leave yourself as much flexibility as possible in the terms of the workout extension. You don't want to set unrealistically short terms that will get the borrower right back in trouble, but you don't want to be too liberal with him or her either. We have discovered several cases emanating from the real estate bust in Florida in the mid-70s in which developers came back faster than we thought they would. As a result, we have some workouts at *very* low interest rates and no principal repayment, for the first three years, with developers who are now in a position to pay both principal and interest at a higher rate. Naturally, they aren't going to pay any more than is required by the terms of the agreement.

Charge-offs

If, in spite of all you can do, you cannot recover all or most of a given problem loan, you need to calculate the cost of continued collection activity versus the additional money you can reasonably expect to recover. If the cost/benefit ratio doesn't look favorable, you may as well wrap up the collection work on that particular loan and put it in mothballs.

You should have written procedures for making this determination, and you should have a standard charge-off procedure. Exhibit 2 is a sample of a charge-off procedure, and Exhibit 3 is an example of a charge-off request form. Charged-off loans should be classified as to their potential for eventual recovery, and Exhibit 4 shows some such classifications. All charged-off loans should be reviewed at regular intervals for any change in the status of the borrower or of any collateral you may have. This review implies that you will have judgments recorded in almost all cases not involving bankruptcy.

Exhibit 2—Sample of a Charge-off Procedure

1. *Criteria for Initiating Charge-off Request*

    a. When a loan has been classified in the "loss" category as a result of a bank examination, or

    b. When it seems apparent to the officer(s) responsible for a loan that it cannot be repaid by the maker, co-maker, or guarantor, and collateral which can be liquidated to repay the loan is insufficient.

2. *Preparation and Review of Charge-off Request*

    a. The officer primarily responsible for the loan will prepare a loan charge-off request (sample form attached).

    b. The completed loan charge-off request and credit file will be reviewed by the officer's department manager and by the commercial loan administrator.

    c. If request is endorsed by the commercial loan administrator and the officer's department manager, the request will be submitted to the senior loan committee.

3. *Action by Senior Loan Committee*

    a. Senior loan committee acts upon request by (1) approving it for complete or partial charge-off, (2) returning it to loan officer for further collection work, or (3) assigning it to another officer or department for further collection effort.

    b. If approved for charge-off, senior loan committee assigns loan to a collection probability category, based on likelihood of ultimate collectibility (see Exhibit 4 for listing of categories).

4. *Charge-off Processing*

    a. Copies of the approved charge-off request will be sent to (1) the loan officer originating the request, (2) the credit department, (3) loan review department, (4) loan and discount department, and (5) auditing department.

    b. Charge-off entries will be made by the loan and discount department.

    c. The charged-off note will remain in the loan and discount department in a special file.

    d. Any collateral retained for future disposal will be held by the collateral department.

5. *Follow-up on Charged-off Loans*

    a. Charged-off loans will be assigned to the central recovery department where they will be worked on immediately or filed and reviewed according to the collection probability number assigned to them.

    b. The manager of the central recovery department will report monthly to bank management on the progress of loans being worked on and will make recommendations for any category changes.

Exhibit 3—Example of Charge-off Request Form

Bank and Trust Co.

Office _____

Date _____
Officer Who
Made Loan _____

Borrower _____

FILES CHECKED FOR:

Address _____

☐ Other Loans

_____

☐ Checking or Savings Acct.

Original Amount $	Original Date	Last Payment Made
Present Balance $	Due Date	Interest Paid to

Original Purpose of Loan

_____

Original Source and Plan of Repayment

_____

Security or Other Collateral	Value at Inception $	Present Value $

_____

Brief Summary of Financial Information on which Loan Was Based

_____

Primary Cause of Loss

_____

Action Taken to Collect or Restore to Satisfactory Basis

_____

Result of Action

_____

Estimate of Eventual Recovery and Suggested Action

_____

Recommendations and Approval   Date

Officer Handling Loan _____

Department Manager _____

Commercial Loan
Administrator _____

Senior Loan Committee _____

Exhibit 4—Collection Probability Categories to Be Assigned to All Charged-off Loans

Category A

Those loans determined to have at least a 50% probability of collection.

  Example: Loans charged off because of delinquency or collateral deterioration presumed to be temporary. Collection efforts to remain current.

Category B

Loans determined to have 24%–50% probability of collection.

  Example: Loan to a bankrupt company with a guarantor who is illiquid because of maker's bankruptcy but presumed to have ability to recoup. Review each six months.

Category C

Loans determined to have 1%–25% probability recovery.

  Example: Loan secured by stock in company which has gone into Chapter XI or loan to individual who has become disabled physically or mentally. Review once each year.

Category D

Loans determined to have virtually no chance of recovery.

  Example: Loan to a borrower discharged in bankruptcy, or loan to borrower who died intestate. Review every three years.

Bankruptcy and how to deal with it is another subject, and I shall not attempt to delve into it except to say that the new bankruptcy law appears to put us, as creditors, at even more of a disadvantage than we already were. From our standpoint, the bankruptcy of a borrower usually represents a sizable defeat.

Loan officer evaluation and problem loans

Let me ask and attempt to answer, or at least stimulate some thought on your part, regarding a couple of other questions.

Income generated

How do you rate loan officers based on business generated and losses taken? It is fairly easy to rate installment lending officers. You can keep a monthly record of loan volume and charge-offs. Over a period of a couple of years, you can generate a very accurate record of your winners and losers. With commercial loan officers, it's not nearly as simple. Their loans don't fit as neatly into reports, and their losses sometimes don't show up until years later. Other factors clouding the picture of commercial loan officers' performance include the wide range of interest rates, compensating balances, and other services performed for the borrower as well as other fees received.

Nevertheless, even with all these complicating factors, I believe it is definitely worthwhile to attempt to rate your commercial loan officers objectively on the basis of loan interest generated, deposit balances obtained, fees received, and losses taken. You can't really hope to get a clear picture in less than about a five-year time frame. But since most loan officers work for you much longer than that, it really is a worthwhile exercise. Wouldn't it be great if all of us could be paid strictly on the basis of our objective worth to our banks? In the long run, this approach would attract the most capable group of bankers we could hope to have.

Losses suffered

What is the real cost of a loan workout? We seldom measure anything more than the cost of the charged off principal and interest. Rarely do we even calculate and report to our boards the cost of unaccrued interest. This unaccrued interest may be the difference between the workout settlement rate and a realistic market rate. Or it may be the cost of a nonaccrual loan or Other Real Estate Owned which stays on our books as long as the regulators allow. That can amount to a very substantial sum of money.

Other substantial costs include fees paid to attorneys, travel expenses, and other out of pocket expenses. You need to keep an accurate record of all of these, just in case a borrower makes a recovery. Many of these collection expenses can be added to the loan balances if you are able to substantiate them.

Harder to calculate, but just as real, are the costs of the time spent by your bank personnel in collection work. A large problem commercial or real estate loan can take hundreds of hours of your executives' time.

Let's assume that a loan officer is paid $25,000 a year. Let's also assume that he works nine hours a day, 240 days a year. That's 2,160 hours a year or a cost to your bank of $11.57 per hour. That doesn't include fringe benefit costs, which add 20-25%, or the cost of the desk or office the loan officer occupies or any equipment he uses. It doesn't include the cost of his secretary, the loan and discount department clerks, the credit department personnel, or any of the other supporting staff. When a loan becomes a problem, it usually requires the attention of several executives within the bank. They may meet for hours at a time to find the best solutions to all the thorny problems related to a bad loan. Their time costs money, sometimes many thousands of dollars which never get charged to that particular bad loan nor to the officer who made it.

To illustrate how much hidden costs a problem loan can generate, I prepared an example (Exhibit 5) using a real estate development loan. This particular

Exhibit 5—The Real Cost of a Problem Loan

Example: A $2,000,000 construction loan at 10% to build a four-story oceanfront condominium building with 40 units. Project begun January 1, 19XX. Almost completed six months later when owner no longer able to pay interest because of rising costs and slack market. Bank places loan on nonaccrual for six months, then converts to OREO. Sales of units completed one year later or 18 months from time loan became non-performing. Units sold at average price of $60,000 per unit or $2,400,000.

1. *Property Maintenance*

   a. Guard service ($100 per day) $ 36,500
   b. Insurance   12,000
   c. Sales commissions and closing costs (10% of sales price)   240,000
   d. Accounting   2,000
   e. Maintenance and repairs   18,000
   f. Advertising   24,000
   g. Property taxes   40,000
   h. Utilities   9,000
   i. Capital expenditures   40,000

                                                                          $421,500

2. *Legal Costs*
   120 hours @$75 $ 9,000

3. *Loan Officer Time ($25,000 per year)*
   40 hours per month times 18 months
   (9-hour days; 240 days per year) $ 8,333

4. *Clerical Time ($10,000 per year)*
   40 hours per month times 18 months $ 3,333

5. *Division Manager Time ($40,000 per year)*
   10 hours per month times 18 months $ 3,333

6. *Chief Executive Officer Time ($75,000 per year)*
   5 hours per month times 18 months $ 3,125

7. *Loss of Interest on Nonaccruing Loan*
   $2,000,000 @10% for 6 months $100,000

8. *Cost of Carrying OREO (Average unsold balance)*
   Outstanding $1,200,000 for 12 months at money cost of 10% $120,000

9. *Total Real Costs* $668,624

10. *Real Direct Loss* $268,624

11. *Indirect Costs Not Included*
    • Fringe benefits to personnel; 20% times salary expenses $ 3,625
    • Lost opportunity cost; return on investment in personnel   ?

loan represents a composite of several loans our bank made in the early 70s. Our real estate workout people came up with the figures shown on this sheet, and I'm satisfied that they are both accurate and typical. Believe me, we had some which were worse.

At any rate, on this particular $2,000,000 loan we suffered a real loss of $268,624, even though the project sold out successfully for $2,400,000.

You'll notice that the last item on the page is a question mark. It's beside the item "Lost opportunity cost; return on investment in personnel." The question mark is there because I frankly don't know how much return we should expect from our investment in a given staff member of our bank. I know that collectively we will have done a good job if we earn a 1% return on assets in a given year. But what if we do better or worse? Shouldn't we be able to reward the high performers and replace the weak performers? We have a long way to go in measuring performance.

Link between problem loans and loan officer performance

You may think that I'm straying from the subject of problem loans, but to me loan officer performance and problem loans are tied inseparably together. Only when we are able to measure the performance of loan officers accurately and objectively will we really have our arms around the problem of loan losses.

Meeting the credit needs of our community while consistently earning a decent return for our shareholders and building a stronger market base and capital structure is tough. The competition we feel from credit unions, S&Ls, and brokerage house cash funds is making it tougher every day.

You need to do some deep thinking about your bank and how you are going to meet these challenges. These are exciting times—I'm enjoying them immensely, and I appreciate the opportunity to share these thoughts with you. □

Assistance to Financially Troubled Companies

by Roger K. Soderberg

WHEN I FIRST CONTEMPLATED THIS TOPIC, I recalled a cold, windy day in January I spent in the city of Buffalo. After a day spent almost entirely in an unheated warehouse going over the remains of a once thriving business, I had a few moments alone with the principal of the company. He complained that, as his business went from bad to worse, and he looked around for assistance, he was faced with a curious dilemma. His friends and associates were, for the most part, successful lawyers, accountants and businessmen, and despite the fact that they were intelligent and capable and possessed all the qualities that would normally make them excellent advisors, they had never had any experience with this kind of problem before. As a result, he found himself in a totally new set of circumstances, unable to cope with them, and unable to find reliable assistance. His dilemma was compounded by the fact that the one advisor who was likely to be most able to give him good assistance at such a time was the one he was least likely to confide in—namely, his banker. In any case, whether the borrower confides in you or not, you are going to be one of the first to recognize what is happening and one of the few people in a position to make the borrower listen to things he probably does not want to hear. Therefore, I thought it would be helpful to discuss some of the kinds of assistance and techniques which are available to a faltering company.

This article is based upon an address by Mr. Soderberg to a meeting of the Buffalo Chapter of RMA.

A "hands-on" approach to a financially troubled company

Our approach to a financially troubled company is an activist approach; a hands-on attitude towards the company and its problems. We are able to take this approach by reason of the fact that our staff, and the staff of any organization like ours, is, of necessity, experienced in and oriented toward day-to-day operational management. A lending institution is probably not going to take such an overall approach directly for several reasons. For one, involvement in a borrower's operations is not the lending officer's function, and time spent in this area is time away from his job of making loans and assisting his good customers. Also, this type of activity is, in fact, not within the loan officer's area of greatest expertise. Even members of a loan review department generally have a financial background as opposed to an operational background. Third, and most important, is the fact that such an approach by a bank exposes it to both legal problems and public criticism. Banks make good defendants.

Even though our overall approach is inappropriate for you to use directly, there are still a number of reasons why I think it would be valuable for you to know more about what we or other companies like us do.

Who should hire the financial service consultant?

First, certain aspects of the things we do and the things we've learned can certainly be employed by an institutional lender, and can be helpful to the loan officer in handling many of the problems he will see. Also, it is perhaps useful for you to know what kind of help is available from outside sources, when to seek it and what to expect from such organizations. In advising your client, there are certain pitfalls that we have learned to look for and about which you might be able to inform him. In some circumstances, the borrower might be able to work his own way out of the problem with the aid of some good guidance from you.

One of the questions that is normally considered is who should hire a consultant—the bank or the borrower? I think that the easiest rule of thumb to follow is that if the bank's principal interest is in working with the customer to rehabilitate the company and have it continue on a sound basis in the future as a good customer, then it is probably appropriate for the bank to urge its customer to hire the consultant. If, however, the bank's aim is, in large measure, simply to get out of an unsatisfactory loan as quickly and as cleanly as possible, then the bank should hire the consultant.

The first step—analyze the problem; the second, formulate a plan to deal with it

I think there are three general areas of activities which are involved in handling problem companies. Although these areas often overlap, it is probably helpful and useful to consider them separately. The three areas are: operations, winding down part or all of a business and, lastly, an outright liquidation.

Ideally, when a consultant is called in, the first thing he should be hired to do is to conduct an independent, objective study and come up with his recommendations. If after such a study it appears that the business can and should be continued, then something should be done to deal with the problems that have created the financial crisis in the first place. I have rarely been in situations where management of the company was not convinced of two facts—the only thing needed to permanently cure their problems is another $200,000 in the bank account and if it hadn't been for the shortsightedness of the banker, they never would have had the problem to begin with. This thinking, in addition to avoiding the real problem, creates one of the first pitfalls which can make the task of rehabilitating a company much more difficult. The worst thing that can happen in this situation is that the company succeeds in borrowing the additional money, thereby obviously increasing its debt and diminishing the possibility for further borrowings. In most cases, it then distributes the proceeds of the new loan to those people who are threatening the most effectively. As a result, in a month the money is gone, a good healthy flow of goods through the business has not been re-established and nothing has been accomplished except that the bank is in deeper and the company has just that much less in the way of resources with which to deal with its problems when it finally gets around to doing so.

If a company has had problems and is trying to convince you that the solution has been found, it should be able to give you a very detailed and specific plan for what it intends to do. I cannot over-emphasize the necessity for planning. Certain obvious exceptions aside, problems do not simply happen to companies. They create and cause their problems. Only an in-depth review of the company and its past, its operations and its management can begin to point the way toward solutions. Past mistakes must be admitted, past failures must be recognized and ineffective people must either be corrected, reassigned or removed. All of these things are difficult for management which must, in most cases, share the responsibility for past mistakes, which may have close personal ties with some people who must leave and who, in some cases, may be impediments to any lasting solution.

After the past problems have been analyzed, a plan must be formulated setting forth the company's objectives and the steps to take in order to accomplish them, with a view toward what the company will be once the plan is accomplished. A plan that cleans up the balance sheet but does not go on to solve operational problems which will prevent future profitable operations has not accomplished a thing.

In all of these analyses, a disciplined effort must be made to base assumptions on known facts and proven formulas. The principal trademark of most poor business managers is their low regard for the necessity of obtaining hard facts. Loose estimates, rough calculations and easy assumptions must be avoided, and any plan which cannot be backed up with hard facts should be rejected. In most businesses mistakes happen and are not disastrous, but in the kind of situation we are discussing the margin of error is perilously small.

Operational tasks to be undertaken

It is difficult to be specific about the operational tasks which must be undertaken. For the most part, I am talking about general business principals; the specifics can only arise when looking at a particular problem. Better receivables collection, reducing overhead, instituting better cost analysis and controls, disciplining staff at all levels and analyzing the company's markets are all typical examples of the basic type of jobs we find must be performed.

I think a major advantage we have is the knowledge that drastic steps can be taken with less adverse affects than one would suspect. If a product is under-priced, buyers will scream about a price increase, but will seldom switch suppliers. If a public debt issue cannot be serviced, it is usually better to default sooner rather than later. If a facility has to be closed, close it—quickly.

Dealing with employees

Re-establishing good control over employees is essential. Low morale, time wasted in worrying about the future, second guessing top management and bad habits learned over an extended period are all factors which must be reversed. This process is sometimes painful, but dealing with people who must perform if success is to be achieved is one of our principal tasks.

Dealing with creditors

One of the most obvious requirements is the establishment of decent relations with the creditors without curing their underlying problem. The most important aspect of dealing with this problem is dealing with trade vendors. It is far easier to convince a creditor to withhold action on his debt than it is to convince vendors that they should continue to ship to the company. The most useful tool in improving relations is candor, total open honesty without impossible promises.

In severe situations, an arrangement of some sort with creditors—worked out voluntarily and out of court—is often a helpful technique. In this regard, we have found that in most cases, it is best to call together a meeting of the largest creditors. Once assembled, give this group as much information about the company as possible together with an outline of the formula for improving the company. If the company has not already borrowed the last dime which it can possibly squeeze out of its bank, it is helpful to condition further advances for initial reduction of trade debt upon some sort of stretch-out or settlement of the balance.

The difficulty with all of these types of arrangements is that the financial difficulties of the company must be explained in sufficient detail so that vendors will be willing to accept what would otherwise be an unacceptable payment plan. At the same time, there must be enough reason for future optimism to cause them to continue to ship. We generally set a cutoff date, which is concurrent with the day of the meeting, stating that all accounts outstanding as of that date will be treated under the plan and that all shipments made after that date will be paid in accordance with regular terms. I should point out that it is not always necessary to deliver to creditors a full plan at the time of the first meeting. Certainly before you can expect anything in the nature of regular shipments, a plan must be set forth showing that the company can be successful. However, in some cases, the first meeting is called largely to forestall any legal action by the creditors, and it may be that this meeting must be held before there has been time to adequately formulate a plan.

It is perhaps surprising how reasonable creditors will be in most situations if they are called together, informed of the current situation with candor and honesty and asked to withhold any legal action for a period of 30, 60 or 90 days while a study is made to determine whether the company should continue in business and, if so, under what plan. When you arrive at a plan, or simply at an understanding to withhold action for the moment, it is generally helpful to ask the group or a small committee made up from its members to prepare and send to all of the other creditors a letter setting forth the results of the meeting and their recommendations. A letter coming from another creditor generally has more impact than one sent by the company or its representative.

Out-of-court arrangements

An out-of-court arrangement with creditors, sometimes involving merely a stretch-out of their indebtedness and sometimes actually involving a compromise of it, is very useful, and people faced with the kind of situation we are discussing should be aware of it and be able to consider its merits in any situation. It has, however, a number of limitations. First, calling together a meeting brings a situation to a head. If you are unable to then resolve the matter, court action will almost certainly follow. Tactful, professional handling of any gathering of creditors is essential. Secondly, there must be careful weighing of the effect such a meeting will have on ongoing shipments. If creditors are screaming but shipments are being made in reasonably good order, a meeting could hurt more than it would help. Almost all businesses require an orderly flow of goods to conduct their operations, but some are certainly more susceptible to this kind of problem than others. I personally have not witnessed any situation in which a retailer successfully called a meeting, worked out even a stretch-out of payments with his vendors and went on to conduct a good business without other drastic action to provide for a source of goods. In one situation involving a retailer, we shut down approximately 80% of the stores and, in effect, funded both ongoing operations and a debt reduction program out of the sales of inventory in stores that were closed. However, as a rule, massive shipments of goods are essential, and delays of even a few weeks can mean missed seasons and lost sales which can never be recouped.

Thirdly, if an out-of-court settlement involves a compromise of debts that are outstanding, the amount of debt forgiveness is taxable income to the company. In a Chapter XI proceeding, for example, this is generally not the case. Of course, in most of these situations, the company has built up a tax loss which it cannot reasonably expect to make full use of through future profits in any case, so this is not too important. However, there are situations in which it is desirable to clean up the company and then sell it. In such a case, the tax loss carry forward could be an important consideration.

In addition, an out-of-court settlement will not permit the distribution of stock in lieu of full payment of creditors' claims. This is because the arrangement then becomes a sale of stock and, in most situations, a registration with the Securities and Exchange Commission would be required. Again, in a Chapter XI proceeding, stock can be distributed as a part of a plan of arrangement without registration.

Any out-of-court arrangement is only binding upon those who actually accept it. Even if 90 percent accept, a significant, discontented creditor can make the whole plan unworkable. In a court proceeding, of course, a majority can impose their will upon a dissenting minority.

Notwithstanding these limitations, the out-of-court settlement of creditors is a very useful tool. It avoids the stigma of bankruptcy and avoids many of the expenses that normally attend the bankruptcy proceeding. While you as a lender would not want to be directly involved in such a situation, you can certainly present it to a financially pressed client as one alternative to be considered.

This and other devices to turn around a company and save it from bankruptcy have a place in anyone's array of tools and, like all of the devices, the real issue is not if, but how, it is employed. This is an area where success rests not with the flashes of brilliance, but with determined, professional execution.

An "unwinding operation"

I would like to get into the subject of what we call an "unwinding operation." This has some aspects of a liquidation, but has some very significant differences, and it is an operation which I think few people fully appreciate.

Pruning off less successful units

There is little question that many companies get into trouble because of a bad acquisition or an expansion that was conducted too quickly. As a result, it is often necessary to get the company out of an operation which it has started. This involves recovering, to the greatest extent possible, its investments in that operation through the sale of inventory or the sale of equipment or the sale of leasehold improvements. It also involves, in most cases, the renegotiation of certain long-term obligations which have been incurred in connection with the operation. This means that settlements have to be made with landlords, employees and unions have to be considered, customers have to be dealt with, vendors have to be reassured and a variety of long-term commitments have to be reassessed.

One of the most frequent things that must be analyzed in this kind of situation is the company's internal systems, including any electronic data processing setup they may have. Often a company which has expanded has, as part of that expansion, undertaken large and expensive computer operations. In a reduced business, they no longer need, nor can they afford, such expensive installations. This means that equipment must be sold or that leases must be eliminated, and it means that new and simpler systems geared to a smaller operation must be installed.

There are considerations even in the sale of assets which you would not have in an outright liquidation. A company which has some brand name identification cannot simply dump a product that did not work out because of the effect it might have on other products carrying the same name. Settlements have to be made with people who will remain creditors after the unwind is over; whereas, in a liquidation, the only aim is to obtain the largest possible dollar recovery for distribution to whoever is entitled to it. Accordingly, in an unwind you might permit vendors to take back inventory which they had shipped to you which will no longer be needed, leasehold improvements might be traded back to the landlord against damages for breaking the lease, and employees, who might otherwise simply be let go, might be reassigned or somehow used in some other capacity.

Finding a purchaser or a merger partner

One of the most desirable solutions to the handling of a problem company is to find an acceptable purchaser or merger partner for the company which will lend it strength that it does not have by itself. However, this is in most cases a vain hope unless and until the company can be cleaned up to a point that a responsible buyer can feel comfortable and confident about what he is buying and his ability to control ongoing losses. For this reason, the steps that we have discussed with regard to operations and an unwind can often be the prelude to a sale, and it is possible that even where your initial review of the company indicates that in fact it cannot survive by itself, you might still go through such operations simply so that the company can be put into shape to be purchased.

The question of liquidation

There is inevitably, in any discussion of the handling of troubled companies, the absolute necessity of considering the problems of liquidation. Many businesses are beyond help when they are first brought to the attention of someone who could help them or are, by their nature, not viable businesses or are owned by management which is unwilling or unable to either admit or correct its mistakes. The most important thing to keep in mind when considering a liquidation is that, even though it represents the end of this particular business, it is in fact a business operation and must be handled in a business-like fashion. Too often, liquidations are left to lawyers or to courts or to others who are not essentially businessmen. The same principals prevail in a liquidation as do in any other situation. You must know and understand what you are selling, you must know and understand the market to which you can sell that product and you must be prepared to demand and expect a fair price for the product. In addition, reasonable control must be established to enable you to know what has been sold and what is still on hand and where it is located. Protection against pilferage must be considered. Packaging, although on a slightly different than normal sense, must be considered. A clean, well lighted, well maintained warehouse will be helpful in selling an inventory even in a liquidation.

The valuation of inventory and equipment

Obviously, a major aspect in the success of a liquidation is going to be the original valuation that was placed on the collateral. Most of you consider and evaluate collateral every day, so I will not go into any of the more obvious considerations and pitfalls, but there are a few that we have come across that are sometimes not given the attention and consideration that they deserve. In the case of both inventory and equipment it is necessary to know something about how the borrower's price for that property was originally arrived at. Particularly in the shortage economy that we are now facing significant differences in the prices various people are paying for the same product can exist. A company which, because of its cash position, must buy in small quantities and which does not have an ideal credit record with a vendor may well pay up to 15% or 20% higher than another customer purchasing the same product. In addition, in many industries, dealers, wholesalers and other middlemen customarily take discounts on their selling prices. However, at present for many types of equipment and inventory, such discounts are no longer available. Accordingly, in a liquidation where a major source of customers may be dealers, you must remember that the dealer's cost for new fresh goods from their suppliers is already 30% below your borrower's cost.

Secondly, many companies refer to items as raw materials which for liquidation purposes should really be considered goods in process. For example, we have done business with a manufacturer of safety toe caps. They buy steel from a service center already slit to a width which they use in their manufacturing operation. They consider coiled steel to be a raw material. However, only they and their one competitor have any efficient use for that particular raw material slit in that particular width. Liquidation prospects would be very slim even though an inventory which consists of true steel raw material should be very saleable. This can be true in a number of other items that we tend to think of as almost commodities.

Preliminaries of liquidation

Before the principal portion of the liquidation can be undertaken, several aspects must be taken care of:

The job of handling a liquidation begins the moment you decide to foreclose and ends when your loan has been repaid. Someone must go directly to the premises to do all of the things required in taking possession, including changing locks, dealing with the local police and fire departments as well as the alarm company, dealing with utilities that must be continued through the term of the liquidation, considering preventative maintenance that should be taken if equipment values are to be maintained while the machinery is not being operated, such as draining cooling systems, oiling equipment, removing harmful chemicals and the like. Also, someone must deal with the landlord, and I might mention that typically we have found the landlord to be the most difficult person to deal with in a liquidation. Both internal and external security protection must be provided. Employees often feel justified in walking off with small tools or other valuables if the only one that is going to suffer is the bank, and an empty building is an invitation to thieves and vandals. Fire and theft and other casualty insurance must be considered. It's likely that the borrower's insurance would have been cancelled for nonpayment of premium, and new insurance must be placed on the equipment. We carry a floater policy for use in these situations and will put equipment under its coverage at the start of a liquidation. Only when all of these details have been taken care of and a system set up for seeing that they continue to be taken care of, can we turn to the central part of the problem, that is, actually selling the property to be liquidated.

Four ways of conducting a liquidation

I would like to discuss four common ways of conducting a liquidation. The first is the sale of inventory to the borrower's regular customers. The highest price which you will be able to get for inventory is the price that the borrower normally gets from his customers. Accordingly, if you can fill orders at regular prices or at small discounts, you can recover a significant amount of your advance against a relatively small amount of inventory. In the liquidation of many manufacturers, a work-out of in-process goods makes sense. Our first step is to analyze the goods in process as well as the components on hand to determine what part of the inventory should be finished. Then we retain a sufficient part of the borrower's work force to complete the inventory on which the finished value will be very high in relation to the costs that must be incurred in finishing it. Generally, we will not incur costs which would be more than 50% of the liquidating sale value of the finished goods, and in most cases, the added value ranges in the area of 15-20%.

Where the defaulted borrower is a distributor of some sort, you often have an excellent chance of selling a significant portion of his inventory to his regular customers. In some cases, where it will not be easy to replace the defaulted customer as a source of supply, it makes sense to send a general mailing to his customers advising that he is going out of business and suggesting that they stock up to the greatest extent possible immediately. We handled the liquidation of an outboard motor manufacturer not too long ago who had a fairly large inventory of spare parts. We wrote to all of the dealers and advised them that they should stock up because it would soon not be possible to purchase parts. We took a full year, but finally sold the inventory at 50% over book value. In situations where the company's goods bear a very high mark up, it is sometimes desirable to let people come in and "cherry pick" the inventory by offering a mark down from the normal selling price, which may still bear a very good relationship to the cost of the goods. In a retail business, we are really talking about a going out of business sale. The same principal can be applied to a wholesaling business and a manufacturing business.

Another desirable way to conduct a liquidation is to find a purchaser who is interested in purchasing the assets for the purpose of conducting a similar business. Other than the company's own customers, this type of purchaser will probably pay the highest price for the collateral you are liquidating. For this reason, I emphasize the necessity of obtaining patents where they are part of a business and, in addition, I would emphasize the necessity of obtaining a lien on all tools, dies and so forth. In selling a facility, you are actually selling a business. Although purchasers will be little interested in the other company's overhead structure or management arrangements, they will be very interested in the cost of goods sold and all of the direct manufacturing costs. Obviously, one of the difficulties of completing this kind of sale is that good cost figures will probably be hard to come by and must often be assembled by the person conducting the sale.

Thirdly, a reasonable method of conducting a liquidation is simply a series of individual sales. You put a good horse trader in the middle of a factory or warehouse, you get the word out that things are for sale, and you work out the best deals you can in each instance. This process is time consuming and requires the services of good people who know the value of what they are selling. The individual people who come in to buy will, in most cases, be very knowledgable about what they are seeking. If the person who is negotiating with them is less knowledgable, he will clearly be taken advantage of.

Lastly, we get to what is probably the least desirable way of conducting a liquidation—namely, an auction. It is not infrequent that both inventory and equipment are put up for sale at an auction. While it is possible that someone once conducted a sale of inventory at auction that made sense, I have never seen one.

With equipment, there is no question but that sometimes an auction becomes necessary and, in certain circumstances, it is a reasonably good way of conducting a liquidation. However, a great care should be used in selecting the auctioneer and in working out an arrangement with him. A variety of deals can be made with auctioneers, and the typical arrangement in which you guarantee to the auctioneer that his expenses and his fee comes out first and you get whatever is left by no means has to be the kind of deal you make. Obviously, auctions are subject to certain things beyond your control, such as weather keeping attendance down, but a well-run, carefully planned auction clearly has a place in the various devices which should be considered in conducting a liquidation.

Summary and conclusion

In all areas of dealing with troubled companies, whether ongoing operations, unwinding operations or liquidations, a high degree of expertise and professionalism is necessary and a little imagination often helps too. There is clearly a financial aspect to dealing with these problems, but there is also a very real operational aspect to handling these situations properly. One cannot deal effectively in this area by reviewing financial statements.

We were asked some time ago to look at a situation to justify a trustee's position in accepting an offer to purchase a division from a bankrupt company. The offer had been made by the manager of the division. When we visited the plant, we found that the man's desk drawer was stuffed full of orders and his warehouses were stuffed full of merchandise ready to fill those orders. We told the trustee that a liquidation would bring more than the offered price. He hired us to do it, and recovered three times more than he had been offered. This, by the way, was a situation that was not being handled by rank amateurs or inexperienced people. It was a major publicly owned company, the lead bank was one of the largest banks in the world and most of the major commercial law firms in New York were involved in the situation. However, none of them had the type of approach or the kinds of people essential to deal with these things well.

Success in handling a problem, whether it be measured in terms of turning the company around and rehabilitating it or in liquidating the company for the maximum possible recovery, will occur only where a number of factors are handled correctly. Management of the company must swallow that inherent difficulty we all have in admitting our limitations and accept such useful assistance as is available. Trade creditors and their lawyers must evidence a desire to cooperate in the resolution of the problem without acrimony or vindictiveness. The lender must maintain the delicate balance of offering constructive help where possible and financial accommodations where reasonable while, at the same time, protecting his lending institution and applying a measure of discipline to the customer.

Lastly, the person handling the situation, whether original management of the company or an outside party, must tie all of the elements together and exhibit enough control and progress to give all of the other parties a new incentive for cooperation. With the right combination of skills, a great deal of hard work and sometimes a little luck as well, many situations can be saved and every situation can be improved. If a liquidation cannot be averted, it at least can be handled well.

The banker's role in this situation is not only difficult but in many cases it is central. The banker not only has to consider his obligation to protect his institution but also his institution's responsibility to and its reputation in the business community. By fully utilizing those tools which are available to him, whether they are resources within his institution or are drawn from outside agencies such as lawyers, accountants, consultants and the like, he can often be the difference between an orderly, sound and constructive approach and utter chaos. ☐

Troubled Debtors: The Fine Line Between Counseling and Controlling

by Margaret Hambrecht Douglas-Hamilton

If you are a lender in control of a financially troubled debtor, you risk exposure to far greater losses than those you might suffer by not having your loan repaid in due course. You might prefer to stay out of trouble by returning to the "simple" relationship of creditor and debtor.

When a corporate borrower gets into financial trouble, its lender will often have a big problem concerning loan repayment. But a lender can have even worse problems if its dealings with a financially troubled debtor would lead a court to conclude that it exercised control over its debtor. Courts have subordinated a controlling lender's debt to other creditors and, in some cases, have charged controlling lenders who interfere with their debtor for losses suffered by other creditors on account of such interference.

There are two important ways a lender can acquire the kind of control over its debtor which may lead to liability. The first is through control of the debtor's management, and the second is through voting control of the debtor's stock. Here are some examples, mostly taken from actual cases, of the type of problems a lender can have with either kind of control over its debtor. Although some of the cases have not been decided, the issues involved represent complaints against lenders who have spent significant amounts of time and money on their defense. If some of the concepts in this discussion seem new, it is better to find out about them in an article than in a complaint which has been filed against you in court. The concepts underlying this form of lender liability have been around for a long time, but suits to impose such liability are part of a fast-growing new trend.

In this article, I am going to try to give a fairly general outline of the current issues in the hope that it will help lenders recognize the control problem when it arises. It is probably safe to say that every troubled loan situation has its own special facts and relationships. Because solutions must be designed to deal with each specific case, I thought it would be more helpful to give a broad view of the major problem areas than to discuss the subtle distinctions which make a solution right in one case and wrong in another. The lender's ability to spot the control problem is very important. In fact, it is my feeling that this is one of those areas where prevention is the best cure.

Management control

By far the most difficult kind of control to identify is the kind which involves improper interference with the debtor's management. You can usually tell whether you have control of your debtor's stock. It is much harder to determine when *suggestions* made by a lender become *demands* or when *help* becomes *interference*. When, for example, does a lender's legitimate interest in a debtor's use of funds result in improper decision making by the lender as to which of the debtor's creditors will be paid?

Lender's control over debtor's sources of financing

Another interesting area where caution is advisable is in drawing up financing agreements. For instance, how far can you go in writing so-called "management clauses?" It is probably unwise to put restrictions on whom will run the debtor company which are too specific or which would interfere with the free election of the debtor's board of directors. This is not to say that a lender is not entitled to place certain financial restrictions on the debtor's management by restrictive covenants which limit additional debt and protect the debtor's assets. However, there are cases where a lender so monopolized a debtor's sources of financing that the lender was considered to be in control of the debtor.

Practically speaking, many lenders have probably found themselves in the position of believing they could turn around a troubled debtor if only they could get some good management into the company. This is a gray area, but there are some definite standards. For example, it is probably all right to make a general suggestion that the debtor consider some changes in management. But it might lead to a liability situation if you dictate specifically who the debtor's officers and directors should be. It is important to remember that a suggestion is something which the debtor is free to accept or reject. A lender should not threaten to call a loan if the suggestion is not followed. In the event that an individual suggested by the lender is in fact employed by the debtor, the lender should be very careful to avoid any appearance that the individual is an agent of the lender or in any way under the control of the lender.

Problems with third parties

Some control problems which lenders have with debtors involve third parties. I already mentioned a lender's very real concern with how its debtor—especially a troubled debtor—will use funds advanced by the lender. How much control should the lender exert over payment of obligations owed by the debtor to third parties? It's one thing to advance limited funds and leave it to the borrower's discretion as to how such funds will be utilized. It's quite another, obviously, to dictate which bills are to be paid and then bounce any checks which don't appear on the approved list. Between the two extremes are a wide variety of situations where the problem can be resolved with greater or lesser degrees of risk.

Another kind of difficulty a lender can have with a troubled debtor results from inducing the debtor not to perform or otherwise to breach an existing contract with a third party. This could happen in a situation where the lender interferes with contracts the debtor may have with its suppliers or employees. It could also happen in cases where a lender obtains a pledge of collateral, such as stock, which violates a negative pledge clause in a prior creditor's agreement.

You may have heard of the Black Watch Farms fraud in upper New York where interests in the same few cows were sold to hundreds of different people. A case growing out of that fraud involved one of the plaintiffs' complaints about the Black Watch creditors. The plaintiff said the creditors knew of their debtor's precarious financial position but concealed this to keep plaintiffs' making payments on the notes for the cows which were pledged to the creditors as collateral. That's an example of another kind of problem a lender can have with third parties, namely, liability for aiding and abetting or conspiring with a debtor.

Voting control

There is a presumption that a lender having voting control over a debtor also has the power to direct the debtor's affairs. Voting control normally means the power to select a majority of the board of directors. A lender may have such power as (1) trustee of a voting trust, (2) holder of an irrevocable proxy, or (3) pledgee of shares with power to vote a controlling block of the debtor's stock.

Federal securities laws and current issues

Liabilities resulting from voting control arise in several contexts. One is in the regulatory context where control, which is often in the form of voting control, exposes a lender to potential liabilities under the Federal securities laws. Although the following outline is far from complete, it does give an idea of the kind of issues which may arise under those laws.

Under the Securities Act of 1933 and the Securities Exchange Act of 1934, an issuer of securities is required to make certain disclosures to the public which buys and sells its securities. Each of those Acts places similar responsibility on anyone who controls the issuer. There are cases indicating that a lender which has control of its debtor could be held responsible for losses suffered by third parties who purchased the debtor's securities based on misrepresentations made to them by the debtor.

An interesting complaint involving a lending bank raised the issue of whether a lender has an obligation to correct misleading or inaccurate statements which its debtor has published in press releases. A lender who controls its debtor would almost certainly have that responsibility. Also, keep in mind that once a lender has control of its debtor (by virtue of stock ownership or otherwise), the lender is subject to most of the same prohibitions as the debtor on selling the debtor's securities. The controlling lender must sell such securities under an effective registration statement or pursuant to some available exemption from the requirements of registration.

If your controlled debtor is either a public utility company which is regulated under the Public Utility Holding Company Act of 1935 or a registered investment company regulated under the Investment Company Act of 1940, you may incur obligations and responsibilities to your debtor under those Acts. Both Acts restrict a controlling lender's ability to improve its financial position at the expense of its controlled debtor. A lender will, for instance, face severe limitations under Section 17 of the Investment Company Act on financial arrangements it may wish to make in workout situations with a troubled debtor. Such arrangements may be void under the Act and also may subject the lender to subordination of its claims to other creditors.

Conflicting obligations under the Trust Indenture Act

One area particularly fraught with danger for bank lenders arises under the Trust Indenture Act. Should a lender serve as indenture trustee for securities issued by its debtor and then acquire control of its debtor's stock, the trustee is obligated to eliminate the conflict of interest or resign within 90 days after discovering the conflict. The Trust Indenture Act, however, provides that resignation become effective only upon acceptance of the appointment by a successor trustee. In a situation involving a financially troubled debtor, it is possible the debtor may have defaulted on the indenture securities, in which case it is often not possible to find a successor trustee. In such cases, it may be virtually impossible for a lender to fulfill both the high obligation of a fiduciary which it has as trustee to the holders of the indenture securities and as controlling person of the debtor *and* the obligation to its own stockholders to be profitable.

Liabilities under other Federal laws

The preceding discussion describes some problem areas for controlling lenders under the Federal securities laws. A lender who acquires control of its debtor may have additional problems relating to control under other regulatory statutes as well. These include the adverse consequences of failing to obtain requisite regulatory approvals before and after assuming control of certain special corporations in regulated industries such as trucking companies, airlines, and insurance companies.

Last, but by no means least, is the liability which will befall a controlling creditor which fails to collect and pay over taxes withheld from wages of its controlled debtor's employees. In any situation in which the lender has "control ... of ... the wages of ... employees" employed by a debtor, the lender will be responsible [under Section 3504 of the Internal Revenue Code] for seeing that the withholding taxes are paid. This is true whether the lender has control over the wages because of the manner in which it finances the debtor or because it exercises management or voting control over the debtor. There is a 100% penalty assessment for failure to collect and pay such taxes.

Manipulation of credit

Another area in which lenders seem particularly vulnerable in controlling stock situations is that in which a lender participates in the manipulation of the credit of a debtor's subsidiary. The usual scenario is one in which a lender takes collateral (which is often controlling stock of the subsidiary) in exchange for a loan to a solvent subsidiary, and the subsidiary then upstreams the loan to its parent company in exchange for intercompany indebtedness of questionable value.

In such cases, the subsidiary's unsecured creditors have successfully argued for equitable subordination of the lender's debt to theirs. Should the subsidiary be a public company, as is the case in a somewhat similar situation involving the Penn Central bankruptcy, the public security holders of the subsidiary may also assert their rights against the lender. The bankruptcy trustee for W. T. Grant Co. has made a similar argument against Grant's 27 lending banks.

A more obvious case is one where the lender manipulates the credit of the debtor corporation whose stock it controls. It is virtually certain that such abusive control will result in subordination of the lender's debt not only to other creditors of the corporation but also to any minority stockholders of the corporation. This principle was established in a case involving the Deep Rock Oil Corporation, and you have probably heard the principle referred to as the "Deep Rock Doctrine."

A lender which acquires control of its debtor is likely to be faced with problems that arise primarily from the restrictions which the fiduciary relation and statutes (becoming operative with control) impose on the lender's dealings with its debtor. Absent such fiduciary responsibility and statutory restraint, a lender—which has no relationship with a corporate borrower other than that of creditor and debtor—is entitled to assert all of its lawful rights as a creditor. Such rights include the right to call a loan when due, to refuse to extend a loan, and lawfully to enforce collection.

Conclusion: guidelines for avoiding control of debtors

I shall conclude with some guidelines as to what a lender might do to avoid control of its debtor.

A lender should—

(1) Avoid any interference with the management of a debtor which suggests that the lender and not the debtor's management runs the company.

(2) Carefully examine the lender's collateral security position with regard to the stock of the debtor and the debtor's subsidiaries.

(3) Exercise extreme caution in making and securing new loans to be certain there is no breach of the rights of existing creditors.

(4) Take care in seeking to improve the lender's position with respect to its outstanding loans to avoid charges by third parties or other creditors that (1) the lender induced the debtor to breach their contractual rights or (2) as was

alleged in the Black Watch Farms case, that the lender aided and abetted or conspired with the debtor in leading others along.

These are fairly general guidelines for keeping out of a quite specific form of trouble. There is, unfortunately, no single or simple answer to the question of what constitutes control of a debtor by a lender. If the trend toward litigation in this area continues, there will no doubt be more answers to that key question. Unfortunately, virtually every answer will be developed at the expense of a lawsuit against some lender. □

VI. Credit Policy and Credit Administration

In contrast to the limited number of articles on problem loans, in recent years the *Journal* has offered its readership a varied menu of essays discussing credit policy and administration. The richness of the literature made selection of a limited number for inclusion in this collection a most difficult task. The opening article, "The Most Challenging Issues Facing Bank Lending" by P. Henry Mueller, provides an overview of the credit policy discipline. He brings together in brief form many of the ideas discussed at length in articles included in earlier sections of this anthology and offers suggestions about how the credit administration process can be structured to help reduce credit risks.

One method of controlling credit risk through sound administration is by the use of sound credit policy. Hubert C. Mott, author of "Establishing Criteria and Concepts for a Written Credit Policy," presents an extensive outline and discussion of what an effective credit policy should encompass. The checklists he provides not only specify the basic contents of a credit policy but also include such topics as the adaptation of a policy to a bank's individual situation and its market area and the establishment of lending authority and loan standards.

Three articles have been included from the many the *Journal* has published on the subject of loan review policies and practices. Cato Ellis, in "Loan Review: An Organizational Dilemma," lays out a number of ways in which the loan review function may be organized and discusses the strengths and weaknesses of the major alternatives. W. Thomas Maloan's article, "Loan Review: A Possible Alternative Method," proposes that loan reviews can effectively be handled by loan officers themselves rather than by a loan review department and offers suggestions about how this approach can be made to work. Articles discussing the loan review department alternative have not been included because the subject is covered in the RMA booklet, *Commercial Loan Review Procedures.**

The final article on the subject of loan review is, "Don't Miss Those Natural Loan Review Opportunities!," by Robert E. Davis. He points out when, during the normal life cycle of a lending relationship, loan reviews can be accomplished efficiently and yet early enough to be effective in identifying credit problems. It is a useful complement to the other articles on this subject, which treat the "who" and the "where" of loan review rather than the "when."

This section of the anthology concludes with an article on a slightly different type of subject. Charles B. Jarrett, Jr., offers guidance, in "Business Ethics and Codes of Conduct," on the question of whether to establish a code of conduct and the specific provisions it might contain. He also discusses how the code might be implemented and what it should *not* attempt to accomplish.

For information about the authors of the articles in Section VI, refer to the List of Contributors on page xi.

---

* P. Graham Conlin, *Commercial Loan Review Procedures* (Philadelphia: Robert Morris Associates, 1978). Softcover, $7.50 (nonmembers).

The Most Challenging Issues Facing Bank Lending

by P. Henry Mueller

P. Henry Mueller believes that the ability of the loan officer is one of the most important elements of the current commercial lending picture. He focuses on the problems and objectives, as well as some of the dos and don'ts, of the lender's job.

Credit quality was once the lending officer's avowed focus. Then banks discovered the budgeting process and profit centers, both necessary and desirable. Today the banker has more profit responsibility than ever before, and his challenge is to manage the risk/reward quotient intelligently so as to optimize earnings while maintaining collectibility.

Recessions may be chastening — and banks are now certainly more deliberate in their lending activities — but contrary to post-recession concerns, there is no evidence that they are unwilling to consider creditworthy loan proposals. In fact, having sustained unusually large loan losses, the restoration of earning power seems center stage. But one thing the recession did was upgrade credit skills.

This article is based on remarks prepared by Mr. Mueller for a panel discussion at RMA's 62nd Annual Fall Conference held in Chicago.

The reconciliation of good credit standards and practices with the profit center concept

I have never underestimated profit center motivation. What I suggest is that management be mindful that human frailties reassert themselves. Such frailties show up in relaxed credit standards and "reaching," especially when an individual's evaluation depends more on budget performance than on ability as a credit officer. It should hardly be necessary to say that a lending officer's job is to act responsibly in the best interest of good credit practice and his institution, regardless of profit center reporting lines. If the market is not growing, standards should not be relaxed in order to maintain growth. Chickens will always come home to roost. And lenders must never forget that integrity and undoubted strength underlie confidence in the commercial banking system. Confidence in any field is hard to gain, but easy to lose.

Management of the credit process and the portfolio

In the credit process, line management creates and manages risk assets. The process is people-driven and starts with a business plan and an appraisal of credit competence opposite the plan. Then it breaks down into specific loan transactions, their evaluation and negotiation, approval, documentation, disbursement, administration, and workouts. Deployment of expertise, an evaluation of the number of borrowing accounts handled by each lending officer, turnover, and training complete the scene.

What makes the process work?

The process requires precise step-by-step definition and responsibilities that are clearly delineated so that conformance can be effectively monitored. Experience shows that loan quality is closely related to how well the process is managed. Put another way, abuse or neglect of such mundane things as documentation, credit records and files, and follow-through, can heighten the risk of perfectly good credit. Recovery efforts, which should have a strategy and a timetable, can also be neglected. Line credit officers should be involved in such efforts and should share responsibility in the institutional credit review process.

The need to recognize and define the interrelationships of the process increases as loan volume rises and as a bank grows organizationally. Without this, undiscovered gaps and deficiencies develop. The challenge demands that lending officers be activists, not passivists, in booking and managing risk assets.

As banks grow, decentralize, and become complex, it remains essential that the bridge be aware of what's going on in the engine room. As in the case of a unit bank, growth of risk assets must be managed so that the portfolio is diversified and liquid in relation to the capital needed to support growth.

Volumes, types of risk, trends, and unused commitments must be reviewed continuously to ensure that they conform to policy bench marks and the overall credit plan established by senior management. The object is to control loan categories and to limit concentrations so that no single occurrence could have a significant adverse impact.

Avoiding the push for market share beyond prudent measures

This challenge boils down to teaching lending officers and their supervisors to use a strategy in extending credit. Some of banking's more serious credit problems can be traced to poor basic market decisions plus the temptation to increase earnings by pushing for bigger market share, often well ahead of historical yardsticks, with insufficient or inexperienced credit officers. When portfolios expand too rapidly, assets may be booked without absorbing the complexities of transactions or without deep thought about their liquidity.

Different markets need different skills

Lending terms for appropriately differentiated risk assets need to be precisely specified and understood for each market. This calls for a business plan which defines the lender's proper markets and the types of borrowers deemed accept-able. The terms on which each category of risk assets will be accepted should be described and the portfolio criteria — size, concentration, maturity — set. Administrative procedures appropriate to the scale of lending activity should be established, the collection aspect included. The professional skills needed for lending and administration, the extent to which they are available, and how they should be deployed must all be determined.

Different markets need different skills, and lenders should engage in credit activities only when they understand the business essentials. They should refrain from extending credit — irrespective of the perceived rewards — when they lack either an understanding of the borrower and the business or the personnel to handle the matter within the anticipated time frame.

The borrower *and* lender must know the business

With this as a backdrop, then, what will be the next categories of problem loans? It would be just as easy to give you a list of stocks that will go up.

I think we would all agree that the quality of art depends upon the quality of the artist. Problems are predictable in any instance in which the borrower or the lender lacks complete familiarity with the business being financed. On this basis, one bank may have problems in a particular loan or loan category and another not. Certainly fads and glamour industries — as in the case of the REIT's — are to be watched, especially where there is a bandwagon effect and where there is some question as to whether normal analysis is being applied. "Sure things" are another area. For good results, a lender must be able and willing to understand the uniqueness of each credit and its market.

Reconciliation of market practices with common sense

Each bank is guided by credit policies and standards it has developed over time. Particularly when breaking into new markets, the argument for a policy exception sometimes goes, "But my situation is different." The challenge here is not to let market practice override common sense. Credit markets are not essentially different, although obviously some variations will have to be accepted. The line must be drawn at the credit comfort level. More than once I have found that the plea for an exception stems from a desire to relax standards to get business, and I have also found local lenders who refused to extend credit on the basis proposed. As a matter of fact, local bank participation is desirable and necessary from the standpoint of money center banks when they lend to local, as opposed to national, borrowers. Local banks usually know more about the credits.

Multi-bank credits

Committed credits and open lines

In a committed credit, the competence of the agent bank and constructive, homogeneous participants who are not fair-weather friends are essential. Also, the banking group should not be large and unwieldy; to take an extreme, more than 100 banks accounted for $50 million of the W. T. Grant credit.

The agent is obviously close to the borrower and responsible for representing his needs. Doing the utmost to achieve a fair and equitable deal, the agent has a fiduciary responsibility to the lending banks. Among other things, this means attentive supervision of the credit, an alertness to problems, and a readiness to move vigorously and quickly. Another primary duty is to keep other lending banks advised of information relating to the loan in question.

Participants in credits need to be well-balanced when trouble strikes, and borrowers should evaluate banks the same way banks try to evaluate management. How will a bank react when up against the wall? What kind of reputation did a bank create for itself in 1974-75? Based on their experience, many borrowers will be quite choosy and select only banks that can be depended upon. Participants have a responsibility to do their own credit analysis and not rely on the mother hen. Be comfortable with the loan or don't participate. If there isn't sufficient time to make a well-reasoned decision, pass.

Domination of steady borrowers

A word now about permitting steady borrowers with a multitude of open lines to divide and conquer. Aren't we kidding ourselves with such an arrangement?

1. There is likely to be no strong leadership, no strong interest in spotting problems early and taking action.

2. Commercial paper backup lines are especially vulnerable. Many banks cut and run at the first sign of trouble and will not put up funds, whereas a committed credit is less likely to walk out.

3. The value of rotational cleanups is dubious. Banks would be better off in a committed credit with well-defined covenants.

The need to take the long, as well as the short, view of credit

A borrowing relationship is not cold-nosed, and a lender is not usually in a position to enter and leave a credit at will. Continued involvement, even in troubled times, is part of the calculus. This is particularly true of borrowers that develop into major "House Accounts." It is easy to be oversentimental about an old relationship, and this may not always be best for either the bank or the borrower. But you have a banking relationship for better or for worse, and you may sometimes be expected to undertake monumental risks.

What the long view entails

A starting point in taking the long view would be a thorough industry analysis and understanding of its structure and economics, its maturity and place in the economy; then, an understanding of the borrower's position in relation to the industry. Ask: What is the company's real business and what must it do well to be successful? What are its thrusts? Credit decisions must be made in the context of ongoing activity and the drift of events, and the hazard of a static approach to lending is great. For example, we can no longer ignore the undermining effect of inflation on our credits.

Look beyond the financials to determine the entity's viability. One of the most difficult aspects of this challenge is that of appraising management. We sometimes find when difficulty develops that we didn't really know and understand the borrower in terms of orientation and quality. Be fully satisfied with the ability and integrity of management; its reputation in the industry; its objectives; the viability of the company; its product, cash flow, and controls. In short, there is no substitute for a well-conceived loan that is well-policed. A good lending officer manages risks rather than vice versa.

The secret of credit

The shift over the past 25 years has been from seasonal lending, where our knowledge had traditionally focused, to the broader, more complex underwriting of term risks, with emphasis on finely tuned cash flow as the way out. This change has often diverted attention from the basic goodness of a credit and its structuring.

We have too often bet heavily on future growth, gone too far in sophisticated cash flow techniques and perhaps accounting techniques and projections, which always seemed to fit perfectly when a loan proposal was presented.

Cash flow is but one of three parts of financial analysis; it must be balanced by *ample liquidity* and *sound leverage*: What is the borrower's profitability versus the industry? How do his dream sheets stand up to sensitivity analysis? What are his total liabilities to equity? We must also distinguish between genuinely complex deals and just poor credits that are camouflaged by complexity.

As we peer ahead, we should not overlook the other classes of creditors involved in our credits. For example, it is safe to assume that, under adverse circumstances, current liabilities and subordinated debt could be on a par with senior debt and trigger bankruptcy as easily as we and other senior creditors could.

The secret of credit is knowing and understanding the risks and then getting protection against them.

Avoiding overgenerosity in amount, terms, and conditions

Easy credit, uneasy creditors. Bankers create their own problems and increase the risk of loss by being overgenerous lenders. It is clear that in the pre-November 1973 era, there were many instances of money being forced upon borrowers. Almost all borrowers that encounter trouble are overleveraged, and have often managed their affairs by the profit and loss statement and not enough by the balance sheet. Trouble starts when earnings fall off.

There is also a point at which overgenerosity to a troubled borrower can impinge on a bank, too, particularly its earnings. Obviously the amount of money involved should always be within the bank's risk-taking capacity. It's wise not to take hog chunks of credits. If you consider that loan reserves must be earned, banks operate at the margin. For example, assume a loan portfolio of $1 million with a 2% net spread which earns $20,000. You make a $10,000 loan that goes bad. This is small in relation to the entire portfolio, but yet your loss is 50% of your portfolio's earnings. In other words, how much, in terms of your profit center earnings, can you afford to lose? Not only the earnings cost of loan losses, but also the cost in talent and other resources to administer weak credits, as well as opportunity cost must be taken into account — these factors make clear that A is the passing grade for lending officer performance. Anything less eats into a bank's primary source of earnings from both a dollar and a people point of view.

Recognition of the importance of non-economic exogenous factors

These are of growing concern and bear on lenders and borrowers. For one thing, with the increased interdependence of economies, we respond as one world to any serious trauma — the energy crisis, for example. But the strongest forces in the world are not always the noisiest and most visible. It is necessary to be as alert and concerned about regulatory, social, political, environmental, and other conditions as about prevailing economic conditions. New regulations, often punitive for us or our borrowers, are always forthcoming. We have seen governmental power stay the enforcement of debt obligations. What about the impact of enforced spending for pollution control? Or unfunded pension liabilities? What about threatened divestiture of certain industries? The inability, because of environmental restrictions, to use natural resources that bear upon a credit can't be changed by covenants in a loan agreement. And not to be overlooked are accounting changes mandated here and abroad.

With all of this overhanging the scene, we must give careful consideration to what a borrower can effectively agree to do. I hope it will never come to pass, but in some instances the very viability of a borrower could be brought into question as a result of decisions made completely outside itself.

Early detection of weakened credit

It is essential to be alert for ambush and to know when steps should be taken to bolster credits. Although lenders should not be precipitous, they need to take timely steps to ensure the return of the funds they lend and, if at all possible, help the borrower to extricate itself from financial difficulty. One-hundred percent early identification of problem credits should be expected of lending officers, and credits must be monitored continuously for possible symptoms of financial ailments.

The far-from-dead business cycle

Despite earlier boasts by some economists that fine tuning could eliminate the business cycle, it is far from dead. Understanding and recognition of its effects on a borrower are necessary so as to be sensitive to changes in leading indicators and other economic signals. Cyclical downturns usually send out advance signals: toleration of excesses by both borrowers and lenders; shortages; shrinking liquidity; speculation, including in low-priced stocks or in stocks being pushed hard by Wall Street; tight money; etc.

There are other symptoms too numerous to cite. They involve management, leverage, and financial factors, as well as external elements. Particularly when a long maturity is involved, many things can and do happen.

Bum loans due to lack of information

Every good credit officer knows that facts make their own decisions, and that most bum loans are made because of a lack of good information. Lenders have a right to this and shouldn't hesitate to ask additional questions if they don't grasp answers. Evasive answers to direct questions concerning recent or projected performance, or arrogance in place of cooperation, could be early warnings. Lending officers should not be swayed by borrower recalcitrance for fear of losing business.

Finally, the most difficult credit decision is whether to put more money into a sick situation. "Hope" and "assurance" of a successful outcome are two different things.

Selection, development, and deployment of lending personnel

People are the guts of lending, and the selection and "care and feeding" of lending officers are one of management's most important tasks, if not the most important. What breeds good credit officers? Who is a good performer and why? There are no easy answers, but we do know the need to have good credit skills at every level of bank management. We also know the importance of continuity and the price we pay when turnover is too rapid.

Curiosity, experience, imagination, and common sense

Four of the ingredients lending officers must possess are curiosity, experience, imagination, and common sense (not to be confused with "smarts" which are obviously important). Business schools have yet to underwrite these, but they are much needed when a credit problem walks off the pages of the textbook.

In recent years when loan volume was accelerating, banks forgot that making a loan is more of an art than a science. Lending is essentially a cottage industry, except for process aspects and perhaps credit scoring as presently used in consumer finance. The idea that credit men or women can be stamped out and credit extended using a factory approach is a dangerous notion unless tightly controlled, as recent loan losses would attest. If we believe this, maybe we have gone too far and should pay more attention to lending as an art.

Credit skill training is sequential, a career process, a melding of experience and formal training at successive levels. It is not cognitive alone, not detached and informational like reading a book or listening to a lecture. Development of good credit officers is part of the daily responsibility of their senior associates. Gaps should not be permitted to develop, and particular attention must be given to retraining and to continuing credit education at all levels.

Accountability goes hand-in-hand with the delegation of credit authority, and reasonable standards and disciplines should be expected. Each lending officer should know exacly what is expected of him or her. Performance should not, of course, be weighed on the basis of factors beyond the individual's control.

Cattle loans aren't made out of Philadelphia

I commented earlier on the need to determine the professional skills necessary for participating in various lending activities and markets. Is your best talent in the slots where it can do the most to support your credit process and prevent abuses and excesses? Is the right type of talent in the right place? You don't make cattle loans out of Philadelphia, so you don't put that kind of talent there. When considering overseas credit assignments, are you turning unknown areas over to relatively junior officers? Remember, your strongest talent is in your familiar home environment.

You can get into trouble in banking faster than in any other business, and this is why I suggest that banking's main emphasis must be on people.   □

Establishing Criteria and Concepts for a Written Credit Policy

by Hubert C. Mott

Written credit policies are a banking tool whose time has come. In this article, Hubert C. Mott discusses policy rationale and defines the general areas that a written policy should cover. He also gets down to specifics by offering sample policy guidelines from a medium-size regional bank.

In any discussion of credit policy, the first question that naturally arises is why have a credit policy at all? Not all banks do, even today, although a far greater percentage have established them in recent years. The number of banks with policies has grown particularly since the supervisory authorities have placed great emphasis lately on banks having a written policy, almost to the point of requiring it. One answer may be found in the following statement:

> The restrictions placed by law, administrative agencies, and bank examiners do not provide answers to many questions regarding safe, sound, and profitable bank lending. Questions regarding the size of the loan portfolio, the maturity of all loans, and the type of loans to be made are left unanswered. Loans may be criticized by the bank

415

examiners it is true, and some loans are prohibited and others limited, but such criticisms and restrictions do not establish a lending policy for a bank. These questions and many others about lending must be answered by each individual bank.[1]

The why, who, and what of a written credit policy

The purpose of a written credit policy

A primary purpose of a written credit policy is to provide a framework of standards and points of reference within which individual lending personnel can operate with confidence, relative uniformity, and flexibility. Lending officers will then be able to make their own decisions within delegated authority, without the necessity for constant referral to higher management.

Without such a written policy, there is a tendency to concentrate all decision making in one or two people at or near the top, with the obvious disadvantages of slower decisions and the inability of loan officers to develop their full potential. The other tendency is to foster a dangerous diversity of lending practices and philosophies within the organization, probably leading ultimately to an inordinate number of problem loans.

In addition to establishing uniform guidelines for loan officers and satisfying the regulatory agencies, a written credit policy can aid bank management in defining the objectives of the bank. Like any other business, the commercial bank establishes particular objectives to be met.

Who should establish credit policy?

One of the questions that should arise in a discussion of loan or credit policy is who should establish the policy.[2] The very importance of the matter requires that the ultimate responsibility be at the highest level in the bank's organization: the board of directors. While it isn't suggested that the statement of loan policy should actually be written by the board, it should be approved by them, and not in a cursory or perfunctory manner, but rather after careful explanation, consideration, and discussion.

The actual drafting will probably be done by the senior lending officer in consultation with the chief executive officer and with contributions from the senior officer's associates and subordinates. Obviously, the level of origin will vary with the size and structure of the organization.

---

[1] Edward W. Reed, *Commercial Bank Management* (New York & London: Harper & Row, 1963), p. 193.

[2] The words loan policy and credit policy will be used interchangeably here since there seems to be no substantive differences in their meaning or common usage.

What should a loan policy include?

Having established the *why* and *who* of loan policy, the other area to consider is *what*. What should a loan policy include? There can be some variations based on the needs of a particular organization, but at least the following areas should be covered in any comprehensive statement of loan policy:

1. **Legal considerations.** The bank's legal lending limit and other legal constraints should be set forth to avoid inadvertent violation of banking regulations.

2. **Delegation of authority.** Each individual authorized to extend credit should know precisely how much and under what conditions he or she may commit the bank's funds. These authorities should be approved, at least annually, by written resolution of the board of directors and kept current at all times.

3. **Types of credit extension.** One of the most substantive parts of a loan policy is a delineation of which types of loans are acceptable and which are not.

4. **Pricing.** In any profit-motivated endeavor, the price to be charged for the goods or services rendered is of paramount importance. Relative uniformity within the same market is necessary. Without it, individuals have few guidelines for quoting rates or fees, and the variations resulting from human nature will be a source of customer dissatisfaction.

5. **Market area.** Each bank should establish its proper market area, based upon, among other things, the size and sophistication of its organization, its ability to service its customers, and its ability to absorb risks. From the bank's capital standpoint, defining one's market area is probably more important in the lending function than in any other aspect of banking.

6. **Loan standards.** This is a definition of the types of credit to be extended, wherein the qualitative standards for acceptable loans are set forth.

7. **Credit granting procedures.** This subject may be covered in a separate manual, and usually is in larger banks. At any rate, it should not be overlooked because proper procedures are essential in establishing sound policy and standards. Without proper procedures for granting credit and constant policing to ensure that these procedures are meticulously carried out, the best conceived loan policy will not function and, inevitably, problems will develop.

Writing a policy that suits the bank involved

Individual variations

The next step after establishing the rationale for and definition of credit policy is to get into the specifics of one's own institution and write the policy that best fits its particular needs.

A word about individual variations. Some areas of credit policy definitely should differ from bank to bank, reflecting the bank's size, asset composition, liability composition, earnings, capital, loan loss reserve, and the abilities of the bank's lending officers and support personnel. The type of market and clientele should also be considered in determining the degree of risk the bank is willing to assume. Although credit policy may vary from bank to bank, sound loan standards and credit granting procedures should not vary appreciably at any given time.

Defining asset management objectives

Defining the bank's asset management objectives is an excellent prelude to writing a specific loan policy. Maximum and optimum loan to deposit ratios should be considered since they bear directly on the size of the loan portfolio.

In establishing the maximum risk that can be assumed, the bank's capital and risk asset ratios should be carefully considered, as well as the size of the loan loss reserve. Earnings history and prospects are also important, since a bank with strong earnings can better withstand loan losses.

The degree of risk in other assets, essentially the investment portfolio, is an important consideration. Recent events highlight this fact. For instance, a portfolio heavy in municipals, selling at large discounts and with real risk of default, adds to the overall loss potential rather than providing a cushion, as a sound investment portfolio does.

Legal considerations

The maximum commitment to any one borrower should be established, if it is to be less than the bank's legal limit. Many banks have so-called "house" limits. There is usually some flexibility, but exceptions should require a very high level of authority and should be carefully controlled. Exact definition of a borrower's total liability to the bank is a necessity in controlling loans within either legal or house limits.

In general, all related liabilities — direct, indirect, and contingent — of borrower, guarantors or endorsers, and related entities should be considered and carefully defined. An example of appropriate language to cover these liabilities might be the following:

> In extending credit, a borrower is considered as including any subsidiary, affiliate or related business, corporation, partnership, a proprietorship, as well as officers of the business, their spouse's or related persons, etc. An officer not having a substantial interest in the corporation may, for lending authority purposes, be considered not related if he does not guarantee or endorse. It is imperative that we do not exceed our lending authority by

grouping loans in this manner, so that the failure of the overall operation could cause numerous problems.

Establishing the bank's market area

The bank's market area should be established and defined, whether it be the town or city, county or region, state, nation, or the world. The economic characteristics of the market a bank serves will influence the composition of the bank's portfolio by type, maturity, and loan repayment plan.

Most important in establishing the market area for loans is the ability of the lending staff to safely and adequately service the portfolio. The greater the distance from the account officer, the less likelihood of frequent, close contact with the borrower and therefore the greater the risk. Certainly it should be a policy that only the strongest credits should be accepted in the outer limits of the bank's geographic area.

Types of credit extension

The distribution of the various types of loans within the overall portfolio is another basic management decision. There are a number of factors which bear directly on the decision as to the desired levels of commercial and industrial loans, real estate loans, and consumer credit. Among these are the nature and stability of deposits, the percentage of time versus demand, and the deposit trends.

A relatively high level of stable time deposits obviously points a bank toward mortgage and other longer term, higher yielding loans than a preponderance of volatile demand deposits. Of course, the needs of the area served and the availability of various types of suitable loans have an impact.

Dollar or percentage limits for loan subcategories

A decision should also be made as to whether it is necessary or desirable to establish dollar or percentage limits for subcategories of loans. For instance, it could be important to establish a limit as to the amount of *nonresidential* real estate mortgage loans the bank is willing to make. Another example might be to establish some relationship between direct and indirect retail installment paper, or a limitation on dealer floor plan lines, or home improvement paper.

Desirable loans

In writing a credit policy, it is usually easier to state categorically those types of loans which are *not* acceptable than to list every nuance of acceptable credit extensions. The statement on acceptable loans can be broader and less specific. It should emphasize the bank's recognized obligation to meet the legitimate credit needs of its trade area and its commitment to do so to the best of its ability.

Examples of desirable loans would include:

1. Short-term working capital loans that are self-liquidating in nature.
2. Loans to experienced farmers where the source of repayment is clear, such as crop loans.
3. Loans to finance the carrying of commodities where the collateral is negotiable warehouse receipts.
4. Nonspeculative construction loans with firm take-out commitments from reliable long-term lenders.
5. Floor plan lending (if it appeals to you).
6. Various kinds of consumer loans.
7. Construction loans on housing.
8. Term and revolving credits.[3]

Other desirable types of loans might be first mortgages on single-family homes with adequate equity, loans secured by accounts receivable, and loans secured by good quality marketable securities that are properly margined.

Unacceptable loans

Unacceptable loans could vary somewhat from one institution to another. However, they should always include loans that are illegal or the purpose of which is illegal and loans solely for speculative purposes.

Other types of unacceptable loans might include:

1. Loans to finance change in business ownership.
2. Construction loans without a firm take-out.
3. Loans secured by second mortgages on real estate.
4. Construction loans on condominiums unless they are presold.
5. Loans to a new business without a track record, unless it is well-collateralized.
6. So-called "bullet" loans or nonamortizing term loans.
7. Unsecured loans for real estate purposes.
8. Loans where the source of payment is solely public or private financing, not firmly committed.
9. Loans based on unmarketable securities.

This list is far from complete and includes only some types of loans that are generally regarded as undesirable for commercial banks. Depending on the type,

---

[3]Robert B. Maloane, "Written Loan Policies," *The Journal of Commercial Bank Lending,* 58 (June, 1976).

location, and size of the bank, other loans which might be included are term loans of more than a certain maturity, nonresidential long-term real estate loans, revolving credits, floor plan lines, loans to second mortgage companies, construction loans, unsecured loans to individuals, and "ship" loans. The list could be expanded, but it should be understood that some or all of these types are perfectly acceptable to some banks, while they would be inappropriate for others.

The need for well-trained, qualified loan personnel

There is one essential condition that should be met for any type of lending, aside from all of the previously mentioned possible constraints, such as deposit mix, capital, loan loss reserve, and earnings. That is the requirement for sufficient qualified people to properly evaluate the risks and follow and collect the loans in a timely manner.

Many forms of lending today require personnel with special knowledge and training. It is most imprudent for a bank to embark on a program of making, say, accounts receivable loans, construction loans, or aircraft loans without having sufficient well-trained and qualified individuals to handle the anticipated volume of this financing.

Delegation of lending authority

The delegation of lending authority is an integral part of loan policy, and it usually exists in some form or other even though the bank may have no aspects of it in writing. Even the smallest bank usually has to delegate some lending authority to one or more of its officers, since the directors normally do not meet frequently enough to properly serve the credit needs of the bank's borrowing customers.

The degree and extent of loan authority delegation by bank boards of directors, as well as forms of lending organization within banks, run the whole gamut from practically nil to almost one hundred percent. This is an entire subject in itself, but suffice it to say that the various systems seem to fall into three broad categories: individual authorities, groups or combinations of two or more individuals, and formal committees. While some banks function with only one of these methods of approving loans, most banks employ a combination of two or more.

Some provisions for loan approval

A typical loan approval function in a medium-sized bank might contain the following provisions:

1. A definition as to what constitutes "secured and unsecured" lending for loan approval purposes.

2. A definition of "borrower's total liability" to protect the bank against maximum extensions of credit to various affiliates, subsidiaries, principals, and related entities all dependent on one basic enterprise. Such a credit extension could be undertaken by an officer or combination of officers lacking the expertise to handle a credit of that magnitude. This is known as the "one ball of wax" principle, and it continues to be a sound one.

3. The establishment of officers' loan committee(s), naming the members, the chairman and secretary, quorum and voting procedures, and the maximum amount of each type of loan the committee may approve. Possible variations may include separate commercial, mortgage, installment, and international loan committees, senior and junior committees, and regional loan committees in the case of extensive branch operations.

4. Establishment of combination authorities, whereby certain individuals, with one or more others, may approve loans up to certain dollar amounts.

5. Listing of individual authorities by name and amount, secured and unsecured, and by type, where appropriate (mortgage officers limited to mortgage loans, for example). The maximum authority would range from very modest amounts for inexperienced individuals and those in junior positions to very large amounts for senior lending officers and executive officers.

How much lending authority should be granted

There are distinctly different philosophies among equally qualified bankers as to how much individual lending authority should be granted.

> Basically, variation arises from different philosophies as to whether individual or collective action should dominate loan decisions. One view is that in order to render prompt decisions and command mutual respect, the individual loan officer should be granted considerable latitude. . . . The other view is that since the capacity of lending officers vary widely, loan authority limits must fit the weakest officer in each bank.[4]

Somewhere between the two extremes

Some banks grant authority up to the bank's legal limit to all lending officers. Others may require that practically all loans be approved by the board of directors. Basically, a bank's loan authority guidelines are influenced by the capacity of lending personnel, the organizational structure of the bank, and the nature of the loan requests.

---

[4]Douglas A Hayes, *Bank Lending Policies, Issues and Practices,* (Ann Arbor: Bureau of Business Research, Graduate School of Business Administration, The University of Michigan, 1964), p. 44.

It is my opinion that for most banks, the best arrangement lies somewhere between the two extremes. It is particularly difficult to believe that any group of individuals are equally qualified to extend the bank's legal limit without undue risk. By the same token, a bank that cannot delegate any authority to its officers must be staffed with inferior personnel, and the directors are derelict in their duty of seeing that the bank is properly staffed!

Pricing

No written loan policy would be complete without guidelines for pricing various types of credit. Without such written guidelines, confusion and uncertainty, inconsistency, and possible unprofitability would exist and be reflected in the decisions of the loan officers.

Interest rate policies

Interest rate policies can range from rather general statements to very specific schedules. The general type would list broad ranges for certain categories of loans. Its goal would be to guide the loan officer in pricing a loan correctly, while allowing the officer sufficient latitude to account for the inherent differences between borrowers, particularly in the commercial field.

Pricing based on total yield

Pricing should recognize and be based upon total yield. It should take into account proper credit for average collected demand balances and related business, as well as the relative credit risk and the term and liquidity of the loan.

In mortgage lending, the quality of the real estate and the percentage of loan to value often give rise to gradations in the rate schedules.

Cost of funds and the risk factor

Each bank's cost of money should be taken into consideration in the pricing of credit. Banks with high average cost of funds should attempt to achieve higher loan yields, with one all-important caveat, however. If their earnings or capital structure is weak, and above normal loan losses would cause an earnings or capital adequacy problem, a high-risk loan portfolio is an almost certain invitation to disaster. It is essential to remember that in pricing a loan, consideration must be given not only to the cost of funds and the cost of administering the loan, but to the important factor of risk.

Price competition among banks

The deterrent to maximum loan pricing is competition. Price competition among banks can at times reach serious proportions, although fortunately the economy has been such in recent years that periods of competition have not been extensive or frequent. They have, nevertheless, fostered loan practices that have been detrimental to the banking industry as a whole, as well as to individual banks.

Perhaps the correct axiom here is that it is proper to meet competition selectively as long as it doesn't have an overall major harmful effect on the bank's balance sheet or income statement. But "don't let the competition make your loans for you." That old adage is everlastingly true!

Interest rate schedules

A detailed schedule of interest rates does have disadvantages. Opportunities or customers may be lost over a quarter of a percentage point, or delays are engendered while a line officer attempts to contact a superior for advice or approval of an exception. If too many exceptions are granted, the schedule becomes meaningless and the uniformity sought is lost. A further disadvantage of a detailed schedule is that it permits no exercise of individual judgment and stifles personal growth, as does too restrictive a lending authority.

Schedules also get out of date rapidly in changing economic times and are useless if not frequently updated, which can be costly in a large organization. It seems, therefore, that reasonably broad but explicit guidelines should be favored over very detailed and rigid price schedules.

Loan standards

To discuss specific principles and standards of loan policy is to get into the "nitty-gritty" of lending, which is not the purpose of this article. Yet a loan policy cannot be fully discussed without becoming involved in this subject to some extent. It is true that the line between policy and administration is often a fine one, but certainly a broad outline of what constitutes an acceptable loan is an integral part of loan policy. It is proper and beneficial in discussing this subject to separate it into the three major types of loans: commercial, real estate mortgage, and consumer installment.

In the commercial area, some banks have set up loan guidelines which supplement the statement of loan policy. These are further broken down into general and specific principles. Thus we move by stages from the general to the specific. The specific principles could be considered as operational instructions and therefore more properly the subject matter of a loan operating manual. But if no such written manual or instructions exist, it is far better to include this material as an adjunct to the loan policy statement than to relegate it to the "pass-on-by-word-of-mouth" category.

Sample loan policy guidelines

A sample statement of loan policy guidelines from a medium-large regional bank follows.[5]

General principles:

1. The bank should not have an undue concentration of loans in any one industry.

2. All *commercial* borrowing customers of the bank should maintain account relationships, and others should be encouraged to do so. If a customer moves out of the bank's trade area, loans should, within a reasonable period of time, be paid or transferred to the bank where the borrower has an account. Commercial borrowers should maintain compensating balances.

3. A credit file should be maintained on each borrowing account with memoranda for each loan showing the basis for the loan, purpose, conditions, rate and terms of repayment, as well as any other pertinent information and the authority for granting the loan.

4. All loans other than those secured by readily marketable liquid collateral should be supported by financial statements, preferably prepared by a certified public accountant. Statements are considered current if they are not more than one-year old. Occasionally a statement may be waived if the borrower is known to be financially strong, or there is other evidence of his unquestioned ability to handle the obligation. A memorandum outlining this evidence should be on file.

5. Loans to closely held companies should carry the endorsements of the principals and, in most cases, that of their spouses.

6. All loans except those secured by passbooks should have a plan of liquidation at the time they are made, and the liquidating program should be documented in the file.

7. Quarterly financial statements, or at a minimum, quarterly sales and earnings figures, should be required on all major lines and loans.

8. Periods of tight money have been frequent occurrences in recent years, and when such periods reoccur, the bank will give priority to the legitimate credit requirements of its existing customers. At the same time, it will discourage credit for speculative ventures and for those ventures which would contribute to inflation.

---

[5]The general and specific principles listed on the following pages are given for illustrative purposes only. Each bank should make its own determination as to which items are applicable and should also make appropriate substitutions for all numbers and percentages given (as, for instance, in item 3 under *Specific principles*).

9. Each lending officer is responsible for following his or her loans, maintaining contact with customers, and protecting the bank when necessary. In addition, a loan review section will review loans on a periodic basis, taking into account such risk factors as the financial condition of the borrower, the value of collateral, agreements concerning repayment, and the borrower's past record.

Specific principles:

1. Short-term loans to business concerns should normally be on notes drawn for a term of not more than ninety days.

2. Loan commitments except for lines of credit and revolving credits, will run for a period of ninety days unless there is a stated expiration date.

3. On secured loans, the following suggested maximum loan to collateral percentages apply:

    a. 97% against our own savings passbooks.
    b. 90% against U. S. Government bonds.
    c. 80% against new vehicles and equipment.
    d. 70%-85% against municipal bonds (depending on their rating).
    e. 70% against convertible debentures.
    f. 70% against stock traded on the NYSE.[6]
    g. 60% against stock traded on the ASE.[6]
    h. 50% against stock traded on the OTC.[6]

4. Lines of credit normally run for a period of one year unless otherwise stated. All lines are subject to annual review.

5. Guidance lines are approved for the internal guidance of the account officer and should not be confirmed either verbally or in writing to the customer.

6. Lines of credit other than revolving lines should normally be cleaned up for thirty days during each twelve-month period.

7. Term loans should be protected by written loan agreement.

8. Loans to directors or businesses in which directors have major interests must be approved by the bank's board of directors.

9. By regulation, all loans to officers must be approved by the board of directors, and loans to officers' spouses must be reported to the board. The maximum amounts are set by the Federal Reserve —

        $ 5,000 — unsecured, secured, or installment
$10,000 — education of children $30,000 — mortgage

---

[6]Provided the stock is selling for more than $10 per share and the number of shares involved does not represent an undue concentration in the total number of shares outstanding of the company.

Officers are required to report to the board any loan they have at another bank within ten days of completion.

10. Before a customer note is accepted for discount, a satisfactory checking should be obtained on the maker from his or her bank of account.

11. The bank should not accept as collateral, securities registered in a street name.

Standards for mortgage lending

The establishment of standards for mortgage lending breaks down naturally into two areas: (1) residential one-to-four family lending and (2) multi-family residential and commercial and industrial loans. The problem is simpler for those banks that engage only in residential mortgage lending. In that case the most important questions concern the geographic area acceptable, maximum ratio of loan to value, minimum credit criteria, appraisal requirements, and prepayment penalties.

The setting of standards for multi-family and commercial and industrial loans is a subject unto itself and one which apparently requires further and continuous study as conditions change. This need has been borne out by the continuing real estate lending debacle that began in 1974.

Construction lending entails a different set of problems. Some general principles of broad applicability to mortgage lending can be established, most of which have been noted before. Specifics should be in operating manuals and administered by qualified specialists. Banks should *resolutely* oppose financing of builder-developers to the extent of one hundred percent or more of value, as well as the idea of capitalizing all interest expense into a construction loan! If they don't, they deserve to suffer.

Sample statement of consumer loan principles

Principles for the extension of consumer loans should be established since they are of equal importance. Some considerations, which might be included in a statement of loan principles, follow.

1. Requirement of spouse's signature on loan in addition to borrower's, subject to limitations of Reg. B.

2. Requirement of current financial statements on loans in excess of a specific amount when on an unsecured or secured basis.

3. Current credit reports from a credit investigating agency and a statement of obligations by borrower.

4. Types of collateral as they influence loan value and maturity guidelines.
   a. New automobiles.
   b. Used automobiles.
   c. Household furniture and appliances.
   d. Sporting equipment, such as boats, campers, or trailers.
   e. Real estate.
   f. Marketable securities.
   g. Maturity limits when loans are secured by cash surrender value of life insurance or savings accounts.

5. Required depository relationship.

6. Dealer-generated loans.
   a. Required financial information from dealer.
   b. Deposit relationship.
   c. Guarantee considerations: full recourse, limited recourse, without recourse, and reserve allocation.
   d. Repossession arrangements.
   e. Income participation.

Credit granting procedures

A natural adjunct to the establishment of a written loan policy is its implementation through effective loan and credit procedures. This is a separate subject, but it is so closely related to loan policy that it deserves at least a brief mention here.

A bare outline of some of the important aspects follows:

1. Written loan memoranda.

2. Financial statement analysis.

3. Credit investigation.

4. Maintenance of credit files.

5. Loan reports and controls.

6. Loan review and workout.

Administration of credit policy

Who has primary responsibility

One final but extremely important aspect of credit policy is its administration. All of the well-written statements of sound lending policy and principles aren't worth the paper they're printed on unless they are adhered to. Whose responsibility is it to see that this is done? There can be no question that the ultimate responsibility rests with the board of directors. The policy statement was approved by them, and they should monitor compliance with it.

Their most direct tool in this regard is the auditor who should report directly to the board. His or her audits should be geared to detect major violations, which should be reported. In addition, the independent auditors should include the checking of compliance with policy in their audit program and report violations to the directors.

Executive officers of the bank also have primary responsibility. By direction of their subordinates and by personal example, they should constantly emphasize to all the staff the importance of operating within the framework of the policy guidelines.

Senior lending officer responsible for day to day administration

The actual day to day administration of loan policy rests with the senior lending officer and his or her staff. It is the senior officer who must set the example and make the difficult decisions. It is important that when the occasional deviation or exception is permitted, the officer explain to all involved the reasons behind the decision. The officer should emphasize that while all rules ought to be somewhat flexible, exceptions should be rare and not frivolously granted.

If the bank is large enough to have a loan review officer or department, the senior lending officer should use this source for detecting and reporting policy violations. The most knowledgable and skilled management will not be successful in maintaining a sound loan portfolio unless there is strict, consistent accountability at all levels.

Loan Review:
An Organizational Dilemma

by Cato Ellis

THERE IS A NEED FOR SOME KIND OF LOAN REVIEW FUNCTION in the large commercial bank today is a statement with which nearly everyone agrees. However, after discussing loan review with bank management and after researching the literature on the subject, it becomes evident that the need for loan review is the only area in which there is anything resembling general agreement.

Loan review is a relatively new field in banking with an increasing amount of emphasis being placed on the function by bank management and by others in the banking industry. As with other new ideas in their infancy, a considerable amount of turmoil is encountered when the new idea grows into adolescence. Discord among those of us in banking as to the how, what, where and why of loan review is a natural result of the growth of an idea. The dilemma is not necessarily bad for the industry since all adolescents strengthen their character by facing and overcoming problems associated with development. Now, let's try to put the dilemma into perspective.

The need for loan review

We shall start with the easiest aspect—the need for loan review. The necessity of some sort of continuous internal review of a bank's loan portfolio has been accepted by most of the country's largest banks since the 1950's. The only disagreement in this area is one of degree—the urgency of the need compared to the amount of time and money management wishes to expend to fulfill it.

The need increases in direct relationship with the growth of a particular banking organization. As the bank's loan portfolio increases in size and diversifies by loan type, it becomes increasingly difficult for top management and/or the bank's directors to maintain a continuous evaluation of the quality of the loan portfolio.

Personnel qualifications

Growth of an organization means change—change that very often is too rapid to deal with effectively. The rapid growth of the early 1970's contributed to a decline in the overall level of experience within most banks. This is especially evident in the lending area. The lending experience of loan officers is relatively minimal compared to an earlier banking era. Management development departments were simply unable to supply the ever-increasing demand for experienced personnel. Today's loan officers may be just as well, and in many ways better, *trained* than the loan officers of yesterday. However, there is no substitute for experience in the field of lending.

Diversification and specialization

Another type of change that accompanies the growth of an organization is the increasing diversification and specialization in the lending field—expansion into such areas as international loans, real estate construction and development loans, lease financing, and accounts receivable financing. Since these areas along with others are so specialized, it is difficult for management to keep abreast of the current trends and policies involved with a particular type of lending situation.

Competitiveness

Today banks are becoming increasingly more aggressive in their attitudes toward business development—a fact which could have an effect on the quality of the loan portfolio. Even though making a loan for any reason other than on the basis of creditworthiness is universally recognized as an unsound credit practice, the fact is that such loans are made to obtain business and meet competition. Modern banking organizations have discarded their myopic attitudes and the competition grows keener with every loan made and every deposit received. Could the result be a deterioration in the quality of the loan portfolio?

Economic and social environment

The last area of change I would like to mention is an external one—our rapidly changing social and economic environment. It is easily realized that when there is an economic downturn, the liquidity of the bank's loan portfolio could suffer. A particular loan may be considered good when made, but six months later this same loan could turn sour. The quality of a loan may be even more vulnerable to deterioration in today's unstable cyclical economy aggravated by alternate periods of inflation, shortages, and recession.

Alvin Toffler so clearly pointed out how the element of rapid change can affect society. The same can be applied to business and to your particular banking organization. Perhaps some form of loan review can prevent "future shock" from occurring within your bank.[1]

Four basic questions

There are four basic questions concerning loan review where disagreement occurs among different banking organizations and among management within the same organization. These questions are:

1. What is the function of loan review?

2. What should be a loan review department's scope of operations?

3. Who should staff the loan review department?

4. Where should loan review be within the organization and to whom should it report?

The answer to the fourth question is most important since the answers to the first three questions can vary depending on the placement of loan review within the organization and the person or persons to whom loan review reports. I will present four basic organizational plans under which the loan review function can be carried out. There are, of course, variations of each plan and even other basic plans which are not covered. However, the organizational designs presented below represent the most prevalent in the industry today, and each plan has its strengths and weaknesses.

Selecting an appropriate plan

The type of plan best suited to a particular organization depends on several factors including the size of the bank in terms of personnel and assets and the

---

[1]Alvin Toffler, *Future Shock*. New York: New York, Random House, 1970.

current quality of the loan portfolio. These factors can be objectively determined, but it is the nebulous or subjective factors which present problems to management when they are trying to tailor a loan review function to their organization.

The most troublesome subjective factor concerns the personalities of the individuals involved. One loan review scheme may work well within one bank, but may not work in another bank of the same size and condition. If the people involved work well together and are able to coordinate their activities, the efficiency of the loan review function will be maximized. In discussing these nebulous factors one writer used the well-known quote, "one man's meat may be another man's poison."[2]

The organizational scheme used by a bank is mainly dictated by the amount of authority that management and/or the board of directors wishes to vest in the loan review function. Loan review, regardless of varying degrees of authority, must maintain its objectivity in determining the quality of a bank's loan portfolio. Because loan review is and should be a staff function, the word authority must be qualified and further defined. "Authority" is not used here in the sense of initiating and taking action on a problem or situation. The "authority" vested in loan review is the relative weight that management and/or the board of directors places on the objective opinions of loan review concerning the loan portfolio. The objectivity and independence vary according to loan review's niche in the organizational plan.

Loan review under the Audit Department

When seeking independence for the loan review function, the natural niche in most large banks today where independence already exists is the Audit Department. Looking at the general organizational chart, the independence from line management is clearly pictured. The Audit Department reports, either directly or indirectly, to the board of directors, although the auditor tries to coordinate his efforts with line management. However, all the work done by the department is eventually reported to the directors. Therefore, the most significant reason for placing loan review under the auditor is the natural independence from line management and the existing channel of information to the board of directors.

The importance placed on independence and a clear, existing channel of information is indication of top management's and/or the directors' desire to obtain an objective opinion of the bank's loan portfolio. It is this determination of

---

[2]Frederick W. Burnham, "Loan Review: A Necessary Exercise in 20-20 Hindsight," in *The Journal of Commercial Bank Lending*, June 1973, page 13.

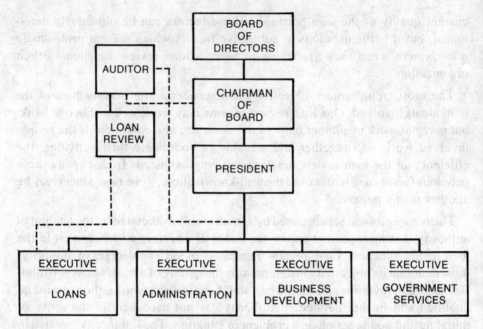

the quality of the bank's loans on a continuing basis that constitutes the broad function of a Loan Review Department.

Objectivity is most important—the loan review officer or officers should be able to give a competent, unbiased opinion concerning loan quality. In other words, loan review under the Audit Department functions as a "watchdog" for the directors over the bank's major asset—its loan portfolio. The ultimate responsibility for the quality of the loan portfolio lies in senior lending management and/or, hopefully, an effective Loan Administration Department.

The Loan Review Department has the responsibility of reporting any variations in the quality and perhaps suggesting ways that quality can be improved through changes in policy or procedures. It is important to remember that under this particular organizational plan loan review cannot dictate policy and procedures, but only recommend changes when after an objective evaluation it feels that changes are justified.

Scope of operations

What should be the scope of a Loan Review Department's operations? The answer to this question obviously depends on several factors including money, personnel, and the degree of examination needed or desired. Under the Audit Department, in general terms, the scope of operations of the loan review function should include four basic elements which are developed below.

• *Review of the bank's loan portfolio, including assignment of grades to loans on a consistent basis:* The degree of review will once again depend on cost–benefit factors. Some banks attempt to review all loans while others satisfy themselves with attempting to review a certain percentage of the total dollar amount of the portfolio. The benefits derived from an extensive loan review program must be weighed against costs, which in many cases may be prohibitive. In considering the scope or degree of review the function of loan review must be reiterated. The board of directors is mainly interested in trends and these trends can be compiled without a 100% review of all loans.

• *Determining that loan policies are generally being followed:* Again, it will be prohibitive for loan review to determine and point out that every loan is within policy. However, through a routine review exceptions to policy will be discovered and investigated, and if in the opinion of loan review these exceptions are considered numerous, they should be reported. A review of the policies can also be conducted, including a discussion with senior lending management concerning possible changes in lending policy.

• *Review of procedures for documentation of loans and collateral and the retention and dissemination of credit information:* The important word here is "review." Loan review must not attempt to be an information bank or, on the other hand, perform a continuous audit of loan documentation and collateral. A review of the procedures will suffice. If loan review is unable to make an objective evaluation of a loan or loans because of poor or nonexistent information in the credit files, and if the collateral supporting a loan is not documented, management must be made aware of these shortcomings. If these problems persist and are intensified, recommendations for improvement should be made to management and an appropriate follow-up conducted.

• *Proper reporting and follow-up procedures:* Although this may on the surface appear to be the least important of the four duties listed, it actually becomes extremely important when you consider one simple concept—communication.[3] If loan review is to function properly, there must be clear and open lines of communication between loan review and all levels of the organization. To achieve the most effective communication a formalized system of reports, replies and follow-up procedures is essential. However, a note of caution must be injected here. Even though there is an excellent system of formal communication, there is no substitute for informal and personal communication. Once again I emphasize the importance of personalities in any organization,

---

[3] *Ibid.*

particularly loan review. In addition, too much reliance on formalized communication can often lead to a slowing-down, if not a reduction, in communication.

Personnel considerations

If a Loan Review Department is to function effectively, it must be staffed by competent personnel trained in credit analysis and familiar with the lending function. It can be especially helpful to have a senior loan review officer with lending experience.

Why is familiarity with the lending function so important? (1) The loan review officer must be able to place himself in the shoes of the loan officer to "avoid proliferating a world of second guessers or purveyors of 20-20 hindsight."[4] He must realize the difficulties in making a loan properly and he must be aware of the things that can go wrong. (2) Communication between the review officer and the loan officer and their mutual respect for each other hopefully will be greater if they are both familiar with the same function—lending. (3) The loan review officer's opinion as to the loan portfolio will possibly be weighed more highly if top management and the directors are aware that he knows what it is like "on the other side of the fence."

Some feel that auditors, former bank examiners, and credit officers could fill the qualifications of the loan review officer, but the majority devote considerable attention to lending experience. The ideal loan review officer would probably have the combined qualities of a loan officer, auditor, bank examiner and credit officer.

Strengths and weaknesses

In general, the strengths and weaknesses of loan review under the Audit Department are these:

Strengths

1. Existing independence
2. Established lines of communication to management and the board of directors
3. Authorized access to all records and information
4. Availability of a pool of staff auditors when needed
5. Formalized system of reporting, replies, and follow-up procedures

Weaknesses

1. Lack of expertise in and understanding of the lending function

---

[4]*Ibid.*

2. Rigidity of structure—lack of informal communication links to senior lending management

3. Suppression of information by line personnel (This is not an acute problem, but it does exist.)

Loan review as an independent staff function

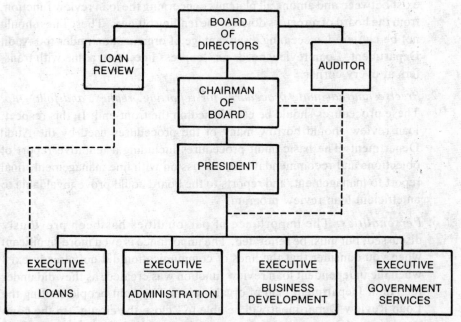

Organization of loan review as an independent staff function will in many ways be similar to organization under the Audit Department. The most noticeable similarity is independence from the normal line positions in the organization. Also, there are many basic tenets that apply to loan review no matter what the organizational design.

Lines and problems of communication

The initial problem encountered when discussing an independent loan review department is where in the organization should it be placed—to whom will it report. Again, the answer will depend on the significance placed on the function by management and the directors. Because independence should be a basic characteristic of loan review, it seems necessary that the natural reporting station should be the board of directors or some committee thereof. This organizational plan is similar to the Audit Department plan in that loan review would be operating as an arm of the board. However, there is one important difference—

the arm is more directly attached. Communication between the board of directors and loan review will hopefully be more direct.

Communication is not just born, it must be established. Effective communication depends on several factors:

1. *Clearly defined lines:* Definite and precise lines of communication should exist between and among all plateaus concerning the loan review function, from the board of directors down to the lending officers. These lines should not be cluttered, a seeming disadvantage of organization under the Audit Department. Loan review needs an "express line," not a line with transfers at every corner.

2. *Precise and adequate procedures for reporting, replies, and follow-up:* These procedures should be established on the front-end. In this respect, loan review should borrow many of the procedures used by the Audit Department. The basic audit procedures including a tentative report of objections and recommendations, discussion with line management, final report to management, and reports to the board could prove invaluable to an efficient loan review program.

3. *Personalities:* The importance of personalities has been previously discussed, but must be reiterated. The importance is even more significant when you consider that the lines of communication did not already exist when the independent loan review function was created, as they did under the Audit Department plan of organization. The right people staffing the Loan Review Department will be able to "close the circuit" in the communication line.

Scope of operations

As an arm of the directors, loan review functions as a guardian over the quality of the loan portfolio. The directors place this responsibility in the hands of loan review because they feel that an independent and objective evaluation of the loan portfolio apart from the senior and executive management will be their most effective tool in protecting themselves from liability. Discussion of loan review under senior lending management will point out that some boards place the responsibility for the loan portfolio in one or more executive officers and depend on their judgment as to the quality. However, whether under audit or independent, the Loan Review Department remains a direct arm of the board of directors.

The operations of the independent Loan Review Department will be similar to operations under the Audit Department. However, the scope of operations may necessarily be smaller because of limitations in staff. The independent department, unless given a large staff and budget, will be unable to accomplish the number or the extent of reviews that it could using the Audit Department's staff pool. Therefore, loan review must concern itself with the quality of its review and possibly limit its review to all loans above a certain dollar amount, depending on the size of the loan portfolio.

Personnel

An independent Loan Review Department must be staffed by personnel experienced in credit analysis and knowledgeable of the lending function. Senior loan review officers should have lending experience or at least be familiar with the lending function, the advantages of which have been presented. In staffing the Loan Review Department communication again becomes important because of the close coordination that is needed between loan review personnel and lending management and officers. An accurate evaluation of loans will depend to a great extent on the flow of information between the loan officer and the loan reviewer. Also, mutual respect and understanding between loan review and the loan officers will aid in the development of a smooth-running and efficient department.

Strengths and weaknesses

In summary, the strengths and weaknesses of loan review as an independent staff function are:

Strengths

1. Independence from lending management—increased objectivity
2. Less rigidity in structure than in the audit department
3. Relative ease in working with lending management
4. Staffed by personnel trained in the lending function
5. Elimination of audit's stigma of being too critical

Weaknesses

1. Lack of existing lines of communication
2. Increases the number of groups reporting to the directors
3. Decreasing scope of review

Loan review under senior lending management

The major consideration concerning loan review reporting to senior lending management is independence. Can the loan review officer make an independent and objective evaluation of the bank's loan portfolio when organized under the executive loan officer or officers? For that matter, do management and the directors wish to have a completely independent and objective evaluation?

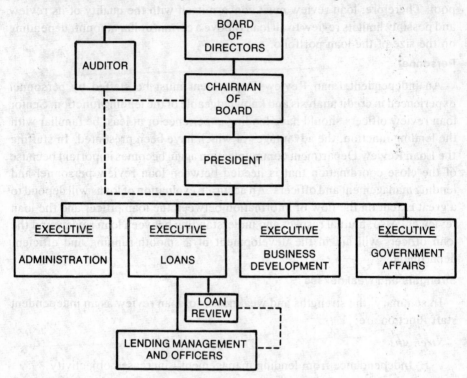

Earlier it was mentioned that by placing loan review under senior lending management, the responsibility for reporting the quality of the loan portfolio is with the executive in charge of loans. One advantage of this organizational design is that responsibility is concentrated in one man. The board of directors in this situation is relying on the competence and the integrity of their executive in charge of loans, and they depend on his judgment of loan portfolio quality.

Importance of personality

I must qualify my meaning in speaking of competence and integrity. Nearly every executive loan officer has competence and integrity, but one should also consider the often hidden ambition and personal ego involved. Since, in effect, the bank's loans are his responsibility, he may be inclined to "paint a rosy picture" concerning the quality of the portfolio to protect his own position in the organization. This is a natural tendency of all individuals, and it is an admirable trait. A loan officer should "stick to his guns" if he feels that one of his loans has been unjustly criticized. However, this same trait could possibly affect the ability of the executive loan officer to present an objective evaluation of the bank's loans.

Factors essential to efficiency

Loan review under senior lending management could work efficiently depending on several factors. One of these factors is the degree of independence that senior lending management gives the loan review officer or officers and the value that is placed on their evaluation. Loan review in this case could become an effective tool of the executive loan officer in making his own evaluation of the loan portfolio. Another important factor, as in the other loan review designs, is the personnel. The executive loan officer has a pool of trained, experienced lending personnel which he could detach to loan review and be completely confident of their evaluation.

If the two above factors could be present in all cases, loan review might logically belong under senior lending management. However, complete independence and objectivity would seemingly be impossible to achieve under this organizational design.

Strengths and weaknesses

Some of the strengths and weaknesses of loan review under senior lending management are:

Strengths

1. Complete and immediate accessibility to all information on loans

2. Personnel trained in the lending function

3. Concentration of responsibility in one center

4. Good communication between loan review and loan officers

Weaknesses

1. Possible lack of objectivity and independence in evaluation of the loan portfolio

2. Possibility of too much reliance on loan review in workout and problem situations

Loan review under the chairman, president or chief executive officer

The effectiveness of any loan review function setup depends to a great extent on the relative importance placed on it by the board of directors and top management. The highest degree of importance placed on the function is demonstrated by having loan review report directly to the chairman, president or chief executive officer. The chief executive officer is the "boss"; he has the ultimate responsibility for the quality of the loan portfolio and authority to take action to maintain or improve this quality. Therefore, he not only has a need for the services of loan review in controlling the quality of the loan portfolio, he can also utilize the findings of loan review in initiating action where it is required.

Like loan review under the independent design there is a direct line of communication to the board of directors. Communication between the Loan Review Department and senior lending management, although not already established, will be relatively free and uncluttered. Essentially the same communication chain utilized in the senior lending management design will simply be taken one step further.

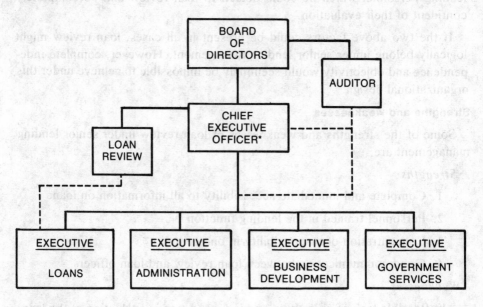

*Chairman or President

Independence potential

Can loan review be independent under this particular design? Although the loss of independence that may be experienced under senior lending management is possible, the probability of it occurring is negligible. Since the quality of the loan portfolio is the CEO's responsibility and the fact is bad loans are impossible to hide forever, the CEO will utilize the loan review officer's findings and recommendations more as a preventive tool than as a cover-up.

Scope of operations

One disadvantage of having loan review report directly to the CEO is that he probably has too many departments reporting to him as it is. It may be that he simply does not have the time to take on this additional task. However, if the CEO has an effective loan review officer whose overall judgment is respected, the benefits of a direct reporting procedure are maximized. The CEO is responsible for the total organization including not only loans, but investments, asset and liability management, operations and marketing. If there are responsible people in the administration of each of these areas, his worries are minimized. Since loans are the bank's major asset, he may benefit from having his own "watchdog" over this area. This "watchdog" would of course indirectly serve the board of directors.

Strengths and weaknesses

Having loan review report to the chairman, president, or CEO combines many of the elements of the independent loan review department and loan review reporting to senior lending management. Some of the strengths and weaknesses of the organizational design are:

Strengths

1. Effective two-way communication both up to the board of directors and down to senior lending management

2. Good probability of an independent evaluation

3. Support both from the board of directors and from senior lending management

4. Demonstration of the importance of loan review

5. More time allocated to the total loan picture, rather than to specific problems

Weakness

1. Increase the number of people reporting to the CEO

2. Necessitates the hiring of separate loan review staff

3. Decreases the scope of review

Elements necessary in any loan review program

I am not going to attempt to recommend the best organizational design for loan review. Too many factors vary from bank to bank, making recommendation impossible.

Loan review truly presents a dilemma for management and directors. Just as it is evident that some form of loan review is needed, it is equally evident that much thought and consideration is needed in developing the most efficient loan review function for a large commercial bank. I am convinced the following elements should be present in any loan review program:

1. Independence and objectivity in evaluation of the loan portfolio

2. Clear and unburdensome lines of communication

3. Personnel trained in credit analysis and familiar with the lending function

4. "Personalities" with the ability to make the program work

5. Support from all areas of management and the board of directors

6. Clearly defined reporting, reply, and follow-up procedures

7. Well defined guidelines, known to all officers, clearly stating loan review's function and scope of operations   □

REFERENCES

Burnham, Frederick W., "Loan Review: A Necessary Exercise in 20-20 Hindsight" in *The Journal of Commercial Bank Lending,* June 1973.

Cooper, P.J., "A Practical Approach to Commercial Loan Review: Liquidity Vs. Collectibility" in *The Journal of Commercial Bank Lending,* 54:12, August 1972.

Harlan, James C., *An Effective Loan Review System For Medium-Sized Banks.* Stonier Graduate School of Banking, 1960.

Jesser, Edward A., Jr., "Effective Loan Administration" in *The Journal of Commercial Banking Lending,* 55:10, June 1973.

Sax, S. W., "Loan Review—Bank Quality Control & R & D" in *Bankers Magazine,* 156:72-6, Spring 1973.

Shea, Jeremiah P., *A Program of Periodic Loan Review for Use in Medium-Sized Banks.* New Brunswick: Graduate School of Banking.

Toffler, Alvin, *Future Shock.* New York: Random House, 1970.

Loan Review:
A Possible Alternative Method

by W. Thomas Maloan

Tom Maloan suggests that loan review be handled by loan officers themselves rather than by a loan review department. He describes a system in which loan officers rate their own loans and produce their own problem loan lists and "corrective" plans of attack. He also points out the benefits and problems with this self-analysis system but leaves the ultimate judgment of the system to you.

Loan review is one of those banking functions which creates the same vision in every banker's mind. The picture is of a staff department operating in conjunction with, and as an adversary to, the line lending officers; the department's charge is quality control over the loan portfolio. In this article, my purpose is neither to criticize nor to elaborate further on the traditional method of loan review. Criticism is unwarranted since this assignment of the loan review function to a special department has worked successfully at numerous banks. Elaboration is unnecessary because of the recent publication by RMA of *Commercial Loan Review Procedures,* a thorough booklet which handles the subject more than adequately.*

Rather, I propose an alternative method for the loan review process which I will discuss along with its benefits and problems. I do not offer this suggestion as a panacea. It is a conceptual change which may stimulate other ideas and

---

* Copies of this booklet are available from the Order Department, Robert Morris Associates, 1616 Philadelphia National Bank Bldg., Philadelphia, PA 19107. $5.00 per copy to RMA member banks; $7.50 to nonmember banks. All orders must be accompanied by payment.

provide the impetus for advancing toward our common goal—a high quality, profitable loan portfolio. If such happens, we will all benefit.

The frequent admonition that "characterization of any person, living or dead, is purely coincidental" is particularly true in this effort. Many bankers' comments over the years have contributed, without their knowledge, to the ideas I'm about to set forth. My thoughts are a distillation of theirs tempered by my own experiences. Consequently, I claim no particular originality, only the responsibility for the conclusions I present.

The basic assumption

I believe any system of loan review is based on one assumption—that the best means of assuring a quality loan portfolio is a sound, well-functioning approval system. Without good initial underwriting and sound credit decisions, no amount of subsequent review can avoid a poor quality portfolio.

Therefore, the first step in the loan review process is an objective, penetrating review of the bank's approval process. A discussion of the various approval systems in existence today is beyond the scope of this article. However, I can identify two factors which should suggest the possible need for either revamping existing methods or adopting entirely new ones:

(1) *Loans which become identified as problems very early in their life.* It is axiomatic that all loans are good when made; however, if they are turning bad during the time between their approval at the loan officer's desk and their finalization at the note teller's window, some questions can be raised about their initial goodness.

(2) *An increase in the number of loans being classified which originated since the most recent examination.* Except for the 1974–75 period when regulatory agencies considered listing only the passed loans in the report, the average classified loan generally originated sometime before the current examination, on the average, two to three years before. If several new loans are classified, this can be a sign that the approval process needs review. (The exact number of new loans is discretionary, but it should be a low number.)

Once the approval process is both sound and well-functioning, the loan review process has a better chance to assist in maintaining the quality of the loan portfolio.

The concept

The alternative I suggest to the traditional loan review process is to require the loan officer himself to rate his own loans. He will identify those loans which he considers a problem. There are several reasons why he is the best equipped to do this:

(1) He has frequent contact with the borrower, and his knowledge is the freshest.

(2) He is the first to know when a borrower overdraws the account, goes past due, or fails to adhere to the established liquidation agreement. All are valid red flags warning of possible trouble.

(3) He usually sees the financial statements first; if he has been in lending longer than 90 days, he makes mental comparisons of liquidity, leverage, and profitability. Any downward changes are also red flags.

(4) He possesses the best early warning system of problems known to man—worry. Any loan which causes him to awaken suddenly at 2:00 a.m. is a problem. Only he has knowledge of this alarm going off.

By having the loan officer identify his problem loans, the loan review system capitalizes on the loan officer's resources.

The procedure

The process begins with each individual loan officer's preparing his list of problem loans, which he discusses with his immediate supervisor.

Review of problem loan list with supervisor

To make the discussion germane and to put it in some reasonable order, I suggest the use of a simple form such as Figure 1. Four main points in the form should be noted:

(1) The brief history and current collateral valuation section is for background for those not as familiar with the account as the handling officer.

(2) The rating section is self-explanatory. If your bank has a loan rating system, this could be used. If you do not, a three-tiered system (unsatisfactory, possible but undetermined loss, probable loss) could be used. Or, easier yet, have one rating only—unsatisfactory. Regardless, the loan officer's rating would be his identification of the problem, and the grading of the severity could be added either by his superior or to the system later after more experience is gained.

(3) The "Why the Loan Is a Problem" section should give the specific reason(s) the loan officer considers the loan a problem.

(4) "Proposed Action" is the plan the loan officer recommends as the proper way to eliminate the problem. This should be detailed enough to provide for the

necessary and anticipated follow-up. Plans could range from additional collateral (type and value should be given) to charge off. If additional advances are recommended, the amount and reasons supporting them should be stated.

The review with a supervisor serves three basic purposes. It starts the process of communications upward regarding problem loans. It requires both supervisor and loan officer agreement that a problem exists. This aids the supervisor in determining if the cause of the problem is the same in each loan (logically, it should not be). Also, the proposed action plan must be jointly accepted as being the best for prompt, satisfactory resolution of the problem. Parenthetically, "best" means from the bank's view and position.

After the discussion between the supervisor and the loan officer has produced an agreed-upon list of problem loans and plans of attack for each one, the supervisor goes over these lists, along with his own problem loans, with *his* supervisor. This "one-over-one" process continues until the bank's chief lending officer (president or someone else) has a complete list for the bank.

Monitoring, declassification, and special reviews

From that point on, the thrust is monitoring these formualted plans. If your bank has a loan review department, it can take over the monitoring responsibility. If not, the supervisors can do it. Monitoring may be formal with periodic written reports or informal with irregular oral reports; the choice would be predicated on managerial technique, magnitude of the problems, and the abilities of the loan officer.

Figure 1
Problem loan write-up sheet

Borrower's Name: _____ Date: _____

Amount of Debt: Outstanding $ _____ Committed: $ _____

Brief History and Current Collateral Valuation:

Rating:

Why the Loan is a Problem:

Proposed Action:

Lending Unit: _____

Loan Officer: _____ Supervisor's Agreement: _____

Ideally, the loan officer should bring a problem loan in for discussion anytime and as soon as he feels he has one. By the same token, he should come back to discuss any one of the previously listed problem loans anytime he feels it is no longer a problem.

Figure 2 could be the basis for the declassification discussion. The declassification procedure is the same as the procedure for classification: It involves a one-over-one consultation and joint agreement. For the system to work at maximum efficiency, the odd-time, as-soon-as-possible discussions are necessary. However, if this optimum cannot be achieved at the start, an acceptable method would be to have the review at regular intervals. Quarterly or semi-annually should suffice.

If the senior credit officer has loans which he handles, he should be included in this process. To exclude him would destroy the system; however, the discussion with another could be made optional as a "perk" of his position.

While this sytem focuses on existing problems, a widely recognized responsibility of loan review is the on-going evaluation of the portfolio to anticipate problems. This system, as described, should meet this need.

However, there are certain loans which, because of their size, may need more formal periodic reviews. These loans are those which would harm earnings or the level of the loss reserves if they went bad and so should be subject to special reviews. They could be conducted by loan review, or the loan officers could review each others' "special" loans. Or one officer could review them all. These special reviews may not be a high priority in every bank, but they do serve to increase the comfort level of both senior management and directors.

Making the self-analysis system work

There are three prime requirements to make "my" loan review system work. First, there must be a change in philosophy regarding the loan officer's mistakes. Under this system, failure to report a problem is a bigger "sin" than making a mistake. This is not to say that mistakes will be condoned more readily under this system than under any other; necessary and corrective action can and should be taken by the line supervisors. However, the loan officer should know that it is far more serious *not* to report a problem than to have a problem. Only when the problem is known can assistance be given to alleviate it.

Second, the supervisors at all levels must be particularly harsh in their criticisms anytime a failure to report a problem is discovered. If the coverup is permitted to exist, this system is destroyed and becomes, in Fred Allen's words, "a treadmill to oblivion."

Figure 2
Problem Loan Declassification Sheet

Borrower's Name: _____ Date: _____

Amount: Outstanding: $_____ Committed: $_____ Classified: $_____

Classification: _____ Classification Date: _____

Reason for Declassification:

Lending Unit: _____ Supervisor's Agreement: _____

Loan Officer: _____ Date: _____

Third, an outside source is needed to verify both the completeness and accuracy of the ratings. For those banks which have it, an internal loan audit system can function as this outside source. However, the most readily available outside source for most banks is the regulatory examination. A full and satisfactory explanation would be required from the loan officer for any loan classified in an examination that was not previously reported in the loan review process. Allowances must be made for honest differences of opinion between examiners and loan officers. But the supervisor must be satisfied with the reason for the loan officer's failure to report the loan.

The benefits of self-analysis

This self-analysis system of loan review should produce some benefits above those of problem loan identification and resolution. These benefits are listed, in order of importance, as follows:

(1) The system reduces staff requirements for the loan review function; no additional people are necessary.

(2) Loan review becomes results-oriented in that a plan of corrective action is required and is predicated on successful completion of the plan to resolve the problem.

(3) The system is based on fresh, immediate information which should produce early identification of problem loans, permitting corrective action at the point when it is usually the most effective. This should reduce both the worry and the time spent on the loan by the loan officer.

(4) The system identifies specific training requirements of individual officers based on their individual needs; as the review process takes place, the super-

visor can note any recurrence of problem types and prescribe remedial action to eliminate their cause.

(5) It eliminates the adversary relationship within the bank between loan review and line lenders.

The problems with the system

As we have all been told many times, "There is no perfect drink to go with a free lunch." This system has built-in difficulties which must be recognized and prepared for at the outset.

Its biggest drawback is the requirement of an action—public confession—which is contrary to human nature. We just don't like "baring our souls" in public; peer pressures in a competitive environment are not conducive to it. However, it is widely acknowledged that managerial support of loan review is mandatory for any reasonable chance of success. Demonstrable managerial support can offset this handicap. Perhaps the senior lending officer can be the first to make his list. This would legitimatize the program in the other officer's eyes. But the easing of tensions caused by the required self-denouncement will have to be reinforced frequently, at least until the loan review system is well established and some benefits to the loan officer are realized.

Another negative factor is the great amount of time required for lending personnel to conduct this review. Loan review is in addition to, rather than in lieu of, the myriad of duties any commercial lending officer has. In reality, however, much of the time spent on this activity would be expended by the loan officer on these loans in most circumstances. To some extent, this system will organize the time. Further, the time required for review should diminish as familiarity with both the system and the loans is increased at all levels.

It is possible the system could falter because of a loan officer's lack of skill in rating loans. A possible solution to this problem was mentioned earlier when rating systems were briefly discussed. Of greater concern is the loan officer who may be deficient in identifying problems. A brief guideline prepared to your bank's specifications which defines when a loan is a problem could assist the loan officer in overcoming this deficiency. For example, the guideline could define a problem as a loan 90 days past due or one which has been renewed three times without reduction. The guideline should assist but should not be a security blanket since there are, as noted, subjective reasons which might cause the loan officer to rate a loan as a problem. In this system, the subjective reasons for problem determination are as important as the objective ones.

Conclusion

Loan review is a needed function. As such, it can be changed but not eliminated. This suggested alternative method moves it to the line from the staff. In this system, the review is done by those who, in reality, are at the best level to know what loans are truly problems. It forces problem solutions to become the focal point of the activity. It should benefit both the bank and the loan officer but not without difficulties and some cost.

Should you try it? Only you can answer that. But I believe it is worth considering.   □

Don't Miss Those Natural Loan Review Opportunities!

by Robert E. Davis

Most articles on loan review have talked about either the concept of loan review or about how to set up an effective loan review system. By contrast, the following article presents what might be a new wrinkle for at least a few bankers, on this oft-written about subject.

The general theme of this article is that it pays to be opportunistic in monitoring and controlling the quality and liquidity of the bank's loan assets. Numerous opportunities are continuously presented to a commercial bank and its loan review section to evaluate the goodness of a loan during its conception and carrying time. The opportunities in question represent natural points of loan *preview* and loan *review*. Generally, they are available prior to loan approval during the decision-making process (preview) and immediately after the loan proceeds have been advanced to the customer or when some action, or lack thereof, prompts an investigation of a seasoned credit (review).

The actual loan review process used within the context of these natural opportunities can be quite different from the review techniques that might be associated with a more formalized and extensive review system. The scope of these particular review procedures, except for the review during the pre-loan approval process, can be limited to the examination of written credit memoranda or to researching specific exceptions that have materialized and prompted an investigation.

The specific review opportunities and procedures suggested here may be sufficient to satisfy the loan review objectives in some banks. However, in other banks, it may be necessary to supplement these opportunities and procedures with a more structured loan review function, one which would generally be a more extensive analysis of the bank's loans and loan portfolios on a regularly scheduled, periodic basis.

Pre-loan review (preview)

When a customer comes into the bank to request a new loan, the banker is presented with his first opportunity to evaluate the quality, liquidity, and appropriateness of the proposed credit. This early pre-loan review or preview opportunity is more important to the banker than any other that might be available later. If the bank is willing to accommodate the customer's credit request, the loan can be structured in the most desirable fashion at the outset. However, if the bank is not inclined to make the loan on any basis, this is the right time to say "no" without having funds advanced and on the line.

Loan officers have been saying for years that "I have never made a bad loan, but, of course, several have gone bad after I initially approved them." The fact is, though, that bad loans do get on the books more than occasionally because the officer does not get enough information, fails to document the loan properly, does not exercise reasonable credit judgment, or simply lacks a sufficient degree of ESP on the particular day the customer first came in.

How can the bank best minimize the possibility of these unwanted credits creeping onto the books? Having qualified and experienced lending personnel is the best method. A loan preview procedure can be another valuable safeguard. Both provide a means of reducing these documentation and judgmental errors experienced prior to the approval and distribution of loan proceeds.

Assistance by loan review staff

Given the fact that in most banks, the members of the loan review staff are highly qualified and have extensive knowledge in the technical areas of lending, they can be of immeasurable assistance to the line officers and can make a valuable contribution to the bank during the pre-loan review process. This assistance can be in the form of—

(1) Analyzing the related financials.

(2) Evaluating the appropriateness of the use of the loan proceeds and of the proposed source and method of repayment.

(3) Comparing the proposed credit to the bank's lending policy.

(4) Assisting with the structuring and documentation of the credit.

(5) Posing credit-oriented questions to the lending officer that might be applicable to the situation.

Before you loan officers become too upset, let me hastily add that I am in no way suggesting that loan review should be given authority for loan approval or that the loan officer should be required to obtain the approval of loan review before making a loan commitment. However, I am suggesting that loan review can provide specialized staff support on at least the larger and more complex credit situations, particularly on those that must be referred to a loan committee or to the board for approval.

Factors affecting degree of loan review's involvement

The degree of loan review's involvement in the initial credit evaluation process is up to bank management and the line officers. For instance, management could require consultation with loan review on all new and restructured loans over a specified amount, which could possibly correspond with that requiring committee approval. Management could also require that loan review evaluate and apply a qualitative loan classification to all credits prior to their presentation to the loan committee.

However, without a definite policy regarding loan review's involvement in the initial evaluation of credits, including smaller credits, the loan review section cannot force itself into the picture. Its position is one of "here we are—call us if we can be of help." There is nothing wrong with that particular posture, as long as it *is* called when its assistance can be of benefit to the bank.

The experience of the bank's lending officers might also influence the degree to which loan review is involved in the initial loan evaluation process. If the general level of lending expertise is low, loan review's involvement should be substantial to ensure that the fundamentals of sound lending are applied and adequate credit information obtained.

Even if the bank is blessed with highly competent and well-trained lending officers, loan review can still provide valuable assistance. By utilizing its expertise in the technical aspects of lending and knowledge of credit fundamentals, along with the line officers' experience and more intimate knowledge of the account, a proper and well-balanced decision will evolve in most cases. Certainly, that must be the bank's goal, for there is no adequate substitute for the right decision up front.

Qualities of good loan preview exercise

In loan preview, the responsiveness of the loan review section to the line officers is of the utmost importance. The loan preview exercise must be prompt, exact, and performed by a qualified individual. The entire function must be designed to ensure that preview does not prolong the decision-making time period or interfere with the effectiveness of the bank's new business development efforts.

As stated previously, I am not suggesting that loan review should be directly involved in the approval process. That involvement would damage and conflict with its objectivity in post-loan review procedures. However, why not utilize the loan review section to its fullest? Solicit its thinking as deemed necessary and beneficial during pre-loan approval evaluations, particularly on large, unusual, or highly complex credit packages.

Post-loan review

After a loan has been approved and advanced, it is quite often productive and beneficial to review the new credit extension one last time before it is sent to file. This post-approval loan review technique, whether it be the sole responsibility of the loan review section or shared by various levels of management, is desirable and can be used to good advantage. The primary objective of this activity is to identify weak credits and to recommend corrective action immediately if that appears necessary. Or those accounts might be marked for special watching to ensure that they are paid in a timely manner and in accordance with terms.

Opportunities provided by post-loan review

This post-loan review technique provides the opportunity for the early detection of credit weaknesses, documentation discrepancies, violations of lending authorities and lending policies, and the initiation of prompt corrective action. In addition, the reviewers have the ability to monitor continuously the general quality and type of newly made loans. Also, this early review gives the bank an opportunity to classify and grade the new credit as to quality and liquidity and to evaluate the individual performance of the bank's lending personnel.

If the bank takes this opportunity to classify or grade new loans, the initial classification should be subject to change when and if the credit is next reviewed. If the initial classification is unfavorable, it should be upgraded when the reasons for that action are cleared to the satisfaction of the loan review section. By utilizing this early grading opportunity, the bank can give those credits initially judged to have less than acceptable risk more attention during their carrying time than might be necessary for loans accorded a higher credit classification rating.

Three methods of structuring post-loan review

At least three possible methods of structuring this type of post-approval loan review procedure are apparent. One would require that new loans, perhaps limited to those over a specified amount for each loan type, be delivered to the loan review section for analysis, accompanied by the loan writeup and credit file. Another method would be to give open publicity to each loan made by circulating complete and comprehensive credit memoranda (loan writeups) on each new credit. These memoranda would be prepared by the loan officer and distributed by the credit department to a designated group of management personnel. The third method would be the issuance by the loan department of a formal daily, weekly, or monthly report on newly extended credits.

Loan referral. The most desirable of these three options would be to have all new line or loan commitments, over a specified amount, referred to the loan review section immediately after approval and recordation in the loan department. With the complete credit file and new loan writeup, the loan review section could perform a full analysis of the loan and could grade that credit for further reference and followup. This method allows loan review to focus on the entire situation, having all of the pertinent information available. Consequently, a more knowledgeable opinion on the soundness of the credit would be rendered.

Loan writeup. The success of monitoring loan quality or performing a post-loan review based on the review of circulating credit memoranda is dependent upon the quality and completeness of the loan writeups. Therefore, it is imperative that the bank clearly establish the type of credit memorandum expected on each new loan—what information is to be included and when it is to be submitted to loan review. Comprehensive and timely credit memoranda can provide a most informative review, and, at the very minimum, can prompt a more thorough review of a particular credit, if something in the writeups sets off a warning signal.

This post-review system may encourage individual loan officers to make more supportable credit decisions and might also improve the quality of the loan writeups. However, it does not necessarily allow for intelligent loan grading or a full evaluation of the credit. A credit memorandum can be written in such a fashion that it can be misleading, or certain essential facts might be omitted or minimized. In either case, an independent judgment of the credit's true quality might be hampered.

Loan report. The other post-loan review possibility is a system whereby the loan department publishes a listing of all new loans made during a given period or at least loans in excess of a specified amount. The report could be distributed to loan review and other management personnel. While the basic data for all loan review functions are obtained on some periodic basis from the loan department, this particular report would have to provide considerably more detailed information than normally required to be of real value. At the minimum, it would have to include the borrower's name, loan amount, rate, terms, collateral, guarantees, purpose, and any other outstanding loans. The report could be reviewed individually by the recipients or more formally by a committee.

Unless the report disclosed full details on each credit, this particular option would not be as effective a means of post-loan review as the others suggested, and it would not allow for an initial grading of loan quality or liquidity. However, it can be a valuable source of information for management and can be used as a means of prompting a detailed review of certain credits that might be included in the report.

Method of communication

All of the suggested post-loan review procedures and any others that might be formulated should be supplemented by a formal method of communication and reporting between loan review, management, and the loan officer. This communication could involve questions, suggestions, or recommendations on new credit commitments directed to the loan officer by loan review or could be simply a solicitation of additional information. In either event, it is essential that the post-loan review effort be effective and productive. It should not be merely a review-for-review's sake. All information developed during the process, including the loan officer's required response to the reviewer's inquiries, should be made a part of the borrower's credit file.

Exception-loan review—warning signals

The realization that storm warnings are being displayed creates another natural opportunity to conduct a review of the credits affected. The initiation of a specific loan review effort, as prompted by the presence of one or more exceptions or symptoms indicative of potential trouble, is basic to any loan review function. The scope of the review should be governed by the seriousness of the particular situation. If the banker is alert to the various warning signals of problems as soon as they become visible, prompt action can be taken in most instances. This action will tend to protect both the bank and its borrower from unnecessary loss or serious injury.

The warning signals presented here may not form an exhaustive list of the potential tipoffs that might set in motion a cursory or complete examination of a particular credit. However, they do represent a number of events that might well point to a deteriorating loan situation. If these and possibly others are used by the loan review section to determine the timeliness of a loan review, it is possible that the result will be the early recognition of a credit problem and at a point where there will still be time to take corrective and protective action.

Declining demand deposit balances and overdrafts

Loan review should monitor the activity and trends on the demand deposit accounts maintained by the bank's borrowing customer. Particular emphasis should be given to the size, frequency, and duration of account overdrafts.

The signal flashed to the banker by unusual demand deposit activity could merely reflect some type of justifiable fluctuation such as changes associated with the customer's normal payment and collection cycle. On the other hand, it is possible that the first sign of a developing or existing credit problem will be reflected by a general decline in the level of account balances. Frequent overdrafts or checks drawn against nonsufficient or uncollected funds are an even stronger signal of impending trouble. At the very minimum, these signals should prompt an inquiry if not a review.

Loan delinquencies

If the borrower develops a habit of being past due on debt obligations to the bank, the lender should assume that a credit problem exists and should not pass this situation off as insignificant. The failure of a borrower to pay a note when it is due reflects an obvious sign of a problem or potential problem.

Using loan delinquencies as a means of monitoring credit quality and of initiating an exception-loan review is particularly useful on retail loans, such as those found in the real estate, installment, and bank card portfolios. Because of the nature of these loans, they often do not receive the same attention from loan review that is normally accorded to short- and intermediate-term commercial loans. Consequently, delinquencies can be a primary means of identifying retail loan problems in the early stages.

In this regard, particular attention should be given to first and second payment delinquencies on these retail credits because that occurrence might well reflect the fact that a bad loan has been put on the books. In an effort to determine the validity of this possibility, the bank's recent consumer loan losses should be reviewed and the ones which were either first or second payment defaults established. You might be surprised to find the answer to be better than 50%.

Noncompliance with terms or loan agreements

Unexpected and excessive loan renewals and partial curtailments on commercial credits and excessive extensions on installment, real estate, and commercial term loan obligations are indications of problematic situations. The same is true for unexpected requests for new and additional credit considerations. These events should be monitored closely and an investigation begun when the situation appears to be reaching a serious level.

It is a fundamental banking principle that all extensions of credit have a clear-cut repayment agreement, one that is satisfactory to the bank and that is consistent with the borrower's ability to pay. Once that agreement has been set, any deviations should be promptly investigated and the reason for the exception clearly identified. If the reason for the nonpayment or partial payment is valid and acceptable, an alternative repayment program can be developed. However, if the exception does not trigger a review, the bank could find itself with a notable crop of illiquid, evergreen credits.

If the bank develops a loan agreement in connection with a particular extension of credit, whether a term loan or some other type of debt arrangement, it is essential to monitor that credit during its carrying time. The borrower's activities and financial progress, or lack thereof, should be watched closely to ensure that the customer adheres to the terms and covenants of that agreement.

Since the guidelines and controls that make up the loan agreement were originally thought to be important to protect the ultimate repayment and quality of the credit, it follows that the bank must insist on compliance with those terms. Any exceptions or deviations that might occur without the bank's knowledge and permission should be promptly reviewed to determine if the original repayment understanding is in jeopardy or the quality of the credit impaired.

Delayed financial statements and statement analysis

The failure of a bank's borrowing customer to submit current financial information to the bank, either when due under a loan agreement or when specifically requested, is a warning signal. The delay could reflect the customer's reluctance to provide the bank with unfavorable financial results or an inability to generate and package a financial report. Both of these reasons provide cause for concern, but whatever the reason, the signal deserves an inquiry by the loan officer or by loan review.

Once a financial statement is received on a borrower, it is not sufficient to simply log it in, after a casual review, and bury it in the credit file. The business statement should be spread and all statements, including personal statements, examined thoroughly. Such examination is a means of identifying any adverse trends or, if a loan agreement exists, any defaults under the provisions of the agreement.

The detailed review and analysis of financial statements are essential if the bank is to have adequate knowledge of the borrower and his financial condition. Without that degree of understanding, how could the bank intelligently judge the appropriateness of the customer's needs or measure the borrower's capacity to service current and future debt obligations?

Economic and competitive factors

Unlike the warning signals available for internal monitoring, the economic and competitive factors that might affect a borrowing relationship are external in nature. Nevertheless, they can be just as reliable in identifying the early signs of financial difficulties. Consequently, the bank must continuously survey the national and local economy and the industrial activities within its market area to discover the positive or negative implications that they might have on any or all of its borrowing customers.

A general downturn in the economy will affect most borrowers, some more severely than others. In addition to a general recessionary cycle, a particular industry could be subjected to adverse conditions for a multitude of reasons.

If competitors of the bank's customer offer new products in the market, withdraw product lines or services, experience rapid growth in volume and profits, or experience untoward difficulties in these areas, the bank should know. These conditions should be compared to the experience of the bank's customer. The objective is to identify any positive or negative implications or conclusions that might be drawn from such an analysis.

The bank must be continually alert to these external factors, noting changes within the economy and specific industries and closely watching the activities of all segments of the market. There may be clues or clear signals visible to those who will just look, ones that could prompt a loan review and prevent a loan loss.

Miscellaneous warning signals

There are a number of other indicators or warning signals that might prompt an inquiry or review of a given credit situation, depending on the circumstances at hand. As with the others noted previously, they do not necessarily and automatically reflect detrimentally on the related credit. One item by itself may be inconclusive. However, a combination of the following symptoms may indicate a problem loan, either now or down the road, and be sufficient evidence to justify at least an exploratory review:*

(1) The death, illness, or unexpected exit of key management personnel.

(2) Marital difficulties of key management personnel.

(3) Unusual or irresponsible behavior by management.

(4) Loss of key sources of revenue or sources of supply.

(5) Substantial growth that strains both production and managerial capacity.

(6) Difficulties in labor relations.

(7) Deteriorating relations with trade suppliers.

(8) Unexpected appearances of other lenders, particularly secured ones.

(9) Unusual and frequent inquiries from other creditors.

(10) Notice of cancellation of insurance.

(11) Notice of lawsuits, tax liens, or other legal actions brought against the borrower.

(12) Notice of security interest being filed against the borrower by other creditors.

(13) The occurrence of natural disasters that would adversely affect the borrower.

(14) The loss of communication or rapport with the borrower.

(15) An overindulgent lifestyle on the part of key personnel.

Summary

Any loan review system, regardless of how simple or how complicated, can be structured to take advantage of the natural points of loan preview and review. One of these natural opportunities is prior to loan approval, during the

---

* Many of these symptoms were taken from material used in Robert Morris Associate's Loan Quality Control Workshop.

decision-making process. Another is at the inception of the loan or immediately after a new loan has been approved or advanced. The third opportunity arises after the loan is on the books, and it is prompted by the occurrence of some event or the recognition of an "exception."

These loan review opportunities represent a means of evaluating and monitoring new credits, or at least new commitments over a specified amount, prior to and after approval. These review techniques allow the banker to judge the quality and liquidity of those credits in a timely manner.

The reviewer examines the loan documentation, the proposed repayment program and the source of repayment, the purpose of the credit, the loan pricing, collateral, and the overall financial conditions of the borrower. All of this is done in an effort to determine conformance with policy and the probability of the timely repayment of the obligation in accordance with the prescribed terms. The early detection of problems will allow for the prompt initiation of corrective measures. The principal motive behind these timely review techniques is clear—identify and correct credit problems early, before it is too late.

Be opportunistic—don't miss those natural loan review opportunities.   □

Business Ethics and Codes of Conduct

by Charles B. Jarrett, Jr.

How does a bank maintain high ethical standards at a time when such standards appear to be highly perishable commodities? Charles Jarrett recommends a written code of conduct as one of the most important ways a bank can preserve (and deserve) its reputation for honesty.

The problem of business ethics is not new. It has long been with us. You need only refer to the Old Testament Book of Deuteronomy where we are cautioned against the charging of usurious rates. Or refer to the New Testament for stories about the money changers in the Temple. Recall Shakespeare's treatment of the money lender Shylock in *The Merchant of Venice* and what that name has come to mean.

In our own time, we have seen the corporate disclosure of improper payments made in the Watergate era. There have been many examples of directors and officers who have been derelict in their duties or, even worse, who have acted in their own self-interest at the expense of their corporation.

Finally, the recent trials and tribulations of Bert Lance have amply demonstrated the results when one's conduct is attacked. The Lance affair is of particular interest to bankers since Mr. Lance's problems arose in the overdraft

---

This article is based on remarks made by the author at the Pennsylvania Bankers Association Lending Officer Institute on December 7, 1977.

and lending areas. This concern over business practices, rightly or wrongly, has given rise to a multiplicity of government agencies whose enforcement activities are geared to ensuring that the ''corporate bad guys'' are exposed and properly chastised. It seems that hardly a day goes by without an investigation by the Securities and Exchange Commission, the Federal Trade Commission, the Federal Reserve, the Comptroller, the Federal Deposit Insurance Corporation, or by multiple state agencies.

New punishments: the passions of our times

How do the courts and the regulators look at the situation? Let me cite a few examples of the great extremes to which some have gone in the recent past to act against companies and individuals who have been found in default:

Item: A manager of a food processing plant in California received a suspended six-month sentence and summary probation after being cited by state food and drug officials for unsanitary conditions at his plant.

Item: A company in Minneapolis was ordered by a Federal judge to select one of its officers to serve a 30-day jail term after the judge ruled that odors coming from its plant did not meet the city's air pollution standards. The order was later rescinded but only on the technicality that none of the officers were individually indicted.

Item: The IRS has admitted to conducting an investigation of 30 major corporations for possible tax frauds based upon unlawful political contributions already disclosed.

Item: The SEC has taken, and sustained in at least one instance, the position that a questionable payment, regardless of amount, is material and must be disclosed in proxy material. In one other instance, the SEC has required a company to appoint an entirely new board of directors, the majority of whom were independent of the company, and to form specified committees of that board.

By imposing or attempting to impose punishments never used before, these actions reflect the passions of our times—that merely keeping up with laws and regulations is not enough.

Take, for instance, a recent decision by the Supreme Court of Oregon. It not only recognized that a corporation could recover profits gained by an officer at the corporation's expense, but it also held that the corporate officer who engaged in such activities was not entitled to any compensation during the period of his wrongdoing. The officer in question was ordered to return to the company over $225,000 in salary which had been paid to him.

The "eleven questions" of the IRS

Recall, too, if you will, the famous (or infamous) "eleven questions" of the IRS promulgated to over 1,200 business corporations, including several banks. These questions dealt with the donating, lending, or otherwise providing of corporate funds for bribes, kickbacks, or political contributions and the maintenance of accounts not reflected on the corporation books or in its financial statements.

The final question was a real winner: "Which other present or former corporate officers, directors, employees, or other persons acting on behalf of the corporation may have knowledge concerning any of the above areas?" How can you answer such a question in the absence of carefully constructed and uniformly applied policies and procedures?

"Sweetheart deals"

Furthermore, the concern is not just for matters which might involve actual violations of laws. The problem may be more acute in those many opportunities we have to take advantage of a relationship or specific knowledge not generally available. There was, for instance, a series of articles in the *Washington Post* dealing with so-called "sweetheart deals" by bankers with other bankers or some of their favored customers—special fees, reduced rates, or free services and the like—nothing necessarily illegal per se, but the sort of thing that can tarnish an image or destroy a reputation or bring about even more burdensome regulation.

Most valued asset: integrity

A financial institution's reputation for integrity is its most valued asset and is largely determined by the conduct of its employees. Each employee must manage his or her own affairs and those of the institution to avoid any situation that might lead to even a suspicion of a conflict of interest.

In this context, it is appropriate to cite the statement of A. W. Clausen, president and chief executive officer of The Bank of America. In announcing a corporate code for full and honest disclosure, he said, "Integrity is not some impractical notion dreamed up by naive do-gooders. Out integrity is the foundation for, the very basis of, our ability to do business. If the market economy ever goes under, our favorite villains—socialists, economists, and government regulators—won't be to blame. We will."[1]

---

[1] *Coopers & Lybrand Newsletter,* April 1977, page 5.

Or as that delightful comic strip character Pogo once said, "We have met the enemy, and they is us."

In a similar vein is the statement of Dr. Gregory H. Adamian, president of Bentley College, Waltham, Massachusetts. While addressing the school's First Annual Conference on Business Ethics, he commented, "Our nation's leaders realize that a healthy ethical climate affects the quality of life in our society. In my judgment, the viability of the uniquely American economic system as we know and appreciate it demands that success in business be achieved by ethical decision-making, *and that profits and ethics are compatible*." (Emphasis added.)[2]

Incidentally, the other speakers at the Bentley Conference were all leaders from the worlds of business, education, politics, and public affairs and diverse in their interests and backgrounds. They almost universally acknowledged the low state to which business has fallen in the eyes of the general public and the need for high ethical corporate standards to reverse this trend.

Need for business to clean up its act

I think that what has been said so far should establish the need for business to set its house in order, to clean up its act, so to speak, and to ensure that its affairs are conducted in a proper manner. Banks are no exception. James H. Higgins, chairman and chief executive officer of my bank, echoed this thought in a letter to a committee of his directors in March 1976: "The banking industry as a whole is very much in the center of public attention these days, and congressional spokesmen in particular are addressing themselves to problems—real or alleged—in the banking industry and the regulatory structure of banking."

We are indeed under the gun. It is incumbent upon us to run our business in a manner above reproach and to be good stewards of the trust placed in us.

Three alternatives for business

What are the courses open to us to achieve this high purpose? I suppose some of us could continue to "play the game"—to look upon our business activities as some sort of a grown-up version of cops and robbers. The underlying theory of this "game" is to get away with as much as we possibly can—to bend the rules to the fullest, to stretch the limits as far as possible.

---

[2] *Reports on Proceedings, The First Annual Conference on Business Ethics, Bentley College,* March 1977, frontispiece.

End of stonewalling days

People do operate in this manner, but I submit that the tenor of the times will not permit this kind of attitude or activity to continue very long. It is precisely this sort of reaction which has created much of the unfavorable business climate existing today. The days of "stonewalling it" are over, and, at least in my opinion, they are not much lamented. To continue to pursue this sort of totally unethical business practice will be, as noted by Mr. Clausen, the real cause of our demise.

The ostrich alternative

The second alternative is to do nothing—to take the position that there are laws on the books and so long as we obey them we need do no more. I suggest this is akin to the ostrich's sticking its head into the sand, hoping the real world will go away. There must be more. Internal self-policing is required and in the long run will be more successful and effective than anything laws and regulations can accomplish.

I also suggest that the absence of self-policing will have the long range effect of more laws, more regulation. For example, in the neighborhood of 250 American companies, including several banks, have notified government regulatory agencies of illegal or questionable payments in the U.S. or abroad. These disclosures have brought increasing demands for legislative and regulatory action and have resulted in new SEC proposals for highly detailed disclosures of corporate practices in many areas.

Notes Leonard A. Wood, executive vice president of the American Institute of Public Opinion (the Gallup Organization): "'An indication of this can be seen in a general public survey conducted for *Newsweek* in February [1977]. In this survey,' said Wood, 'those interviewed were asked what groups they thought would gain influence in the Carter Administration and which would lose influence. The groups most often mentioned as losing influence were lobbyists and business corporations.' Despite this, Wood said that 'public sentiment for more controls on business can be expected to continue, if not increase.'"[3]

Closer to home, the banking industry is facing the prospect of considerable new legislation at least partially as a reaction to the Lance affair. The bills under consideration are long and complex and include similar but stricter provisions to many of those in the Financial Institutions Supervisory Bill (S. 71) introduced by Senator Proxmire. Of particular interest to bankers are the severe limitations on "insider" loans involving directors, officers, 5% sharehol-

---

[3] Ibid. p. 5.

ders and all their companies, political committees, and family members: 5% of capital accounts per borrower and a 50% aggregate limit on all insiders, their affiliated companies, political committees, and family members. These limitations could have a devastating effect on a bank with a large number of outside directors who, or whose companies, are large borrowers.

There are many other equally restrictive and burdensome features. While it appears no action is imminent, these proposals reflect a strong segment of congressional thought. We cannot, in view of these sorts of responses to business and banking activities, take the position that mere compliance with existing law is enough. We must settle our own affairs internally to avoid further restrictive measures.

In short, we may wait for governmental action, making specific acts unlawful and perhaps restricting legitimate business activity, or we can conduct our own investigations and monitor our own activities.

Preventive measures

Our third and more viable alternative, then, seems to be the establishment of preventative measures. These would include a statement of corporate policy, a heightening of management awareness, internal controls, and internal audit. All of these are very important, but I would like more to deal particularly with the statement of corporate policy—a code of conduct, if you will.

I recently attended a conference of attorneys dealing with the question of directors' duties, responsibilities, and liabilities. Almost without exception, the panelists agreed that a cornerstone of any corporate endeavor in this area was the formulation and implementation of a policy statement. Such a statement should set forth a high ethical standard, which, among other things, would protect the corporation from claims by employees or agents that they did not know what the standards were or that they even existed.

In general terms, the statement of policy should do three things:

(1) Establish criteria for standards of business ethics.

(2) Define and monitor conflicts of interest.

(3) Provide for a system of compliance, including the control and reporting of fraudulent acts to the proper persons.

Who drafts the code

Before going into the details of these three areas, we should respond to the question, "Who is going to do it?" Obviously, no code is going to be very effective without the full support of the top management of the bank. The chief executive officer must actively favor it and give unlimited support to those working on the code.

He cannot write it himself; he has neither the time nor, in many instances, the expertise to deal with many of the technical and legal points which are covered. However, the CEO must endorse the finished product and let the world know in no uncertain terms that it has his full and complete blessing.

The actual mechanics of drafting a corporate code are best left to a group of senior management people: the bank's legal counsel, chief financial officer, and chief personnel officer. Of course, considerable data are required from many, many other areas including lending, credit policy, operations, trust, etc. But it is these three, and particularly legal counsel, who are best able to see the code from an overall corporate point of view. They are in the best position to know what the law requires or permits, what are the applicable financial and accounting principles, what are the personnel considerations that must be taken into account, and how we can blend all this into a viable, workable program.

Guidelines for preparing the code

There are a lot of examples of codes available. Many banks have long had statements covering some phases of their operations. Today, many more are expanding these into full-blown codes covering all aspects of the banking world. BAI has prepared and circulated to all its members *Guides for Management on Bank Business Ethics and Conflicts of Interest*. This is not a rigid document telling the bank exactly how it should be. Rather it sets forth as guides various ways of dealing with the many problems.

As stated in the foreword to that booklet, "Recognizing that banks should set their own standards of conduct based on their particular values, beliefs, and public obligations, the institution has made no attempt to set forth a definitive code or policy for the industry. Instead, its objective is to provide a guide of sample written statements of policies now in effect in many banks throughout the United States."[4]

I had the privilege and pleasure of serving on the BAI task force that drafted those guides, and they are simply that—statements or compilations of various ways in which problems of business ethics and conflicts of interest may be treated. None of us can dictate to all banks what should or should not be in their code. But we can offer suggestions and guidelines, and we can point out areas of real concern. With that in mind, let's turn to some of the specifics that should be covered in a policy statement.

---

[4] Bank Administration Institute, *Bank Business Ethics and Conflicts of Interest*, June 1977, page vii.

Main points to cover: business ethics

As I noted earlier, the first thing is establishing criteria for ethical standards. What is included will vary from bank to bank, but there are some specific areas which seem indispensible.

Privileged information

First, the code should state that information about a customer is privileged and must be held in the strictest confidence. It should be used for corporate purposes only and under no circumstances for personal gain. Misuse of customer confidential information could have a material adverse effect on the customer, subjecting the bank to liability for damages.

Similarly, information about the bank itself should not be released unless it is published in reports to shareholders or otherwise made available to the public. Any questions concerning disclosure should be approved by legal counsel and the chief financial officer. Furthermore, the use of confidential information quite often is subject to Federal or state securities laws and could result in severe penalties for misuse.

Gifts

Next, the area of gifts to or from customers, suppliers, or public officials should be carefully scrutinized. The policy should emphasize the necessity for discretion and common sense. Obviously, gifts of a nominal value on special occasions or legitimate entertainment for proper business purposes are perfectly all right. But they should not be of such value or frequency so as to be subject to interpretation as a gratuity for doing business with the bank.

The same restrictions would apply to accepting a legacy by way of a will. There are, of course, exceptions, such as a gift or legacy based upon a family relationship. Remember, too, it is a crime under Federal statutes for any employee of a federally-insured bank to require or accept any gift or commission for granting an extension of credit.

Limitations on political activity

Third, the policy statement should also set forth clearly and precisely the limitations on political activity. We all know it is illegal under U.S. law and many state laws to use corporate funds for campaign contributions or other political purposes. But what constitutes "political activity," and what constitutes "corporate funds?" Questions concerning employees' time, use of office equipment, advertising, and so forth must be carefully considered and precisely answered. The policy of the bank on granting leaves of absence for political purposes should be spelled out, as well as its attitude on political action committees.

The statement should make it clear that no attempt to circumvent the law will be condoned, and even those activities legally permissible will be carefully delineated. This whole area of political activity has been one of the major bones of contention and must be given utmost consideration.

Loans to officers, directors, and employees

Of equal importance is the next area: loans to officers, directors, and employees and rates of interest charged for such loans. Subject to the limitations imposed by regulation on the amounts which a bank may lend to its executive officers, there really is no restriction on loans to or rates charged employees. Nevertheless, the bank should have in place a policy applying uniform standards on loans to *all* officers and employees as to amount, rate, and credit considerations.

Recognizing that special rates may be given as a part of overall employee benefits, those special rates must be the same for all employees. Similar criteria should be established for loans to directors and to companies they head. Under no circumstances should directors participate in decisions on loans to them or to their companies. Such loans should carry an interest rate equal to comparable credit risks.

Separation of trust and commercial departments

Finally, of paramount importance in any statement is the necessity for separation of the trust and commercial departments. It is not sufficient to say that a "Chinese wall" exists. It must be emphasized that the credit and related information available to lending officers not be given to trust personnel who are making investment decisions. Each group must be responsible for its own decisions arrived at independently.

The code must make it clear that a bank acting in a fiduciary capacity administers trust assets *solely* in the best interests of the beneficiaries. This policy requires a higher standard and cannot be colored by a divided loyalty.

Other considerations

There are many more areas which are properly included in a statement of business ethics. Among them are charitable contributions, indemnification of directors and officers, reciprocity with other financial institutions, advertising and public relations, employment of relatives, and community responsibilities. Each of these is to be considered, and, once again, each institution must decide for itself what is necessary in view of its own activities, goals, and community situation.

Main points to cover: conflicts of interest

Leaving the area of business ethics, let's turn to the second major area of our code, conflicts of interest. There are again innumerable topics which can be covered, but I shall limit myself to some of the more important and obvious ones. These include outside interests and personal investments, business opportunities of the bank, referral of customers to attorneys, accountants and the like, borrowing from customers, and purchase of assets from the bank.

Outside interests and personal investments

Officers and employees can and should have outside interests, but none which would conflict with the interests of the bank or its customers. There is nothing wrong with a bank employee serving as a director of another company or having a financial interest in a family business. But that relationship must be disclosed, and such employee should not represent that company in its dealings with the bank. Certainly, employees should not engage in activities which are in competition with the bank.

Similarly, investments by an employee should be disclosed if they are in an entity which is a customer, borrower, supplier, or competitor of the bank. An employee cannot make an investment in a security under circumstances which would indicate reliance on information obtained in the course of his or her employment and which is not generally known or available. In the course of employment, we often learn of business opportunities offered to the bank. It must be absolutely clear that the employee cannot take advantage of such knowledge for his or her own benefit.

Referral of customers to outside experts

Very often bank employees are asked to render legal or tax advice or to refer a customer to attorneys, tax experts, accountants, stockbrokers, or real estate agents. The law limits the bank in these kinds of services it can provide for a customer, but it does permit the bank to refer a customer to experts in these various fields. However, the bank's code should provide that customers be furnished with a list of several persons to avoid the appearance of influencing recommendations made by bank employees.

Borrowing from customers

Another point—under no circumstances should an employee borrow from a customer of the bank unless that customer is a recognized lending institution or a business concern offering credit sales to the public generally, such as a department store or an oil company. Needless to say, any such authorized borrowing must be on the same terms and conditions as offered to all customers of that lender. In a similar vein, there must be strict limitations on the sale to or purchase from the bank of assets. Such sales can be only at a public auction or sale or pursuant to court approval.

The list goes on. But the essence is that the bank must determine those areas of employee activity which could present the possibility of conflict or pressure on an employee in a manner adverse to the high performance of his or her duties. The code must set forth these areas of conflict and clearly and concisely state the bank's position and policies.

Implementation of the code

Finally, the third concern of the code is implementation. It does little good to have a code without provision for bank-wide dissemination and periodic review.

The code must contain in its provisions a satisfactory means of disclosure of any of the covered items. All persons who receive the code should be required not only to acknowledge receipt but to state they have read and understood its contents.

In addition, those in supervisory or particularly sensitive positions should be required to provide a periodic statement that they have reviewed the code with their staff and are unaware of any violations in their area of operations. The results of this review are submitted to the person or persons charged with its implementation: legal council, the bank's comptroller, the audit committee of the board, or perhaps some other person specifically designated to handle compliance matters.

It goes without saying that there should be an immediate investigation and resolution of any situation in which a manager cannot answer "no violation" or in which an actual violation has been uncovered. As in medicine, the best cure here is prevention, and people must realize not only the necessity for compliance but the severe results of compromising the standards.

What should these severe results be? The punishment should fit the crime, and if it is serious enough, one's job could be on the line. Of course, there are lesser sanctions, such as reprimand or suspension, but much of this must be left to the discretion of bank management. I don't think you have to be told what to do with an employee who refuses to cooperate or deliberately evades the provisions of the code.

What the code should not do

What are some things a code should *not* do? First of all, it should not create absolute, rigid, or dogmatic criteria. There must be room for some interpretation, some flexibility. A good code will be an everchanging document with revision and interpretation—if you will, much like the Constitution of the United States.

I would interject that while the code must be somewhat flexible and capable of interpretation, its enforcement cannot permit exception. It must set forth the clear understanding that the proscribed conduct simply will not be tolerated. We are at risk here, and we must be able to justify our conduct to our board of directors and shareholders—or suffer the consequences.

Second, the code should not bring about *1984* conditions or create a Gestapo. We do not want to impose an aura of such fear and trepidation that employees are too frightened to do their jobs. We cannot take away an individual's pride, initiative, or integrity or destroy his or her right to privacy. We are creating standards which we strive to meet. While there are penalties for failure, we must be realistic in our application.

Finally, the code should not be an excuse to withdraw from the world. It can't be the vehicle by which management washes its hands of any community or political involvement. As was stated by Jayne Baker Spain, a senior vice president of Gulf Oil Corporation (certainly a company much in the limelight in this area): "'Rather than shrinking from the political arena, as many would have us do, we will continue to speak out, openly and candidly, for those principles and policies that we think best for us, for our customers and shareholders, and the nation,' she said. 'And with equal vigor, we will speak out against those we judge to be harmful.'"[5]

Conclusion

One final question—will it work? I, for one, think so. I reject the theory that there are no ethics left in this country, that we are so diverse that there is no overall set of standards or sense of value. People, businessmen, and bankers want to do what is right. But what has been largely missing are concrete, specified standards needed in this complex world of ours.

A code will help fill this gap, but bear in mind it offers no panacea, no cure-all, no guarantee that all will be well with us and the world. But what it will do is show that we have set standards, that we are striving to cure our problems and to respond to our attackers and that we are prepared to act quickly in events of wrongdoing without the need for government or other outside supervision.

I recommend that each of you take the existing codes and guides available and review them for areas to be covered and for appropriate language. Consider the specific needs of your bank, charge the proper persons with creating and implementing the code, and have at it. ☐

---

[5] *Reports on Proceedings, The First Annual Conference on Business Ethics, Bentley College,* March 1977, p. 25.

VII. Aspects of International Lending

The criterion used in selecting articles for this section of the book was whether the subject was of central importance to the general practitioner of lending rather than of use to the specialist. This approach helped reduce the candidate articles to a manageable number. For additional insights, the reader should refer to *Offshore Lending by U.S. Commercial Banks,* the second edition of which was recently published jointly by RMA and the Bankers Association for Foreign Trade.*

Even though it was originally published in 1972, P. Henry Mueller's "Sighting In On International Lending" remains a relevant as well as articulate summary of the problems that can arise from incautious and uninformed participation in the international lending arena. He reviews major categories of borrowers, suggests methods of developing adequate information for proper credit judgment, and offers advice on loan structure and credit policy planning.

Nancy Seawahl has provided an industry resource with her bibliographical article, "Getting Started in International Lending—A Guide to Sources of Printed Information." Although there have been useful books printed since 1978 when Seawahl's article appeared in the *Journal* and new magazines and reports have been started since then, the major sources of information she identifies and reviews remain the important ones for today's bankers.

Once the appropriate, relevant data have been located, Christopher Korth's article, "Developing a Country-Risk Analysis System," suggests how they can be organized into a meaningful country analysis. He also discusses the preparation of a risk rating for a country and the establishment of lending limits.

Many banks make their first international loans in the form of placements with foreign banks. These lines continue to make up a significant portion of the international portfolio even after other relationships have been established. Thus, the article by Charles F. Mansfield, Jr., "An Approach to Evaluating Foreign Bank Credit Risk," is of particular relevance. It is the only article on lending to a specific borrower category included in this anthology.

The legal field moves rapidly, and it often moves especially rapidly with respect to international lending practices. Nevertheless, the article by C. Thorne Corse, "International Term Loan Agreements and Loan Syndications," has worn well enough to justify being included. Corse's comments, which include observations on such topics as choice of law, documentation, sovereign immunity, and syndication procedures, are particularly relevant for the regional bank which is participating in such agreements.

For information about the authors of the articles in Section VII, refer to the List of Contributors on page xi.

---

* F. John Mathis, ed., *Offshore Lending by U.S. Commercial Banks,* 2nd ed. (Philadelphia: Bankers' Association for Foreign Trade and Robert Morris Associates, 1981). Hardcover, $22.00.

Sighting in on International Lending

by P. Henry Mueller

WHAT YOU SEE IS WHAT YOU GET," goes a popular TV comic's line. Bankers, still smarting from 1970's loan losses, would add, "but what you don't see—or, better still, notice—is what gets you."

Sparked by the credit and monetary developments of the past two years, the problem of perception—what we see and what we don't[1]—has become the central theme of a soul search into standards of international lending by bankers around the world. Thoughts of Penn Central, Intrabank, and Rolls Royce—to mention a few—linger on.

So, too, does the reminder that the credit and financial world is increasingly orienting itself *supra*nationally. Wherever we are based, we are but part of one financial market; our own problem can easily translate into someone else's. As one observer has expressed it: "Financial sovereignty is becoming blurred."

Isn't this, then, a good time to pull up our socks and, perhaps, rethink lending policies? Little has been written on international lending and credit standards as such.

---

[1] Three particularly critical areas in international lending are: 1—country risk (market uncertainties as well as cross-currency and sovereign risks); 2—knowledge and understanding of the borrower by the lender; and 3—the extent of the borrower's sophistication in terms of financial management (e.g., planning, budgeting, forecasting).

Reprinted from Overseas Citibanker, Number 1, 1972.

Even as the literature is extended, individual experience and the development of an intuitive grasp of what makes sense and what doesn't will remain basic ingredients of successful practice.

Although the question of standards is usually discussed in a general, "broad-brush" way, the international credit market actually has five major components. Each involves credit extended by home offices, foreign branches, subsidiaries or affiliates of domestic banks in the form of U.S. dollars or other currencies. These categories, which contain an infinite variety of approaches, practices and criteria, include: 1) loans or placements (deposits) to foreign banks or to overseas branches of domestic banks; 2) loans to governments or to governmental entities; 3) loans to foreign branches, subsidiaries or affiliates of domestic companies under parent guarantee or other form of undertaking; 4) loans to foreign multinational companies; and 5) credit extension to local concerns, including unguaranteed loans to subsidiaries and affiliates of domestic or foreign multinational companies (by home offices or by foreign branches, subsidiaries or affiliates of domestic banks).

Caselettes on the problem of credit standards

In pursuing the question of standards, it may be useful to examine these types of loans more closely. I have introduced each category with a "caselette" based on an actual credit which—in the manner of an Aesop fable—illustrates one or more problems. While the credits are international, they also have domestic lending flavor. Following the "caselette" are the essentials germane to the category.

Loans or placements to foreign banks or to overseas branches of domestic banks.

> A New York banker was hustled from his plane by his local representative to visit a major foreign commercial bank, in follow-up of an approach made by this prospect for a credit facility. Luckily, despite his representative's high enthusiasm for the business potential, the New Yorker was able to ascertain the true state of affairs, later depicted in a leading newspaper: *"The Government is planning to reopen the bankrupt Banco [X] which closed its doors last June 30, leaving thousands of depositors and about 50 foreign banks holding worthless passbooks and commercial paper . . . banks in the United States would probably convert a portion of the defaulted loans they hold into stock of the reopened bank. Overall, however, the outlook for recovery on the losses was said to be 'grim,' . . . foreign lenders knew full well that Banco [X] was operating in a fast and loose manner. . . . "*

The message? Obtain and heed the facts; then exercise sound, independent credit judgment.

The growth of the Eurodollar market has given impetus to placements of deposits with other banks, and interest-differential banking has bred the feeling that so long as a spread can be made, the cost of money matters little. In a period of escalating interest rates, however, a squeeze sets in as more and more marginal lenders and borrowers become involved. Weak borrowers become unable to service debt, and weak lenders lack the ability to absorb more than normal credit or exchange losses. This often transmits direct or indirect strain of varying degrees to other market participants, as illustrated by the famous "Salad Oil Scandal"[2] of a few years ago and by the more recent collapse of Penn-Central with its ensuing shock waves.

The bank making a placement expects liquidity from its deposit and, for this liquidity to be real, the credit of the recipient bank must be beyond question. Yet bank figures typically are inadequate for analysis of this sort except on a broad comparative-ratio basis—e.g., positions can be "squared" for statement purposes. One encounters a variety of accounting practices and legal reporting requirements. Terms and definitions vary in meaning or broad general terms are used. "Reserve" accounts may hide sins or accomplishments. A financial statement is, after all, but a snapshot of the bank (or company for that matter) taken at a given point in time. If you doubt what little information bank figures typically disclose, look at any U.S. bank statement as if it were the sole ingredient for productive analysis.

While comparative-ratio analysis thus provides no definite answers in and by itself, it does help as an initial measure of liquidity and the use of debt, profitability and asset use. Such an analysis pinpoints areas to be probed in discussions with management, an essential requirement. Qualitative analysis is more essential in evaluating banks than in many industries, not only because figures *per se* are difficult to interpret, but because bank assets and liabilities shift character rapidly.

Judgment of a bank's management (its competence, integrity and reputation) and its liquidity consciousness (ability to meet demands for funds) are the key elements. Unlike a manufacturer who, even with poor management, can temporarily prosper from a good idea or invention in a rising market, the banker possesses little technological superiority. A bank's track record, its history and soundness of growth, its investment policies, access to discount facilities or other sources of liquidity, ownership, board reputation, and market influences are, of course, among other factors that must also be assayed if the analysis is to be valid. The variance of regulatory standards

---

[2] Anthony DeAngelis, president of the Allied Stock Vegetable Oil Refining Corp., speculated in vegetable oil futures contracts on a large scale during the early 1960s. His speculation was accomplished with $150 to $175 million of borrowed money, using the salad oil stored in his company's tanks in New Jersey as collateral for the loans. In 1963, DeAngelis' firm went bankrupt and the salad oil tanks were found empty. Commodity prices tumbled, an old-line Wall Street house collapsed and the reputation of a major American corporation which had guaranteed the existence of the salad oil was tarnished.

from country to country and their influence on the reliability of bank guarantees or other undertakings is another factor which should not be overlooked.

In some instances, a government or central bank may provide support (to a greater or lesser degree) because banking is regarded as an activity of public interest. For example, since 1934 no depositor in Italy has lost a lire, even though banks have been liquidated. In some countries—although not in Italy—where banks are agencies of, or owned by, the government, money costs may be lower than those incurred by the private banker. The latter then finds pricing difficult; government-oriented lenders, being instruments of policy rather than of profit, may lack the private banker's profit motivation.

Many countries are still underdeveloped when it comes to data, and the borrower holds the trump cards on giving out information. (All the more reason to be able to *lead* with solid questions which will "get the trumps out.") It could, in fact, be argued that standards for international lending should be more stringent than those observed domestically because there is, in more cases than not, less to go on and more uncertainty.

The best and really only source of qualitative information is regular, in-depth calling (once a year is not enough), plus accurately directed inquiry of competitors and others in the local market, i.e., what does the "Street" think? A network of personal contacts is a must, as these disclose a management's wisdom, its goals, and the policies and actions needed to attain them. But while it takes some sleuthing to develop information and follow the thread, the facts can usually be unraveled on a personal-contact basis if one knows how to go about getting them and the informant has confidence in the inquirer. Statement analysis is difficult without this additional insight.

The Bank of Sark[3] is a case in point, albeit extreme. As you may recall, the Bank of Sark wasn't a bank at all, although a supposedly audited financial statement showed assets of $72,500,001.39. An insurance company, other businesses—some well known —and presumably banks suffered losses.

---

[3] Documents from a "Bank of Sark" were used in a series of international swindles, involving two hundred fictitious or "shell" companies, which resulted in a loss of some $40 million for creditors. In one type of swindle, Bank of Sark paper was taken to a U.S. bank and cashed or used as collateral for a loan. The depositor would draw on his account during the three months it took for the Guernsey-based "bank" to bounce the check. Then the depositor would disappear. Another common "Bank of Sark" scheme involved insurance companies and mutual funds which were drawn up fat with "assets." These assets often consisted of stock shares in shell corporations, worthless mining shares, land of uncertain ownership and "millions" deposited in the Bank of Sark. Insurance policies and fund shares were then sold. The companies went out of business when the first sizable claims appeared.

A bank's financial statement is but the departure point for discussions which will lead to sound credit appraisal. The figures provide a useful source of profitable questions. Their value in this sense is all too often overlooked.

Loans to governments
or to governmental entities.

In 1954, fifteen U.S. Banks provided a central bank (then fiscal agent for its government) with a $200 million five-year term loan secured by gold lodged with the Federal Reserve Bank of New York. The purpose of the loan was to bolster the country's exchange position which had been drastically affected by sagging commodity prices. The nation, at the time, held about $270 million in gold as reserves, but was reluctant to dispose of it.

Hopes for export recoveries did not materialize and the payment schedule could not be met. This led to a series of refundings, terminating in a third refunding agreement of June 1961. When the initial payment under this final agreement was about to fall due and circumstances indicated another refunding in the offing, the lead bank prevailed upon the government to consider the sale of the gold to liquidate the loan, thereby saving an annual interest outlay of some $10 million in exchange, which the borrower could ill afford. The government took this advice, disposed of the gold and liquidated the loan.

The message? Structure loans to governments or their entities in such a way that they will survive the vagaries of political and economic change and still ensure repayment (obtaining gold as security is often not possible). Foster a working relationship with officials which engenders mutual respect.

Governments come and go, but borrowing resolutions and other durable supporting documentation, which will be honored regardless of change, are essential. This means not only legal validity of instruments but financial ability to abide by provisions. For instance, where does the jurisdiction of the loan agreement lie? If in the lender's country, he can attach assets if need be and generally take more fruitful action.

It is sounder practice to lend to a central bank or to an operating government entity that will have continuity—and hopefully cash flow—on its own than to a government *per se.* Preferably, loans should be made for specific projects or purposes that will generate cash for repayment (otherwise short maturities may be more desirable). This is not always possible, but as a minimum, credit should be extended to entities whose appropriations include debt-repayment capacity, budgeted and approved by the legislature or other valid authority.

It is desirable, when considering a specific loan proposal, to look at all exposure in the country and not to approve credits in a vacuum. There are additional factors to consider. Among them: reserves—gold, foreign exchange and SDR's; foreign debt schedule; the balance of payments position; government budget and cash flow; goods and services account, which includes the trade balance; IMF status, and IMF or other foreign credit available (when feasible, tie loans to IMF covenants and provide for repayment prior to IMF); and whether or not export or other forms of guarantee are involved. Then, too, the economies of developing nations, being more vulnerable to internal and external factors, tend to fluctuate more than those of developed countries. Thus, the examination should take into account the governmental plans and how these square with the systems and manpower available to carry them out.

Loans to foreign branches, subsidiaries or affiliates of domestic companies under parent guarantee or other form of undertaking.

> This "caselette," about guarantees, didn't involve an undertaking. It was a Cuban credit that resulted in a sizable charge-off. The feasibility of the project, an ore operation with a processing mill in the U.S., was unquestioned from both an operating and an economic viewpoint. The bank told itself that no successor to Batista would prevent ore shipments because they would be of no use on their own. Castro undid the assumption.

The message? Don't be half safe. There is no such thing as a sure thing. Don't put too much into one basket. There is no substitute for documented parent support in lending to a subsidiary, especially when the assets against which you lend are abroad.

Should it develop that a facility may stand or fall on the creditworthiness of the sponsor, lending under parent guarantee or other undertaking is the same as lending the parent directly. In the absence of a formal guarantee, repayment hinges on the moral fiber of the parent. Should the parent be unwilling or unable to honor the undertaking (possibly because the size of the credit in relation to the parent's net worth arouses fear of stockholder suit), the arrangement could prove tenuous.

To the extent possible, the loan should be structured to stand on its own so that resort to a guarantee or other form of sponsorship will be unnecessary. This means that the basic questions of purpose and method of repayment must be satisfactorily resolved. Loans usually are for working capital (and should be temporary) or for the acquisition of fixed assets. While many are based only on asset value, these should be discouraged. Working-capital loans should be self-liquidating, which means that the true worth of receivables and inventory must be known. Loans to acquire fixed assets should be based on realistic earnings projections which ensure that the borrower will generate sufficient overall cash flow to cover scheduled repayments. Term loans structured on the basis of future projections which are not consistent with historical performance should be avoided unless they are justified by extensive analysis.

As a by-product of the analysis which determines the structure of the loan, an assessment should be made of the likelihood of contingencies which would force a fall-back on the sponsorship. (You seldom keep a friend by calling on a guarantee.) This should be explicity covered during the negotiation, to avoid later surprises and embarrassments. Frank discussion at the outset obviates many a future argument. Lastly, a guarantee should preferably be set up so that it is effective without exhausting all other remedies.

Loans to foreign multinational companies.

A prized eastern hemisphere-based multinational client, long an industry leader, had been borrowing $1 million on a 90-day note basis for some years. One day an account officer, not involved in handling this particular account relationship and located across the world, chanced to hear from a company contact that the borrower might face a rocky road ahead. This was passed on to New York and, somewhat skeptically, the bank asked its eastern hemisphere branch to check it out. A customer call revealed the management team's eroding ability to develop new programs to meet tough new product competition. The branch asked for financial figures and, when these were not delivered as promised, the loan was called and repaid.

Five days later a newspaper story revealed that the company was indeed in trouble. While it should eventually surmount its difficulties, the remaining banks will be locked in for many years to come. The branch's timely escape obviated considerable anguish and expense.

The message? Stay on top of all accounts, even the so-called "blue chips"; check out unfavorable news promptly, no matter how improbable; be extremely wary of management which will not or cannot produce financial figures, also of executives who seem mired in past glories and cannot offer realistic plans, much less produce forecasts.

Credit extension to local concerns,
including unguaranteed loans to
subsidiaries and affiliates of domestic or foreign multinational companies by home
offices (or by foreign branches, subsidiaries or affiliates of domestic banks).

In XYZ country, the branch of a U.S. bank assumed a lead role in financing the imports, inventory and collections of a dealer that sold automobile and earthmoving equipment manufactured by two major corporations. Overdraft facilities were also extended. Despite sketchy financial statements and a minimum of informed discussion on financial matters, substantial deposit balances and dynamic business volume convinced the bank that all was well with the well-positioned client.

The bank realized too late that the company's growth was faster than it could comfortably digest. Financial planning was non-existent. Management was overcentralized, and the firm became overextended. Controls broke down on both inventory and collections.

The bank's controls were also lacking. The firm's import facilities were liquidated by overdrafts which also financed real-estate ventures. At the same time the manufacturers were extending substantial credit.

The result: a negotiated settlement with the U.S. bank and the two manufacturers holding a lot of paper. The bank's erstwhile client was in control of sizable pieces of unattachable real estate, but blessed few marketable pieces of the equipment that had been financed.

The message? Growth can grab you. Check the plans of growing companies against what can be ascertained from available figures and regular customer contact; tie facilities to identifiable and appropriate financial needs (avoid open-ended overdrafts); don't assume that manufacturers are monitoring closely—their profits on sales sometimes have a way of obscuring credit considerations, much as a bank's sizable balances may put it to sleep for too long.

From a credit standpoint, categories four and five are similar; they differ in scale and complexity. If, as is sometimes alleged, a double standard is applied in domestic and foreign lending, it is here that the issue comes into sharp focus.

Common anchor

It is generally accepted that in the U.S. availability of credit information and lending sophistication—such as the application of cash-flow lending techniques and use of capital markets—are further advanced than they are elsewhere. (Parenthetically, the latter may be more of a truism than the former—available information didn't tip anybody on a number of the names now being written off the books of many of our banks.) A basic difference between domestic and international lending is, of course, that political and cross-currency risks are key considerations in evaluating overseas risks. But, as long ago as 1922, an international banker pointed out: "There is no mystery about banking in the Orient or South America any more than there is about banking in the United States. The governing principles are the same and there should, generally speaking, be but slight variance in practice." In other words, if one applies sound principles to international credits, and takes care to ask the same questions he would ask domestically, sifting out the "easy" answers, he will have little to worry about in his overseas loan portfolio.

Time-tested principles and standards form the template to be placed against any credit. It is when the credit officer finds it necessary to deviate that the issue of quality of domestic vs. foreign lending standards emerges. The emphasis he gives to the various elements of the proposal at hand, which exist not in isolation but only as part of the whole, is the critical area of his judgment—the point at which the right choice must be made among alternatives. The analysis and weighing of criteria, then, not the standards or the approach, are the variables which alter with circumstances. Volkswagen is subject to differing safety requirements in some sixty countries, yet these do not alter the company's standards of engineering or quality control.

Sound principles and standards could be likened to an anchor from which a boat swings with wind and tide. While its position shifts in response to changing circumstances, the boat never breaks its tie with the ground tackle.

For instance, current ratios, inventory vs. sales ratios and other industry benchmarks which are applied in the U.S. may well be counter productive when applied rigidly elsewhere (in a highly inflationary economy, inventory buildup, particularly of imported raw materials, may be prudent). Also, a credit decision may be colored by having a presence (e.g., branch) in the country. Or, a parent company may prefer to minimize country exposure by leveraging its subsidiaries; under these circumstances, a letter of support or other understanding may suffice in lieu of a guarantee. In short, credit is behavioral in nature, not mechanistic, and can't be regarded as a geometric exercise.

Eurodollar practices

One of the significant developments of recent years has been the internationalization of business and banking. We find ourselves increasingly outward-looking, taking a world view. The imposition of capital controls such as OFDI (the Office of Foreign Direct Investment) regulations and the Voluntary Foreign Credit Restraint Program in the U.S. encouraged the use of the Eurodollar which, financially at least, has unified the free world. It has overridden the parochialism of national markets, yielding what has often seemed to be a limitless ocean of funds to be loaned at a spread—developments which "are both welcome and worrisome," according to J. L. Robertson, Vice Chairman of the Federal Reserve Board of Governors.

A glance at the practices which have developed in the Eurodollar market is a good jumping off place for a closer examination of standards. The June 28th issue of *Barron's,* in reporting the collapse of Fribgest,[4] states:

---

[4] Societe Continentale de Gestion Financiere S. A. (Fribgest) was a Lausanne-based company which bought mortgages and invested in real estate, financing with three- to six-month loans in the Eurodollar market. When Eurodollar interest rates soared in 1970, the cost of servicing the debts exceeded the income from the company's investments. To refinance these debts, Fribgest took on additional short-term loans and by mid-1971 95% of its borrowings were well under twelve months while 80% of its investments were tied up. The company had commitments of over $60 million when paid-up capital was only $1.4 million. Yet Fribgest enjoyed unquestioned lines of credit at Eurodollar banks, the only security required was mention of its parents—Continental Grain Company of New York (44%) and Banque de l'Indochine (39%). When the crunch came, the parents disavowed Fribgest, leaving Eurodollar creditors with $68 million in loan losses.

The harsh light of inquiry confirms that this (the Eurodollar market) is a very different animal from any domestic credit market. In it there are no normal banker-customer relationships. Credit is traded wholesale, in $100,000 and $1 million lots, over the telex and telephone. There are no security, no collateral, no mortgages, no explicit guarantees. There is scant consideration for underlying assets. There is only trust, based on names. Significantly, one bank officer who told *Barron's* he had lent Fribgest several million dollars because of its parents' names, thought that the latter was called Colonial Grain and didn't know that Fribgest never had been listed by Indochine as a subsidiary.

This free-and-easy atmosphere helps explain why the Eurodollar market has mushroomed while Western economies have suffered a downtick. Many banks in fact, have been trading too feverishly, which is why they were caught lending to Fribgest. They have accepted all the Eurodollar deposits they can, without knowing what they will do with them. Once stocked up, these institutions phone and telex all over Europe, looking for turns of as little as one-quarter or even three-sixteenths of a point. Bank treasurers who find they are bulging with Eurodollars take unconsidered risks, usually via a money broker, just to put their money to work. One of Fribgest's last loans of $1.25 million, was taken from a bank officer who had been in Europe less than two weeks, who had never heard of Fribgest but had been told the money broker was "okay."

Lack of normal prudence is shown by the fact that, as Fribgest sank deeper and deeper into trouble this year, it began offering one point and even 1¼% over the market rate without arousing bankers' suspicions.

For credit officers accustomed to practicing "normal prudence," bandwagon psychology is frightening: the thought of banker/customer relationships, so key to evaluation, being nonexistent and the perversion of commercial banking to a brokering or commission merchant operation; failure to relate debt repayment to ability to service; betting on the opinion of others, or a "sure thing"; the lack of factual analysis because of the misapprehension that in a wholesale market all risks, especially big names, are of prime stature; the "take it or leave it" technique of forming syndicates.

Seemingly, lending in the Eurodollar market has developed a subculture among lenders hungry enough to ignore prudent credit practice. But following fads in lending can sometimes lead to trouble. Actually, the customers that participate in the Eurodollar market should be stronger and better financed than others.

In lending to foreign multinational companies, it should be possible, through direct involvement and analysis, to develop knowledge sufficient not to compromise acceptable lending standards as we know them domestically. Short of this, much is left to conjecture and the lending "opportunity" might better be passed by.

Role of the loan officer

From the viewpoint of maintaining acceptable credit standards, the most difficult part is played by the lending officer of a foreign branch, subsidiary or affiliate of a domestic bank or a domestic-based department of a bank ambitious enough to lend to enterprises of various sizes overseas, to subsidiaries and affiliates of domestic or foreign companies on an unguaranteed or otherwise unsponsored basis, and to public or state-controlled companies. He must compete with banks that have been on the scene for generations and which traditionally have been prepared to extend credit on limited information and to lend against a name and/or assets rather than on a self-liquidating or on an amortized cash-flow basis. He may also find himself plagued by an environment of efficient industry but inefficient bureaucracy.

Generalizations can be wrong on a case-by-case basis, but here are the three virtually universal categories of borrowing the lending officer encounters:

1. The "one-man show." Long on production and marketing skills rather than on financial management and planning, he tends to borrow short term on his reputation, personal guarantee or pledge of assets.

2. The important family-group company. The family seldom recognizes the need for professional management. Secrecy in financial data prevails. Borrowings are usually short term based on "name" and on the "gut feel" of the lender. There is a tendency for borrowers in this group to rest on past glories. There is also a particular inability (or unwillingness because of possible ownership dilution) to raise new capital.

3. The large listed companies. Considered prime, they borrow on financial standing that is based on published reports of varying degrees of quality. They tend to operate on a perpetual credit-line basis. Facilities may go on for years, "good until canceled." Multiple (ten, twenty, thirty perhaps) line banks are used and sometimes played off against each other. Terms may be dictated to small banks. Medium-term borrowings are also used. Local banks frequently control large blocks of stock, receive the dividends and, figuratively speaking, act as mother and father.

In varying degrees, these categories share certain characteristics: an information gap, lack of financial planning, high leverage, borrowing short for long-term purposes and lack of a meaningful capital market.

Domestic banks often may not be an important influence in an overseas marketplace. Perhaps neither their size nor their lending capacities enable them to dominate the market or to place themselves in a position to be a "necessary lender." In these cases it is not easy for the bank to impose its own credit standards. Nonetheless, the impact of financial reversals of several old line names, the influence of American subsidiaries on accounting practice, the discipline of good input required by computer credit analysis and the growing need for money which, in turn, demands more in the way of financial information, are serving to upgrade credit standards. The art of concealing figures is on the decline (even the most secretive company treasurers find it impossible to hide a trend over any period of time).

Under these circumstances, the credit officer must decide which standards are his "anchor"—and hence immutable—and which standards he can adapt to his lending environment. *The two elements that must always be the "anchor" are: (1) sufficient facts about the borrower and (2) a self-liquidating or cash flow approach to repayment (with ample asset protection) as opposed to "name" or "hock shop" lending.* These largely determine success in extending credit anywhere, and they should be the targets of credit strategy. Several factors remain: competitive practices; differing term-loan patterns; environmental factors such as the economic and political climate (where does the borrower stand if the opposition wins?); cross-currency and sovereign risk exposures, exchange controls, devaluation or revaluation threats, *inter alia.* Some of these permit greater flexibility than others.

Faced with varying circumstances, the credit officer who rigorously applies himself to getting the facts, familiarizing himself with the economic environment and the institutions that produce the figures, and identifying the cash flow required for repayment—and this does require considerable effort and ingenuity—can intelligently adjust to market practice in such things as permitting overdrafts, lending on a longer basis than is generally done elsewhere and adapting to other environmental factors. His analysis and weighing of factors may vary from what he is accustomed to domestically but, with skill, he can always maintain standards at an acceptable level. Finally, profits are the acid test for, as all credit men know, the best clue to good management is the bottom line.

Developing data

Samuel Butler's comment about life being the art of drawing sufficient conclusions from insufficient premises takes on special meaning when credit officers encounter an information gap. Relatively speaking, the availability of data in some markets is woefully lacking when compared with what is normally available in, say, the U.S.

Mercantile information tends to be inaccurate and out of date, and trade checkings poor. The relative lack of published financial information may make it difficult to obtain figures on even a broad industry basis. When this is available, certain doubts are raised as to reliability.

Bank checkings are frustrating. There is a reluctance to share information beyond basic data, sometimes to the point where the data obtained is meaningless. The extent to which a borrower is indebted to other banks is not always easy to determine.

In some countries the practice of preparing several different sets of financial statements is not uncommon (sometimes up to five: for the tax collector, the banker, the major stockholders, the minority stockholders and the security analysts). Emphasis is on balance sheets rather than operating statements. Profit figures do not necessarily represent real profits. Many major companies are privately held, not traded on public exchanges. Reported operating figures may be bound up with the prevailing tax situation via expensing and profit reserves. In Japan, Europe and some other areas, reported profits are not considered the most important measurement of business success —total turnover, market share, total assets and capital base are frequently more important indices.

Audited figures can mean many things in different countries. There is not always a Securities & Exchange Commission to dictate format and disclosure. In Asia particularly, financial statements may not reflect the true position of the borrower. Accounting principles, even as we know them in the U.S., have rubber in them. When one looks elsewhere they are frequently nonexistent. Consequently, each audited statement must be interpreted in the environment of the country involved. The variety in accounting principles stems from historical influences—influence of the British in the commonwealth countries, the continental influence in Europe and its colonies or possessions and the American influence which spreads to Mexico and to some parts of Latin America. Principles also tend to overlap.

In a talk before last year's annual meeting of the Bankers' Association for Foreign Trade, Joseph P. Cummings, a partner of Peat, Marwick, Mitchell & Co., enumerated several problems with local audits: the nonconsolidation of statements (including omission of loss subsidiaries); equalization of earnings year to year—by use of contingency reserves or inventory adjustment—which makes poor years look good; omission of proper accruals for pension and other costs; lack of contingent liability disclosure; lack of allocation for income tax (you may be seeing income before the government takes the tax).

One message that comes through is that very often the audit may be performed by someone with far lower standards than one is accustomed to. Another is the need for greater use of source and application of funds statements for each year that a balance sheet and a profit and loss statement are available. Nonetheless, to repeat an earlier point, it is impossible to hide a trend. No matter how imperfect, statements do raise very useful questions even though they don't provide the answers.

Lack of financial planning, particularly on the part of family-owned enterprises and small- to medium-sized companies, is a further problem. Too much reliance is placed on the "old school tie" and on the historical reputation of individuals and family groups. More often than not, market budgets and forecasts (though not financial) are available. The importance of reliable detailed audits is highlighted when one realizes that the business environment in most of the world is somewhat like that of the U.S. in the 1940s and 1950s. Rising costs, the need for additional capital, the need for management and keener competition are forcing smaller firms to merge or to go out of business. Good operating information is critical to credit judgment, and a banker is shortsighted is he is lured into thinking he can neglect accepted lending data and principles because the interest return is high or that he must be more lenient to justify his presence in the local market. In time he will find that as a result of the effort and expense required to keep his portfolio healthy—or, if he is unlucky, to collect it—any anticipated benefit was a mirage.

Structuring loans

Despite informational shortcomings, a competent lending officer who starts with what is available should have the resourcefulness to develop what he feels he needs to reach a good decision and to structure the credit proposal in a way that will suit the bank as well as the borrower. The starting point is to sit down with the borrower, uncover the real purpose of the loan ("for general working capital needs" is unacceptable) and, once that is done, make a judgment as to whether the investment will generate the repayment.

Psychological factors become part of the scenario, too, in negotiating and in calculating how managers may behave under varying economic circumstances. For instance, when seeking information, the loan officer may encounter what might be called a charisma problem. Because of an account relationship or the pursuit of what is thought to be a choice piece of new business, the power the borrower wields over the lender in shaping credit patterns might surface. (Sometimes it's an early warning signal that someone is trying to conceal unfavorable data.) In these circumstances a banker is not always master of his fate and the cost of mastering it could be high.

Many corporate treasurers have learned how to divide and conquer. Everyone's problem becomes nobody's problem when each bank has only a minor share of a credit and there is no single agent or bank big enough in the credit to oblige the treasurer to pay attention.

Important clients may try to dictate, and frequently get, what they think they should have in the way of credit and terms even if these are inappropriate and unsound. This stems from conceptual misunderstandings of bank credit limitations, from pride and a desire to drive the best deal. Everyone is different and thinks his own problem is a justifiable exception to whatever policy one is seeking to make effective. By sorting out the proposal and placing it on a basis he believes reasonable, the banker risks losing the business to a competitor. The latter sees a rare opportunity to grab it, and this then becomes the rationale for stretching his lending standards. This situation, called "grandstanding," may well signal the time to let the "opportunity" go by.

Generally speaking, even the "toughest" clients are reasonable once they understand why a bank must maintain certain standards and requirements. Good two-way banking relationships—and all sound business relationships are built on mutuality of interest—can be constructed only on a mutual basis involving two-way respect. (No borrower respects, or takes seriously, the dicta of the "giveaway banker." Likewise, all bankers should be wary of the borrower who is willing to pay "giveaway" prices for funds—the rates Fribgest was willing to pay should have been the clue that something was awry in the company.)

There are also occasions when the lending officer himself has a blind spot in the face of an unsound or unreasonable request from a borrower whose balances and interest income are of primary importance to him. Living closely with a situation over a period of years sometimes blinds him to the realities and risks involved.

Cash-flow planning

From the lender's viewpoint, the wherewithal to repay is what credit is all about. We can talk about collateral and loans against assets, but assured cash flow is *de rigueur*. If assets or collateral are to be sold, there is the chance that the market will be unfavorable—and liquidation as a primary way out of a loan is hardly the way to develop a banking relationship. It can serve perhaps as a second way out since assets or collateral usually commit management to continue as a going entity and thereby bolster its sense of responsibility.

When we talk cash flow, we are really talking about a future-oriented approach to lending. The lender's span of exposure may run to several years, and this necessitates financial planning on the part of both borrower and lender. Appropriately, we relate debt repayment to a flow of funds which will permit regular amortization rather than repayment from refinancing or sale of assets.

This can be a difficult undertaking because some markets lack a variety of financial alternatives, and financial planning is thereby vitiated. Especially in less-developed countries, borrowers rely on bank financing for the entire range of their financial needs as there is no long-term capital market available, using 90-day note borrowings that should be on a term basis. This can cause severe balance-sheet distortions, especially in the area of liquidity management, and the lending officer is forced to focus carefully on the ability of the borrower (as well as perhaps his own capability) to roll over high volumes of short-term financing.

Many of the credit problems of the past couple of years have stemmed from borrowers borrowing short for long-term purposes. A borrower's lack of planning, and/or the ability to implement it, imposes a tremendous burden on the banking structure. It is natural under these circumstances for companies to use the simplest form of debt, perhaps an overdraft continually outstanding. This works to the detriment of both borrower and lender in that financing is poorly structured, possibly costlier than it should be, and the bank is placed in a difficult cash-management position.

Key questions that the international banker must also always ask himself are to what extent the borrower can withstand the impact of currency devaluation or, for that matter, reevaluation, and what risk the bank takes in terms of various types of governmental controls freezing loan repayment. These are not insuperable obstacles to sound credit; they are simply additional risks that must be considered in the overall structuring of a loan. Implicit is the need for the legal side of a transaction to be properly buttoned up. It is up to the banker to judge the credit risk, but a lawyer must couch the terms and conditions in protective language based on the laws of the country and provide closing opinions. There are areas in which even this is difficult. In the Trucial States, for example, foreign banks are not permitted to own property and are thus precluded from utilizing mortgages as security. In fact, there is no *commercial* law or code: the only courts are those which render decisions based on interpretation of the Koran.

Planning credit policy

This "coloring book" of bank involvement in international lending hopefully illustrates the variety of local practice and the abiding need to operate within a framework of reliable standards. Indeed, except for country risk, the approach to lending in Timbuktu doesn't differ from that in Des Moines.

The starting point in setting standards for credit extension internationally should be a careful look at one's own bank's direction. One then determines his appetite for types of exposure (including size of participation in individual deals) and chooses the lending areas that are profitable with reasonable risk. Risk diversification and the maintenance of a reasonable relationship between risk and capital reserves are also part of the question. It would make most sense for a bank to restrict its lending to sectors of the credit market in those geographical areas where it can operate comfortably.

Credit quality is influenced by management, competition, technology and by change itself. While credit principles are universal, it is the lender who becomes the market and sets the standards. It is his interplay with circumstances that produces good or bad decisions. In turn, he should have the benefit of policy guidance in writing—spelled out in his bank's policy manual or credit handbook.

As to the individual credit officer's role, the credit ecology is now such that he must anticipate, not react—a costly stance in the past. He needs to be forward-looking, informed on industry generally in selected markets and able to identify those names within an industry that are worthwhile. He must develop strategy and tactics in a sound and creative fashion that will match the borrower's needs, as well as those of his bank. Problems are easier when one takes the initiative. Credit is not an abstraction—it involves dealing with people, and each proposition is as unique as the borrower's fingerprint.

An eminent credit officer, the late D. A. Forward,[5] observed: "The difference between a smart lending officer and one who is not is that the former has the intelligence and takes the time to obtain all of the pertinent facts before he reaches his decision."

After defining the risk, the starting points for negotiation are adequate knowledge and understanding of the borrower and assurance of cash generation rather than refinancing as a source of payout. As a basis for his determination, the banker has hopefully formulated strategy beforehand. If reasonable standards can't be met, he "passes," confident that unsound compromise would be no favor to either borrower or lender.

Another "must" is to review credits continuously and to follow up on terms of loan agreements, being sensitive to when steps should be taken to strengthen them. Heavy weather can sink the best credits if we fail to inspect our primary and secondary protection, and inspect them regularly.

Looking back, the Penn Central derailment seemed to mark the end of one credit era and the beginning of another. Protracted prosperity had encouraged practices which led to the abdication of well-tested standards. Banks found that corporate bigness doesn't necessarily add strength and, in some cases, can create complexity with which it isn't easy to cope. The world reached a point where it was increasingly borrowing short for long-term purposes—and then scrambling to refinance short maturities.

Professor M. Colyer Crum of Harvard has detected an even more basic change: "Over the last 25 years, we have moved from a capital-surplus economy to a capital-scarce economy . . . . In their strategy planning, both large and small companies and governmental units could almost ignore the question of where the money was coming from and what it would cost."

The 1970s should be exacting years for credit officers worldwide. It's certainly fair to say that our area of activity is rated "X"—for mature lenders only! May we, like

---

[5] Vice Chairman of First National City Bank until his retirement in 1959, Mr. Forward was in charge of credit policy supervision.

Sherlock Holmes, who surprised a stranger with his power of perception, be able to say: "I see no more than you, but I have trained myself to notice what I see."

No article on credit, domestic or foreign, can cover all situations. Nor can the simple digestion of pertinent material develop a broad, sound lending banker. If I have done no more than wave a few danger signals, run up a few storm-warning flags, my purpose will have been served. Constant exposure to changing patterns, willingness to innovate and a mind open to learning are essential. The best banker is often the first to admit that he still has much to learn. ☐

Getting Started in International Lending— A Guide to Sources of Printed Information

by Nancy Seawahl

Having ready sources of country by country statistics and other financial data are musts for those starting to work in the area of international lending. Nancy Seawahl provides a comprehensive list of such sources which should prove useful for the novice—and perhaps for the more experienced as well.

Problems in evaluating a country's credit worthiness are varied and complex and are even more so when dealing with lesser developed nations. The country's external financial position—which includes an analysis of the balance of payments, foreign trade position, capital flows, international reserve position, and so forth—must be assessed. In addition, the strengths and weaknesses of the nation's domestic economy and socio-political stability must be evaluated.

At first glance, this might appear to be a formidable task. However, there is a great deal of information available that analysts can utilize in developing an evaluation of a country's "credit" rating. The purpose of this article is to provide those interested in getting started in international lending with a general guide to the types of information which are available to them.[1]

Initial sources of background information

As a good starting point for our background research, it is suggested that a brief history of the country, its economy, and political systems be obtained and carefully studied. The U.S. State Department publishes a series of *Background Notes* which contain basic background information covering a particular country's history, political system, and economy. Furthermore, each series presentation includes a short bibliography of other data sources which may prove helpful.

There are also a number of general yearbooks and almanacs available that provide additional basic information about a great many countries. Two good examples of these types of yearbooks which cover the world are *Statesman's Yearbook* and *Europa Year Book*. In addition, there are yearbooks which are published that only contain information about a particular region or individual country. These provide a more detailed review of the country's developments. Typical examples are *Africa South of the Sahara*, the *Asia Yearbook*, and the *Arab Business Yearbook*.[2]

Gathering current information

Armed with basic background information, the next step is to proceed to the current published material. There are a number of excellent sources that provide a brief summary of up-to-date facts relating to economic conditions and trends on a global scale. For example, the Economist Intelligence Unit publishes a series of *Quarterly Economic Reviews* covering economic and business conditions for some 150 countries. In addition to a brief discussion of current economic and business trends within a country, these quarterly reviews also highlight political situations, development plans, and major investment projects occurring there. Each issue also contains selected economic indicators and foreign statistics.

---

[1] Obviously, in an article designed to serve only as an introduction to the subject, it is inappropriate to list all of the numerous possible sources of foreign economic and financial information which can be used as the basis for an accurate evaluation of a country. The publications cited at the end of this article are intended to serve only as examples of the possible types of material available which an analyst could utilize.

[2] In addition to the above titles, there are numerous yearbooks published by individual nations which provide a more detailed review of the country's economic and political development. Typical examples would be the *Japan Economic Yearbook*, the *Canada Year Book*, and *Denmark: An Official Handbook*.

Along these same lines, the U.S. Bureau of International Commerce also publishes a series of annual and semi-annual reviews entitled *Foreign Economic Trends and Their Implications for the United States*. Compiled by the various U.S. embassies overseas, they cover current business and economic developments. They also include a table of key economic indicators.

Other sources of current general information which can be quite helpful are annual economic surveys such as the ones published by the Organization for Economic Cooperation and Development (OECD) on their member countries. Similarly, the United Nations publishes regional economic surveys covering developments within its member countries.

There are also private organizations which specialize in international business activities and which publish magazines, pamphlets, and special reports. These contain articles covering a great many countries and a broad spectrum of topics. Some examples of these types of publications are *Rundt's Weekly Intelligence,* Business International's series of weekly reports, and Predicast's *Worldcasts*.

In addition, there are numerous periodicals and newspapers which cover international developments. For example, the *Economist* magazine is well-known for its evaluation of foreign economic and political events. Besides general news, the *New York Times,* the *Financial Times,* and the international edition of the *Herald Tribune* all report significant international economic and political developments. Finally, the *Christian Science Monitor* is quite well-known for its review of foreign political events.

Sources of statistical data

For statistical data, one of the most comprehensive and up-to-date sources is *International Financial Statistics* published by the International Monetary Fund. It reports current data on foreign exchange rates, international reserves, data on prices and production, interest rates, and international trade and balance of payments statistics for the IMF's member countries. Other standard statistical sources include the OECD's *Main Economic Indicators* and the *Monthly Bulletin of Statistics* published by the United Nations.

Perhaps one of the most important sources of statistical data and other information which should not be overlooked is the material published by a country's central bank. Not only is this material the primary source for that country's current banking and monetary statistics, but the central bank's monthly bulletins also include other basic economic data such as employment levels, domestic price indices, cost of living indices for major cities, retail sales, residential construction, energy consumption, industrial production, balance of payments, foreign exchange rates, and so forth, as well as additional international statistics.

Information available about each country

In addition, there are other available resources that provide information about each country. As mentioned earlier, most foreign governments publish yearbooks which are quite useful because they contain general reviews of recent economic, social, and political developments. Along these same lines, numerous foreign governments also publish statistical annuals similar to the *Statistical Abstract of the United States*. Furthermore, many publish periodic reviews that provide monthly and quarterly data much like the *Survey of Current Business* or *Business Conditions Digest* published by the U.S. Government.

Financial institutions can also be a good source of current data. Many banks, both foreign and domestic, publish bulletins or letters which analyze current economic and financial trends. Many of these also contain relevant statistical data.

Additional information can be found in magazines published and sold in the country being evaluated. These discuss current economic, commercial, and political developments similar to coverage provided by *Fortune, Business Week, Newsweek,* or *Time.*

Major local newspapers are also good sources for current information. Although their candidness is tempered by the amount of press censorship in a given nation, they are an invaluable aid to the analyst in developing a "feel" for a particular country.

Firsthand knowledge

Part of the fact-gathering process should include discussions with people who have firsthand knowledge of the country. Both the U.S. Departments of State and Commerce have country specialists who are willing to share their expertise with businessmen. This is also true of the specialists working at the U.S. Export-Import Bank, the World Bank, and the International Monetary Fund.

The larger U.S. commercial banks all have international loan officers and economists who are quite knowledgeable and usually willing to sit down and discuss a particular country's economic situation with an analyst. Other potential sources of information are business people, members of the academic community, and the foreign government's embassy in Washington, D.C.

When all of the research has been completed, plan a visit to the country. It is virtually impossible to gain a comprehensive understanding of a foreign country without having visited it.

Getting to know the country "managers"

The key question in country risk analysis is how financially well-managed is the country. And while an analyst has to carefully study the facts and figures, it is also imperative to get to know the "managers"—the people who not only make but also implement the economic decisions. This includes talking to government officials and economists at the ministry of finance, those responsible for economic planning, and also officials at the central bank. Obtain their views on the economy and its "weak" spots, the role of foreign borrowings, and so on.

Discuss economics and politics with local bankers and business people as well as foreigners living there. Visit the economic, political, or treasury attachés at the U.S. Embassy. The local residents can also be important sources of information.

Making recommendations based on the data accumulated

Once these tasks are completed, the analyst has acquired the prerequisites for intelligently evaluating a particular country's credit worthiness. Past performance and current data provide only the foundation for country risk analyses. The international lender must now develop a model which projects the country's future prospects based upon all of the data the lender has accumulated. If the lender has done the research work well and truly understands the implications of the accumulated data, the bank's management should feel confident about accepting the lender's suggestion to make or deny loans within a country.

As mentioned earlier, evaluating a country's credit worthiness is not an exact science. It depends upon the interaction of various and often complex factors. The same is true regarding the sources of information which are available. It is hoped that the lists of sources which follow will provide a starting point upon which the analyst can begin building a personal data bank that will ultimately lead to an understanding of the risks involved in making loans within a particular country or an area of the world.

Basic statistical sources

International

(1) International Monetary Fund, Washington, D.C. 20431

International Financial Statistics. Published monthly with annual supplements. A standard source of statistics on all aspects of domestic and international finance. For each member nation, it reports current world data on foreign exchange rates, international reserves, prices, production, interest rates, government finance, foreign trade, and balance of payments.

(2) United Nations, New York, N.Y. 10017

Monthly Bulletin of Statistics. It provides statistics on a wide range of economic and social subjects from over 200 countries and territories to update the *Statistical Yearbook.*

Statistical Yearbook. It presents annual data on population, agriculture, trade, and balance of payments, to name a few, for about 270 countries.

(3) World Bank, Washington, D.C. 20433

World Tables—1976. Published irregularly by Johns Hopkins University Press. It provides time series for a number of basic economic data, together with derived economic indicators for selected periods to facilitate comparison among countries.

Europe

(1) Federal Reserve Bank of St. Louis, Research Department, P.O. Box 442, St. Louis, Mo. 63166

Rates of Change in Economic Data for Ten Industrial Countries. Published quarterly with an annual supplement. The quarterly contains rates of change for money supply, price indices, employment, measures of output, and international trade over a five-year period. The annual supplement gives historical data for the same series covering a 20-year period. European countries included are Belgium, France, Germany, Italy, Netherlands, Switzerland, and the United Kingdom. Other countries included are Canada, Japan, and the United States.

(2) International Currency Review, 11 Regency Place, London SW1P 2EA, England

Economic Data Service. Published monthly in loose-leaf form. It contains a wide range of statistics on a country-by-country basis for 20 leading economies. European countries included are Germany, United Kingdom, France, Netherlands, Belgium, Switzerland, Italy, Austria, Spain, Norway, Sweden, Denmark, and Finland. Other countries are the United States, Japan, Canada, Australia, New Zealand, South Africa, and Hong Kong.

(3) Organization for Economic Cooperation and Development, Paris, France. In the U.S. address subscription requests to OECD, 1750 Pennsylvania Avenue, N.W., Washington, D. C. 20006

Main Economic Indicators. Published monthly. It is a current guide to key economic indicators for the OECD countries. A quarterly supplement provides background material on industrial production. There is a separate biannual companion volume of historical statistics titled *Main Economic Indicators: Historical Statistics*.

(4) Statistical Office of the European Communities, Brussels, Belgium

Eurostat. Published monthly. It includes data on population, labor force, national accounts, industrial production, foreign trade, prices and wages, and balance of payments for the present European Economic Community (EEC) member nations.

(5) United Nations, Economic Commission for Europe (ECE), New York, N.Y. 10017

Statistical Indicators of Short Term Economic Changes in ECE Countries. Published monthly. Economic and financial indicators presented on a country-by-country basis for the 32 ECE countries.

(6) U.S. Domestic and International Business Administration, Department of Commerce, Washington, D.C. 20230

International Economic Indicators and Competitive Trends. Published quarterly by the U.S. Government Printing Office. It presents comparative economic data for the U.S. and its seven principal industrial competitors. Data covered includes real gross national product, industrial production, capacity utilization price indicators, and trade indicators.

Far East and Australasia

(1) Agency for International Development, Statistics and Reports Division, Washington, D.C. 20523

East Asia Economic Growth Trends; Near East and South Asia Economic Growth Trends. Published annually. Together, they provide a summary of basic economic and social data for the region.

(2) Federal Reserve Bank of San Francisco, Public Information Section, P.O. Box 7702, San Francisco, Calif. 94120

Pacific Basin Economic Indicators. Published quarterly. It contains rates of change for money supply, price indices, employment, measures of output, and international trade over a five-year period.

(3) United Nations, Economic and Social Commission for Asia and the Pacific, New York, N. Y. 10017

Statistical Yearbook for Asia and the Pacific. It details basic economic and social statistics for the region. A list of principal sources is included.

Latin America

(1) Agency for International Development, Statistics and Reports Division, Washington, D.C. 20523

Latin America Economic Growth Trends. Published annually. It provides a summary of basic economic and social data covering 22 Latin American countries.

(2) Latin American Center, University of California, Los Angeles, Calif. 90024

Statistical Abstract of Latin America. Published annually. It contains demographic, economic, social, and political data arranged by country.

(3) Organization of American States, Washington, D.C. 20006

America en Cifras. Published biannually. It details basic economic, demographic, social, and cultural statistics in a multivolume work.

(4) United Nations, Economic Commission for Latin America, New York, N.Y. 10017

Statistical Yearbook for Latin America. A one-volume annual work, containing regional and national statistics on the economy, population, mining, manufacturing, construction, electricity, transportation, and trade.

Foreign economic conditions

International

(1) Business International Corporation, One Dag Hammarskjold Plaza, New York, N.Y. 10017

Business International. Published weekly. It provides a comprehensive analysis of important global economic and political developments. BI also publishes these weekly regional reports: *Business Asia, Business Eastern Europe, Business Europe,* and *Business Latin American* which give more in-depth coverage of economic and political developments.

(2) Economist Intelligence Unit Ltd., Spencer House, 27 St. James Place, London SW1A INT, England

Quarterly Economic Reviews. Published quarterly with an annual supplement. Each edition reviews current economic and business conditions and prospects, backed by comment and statistical analysis for 150 countries. Each also discusses the current political scene and assesses the current economic situation and economic plans and policies.

(3) S. J. Rundt and Associates, 130 East 63rd Street, New York, N.Y. 10021

Rundt's Weekly Intelligence. It reviews important current world business, economic, and political developments. It is arranged alphabetically by country. Also included are statistical tables on eurocurrency deposit rates and foreign exchange market quotations for major currencies as well as Latin American currencies.

(4) United Nations, Department of Economic and Social Affairs, New York, N.Y. 10017

World Economic Survey. Published annually. It surveys current trends in the world economy, with emphasis on international trade, payments, and production.

(5) U.S. Bureau of International Commerce, Department of Commerce, Washington, D.C.

Foreign Economic Trends and Their Implications for the United States. Published semiannually or annually. A series of 150 reports from U.S. embassies overseas which cover current business and economic conditions, with their implications for the United States.

Europe

(1) Commission of the European Communities, Directorate-General for Economic and Financial Affairs, Rue de la Loi 200, Brussels 1049, Belgium

The Economic Situation in the Community. Published quarterly. It reviews the recent developments in and outlook for the economic situation in the EEC as a whole and in each member nation.

(2) Economist Intelligence Unit Ltd., Spencer House, 27 St. James Place, London SW1A INT, England

European Trends. Published quarterly. It reports current news about policies and issues concerning the region.

(3) Euromoney Research Bureau, 20 Tudor Street, London EC4Y OJS, England

Euromoney Monthly Economic Survey. It provides a thorough, concise review of ten economies each month, plus a weekly diary of significant economic events. The European countries covered are Belgium, France, Germany, Netherlands, and the U.K. Other countries include Australia, Canada, Japan, South Africa, and the U.S.

(4) Organization for Economic Cooperation and Development, Paris, France. In the United States, address subscription requests to OECD, 1750 Pennsylvania Avenue, N.W., Washington, D.C. 20006

OECD Economic Outlook. Published semiannually. It surveys recent developments and assesses future prospects for the region. It publishes separate reviews on each of the member nations throughout the year which provide an in-depth discussion of economic policy, recent trends, and the outlook for the coming year.

(5) Economic Commission for Europe, United Nations, New York, N.Y. 10017

Economic Survey for Europe. Published annually. It is a review of the past year's economic developments in the ECE member nations—Eastern European countries are included.

Far East and Australasia

(1) Asian Finance Publications, Suite 9D, Hyde Centre, 223 Gloucester Road, Hong Kong

Asian Finance. Published monthly. It reviews developments that pertain to Asian finance and industry.

(2) Business International Corporation, One Dag Hammarskjold Plaza, New York, N. Y. 10017

Business Asia. Published weekly. It contains a comprehensive analysis of important economic and political developments in Asia and the Pacific.

(3) Far Eastern Economic Review, Circulation Department, GPO Box 47, Hong Kong

Far Eastern Economic Review. Published weekly. It features articles on economic, political, business, and financial trends.

(4) Pacific Magazines, Ltd., 5th Floor, 257 Gloucester Road, Hong Kong

Insight: For Decision Makers in Asia. Published monthly. It covers business and financial developments in Asia and the Pacific.

(5) United Nations, Economic Commission for Asia and the Pacific, New York, N.Y. 10017

Economic Survey of Asia and the Pacific. Published annually. A survey of economic conditions in the region as a whole. This is supplemented by *Economic Bulletin for Asia and the Far East* which is published tri-annually.

Statistical Yearbook for Asia and the Pacific. Annual statistics are arranged by country and cover key demographic, economic, financial, and social indicators. A list of principal sources is given at the end.

Latin America

(1) The Andean Report, Apartado 2484, Lima, Peru

The Andean Report. Published monthly. It provides a concise summary of the month's economic and commercial developments, plus specific reports on particular subjects and legal and tax regulations affecting the business climate.

(2) Business International Corporation, One Dag Hammarskjold Plaza, New York, N.Y. 10017

Business Latin America.   Published weekly. It provides a comprehensive analysis of important economic and political developments in Latin America.

(3) Inter-American Development Bank, Washington, D.C.

Economic and Social Progress in Latin America.   Published annually. Divided into two parts: The first contains a regional description of general and sectoral trends, and the second contains a country-by-country analysis.

(4) Latin American Newsletters, Ltd., 90-93 Cowcross Street, London, England. In the U.S., address subscription requests to William Holub, 432 Park Avenue South, New York, N.Y.

Latin American Economic Report.   Published 50 times a year. It provides news coverage on recent economic, political, and social events on a country-by-country basis.

Latin America Weekly Political Report.   It provides news coverage on political events in Latin America on a country-by-country basis.

(5) Lloyds Bank International Ltd., 40-66 Queen Victoria Street, London EC4P 4EL, England

Bank of London and South America Review (BOLSA).   Published monthly. It reviews current economic and commercial developments on a country-by-country basis, plus selected statistical indicators.

(6) United Nations, Economic Commission for Latin America, New York, N.Y. 10017

Economic Survey of Latin America.   Published annually. A multi-volume set containing general background information on the world economy, an overview of Latin America's economy during the preceding year, and individual country reports with a detailed presentation of the economy together with relevent statistical tables. This is supplemented by the *Economic Bulletin for Latin America* which is published biannually.

Africa and the Middle East

(1) The Arab Economist, Gefinor Center, P.O. Box 6068, Beirut, Lebanon

The Arab Economist.   Published monthly. It surveys the Arab economies, highlighting significant economic developments and including statistical indicators.

(2) New African Development, 63 Long Acre, London WC2E 9JH, England
   New African Development.   Published monthly. It analyzes economic
   and trade developments in the area and features economic surveys on
   individual countries.

(3) United Nations, Economic Commission for Africa, New York, N.Y. 10017
   Economic Survey of Africa.   Published annually. It reviews economic
   growth in development in Africa. This is supplemented by *Economic
   Bulletin for Africa* published twice yearly.

Selected sources on foreign currency and exchange regulation

(1) Business International Corporation, One Dag Hammarskjold Plaza, New
   York, N.Y. 10017
   Money Report.   Published weekly. It provides a weekly analysis of
   developments in the world's financial and currency markets, including
   foreign exchange forecasts.

(2) International Currency Review, 11 Regency Place, London SW1P 2EA,
   England
   Interest Rate Service.   Published in loose-leaf form, 20 times a year. It
   provides a running commentary, accompanied by interest rate charts
   on interest rate and yield developments in 11 countries.

   International Currency Review.   Published every two months. It
   specializes in analyzing economic developments and monetary affairs
   and is aimed at the reader who is interested in the implications for the
   foreign exchange market.

   London Currency Report.   Published bi-weekly. Reviewing some 20
   currencies and countries regularly, the service deals with currency,
   monetary, economic, and political developments which are relevant to
   international currency forecasting and analysis.

   Middle East Currency Reports.   Published in loose-leaf form. It is a
   prime source of information regarding the developing currency and
   monetary systems of the region.

(3) International Monetary Fund, Washington, D.C. 20431
   Annual Report on Exchange Regulations.   It provides a country-by-
   country description of exchange systems and related regulations in
   operation in most countries of the world.

(4) International Reports, Inc., 200 Park Avenue South, New York, N.Y.
   10003
   International Reports.   Published weekly. It surveys the world financial markets and includes foreign exchange market projections.

(5) Pick Publishing Corporation, New York, N.Y.
  Pick's Currency Yearbook.   It gives a complete description of each currency, including history, transferability, administration, and statistics on official exchange rates.

Selected sources of company information

International

(1) Dun and Bradstreet, New York, N.Y.
  Principal International Businesses.   Published annually. It details selected financial information arranged alphabetically by country, together with indexes by SIC number and by company.
(2) Financial Times, 10 Bolt Court, Fleet Street, London EC4A 3HL, England
  International Business Year Book.   It details essential information on 700 of the world's top companies. Also included are very brief descriptions of the country as well as important facts on international markets and economic groups.
(3) Standard and Poor's Corporation, New York, N.Y.
  International Stock Report.   Published monthly. It analyzes some of the top foreign companies, giving relevant financial information and recent developments.

Europe

(1) Dun and Bradstreet International, London, England
  Europe's 5000 Largest Companies.   Published annually. It presents selected financial information on the 5000 largest industrials and 1000 largest trading companies of Western Europe.
(2) Extel Statistical Services, Ltd., London, England
  Extel European Country Service.   It is a comprehensive financial system covering 400 major companies whose stocks are quoted on European stock exchanges. There is a similar service for British companies titled *Extel British Company Service*.
(3) F. Watts, New York, N.Y.
  Jane's Major Companies of Europe.   Published annually. Selected financial information on 1000 western European companies. It is arranged by industry with indexes by country and by company.

Foreign trade and balance of payments statistics

(1) International Monetary Fund, Washington, D.C. 20431
  Balance of Payments Yearbook.   Published monthly in loose-leaf sections as information becomes available. It presents the balance of

payments transaction in standard form together with explanatory notes.

Direction of Trade. Published monthly. It contains the latest available information on each country's direction of trade with comparative data for the preceding year, plus quarterly summaries for various areas of the world.

(2) Organization for Economic Cooperation and Development, Paris, France. In the U.S., address subscriptions to OECD, 1750 Pennsylvania Avenue, N.W., Washington, D.C. 20006

Statistics of Foreign Trade.

Series A. Monthly Bulletin. It contains an overall picture of total trade of OECD countries, analyzed into flows with country and country groupings of origin and destination. It also includes summary monthly tables showing a breakdown of overall trade by main commodity categories and available indices of foreign trade unit values and volumes.

Series B. Trade by Commodities, Country Summaries. Published quarterly. It analyzes total trade of the OECD area by main commodity categories and partner areas and countries. It is more generalized than Series A.

(3) United Nations, New York, N.Y. 10017

Yearbook of International Trade Statistics. It provides annual summaries of trade by large commodity classes and by principal regions and countries.

Forecasting services

(1) Business International Corporation, One Dag Hammarskjold Plaza, New York, N.Y. 10017

BI/Data. It is an on line data base with annual data on selected key indicators for some 70 key countries, plus short-term forecasts for 35 leading markets. Other BI forecasting services include a *Latin American Forecasting Study, Asia/Pacific Forecasting Study,* and the *European Forecasting Study,* each of which provide a five-year outlook.

(2) Eurofinance, 9, Avenue Hoche, 75008 Paris, France

Euroeconomics. It is a comprehensive economic and financial forecasting service, with primary focus on European economies. It assesses the impact of recent or anticipated economic and political events on the overall economy, selected sectors and markets, both quantitatively and qualitatively.

(3) Predicasts, Inc., Cleveland, Ohio

> **World-Regional-Casts.** Published quarterly. It abstracts published forecasts by country for all countries, except the U.S., providing a summary sheet for each which contains the historical data and a consensus forecast for various series to 1985.

Financial statistics

(1) Organization for Economic Cooperation and Development, Paris, France
In the U.S., address subscription requests to OECD, 1750 Pennsylvania Avenue, N.W., Washington, D.C. 20006

> **Financial market trends.** Published five times a year. It contains statistics and charts on current developments in the international and national financial markets and brief summaries of recent events in major market sectors.

> **OECD Financial Statistics.** Published annually, with updating supplements issued every two months. It provides information on the financial markets in the OECD area countries. Topics covered include capital operations and financial transactions of the main sectors of the economy, financial transactions with foreign countries, interest rates for key financial instruments in each country, interest rates on the Eurodollar markets, and medium- and long-term international bank loans.

(2) World Bank, Publications Office, 1818 H Street, N.W., Washington, D.C. 20043

> **Borrowing in International Capital Markets.** Published quarterly. It lists foreign and international bond issues and publicized eurocurrency credits for selected countries.

> **World Debt Tables.** Published annually with updating supplements issued irregularly during the year. It is a standard source of data on external public debt for developing countries.

National income statistics

(1) Organization for Economic Cooperation and Development, Paris, France
In the U.S., address subscription requests to OECD, 1750 Pennsylvania Avenue, Washington, D.C. 20006

> **National Accounts Statistics.** Published annually. It reports time series for national account aggregates by country, plus separate tables showing rates of change for selected series.

(2) United Nations, New York, N.Y. 10017
Yearbook of National Account Statistics.   It contains detailed estimates of national income and related measures for some 100 countries.

Worldwide comparative cost of living statistics

(1) Union Bank of Switzerland, Bahnhofstrass 45, Zurich, Switzerland
Prices and Earnings Around the Globe.   Published annually. It discusses and compares purchasing power in 37 cities around the world and includes tables giving comparative prices for food, clothing, housing, household appliances, services, restaurant and hotel prices, and automobile prices. It also includes tables on gross annual earnings for various occupations.

(2) United Nations, New York, N.Y. 10017
Monthly Bulletin of Statistics.   The February and August issues each year contain a cost-of-living index by country with New York City being the base city.

(3) United States Department of Labor, Washington, D.C. 20212
Indexes of Living Costs Abroad and Quarters Allowances.   Published quarterly. It is a cost-of-living index by country with Washington, D.C. being the base city.

Government finance statistics

(1) International Monetary Fund, Washington, D.C. 20431
Government Finance Statistics Yearbook, Volume I.   Published annually. It provides internationally comparable data on government operations for one to three years on about 90 countries.

Selected periodicals and newspapers
General

(1) **The Banker.**   Published monthly. It covers banking and financial trends throughout the world, with emphasis on the United Kingdom.
For subscription information, write The Banker Division, Financial Times, Ltd., Bracken House, 10 Cannon Street, London EC4P 4BY, England

(2) **Columbia Journal of World Business.**   Published bi-monthly. It features in-depth articles on topics of interest to the business and financial community.
For subscription information, write Columbia University, 408 Uris, New York, N.Y. 10027

(3) **The Economist.** Published weekly. It contains feature articles on economic and political trends, focusing primarily on the U.K. but also covering Europe, the international scene, and the United States.

For subscription information, write Subscription Department, The Economist Newspaper, Ltd., P.O. Box 190, 23a St. James Street, London SW1A HF, England

(4) **Euromoney.** Published monthly. It features an analysis of the international money markets and financial trends.

For subscription information, write Euromoney Publications, Ltd., 20 Tudor Street, London EC4Y OJS, England

(5) **Financial Times.** Published daily. It provides extensive coverage of world political and economic events.

For subscription information, write Subscription Department, Financial Times, Bracken House, 10 Cannon Street, London EC4P 4BY, England

(6) **IMF Survey.** Published twice a month. It features articles on international financial and economic developments plus coverage of the International Monetary Fund's activities.

For subscription information, write Secretary, International Monetary Fund, Washington, D.C. 20431

(7) **The International Executive.** Published three times a year. It reviews books of interest to the international executive and gives a subject listing of timely periodical articles.

For subscription information, write Foundation for the Advancement of International Business Administration, Inc., 64 Ferndale Drive, Hastings-on-Hudson, N.Y. 10706

(8) **Institutional Investor: International Edition.** Published monthly. It features articles dealing with international finance and investment.

For subscription information, write Institutional Investor Systems, Inc., 488 Madison Avenue, New York, N.Y. 10022

(9) **International Finance.** Published bi-weekly. It reviews international economic and financial developments.

For subscription information, write Economics Group, One Chase Manhattan Plaza, New York, N.Y. 10015

(10) **Petroleum Economist.** Published monthly. It provides comprehensive coverage of oil and energy developments in every country of the world, plus up-to-date statistics on production, consumption, and prices.

For subscription information, write Petroleum Economist, 5 Pemberton Row, Fleet Street, London EC4A 3DP, England

(11) **World Financial Markets.** Published monthly. It analyzes international economic and financial developments.

> For subscription information, write Morgan Guaranty Trust Company of New York, 23 Wall Street, New York, N.Y. 10015

Foreign accounting principles and reporting practices

In addition to the general publications listed below, several of the large accounting firms publish a series of information booklets summarizing accounting methods and financial reporting practices for the countries in which they do business.

(1) **Accounting in Europe** by Michael Lafferty, Nichols Publishing Company, New York, N.Y., 1975.

(2) **Guide for the Reader of Foreign Financial Statements** by Price Waterhouse and Company, New York, N.Y., 1975.

(3) **Professional Accounting in 30 Countries** by American Institute of Certified Public Accountants, International Practice Executive Committee, New York, N.Y., 1975.

(4) **A Survey in 46 Countries—Accounting Principles and Reporting Practices** by Price Waterhouse and Company, New York, N.Y., 1975.

Yearbooks

(1) **Arab Business Yearbook.** It contains basic economic and financial information as well as brief descriptions of foreign investment regulations, tariffs and trade regulations, corporate and personal taxation, and accounting principles relating to the Arab world. It also includes a listing of public holidays and other useful information for the business traveler.

> It is available from Graham and Trotman, Ltd., 20 Fouberts Place, Regent Street, London, W1V 1HH, England.

(2) **Asia Yearbook.** It gives a regional overview of the past year's major economic and political events as well as a more lengthy discussion of each country's political and economic developments.

> It is available from Far Eastern Economic Review, South China Building, 12th Floor, 1-3 Wyndham Street, Hong Kong.

(3) **Europa Year Book.** It is a two-volume set with Volume I covering international organizations and Europe and Volume II covering Africa, the Americas, Asia, and Australasia. For each country, it includes information on recent history, the government, and basic economic data plus listing major business enterprises, trade and industrial organizations, and financial

institutions. Europa also publishes three regional yearbooks: *The Far East and Australasia, The Middle East and North Africa,* and *Africa South of the Sahara.* These cover much the same information as the *Europa Year Book* but in more depth. A "who's who" section on prominent people is also included for the countries covered.

Published by Europa Publications, London, England, it is distributed in the United States by Gale Research, 1249 Washington Blvd., 800 Book Building, Detroit, Mich. 48231.

(4) **International Petroleum Encyclopedia.** It contains an international economic overview of the petroleum industry. It includes annual developments of the industry on a regional and individual country basis.

It is available from Petroleum Publishing, Box 1260, Tulsa, Okla. 74101.

(5) **Political Handbook and Atlas of the World.** Information for each country includes basic background data on the government, political party programs and leaders, the press, and diplomatic representation.

It is published by and available from McGraw-Hill Book Company, 1221 Avenue of the Americas, New York, N.Y. 10020.

(6) **Statesman's Yearbook.** A concise manual giving brief data about the governments of the world and international organizations. Information includes facts about the constitution, economic conditions, education, religion, national defense, agriculture, and commerce.

It is published by MacMillan Press, Ltd., London, England, and distributed in the United States by St. Martin's Press, 175 5th Avenue, New York, N.Y. 10010.

Don't overlook

(1) **Area Handbook Series.** Published by the U.S. Department of the Army, this series provides basic information concerning a country's social, political, economic, and military institutions.

(2) **Background Notes.** It is a series of 4–12 page summaries of basic data on approximately 164 countries. Each contains information on the country's land, people, history, government, political conditions, economy, and foreign relations. It includes a map and brief bibliography.

Available individually or as a complete set from Superintendent of Documents, U.S. Government Printing Office, Washington, D.C. 20402.

(3) **Country Experts in the Federal Government.** This lists country specialists in various U.S. governmental agencies who have responsibility for follow-

ing a particular aspect or aspects of a specific country. It is arranged by country, and telephone numbers are given for each analyst.

It is available from Washington Researchers, 910 Seventeenth Street, N.W., Washington, D.C. 20006.

(4) **International Economic Report of the President.** It is published annually by the Council on International Economic Policy and is available from the Superintendent of Documents.   □

Developing a Country-Risk Analysis System

by Christopher M. Korth

Formerly employed at The First National Bank of Chicago, Christopher Korth had a large role in developing and implementing a country-risk analysis system which at one time was in effect at the First. In the following article, Mr. Korth discusses that system's method of country risk and size ratings after first reviewing the principal variables which can affect international lending risk.

U.S. banks play a major, unique, and vital role in international finance, reflecting several important factors:

(1) The scale of U.S. international trade.

(2) The significant role played by U.S. customers as investors in foreign countries.

(3) The use of the U.S. dollar as the major reserve currency for international official liquidity purposes.

(4) The dollar's role as the principal vehicle currency for most international trade and capital flows.

Such factors have forced American banks to the forefront of the world financial arena.

The need for risk analysis

Because of large scale foreign loan exposure and legitimate concern about the safety of loans to many countries, lenders should exercise great care in evaluating, allocating, and limiting foreign loans.

While the U.S. economy is one of the least regulated in the world, the U.S. banking system is one of the most regulated of the world's major financial centers. Regulation thus enforces a rather high overall level of safety which greatly reduces (although it certainly does not totally eliminate) the opportunity for serious banking problems.

However, the high degree of federal control which characterizes the domestic operations of U.S. banks does not hold true for their international operations. For example, although federal regulations exist which limit the amount that a national bank can lend to an individual borrower,[1] either in the U.S. or abroad, no comparable limit exists for lending to an entire country. Thus, ironically, a bank has an absolute ceiling on its loans to a company such as General Motors or AT&T but has none on its total loans (both government and private sectors) to a country such as Zaire, Peru, or Indonesia. Even for loans to foreign governments, especially Communist countries where all the financial strings are essentially controlled by a single authority, the legal lending limit has been liberally interpreted to permit lending to a variety of government agencies. All that is required is the demonstration that the borrowing entity could finance the obligation on its own if it had control over its own finances (the so-called "means" test) and that the use of the funds is for that entity's use (the "purpose" test).[2] Since the legal lending limit was never really envisioned as a limit on lending to national governments, a flexible interpretation is not unwarranted; the problem arises from the degree of flexibility.

Some degree of supervision has, of course, been exercised—by the Federal Reserve and Comptroller of the Currency's Office especially. However, that supervision has often tended to be ill-defined and rather liberal. Recognizing this, the U.S. federal authorities have proposed a more thorough and systematic approach to the supervision of international banking.[3] Also, the Comptroller's Office now uses a concentration of credit risk report which identifies countries in which a bank has made loans exceeding "25% or more of the bank's capital structure." However, even these approaches are intended as normative rather than statutory controls. No country-loan limits will be set for individual banks. Nor will official credit ratings for countries be given. Rather, stress is being placed upon encouraging banks to diversify their foreign loan portfolios and to develop and maintain "adequate internal mechanisms for monitoring and controlling country exposure."[4]

---

[1] The lending limit is essentially equal to 10% of the bank's paid-in capital and surplus plus retained earnings.

[2] News Release, "Final Ruling—12USC84 (Loans to Foreign Govts, Their Agencies and Instrumentalities)," Office of the Comptroller of the Currency, April 12, 1979.

[3] "A New Supervisory Approach to Foreign Lending," *Quarterly Review,* Federal Reserve Bank of New York, Spring 1978; pp. 1–6.

[4] *Ibid,* p. 6.

Thus, U.S. commercial banks are basically being permitted to rely upon their own procedures for discipline and control—although with a moderate degree of governmental prodding. However, this freedom is only as good for the individual bank and the entire banking system as is the use that is made of it.

Significant latitude is being permitted in determining a bank's monitoring and control procedures. The remainder of this article is directed toward examining the process whereby a bank can develop such procedures.

Considerations in country-risk analysis for bank loans

The basic goal of analyzing the quality of foreign loans is to minimize the risk in the bank's foreign portfolio. Risk, for our purposes, is country-risk, the likelihood of the occurrence of default, moratorium, forced rescheduling, or merely excessive delays in the repayment of principal and interest on a national rather than individual company level. There are other types of risk to which foreign lending exposes a bank. However, they are the objects of different kinds of risk analysis and do not concern us here. Foremost among these are commercial risk, which is generally quite analogous to its domestic counterpart, and foreign-exchange risk, which requires a separate type of economic and political analysis.

Needs of individual banks

The analytical system which a bank employs should reflect the character of the bank and the nature of its foreign lending. For example, a bank may refuse to lend to certain countries on philosophical grounds. Likewise, a large, diversified bank with only a modest-sized portfolio of foreign loans might approach sovereign-risk analysis very differently than a bank whose foreign loans comprise a sizable share of its total loans.

Table 1 indicates the significance of foreign deposits for major groups of the 50 largest U.S. banks and for those individual major banks for whom foreign deposits are at least 38% of their total deposits. Since foreign loans are largely funded abroad, foreign deposits as a share of total deposits is a valid indicator of the relative role played by foreign loans in the banks' portfolios. As shown in Table 1, the major New York and Chicago banks are most heavily committed to international lending. Thus, these two groups of banks would have the greatest need for an accurate reading of international lending risk. Most of them have developed some formal review system in recent years—but some do not actually use it. Senior bank officers are strongly tempted to operate intuitively in international lending, but the complexities are too great to justify it.

Table 1—U.S. Bank Reliance on Foreign Deposits

Bank's Rank in Size (by total assets)	Foreign Deposits as Percent of Total Deposits
A. Groups of Banks	
10 largest U.S. banks	43
11–30	23
31–50	8
B. Individual Banks	
2. Citicorp	68
3. Chase Manhattan	56
17. First National of Boston	53
5. J. P. Morgan	50
1. Bank of America	46
10. First National of Chicago	44
7. Continental of Illinois	43
6. Chemical of New York	40
9. Bankers Trust	39
4. Manufacturers Hanover	38

Source: "How the Top 200 Banks Performed in 1978," *Business Week*, April 23, 1979; pp. 93–107.

A total of 25 U.S. banks have foreign deposits (and presumably loans) of at least $1 billion each. These banks, as well as many banks with even less foreign deposits, also have a strong need to understand fully their foreign lending risk. And these banks are far less likely to be very sophisticated about country-risk analysis at the present time.

Nature of foreign lending

Also, the nature of foreign lending differs between banks. For example, guarantees of foreign loans are much more significant internationally than they are domestically. Banks whose foreign loans are mostly guaranteed by an agency of the U.S. Government, such as the Export-Import Bank or the Commodity Credit Corporation; international agencies, such as the World Bank; or a U.S. company have relatively little sovereign risk. Likewise, third-country guarantees can shift the ultimate risk from relatively high-risk countries to those with relatively low risk. A German company's guarantee of a loan to its Brazilian subsidiary or a Saudi Arabian guarantee of a loan to the government of Sudan would be examples of such situations.

If a bank lends to only a few countries or only to countries in one part of the world, then its risk will also be greater. It will be losing the self-insurance which a well-diversified portfolio can provide. That would be analogous to a bank which had made a large portion of its loans to a limited category of domestic borrowers, such as to farmers or to the auto industry. Banks involved in this restricted type of international lending can use a more limited format of country loan-risk analysis. Nevertheless, the need for careful analysis of the small number of countries involved remains very strong.

Goals of the country-risk evaluation process

One of the principal functions of a well-designed and implemented foreign-loan risk review system is to provide the discipline of careful and periodic analysis of loans to individual countries and in relation to the entire portfolio. Many banks drifted, or were dragged, into foreign lending. Not only do many of them not have adequate systems of country-risk analysis but many have done a poor job of simply analyzing the balance within their foreign portfolios between loans to different countries. One multibillion dollar bank has as its largest foreign commitment a large exposure to Peru—a position open to serious question.

It is extremely important that a bank clearly differentiate the goals of the country-risk evaluation process from those of the loan marketing process. In the evaluation, it will be attempting to measure risk and, with this as a guide, suggesting loan limits for countries of different economic sizes and potential. For this purpose we will be analyzing economic, sociological, and political factors which can affect risk together with overall market attractiveness (that is, GNP and growth potential).

We are *not* interested in such marketing-related factors as the existence of a bank branch in the country (and the corresponding need to cover the expenses of the branch, provide it with adequate business, or even to justify its existence), the desire to maintain or enhance market position, the existence of special relationships with a government or the local business community, the promise of new business opportunities, or even attractive loan spread. Any or all of these can be very valid factors in a bank's decision regarding a proposed foreign loan. However, they should not affect a country-risk analysis; they would interfere with the process. *After* a risk assessment has been made, these factors can serve as additional valuable considerations in making the ultimate loan decision. For example, the proposed loan spread would be an obvious factor to use in conjunction with risk. So also would efforts to gain access to or to consolidate and expand a bank's involvement in a foreign market be an additional rational criteria. For example, several years ago, shortly after the government of the Perons left office and while the country's credit rating remained fairly low, Argentina was able to borrow $1 billion internationally on very favorable terms. Most of the banks realized the risk but were anxious to get a foot in the door of a potentially promising market.

The process of country-risk analysis for bank loans

The procedure which is about to be described is designed for the broadest possible application in the area of country-risk analysis. It is broad enough to be used for evaluations of any type of economic and political system. Moreover, it is designed so as to permit easy comparison between any two countries of the world. Through the use of this system, called the Country Loan Risk Evaluation System (CLRES), a bank can, if it desires, compare alternative investment opportunities in one geographical area of the world, such as between France and Italy. And it can also compare opportunities between any two or more areas of the world, such as between France, Mexico, and Thailand.

Need for open-mindedness

In approaching sovereign risk analysis, the analyst should be very open-minded; he should not prejudge solely on the basis of the general nature of a country's economic, political, or social system, such as in Eastern Europe, South Africa, or Chile. A wide variety of economic, political, and social systems can provide attractive loan opportunities as long as there is a high probability of repayment of principal and interest on schedule. Therefore, moral judgments are to be avoided—as does indeed appear to be the case with most large American banks. However, as was noted previously and will be discussed at the end of this article, moral judgments can play a legitimate role in a bank's ultimate lending decision: They simply are not reasons for sharply downgrading certain countries in terms of lending risk.

Similarly, it should be assumed that most governments, regardless of their political persuasion and even public rhetoric (such as Libya's), will honor international financial commitments if reasonably able to do so. However, the analyst is not required to assume high moral principles, from his perspective, but only to assume that foreign countries recognize that it is in their own self-interest, in terms of trade financing as well as bank financing, to maintain a good credit rating. Even radicals, such as Libya's Colonel Qadhafi, who have recommended declarations of debt moritoriums on some of the poorest countries, have been very careful never to give any hint that they themselves might follow their own ill-chosen advice. Nevertheless, a radical change of government which could lead to the renunciation of many debts of the previous government is still cause for careful attention. For instance, some Eastern European countries renounced their debts after World War II.

The analyst also needs to bear in mind that stable, as well as unstable, economic and political systems can be risky for lenders. In recent years, Tur-

key, Jamaica, and North Korea have provided examples of relatively stable but
still high-risk situations.

Political factors

The analysis of the risk itself, as has been noted, involves a careful evaluation of a large number of economic, political, and sociological factors. Table 2
outlines many of the principal political variables that ought to be considered in
making a foreign loan risk analysis. The list is not exhaustive. However, the
factors which are listed warrant careful analysis even if there is a presumption
that a particular variable is irrelevant for a particular country. Many sad loan
experiences have resulted from failure to weigh important variables
adequately.

As can be seen in Table 2, the variables are subdivided into domestic and
international. Most of the relevant political variables are inherently domes-

---

Table 2—Political Factors Affecting Sovereign Risk for
International Bank Loans

A. Domestic
   1. The political system
      a. Its basic strength
      b. Its resiliency—capacity for change without disruptive conflict
      c. Likelihood of system-disrupting conflict arising from within the country
         (1) Strength of opposition groups
         (2) Philosophies of strong opposition groups

   2. The group in power
      a. Philosophy
      b. Policies
      c. Government officials
         (1) Ability; number of qualified officials
         (2) Willingness and capability for making tough decisions
      d. Strength; capability of implementing plans

   3. The governmental system
      a. Efficiency; "red tape"
      b. Flexibility

B. International
   1. Likelihood of system-disrupting conflict arising from outside the country
      a. Due to country's own problems
      b. Due to treaty or other obligations
   2. Relations with major trading partners
   3. Relations with U.S.

---

tic—although some of them, such as the philosophy and policies of the government and the quality of government officials, can strongly affect international events as well. Nevertheless, the "domestic" political factors directly affect local as well as international participants.

The domestic political factors can be generally grouped into three categories: the political system, the group in power, and the governmental system. Variables affecting the basic political system include its basic strength and its ability to adjust to changing forces without breaking down.

Concerning the group in power, factors of primary concern are its philosophy, policies, and the ability of its officials. A country with a clear-cut philosophy, relatively unified policies, and a strong government bureaucracy would warrant a lower risk, despite perhaps the threat of war with a neighboring country, than would a government with less unity of policies and fewer qualified bureaucrats.

The governmental system itself is an important variable since bureaucracies tend to have lives of their own. As a result, they are often hard for the administration to control. A good example is Egypt where, despite clear-cut government policies designed to facilitate an inflow of foreign investment, the policy has never been successfully implemented in many parts of the bureaucracy; as a result, the bureaucracy serves as an effective barrier to the implementation of government policy.

On the international side, concern is focused on both favorable international ties, such as the European Common Market, which improve the outlook and reduce risk and those which threaten conflict—either directly or through international obligations.

Socio-cultural factors

Table 3 outlines sociological factors which can affect international lending risk. As with the political factors, they are divided between their essentially domestic and international components. The domestic factors include considerations of such variables as the homogeneity and cohesiveness of major social groups and their general psychology, political activism, unemployment, and the extent of social unrest. In general, a homogeneous, or at least acquiescent, population suggests greater stability and less risk. Such a population would be the Indians of Mexico. While they make up a majority of the population and are little, if any, better off 60 years after the revolution, they remain politically inactive.

Internationally, socio-cultural factors are relevant only if they offer favorable or unfavorable influences on political stability and economic strength. An

Table 3—Socio-Cultural Factors Affecting Soverign Risk for International Bank Loans

A. Domestic
  1. Social groups
     a. Homogeneity of population
        (1) Ethnic
        (2) Religious
        (3) Linguistic
        (4) Class
     b. Extent of cohesiveness or divisiveness
  2. General psychology of population; work ethic
  3. Political activism of population
  4. Unemployment
  5. Extent of social unrest
     a. Strikes
     b. Riots
     c. Insurgency

B. International
  1. Cross-border ties
     a. Ethnic
     b. Religious
     c. Linguistic
     d. Historical
  2. Cross-border antagonisms
     a. Ethnic
     b. Religious
     c. Historical

example would be the generally favorable influence of the U.S. on the Canadian economy in contrast to the religious bitterness between India and Pakistan. Obviously, these and the other examples I have given represent only one analyst's view of conditions in different countries. The reader may disagree with the evaluation, but that doesn't invalidate or weaken the basic methodology.

Economic factors

Table 4's list of economic variables which can affect international lending risk is the longest of the three tables of variables. Table 4 is also subdivided into domestic and international components. However, unlike Tables 2 and 3, the list of international factors is much longer than the domestic. Nonetheless, the domestic factors, such as economic growth, inflation, governmental policies, and the strength of financial infrastructure, are vitally important to international lending risk. For example, significant cyclicality of major industries (the effect of fickle monsoon rains upon crops) or of unwise monetary and fiscal policies (the Chilean and Argentine governments in the early 1970s) can very seriously affect the risk for international lenders to such countries.

On the international side, the principal focus is on the balance of payments, currency strength, foreign debt, and the availability of international financial

Table 4—Economic Factors Affecting Sovereign Risk for International Bank Loans

A. Domestic
  1. Economic growth; investment trends
  2. Cyclicality of economy; economic diversification
  3. Inflation
     a. Monetary policy
     b. Fiscal policy; budget deficits
  4. Strength of local financial markets; portion of total investment financed locally

B. International
  1. Balance of payments
  2. International trade
     a. Importance of trade in GNP
     b. Stability of trade earnings
        (1) Diversity of exports
        (2) Elasticity of export demand
        (3) Elasticity of import demand
            (a) Capital equipment
            (b) Necessities
                1) Degree of self-reliance in food
                2) Reliance on imported energy
                3) Luxuries
     c. International trade ties; proximity to major markets
     d. Extent of trade controls

  3. International capital
     a. Currency
        (1) Strength
        (2) Stability
        (3) Quality of exchange markets
        (4) Depth of exchange markets
        (5) Extent of controls over exchange markets
     b. Debt
        (1) Total
        (2) Short-term as share of total
        (3) Debt service ratio
        (4) Debt service schedule
     c. International financial resources
        (1) International resources; gold valued at market
        (2) International borrowing capacity
            (a) History of debt repayment
            (b) Credit rating
        (3) Autonomous capital inflows
     d. Share of total investment financed from abroad

resources. Of course, these are all closely intertwined, but together they paint a picture of a country which may have difficulties meeting its scheduled or proposed debt obligations. For example, an increasing chorus of concern continues regarding the ability of Eastern European countries to service their foreign long-term debt obligation of almost $50 billion. (Long-term lending to Eastern Europe by U.S., banks had reached almost $7 billion by the end of 1977. However, as already discussed, the brunt of the worry falls upon Western Europe where commercial banks have more than $20 billion outstanding in Eastern Europe.)

To summarize, country risk for an international lender may arise as a result of political, social, or economic factors—either domestic or international. The analyst must be prepared to dig into all possible problem areas. The international lending area is fascinatingly and frustratingly diverse and demands a high degree of flexibility, open-mindedness, and insight on the part of the analyst.

The risk rating

The previous section surveyed the array of principal variables which can affect international lending risk. However, it did not say what form the results of this evaluation process (that is, the risk rating) would take.

Several different approaches have been developed.[5] Essentially they differ in the degree of flexibility permitted in the structure of the system. The most rigid systems are the essentially quantitative ones such as checklists with weights assigned to the different variables. Since many of the factors which we wish to analyze—the extent of exchange controls, political stability, and so forth—do not conveniently lend themselves to being quantified and since many of the important quantitative variables are not current enough for many countries, we chose to seek a more qualitative system.

At the opposite end of the spectrum of possible approaches is the fully qualitative type of system which is based upon unstandardized qualitative reports. However, this approach would not permit adequate comparability between the more than 120 countries on a convenient basis. Therefore, we also rejected this approach.

The other two types of systems rely upon a structured qualitative system— one coupled with a structured checklist but without quantitative weightings.

---

[5] "A Survey of Country Evaluation Systems in Use," Report of the Policy Analysis Staff, Export-Import Bank of the U.S., December 22, 1976. Also, "The Analysis of Country Loan-Risk for Less-Developed Countries," Christopher M. Korth, Center for International Business Studies, College of Business, University of South Carolina, Paper No. 77–16, October 1977.

We felt that the greater restrictiveness of the checklist approach and the ever-present problem of inadequate availability of up-to-date quantitative information were important limitations of this approach.

As indicated previously, we chose the so-called "structured qualitative" approach. We felt very strongly that a wide range of variables needed to be systematically analyzed. However, we preferred to weigh and compare them qualitatively. Granted, this approach only permits very general categorization of risk. However, this is quite acceptable—indeed desirable. It is very difficult—if indeed possible or even necessary—to quantify many of the variables.

The country-risk analysis was used to assign countries into a five-point risk index, ranging from A, very safe, to E, very risky (see Table 5). Some observers have recommended more than five categories. However, the greater the number of categories, the greater the degree of confidence that is implied in one's ability to differentiate between the risk of different countries; this can be very misleading. Also, statisticians indicate that five is an optimal number for most types of categorization. It is, accordingly, the most common and the one with which most people are the most familiar. Finally, since this index will be combined with another index for setting loan limits, a greater number of categories could become quite unwieldy. It is important that a system such as

---

Table 5—Country Risk Ratings

A. *An excellent risk.* Very stable politically with strong, resilient system. Also, strong and stable economically with little likelihood of severe disruption. Highly unlikely that loans and interest would not be repaid in full and on schedule.

B. *A good risk.* Political system is basically strong but less resilient than for "A"; system-disrupting conflicts possible but not likely in short to medium term. Although the economy is basically stable, problems such as inflation, cyclicality, and payments deficits and foreign debt could cause difficulties. Nevertheless, the problems are not likely to become too serious, and there is a high probability of repayment on schedule.

C. *A fair risk.* Presently stable though basic political structure is weak; destablizing pressures could easily develop. Some economic problems causing serious strains. Should be carefully monitored, since repayment problems are quite possible.

D. *A poor risk.* Politically unstable with a high degree of conflict; substantial change in the system very possible. Marked instability and weakness in the economic system. Relatively great risk of loans not being repaid on schedule; significant possibility of default or moritorium.

E. *Very poor risk.* Highly unstable. High possibility of repayment problems.

---

this be simple enough to be readily understood and easily employed by the many different people who are involved in the international lending process.

Lending limits

As already stressed, a country-risk analysis should be as objective as possible. It should identify the *risk* of a loan in a particular country. As such, it bears little relationship to such factors as the country's GNP or long-term economic potential or the bank's economic position and goals in that country. Country-risk analysis should only concentrate on questions of the risk of lending to that country. (In a similar vein, credit-risk analysis should examine only the *risk* of the credit—not how much business the bank can do with that customer.)

The next step is for a bank to set its own country lending limits. As was mentioned at the start of this article, bank regulatory agencies do not mandate lending limits. However, it is very important that the bank set such limits for itself.

Not only should a country lending limit be a function of country risk, it should also be a function of country size. Quite obviously, an economy which is the size of the Netherlands' would not generally warrant as large a proportion of a bank's foreign lending as would Germany. The setting of specific country limits prevents excessive concentration in individual countries (with concentration being measured by both country risk and size)—as with the bank whose major foreign commitment was in Peru. The use of lending limits also encourages a balance in the distribution of foreign loans among foreign countries. Even if a bank limits its lending geographically to, say, Europe, prudent lending policy requires that "all of the bank's eggs not be in one basket."

Accordingly, my bank uses country size as well as country risk as bases for the allocation of foreign loans. Table 6 outlines the five-point index for country size. (A size "5" country would be among the world's smallest while a size "1" would be among the world's seven or eight largest.) Again, the number of categories could have been greater. However, the system would become increasingly unwieldy. Also, different analysts could readily, and with good reason, choose different ranges of GNP; the choice of the GNP ranges is merely a personal or corporate decision and does not change the value of the index at all.

Combined risk and size ratings

Thus far, each country has been assigned a risk rating (A–E) and an economic-size rating (1–5). The combination of these two ratings (Table 7) produces 25 possible alpha-numeric ratings (such as C-2 or A-5) into which *all* countries of the world can be assigned. (If the indexes had had seven or ten

Table 6—Country Economic-Size Ratings

Gross National Product (GNP) (in billions)	Economic-Size Rating
$175+	1
$ 50–175	2
$ 20–50	3
$ 5–20	4
$ 0–5	5

elements, the resulting 7 × 7 or 10 × 10 matrixes would have 49 or 100 different alpha-numeric categories respectively—rather unwieldy.) This combination of the two ratings comprise the core of what we call the Country Loan-Risk Evaluation System (CLRES).

If the analysis has been accurate, the countries in any particular square will be reasonably comparable in risk and economic size. Thus, there ought to be a logical consistency in loan limits between them. (Indeed, the CLRES is de-

Table 7—The Country Loan-Risk Evaluation System (CLRES) Matrix
Economic Size*
(in billions)

		1 ($175+)	2 ($50–175)	3 ($20–50)	4 ($5–20)	5 ($0–5)
R I S K	A					
	B					
R A T I N G S	C					
	D					
	E					

* The numbers in parenthesis are GNP ranges in billions of dollars.

signed to ensure that consistency in loan limits can be created between *all* countries.)

With this breakdown of countries into different categories, a bank has a convenient basis for the setting of loan limits. First, senior management must set the *maximum lending limit* which it will accept for *any* country. This will serve as the reference point from which *ranges* of lending limits (LL) can be set for each of the 25 alpha-numeric categories. Ranges are used to permit greater flexibility. For example, differences in LLs between different countries with the same alpha-numeric rating (for example, B-3)—as between two countries with GNPs of $25 billion and $45 billion—could vary by a significant margin. The use of ranges also leaves room for future increases in lending limits up to the maximum for that rating. Naturally, the ranges decline from left to right on the table as economic size declines and from top to bottom as risk increases. We suggested mandatory lending limits of $0 for all E, D-4, and D-5 countries. With D-1, D-2, and D-3 countries, the economic size and future economic potential were sufficient to warrant taking a chance and establishing a limited lending position in the country although the country risk was high.

Exceptions from the ratings due to subjective factors

Thus far, the CLRES review process has shown how individual banks can systematically determine risk and size ratings for foreign countries and how, with this information, lending limits can be set on a relatively objective basis. Subjective factors are sometimes employed to distort this process. This can be quite logical and need not violate the system. What is important is that through the discipline of the system, the rationale for the exceptions be clearly noted. Classic examples of such exceptions might involve lower lending limits for Communist countries (or perhaps a supplementary regional sublimit for all of Eastern Europe) or more generous lending limits for some oil exporters.

Marketing considerations

Also, marketing considerations have deliberately been excluded thus far in our study. It is extremely important that the risk analysis not be distorted by such factors. However, marketing considerations can indeed be important but additional factors in the final loan decision. As was suggested regarding the $1 billion Argentine loan, such factors as the desire to penetrate a new market, maintain market prominence, special relationships with a government, or the existence of bank offices within that country can well affect a bank's decision about lending limits or an individual loan. But at least bank management will be aware in advance of the extra degree of risk being assumed. The important thing is that *all* of the relevant factors get appropriate consideration and that the bank has a true picture of all risks involved in the decision.

Conclusions

The CLRES is a rational, effective, and very flexible approach to satisfying the need for careful country-risk analysis and the setting of country loan limits. What has been described here, however, is only the simplest application of the system. Further logical refinements provide guidelines for acceptable interest-rate spreads, separate long- and short-term limits, separate government and private-sector limits, and separate local-currency and cross-border limits. Lending officer guidelines can also be provided to keep pace with the increase of loan portfolios in an individual country and to maintain a balanced loan-payoff pattern so that new funds are constantly becoming available.

A systematic approach such as CLRES has several important contributions to make:

1. Risk appraisal.
2. Recognition of opportunity.
3. Balanced allocation of assets between countries (that is, self-insurance).
4. Tying loan spreads to risk.
5. The overall discipline of preview and review.

An Approach to Evaluating Foreign Bank Credit Risk

by Charles F. Mansfield, Jr.

Whether the subject of a credit analysis is a U.S., French, or Japanese bank, it may be thoroughly evaluated, according to Charles Mansfield, by following the same basic procedure: Identify the critical financial variables and structure an analysis to examine them, both individually and in relation to other factors. The author focuses on six such variables and explains how to use them in analyzing foreign credit risks.

Many corporate officers and international bankers have recently come to scrutinize more carefully the nature and quality of the financial institutions with which their firms do business. Generally speaking, this renewed emphasis derives from the 1974-75 global recession, but it can also be traced to such specific events as the Herstatt failure.

"The winds and waves are always on the side of the ablest navigator," wrote Gibbon. In a changing or problematic environment, therefore, it is imperative to recognize and reaffirm those fundamentals which either require the highest priority or should not be altered without sufficient justification. In exactly such a context, the importance of the credit function and of the credit process as its guide should be acknowledged and reaffirmed. I hope that the following ideas will provide some renewed incentive for greater introspection and the refinement of practices for maintaining a healthy portfolio.

State of the art of international interbank lending

Concerning credit extensions to financial institutions, a recent article in *The Journal of Commercial Bank Lending* contained a simple statement worth remembering: "If you have a 'Due From' ledger, you are extending credit."

In recent years, interbank lending has expanded rapidly, thereby increasing substantially the demand for funds. From a rather modest $6.9 billion of syndicated bank loans in 1972, the Euromarket arranged $21.9 billion of loans in 1973 and a phenomenal $29.3 billion in 1974. The total in 1975 dipped to just below $21 billion, but it is clearly on the rise again. Some $20.4 billion worth of credits was announced during just the first ten months of 1976. Yet, many of these credits and many interbank transactions, as well, were granted casually with inadequate scrutiny of how the proceeds were to be used.

By supplying credit and creating international liquidity, commercial banks, mostly American, have partially assumed some functions that formerly were the domain of official international institutions such as the International Monetary Fund (IMF). Moreover, it is becoming increasingly clear that such credits and interbank placements represent potential risks and, therefore, should not be considered with any less stringent standards than would be applied in assessing the risks associated with other prospective credit extensions. Accordingly, lenders must consider the basic elements in any credit decision as the criteria for evaluating international interbank credits.

For most international banks today, interbank credits comprise the largest portion of their overseas loan portfolios. It is readily recognized that if one includes Eurocurrency placements, the total obligations among banks in different countries sum to a staggering figure: Total Euromarket loans and deposits have been estimated at $215 billion! According to a recent survey, the total external debt of the non-OPEC developing countries totaled $150 billion at the end of 1975, of which $100 billion was lent to or guaranteed by the public sector. An estimated $59.3 billion of the total was owed to commercial banks, and $38.5 billion — or 65% of this bank debt — was owed to banks in the United States or their foreign branches.

Despite this unprecedented financial growth, little has been written until recently on the nature, practices, and problems of interbank credit. The rules and procedures that prudent lenders should follow when considering a credit extension to or the placement of funds with a bank in a foreign country have also been neglected.

Increased attention to foreign risk evaluation

The events of recent years have clearly caused interbank lending, once regarded as risk-free, to be analyzed much more carefully than before. Even short-term foreign exchange transactions have become significantly more susceptible to variation and thus riskier under the current floating rate system. Quite properly, then, overall risk evaluation requires and is receiving increased attention.

In the future, penetration of markets by commercial banks must have a solid base in terms of credit factors because there may be, according to many observers, more frequent and turbulent cyclical economic movements than in the past. In short, interbank lending, particularly overseas, is in a new environment. Renewed emphasis must be placed on the following:

1. Clear identification and precise measurement of market risks.

2. Selection of acceptable risk criteria.

3. Ensuring that the credit process is suited to the characteristics of each risk asset category.

4. Reinforcement of the credit, managerial, and marketing skills needed to serve particular markets.

U.S. domestic analysis techniques applicable to foreign credit

In some U. S. banks, good progress has been made in updating and refining credit analysis techniques for domestic commercial banks. However, specific ratios used in the U. S. do not always have ready application to foreign bank analyses. Nevertheless, they do provide a framework within which an analyst, who knows what information he wants, can make sound decisions with respect to a given institution's soundness and creditworthiness.

Getting the desired type and amount of information on banks located in foreign countries may involve difficulty and frustration. In contrast, the uniformity and comparative wealth of information available on U. S. banks have facilitated the development of an analytical methodology. Despite variations in both accounting techniques and banking practices among the various countries, this methodology can be useful to account managers and credit analysts overseas.

Much of the difficulty and frustration in analyzing foreign credit risk can be overcome provided the individual manager becomes attuned to his particular marketplace. This demands knowledge of the liquidity position and types of loans that his client bank is making and the ability to assess whether sources of funds and portfolio quality are good or otherwise. This can best be achieved by frequent checking with the marketplace through reliable sources, not the least of which should be the manager's own foreign exchange traders.

Risk selection and analysis

An honest assessment of risk versus return remains the true test of sound credit extension. Three basic aspects are involved. Bankers must —

1. Understand the risks being taken. In the international area, these include the political and economic risks of a particular country as well as the commercial or financial risks of dealing with a particular borrower.

2. Evaluate each credit in terms of total compensation. Adequate pricing is essential if banks are to generate sufficient new capital through retained earnings.

3. Consider now only the adequacy of pricing on a particular credit but also what each transaction means in terms of a broader, long-term relationship.

In short, the idea is to identify the critical financial variables and to structure an analysis that will examine them, both by themselves and in relation to other important factors.

Risk measurement and acceptance depend on several factors, the most important of which are the type of credit extended and the standing of the obligor bank. The fact that risk increases with time strongly influences the first factor; the quality of management is the crucial element in assessing the second. The following list provides the main areas of focus when analyzing the credit risk associated with foreign banks:

1. Management
2. Earnings
3. Asset quality
4. Liquidity
5. Capitalization/capital adequacy
6. Cross-border risk

Management

Any analysis of a bank must begin with bank management, its integrity and competence, and how the management process itself works in that organization.

No bank is better than its management. A bank's decision-makers should be well-trained professionals; indeed, management is the key to the sometimes conflicting requirements of liquidity and capital adequacy. Its board of directors should be comprised of responsible individuals of sound reputation. Key department heads, especially those responsible for international business, should know their jobs and responsibilities well.

It is useful to identify individuals at several levels of a bank's management who are well informed about the bank and willing to discuss it, especially in regard to such critical areas as asset quality and earnings composition. Knowledge of the management process is vital and should include answers to the following key questions:

1. **Internal control systems:** Does the bank have an internal auditing function?

2. **Accounting policies:** Are earnings on an accrual or cash basis? Is income front-ended? What is the policy for recognizing loan losses? Who controls this? Have outside auditors been retained? How good are they?

3. **Internal Management Information System (MIS):** What information does management have about its business? How frequently is it updated? How is it used? Is there a formal budgeting process?

4. **Personnel policies:** Is management the career-professional type, or is it staffed by politicos? What training programs are required? Does management tolerate conflicts of interest? Are account officers paid commissions for generating loans?

5. **Reputation:** What does the market think of officers and directors? What are the rumors about the bank? What is the general perception of management compared with its competition?

Earnings

Since bank profitability typically shows the first sign of weakness when problems arise, risk is traditionally measured by the variability of earnings. Thus, over the long run, the quality of a bank's earnings is the best single indicator of the quality of management. Problems may develop in earnings and in asset quality which soon enough affect earnings. When they do, the analyst must look to liquidity and capital as defenses.

Perhaps the best indicator of earnings performance is the rate of return on average assets. This is a period's earnings divided by average assets managed during the period. If this figure is high in relation to that of other banks of comparable size and type in the same country and relatively consistent or rising over time, it indicates that the bank is able to add to its capital base through retained earnings. It also indicates that the bank has a cushion against mistakes, difficult economic conditions, or poor luck. If the figure is low or declining rapidly, it could indicate that the bank is paring its margins dangerously thin to get loan business or is engaging in increasingly risky lending.

The profit margin ratio is an exceptionally reliable measurement of management control over expenses as well as maintaining "spreads." Technically, the profit margin is simply earnings before taxes expressed as a percent of the total income of the bank less the interest expense. In other words, the profit margin or spread is the end result of gathering deposits at one rate and then lending them at a higher rate.

In banks of comparable size, business, and location, the bank with the wider profit margin is usually acknowledged to be the best managed. However, in some management-owned banks, higher salaries may lessen the significance of this ratio. In such cases, one must look closely at the nonsalary expenses related to other similar banks. Incidentally, the profit margin ratio tends to favor the wholesale banks because of their lower overhead.

Accounting practices must be thoroughly understood. It is sometimes difficult to recognize earnings which might be hidden in other accounts. In short, it is important to know the derivation of the figures.

Asset quality

Information on the quality of a bank's loan portfolio is often sparse in the U.S., and such qualitative data are in many instances even more difficult to obtain from foreign financial institutions.

A lender can predict, to a degree, a given bank's loan losses using historical loss experience, an awareness of management quality, reasonably accurate economic forecasts, and sound judgment concerning credit exposure in certain areas. With this forecast in mind, managers must strive to obtain as much information as possible concerning asset quality. The following approach is recommended:

1. Look for large concentrations of credit in single areas. A bank should limit concentrations so that no single occurrence can have a significant adverse impact.

2. Look for significant changes in the loan portfolio. History teaches that when any bank or other business becomes rapidly and heavily involved in a new field, there are ultimate costs to be borne in connection with handling unforeseen problems (for example, REIT's).

3. Compare the loan portfolio with the economic outlook for the bank's country or market segments. Economic trends should be observed and carefully analyzed. Good performance under adverse conditions is the best indicator of the quality of both management and the loan portfolio.

4. Above all, ask direct questions about any potential concerns regarding the quality of the loan portfolio. (This brings to mind a comment by a

distinguished credit officer and colleague: "Credit has not three 'C's' but only one: curiosity.")

Loan loss coverage is a valuable ratio that links asset quality and earnings. In U.S. bank terminology, it is the ratio of pretax income before securities gains (losses) and before the provision for possible loan losses to total net loan losses. In overseas situations, an appropriate analogue should be developed. Ideally, the numerator in the fraction should "cover" the denominator, net loan losses, by a healthy margin. The beauty of this ratio is that it gives a true picture of a bank's gross earnings generation compared with a true picture of its current loan losses and recoveries.

No bank that depends on other financial institutions and external market sources for a significant portion of its funding can afford a loss. A loss by a bank causes a "red flag" bearing its name to be unfurled immediately in full view of all its potential funds suppliers. Ultimately, it may force such a bank to go to its central bank as the lender of last resort, or it may force a merger or even liquidation.

Liquidity

A bank's liquidity may be defined as its ability to meet demands for funds. It is a key element in any qualitative evaluation of a bank because of the rapidly shifting character of a bank's assets and liabilities. This position is necessarily modified from time to time to maintain adequate levels of operating cash, legal reserves, accounts with correspondent banks, and vault cash. In other words, liquidity means maintaining sufficient reserves to meet both daily and seasonal deposit swings, long-term deposit trends, and customer loan demand.

The idea is to operate within these constraints without unduly disturbing the loan portfolio, incurring excessive investment losses through the sale of securities, or resorting to borrowings except for temporary periods. If strains on liquidity persist, bank credit must be allocated and, perhaps, applications for new loans curtailed or declined.

Over the past fifteen years, there has been a change in banking resources and their management which has introduced new controversy into bank liquidity concepts. It is the increased importance of purchased money in banks' daily operations.

Revolution in the management of bank resources. — Any discussion of sources of funds management must emphasize that the past several years have witnessed a revolution in the management of commercial banking resources. Sources of funds used to be more limited, and the basic problem was simply to manage assets. In contrast, banks nowadays are using many recent innovations which have expanded the scope of resources management to embrace the entire mix of assets and liabilities. Furthermore, the scramble for money which gave rise to the changes is still going on. Indeed, as we look ahead, virtually all forecasters agree that we are in an era of presistent large demand for funds.

As a consequence, liquidity today is largely governed by cash inflow and outflow rather than by balance sheet ratios alone. Despite the credit squeezes of recent years (1966, 1969-70, and 1974) and the concomitant inability to sell assets without sustaining deep discounts, banks found that balanced interest differentials (adjustments of interest paid and interest charged) could keep them in the lending business. Thus bankers perceived that they could still accommodate borrowers' demands by buying lendable funds.

For the large metropolitan and regional banks, liquidity can be described as the ability of a particular bank to acquire funds through the issuance or acceptance of a liability by the bank. Each bank must manage its affairs so that it can respond to the needs of its customers seeking credit and other financial services. Its ability to attract funds from the market, the large industrial corporations, insurance companies, and other financial institutions and to borrow is determined by its ability to pay a competitive rate of return. In a very real sense, then, each bank operates within the context of its own given market — be it international, national, or regional — and its customers' needs.

Bank reliance on purchased funds. — Because no two banks will have identical requirements, liquidity is not a fixed concept, and there is no single measure or ratio for it. This is also true because in many banks the change in deposit mix, demand versus time deposits and different reserve requirements, has operated to make total liquidity ratios invalid. Accordingly, since the liquidity game has changed, it is necessary to look beyond liquid assets to a given bank's reliance on purchased funds.

Often dubbed the "hot money" ratio, the ratio of basic market-sensitive liabilities to loans or loans and investments illustrates a bank's reliance on purchased funds. The majority of a bank's funds may be very stable deposits associated with longstanding customer relationships. However, in some banks, funds represent largely bought or borrowed money which can be highly volatile.

Other liquidity ratios in common use are the loan-to-deposit and quick-asset-to-deposit ratios. While there are many other more sophisticated ratios, these require more detailed breakdowns of balance sheet numbers than most banks can reasonably anticipate receiving from their clients within the next few years.

Because of its liquidity and sovereign (country, cross-border) risk implications, a key consideration in assessing foreign bank credit risk is ownership: government, such as in France and Italy or private, such as in England and Japan. A government bank should have the government's legal and moral commitment; if this is assured, the credit risk reduces to government or sovereign risk. Some private commercial banks may have "national importance," the test being what economic and political consequences would follow if they became insolvent.

In time of financial crisis, the central bank would probably function as the lender of last resort to a given bank or the whole banking system. That is, the central bank would carry out its basic and traditional role as the supplier of supplementary liquidity. While governments come and go for a variety of reasons, the central bank is generally regarded as a perpetual institution by virtue of both its role and its tie to the IMF.

In sum, the extent to which a sovereign government can be expected to support a given bank in time of crisis is a critical factor in the foreign bank credit decision.

Capitalization and capital adequacy

In the last few years, the question of bank capital adequacy has been the subject of acrimonious debate, especially in the U. S. This disagreement is an outgrowth of numerous adverse developments which included at least three prominent bank failures. Intelligent efforts to develop a precise definition of what constitutes adequate bank capital, principally by means of ratio analysis, have invariably yielded only inexact and less than satisfactory results. While it is not suggested that analytical methods be ignored in assessing the soundness of banks, particularly those in foreign countries, it is maintained that capital adequacy reduces to what local banking regulations require or what is considered normal for similar (leading) banks in the same country.

In response to a question at the American Bankers Association Correspondent Banking Conference in November 1976, Citicorp Chairman Walter B. Wriston went to the heart of the matter. "You have capital adequacy," he said, "when you give the marketplaces of your area, or country, or the world, confidence that their needs will be met with enough margin for error to take care of the mistakes that we're all going to make." Implicit here are the ideas that banks function as intermediaries of financial resources and assume risk and in doing so, will experience credit losses. Continued Mr. Wriston, "...the hallmark of any business is the ability to keep your risk within your risk-taking capabilities. It's just that simple. Risk taking capability [that is, capital adequacy] has to be defined as the ability to absorb losses in your earnings stream."

A number of capital ratios are used, including loans to capital and capital to risk assets/earning assets/total assets; however, the measurement that relates a bank's earning power to its net loan losses is probably the most meaningful. In the final analysis, the answer to what constitutes adequate capital lies in a bank's profitability, the quality of its loan portfolio, and its liquidity. Only after these analyses are complete should one rely on traditional capital adequacy ratios.

Cross-border risk

In judging the credit of a particular country, there are many factors, too numerous to treat thoroughly here, that demand serious consideration and analysis. First, a creditor must closely monitor conditions in the country. These include the current economic situation as well as the related outlook and policies. In addition, the trends and prospects for a country's principal economic sectors must be examined. In the same context, the actual and potential flow of funds and financial intermediation, both internal and external, must be understood.

Second, other elements such as political and social conditions and their outlook, as well as the country's international position and relations, are critical elements in the credit decision.

Third, statistical indicators such as debt service ratios (for example, debt service to GNP or to export receipts), export growth, diversification, and earnings variability, as well as imports in relation to GNP, monetary reserve changes, and growth in external debt must be analyzed and understood if national creditworthiness is to be judged properly.

Also to be considered are factors that reduce country risk such as scheduling maturities (risk increases with the length of the obligation), transactions that are self-liquidating, and having loans guaranteed by the government or the central bank. To emphasize this last point, Citicorp, in its 1975 Annual Report, reported that it "has never in its history experienced a loss where a loan has been guaranteed by a central bank."

Various warning signals normally appear before a nation's economy experiences material adverse changes. Careful monitoring by a creditor generally enables him to protect his position by taking corrective action in timely fashion. Diversification of risk is the guiding principle, and profit opportunities must always be subordinated to the principle of avoiding excessive country risk.

Ratio analysis appraised

Detailed studies have shown that ratios have had little bearing on bank failures over recent history. Hence, ratio analysis should be only one tool in a large tool box. In other words, it can at best provide only a surface look at a bank or group of banks and should never be the sole basis of decision-making.

The use of ratios in analysis is limited by variations in accounting standards, and the complex array of ratios sometimes used by bank analysts in the U. S. is often of little value when analyzing a foreign bank's statement. Ratio analysis should be used only to compare similar banks or to follow the progress of a given bank over a period of years.

Once calculated, ratios must be related to some bench marks that the lender considers appropriate for a particular situation, such as similar type banks in the same country. Yet, because banks are not usually comparable in any precise sense, it is important not to draw hasty conclusions when a bank's statement differs from the norm. However, it is absolutely essential to probe more deeply to ask why the statement differs. A second source of standards is a creditor bank's own experience and judgment of what constitutes acceptable norms of overall performance and financial condition.

Analysis of financial statements over a period of years ultimately does give some indication of the direction in which a given institution is heading. Over time, a reasonable portion of a bank's earnings should be retained, and capital should grow proportionately with assets and liabilities. This may be the most valuable objective of statement and ratio analysis.

Conclusion

Charles M. Williams, Harvard University's George Gund Professor of Commercial Banking, observed the following in the Robert Morris Associates' text, *Offshore Lending by U.S. Commercial Banks:* Any significant and sustained downturn after a long period of enthusiastic expansion and optimism is almost certain to lead to increased loan losses and concern for credit quality and to feed a management mood of 'back to sound lending'." Since this observation was committed to writing, it has proved correct; its pertinence, therefore, is unquestionable. "Old-time religion" has imbued the commercial lending culture once more, and the recent mood clearly has been one of "back to basics." Though "caution" is still the password of bankers, there is no reason why growth cannot still be achieved. However, if this is to be accomplished, it can only be done without the overly imaginative lending that induced the much lamented losses of the past two years. In this connection, it is appropriate to recall the wisdom of the Dutch proverb: "In prosperity, caution; in adversity, patience."

Another observation, this one by the late D. A. Forward, an eminent credit officer and a former Vice Chairman of Citibank, is worthy of note: "The difference between a smart lending officer and one who is not is that the former has the intelligence and takes the time to obtain all of the pertinent facts before he reaches his decision."[1]

_____
[1] Vice Chairman of First National City Bank until his retirement in 1959, Mr. Forward was in charge of credit policy supervision.

No matter how carefully a general information package is assembled by a creditor, there will always be the need for creativity on the part of lending officers in judging a particular borrower's situation. No generalized system can substitute for creditor judgment as to what data may be necessary since each borrower has some unique characteristics. The creativity and talent of the lending officer in developing this individual information package are vital.

Looking ahead, let us keep in mind the following:

1. We must recognize and understand thoroughly the risks when extending credit to foreign financial institutions.

2. Our degree of understanding will be a function of (a) the type and quality of data that we obtain from borrowers and (b) our skill in deriving meaningful information from the data through quality credit analysis and review.

3. We should request only the data we want to review, and we should request it the first time around.

4. No one element of analysis is sufficient in itself; rather, each must be considered in relation to other variables. Moreover, the analysis system must vary with each sovereignty.

In 1972, P. Henry Mueller, Chairman Credit Policy Committee of Citicorp and Citibank, N.A., made a significant point which many international bankers today have seemingly failed to consider: "Credit quality is influenced by management, competition, technology and by change itself. While credit principles are universal, it is the lender who becomes the market and sets the standards. It is his interplay with circumstance that produces good or bad decisions."[2]

There will always be a fine balance to be struck between too much credit and too little, between risk and reward, with earnings luring lenders away from proven principles. Yet it is essential that bankers use common sense in lending and remain alert and adaptable to changing circumstances: Continuous exposure to change, willingness to innovate within the basic banking framework, and openness of mind are required. Lastly, it is still true that the best banker is often the first to admit that he still has much to learn. □

---

[2]P. Henry Mueller, "Sighting In On International Lending," *The Journal of Commercial Bank Lending,* November 1972.

International Term Loan Agreements and Loan Syndications

by C. Thorne Corse

An expert on the legalities involved in international lending discusses such topics as the choice of law and forum for international transactions, sovereign immunity, and the problems associated with international loan syndications.

The first part of the title of this article is something of a misnomer. I do not propose to discuss in any detail the construction or drafting of a term loan agreement. For one thing, I must assume that the readers of this article have adequate expertise in this general area. For another—perhaps a more realistic consideration—there isn't space. Accordingly, in general, I shall allude to drafting problems only in those contexts which are particularly relevant to international loans or to loan syndications.

I should, however, like to pass on to you one word of general advice: Keep the agreement as short and simple as possible. Apart from any other excellent reasons for so doing, in international transactions you are likely to be dealing with borrowers and other banks, not to mention their respective lawyers, whose grasp of the English language may be shaky at best. I can assure you

---

This article is based on a presentation made by the author at the Practising Law Institute International Banking course held in San Francisco and New York in March and April, 1977.

from bitter personal experience that an incomprehensible clause in English becomes even more so when translated into any other language.

My presentation, unlike Gaul, will generally be divided into two parts, with, however, considerable overlap. I propose first to discuss particular problems that may arise in international lending, whether there is a single lender or many, and then to go into problems involved in multi-lender transactions.

International lending—general

Choice of law

The problem of what law should be, by contract or otherwise, applicable to international lending transactions has received increasing attention over the past few years for two main reasons. First, with the recent worldwide recession, lenders have naturally had increased concern with the legal enforceability of lending transactions. This has in turn led to a more profound legal analysis of the problem. Second, more and more countries, particularly in Latin America, have been urging, or sometimes insisting on, choice of their own law.

In fall 1976, a decision was handed down by the Supreme Court of Colombia to the effect that a choice of foreign law or a choice of foreign forum provision in a contract entered into by a Colombian entity, whether public or private, is in violation of the Colombian Constitution and is therefore unenforceable. In fact, the decision went so far as to hold that even arbitration proceedings must be held in Colombia with Colombian arbitrators. Based on this decision, Colombian borrowers currently refuse to accept documentation containing provisions making applicable any foreign law or submitting to any foreign jurisdiction.

For another example, I am informed by Mexican counsel that in a law suit brought in a Mexican court against a Mexican borrower, contractual choice of a foreign law will not be recognized, and the Mexican courts will willy-nilly apply Mexican law.

It is my personal opinion that the incidence of borrowers or their courts applying their own law is more likely to increase than to diminish. From this it follows that even when a borrower is willing to accept the applicability of foreign law, one should always ensure that the agreement is also enforceable under the borrower's (or, if applicable, the guarantor's) own law.

It has always been my own feeling, for what it is worth, that the applicable law should not be a matter of major concern as long as the jurisdiction chosen has a sufficiently sophisticated body of substantive law to deal with whatever may be the complications of the particular transaction and is reasonably susceptible of proof in a foreign forum. This approach, however, is not always shared by our clients, who, perhaps justifiably, feel more comfortable with their own law, or at least one with which they are generally familiar.

Assuming that one is not stuck with a particular law, such as in Mexico or Colombia, one must take into account in selecting a law to be applicable to a transaction at least the following factors:

(1) If the jurisdiction in which the contract is likely to be enforced subscribes to the reasonable nexus doctrine in relation to choice of law, one must obviously be able to establish such nexus.

(2) If the law is other than that of the likely forum, one must explore the degree of difficulty and the methods prescribed for proof of foreign law, since in almost all jurisdictions, it must be proved as a question of fact.

(3) Although this is a point which is often overlooked, it is vital to explore the usury provisions of the law chosen, particularly in periods of high interest rates.

In this connection, one should bear in mind that in many civil law jurisdictions, a unilateral setting of an interest rate by the lender may result in inability to collect any interest. This fact becomes particularly relevant when, for example, the interest rate is based upon the lender's London interbank offered rate (LIBOR). There is at least some risk of the same problem arising if the rate is tied to the lender's prime.

Choice of forum

When one is faced with a situation such as that in Colombia, one obviously, has no choice. The client must decide whether as a matter of business judgment he is willing to submit to the prescribed forum. The lawyer's function in assisting the client in this decision, as I see it, is to determine, as pointed out above, the sophistication of the law of the forum which may, as a practical matter, be applied whether or not there has been a choice of a different body of substantive law. Perhaps more important, the lawyer's function is to determine the sophistication and integrity of the judicial system of the prescribed forum.

Where the choice is open, the following factors should be taken into account:

(1) To the extent applicable, again one must consider the reasonable nexus doctrine.

(2) In addition, even if there is both subject matter and personal jurisdiction, there is a risk of the application of the forum non conveniens doctrine. I am told, for example, that there is authority in New York law that despite a submission to the jurisdiction by a potential defendant, a New York court may on its own motion dismiss the proceeding on the basis of that doctrine.

(3) In some jurisdictions, a choice of forum provision is, as a matter of law, exclusive. Consider, for example, the situation in Chile. If an agreement contains a clause submitting to the jurisdiction of the Chilean courts, the latter will not recognize a foreign judgment in respect thereof even though there was both subject matter and personal jurisdiction under the law of the forum where the judgment was entered. Accordingly, unless one can find assets of the borrower involved outside of Chile, or any other country with a similar doctrine, a foreign judgment is of no value.

Obviously a submission to the jurisdiction clause must incorporate the appointment of an agent for service of process. One must not forget to obtain the agreement of the agent appointed so to act.

Documentation

As I indicated in the introduction, I do not propose to discuss drafting problems. One must determine, however, whether it is appropriate or desirable in a particular case to have the borrower's obligations evidenced by promissory notes or whether entries on a loan account would be more appropriate.

In many civil law countries, there is an advantage in having promissory notes which are "negotiable instruments" under the local law since it is possible procedurally to move more expeditiously, through what is usually called "executive procedure," in the enforcement of a note than in the enforcement of an obligation otherwise evidenced. The availability or not of executive procedure is a procedural matter, not substantive, and, accordingly, is not affected by any choice of law provision. There are, however, disadvantages to using notes:

(1) In some jurisdictions, they will attract stamp tax which, even though it normally would be for the borrower's account, is undesirable.

(2) In addition, in many jurisdictions the obtaining of promissory notes is operationally extremely burdensome. For example, a promissory note in some jurisdictions is unenforceable if it is in installment form. This form means that one must obtain a separate note for each maturity of each advance.

If one has a multi-advance, multi-lender transaction, this obviously results in a mountain of paper. In addition, some jurisdictions do not regard an interest-bearing note as negotiable. In this case, one must not only obtain a note for each maturity of each advance but for each installment of interest. If, as in most cases, one is working with a floating rate over LIBOR or even over prime, this situation results not only in an even higher mountain but in an operational nightmare.

Sovereign immunity

With the increasing volume of loans made to, or guaranteed by, foreign governments or to or by foreign governmental entities, the question of sovereign immunity has become of greater and greater concern. It should be noted that the question arises in two areas: whether the foreign government or entity is subject to suit in the first place and, assuming that it is subject to suit, whether its property is subject to execution in implementation of any resulting judgment.

In the United States.   Before January 19, 1977, the following cases in the U.S. generally recognized international law doctrine and have drawn a distinction between a government acting in its sovereign capacity and a government acting in a commercial capacity. They have generally held that when the activity was sovereign, sovereign immunity attached, but when it was commercial, it did not.

The situation was complicated, however, by the interjection of the U.S. State Department, under the terms of the so-called Tate letter of 1952. The terms of the letter stipulate that upon application to the Department by the foreign government or entity involved, a political determination was made by that Department, generally based on the dichotomy discussed above, which was then followed by the courts.

In addition, before January 19, there was no prescribed method by which process could be served on a foreign government or foreign entity. In a very large number of the cases which arose, jurisdiction was sought to be obtained by attachment of property located in the U.S. belonging to the government or entity concerned. In fact, the majority of determinations by the State Department under the Tate letter involved this situation.

The Tate letter and the cases decided thereunder are no longer relevant because of the statute referred to below. Therefore, I do not propose a detailed discussion of the state of the law on this question before January 19.

On October 21, 1976, the President signed Public Law No. 94-583, The Foreign Sovereign Immunities Act of 1976, which became effective January 19, 1977. In general, this Act has brought about the following major results:

(1) Decisions on sovereign immunity are now to be made exclusively by the courts without State Department involvement. However, the State Department has reserved the right to appear as amicus in court proceedings which it regards as involving issues significant to the conduct of the foreign policy of the U.S.*

---

* See the letter from the State Department to the Attorney General dated November 10, 1976.

(2) The Act confers jurisdiction over an action against a foreign state or foreign entity on the U.S. District courts irrespective of the amount in controversy.

(3) The Act establishes means by which service of process may be made upon a foreign state or entity.

(4) The distinction referred to above between sovereign activities and commercial activities has been codified. However, it can be argued that there are some definitional ambiguities in the codification. For example, a commercial activity is defined as "either a regular course of commercial conduct or a particular commercial transaction or act. The commercial character of an activity shall be determined by reference to the nature of the course of conduct or particular transaction or act, rather than by reference to its purpose." Without discussing this definition in detail, it is obvious that one must look elsewhere for the meaning of "commercial," which could present problems.

I do not propose to furnish to you a detailed analysis of the Act, but for our purposes, the following points are significant:

(1) Sovereign immunity from suit shall not exist if it has been waived, explicitly or by implication, and notwithstanding any attempted withdrawal of such waiver (see below). Sovereign immunity shall also be nonexistent if the action is based upon a commercial activity carried on in the U.S. or upon an act performed in the U.S. in connection with a commercial activity elsewhere or an act performed elsewhere in connection with a commercial activity elsewhere if the act "causes a direct effect in the United States."

(2) Property in the U.S. shall not be exempt from execution if immunity has been waived notwithstanding any withdrawal, if the property is or was used for the commercial activity which was the subject of the action, and in the case of a foreign entity other than the state itself, if the judgment is on a claim arising from a commercial activity.

Of course, there remains the question as to the degree to which a foreign government will recognize a judgment entered in the U.S. in conformity with the Act. Accordingly, the collectability of such a judgment in the absence of property upon which execution can be levied in the U.S. is still problematical.

Outside the United States. I am not in a position to give you a country by country rundown of the laws of all the countries of the world on this subject. To a greater or lesser degree, however, the dichotomy between commercial and sovereign activities is recognized in respect to immunity claims by foreign governments.

In some jurisdictions, however, a waiver in advance, in, for example, a loan agreement, of either jurisdiction or execution can be withdrawn and, accordingly, is not enforceable. This is the present law in England, although a recent opinion of the Queen's Counsel received in another context prophesies that the English courts or Parliament will move closer to the U.S. approach.

There are also jurisdictions where it has been held constitutionally beyond the power of the sovereign to waive immunity to either jurisdiction or execution or to both. In each case, one must obviously look to the law of the borrower or guarantor involved.

Generally, I think that the whole problem of sovereign immunity is given a little bit more importance than perhaps it deserves. Except on the rare occasions when it is possible to execute against property in this country, the realities of life are that if a sovereign government elects not to live up to its obligations, it probably can get away with it. Accordingly, I suggest that the collectability of loans to or guaranteed by governmental entities is more dependent upon the need of the government involved to maintain its reputation for integrity in the world financial community than it is upon the applicability of sovereign immunity.

Loan syndications

Pre-closing problems

Until recently, little attention has been focused on the risks involved in the activities prior to actual documentation of a transaction of that lender or those lenders who are putting together a multi-lender loan. The recent heightened interest has arisen primarily from the greatly increased size of individual transactions which, in turn, has complicated their organization and structure.

Until a few years ago, the sum of say $50,000,000 was regarded as a very large loan and usually did not require or justify the participation of more than a relatively limited number of lenders. Most, if not all, of these lenders were likely to be among the larger and more sophisticated institutions with adequate facilities of their own to investigate and appraise the credit worthiness of the transaction.

In addition, communication among a relatively few lenders obviously is easier than when many are involved. Accordingly, individual lenders were probably able to exercise more influence on the lead lender(s) regarding the terms and conditions contained in the final documentation.

The size of individual transactions has increased greatly, and up to $1,000,000,000 is now not uncommon. This increase has created an obvious necessity for the inclusion of a very large number of lenders in individual transactions. Communication among lenders has thus become more difficult and more formal. As a result, lenders who do not have the sophistication or the facilities independently to investigate and appraise the credit worthiness of the transaction have been included in syndicates.

Accordingly, whether the lead lenders like it or not, it is unquestionably a fact of life that more and more of the members of a multi-lender group are relying very heavily on the judgmental decisions of the leads. Further, the multiplicity of lenders has resulted in the practical necessity of the preparation by the lead(s) of "offering memoranda"—never, never called prospectuses!

Obviously, if one puts matters involving one's judgment of the project's credit worthiness into written form, it is a great deal more likely that what one says will come home to haunt one. Various devices have been developed in an attempt to minimize this danger. They are discussed in somewhat more detail in the following section of this article. I shall merely point out here that I have serious misgivings as to their effectiveness.

Closing problems

In international transactions, the problems involved in closing documentation for a multi-lender transaction are essentially those problems which I have already discussed plus, of course, all those additional problems which may arise in any multi-party transaction, be it domestic or international.

The situation is further complicated, however, by substantial differences of opinion among lenders and among lenders' lawyers as to the importance of the various problems discussed and as to the appropriate solutions. It has been my general experience that lead lenders and their lawyers have an unshakable conviction that syndicate members and their lawyers are a nitpicking group of idiots. On the other hand, syndicate members and their lawyers are convinced that their colleagues in or associated with the lead lenders bear resemblance to Idi Amin.

There is obviously no easy solution to this primarily psychological problem. The only constructive suggestion that I can make is that all parties involved make a conscious effort to exude sweet reasonableness.

One additional word of advice, however. With respect to drafting or other strictly legal problems (as opposed to business problems), every effort should be made to put negotiations on a lawyer to lawyer basis rather than permitting them to be channeled through the respective clients. I have never known a lawyer's communication to another lawyer not to suffer in translation when passed on through one or more laymen.

Post-closing problems

In the context of this article, the principal problem, it seems to me, involves the relationship of the lead lender(s) to the participating lenders and the responsibilities of the former to the latter. I find great difficulty in reaching a conclusion other than that the lead has at least a quasi-fiduciary responsibility toward the others, both at common (or, for that matter, civil) law, and, where they are applicable, under the U.S. Securities Acts.

Obviously, as long as all is going well and the loan is being paid, there is not likely to be a problem. If, however, something goes wrong, it is obvious that the participating lenders would like to pass on their loss, if any, to the lead(s). The issue then becomes whether the lead(s) has(ve) handled the administration of the loan properly. For a further discussion of this issue in connection with the Colocotronis litigation, see the article in the January 1978 issue of *The Journal of Commercial Bank Lending* entitled, "The Colocotronis Case: Considerations for Multi-bank Lenders."

In this situation, inquiry is focused on two areas: The first is whether adequate and accurate disclosure has been made on information concerning the borrower which has come, or conceivably which, in the exercise of reasonable precautions, should have come, to the notice of the lead(s). My general advice is to err on the side of disclosure and, of course, to be as certain of one's facts as possible.

That advice, however, is not as easy to follow as it sounds. In the first place, the volume of paper work involved in informing a large syndicate that, for example, the president of the borrower is sleeping with his secretary is horrendous. Lending officers justifiably feel that they have a great many more important things to do. In the second place, there is almost invariably considerable pressure from the borrower not to reveal certain items which may come to the attention of the lead(s). This may be very difficult to resist, particularly if there is serious doubt that the information involved is material within the meaning of the Securities Acts or, for that matter, common law.

The second area of concern, of course, is the administration of the loan itself. Leaving aside the purely ministerial functions such as distributing payments received, the question is when and under what circumstances should the lead(s) act or refrain from acting under the terms of the loan agreement.

This is one area in which I can give you some small degree of comfort. It is possible to provide in the documentation that the lead(s) will act upon the direction or authorization of some minimum number of the other lenders. This itself, however, can present difficulties and may not be completely desirable. It may be that under particular circumstances prompt action for the protection of the lenders is necessary and could prove to be impossible if elaborate consultation were a condition precedent.

Exculpation

Attempts are made to avoid the problems just described by the insertion in offering memoranda and in loan documentation of exculpatory clauses. In an offering memorandum, the usual form is a statement to the effect that the lead lender(s) has(ve) received the information contained in the memorandum from the borrower and from various public sources (preferably naming them) and assume(s) no responsibility for either the accuracy or completeness of the information furnished.

In loan documentation, a typical disclaimer is that the lead lender(s) make(s) no representation or warranty as to the validity, enforceability, or any other matter with respect to the documentation and assume(s) no responsibility or liability in connection with the administration of the loan except for its willful misconduct or gross negligence.

A further clause which is becoming more common is a representation on the part of the participating lenders that they have made an independent investigation of the affairs of the borrower and the circumstances of the loan and in making their decision to participate therein have not relied upon any representation of or information received from the lead lender(s).

I suggest to you that all of these provisions are likely to be whistling in the wind.

With respect to the disclaimer in the offering memorandum, I think that there is a distinct risk both under the Securities Acts and under general fiduciary doctrines that the lead(s) would be held, despite the disclaimer, to a duty of reasonable investigation.

As far as the willful misconduct/gross negligence wording in the loan documentation is concerned, in the first place, I have never found anyone who could tell me the distinction between gross negligence and simple negligence. In the second place, the determination, of course, will be made by a court with 20/20 hindsight.

So far as the disclaimer of reliance by participating lenders is concerned, I cannot gain much comfort from such a self-serving declaration when I know as a fact that among the participants is the First National Bank of East Earwax, which has footings of $20,000,000 and a lending staff consisting of its president and his part-time secretary and when the transaction being financed involves, for example, the construction of a nuclear plant in Timbuktu.

There has been, to my mind, a regrettable tendency recently to expand exculpatory clauses and to include a laundry list of items in respect of which the lead(s) accept(s) no responsibility. I think that such an expansion is highly dangerous.

If a court, taking into account the relative sophistication of the lead(s) and First of East Earwax, elects to apply the doctrine that one cannot relieve himself from the consequences of his own wrongdoing, one runs the serious risk of having put ideas in the mind of the court. The court might then find grounds for holding the lead(s) responsible for actions or failures to act which would never otherwise have occurred to the court or any one else other than the imaginative lawyer who dreamed up the list.   □